Outlines of Theology

A. A. HODGE
OUTLINES
OF
THEOLOGY

FOR
STUDENTS
AND
LAYMEN

**ZONDERVAN
PUBLISHING HOUSE** OF THE ZONDERVAN CORPORATION
GRAND RAPIDS, MICHIGAN 49506

ZONDERVAN PUBLISHING HOUSE
Grand Rapids, Michigan 49506, U.S.A.

•

First published 1860
Rewritten and enlarged edition 1879
*This edition reprinted
from the* 1879 *edition* 1972
Reprinted 1973

Sixth printing 1980
ISBN 0-310-26200-3

•

PREFACE TO FIRST EDITION.

In introducing this book to the reader, I have only a single word to say upon two points: *first*, as to the uses which I regard this form of exhibiting theological truth as being specially qualified to subserve; and, *secondly*, as to the sources from which I have drawn the materials composing these "Outlines."

As to the first point, I have to say, that the conception and execution of this work originated in the experience of the need for some such manual of theological definitions and argumentation, in the immediate work of instructing the members of my own pastoral charge. The several chapters were in the first instance prepared and used in the same form in which they are now printed, as the basis of a lecture delivered otherwise extemporaneously to my congregation every Sabbath night. In this use of them, I found these preparations successful beyond my hopes. The congregation, as a whole, were induced to enter with interest upon the study even of the most abstruse questions. Having put this work thus to this practical test, I now offer it to my brethren in the ministry, that they may use it, if they will, as a repertory of digested material for the doctrinal instruction of their people, either in Bible classes, or by means of a congregational lecture. I offer it also as an attempt to supply an acknowledged public want, as a syllabus of theological study for the use of theological students generally, and for the use of those many laborious preachers of the gospel who can not command the time, or who have not the opportunity, or other essential means, to study the more expensive and elaborate works from which the materials of this compend have been gathered.

The questions have been retained in form, not for the purpose of adapting the book in any degree for catechetical instruction, but as the most convenient and perspicuous method of presenting an "outline of theology" so condensed. This same necessity of condensation I would also respectfully plead as in some degree an excuse for some of the instances of obscurity in definition and meagreness of illustration, which the reader will observe.

In the second place, as to the sources from which I have drawn the materials of this book, I may for the most part refer the reader to the several passages, where the acknowledgment is made as the debt is incurred.

In general, however, it is proper to say that I have, with his permission, used the list of questions given by my father to his classes of forty-five and six. I have added two or three chapters which his course did not embrace, and have in general adapted his questions to my new purpose, by omissions, additions, or a different distribution. To such a degree, however, have they directed and assisted me, that I feel a confidence in offering the result to the public which otherwise would have been unwarrantable. In the frequent instances in which I have possessed his published articles upon the subjects of the following chapters, the reader will find that I have drawn largely from them. It is due to myself, however, to say, that except in two instances, " The Scriptures the only Rule of Faith and Judge of Controversies," and the " Second Advent," I have never heard delivered nor read the manuscript of that course of theological lectures which he has prepared for the use of his classes subsequently to my graduation. In the instances I have above excepted, I have attempted little more, in the preparation of the respective chapters of this book bearing those titles, than to abridge my father's lectures. In every instance I have endeavored to acknowledge the full extent of the assistance I have derived from others, in which I have, I believe, uniformly succeeded, except so far as I am now unable to trace to their original sources some of the materials collected by me in my class manuscripts, prepared fourteen years ago, while a student of theology. This last reference relates to a large element in this book, as I wrote copiously, and after frequent oral communication with my father, both in public and private.

A. A. Hodge.

Fredericksburg, May, 1860.

PREFACE TO REVISED AND ENLARGED EDITION.

The Preface to the original edition gives a perfectly accurate and somewhat circumstantial account of the origin of this work. Since its first publication the evidences of the fact that it met a public need have been multiplying. Its sale in America and Great Britain has continued. It has been translated into Welsh and Modern Greek, and used in several theological training schools.

The author, in the meantime, has been for fourteen years engaged in the practical work of a theological instructor. His increased knowledge and experience as a teacher have been embodied in this new and enlarged edition, which has grown to its present form through several years in connection with his actual class instructions.

The new edition contains nearly fifty per cent more matter than the former one. Two chapters have been dropped, and five new ones have been added. Extracts from the principal Confessions, Creeds, and classical theological writers of the great historical churches have been appended to the discussions of the doctrines concerning which the Church is divided. Several chapters have been entirely rewritten, and many others have been materially recast, and enlarged. And the Appendix contains a translation of the CONSENSUS TIGURINUS of Calvin, and of the FORMULA CONSENSUS HELVETICA of Heidegger and Turretin, two Confessions of first class historical and doctrinal interest to the student of Reformed theology, but not easily accessible.

The work is again offered to the Christian Church, not as a complete treatise of Systematic Theology, for the use of the proficient, but as a simple Text Book, adapted to the needs of students taking their first lessons in this great science, and to the convenience of many earnest workers who wish to refresh their memories by means of a summary review of the ground gone over by them in their earlier studies.

PRINCETON, N. J., August 6th, 1878.

CONTENTS.

CHAPTER I.

CHAPTER II.

CHAPTER III.

CHAPTER IV.

CHAPTER V.

CHAPTER VI.

CHAPTER VII.

CHAPTER VIII.

CHAPTER IX.

CHAPTER X.

CHAPTER XI.

CHAPTER XII.

CHAPTER XIII.

CHAPTER XIV.

CHAPTER XV.

CHAPTER XVI.

CHAPTER XVII.

CHAPTER XVIII.

CHAPTER XIX.

14   *CONTENTS.*

OUTLINES OF THEOLOGY.

CHAPTER I.

CHRISTIAN THEOLOGY; ITS SEVERAL BRANCHES; AND THEIR RE-
LATION TO OTHER DEPARTMENTS OF HUMAN KNOWLEDGE.

1. *What is Religion? And what Theology in its Christian
sense?*

Religion, in its most general sense, is the sum of the relations which man sustains to God, and comprises the truths, the
experiences, actions, and institutions which correspond to, or
grow out of those relations.

Theology, in its most general sense, is the science of
religion.

The Christian religion is that body of truths, experiences,
actions, and institutions which are determined by the revelation
supernaturally presented in the Christian Scriptures. Christian Theology is the scientific determination, interpretation,
and defence of those Scriptures, together with the history of
the manner in which the truths it reveals have been understood, and the duties they impose have been performed, by all
Christians in all ages.

2. *What is Theological Encyclopædia? and what Theological
Methodology?*

Theological Encyclopædia, from the Greek ἐγκυκλοπαιδεία
(the whole circle of general education), presents to the student
the entire circle of the special sciences devoted to the discovery, elucidation, and defence of the contents of the supernatural
revelation contained in the Christian Scriptures, and aims to
present these sciences in those organic relations which are
determined by their actual genesis and inmost nature.

Theological Methodology is the science of theological
method. As each department of human inquiry demands a
mode of treatment peculiar to itself; and as even each subdivision of each general department demands its own special

modifications of treatment, so theological methodology provides
for the scientific determination of the true method, general
and special, of pursuing the theological sciences.   And this includes two distinct categories: (*a*) The methods proper to the
original investigation and construction of the several sciences,
and (*b*) the methods proper to elementary instruction in the
same.

All this should be accompanied with critical and historical
information, and direction as to the use of the vast literature
with which these sciences are illustrated.

3. *How far is the scientific arrangement of all the theological
sciences possible?   And on what account is the attempt desirable?*

Such an arrangement can approach perfection only in proportion as these sciences themselves approach their final and
absolute form.   At present every such attempt must be only
more or less an approximation to an ideal unattainable in the
present state of knowledge in this life.   Every separate attempt
also must depend for its comparative success upon the comparative justness of the general theological principles upon which
it is based.   It is evident that those who make Reason, and
those who make the inspired Church, and those who make the
inspired Scriptures the source and standard of all divine knowledge, must severally configure the theological sciences to the
different foundations on which they are made to stand.

The point of view adopted in this book is the evangelical
and specifically the Calvinistic or Augustinian one, assuming
the following fundamental principles: 1st. The inspired Scriptures are the sole, and an infallible standard of all religious
knowledge.   2d. Christ and his work is the centre around
which all Christian theology is brought into order.   3d. The
salvation brought to light in the gospel is supernatural and of
Free Grace.   4th. All religious knowledge has a *practical end*.
The theological sciences, instead of being absolute ends in themselves, find their noblest purpose and effect in the advancement
of personal holiness, the more efficient service of our fellow-
men, and THE GREATER GLORY OF GOD.

The advantages of such a grouping of the theological sciences are obvious, and great.   The relations of all truths are
determined by their nature, whence it follows that their nature is revealed by an exhibition of their relations.   Such an
exhibition will also tend to widen the mental horizon of the
student, to incite him to breadth of culture, and prevent him
from unduly exalting or exclusively cultivating any one special
branch, and thus from perverting it by regarding it out of its
natural limitations and dependencies.

4. *What are the fundamental questions which all theological science proposes to answer, and which therefore determine the arrangement of the several departments of that general science?*

1st. Is there a God? 2d. Has God spoken? 3d. What has God said? 4th. How have men in time past understood his word and practically, in their persons and institutions, realized his intentions?

5. *What position in an encyclopædia of theological sciences must be given to other branches of human knowledge?*

It is evident that as the Supernatural Revelation God has been pleased to give has come to us in an historical form, that history, and that of the Christian Church, is inseparably connected with all human history more or less directly. Further, it is evident that as all truth is one, all revealed truths and duties are inseparably connected with all departments of human knowledge, and with all the institutions of human society. It hence follows that theological science can at no point be separated from general science, that some knowledge of every department of human knowledge must always be comprehended in every system of Theological Encyclopædia as *auxiliary* to the Theological sciences themselves. Some of these auxiliary sciences sustain special relations to certain of the theological sciences, and are very remotely related to others. It is, however, convenient to give them a position by themselves, as in general constituting a discipline preparatory and auxiliary to the science of theology as a whole.

6. *State the main divisions of the proposed arrangement of the theological sciences.*

I. *Sciences Auxiliary* to the study of theology.

II. *Apologetics*—embracing the answers to the two questions—Is there a God? and Has God spoken?

III. *Exegetical Theology*—embracing the critical determination of the *ipsissima verba* of the Divine Revelation, and the Interpretation their meaning.

IV. *Systematic Theology*—embracing the development into an all-embracing and self-consistent system of the contents of that Revelation, and its subsequent elucidation and defence.

V. *Practical Theology*—embracing the principles and laws revealed in Scripture for the guidance of Christians (*a*) in the promulgation of this divine revelation thus ascertained and interpreted, and thus (*b*) in bringing all men into practical obedience to the duties it imposes and (*c*) into the fruition of the blessings it confers.

VI. *Historical Theology*—embracing the history of the actual development during all past ages and among all people of the theoretical and practical elements of that revelation (1) in the faith and (2) in the life of the Church.

7. *State the chief departments of human knowledge auxiliary to study of Theology.*

1st. As underlying and conditioning all knowledge, we have *Universal History*, and as auxiliary to theological science especially the Histories of Egypt, Babylonia, Assyria, Greece, Rome and of Mediæval and Modern Europe.

2d. *Archæology* in its most comprehensive sense, including the interpretation of inscriptions, monuments, coins, and remains of art, and the illustrations gathered thence and from all other available sources, of the geographical distribution and physical conditions, and of the political, religious, and social institutions and customs of all peoples, of all ages.

3d. *Ethnology*—the science of the divisions of the human family into races and nations, and of their dispersion over the world—which traces their origin and affiliations and their varieties of physical, intellectual, moral, and religious character, and the sources and modifying conditions of these variations.

4th. *Comparative Philology*, the science which starting from the natural groups of human languages, traces the relations and origins of languages and dialects, and transcending the first dawn of human history, traces the unity of races now separated, and the elements of long extinct civilizations, and the facts of historic changes otherwise left without record.

5th. *The Science of Comparative Religion*, the critical study and comparison of the history, beliefs, spirit, principles, institutions, and practical character of all the Ethnic religions, tracing the light they throw upon (*a*) human nature and history, (*b*) the moral government of God, and (*c*) the supernatural revelation recorded in Scripture.

6th. *Philosophy*, the ground and mistress of all the merely human sciences. This will include the history of the origin and development of all the schools of philosophy, ancient, mediæval, and modern—a critical study and comparison of their principles, methods, and doctrines, and the range and character of their respective influence upon all other sciences and institutions, especially upon those which are political and religious, and more especially upon those which are definitely Christian.

7th. *Psychology*, or that department of experimental science which unfolds the laws of action of the human mind under normal conditions, as exhibited (*a*) in the phenomena of individual consciousness and action, and (b) in the phenomena of social and political life.

8th. *Æsthetics*, or the science of the laws of the Beautiful in all its forms of Music, Rhetoric, Architecture, Painting, etc., and the principles and history of every department of art.

9th. The *Physical Sciences*, their methods, general and special; their history, genesis, development, and present tendencies; their relation to Philosophy, especially to Theism and natural religion, to civilization, to the Scriptural records historically and doctrinally.

10th. *Statistics*, or that department of investigation which aims to present us with a full knowledge of the present state of the human family in the world, in respect to every measurable variety of condition—as to numbers and state, physical, intellectual, religious, social, and political, of civilization, commerce, literature, science, art, etc., etc.; from which elements the immature forms of social science and political economy are being gradually developed.

8. *What particulars are embraced under the head of Apologetics?*

This department falls under two heads: (1.) Is there a God. (2.) Has He spoken; and includes—

1st. The proof of the being of God, that is of an extramundane person transcendent yet immanent, creating, preserving, and governing all things according to his eternal plan. This will involve the discussion and refutation of all Antitheistic systems, as Atheism, Pantheism, Naturalistic Deism, Materialism, etc.

2d. The *Development of Natural Theology*, embracing the relation of God to intelligent and responsible agents as Moral Governor, and the indications of his will and purpose, and consequently of the duties and destinies of mankind, as far as these can be traced by the light of Nature—

3d. The *evidences of Christianity*, including—

(1.) The discussion of the proper use of reason in religious questions.

(2.) The demonstration of the *à priori* possibility of a supernatural revelation.

(3.) The *necessity* for and the *probability* of such a revelation, the character of God and the condition of man as revealed by the light of nature, being considered.

(4.) The positive proof of the *actual fact* that such a revelation has been given (a) through the Old Testament prophets, (b) through the New Testament prophets, and (c) above all in the person and work of Christ. This will involve, of course, a critical discussion of all the evidence bearing on this subject, external and internal, historical, rational, moral, and spiritual, natural and supernatural, theoretical and practical, and a refutation of all the criticism, historical and rational, which has been brought to bear against the fact of revelation 'or the integrity of the record.   Much that is here adduced will of course necessarily be also comprehended under the heads of Systematic and of Exegetical Theology.

9. *What is embraced under Exegetical Theology?*

If the facts (1) That there is a God, and (2) that he has spoken, be established, it remains to answer the question, "*What has God said?*" Exegetical Theology is the general title of that department of theological science which aims at the Interpretation of the Scriptures as the word of God, recorded in human language, and transmitted to us through human channels; and in order to this, Interpretation aims to gather and organize all that knowledge which is necessarily introductory thereto.   This includes the answer to two main questions: (1) What books form the canon, and what were the exact words of which the original autographs of the writers of these several books consisted, and (2) What do those divine words, so ascertained, mean.

The answers to all questions preliminary to actual Interpretation, come under the head of *Introduction*, and this is divided (1) into *General Introduction*, presenting all that information, preliminary to interpretation, which stands related in common to the Bible as a whole, or to each Testament as a whole, and (2) into *Special Introduction*, which includes all necessary preparation for the interpretation of each book of the Bible in detail.

A. GENERAL INTRODUCTION includes—

1st. The Higher Criticism or the canvass of the extant evidences of all kinds establishing the authenticity and genuineness of each book in the sacred canon.

2d. The Criticism of the Text, which, from a comparison of the best ancient manuscripts and versions, from internal evidence, and by means of a critical history of the text from its first appearance to the present, seeks to determine the *ipsissima verba* of the original autographs of the inspired writers.

3d. *Biblical Philology*, which answers the questions: Why were different languages used in the record? and why Hebrew and Greek?   What are the special characteristics of the dialects of those languages actually used, and their relation to the families of language to which they belong?   And what were the special characteristics of dialect, style, etc., of the sacred writers individually.

4th. *Biblical Archæology*, including the physical and political geography of Bible lands during the course of Bible history, and determining the physical, ethnological, social, political, and religious conditions of the people among whom the Scriptures originated, together with an account of their customs and institutions, and of the relation of these to those of their ancestors and of their contemporaries.

5th. *Hermeneutics*, or the scientific determination of the principles and rules of Biblical Interpretation, including (1) the logical and grammatical and rhetorical principles determining the interpretation of human language in general, (2) the modification of these principles appropriate to the interpretation of the specific forms of human discourse, *e. g.*, history, poetry, prophecy, parable, symbol, etc., and (3) those further modifications of these principles appropriate to the interpretation of writings supernaturally inspired.

6th. Apologetics having established the fact that the Christian Scriptures are the vehicle of a supernatural revelation, we must now discuss and determine the nature and extent of *Biblical Inspiration* as far as this is determined by the claims and the phenomena of the Scriptures themselves.

7th. The *History of Interpretation*, including the history of ancient and modern versions and schools of interpretation, illustrated by a critical comparison of the most eminent commentaries.

B. Special Introduction treats of each book of the Bible by itself, and furnishes all that knowledge concerning its dialect, authorship, occasion, design, and reception that is necessary for its accurate interpretation.

C. Exegesis proper is the actual application of all the knowledge gathered, and of all the rules developed, in the preceding departments of Introduction to the Interpretation of the sacred text, as it stands in its original connections of Testaments, books, paragraphs, etc.

Following the laws of grammar, the *usus loquendi* of words, the analogy of Scripture, and the guidance of the Holy Ghost, Exegesis seeks to determine the mind of the Spirit as expressed in the inspired sentences as they stand in their order.

There are several special departments classed under the general head of Exegetical Theology, which involve in some degree that arrangement and combination of Scripture testimonies under topics or subjects, which is the distinctive characteristic of Systematic Theology.

These are—

1st. *Typology*, which embraces a scientific determination of the laws of Biblical symbols and types, and their interpretation, especially those of the Mosaic ritual as related to the person and work of Christ.

2d. *Old Testament Christology*, the critical exposition of the Messianic idea as it is developed in the Old Testament.

3d. *Biblical Theology*, which traces the gradual evolution of the several elements of revealed truth from their first sugges-tion through every successive stage to their fullest manifesta-tion in the sacred text, and which exhibits the peculiar forms and connections in which these several truths are presented by each inspired writer.

4th. The Development of the principles of Prophetical In-terpretation and their application to the construction of an outline of the Prophesies of both Testaments.—"Notes on New Testament Literature," by Dr. J. A. Alexander.

10. *What is embraced under the head of Systematic Theology.*

As the name imports, Systematic Theology has for its object the gathering all that the Scriptures teach as to what we are to believe and to do, and the presenting all the elements of this teaching in a symmetrical system. The human mind must seek unity in all its knowledge. God's truth is one, and all the contents of all revelations natural and supernatural must constitute one self-contained system, each part organically re-lated to every other.

The method of construction is inductive. It rests upon the results of Exegesis for its foundation. Passages of Scripture ascertained and interpreted are its data. These when rightly interpreted reveal their own relations and place in the system of which the Person and work of Christ is the centre. And as the contents of revelation stand intimately related to all the other departments of human knowledge, the work of Systematic Theology necessarily involves the demonstration and illustra-tion of the harmony of all revealed truth with all valid science, material and psychological, with all true speculative philosophy, and with all true moral philosophy and practical philanthropy.

It includes—(1.) The construction of all the contents of revelation into a complete system of faith and duties. (2.) The history of this process as it has prevailed in the Church during the past. (3.) Polemics.

I. The construction of all the contents of revelation into a complete system. This includes the scientific treatment (*a*) of all the matters of faith revealed, and (*b*) of all the duties enjoined.

In the arrangement of topics the great majority of theolo-gians have followed what Dr. Chalmers calls the synthetical method. Starting with the idea and nature of God revealed in the Scriptures, they trace his eternal purposes and temporal acts in creation, providence, and redemption to the final consummation. The Doctor himself prefers what he calls the analytic method, and starts with the facts of experience and the light of nature, and man's present morally diseased condition, leads upward to redemption and to the character of God as revealed therein.

Following the former of these methods all the elements of the system are usually grouped under the following heads:

1st. Theology proper: including the existence, attributes, triune personality of God, together with his eternal purposes, and temporal acts of creation and providence.

2d. Anthropology: (doctrine of man) including the creation and nature of man, his original state, fall, and consequent moral ruin. This embraces the Biblical Psychology, and the Scriptural doctrine of sin, its nature, origin, and mode of propagation.

3d. Soteriology: (doctrine of salvation) which includes the plan, execution, and application and glorious effects of human salvation. This embraces Christology (the doctrine of Christ), the incarnation, the constitution of Christ's person, his life, death, and resurrection, together with the office-work of the Holy Ghost, and the means of grace, the word and sacraments.

4th. Christian Ethics: embracing the principles, rules, motives, and aids of human duty revealed in the Bible as determined (a) by his natural relations as a man with his fellows, and (b) his supernatural relations as a redeemed man.

5th. Eschatology (science of last things) comprehending death, the intermediate state of the soul, the second advent, the resurrection of the dead, the general judgment, heaven and hell.

6th. Ecclesiology (science of the Church); including the scientific determination of all that the Scriptures teach as to the Church visible and invisible, in its temporal and in its eternal state; including the Idea of the Church—its true definition—its constitution and organization, its officers and their functions. A comparison and criticism of all the modifications of ecclesiastical organization that have ever existed, together with their genesis, history, and practical effects.

II. Doctrine-History, which embraces the history of each of these great doctrines traced in its first appearance and subsequent development, through the controversies it excited and the Confessions in which it is defined.

III. Polemics, or Controversial Theology, including the defence of the true system of doctrine as a whole and of each constituent element of it in detail against the perversions of heretical parties within the pale of the general Church. This embraces—(1.) The general principles and true method of religious controversies. (2.) The definition of the true *Status Quæstionis* in each controversy, and an exposition of the sources of evidence and of the methods, defensive and offensive, by which the truth is to be vindicated. (3.) The history of controversies.

11. *What is embraced under the head of Practical Theology?*

Practical Theology is both a science and an art. As an art it has for its purpose the effective publication of the contents of revelation among all men, and the perpetuation, extension, and edification of the earthly kingdom of God. As a science it has for its province the revealed principles and laws of the art above defined. Hence as Systematic Theology roots itself in a thorough Exegesis at once scientific and spiritual, so does Practical Theology root itself in the great principles developed by Systematic Theology, the department of Ecclesiology being common ground to both departments: the product of the one, and the foundation of the other.

It includes the following main divisions—

1st. The discussion of the Idea and Design of the Church, and of its divinely revealed attributes.

2d. The determination of the divinely appointed constitution of the Church, and methods of administration, with the discussion and refutation of all the rival forms of Church organization that have prevailed, their history, and that of the controversies which they have occasioned.

3d. The discussion of the nature and extent of the discretion Christ has allowed his followers in adjusting the methods of ecclesiastical organization and administration to changing social and historical conditions.

4th. Church membership, its conditions, and the relation to Christ involved, together with the duties and privileges absolute and relative of the several classes of members. The relation of baptized children to the Church, and the relative duties of Parents and of the Church in relation to them.

5th. The Officers of the Church—extraordinary and temporary; ordinary and perpetual.

(1.) Their call and ordination; their relations to Christ and to the Church.

(2.) Their functions—

A. As Teachers—including—

(*a.*) Catechetics, its necessity, principles, and history.

(*b.*) Sunday-schools. The duties of parents and of the Church in respect to the religious education of children.

(*c.*) Sacred Rhetoric. Homiletics and pulpit elocution.

(*d.*) Christian literature. The newspaper, and periodicals and permanent books.

B. As Leaders of Worship, including—

(*a.*) Liturgies, their uses, abuses, and history.

(*b.*) Free forms of prayer.

(*c.*) Psalmody, inspired and uninspired, its uses and history.

(*d.*) Sacred Music, vocal and instrumental uses and history.

C. As Rulers—

(*a.*) The office, qualification, duties and Scriptural Warrant of Ruling Elders—

(*b.*) The office, qualification, duties, mode of election, and ordination, and Scriptural Warrant of the New-Testament Bishop or Pastor.

(*c.*) The Session, its constitution and functions. The theory and practical rules and methods of Church discipline.

(*d.*) The Presbytery and its constitution and functions. The theory and practical rules and precedents regulating the action of Church courts, in the exercise of the constitutional right of Review and Control in the issue and conduct of trials, complaints, appeals, etc., etc.

(*e.*) The Synod and General Assembly and their constitution and functions. The Principles and policy of Committees, Commissioners, Boards, etc., etc.

This leads to the functions of the Church as a whole, and the warrant for and the uses and abuses of Denominational distinctions, and the relations of the different Denominations to one another.

1st. Church Statistics, including our own Church, other Churches, and the world.

2d. Christian, social, and ecclesiastical economics, including the duties of Christian stewardship, personal consecration, and systematic benevolence. The relation of the Church to the poor and to criminals, the administration of orphan asylums, hospitals, prisons, etc. The relation of the Church to voluntary societies, Young Men's Christian Associations, etc., etc.

3d. The education of the ministry, the policy, constitution and administration of theological seminaries.

4th. Domestic Missions, including aggressive evangelization, support of the ministry among the poor, Church extension and Church erection.

5th. The relation of the Church to the state, and the true relation of the state to religion, and the actual condition of the common and statute law with relation to Church property, and the action of Church Courts in the exercise of discipline, etc. The obligations of Christian citizenship. The relation of the Church to civilization, to moral reforms, to the arts, sciences, social refinements, etc., etc.

6th. Foreign Missions in all their departments.

See "Lectures on Theological Encyclopædia and Methodology," by Rev. John M'Clintock, D.D., LL.D., edited by J. T. Short, B.D.; and "Bibliotheca Sacra," Vol. 1, 1844; "Theological Encyclopædia and Methodology," from unpublished lecture of Prof. Tholuck, by Prof. E. A. Park.

12. *What is embraced under the head of* HISTORICAL THEOLOGY ?

According to the logical evolution of the whole contents of the theological sciences, the Interpretation of the letter of Scripture, and the construction of the entire System of related truths and duties revealed therein, must precede the History of the actual development of that revelation in the life and faith of the Church. Just as the fountain must precede the stream which flows from it. Yet, as a matter of fact, in the actual study of the family of theological sciences, History must precede and lay the foundation for all the rest. History alone gives us the Scriptures in which our revelation is recorded, and the means whereby the several books and their *ipsissima verba* are critically ascertained. We are indebted to the same source for our methods of interpretation, and for their results as illustrated in the body of theological literature accumulated in the past; also for our creeds and confessions and records of controversies, and hence for the records preserving the gradual evolution of our system of doctrine. In the order of production and of acquisition History comes first, while in the order of a logical exposition of the constituent theological sciences in their relations within the system, History has the honor of crowning the whole series.

Historical Theology is divided into *Biblical* and *Ecclesiastical*. The first derived chiefly from inspired sources, and continuing down to the close of the New Testament canon. The latter beginning where the former ends, and continuing to the present time.

Biblical History is subdivided into—1st. Old Testament History, including (1) the Patriarchal, (2) Mosaic, and (3) Prophetical eras, together with (4) the history of the chosen people during the interval between the close of the Old and the opening of the New Testament. 2d. New Testament History, including (1) the life of Christ, (2) The founding of the Christian Church by the Apostles down to the end of the first century.

With respect to *Ecclesiastical History* several preliminary departments of study are essential to its prosecution as a science.

1st. Several of the auxiliary sciences already enumerated must be cited as specifically demanded in this connection.

These are—(1.) Ancient, Mediæval, and Modern Geography. (2.) Chronology. (3.) The Antiquities of all the peoples embraced in the area through which the Church has at any period extended. (4.) Statistics, exhibiting the actual condition of the world at any particular period. (5.) The entire course of General History.

2d. The Sources from which Ecclesiastical History is derived should be critically investigated. (1.) Monumental sources, such as (*a*) buildings, (*b*) inscriptions, (*c*) coins, etc. (2.) Documental, which are—(*a.*) Public, such as the Acts of Councils, the briefs, decretals, and bulls of Popes; the archives of governments, and the creeds, confessions, catechisms, and liturgies of the Churches, etc., etc. (*b.*) Private documents, such as contemporary literature of all kinds, pamphlets, biographies, annals, and later reports and compilations.

3d. The History of the literature of ecclesiastical history from Eusebius to Neander, Kurtz, and Schaff. The methods which have been and which should be followed in the arrangement of the material of Church History.

The actual Method always has been and probably always will be a combination of the two natural methods—(*a*) chronological, and (*b*) topical.

The fundamental principle upon which, according to Dr. M'Clintock, the materials of Church History should be arranged, is the distinction between the life and the faith of the Church. The two divisions therefore, are (1) History of the life of the Church, or Church History proper, and (2) History of the thought of the Church, or Doctrine-History.

1st. The History of the Life of the Church deals with persons, communities, and events, and should be treated according to the ordinary methods of historical composition.

2d. The History of the Thought of the Church comprises—

(1.) Patristics, or the literature of the early Christian Fathers; and Patrology, or a scientific exhibition of their doctrine.

These Fathers are grouped under three heads—(*a*) Apostolical, (*b*) Ante-Nicene, and (*c*) Post-Nicene, terminating with Gregory the Great among the Latins, A. D. 604, and with John of Damascus among the Greeks, A. D. 754. This study involves the discussion of (*a*) the proper use of these Fathers, and their legitimate authority in modern controversies; (*b*) a full history of their literature, and of the principal editions of their works; and (*c*) the meaning, value, and doctrine of each individual Father separately—

(2.) Christian Archæology, which treats of the usage, worship, discipline of the early Church, and the history of Christian worship, art, architecture, poetry, painting, music, etc., etc.

(3.) Doctrine-History, or the critical history of the genesis and development of each element of the doctrinal system of the Church, or of any of its historical branches, with an account of all the heretical forms of doctrine from which the truth has been separated, and the history of all the controversies by means of which the elimination has been effected. This will, of course, be accompanied with a critical history of the entire Literature of Doctrine-History, of the principles recognized, the methods pursued, and the works produced.

(4.) Symbolics, which involves—(a.) The scientific determination of the necessity for and uses of public Creeds and Confessions. (b.) The history of the occasions, of the actual genesis, and subsequent reception, authority, and influence of each one of the Creeds and Confessions of Christendom. (c.) The study of the doctrinal contents of each Creed, and of each group of Creeds separately, and (d.) Comparative Symbolics, or the comparative study of all the Confessions of the Church, and thence a systematic exhibition of all their respective points of agreement and of contrast.

M'Clintock's "Theological Encyclopædia"; "Notes on Ecclesiastical History," by Dr. J. A. Alexander, edited by Dr. S. D. Alexander.

CHAPTER II.

ORIGIN OF THE IDEA OF GOD AND PROOF OF HIS EXISTENCE.

1. *What is the distinction between a* NOMINAL, *and a* REAL *definition? and give the true definition of the word God.*

A nominal definition simply explains the meaning of the term used, while a real definition explains the nature of the thing signified by the term.

The English word God is by some derived from "good." Since, however, its various forms in cognate languages could not have had that origin, others derive it from the Persic *Choda* —*dominus,* "possessor." The Latin *Deus,* and the Greek Θεός have been commonly derived from the Sanscrit *div* to give "light." But Curtius, Cremer, and others derive it from θεσ in θέσσασθαι "to implore." Θεός is "He to whom one prays."

The word God is often used in a pantheistic sense, for the impersonal, unconscious ground of all being, and by many for the unknowable first cause of the existent world. It is for this reason that so many speculators, who actually or virtually deny the existence of the God of Christendom, yet indignantly repudiate the charge of atheism, because they admit the existence of a self-existent substance or first cause to which they give the name God, while they deny to it the possession of the properties generally designated by the term.

But, as a matter of fact, in consequence of the predominance of Christian ideas in the literature of civilized nations for the last eighteen centuries, the term "God" has attained the definite and permanent sense of a self-existent, eternal, and absolutely perfect free personal Spirit, distinct from and sovereign over the world he has created.

The man who denies the existence of such a being denies God.

2. *How can a "real" definition of God be constructed?*

Evidently God can be defined only in so far as he is known to us, and the condition of the possibility of our knowing him

is the fact that we were created in his image. Every definition
of God must assume this fact, that in an essential sense he and
his intelligent creatures are beings of the same genus. He is
therefore defined by giving his genus and specific difference.
Thus he is as to genus, an intelligent personal Spirit. He is,
as to his specific difference, as to that which constitutes him
God, infinite, eternal, unchangeable in his being, in his wisdom,
in his power, in his holiness, and in all perfections consistent
with his being.

3. *To what extent is the idea of God due to Tradition?*

It is evident that the complete idea of God presented in the
foregoing definition has been attained only by means of the
supernatural revelation recorded in the Christian Scriptures.
It is a fact also that the only three Theistic religions which
have ever prevailed among men (the Jewish, Mohammedan
and Christian) are historically connected with the same revelation. It is also, of course, in vain to speculate as to what
would be the action of the human mind independent of all
inherited habits, and of all traditional opinions. We are entirely without experience or testimony as to any kind of knowledge attained or judgments formed under such conditions. It
is moreover certain that the form in which the theistic conception is realized, and the associations with which it is accompanied, are determined in the case of each community by the
theological traditions they have inherited from their fathers.

It is, on the other hand, indubitably certain that all men
under all known, and therefore under all truly natural conditions, do spontaneously recognize the divine existence as
more or less clearly revealed to them in the constitution and
conscious experience of their own souls, and in external nature.
The theistic conception hence is no more due to authority, as
often absurdly charged, than the belief in the subjective reality
of spirit or in the objective reality of matter formed under the
same educational conditions. The recognition of the self-man-
ifest God is spontaneous, and universal, which proves the evidence to be clear and everywhere present, and convincing to
all normally developed men.

4. *Is the idea of God* INNATE? *And is it an* INTUITIVE *truth?*

That depends upon the sense in which the respective terms
are taken. It is evident that there are no "innate" ideas in
the sense that any child was ever born with a conception of
the divine being, or any other conception already formed in his
mind. It is also certain that the human mind when developed
under purely natural conditions, in the absence of all super-

natural revelation, can never attain to an adequate conception of the divine nature. On the other hand, however, all history proves that the idea of God is innate in the sense that the constitutional faculties of the human soul do, under all natural conditions, secure the spontaneous recognition, more or less clear, of God as the ultimate ground of all being, and as the Lord of conscience, self-manifested in the soul and in the world. It is innate in so much as the evidence is as universally present as the light of day, and the process by which it is apprehended is constitutional.

If the term "intuition" is taken in its strict sense of a direct vision of a truth, seen in its own light to be necessary, by an intellectual act incapable of being resolved into more elementary processes of thought, then the existence of God is not a truth apprehended intuitively by men. The process whereby it is reached, whether spontaneously or by elaborate reasoning, embraces many indubitable intuitions as elements, but no man apprehends God himself by a direct intuition.

Because—(1.) Although the recognition of the divine existence *is* necessary in the sense that the great majority of men recognize the truth, and are unable to disbelieve it even when they wish, and no one can do so without doing violence to his nature, yet it is *not* necessary to thought in the sense that the non-existence of God is unthinkable. (2.) Because God manifests himself to us not immediately but mediately through his works, and there is always present, at least implicitly, an inference in the act whereby the soul recognizes his presence and action. (3.) The true idea of God is exceedingly complex, and is reached by a complex process, whether spontaneous or not, involving various elements capable of analysis and description.

On the other hand it is true that God manifests himself in his working in our souls and in external nature just as the invisible souls of our fellow-men manifest themselves, and we spontaneously recognize him just as we do them. We recognize them because (*a*) we are generically like them, and (*b*) their attributes are significally expressed in their words and actions. And we recognize God because (*a*) we have been made in his image, which fact we spontaneously recognize (*b*) from his self-revelations in consciousness, especially in conscience, and from the characteristics of the external world.

"While the mental process which has been described—the theistic inference—is capable of analysis, it is itself synthetic. The principles on which it depends are so connected that the mind can embrace them all in a single act, and must include and apply them all in the apprehension of God. Will, intelligence, conscience, reason, and the ideas which they supply;

cause, design, goodness, infinity, and the arguments which rest on these ideas—all coalesce into this one grand issue."—"Theism" by Prof. Flint, pp. 71, 72.

5. *If the existence of God is spontaneously recognized by all men under normal conditions of consciousness, what is the value of formal arguments to prove that existence? And what are the arguments generally used?*

1st. These arguments are of value as analyses and scientific verifications of the mental processes implicitly involved in the spontaneous recognition of the self-manifestations of God. 2d. They are of use also for the purpose of vindicating the legitimacy of the process against the criticisms of skeptics. 3d. Also for the purpose of quickening and confirming the spontaneous recognition by drawing attention to the extent and variety of the evidence to which it responds. 4th. The various arguments are convergent rather than consecutive. They do not all establish the same elements of the theistic conception, but each establishes independently its separate element, and thus is of use (*a*) in contributing confirmatory evidence *that* God is, and (*b*) complementary evidence as to *what* God is.

They constitute an organic whole, and are the analysis and illustration of the spontaneous act whereby the mass of men have always recognized God. "Although causality does not involve design, nor design goodness, design involves causality, and goodness both causality and design. The proofs of intelligence are also proofs of power; and the proofs of goodness are proofs of both intelligence and power. The principles of reason which compel us to think of the Supreme Moral Intelligence as self-existent, eternal, infinite, and unchangeable Being, supplement the proofs from other sources, and give self-consistency and completeness to the doctrine of theism."—"Theism," Prof. Flint, pp. 73, 74.

The usual arguments will be examined under the following heads:

1st. The Cosmological Argument, or the evidence for God's existence as First Cause.

2d. The Teleological Argument, or the evidence of God's existence afforded by the presence of order and adaptation in the universe.

3d. The Moral Argument, or the evidence afforded by the moral consciousness and history of mankind.

4th. The evidence afforded by the phenomena of Scripture and the supernatural history they record.

5th. The *A priori* Argument, and the testimony afforded by reason to God as the Infinite and Absolute.

6. State the Cosmological Argument.

It may be stated in the form of a syllogism, thus—

Major Premise.—Every new existence or change in any thing previously existing must have had a cause pre-existing and adequate.

Minor Premise.—The universe as a whole and in all its parts is a system of changes.

Conclusion.—Hence the universe must have a cause exterior to itself, and the ultimate or absolute cause must be eternal, uncaused, and unchangeable.

1st. As to the major premise; the causal judgment is intuitive and absolutely universal and necessary. It has been denied theoretically by some speculators, as Hume and Mill, but it is always used by them and all others in all their reasoning as to the origin of the world, as well as of all things it contains. The judgment is unavoidable; the opposite is unthinkable. Something exists now, therefore something must have existed from eternity, and that which has existed from eternity is the cause of that which exists now.

It has been claimed that the causal judgment leads to an infinite regressive series of causes and effects. But this is absurd. (1.) The judgment is not that every thing must have a cause, but that every new thing or change must have been caused. But that which is eternal and immutable needs no cause. (2.) An infinite series of causes and effects is absurd, for that is only a series of changes, which is precisely that which demands a cause, and all the more imperatively in proportion to its length. A real cause, on the other hand,—that in which the causal judgment can alone absolutely rest,—must be neither a change nor a series of changes, but something uncaused, eternal and immutable.

As a matter of fact all philosophers and men of science without exception assume the principles asserted. They all postulate an eternal, self-existent, unchangeable cause of the universe, whether a personal spirit, or material atoms, or a substance of which both matter and spirit are modes, or an unconscious intelligent world-soul in union with matter.

2d. As to the minor premise. The fact that the universe as a whole and in all its parts is a system of changes is emphasized by every principle and lesson of modern science. Every discovery in the fields of geology and astronomy, and all speculation—as the nebular hypothesis and the hypothesis of evolution—embody this principle as their very essence.

But John Stuart Mill in his "Essay on Theism," pp. 142, 143, says: "There is in nature a permanent element, and also a

changeable: the changes are always the effects of previous
changes; the permanent existences, so far as we know, are not
effects at all. . . . There is in every object another and
permanent element, viz., the specific elementary substance or
substances of which it consists, and their inherent properties.
These are not known as beginning to exist; within the range
of human knowledge they had no beginning, consequently no
cause; though they themselves are causes or concauses of every
thing that takes place." "Whenever a physical phenomenon
is traced to its cause, that cause when analyzed is found to be
a certain quantum of force, combined with certain collocations.
. . . The force itself is essentially one and the same, and
there exists of it in nature a fixed quantity, which (if the theory of the conservation of forces be true) is never increased
or diminished. Here then we find in the changes of material
nature a permanent element, to all appearance the very one
of which we are in quest. This it is apparently to which, if to
any thing, we must assign the character of First Cause."—
"Essay on Theism," pp. 144, 145.

WE ANSWER—(1.) The existence of "Energy" in any of its
convertable forms dissociated from matter is absolutely unthinkable. This is recognized as an unquestionable scientific
truth by Stewart and Tait ("Unseen Universe," p. 79). (2.) It
is an obvious fact "that all but an exceedingly small fraction of the light and heat of the sun and stars goes out into
space, and does not return to them. In the next place the visible motion of the large bodies of the universe is gradually
being stopped by something which may be denominated etherial friction," and at last they must fall together, and constitute
by successive aggregations one mass. "In fine the degradation
of Energy of the visible universe proceeds, *pari passu*, with
the aggregation of mass. The very fact, therefore, that the
large masses of the visible universe are of finite size, is sufficient to assure us that the process can not have been going on
forever, or in other words that the visible universe must have
had an origin in time"—since (*a*) Energy remains aggregated
in finite quantities yet undiffused, and (*b*) since the matter of
the universe still remains in separate masses. Thus the very
law of the correlation of Energy to which Mill appeals proves,
when really tested, that the visible universe had a beginning
and will have an end. Stewart and Tait ("Unseen Universe,"
p. 166). (3.) His assumption, also, that the matter of the universe is in its ultimate atoms eternal and unchangeable, is un-
proved and contrary to scientific analogy. Clark Maxwell (in
his address as President of the British Association for Advancement of Science, 1870) says: "The exact equality of each mole-

cule to all others of the same kind gives it, as Sir John Herschell has well said, the essential character of a manufactured article, and precludes the idea of its being eternal and self-existent." (4.) As a matter of fact all evolution theories as to the genesis of the universe necessarily postulate a commencement in time, and a primordial fire-mist. But this fire-mist can not be the First Cause the causal judgment demands, because it is not eternal and immutable. If eternal it would be fully developed. If fully developed it could not develop into the universe. If immutable it could not pass into change. If not immutable it is itself, like the universe which issues from it, a transient condition of matter, like all other change demanding for itself a cause.

7. *State the Teleological Argument.*

Teleology from τέλος, end, and λόγος, discourse, is the science of final causes, or of purposes or design as exhibited in the adjustments of parts to wholes, of means to ends, of organs to uses in nature. It is also familiarly called the Argument from Design; and is ultimately based upon the recognition of the operations of an intelligent cause in nature. It may be profitably stated in two forms based respectively on the more general and the more special manifestations of that intelligence.

FIRST FORM. *Major Premise.*—Universal order and harmony in the conspiring operation of a vast multitude of separate elements can be explained only by the postulate of an intelligent cause.

Minor Premise.—The universe as a whole and in all its parts is a fabric of the most complex and symmetrical order.

Conclusion.—Therefore the eternal and absolute cause of the universe is an intelligent mind.

SECOND FORM. *Major Premise.*—The adjustment of parts and the adaptation of means to effect an end or purpose can be explained only by reference to a designing intelligence and will.

Minor Premise.—The universe is full of such adjustments of parts, and of organisms composed of parts conspiring to effect an end.

Conclusion.—Therefore the First Cause of the universe must be an intelligent mind and will.

These arguments if valid amount to proving that God is an eternal self-existing Person. For the assumption of an unconscious intelligence, or of an intelligence producing effects without the exercise of will is absurd. These phrases represent no possible ideas. And intelligence and will together constitute personality.

As to the first form of the argument it is evident that the

very fact that science is possible is an indubitable proof that
the order of nature is intellectual.   Science is a product of the
human mind, which is absolutely incapable of passing beyond
the laws of its own constitution.   Intuitions of reason, logical
processes of analysis, inductive or deductive inference, imagination, invention, and all the activities of the soul organize the
scientific process.   To all this external nature is found perfectly
to correspond.   Even the most subtle solutions of abstract
mathematical and mechanical problems have been subsequently
found by experiment to have been anticipated in nature.   The
laws of nature are expressions of numerical and geometrical
harmonies, and are instinct with reason and beauty.   Yet these
laws although invariable under invariable conditions, are neither eternal nor inherent in the elementary constitution of the
universe.   The properties of elemental matter are constant,
but the laws which organize them are themselves complicated
effects resulting from antecedent adjustments of these elements
themselves under the categories of time, place, quantity, and
quality.   As these adjustments change the laws change.   These
adjustments, therefore, are the cause of these laws, and the adjustments themselves must be the product either of chance,
which is absurd, or of intelligence, which is certain.

This intellectual order of nature is the first necessary postulate of all science, and it is the essence of all the processes of
the universe from the grouping of atoms to the revolution of
worlds, from the digestion of a polyp to the functional action
of the human brain.

As to the second form of this Argument.—The principle of
design presupposes the general intellectual order of the universe and her laws, and presents in advance the affirmation
that the character of the First Cause is further manifested by
the everywhere present evidence that these general laws are
made to conspire by special adjustments to the accomplishment
of ends evidently intended.   This principle is illustrated by
the mutual adjustments of the various provinces of nature, and
especially by the vegetable and animal organisms, and the relations they involve, of organ to organism, of organism to instinct, and of single organisms and classes of organisms to
each other and to their physical surroundings.   In many cases
the intention of these special adjustments is self-evident and
undeniable, as in the case of the parts of the eye to the purpose of vision.   In other cases it is more obscure and conjectural.   In the present condition of science we can understand
only in part, but from the beginning the evidence of intelligent purpose has been transparent and overwhelming.   A
single sentence proves intelligence, although the context is

undecipherable. But every advance of science discloses the same evidence over wider areas and in clearer light.

8. *State and answer the objections to the theistic inference from the evidences of special design.*

1st. Hume ("Dialogues on Natural Religion," Pt. VII., etc.,) argues that our conviction that adaptation implies design is due to experience and cannot go beyond it. That our judgment that natural organisms imply design in their cause is an inference from the analogy of human contrivance, and its effects. He argues further that this analogy is false because—(1.) The human worker is antecedently known to us as an intelligent contriver, while the author of nature is antecedently unknown, and the very object sought to be verified by the theistic inference. (2.) The processes of nature are all unlike the processes by which man executes his contrivances, and the formation of the world, and the institution of the processes of nature are peculiar effects of the like of which we have no experience.

We answer—(1.) The argument rests upon a false assumption of fact. The human contriver, the soul of our fellow-man, is *not* antecedently known to us, nor is ever in any way known except by the character of the works by which he manifests himself. And precisely in the same way and to the same extent is the Author of nature known. (2.) It rests on a false assumption of principle. The analogy of human contrivances is not the ground of our conviction that order and adaptation imply intelligence. It is a universal and necessary judgment of reason that order and adaptation can only spring from an intelligent cause, or from accident, and that the latter supposition is absurd.

2d. Some men of science, who have become habituated to the consideration of the universe as an absolute unit, all the processes of which are executed by invariable general laws (a mode of thought in which for centuries science was anticipated by Augustinian Theology), object that in inferring intention from the adjustment of parts in special groups or systems, the natural theologian had mistaken a part for a whole, and an incidental effect of a general law, resulting from special and temporary conditions, for the real end of the law itself. They hold that if even the First Cause of the universe were intelligent, it were infinitely absurd for men to presume to interpret his purpose from what we see of the special results of the working of laws working from infinite past time, through infinite space, and over an infinite system of conspiring parts.

We answer—(1.) It is self-evident that the relations of the parts of a special whole conspiring to a special end may be

fully understood, while the relations of that special whole to
the general whole may be entirely unknown, although strong
light is thrown even on this side by reason and revelation. A
single bone of an unknown species of animal gives undeniable
evidence of special adaptation, and may even, as scientists justly
claim, throw light beyond itself upon the constitution of that
otherwise unknown whole to which it belonged. (2.) We confess that this criticism, although failing as to the argument
from design, has force relatively to the mode in which that
argument has often been conceived. The older natural theologians did often to too great a degree abstract individual organisms from the great dynamic whole of which they are
products as well as parts. Dr. Flint ("Theism," p. 159) well
distinguishes between the *intrinsic*, the *extrinsic*, and the *ultimate* ends of any special adjustment. Thus the intrinsic end
of that special adjustment of parts called the eye is vision. Its
extrinsic ends are the uses it serves to the animal it belongs
to, and all the uses he serves to all he stands immediately or
remotely related to. Its ultimate end is the end of the universe itself. "Theism," p. 163—"When we affirm, then, that
final causes in the sense of intrinsic ends are in things, we
affirm merely that things are systematic unities, the parts of
which are definitely related to one another, and co-ordinated
to a common issue; and when we affirm that final causes in
the sense of extrinsic ends are in things, we affirm merely that
things are not isolated and independent systems, but systems
definitely related to other systems, and so adjusted as to be
parts or components of higher systems, and means to issues
more comprehensive than their own."

It is true indeed that a man can not discern the ultimate
end of a part until he discerns the ultimate end of the whole,
and that he can not discern *all* the extrinsic ends of any special system until he knows all its relations to all other special
systems. Nevertheless, as a man who knows nothing of the
relation of a given plant or animal to the flora or fauna of a
continent, may be absolutely certain of the functions of the
root or the claw in the economy of the plant or beast, so the
manner in which all the parts which conspire to make a special whole are adapted to effect that end may be perfectly understood, while we know nothing as yet of the extrinsic relation
of that special whole to that which is exterior to itself.

3d. It has been claimed in recent times by a certain class
of scientists that evidence for the existence of God afforded by
the order and adaptation exhibited in the processes of nature
has been very much weakened, if not absolutely invalidated,
by the assumed probability of the alternative hypothesis of

Evolution. There are many theories of Evolution, but the term in the general sense denotes the judgment that the state of the universe as a whole and in all its parts any one moment of time, has its cause in its state the immediately preceding moment, and that these changes have been brought about through the agency of powers inherent in nature, and that they may be traced back from moment to moment without any break of causal continuity through all past time.

All possible theories of Evolution, considered in their relation to theology, may be classified thus: (1.) Those which neither deny nor obscure the evidence which the order and adaptation observed in nature afford to the existence of God, and his immanence in and providential control of his works. (2) Those which, while recognizing God as the original source in the remote past, to which the origination and the primary adjustments of the universe are to be referred, yet deny his immanence and constant providential activity in his works. (3.) Those which professedly or virtually obscure or deny the evidence afforded by the order and adaptation of the universe for the existence and activity of God alike as Creator and as Providential Ruler.

With the *first* class of Evolution theories the Natural Theologian has, of course, only the most friendly interest.

As to the *second* class, which admits that a divine intelligence contrived and inaugurated the universe at the absolute beginning, yet deny that any such agent is immanent in the universe controlling its processes, WE REMARK—(1.) That the point we have at present to establish is the eternal self-existence of an intelligent First Cause; and not the mode of his relation to the universe. The latter question will be treated in subsequent chapters. (2.) It is far more philosophical, and more in accordance with a true interpretation of the scientific principle of continuity, to conceive of the First Cause as immanent in the universe, and as organically concurring with all unintelligent second causes in all processes exhibiting power or intelligence. This is recognized by that large majority of scientific men who are either orthodox Theists, or who refer all the phenomena of the physical universe to the dynamic action of the divine will. (3.) The evidence afforded by man's moral consciousness and history and ·by revelation, to the immanence and effective agency of God in all his works, is unanswerable.

As to the *third* class of Evolution theories, which do either professedly or virtually obscure or deny the evidence afforded by order or contrivance to an intelligent First Cause of the Universe, as for example the theory of Darwin as to the differentiation of all organisms through *accidental* variations occurring through unlimited time, WE REMARK—

1st. Every such scheme, when it is proposed as an account of the existing universe, must furnish a probable explanation of *all* classes of facts. It is notorious that every theory of purely natural Evolution fails utterly to explain the following facts: (1.) The origination of life. It could not have existed in the fire-mist. It could not have been generated by that which has no life. The mature decision of science to-day (1878) is expressed in the old axiom *omne vivum ex vivo*. (2.) The origin of sensation. (3.) Also of intelligence and will. (4). Also of conscience. (5.) The establishment of distinct logically corrolated and persistent types of genera and species, maintained by the law of hybridity. (6.) The origin of man. Prof. Virchow of Berlin, in his recent address at the German Association of Naturalists and Physicians at Munich, says, "You are aware that I am now specially engaged in the study of anthropology; but I am bound to declare that every positive advance which we have made in the province of prehistoric anthropology has actually removed us further from the proof of such connection (*i. e.*, the descent of man from any lower type)."

2d. But even if continuous evolution could be proved as a fact, the significance of the evidence of intelligent order and contrivance would not be in the least affected. It would only establish a method or system of means, but could in no degree alter the nature of the effect, nor the attributes of the real cause disclosed by them. (1.) The laws of abiogenesis, of reproduction, of sexual differentiation and reproduction, of heredity, of variation, such as can evolve sensation, reason, conscience, and will out of atoms and mechanical energy, would all still remain to be accounted for. (2.) Laws are never causes, but always complicated modes of action resulting from the co-action of innumerable unconscious agents. Instead, therefore, of being explanations they are the very complex effects for which reason demands an intellectual cause. (3.) All physical laws result from the original properties of matter acting under the mutual condition of certain complicated adjustments. Change the adjustments and the laws change. The laws which execute evolution, or rather into which the process of evolution is analyzed, must be referred back to the original adjustments of the material elements of the fire-mist. These adjustments, in which all future order and life is by hypothesis latent, must have been caused by chance or intelligence. Huxley in his "Criticisms on Origin of Species," p. 330, founds the whole logic of Evolution on chance thus: It has been "demonstrated that an apparatus thoroughly well-adapted to a particular purpose, may be the result of a method of trial and error worked out by unintelligent agents, as well as of the direct application of the means appropriate to that end by an intelligent agent." "According to Teleology, each organism is like a rifle bullet fired straight at a mark; according to Darwin organisms are like grape-shot, of which one hits something and the rest fall wide." The modern scientific explanation of the processes of the universe by physical causes alone, to the exclusion of mind, differs from the old long-exploded chance theory, only by the accidents (a) of the juggling use of the words "laws of nature," (b) and the assumption that chance operating through indefinate duration can accomplish the work of intelligence. But as no man can believe that any amount of time will explain the form of flint knives and arrow heads, in the absence of human agents, or that any number of throws could cast a font of type into the order of letters in the plays of Shakespeare, so no man can rationally believe that the complicated and significantly intellectual order of the universe sprang from chance. (4.) In artificial breeding man selects. In "natural selection" nature selects. Hence, if the results are the most careful adjustments to effect purpose, it follows that that characteristic must be stamped upon the organisms by nature, and hence nature itself must therefore be intelligently directed, either (a) by an intelligence immanent in her elements, or in her whole as organized, or (b) by the original adjustment of her machinery by an intelligent Creator.

9. *State the Moral Argument, or the Evidence afforded by the Moral Consciousness and History of mankind.*

The Cosmological argument led us to an eternal self-existent First Cause. The argument from the order and adaptation discovered in the processes of the universe revealed this great First Cause as possessing intelligence and will; that is, as a personal spirit. The moral or anthropological argument furnishes new data for inference, at once confirming the former conclusions as to the fact of the existence of a personal intelligent First Cause, and at the same time adding to the conception the attributes of holiness, justice, goodness, and truth. The argument from design includes the argument from cause, and the argument from righteousness and benevolence includes both the arguments from cause and from design, and adds to them a new element of its own.

This group of arguments may be stated thus:

1st. Consciousness is the fundamental ground of all knowledge. It gives us immediately the knowledge of self as existing and as the subject of certain attributes, and the agent in certain forms of activity. These souls and all their attributes must be accounted for. They have not existed from eternity. They could not have been evolved out of material elements, because—(1.) Consciousness testifies to their unity, simplicity, and spirituality. (2.) The laws of reason and the moral sense can not be explained as the result of transformed sense impressions modified by association derived by heredity (Mill and Spencer); for, (a) they are universally the same, (b) incapable of analysis, (c) necessary, and (d) sovereign over all impulses. Therefore the human soul must have been created, and its Creator must have attributes superior to his work.

2d. Man is essentially and universally a religious being. The sense of absolute dependence and moral accountability is inherent in his nature, universal and necessary. Conscience always implies responsibility to a superior, in moral authority, and therefore in moral character. It is especially implied in the sense of guilt which accompanies every violation of conscience. God is manifested and recognized in conscience as a holy, righteous, just, and intelligent will; i. e., a holy personal spirit.

3d. The adaptations of nature, as far as we can trace their relations to sentient beings, are characteristically beneficent, and evidence a general purpose to promote happiness, and to gratify a sense of beauty. This implies design, and design of a special esthetic and moral character, and proves that the First Cause is benevolent and a lover of beauty.

4th. The entire history of the human race, as far as known, discloses a moral order and purpose, which cannot be explained by the intelligence or moral purpose of the human agents concerned, which discovers an all-embracing unity of plan, comprehending all peoples and all centuries. The phenomena of social and national life, of ethnological distribution, of the development and diffusion of civilizations and religions can be explained only by the existence of a wise, righteous, and benevolent ruler and educator of mankind.

10. *State and answer the objections to the Moral Argument.*

These objections are founded—1st. On the mechanical invariability of natural laws, and their inexorable disregard of the welfare of sentient creatures. 2d. The sufferings of irrational animals. 3d. The prevalence of moral and physical evils among men. 4th. The unequal apportionment of providential favors, and the absence of all proportion between the measure of happiness allotted, and the respective moral characters of the recipients.

These difficulties, more or less trying to the faith of all, are the real occasion in the great majority of instances, of skeptical atheism. John Stewart Mill in his "Essay on Nature" ("Three Essays on Religion") describes it as the characteristic of "Nature" ruthlessly to inflict suffering and death, and affirms that the cause of nature, if a personal will, must be a monster of cruelty and injustice. In his "Essay on Theism," Pt. ii., he argues that the attempt to maintain that the author of nature, such as we know it, is at once omniscient and omnipotent and absolutely just and benevolent is abominably immoral. That he can be excused of cruelty and injustice only on the plea of limited knowledge or power, or both. He sums up his conclusion from the evidence thus: "A Being of great but limited power, how or by what limited we cannot even conjecture; of great and perhaps unlimited intelligence, but perhaps also more narrowly limited than his power: who desires and pays some regard to the happiness of his creatures, but who seems to have other motives of action which he cares more for, and who can hardly be supposed to have created the universe for that purpose only." In his "Autobiography," ch. ii., he says of his father, James Mill, "I have heard him say, that the turning point of his mind on the subject was reading Butler's Analogy. That work, of which he always continued to speak with respect, kept him, as he said, for some considerable time, a believer in the divine authority of Christianity; by proving to him, that whatever are the difficulties of believing that the Old and New Testaments proceed from, or record the acts of, a perfectly wise and good being, the same and still greater difficulties stand in the way of the belief, that a being of such a character can have been the Maker of the universe. He considered Butler's argument as conclusive against the only opponents for whom it was intended. Those who admit· an omnipotent as well as perfectly just and benevolent Maker and Ruler of such a world as this, can say little against Christianity but what can with at least equal force be retorted against themselves. Finding, therefore, no halting place in Deism, he remained in a state of perplexity, until, doubtless after many struggles, he yielded to the conviction, that concerning the origin of things nothing whatever can be known."

WE ANSWER—1st. ·It is unquestionably true that God has not created the universe for the single purpose, or even for the chief purpose, of promoting the happiness of his creatures. Our reason and observation, and the Christian Scriptures, unite in revealing as far higher and more worthy ends of divine action the manifestation of his own glory, and the promotion by education and discipline of the highest excellence of his intelligent

moral creatures. It is evident that the operation of inexorable
general laws, and the mystery and sufferings incident to this
life, may be the most effective means to promote those ends.
2d. The direct intention of all the organs with which sensitive creatures are endowed is evidently to promote their well-
being; pain and misery are incidental. Even the sudden violent deaths of irrational animals probably promote the largest
possible amount of sentient happiness. 3d. Conscience has
taught men in all ages that the sufferings incident to human
life are the direct and deserved consequences of human sin,
either penalties, or chastisements benevolently designed for
our moral improvement. 4th. The origin of sin is a confessed
mystery, relieved however by the consideration, that it results
from the abuse of man's highest and most valuable endowment,
responsible free agency, and by the fact revealed in the Christian Scriptures that even sin will be divinely overruled to the
fuller manifestation of the perfections of God, and to the higher
excellence and the more perfect happiness of the intelligent
creation. 5th. The inequalities of the allotments of providence,
and the disproportion between the well-being and the moral
characters of men in this life, results from the fact that it is
not the scene of rewards and punishments, and that different
characters and different destinies require a different educational
discipline, and it points to future readjustments revealed in the
Bible (Ps. lxxiii.). 6th. Neither the teleological nor the moral
argument involves the assertion that with our present knowledge we are able to discern in the universe the evidences of
either infinite or perfect wisdom or goodness. These are both
indicated as matters of fact, and general characteristics of nature. But our discernment of both is necessarily limited by the
imperfections of our knowledge. Even in the judgment of reason alone the infinite probability is that what appears to us
anomalous, inconsistent either with perfect wisdom or perfect
goodness, will be found, upon the attainment of more adequate
information on our part, to illustrate those very perfections
which we have been tempted to think they obscure.

11. *State the Scriptural Evidence.*

Since man is a finite and guilty and morally corrupt
creature it is unavoidable that the self-manifestations of God
in nature should be imperfectly apprehended by him. That
supernatural revelation which God has disclosed through an
historical process of special interventions in chronological successions, interpreted by a supernaturally endowed order of
prophets, and recorded in the Christian Scriptures, supple-
ments the light of nature, explains the mysteries of provi-

dence, and furnishes us with the principles of a true theodice. The God whom nature veils while it reveals him, stands before us unveiled in all the perfection of wisdom, holiness, and love in the person of Christ. He who hath seen Christ hath seen the Father. The truth of Theism is demonstrated in his person, and henceforth will never be held except by those who loyally acknowledge his Lordship over intellect and conscience and life.

12. *State the principle upon which the A priori arguments for the existence of God rest, the value of the principle, and the principal forms in which they have been presented.*

An *à posteriori* argument is one which logically ascends from facts of experience to causes, or principles. Thus by means of the preceding arguments we have been led from the facts of consciousness and of external nature to the knowledge of God as an intelligent and righteous personal spirit, the powerful, wise, and benevolent First Cause and Moral Governor. An *à priori* argument is one which proceeds from the necessary ideas of reason to the consequences necessarily deduced from them, or the truths necessarily involved in them.

It is certain that the intuitions of necessary truth are the same in all men. They are not generalizations from experience, but are presupposed in all experience. They bear the stamp of universality and necessity. They have objective validity, not depending upon the subjective state of personal consciousness, nor depending upon the nature of things, but anterior and superior to all *things*. What then can be the ground of eternal, necessary, universal, unchangeable truth, unless it be an infinite, eternal, self-existent, unchangeable nature, of whose essence they are.

We have seen that our reasons can rest only in a cause itself uncaused. An uncaused cause must be eternal, self-existent, and unchangeable. We have in our minds ideas and intuitions of infinity and perfection, as well as of eternity, self-existence, and immutability. "These, unless they are wholly delusive—which is what we are unable to conceive—must be predicable of some being. The sole question is, Of what being? It must be of him who has been proved to be the First Cause of all things, the source of all the power, wisdom, and goodness displayed in the universe. It can not be the universe itself, for that has been shown to be but an effect, to have before and behind it a Mind, a Person. It can not be ourselves, or any thing to which our senses can reach, seeing that we and they are finite, contingent, and imperfect. The author of the universe alone—the Father of our spirits, and the Giver of every good and perfect gift—can be uncreated, and unconditioned, infinite, and perfect. This completes the idea of God so far as it can be reached or formed by natural reason. And it gives consistency to the idea. The conclusions of the *à posteriori* arguments fail to satisfy either the mind or the heart until they are connected with and supplemented by, the intuition of the reason—infinity. The conception of any other than an infinite God—a God unlimited in all his perfections—is a self-contradictory conception which the intelligence refuses to entertain."—Dr. Flint, "Theism," p. 291.

1. Anselm, Archbishop of Canterbury (1093–1109), in his "*Monologium and Proslogium,*" states the argument thus: We have the idea of an infinitely perfect being. But real existence is a necessary element of infinite perfection. Therefore an infinitely perfect being exists, otherwise the infinitely perfect as we conceive it would lack an essential element of perfection. 2. Des Cartes (1596–1650) in his "*Meditationes de prima philosophia,*" prop. 2, p. 89, states it thus: The idea of an infinitely perfect being which we possess could not have originated in a finite source, and therefore must have been communicated to us by an infinitely perfect being. He also in other connections claims that this idea represents an objective reality, because (1) it is pre-eminently clear, and ideas carry conviction of correspondence to truth in proportion to their clearness, and (2) it is necessary. 3. Dr. Samuel Clarke, in 1705, published his "Demonstration of the Being and Attributes of God." He argues that time and space are infinite and necessarily existent. But they are not substances. Therefore there must exist an eternal infinite substance of which they are properties.

THE PRINCIPAL ANTI-THEISTIC THEORIES.

13. *What is Atheism?*

Atheism, according to its etymology, signifies a denial of the being of God. It was applied by the ancient Greeks to Socrates and other philosophers, to indicate that they failed to conform to the popular religion. In the same sense it was applied to the early Christians. Since the usage of the term Theism has been definitely fixed in all modern languages, atheism necessarily stands for the denial of the existence of a personal Creator and Moral Governor. Notwithstanding that the belief in a personal God is the result of a spontaneous recognition of God as manifesting himself in consciousness and the works of nature, atheism is still possible as an abnormal state of consciousness induced by sophistical speculation or by the indulgence of sinful passions, precisely as subjective idealism is possible. It exists in the following forms: 1. Practical, 2. Speculative. Again Speculative Atheism may be (1) Dogmatic, as when the conclusion is reached either (*a*) that God does not exist, or (*b*) that the human faculties are positively incapable of ascertaining or of verifying his existence (*e. g.*, Herbert Spencer, "First Principles," pt. 1). (2.) Skeptical, as when the existence is simply doubted, and the conclusiveness of the evidence generally relied upon is denied. (3.) Virtual, as when (*a.*) principles are maintained essentially inconsistent with the existence of God, or with the possibility of our knowledge of him : *e. g.*, by materialists, positivists, absolute idealists. (*b.*) When some of the essential attributes of the divine nature are denied, as by Pantheists, and by J. S. Mill in his "Essays on Religion." (*c.*) When explanations of the universe are given which exclude (*a¹*) the agency of an intelligent Creator and Governor, (*b¹*) the moral government of God, and the moral freedom of man, *e. g.*, the theories of Darwin and Spencer, and Necessitarians generally. See Ulrici, "God and Nature" and "Review of Strauss"; Strauss, "Old and New"; Buchanan, "Modern Atheism"; Tulloch, "Theism"; Flint, "Theism."

14. *What is Dualism?*

Dualism, in philosophy the opposite of Monism, is the doctrine that there are two generically distinct essences, Matter and Spirit in the universe. In this sense the common doctrine of Christendom is dualistic. All the ancient pagan philosophers held the eternal independent existence of matter, and consequently all among them who were also Theists were strictly cosmological dualists. The religion of Zoroaster was a mythological dualism designed to account for the existence of evil. Ormuzd and Ahriman, the personal principles of good and evil, sprang from a supreme abstract divinity, Akerenes. Some of the sects of this religion held dualism in its absolute form, and referred all evil to ὕλη, self-existent matter. This principle dominated among the various spurious Christian Gnostic sects in the second century, and in the system of Manes in the third century, and its prevalence in the oriental world is manifested in the ascetic tendency of the early Christian Church. See J. F. Clarke, "Ten Religions"; Hardwicke, "Christ and other Masters"; Neander's "Church History"; Pressensé, "Early Years of Christianity"; Tennemann, "Manual Hist. Philos."

15. *What is Polytheism?*

Polytheism (πολύς and θεός) distributes the perfections and functions of the infinite God among many limited gods. It sprang out of the nature-worship represented in the earliest Hindu Veds, so soon and so generally supplanting primitive monotheism. At first, as it long remained in Chaldea and Arabia, it consisted in the worship of elements, especially of the stars and of fire. Subsequently it took special forms from the traditions, the genius, and the relative civilizations of each nationality. Among the rudest savages it sank to Fetichism as in western and central Africa. Among the Greeks it was made the vehicle for the expression of their refined humanitarianism in the apotheosis of heroic men rather than the revelation of incarnate gods. In India, springing from a pantheistic philosophy, it has been carried to the most extravagant extreme, both in respect to the number, and the character of its deities. Whenever polytheism has been connected with speculation it appears as the exoteric counterpart of pantheism. Carlyle, "Hero-worship"; Max Müller, "Compar. Myth.," in Oxford Essays; Prof. Tyler, "Theology of Greek Poets."

16. What is Deism?

Deism, from *deus*, although etymologically synonymous with theism, from θεός, has been distinguished from it since the middle of the sixteenth century, and designates a system admitting the existence of a personal Creator, but denying his controlling presence in the world, his immediate moral government, and all supernatural intervention and revelation. The movement began with the English Deists, Lord Herbert of Cherbury (1581–1648), Hobbes (†1680), Shaftesbury, Bolingbroke (1678–1751), Thomas Paine (†1809), etc. It passed over to France and was represented by Voltaire and the Encyclopædists. It passed over into Germany and was represented by Lessing and Reimarus ("*Wolfenbüttel Fragmentist*"), and invading Church and Theology, it was essentially represented by the old school of naturalistic rationalists, who admitted with it a low and inconsequent form of Socinianism, *e. g.*, Eichhorn (1752–1827), Paulus (1761–1851), Wegscheider (1771–1848). It has been represented in America by the late Theodore Parker, and the extreme left of the party known as "Liberal Christians." In Germany mere deistical naturalism gave way to pantheism, as the latter has recently given way to materialistic atheism, *e. g.*, Strauss. See Leland, "View of Deistical Writers"; Van Mildert's "Boyle Lectures"; Farrar, "Critical Hist. of Freethought"; Dorner, "Hist. Protest. Theology"; Hurst, "Hist. of Rationalism"; Butler's "Analogy."

17. What is Idealism?

"Idealism is the doctrine that in external perceptions the

objects immediately known are ideas. It has been held under various forms."—See Hamilton's "Reid," Note C.

"Some of the phases of modern *Idealism* among the Germans, may be seen in the following passage from Lewes:—'I see a tree. The common psychologists tell me that there are three things implied in this one fact of vision, viz.: a tree, an image of that tree, and a mind that apprehends that image. Fichte tells me that it is I alone who exist. The tree and the image of it are one thing, and that is a modification of my mind. This is *subjective idealism.* Schelling tells me that both the tree and my *ego* (or self), are existences equally real or ideal; but they are nothing less than manifestations of the absolute, the infinite, or unconditioned. This is *objective idealism.* But Hegel tells me that all these explanations are false. The only thing really existing (in this one fact of vision) is the idea, the relation. The *ego* and the tree are but two terms of the relation, and owe their reality to it. This is *absolute idealism.* According to this, there is neither mind nor matter, heaven or earth, God or man.' The doctrine opposed to Idealism is Realism."—"Vocabulary of the Philosophical Sciences," by C. P. Krauth, D.D., 1878.

18. *What is Materialism?*

As soon as we begin to reflect we become conscious of the presence of two everywhere interlaced, but always distinct classes of phenomena—of thought, feeling, will on the one hand, and of extension, inertia, etc., on the other. Analyze these as we may, we never can resolve the one into the other. The one class we come to know through consciousness, the other through sensation, and we know the one as directly and as certainly as the other; and as we can never resolve either into the other, we refer the one class to a substance called spirit, and the other class to a substance called matter.

Materialists are a set of superficial philosophers in whom the moral consciousness is not vivid, and who have formed the habit of exclusively directing attention to the objects of the senses, and explaining physical phenomena by mechanical conceptions. Hence they fall into the fundamental error of affirming—(1.) That there is but one substance, or rather that *all* the phenomena of the universe can be explained in terms of atoms and force. (2.) That intelligence, feeling, conscience, volition, etc., are only properties of matter, or functions of material organization, or modifications of convertible energy. Intelligence did not precede and effect order and organization, but order and organization developed by laws inherent in matter develop intelligence. The German Darwinists style that system the "*mechanico-causal*" development of the universe; Huxley says life, and hence organization results from the "molecular mechanics of the protoplasm."

WE ANSWER—1st. This is no recondite theory, as some pretend, concerning substance. If the phenomena of consciousness are resolved into modifications of matter and force, *i. e.*, ultimately into some mode of motion, then all ultimate and necessary truth is impossible, duty has no absolute obligation, conscience is a lie, consciousness a delusion, and freedom of will absurd. All truth and duty, all honor and hope, all morality and religion, would be dissolved.

2d. The theory is one-sided and unwarrantable. In fact our knowledge of the soul and of its intuitions and powers are more direct and clear than the scientist's knowledge of matter. What does he know of the real nature of the atom, of force, of gravity, etc.

3d. The explanation of matter by mind, of force and order by intelligence and will, is rational. But the explanation of the phenomena of intelligence, will, and consciousness as modes of matter or force is absurd. The reason can rest in the one and can not in the other. The soul of man is known to be an absolute cause—matter is known not to be, to be but the vehicle of force, and force to be in a process of dispersion. Intelligence is known to be the cause of order and organization, organization can not be conceived to be the cause of intelligence.

Tyndal ("Athenæum" for August 29, 1868) says: "The passage from the physics of the brain to the corresponding facts of consciousness is unthinkable. Granted that a definite thought and a definite molecular action in the brain occur simultaneously: we do not possess the intellectual organ, nor apparently any rudiment of the organ, which would enable us to pass, by a process of reasoning, from the one phenomenon to the other. . . . In affirming that the growth of the body is mechanical, and that thought as exercised by us has its correlative in the physics of the brain, I think the position of the Materialist is stated as far as that position is a tenable one. I think the Materialist will be able finally to maintain this position against all attacks; but I do not think as the human mind is at present constituted, that he can pass beyond it. I do not think he is entitled to say that his molecular grouping and his molecular motions explain every thing. In reality they explain nothing."

19. *What is Pantheism?*

Pantheism ($\pi\tilde{\alpha}\nu$ θεός) is absolute monism, maintaining that the entire phenomenal universe is the everchanging existence-form of the one single universal substance, which is God. Thus God is all, and all is God. God is τό ὄν, absolute being, of which every finite thing is a differentiated and transient form. This doctrine is, of course, capable of assuming very various forms. (1.) The one-substance pantheism of Spinoza. He held that God is the one absolute substance of all things, possessing two attributes, thought and extension, from which respectively the physical and intellectual worlds proceed by an eternal, necessary, and unconscious evolution. (2.) The material pantheism of Strauss, "Old and New Faith." (3.) The idealistic pantheism of Schelling, maintaining the absolute identity of subject and object; and of Hegel, maintaining the absolute identity of thought and existence as determinations of the one absolute Spirit.

It is obvious that pantheism in all its forms must either deny the moral personality of God, or that of man, or both. Logically it renders both impossible. God comes to self-consciousness only in man; the consciousness of free personal self-determination in man is a delusion; moral responsibility is a prejudice; the supernatural is impossible and religion is superstition. Yet such is the flexibility of the system, that in one form it puts on a mystical guise, representing God as the all-person absorbing the world into himself, and in the opposite form it puts on a purely naturalistic guise, representing the world as absorbing God, and the human race in its ever-culminating development the only object of reverence or devotion. The same Spinoza who was declared by Pascal and Bossuet to be an atheist, is represented by Jacobi and Schleiermacher to be the most devout of mystics. The intense individuality of the material science of this century has reacted powerfully on pantheism, substituting materialism for idealism, retiring God, and elevating man, as is seen in the recent degradation of pantheism into atheism in the case of Feuerbach and Strauss, etc.

The most ancient, persistent, and prevalent pantheism of the world's history is that of India. As a religion it has moulded the character, customs, and mythologies of the people for 4,000 years. As a philosophy it has appeared in three principal forms—the Sanckhya, the Nyaya, and the Vedanta. Pantheistic modes of thought more or less underlay all forms of Greek philosophy, and especially the Neo-Platonic school of Plotinus (†205–270), Porphyry (233–305), and Jamblicus (†333). It reappeared in John Scotus Erigena (b. 800), and with the Neo-Platonists of the Renaissance—*e. g.*, Giordano Bruno (†1600). Modern pantheism began with Benedict Spinoza (1632–1677), and closes with the disciples of Schelling and Hegel.

Besides pure pantheism there has existed an infinite variety of impure forms of virtual pantheism. This is true of all systems that affirm the impersonality of the infinite and absolute, and which resolve all the divine attributes into modes of causality. The same is true of all systems which represent providential preservation as a continual creation, deny the real efficiency of second causes, and make God the only agent in the universe, e. g., Edwards on "Original Sin," pt. 4, ch. 3, and Emmons. Under the same general category falls the fanciful doctrine of Emanations, which was the chief feature of Oriental Theosophies, and the Hylozoism of Averröes (†1198), which supposes the co-eternity of matter and of an unconscious plastic *anima mundi.* See Hunt, "Essay on Pantheism," London, 1866; Saisset, "Modern Pantheism," Edinburgh, 1863; Cousin, "History of Modern Philosophy"; Ritter's "Hist. Ancient Philos."; Buchanan, "Faith in God," etc.; Döllinger, "Gentile and Jew," London, 1863; Max Müller, "Hist. Anc. Sancrit Lit."

CHAPTER III.

THE SOURCES OF THEOLOGY.

A general definition of Theology, Chap. I., Ques. 1.

1. *What are the two great departments into which Theology is divided?*

1st. Natural Theology, which is the science which proposes to itself these two questions: (1.) Can the real objective existence of God as a personal extramundane Spirit be established by satisfactory evidence? (2.) What may be legitimately ascertained concerning the true nature of God in himself, and concerning his relations to the universe, and especially to man, by the light of nature alone. A distinction here must be carefully observed between that knowledge of God which can be reached from the evidences afforded in his works by the powers of human reason independently of all suggestions afforded by supernatural revelation, *e. g.*, the theology of Plato and Cicero; and on the other hand, that knowledge of God which the human faculties are *now* able to deduce from the phenomena of nature under the borrowed, if unacknowledged, light of a supernatural revelation, *e. g.*, the theology of Modern Rationalists.

2d. Revealed Theology is that science which, Natural Theology presupposed, comprehends as its province all that has been revealed to us concerning God and his relation to the universe, and especially to mankind, through supernatural channels.

2. *What extreme views have been entertained as to the possibility and validity of Natural, and as distinguished from Revealed Theology?*

1st. That of Deists or naturalistic Theists, who deny either the possibility or the historical fact of a supernatural revelation, and maintain that Natural Theology discovers all that it is either possible or necessary for man now to know about God, or his relation to us. Many German supernaturalistic rationalists, while they admit the historical fact of a supernatural revelation, hold that its only office is to enforce and illustrate the truths already given in Natural Religion, which are sufficient in themselves, and need re-enforcement only because they are not sufficiently attended to by men.

This is disproved below, Ques. 7–10.

2d. The opposite extreme has been held by some Christians, that Natural Theology has no real existence; but that we are indebted to supernatural revelation for our first valid information that God exists. This is disproved—(1.) By the testimony of Scripture, Rom. i. 20–24, and ii. 14, 15, etc. (2.) By the testimony of experience, e. g., the knowledge of God attained by the more eminent heathen philosophers, however imperfect. (3.) The validity of the Theistic inference from the phenomena of consciousness and of the external world has been vindicated in Chapt. II. (4.) It is self-evident that some knowledge of God is logically presupposed in the recognition of a supernatural revelation as coming from him.

3. *State the principal answers given to the question, " What is the Source or Standard of Knowledge in Theology?"*

1st. The Theory of Schleiermacher and the Transcendental school. He was preacher and professor in Halle and Berlin from 1796 to 1834, and was the author of the "Mediation Theology," and inaugurated the movement by his "Discourses on Religion, addressed to the Educated among its Despisers," 1799, and his "Christian Faith on the Principles of the Evangelical Church," 1821.

He considered religion to be a form of feeling, and to be grounded on our constitutional God-consciousness, which consists, on the intellectual side, of an intuition of God, and on the emotional side, of a feeling of absolute dependence. Christianity consists of that specific form of this constitutional religious consciousness which was generated in the bosom of his disciples by the God-man Christ. And as human consciousness in general is generated in every individual by his social relations, so Christian consciousness is generated in communion with that society (the Church) which Christ founded and of which he is the centre of life. And as the common intuitions of men are the last appeal in all questions of natural knowledge, so the common Christian consciousness of the Church is the last appeal in all questions of Christian faith, which in its totality is the rule of Faith, and not the Scriptures.

OBJECTION. (1.) This view is inconsistent with the nature of Christianity, which as a remedial scheme rests upon certain *historical facts*, which must be known in order to be effective, and which can be authoritatively made known only by means of a supernatural revelation. No form of intuition can reach them. (2.) It is inconsistent with the uniform conviction of Christians that Christianity is a system of divinely revealed facts and principles. (3.) It affords no criterion of truth. It must regard all the doctrines of the various Church parties as reconcilable variations of the same fundamental truth. (4.) It is inconsistent with the claims of Scripture as the word of God, and with its explicit teaching, as to the nature of revelation communicating objective truth, and as to the necessity of the knowledge of the truth so conveyed in order to salvation.

2d. The Mystic Doctrine of the Inner Light, or the General Inspiration of all Men, or at least all Christians, as held by the Quakers. This view differs from Rationalism because it makes the feelings rather than the understanding the organ of religious truth, and because it regards the "inward light" as the testimony of God's Spirit to and within the human spirit. It differs from our doctrine of Inspiration because it is the practical guidance and illumination of the divine Spirit in the hearts of all believing men, and not confined to the official Founders and First Teachers of the Church. It differs from spiritual illumination, which we believe to be experienced by all truly regenerated believers only, because (1) it leads to the knowledge of truth independently of its revelation in Scripture, and (2) it belongs to all men who are willing to attend to and obey it.

OBJECTION. (1.) This view contradicts Scripture. (*a.*) Which never promises an illumination which will carry men beyond, or make men independent of its own teaching. (*b.*) They teach the absolute necessity for salvation of the objective revelation given in the written word (Rom. xi. 14–18). (2.) Is disproved by experience, which (*a*) testifies that the "inner light" affords no criterion to determine the truth of different doctrines. (*b*) that it has never availed to lead any individual or community to the knowledge of saving truth independently of the objective revelation, and (*c*) that it has always led to an irreverent depreciation of the word, and in the long run to disorder and confusion.

III. The Theory of an Inspired Church, that is inspired in the persons, or at least the official teaching, of its chief pastors and teachers. This view is refuted Chapter V.

IV. The common postulate of all Rationalists, that Reason is the source and measure of all our knowledge of God. This view is considered and refuted below, Questions 7–10.

V. The true and Protestant Doctrine. That the Scriptures of the Old and New Testaments, being given by the Inspiration of God, are his words to us, and an infallible and authoritative Rule of Faith and Practice, and to the exclusion of all others, the one source and standard of Christian Theology.

4. *What is the precise sense in which the term " Reason" is used by those who contrast it to Faith as the source of Religious Knowledge?*

The term "Reason" is used in various senses by different classes of Rationalists. By some it is used as the organ of the higher institutions apprehending necessary and ultimate truth, Such is the God-consciousness of Schleiermacher, and the intuition of the infinite of Schelling and Cousin, and such, in effect, are the moral intuitional feelings of Newman and Parker. By others "Reason" stands for the understanding, or logical faculty of observing, judging, and drawing inferences in the sphere of experience. Hence it comprehends as its ground and standard the mass of the accredited knowledge and opinion of the day. Practically all men designate by the respectable name of reason their own permanent habit and attitude of mind, with the organized mass of knowledge, opinion, and prejudice with which their minds are full. That is said to stand to reason which is congruous to that habit, or to that mass of accepted opinion.

In this controversy, however, we designate by the term "Reason" man's entire natural faculty of ascertaining the truth, including intuitions, understanding, imagination, affections and emotions, acting under natural conditions, and independently of supernatural assistance.

5. *What is Rationalism?*

A "Naturalist" is one who holds that Nature is a complete self-contained, self-supported sphere in itself, and hence denies either the reality of the supernatural, or that it can be an object of human knowledge; and hence denies the necessity, or possibility, or actual fact, of a supernatural revelation. The term "Rationalist" is more general. It includes the Naturalist of every grade, and also all those who while admitting the fact of a divine revelation, yet maintain that revelation, its doctrines and records, are all to be measured and accredited or rejected and interpreted by human reason as ultimate arbiter. With the Rationalists Reason is the ultimate ground and measure of faith.

In its historical sense Rationalism, as a mode of freethinking springing up in the midst of the Christian Church itself, giving rise to an illegitimate use of reason in the interpretation of the Scriptures and their doctrines, has always been active in some form, and in one degree or another, and has been signally manifest in a class of the Mediæval schoolmen, and in the disciples of Socinus. Its modern and most extreme form originated in Germany in the middle of the last century. The causes to which it is to be attributed were—(*a.*) The low state of religion pervading all Protestant countries. (*b.*) The influence of the formal philosophy and dogmatism of Wolf, the disciple of Leibnitz. (*c.*) The influence of the English Deists. (*d.*) The influence of the French infidels collected at the court of Frederick the Great of Prussia. The father of critical rationalism was Semler, Prof. at Halle (b. 1725, and d. 1791). Although personally devout, he arbitrarily examined the canonicity of the books of Scripture, neglecting historical evidence, and substituting his own subjective sense of fitness. He introduced the principle of "accommodation" into Biblical interpretation, holding that besides much positive truth, Christ and his apostles taught many things in "accommodation" to the ideas prevailing among their contemporaries.—Hurst, "History of Rationalism."

This tendency, afterwards greatly aggravated through the influence of Lessing and Reimarus the Wolfenbüttel Fragmentist, penetrated the mass of German theological literature, and culminated in the last years of the eighteenth and first years of the nineteenth century. Among its principal representatives were Bretschneider, Eichhorn, and Paulus in Biblical, and Wegscheider in dogmatic theology. The two last especially, while admitting the fact that Christianity is a supernatural revelation, yet maintained that it is merely a republication of the elements of natural religion, and that Reason is the supreme arbiter as to what books are to be received as canonical, and as to what they mean. Miracles were regarded as unworthy of belief. The narratives of miracles recorded in the Scriptures were referred to the ignorance, superstition, or partiality of the writers, and the miracles themselves were referred to natural causes. Jesus was regarded as a good man, and original Christianity as a sort of philosophical Socinianism. This is what has been historically designated in Germany by the title *Rationalism*, and more specifically as the *Rationalismus Vulgaris*, the old, or *common-sense* Rationalism.

After the rise of the philosophies of Fichte, Schelling and Hegel, a new impulse was given to theological ˙speculation, and to Biblical interpretation. This gave rise on the one hand to a reaction towards orthodoxy through the "Mediation Theology" of Schleiermacher, and on the other to a new school of Transcendental Rationalism, the basis of which is a pantheistic mode of thought. It necessarily denies the supernatural, and postulates the fundamental principle that miracles are impossible. This school, whose head-quarters was Tubingen, has been most prominently represented by Christian Baur with his *Tendency* Theory, Strauss with his *Mythical* theory, and Renan with his *Legendary* theory, to account for the origin of the New Testament writings, while denying their historical basis of fact.

This tendency, in various degrees of force, is manifested in the state of theological opinion in England and America, principally in the School of Coleridge, Maurice, Stanley, Jowett and Williams, and the Broad Church party generally; in Scotland in Tulloch; in America by the late Theodore Parker, the school of liberal Christians, and in the general relaxation of faith discernible on every side.

"German Rationalism," Hagenbach, Clarke Edinburg Library; "History of German Protestantism," Kahnis, Clarke Ed. Lib.; "Critical History of Free Thought," A. S. Farrar, New York, D. Appleton & Co.; "Germany, its Universities, Theology, and Religion," Philip Schaff, D.D.; "History of Rationalism," President Hurst, C. Scribner, New York.

6. *Into what two classes may all the argumentative grounds of opposition to historical Christianity be grouped?*

1st. *A priori* grounds. These rest upon a false view of the being and nature of God, and of his relation to the world. Thus the Positivist, who confines man's knowledge to Phenomena, and their laws of co-existence and sequence; the Deist, who denies the immanence of God in his works, and denies or renders remote and obscure his relation to us as Moral Governor, and spiritual Father; and the Pantheist, who denies his personality; and the scientific naturalist, who sees in nature only the operation of invariable self-executing physical laws;—must all alike deny the possibility and credibility of miracles, must resolve inspiration into genius, and in some way or other explain away the Scriptures, as historical records of fact. This class of questions has been discussed above, Chapter II.

2d. Historical and Critical grounds. These all rest on the assumed defect in the historical evidence for the genuineness and authenticity of the several books of the canon, and in the alleged discrepancies, and historical and scientific inaccuracies, found in Scripture. This class of questions must be met in the departments of Biblical Introduction, and Exegesis.

7. *State the grounds upon which it is evident that Reason is not the ultimate source and measure of religious ideas.*

These are in general three: (1.) *A priori.* Reason, considering man's present condition of ignorance, moral degradation, and guilt, has no qualities which render it competent to attain either (*a*) certainty or (*b*) sufficient information for man's practical guidance, as to God's existence, or character, or relation to us, or purposes with regard to us. (2.) From universal experience; unassisted reason has never availed for these ends, but when unduly relied upon has always led men, in spite of a neglected revelation, to skepticism and confusion. (3.) As a matter of fact an infallible record of a supernatural revelation has been given, which conveys, when interpreted with the illuminating assistance of the Holy Spirit, information, the knowledge of which is essential to salvation, which reason could by no means have anticipated.

To establish this argument the following points must be separately established in their order:

1st. A supernatural revelation is necessary for man in his present condition.

2d. A supernatural revelation is possible alike *á parte Dei* and *á parte hominis.*

3d. From what Natural Theology reveals to us of the Attributes of God, of his relations to men, and of our moral condition, a supernatural revelation is antecedently probable.

4th. It is an historical fact that Christianity is such a supernatural revelation.

5th. It is also an historical fact that the present Canon of the Old and New Testaments consist only of and contain all the extant authentic and genuine records of that revelation.

6th. That the books constituting this canon were supernaturally inspired, so as to be constituted the word of God, and an infallible and authoritative rule of faith and practice for men.

8. *Prove that a supernatural revelation is necessary for men in their present condition.*

1st. Reason itself teaches—(1) that as a matter of fact man's moral nature is disordered, and (2) his relations to God disturbed by guilt and alienation. Reason is capable of discovering the fact of sin, but makes no suggestions as to its remedy. We can determine *à priori* God's determination to punish sin, because that as a matter of Justice rests on his unchangeable and necessary nature, but can so determine nothing with respect to his disposition to provide, or to allow a remedy, because that, as a matter of grace, rests on his simple volition.

2d. A spontaneous religious yearning, natural and universal, for a divine self-revelation and intervention on the part of God, and manifest in all human history, proves its necessity.

3d. Reason has never in the case of any historical community availed to lead men to certainty, to satisfy their wants, or
to rule their lives.

4th. Rationalism is strong only for attack and destruction.
It has never availed in any considerable degree in the way of
positive construction. No two prominent Rationalists agree as
to what the positive and certain results of the teaching of reason are.

9. *Prove that a supernatural revelation is possible both à parte
Dei, and à parte hominis.*

As to its being possible on God's side, if Theism be true, if
God be an infinite extramundane person, who yet controls the
operation of the laws he has ordained as his own methods, and
has subordinated the physical system to the higher interests of
his moral government—then obviously to limit him as to the
manner, character, or extent of his self-manifestations to his
creatures is transcendently absurd. All the philosophical presumptions, which render a supernatural revelation on the part
of God impossible, are based on Deistic, Materialistic, or Pantheistic principles. We have exhibited the argument for Theism in Chapter II.

As to its being possible on man's side, it has been argued
by modern transcendental rationalists that the communication
of new truth by means of a "book revelation" is impossible.
That words are conventional signs which have power to excite
in the mind only those ideas which, having been previously
apprehended, have been conventionally associated with those
words.

WE ANSWER—1st. We admit that simple ultimate ideas
which admit of no analysis, must in the first instance be apprehended by an appropriate organ in an act of spontaneous intuition. No man can attain the idea of color except through the
act of his own eyes, nor the idea of right except by an intuitive
act of his own moral sense. But, 2d, the Christian revelation
involves no new simple ultimate ideas incapable of analysis.
They presuppose and involve the matter of all such natural
intuitions, and they excite the rational and moral intuitions
to a more active and normal exercise by association with new
aspects of our divine relations, but for the most part they nar-
rate objective and concrete facts, they explain the application
of intuitive principles to our actual historical condition and
relations; they state the purposes, requirements, and promises
of God. But, 3d, even new simple ideas may be excited in the
mind by means of a supernatural inward spiritual illumination
acting on the minds of the subject of religious experience. The

work of the Holy Spirit accompanying the written word completes the revelation. An experienced Christian, under the teaching of the Holy Spirit through the word, has as clear and certain a knowledge of the matter involved in his new experience, as he has of the matter of his perceptions through his bodily senses.

10. *Show from the data of Natural Theology that in the present state of human nature a supernatural revelation is antecedently probable.*

As shown in Chapt. II., Natural Theology ascertains for us an infinite, eternal, wise, and absolutely righteous and benevolent personal God. It ascertains also that man created in the divine image is morally corrupt and judicially condemned. It reveals to us man needing divine help, yearning and hoping for it, and therefore not incapable of it, as are the finally lost demons. Therefore all the perfections of God, and all the miseries of men, lead to the rational hope that at some time and in some way God may be graciously disposed to intervene supernaturally for man's help, and reveal his character and purposes more fully for man's guidance.

11. *How may it be proved that it is an historical fact that Christianity is such a supernatural revelation?*

The reader must here be referred to the many and excellent treatises on the Evidences of Christianity.

Paley's, Chalmers', Erskine's, and Alexander's works on the Evidences; A. S. Farrar's "Critical History of Free Thought"; Hopkins's "Evidences of Christianity"; Barnes's "Evidences of Christianity in the Nineteenth Century"; G. Wardlaw's "Leading Evidences of Christianity"; Hetherington's "Apologetics of the Christian Faith"; Leathes's "Grounds of Christian Hope"; Row's "Supernatural in the New Testament"; Rogers's "Superhuman Origin of the Bible"; Christlieb's "Modern Doubt and Christian Belief"; Rawlinson's "Historical Evidence of the Truth of the Scripture Records"; Wace's "Christianity and Morality"; Titcomb's "Cautions for Doubters"; Pearson's "Prize Essay on Infidelity"; F. W. Farrar's "Witness of History to Christ."

12. *How can it be proved that the accepted Canon of the Old and New Testament consists only of, and contains all the authentic and genuine records of the Christian Revelation?*

Here also the reader must be referred to the best treatises on the Canon of holy Scriptures. B. F. Westcott, on "The Canon" and on "Introduction to the Study of the Gospels"; Tischendorf, "When were our Gospels composed?" E. Cone Bissell, "Historic Origin of the Bible"; Prof. George P. Fisher, "The Supernatural Origin of Christianity," and "The Beginnings of Christianity."

13. *What is the Nature and Extent of the Inspiration of the Christian Scriptures?*

See below, Chapter IV.

14. *What is the legitimate office of Reason in the sphere of Religion?*

1st. Reason is the primary revelation God has made to man, necessarily presupposed in every subsequent revelation of whatever kind. 2d. Hence Reason, including the moral and emotional nature, and experience, must be the organ by means of which alone all subsequent revelations can be apprehended and received. A revelation addressed to the irrational would be as inconsequent as light to the blind. This is the *usus organicus* of reason. 3d. Hence no subsequent revelation can contradict reason acting legitimately within its own sphere. For then (1) God would contradict himself, and (2) faith would be impossible. To believe is to assent to a thing as true, but to see that it contradicts reason, is to see that it is *not* true. Hence the Reason has the office in judging the Evidences or in interpreting the Records of a supernatural revelation, of exercising the *judicium contradictionis.* Reason has therefore to determine two questions: 1st. Does God speak? 2d. What does God say? This, however, requires (*a*) the co-operation of all the faculties of knowing, moral as well as purely intellectual, (*b*) a modest and teachable spirit, (*c*) perfect candor and loyalty to truth, (*d*) willingness to put all known truth to practice, (*e*) the illumination and assistance of the promised Spirit of truth.

This is the old distinction between what is contrary to reason, and what is above it. It is evident that it is the height of absurdity for reason to object to an otherwise accredited revelation that its teaching is incomprehensible, or that it involves elements apparently irreconcilable with other truths. Because—(1.) This presumes that human reason is the highest form of intelligence, which is absurd. (2.) In no other department do men limit their faith by their ability to understand. What do men of science understand as to the ultimate nature of atoms, of inertia, of gravity, of force, of life? They are every moment forced to assume the truth of the impossible, and acknowledge the inexplicability of the certain.

All speculative infidelity springs out of the insane pride of the human mind, the insatiate rage for explanation, and, above all, for the resolution of all knowledge to apparent logical unity. Common sense, and the habit of reducing opinions to actual practice, leads to health of mind and body, and to religious faith.

15. *What is Philosophy, and what is its relation to Theology?*

Philosophy, in its wide sense, embraces all human knowledge, acquired through the use of man's natural faculties, and consists of that knowledge interpreted and sytematized by the reason. Science is more specific, relating to some special department of knowledge thoroughly reduced to system. In later days the word Science is becoming more and more definitely appropriated to the knowledge of the physical phenomena of the universe. In this sense Science has for its task the determination of phenomena in their classifications of likeness and unlikeness, and their laws or order of co-existence and succession, and does not inquire into substance, or cause, or purpose, etc. Philosophy is presupposed, therefore, in science as the first and most general knowledge. It inquires into the soul and the laws of thought, into intuition and ultimate truth, into substance and real being, into absolute cause, the ultimate nature of force and will, into conscience and duty.

As to its relations to Theology it will be observed—

1st. The first principles of a true philosophy are presupposed in all theology, natural and revealed.

2d. The Holy Scriptures, although not designed primarily to teach philosophy, yet necessarily presuppose and involve the fundamental principles of a true philosophy. Not the inferences of these principles drawn out into a system, but the principles themselves, as to substance and cause, as to conscience and right, etc.

3d. The philosophy prevalent in every age has always and will necessarily react upon the interpretation of Scripture and the formation of theological systems. This has been true as to the early Platonism, and the Neo-Platonism of the second age; as to the Aristotelian philosophy of the middle ages; as to the systems of Des Cartes and Leibnitz; of Kant, Fichte, Schelling, and Hegel on the continent, and the systems of Locke, Reid, Coleridge, etc., in Britain.

4th. The devout believer, however, who is assured that the Bible is the very word of God, can never allow his philosophy, derived from human sources, to dominate his interpretation of the Bible, but will seek with a docile spirit and with the assistance of the Holy Spirit, to bring his own philosophy into perfect harmony with that which is implicitly contained in the word. He will, by all means, seek to realize a philosophy which proves itself to be the genuine and natural handmaid of the religion which the word reveals.

All human thought, and all human life, is one. If therefore God speaks for any purpose, his word must be supreme, and in so far as it has any bearing on any department of human opinion or action, it must therein be received as the most certain informant and the highest Law.

The various departments of Christian Theology have been ennumerated in Chapter I.

CHAPTER IV.

THE INSPIRATION OF THE BIBLE.

NECESSARY PRESUPPOSITIONS.

1. *What are the necessary presuppositions, as to principles, and matters of fact, which must be admitted before the possibility of inspiration, or the inspiration of any particular book can be affirmed?*

1st. The existence of a personal God, possessing the attributes of power, intelligence, and moral excellence in absolute perfection.

2d. That in his relation to the universe he is at once immanent and transcendant. Above all, and freely acting upon all from without. Within all, and acting through the whole and every part from within, in the exercise of all his perfections, and according to the laws and modes of action he has established for his creatures, sustaining and governing them, and all their actions.

3d. His moral government over mankind and other intelligent creatures, whereby he governs them by truth and motives addressed to their reason and will, rewards and punishes them according to their moral characters and actions, and benevolently educates them for their high destiny in his communion and service.

4th. The fact that mankind, instead of advancing along a line of natural development from a lower to a higher moral condition, have fallen from their original state and relation, and are now lost in a condition involving corruption and guilt, and incapable of recovery without supernatural intervention.

5th. The historical integrity of the Christian Scriptures, their veracity as history, and the genuineness and authenticity of the several books.

6th. The truth of Christianity in the sense in which it is set forth in the sacred record.

All of these necessary presuppositions, the truth of which is involved in the doctrine that the Scriptures are inspired, fall under one of two classes—

(1.) Those which rest upon intuition and the moral and spiritual evidences of divine truth, such as the being and attributes of God, and his relations to world and to mankind, such as the testimony of conscience and the moral consciousness of men as sinners justly condemned, and impotent.

(2.) Those which rest upon matters of fact, depending upon historical and critical evidence as to the true origin and contents of the sacred books.

If any of these principles or facts are doubted, the evidence substantiating them should be sought in their appropriate sources, *e. g.*, the department of Apologetics—the Theistic argument and Natural Theology, the evidences of Christianity, the Historic Origin of the Scriptures, the Canon, and Criticism and Exegesis of the Sacred Text.

STATEMENT OF THE CHURCH DOCTRINE OF INSPIRATION.

2. *In what sense and to what extent has the Church universally held the Bible to be inspired?*

That the sacred writers were so influenced by the Holy Spirit that their writings are as a whole and in every part God's word to us—an authoritative revelation to us from God, indorsed by him, and sent to us as a rule of faith and practice, the original autographs of which are absolutely infallible when interpreted in the sense intended, and hence are clothed with absolute divine authority.

3. *What is meant by "plenary inspiration"?*

A divine influence full and sufficient to secure its end. The end in this case secured is the perfect infallibility of the Scriptures in every part, as a record of fact and doctrine both in thought and verbal expression. So that although they come to us through the instrumentality of the minds, hearts, imaginations, consciences, and wills of men, they are nevertheless in the strictest sense the word of God.

4. *What is meant by the phrase "verbal inspiration," and how can it be proved that the words of the Bible were inspired?*

It is meant that the divine influence, of whatever kind it may have been, which accompanied the sacred writers in what they wrote, extends to their expression of their thoughts in language, as well as to the thoughts themselves. The effect being that in the original autograph copies the language expresses the thought God intended to convey with infallible accuracy, so that the words as well as the thoughts are God's revelation to us.

That this influence did extend to the words appears—1st, from the very design of inspiration, which is, not to secure the infallible correctness of the opinions of the inspired men themselves (Paul and Peter differed, Gal. ii. 11, and sometimes the prophet knew not what he wrote), but to secure an infallible record of the truth. But a record consists of language.

2d. Men think in words, and the more definitely they think the more are their thoughts immediately associated with an exactly appropriate verbal expression. Infallibility of thought can not be secured or preserved independently of an infallible verbal rendering.

3d. The Scriptures affirm this fact, 1 Cor. ii. 13; 1 Thess. ii. 13.

4th. The New Testament writers, while quoting from the Old Testament for purposes of argument, often base their argument upon the very words used, thus ascribing authority to the word as well as the thought.—Matt. xxii. 32, and Ex. iii. 6, 16; Matt. xxii. 45, and Psalms cx. 1; Gal. iii. 16, and Gen. xvii. 7.

5. *By what means does the Church hold that God has effected the result above defined?*

The Church doctrine recognizes the fact that every part of Scripture is at once a product of God's and of man's agency. The human writers have produced each his part in the free and natural exercise of his personal faculties under his historical conditions. God has also so acted concurrently in and through them that the whole organism of Scripture and every part thereof is his word to us, infallibly true in the sense intended and absolutely authoritative.

God's agency includes the three following elements:

1st. His PROVIDENTIAL agency in producing the Scriptures. The whole course of redemption, of which revelation and inspiration are special functions, was a special providence directing the evolution of a specially providential history. Here the natural and the supernatural continually interpenetrate. But, as is of necessity the case, the natural was always the rule and the supernatural the exception; yet as little subject to accident, and as much the subject of rational design as the natural itself. Thus God providentially produced the very man for the precise occasion, with the faculties, qualities, education, and gracious experience needed for the production of the intended writing. Moses, David, Isaiah, Paul, or John, genius and character, nature and grace, peasant, philosopher, or prince, the man, and with him each subtile personal accident, was providentially prepared at the proper moment as the necessary instrumental precondition of the work to be done.

2d. REVELATION of truth not otherwise attainable. Whenever the writer was not possessed, or could not naturally become possessed, of the knowledge God intended to communicate, it was supernaturally revealed to him by vision or language. This revelation was supernatural, objective to the recipient, and assured to him to be truth of divine origin by appropriate evidence. This direct revelation applies to a large element of the sacred Scriptures, such as prophecies of future events, the peculiar doctrines of Christianity, the promises and threatenings of God's word, etc., but it applies by no means to all the contents of Scripture.

3d. INSPIRATION. The writers were the subjects of a plenary divine influence, called inspiration, which acted upon and through their natural faculties in all they wrote, directing them in the choice of subject and the whole course of thought and verbal expression, so as while not interfering with the natural exercise of their faculties, they freely and spontaneously produce the very writing which God designed, and which thus possesses the attributes of infallibility and authority as above defined.

This inspiration differs, therefore, from revelation—(1.) In that it was a constant experience of the sacred writers in all they wrote, and it affects the equal infallibility of all the elements of the writings they produced. While, as before said, revelation was supernaturally vouchsafed only when it was needed. (2.) In that revelation communicated objectively to the mind of the writer truth otherwise unknown. While Inspiration was a divine influence flowing into the sacred writer subjectively, communicating nothing, but guiding their faculties in their natural exercise to the producing an infallible record of the matters of history, doctrine, prophecy, etc., which God designed to send through them to his Church.

It differs from spiritual illumination, in that spiritual illumination is an essential element in the sanctifying work of the Holy Spirit common to all true Christians. It never leads to the knowledge of new truth, but only to the personal discernment of the spiritual beauty and power of truth already revealed in the Scriptures.

Inspiration is a special influence of the Holy Spirit peculiar to the prophets and apostles, and attending them only in the exercise of their functions as accredited teachers. Most of them were the subjects both of inspiration and spiritual illumination. Some, as Balaam, being unregenerate were inspired, though destitute of spiritual illumination.

The Proof of the Church Doctrine of Inspiration.

6. *From what sources of evidence is the question as to the nature and extent of the Inspiration of the Scriptures to be determined?*

1st. From the statements of the Scriptures themselves.

2d. From the phenomena of Scripture when critically examined.

The Statements of the Scriptures as to the Nature of their own Inspiration.

7. *How can the propriety of proving the Inspiration of the Scriptures from their own assertions be vindicated?*

We do not reason in a circle when we rest the truth of the inspiration of the Scriptures on their own assertions. We come to this question already believing in their credibility as histories, and in that of their writers as witnesses of facts, and in the truth of Christianity and in the divinity of Christ. Whatever Christ affirms of the Old Testament, and whatever he promises to the Apostles, and whatever they assert as to the divine influence acting in and through themselves, or as to the infallibility and authority of their writings, must be true. Especially as all their claims were indorsed by God working with them by signs and wonders and gifts of the Holy Ghost. It is evident that if their claims to Inspiration and to the infallibility and authority of their writings are denied, they are consequently charged with fanatical presumption and gross misrepresentation, and the validity of their testimony on all points is denied. When plenary inspiration is denied all Christian faith is undermined.

8. *How may the Inspiration of the apostles be fairly inferred from the fact that they wrought miracles?*

A miracle is a divine sign ($\sigma\eta\mu\epsilon\tilde{\iota}o\nu$) accrediting the person to whom the power is delegated as a divinely commissioned agent, Matt. xvi. 1, 4; Acts xiv. 3; Heb. ii. 4. This divine testimony not only encourages, but absolutely renders belief obligatory. Where the sign is God commands us to believe. But he could not unconditionally command us to believe any other than unmixed truth infallibly conveyed.

9. *How may it be shown that the gift of Inspiration was promised to the apostles?*

Matt. x. 19; Luke xii. 12; John xiv. 26; xv. 26, 27; xvi. 13; Matt. xxviii. 19, 20; John xiii. 20.

10. *In what several ways did they claim to have possession of the Spirit?*

They claimed—

1st. To have the Spirit in fulfilment of the promise of Christ. Acts ii. 33; iv. 8; xiii. 2–4; xv. 28; xxi. 11; 1 Thes. i. 5.

2d. To speak as the prophets of God.—1 Cor. iv. 1; ix. 17; 2 Cor. v. 19; 1 Thes. iv. 8.

3d. To speak with plenary authority.—1 Cor. ii. 13; 1 Thes. ii. 13; 1 John iv. 6; Gal. i. 8, 9; 2 Cor. xiii. 2, 3, 4. They class their writings on a level with the Old Testament Scriptures.— 2 Pet. iii. 16; 1 Thes. v. 27; Col. iv. 16; Rev. ii. 7.—Dr. Hodge.

11. *How was their claim confirmed?*

1st. By their holy, simple, temperate, yet heroic lives.

2d. By the holiness of the doctrine they taught, and its spiritual power, as attested by its effect upon communities and individuals.

3d. By the miracles they wrought.—Heb. ii. 4; Acts xiv. 3; Mark xvi. 20.

4th. All these testimonies are accredited to us not only by their own writings, but also by the uniform testimony of the early Christians, their contemporaries, and their immediate successors.

12. *Show that the writers of the Old Testament claim to be inspired.*

1st. Moses claimed that he wrote a part at least of the Pentateuch by divine command.—Deut. xxxi. 19–22; xxxiv. 10; Num. xvi. 28, 29. David claimed it.—2 Sam. xxiii. 2.

2d. As a characteristic fact, the Old Testament writers speak not in their own name, but preface their messages with, "Thus saith the Lord," "The mouth of the Lord hath spoken it," etc.— Jer. ix. 12; xiii. 13; xxx. 4; Isa. viii. 1; xxxiii. 10; Mic. iv. 4; Amos iii. 1; Deut. xviii. 21, 22; 1 Kings xxi. 28; 1 Chron. xvii. 3.—Dr. Hodge.

13. *How was their claim confirmed?*

1st. Their claim was confirmed to their cotemporaries by the miracles they wrought, by the fulfilment of many of their predictions (Num. xvi. 28, 29), by the holiness of their lives, the moral and spiritual perfection of their doctrine, and the practical adaptation of the religious system they revealed to the urgent wants of men.

2d. Their claim is confirmed to us principally—(1.) By the remarkable fulfillment, in far subsequent ages, of many of their prophesies. (2.) By the evident relation of the symbolical religion which they promulgated to the facts and doctrines of Christianity, proving a divine preadjustment of the type to the antitype. (3.) By the indorsement of Christ and his apostles.

14. *What are the formulas by which quotations from the Old Testament are introduced into the New, and how do these forms of expression prove the inspiration of the ancient Scriptures?*

"The Holy Ghost saith," Heb. iii. 7. "The Holy Ghost this signifying," Heb. ix. 8. "God saith," Acts ii. 17, and Isa. xliv. 3; 1 Cor. ix. 9, 10, and Deut. xxv. 4. "The Scriptures saith," Rom. iv. 3; Gal. iv. 30. "It is written," Luke xviii. 31; xxi. 22; John ii. 17; xx. 31. "The Lord by the mouth of his servant David says," Acts iv. 25, and Ps. ii. 1, 2. "The Lord limiteth in David a certain day, saying," Heb. iv. 7; Ps. xcv. 7. "David in spirit says," Matt. xxii. 43, and Ps. cx. 1.

Thus these Old Testament writings are what God saith, what God saith by David, etc., and are quoted as the authoritative basis for conclusive argumentation; therefore they must have been inspired.

15. *How may the Inspiration of the Old Testament writers be proved by the express declarations of the New Testament?*

Luke i. 70; Heb. i. 1; 2 Tim. iii. 16; 1 Pet. i. 10–12; 2 Pet. i. 21.

16. *What is the argument on this subject drawn from the manner in which Christ and his apostles argue from the Old Testament as of final authority?*

Christ constantly quotes the Old Testament, Matt. xxi. 13; xxii. 43. He declares that it can not be falsified, John vii. 23; x. 35; that the whole law *must* be fulfilled, Matt. v. 18; and all things also foretold concerning himself "in Moses, the prophets, and the Psalms," Luke xxiv. 44. The apostles habitually quote the Old Testament in the same manner, "That it might be fulfilled which was written," is with them a characteristic formula, Matt. i. 22; ii. 15, 17, 23; John xii. 38; xv. 25; etc. They all appeal to the words of Scripture as of final authority. This certainly proves infallibility.

The Phenomena of Scripture considered as Evidence of the Nature and Extent of its Inspiration.

17. *What evidence do the Phenomena of the Scriptures afford as to nature and extent of the human causes conspiring to produce them?*

Every part of Scripture alike bears evidence of a human origin. The writers of all the books were men, and the process of composition through which they originated was characteristically human. The personal characteristics of thought and feeling of these writers have acted spontaneously in their literary activity, and have given character to their writings in a manner precisely similar to the effect of character upon writing in the case of other men. They wrote from human impulses, on special occasions, with definite design. Each views his subject from an individual standpoint. They gather their material from all sources,—personal experience and observation, ancient documents, and contemporary testimony. They arrange their material with reference to their special purpose, and draw inferences from principles and facts according to the more or less logical habits of their own minds. Their emotions and imaginations are spontaneously exercised, and flow as co-factors with their reasoning into their compositions. The limitations of their personal knowledge and general mental condition, and the defects of their habits of thought and style, are as obvious in their writings as any other personal characteristics. They use the language and idiom proper to their nation and class. They adopt the *usus loquendi* of terms current among their people, without committing themselves to the philosophical ideas in which the usage originated. Their mental habits and methods were those of their nation and generation. They were for the most part Orientals, and hence their writings abound with metaphor and symbol; and although always reliable in statement as far as required for their purpose, they never aimed at the definiteness of enumeration, or chronological or circumstantial narration, which characterizes the statistics of modern western nations. Like all purely literary men of every age, they describe the order and the facts of nature according to their appearances, and not as related to their abstract law or cause.

Some of these facts have, by many careless thinkers, been supposed to be inconsistent with the asserted fact of divine guidance. But it is evident, upon reflection, that if God is to reveal himself at all, it must be under all the limits of human modes of thought and speech. And if he inspires human agents to communicate his revelation in writing, he must use them in a manner consistent with their nature as rational and spontaneous agents. And it is evident that all the distinctions between the different degrees of perfection in human knowledge, and elegance in human dialect and style, are nothing when viewed in the light of the common relations of man to God. He obviously could as well reveal himself through a peasant as through a philosopher; and all the better when the personal characteristics of the peasant were providentially and graciously preadjusted to the special end designed.

18. *What evidence do the Phenomena of the Scriptures afford as to the nature and extent of the divine agency exercised in their production?*

1st. Every part of Scripture affords moral and spiritual evidence of its divine origin. This is, of course, more conspicuous in some portions than in others. There are transcendant truths revealed, a perfect morality, an unveiling of the absolute perfections of the Godhead, a foresight of future events, a heart-searching and rein-trying knowledge of the secrets of the human soul, a light informing the reason and an authority binding the conscience, a practical grasp of all the springs of human experience and life, all of which can only have originated in a divine source. These are characteristics of a large portion of the Scriptures, and of the Scriptures alone in all literature, and together with the accompanying witness of the Holy Ghost, these are practically the evidences upon which the faith of a majority of believers rests.

2d. But another characteristic of the Scriptures, taken in connection with the foregoing, proves incontestibly their divine origin as a whole and in every part. The sacred Scriptures are an organism, that is an whole composed of many parts, the parts all differing in matter, form, and structure from each other, like the several members of the human body, yet each adjusted to each other and to the whole, through the most intricate and delicate correlations mediating a common end. Scripture is the record and interpretation of redemption. Redemption is a work which God has prepared and wrought out by many actions in succession through an historical process occupying centuries. A supernatural providence has flowed forward evolving a system of divine interventions, accompanied and interpreted by a supernaturally informed and guided order of prophets. Each writer has his own special and temporary occasion, theme, and audience. And yet each contributed to build up the common organism, as the providential history has advanced, each special writing beyond its temporary purpose

taking its permanent place as a member of the whole, the
gospel fulfilling the law, antitype has answered to type and
fulfilment to prophecy, history has been interpreted by doctrine, and doctrine has given law to duty and to life. The
more minutely the contents of each book are studied in the
light of its special purpose, the more wonderfully various and
exact will its articulations in the general system and ordered
structure of the whole be discovered to be. This is the highest
conceivable evidence of design, which in the present case is
the proof of a divine supernatural influence comprehending the
whole, and reaching to every part, through sixteen centuries,
sixty-six distinct writings, and about forty co-operating human
agents. Thus the divine agency in the genesis of every part
of Scripture is as clearly and certainly determined as it is in
the older genesis of the heavens and the earth.

19. *What is the objection to this doctrine drawn from the free
manner in which the New Testament writers quote those of the Old
Testament, and the answer to that objection?*

In a majority of instances the New Testament writers quote
those of the Old Testament with perfect verbal accuracy. Sometimes they quote the Septuagint version, when it conforms to the
Hebrew; at others they substitute a new version; and at other
times again they adhere to the Septuagint, when it differs from
the Hebrew. In a number of instances, which however are
comparatively few, their quotations from the Old Testament
are made very freely, and in apparent accommodation of the
literal sense.

Rationalistic interpreters have argued from this last class
of quotations that it is impossible that both the Old Testament
writer quoted from, and the New Testament writer quoting,
could have been the subjects of plenary inspiration, because,
say they, if the *ipsissima verba* were infallible in the first instance, an infallible writer would have transferred them unchanged. But surely if a human author may quote himself
freely, changing the expression, and giving a new turn to
his thought in order to adapt it the more perspicuously to his
present purpose, the Holy Spirit may take the same liberty
with his own. The same Spirit that rendered the Old Testament writers infallible in writing only pure truth, in the very
form that suited his purpose then, has rendered the New Testament writers infallible in so using the old materials, that
while they elicit a new sense, they teach only the truth, the
very truth moreover contemplated in the mind of God from
the beginning, and they teach it with divine authority.—See
Fairbairn's "Herm. Manual," Part III. Each instance of such

quotation should be examined in detail. as Dr. Fairbairn has done.

20. *What objection to the doctrine of Plenary Inspiration is drawn from the alleged fact that "Discrepancies" exist in the Scriptural Text? and how is this objection to be answered?*

It is objected that the sacred text contains numerous statements which are inconsistent with other statements made in some part of Scripture itself, or with some certainly ascertained facts of history or of science.

It is obvious that such a state of facts, even if it could be proved to exist, would not, in opposition to the abundant positive evidence above adduced, avail to disprove the claim that the Scriptures are to some extent and in some degree the product of divine inspiration. The force of the objection would depend essentially upon the number and character of the instances of discrepancy actually proved to exist, and would bear not upon the fact of Inspiration, but upon its nature and degree and extent.

The fact of the actual existence of any such "discrepancies," it is evident, can be determined only by the careful examination of each alleged case separately. This examination belongs to the departments of Biblical Criticism and Exegesis. The following considerations, however, are evidently well-grounded, and sufficient to allay all apprehension on the subject.

1st. The Church has never held the verbal infallibility of our translations, nor the perfect accuracy of the copies of the original Hebrew and Greek Scriptures now possessed by us. These copies confessedly contain many "discrepancies" resulting from frequent transcription. It is, nevertheless, the unanimous testimony of Christian scholars, that while these variations embarrass the interpretation of many details, they neither involve the loss nor abate the evidence of a single essential fact or doctrine of Christianity. And it is moreover reassuring to know that believing criticism, by the discovery and collation of more ancient and accurate copies, is constantly advancing the Church to the possession of a more perfect text of the original Scriptures than she has enjoyed since the apostolic age.

2d. The Church has asserted absolute infallibility only of the original autograph copies of the Scriptures as they came from the hands of their inspired writers. And even of these she has not asserted infinite knowledge, but only absolute infallibility in stating the matters designed to be asserted. A "discrepancy," therefore, in the sense in which the new critics affirm and the Church denies its existence, is a form of statement existing in the original text of the Hebrew and Greek Scriptures evidently designed to assert as true that which is in plain irreconcilable contradiction to other statements existing in some other portions of the same original text of Scripture, or to some other certainly ascertained element of human knowledge. A "discrepancy" fulfilling in every particular this definition must be proved to exist, or the Church's doctrine of plenary verbal inspiration remains unaffected.

3d. It is beyond question, that, in the light of all that the Scriptures themselves assert or disclose as to the nature and the extent of the divine influence controlling their genesis, and as to their authority over man's conscience and life as the voice of God, the existence of any such "discrepancies" as above defined is a violent improbability. Those who assert the existence of one or more of them must bring them out, and prove to the community of competent judges, that all the elements of the above definition meet in each alleged instance, not probably merely, but beyond the possibility of doubt. The *onus probandi* rests exclusively on them.

4th. But observe that this is for them a very difficult task to perform, one in any instance indeed hardly possible. For to make good their point against the vast presumptions opposed to it, they must prove over and over again in the case of each alleged discrepancy each of the following points: (1.) That the alleged discrepant statement certainly occurred in the veritable autograph copy of the inspired writing containing it. (2.) That their interpretation of the statement, which occasions the discrepancy, is the only possible one, the one it was certainly intended to bear. The difficulty of this will be apprehended when we estimate the inherent obscurity of ancient narratives, unchronological, and fragmentary, with a background and surroundings of almost unrelieved darkness. This condition of things which so often puzzles the interpreter, and prevents the apologist from proving the harmony of the narrative, with equal force baffles all the ingenious efforts of the rationalistic critic to demonstrate the "discrepancy." Yet this he must do, or the presumption will remain that it does not exist. (3.) He must also prove that the facts of science or of history, or the Scriptural statements, with which the statement in question is asserted to be inconsistent, are real facts or real parts of the autograph text of canonical Scripture, and that the sense in which they are found to be inconsistent with the statement in question is the only sense they can rationally bear. (4.) When the reality of the opposing facts or statements is determined, and their true interpretation is ascertained, then it must, in conclusion, be shown not only that they appear inconsistent, nor merely that their reconciliation is impossible in our present state of knowledge, but that they are in themselves essentially incapable of being reconciled.

5th. Finally it is sufficient for the present purpose, to point to the fact that no single case of "discrepancy," as above defined, has been so proved to exist as to secure the recognition of the community of believing scholars. Difficulties in interpretation and apparently irreconcilable statements exist, but no "discrepancy" has been proved. Advancing knowledge removes some difficulties and discovers others. It is in the highest degree probable that perfect knowledge would remove all.

21. *Explain the meaning of such passages as* 1 Cor. vii. 6 and 12 and 40, Rom. iii. 5 and vi. 19, and Gal. iii. 15, *and show their perfect consistency with the fact of the plenary inspiration of the whole Bible.*

"I speak as a man," is a phrase occurring frequently, and its sense is determined by the context. In Romans iii. 5, it signifies that Paul was, for argument's sake, using the language common to men; it was the Jews' opinion, not his own. In Rom. vi. 19, it signifies "in a manner adapted to human comprehension," and in Gal. iii. 15, it signifies "I use an illustration drawn from human affairs," etc.

"I speak this by permission, not of commandment."—1 Cor. vii. 6, refers to verse ii. Marriage was always permitted, but under certain circumstances inexpedient.

"And unto the married I command, *yet* not I but the Lord." "But to the rest speak I, not the Lord."—1 Cor. vii. 10 and 12. Reference is here made to what the "Lord," that is Christ, taught in person while on earth. The distinction is made between what Christ taught while on earth, and what Paul teaches. As Paul puts his word here on an equal basis of authority with Christ's word, it of course implies that Paul claims an inspiration which makes his word equal to that of Christ in infallibility and authority.

"And I think also that I have the Spirit of God."—1 Cor. vii. 40. "*I think* (δοκῶ) *I have*, is only, agreeably to Greek usage, an urbane way of saying, *I have* (comp. Gal. ii. 6, 1 Cor. xii. 22). Paul was in no doubt of his being an organ of the Holy Ghost." Hodge, "Com. on First Corinthians."

DEFECTIVE STATEMENT OF THE DOCTRINE.

22. *State what is meant by theological writers by the inspiration " of superintendence," " of elevation," " of direction," and " of suggestion."*

Certain writers on this subject, confounding the distinction between inspiration and revelation, and using the former term to express the whole divine influence of which the sacred writers were the subjects, first, in knowing the truth, second, in writing it, necessarily distinguish between different degrees of inspiration in order to accommodate their theory to the facts of the case. Because, *first*, some of the contents of Scripture evidently might be known without supernatural aid, while much more as evidently could not; *second*, the different writers exercised their natural faculties, and carried their individual peculiarities of thought, feeling, and manner into their writings.

By the "inspiration of superintendence," these writers meant precisely what we have above given as the definition of inspiration. By the "inspiration of elevation," they meant that divine influence which exalted their natural faculties to a degree of energy otherwise unattainable.

By the "inspiration of direction," they meant that divine influence which guided the writers in the selection and disposition of their material.

By the "inspiration of suggestion," they meant that divine influence which directly suggested to their minds new, and otherwise unattainable truth.

23. *What objections may be fairly made to these distinctions?*

1st. These distinctions spring from a prior failure to distinguish between revelation the frequent, and inspiration the constant, phenomenon presented by Scripture; the one furnishing the material when not otherwise attainable, the other guiding the writer at every point, (1) in securing the infallible truth of all he writes; and (2) in the selection and distribution of his material.

2d. It is injurious to distinguish between different degrees of inspiration, as if the several portions of the Scriptures were in different degrees God's word, while in truth the whole is equally and absolutely so.

False Doctrines of Inspiration.

24. *What Principles necessarily lead to the denial of any supernatural Inspiration?*

All philosophical principles or tendencies of thought which exclude the distinction between the natural and the supernatural necessarily lead to the denial of Inspiration in the sense affirmed by the Church. These are, for example, all Pantheistic, Materialistic, and Naturalistic principles, and of course Rationalistic principles in all their forms.

25. *In what several forms has the doctrine of a Partial Inspiration of the Scriptures been held?*

1st. It has been maintained that certain books were the subjects of plenary inspiration, while others were produced with only a natural providential and gracious assistance of God. S. T. Coleridge admittted the plenary inspiration of "the law and the prophets, no jot or tittle of which can pass unfulfilled," while he denied it of the rest of the canon.

2d. Many have admitted that the moral and spiritual elements of the Scriptures, and their doctrines as far as these relate to the nature and purposes of God not otherwise ascertainable, are products of inspiration, but deny it of the historical and biographical elements, and of all its allusions to scientific facts or laws.

3d. Others admit that the inspiration of the writers controlled their thoughts, but deny that it extended to its verbal expression.

In one, or in all of these senses, different men have held that the Scriptures are only "partially" inspired. All such deny that they "ARE the word of God" as affirmed by the Scriptures themselves and by all the historical Churches, and admit merely that they "*contain* the word of God."

26. *State the doctrine of Gracious Inspiration.*

Coleridge, in his "Confessions of an Inquiring Spirit," Letter vii., holds that the Scriptures, except the Law and the Prophets, were produced by their writers assisted by "the highest degree of that grace and communion with the Spirit which the Church under all circumstances, and every regenerate member of the Church of Christ, is permitted to hope and instructed to pray for." This is the doctrine of Maurice ("Theological Essays," p. 339) and virtually that of Morell ("Philosophy of Religion," p. 186) and of the Quakers. These admit an objective supernatural revelation, and that this is contained in the Scriptures, which are highly useful, and in such a sense an authoritative standard of faith and practice; that no pretended revelation which is inconsistent with Scripture can be true, and that they are a judge in all controversies between Christians. Nevertheless they hold that the Scriptures are only "a secondary rule, subordinate to the Spirit from whom they have all their excellency," which Spirit illumes every man in the world, and reveals to him either with, or without the Scriptures, if they are unknown, all the knowledge of God and of his will which are necessary for his salvation and guidance, on condition of his rendering a constant obedience to that light as thus graciously communicated to him and to all men. "Barclay's Apology, Theses Theological," Propositions i., ii., and iii.

AUTHORITATIVE STATEMENTS.

ROMAN CATHOLIC.—"*Decrees of Council of Trent*," Sess. iv. "Which gospel . . . our Lord Jesus Christ, the Son of God, first promulgated with his own mouth, and then commanded to be preached by his apostles to every creature, . . . and seeing clearly that this truth and discipline are contained in the written books, and the unwritten tradition, which received by the apostles from the mouth of Christ himself, or from the apostles themselves, the Holy Ghost dictating, have come down even unto us, transmitted as it were from hand to hand : [the Synod] following the example of the orthodox Fathers, receives and venerates with an equal affection of piety and reverence, all the books both of the Old and of the New Testament—seeing God is the author of both—as also the said traditions, as well those appertaining to faith as to morals, as having been dictated, either by Christ's own word of mouth, or by the Holy Ghost, and preserved in the Catholic Church by a continuous succession."

"*Dogmatic Decrees of the Vatican Council*," 1870, Sess. iii., Ch. ii. "Further this supernatural revelation, according to the universal belief of the Church, declared by the sacred Synod of Trent, is contained in the written books and unwritten traditions which have come down to us, having been received by the apostles from the mouth of Christ himself, or from the apostles themselves, by the dictation of the Holy Spirit, have been transmitted as it were from hand to hand. And these books of the Old and New Testament are to be received as sacred and canonical, in their integrity, with all their parts, as they are enumerated in the decree of the said Council, and are contained in the ancient Edition of the Vulgate. These the Church holds to be sacred and canonical, not because having been carefully composed by mere human industry, they were afterwards approved by her authority, nor merely because they contain revelation with no admixture of error; but because, having been written by the inspiration of the Holy Ghost, they have God for their author, and have been delivered as such to the Church herself."

LUTHERAN.—"*Formula Concordiæ Epitome.*" 1. "We believe, confess, and teach that the only rule and norm, according to which all dogmas and all doctors ought to be esteemed and judged, is no other whatever than the prophetic and apostolic writings of the Old and New Testament, as it is written, Ps. cxix. 105, and Gal. i. 8."

REFORMED.—"*Second Helvetic Confession*," Ch. i. Concerning Holy Scripture. "We believe and confess, that the canonical Scriptures of the holy prophets and apostles of each Testament are the true word of God, and that they possess sufficient authority from themselves alone and not from man. For God himself spoke to the fathers, to the prophets, and to the apostles, and continues to speak to us through the Holy Scriptures."

"*The Belgic Confession*," Art. iii. "We confess that this word of God was not sent nor delivered by the will of man, but that *holy men of God spake as they were moved by the Holy Ghost*, as the apostle Peter saith. And that afterwards God, from a special care which he has for us and our salvation, commanded his servants, the prophets and apostles, to commit his revealed word to writing, and he himself wrote with his own finger the two tables of the law. Therefore we call such writings holy and divine Scriptures."

"*Westminster Confession of Faith,*" Chap. i. "Therefore it pleased the Lord, at sundry times and in divers manners, to reveal himself and to declare his will unto his Church; and afterwards, for the better preserving and propagating of the truth, and for the more sure establishment and comfort of the Church against the Corruption of the flesh and the malice of Satan and of the world, to commit the same wholly unto writing." "The authority of the Holy Scripture, for which it ought to be believed and obeyed, dependeth not upon the testimony of any man or church, but wholly upon God (who is truth itself) the Author thereof; and therefore it is to be received because it is the word of God."

CHAPTER V.

THE RULE OF FAITH AND PRACTICE.

THE SCRIPTURES OF THE OLD AND NEW TESTAMENTS, HAVING BEEN GIVEN BY INSPIRATION OF GOD, ARE THE ALL-SUFFICIENT AND ONLY RULE OF FAITH AND PRACTICE, AND JUDGE OF CONTROVERSIES.

(This chapter is compiled from Dr. Hodge's unpublished "Lectures on the Church.")

1. *What is meant by saying that the Scriptures are the only infallible rule of faith and practice?*

Whatever God teaches or commands is of sovereign authority. Whatever conveys to us an infallible knowledge of his teachings and commands is an infallible rule. The Scriptures of the Old and New Testaments are the only organs through which, during the present dispensation, God conveys to us a knowledge of his will about what we are to believe concerning himself, and what duties he requires of us.

2. *What does the Romish Church declare to be the infallible rule of faith and practice?*

The Romish theory is that the complete rule of faith and practice consists of Scripture and tradition, or the oral teaching of Christ and his apostles, handed down through the Church. Tradition they hold to be necessary, 1st, to teach additional truth not contained in the Scriptures; and, 2d, to interpret Scripture. The Church being the divinely constituted depository and judge of both Scripture and tradition.—"Decrees of Council of Trent," Session IV, and "Dens Theo.," Tom. II., N. 80 and 81.

3. *By what arguments do they seek to establish the authority of tradition? By what criterion do they distinguish true traditions from false, and on what grounds do they base the authority of the traditions they receive?*

1st. Their arguments in behalf of tradition are—(1.) Scripture authorizes it, 2 Thess. ii. 15; iii. 6. (2.) The early fathers asserted its authority and founded their faith largely upon it. (3.) The oral teaching of Christ and his apostles, when clearly ascertained, is intrinsically of equal authority with their writings. The Scriptures themselves are handed down to us by the evidence of tradition, and the stream can not rise higher than its source. (4.) The necessity of the case. (*a.*) Scripture is obscure, needs tradition as its interpreter. (*b.*) Scripture is incomplete as a rule of faith and practice; since there are many doctrines and institutions, universally recognized, which are founded only upon tradition as a supplement to Scripture. (5.) Analogy. Every state recognizes both written and unwritten, common and statute law.

2d. The criterion by which they distinguish between true and false traditions is Catholic consent. The Anglican ritualists confine the application of the rule to the first three or four centuries. The Romanists recognize that as an authoritative consent which is constitutionally expressed by the bishops in general council, or by the Pope ex-cathedra, in any age of the church whatever.

3d. They defend the traditions which they hold to be true. (1.) On the ground of historical testimony, tracing them up to the apostles as their source. (2.) The authority of the Church expressed by Catholic consent.

4. *By what arguments may the invalidity of all ecclesiastical tradition, as a part of our rule of faith and practice, be shown?*

1st. The Scriptures do *not*, as claimed, ascribe authority to oral tradition. Tradition, as intended by Paul in the passage cited (2 Thess. ii. 15, and iii. 6), signifies all his instructions, oral and written, communicated *to those very people themselves*, not handed down. On the other hand, Christ rebuked this doctrine of the Romanists in their predecessors, the Pharisees, Matt. xv. 3, 6; Mark vii. 7.

2d. It is improbable *à priori* that God would supplement Scripture with tradition as part of our rule of faith. (1.) Because Scripture, as will be shown below (questions 7–14), is certain, definite, complete, and perspicuous. (2.) Because tradition, from its very nature, is indeterminate, and liable to become adulterated with every form of error. Besides, as will be shown below (question 20), the authority of Scripture does not rest ultimately upon tradition.

3d. The whole ground upon which Romanists base the authority of their traditions (viz., history and church authority) is invalid. (1.) History utterly fails them. For more than three hundred years after the apostles they have very little, and that contradictory, evidence for any one of their traditions.

They are thus forced to the absurd assumption that what was taught in the fourth century was therefore taught in the third, and therefore in the first. (2.) The church is not infallible, as will be shown below (question 18).

4th. Their practice is inconsistent with their own principles. Many of the earliest and best attested traditions they do not receive. Many of their pretended traditions are recent inventions unknown to the ancients.

5th. Many of their traditions, such as relate to the priesthood, the sacrifice of the mass, etc., are plainly in direct opposition to Scripture. Yet the infallible church affirms the infallibility of Scripture. A house divided against itself can not stand.

5. *What is necessary to constitute a sole and infallible rule of faith?*

Plenary inspiration, completeness, perspicuity, and accessibility.

6. *What arguments do the Scriptures themselves afford in favor of the doctrine that they are the only infallible rule of faith?*

1st. The Scriptures always speak in the name of God, and command faith and obedience.

2d. Christ and his apostles always refer to the written Scriptures, then existing, as authority, and *to no other rule of faith whatsoever.*—Luke xvi. 29; x. 26; John v. 39; Rom. iv. 3; 2 Tim. iii. 15.

3d. The Bereans are commended for bringing all questions, even apostolic teaching, to this test.—Acts xvii. 11; see also Isa. viii. 16.

4th. Christ rebukes the Pharisees for adding to and perverting the Scriptures.—Matt. xv. 7–9; Mark vii. 5–8; see also Rev. xxii. 18, 19, and Deut. iv. 2; xii. 32; Josh. i. 7.

7. *In what sense is the completeness of Scripture as a rule of faith asserted?*

It is not meant that the Scriptures contain every revelation which God has ever made to man, but that their contents are the only supernatural revelation that God does now make to man, and that this revelation is abundantly sufficient for man's guidance in all questions of faith, practice, and modes of worship, and excludes the necessity and the right of any human inventions.

8. *How may this completeness be proved from the design of Scripture?*

The Scriptures profess to lead us to God. Whatever is necessary to that end they must teach us. If any supplementary rule, as tradition, is necessary to that end, they must refer us to it. "Incompleteness here would be falsehood." But while one sacred writer constantly refers us to the writings of another, not one of them ever intimates to us either the necessity or the existence of any other rule.—John xx. 31; 2 Tim. iii. 15–17.

9. *By what other arguments may this principle be proved?*

As the Scriptures profess to be a rule complete for its end, so they have always been practically found to be such by the true spiritual people of God in all ages. They teach a complete and harmonious system of doctrine. They furnish all necessary principles for the government of the private lives of Christians, in every relation, for the public worship of God, and for the administration of the affairs of his kingdom; and they repel all pretended traditions and priestly innovations.

10. *In what sense do Protestants affirm and Romanists deny the perspicuity of Scripture?*

Protestants do not affirm that the doctrines revealed in the Scriptures are level to man's powers of understanding. Many of them are confessedly beyond all understanding. Nor do they affirm that every part of Scripture can be certainly and perspicuously expounded, many of the prophesies being perfectly enigmatical until explained by the event. But they do affirm that every essential article of faith and rule of practice is clearly revealed in Scripture, or may certainly be deduced therefrom. This much the least instructed Christian may learn at once; while, on the other hand, it is true, that with the advance of historical and critical knowledge, and by means of controversies, the Christian church is constantly making progress in the accurate interpretation of Scripture, and in the comprehension in its integrity of the system therein taught. Protestants affirm and Romanists deny that private and unlearned Christians may safely be allowed to interpret Scripture for themselves.

11. *How can the perspicuity of Scripture be proved from the fact that it is a law and a message?*

We saw (question 8) that Scripture is either complete or false, from its own professed design. We now prove its perspicuity upon the same principle. It professes to be (1) a law to be obeyed; (2) a revelation of truth to be believed, to be received by us in both aspects upon the penalty of eternal death. To suppose it not to be perspicuous, relatively to its design of commanding and teaching, is to charge God with dealing with us in a spirit at once disingenuous and cruel.

12. *In what passages is their perspicuity asserted?*

Ps. xix. 7, 8; cxix. 105, 130; 2 Cor. iii. 14; 2 Pet. i. 18, 19; Hab. ii. 2; 2 Tim. iii. 15, 17.

13. *By what other arguments may this point be established?*

1st. The Scriptures are addressed immediately, either to all men promiscuously, or else to the whole body of believers as such.—Deut. vi. 4–9; Luke i. 3; Rom. i. 7; 1 Cor. i. 2; 2 Cor. i. 1; iv. 2; Gal. i. 2; Eph. i. 1; Phil. i. 1; Col. i. 2; James i. 1; 1 Peter i. 1; 2 Peter i. 1; 1 John ii. 12, 14; Jude i. 1; Rev. i. 3, 4; ii. 7. The only exceptions are the epistles to Timothy and Titus.

2d. All Christians promiscuously are commanded to search the Scriptures.—2 Tim. iii. 15, 17; Acts xvii. 11; John v. 39.

3d. Universal experience. We have the same evidence of the light-giving power of Scripture that we have of the same property in the sun. The argument to the contrary is an insult to the understanding of the whole world of Bible readers.

4th. The essential unity in faith and practice, in spite of all circumstantial differences, of all Christian communities of every age and nation, who draw their religion directly from the open Scriptures.

14. *What was the third quality required to constitute the Scriptures the sufficient rule of faith and practice?*

Accessibility. It is self-evident that this is the pre-eminent characteristic of the Scriptures, in contrast to tradition, which is in the custody of a corporation of priests, and to every other pretended rule whatsoever. The agency of the church in this matter is simply to give all currency to the word of God.

15. *What is meant by saying that the Scriptures are the judge as well as the rule in questions of faith?*

"A rule is a standard of judgment; a judge is the expounder and applier of that rule to the decision of particular cases." The Protestant doctrine is—

1st. That the Scriptures are the only infallible rule of faith and practice.

2d. (1.) Negatively. That there is no body of men who are either qualified, or authorized, to interpret the Scriptures, or to apply their principles to the decision of particular questions, in a *sense binding upon the faith of their fellow Christians.*

(2.) Positively. That Scripture is the only infallible voice in the church, and is to be interpreted, in its own light, and with the gracious help of the Holy Ghost, who is promised to every Christian (1 John ii. 20–27), by each individual for himself, with the assistance, though not by the authority, of his fellow Christians. Creeds and confessions, as to form, bind only those who voluntarily profess them, and as to matter, they bind only so far as they affirm truly what the Bible teaches, and because the Bible does so teach.

16. *What is the Romish doctrine as to the authority of the church as the infallible interpreter of the rule of faith and the authoritative judge of all controversies?*

The Romish doctrine is that the church is absolutely infallible in all matters of Christian faith and practice, and the divinely authorized depository and interpreter of the rule of faith. Her office is not to convey new revelations from God to man, yet her inspiration renders her infallible in disseminating and interpreting the original revelation communicated through the apostles.

The church, therefore, authoritatively determines—1st. What is Scripture? 2d. What is genuine tradition? 3d. What is the true sense of Scripture and tradition, and what is the true application of that perfect rule to every particular question of belief or practice.

This authority vests in the pope, when acting in his official capacity, and in the bishops as a body; as when assembled in general council, or when giving universal consent to a decree of pope or council.—"Decrees of Council of Trent," Session iv.; "Deus Theo.," N. 80, 81, 84, 93, 94, 95, 96. "Bellarmine," Lib. III., de eccles., cap. xiv., and Lib. II., de council., cap. ii.

17. *By what arguments do they seek to establish this authority?*

1st. The promises of Christ, given, as they claim, to the apostles, and to their official successor, securing their infallibility, and consequent authority.—Matt. xvi. 18; xviii. 18–20; Luke xxiv. 47–49; John xvi. 13; xx. 23.

2d. The commission given to the church as the teacher of the world.—Matt. xxviii. 19, 20; Luke x. 16, etc.

3d. The church is declared to be "the pillar and ground of the truth," and it is affirmed that "the gates of hell shall never prevail against her."

4th. To the church is granted power to bind and loose, and he that will not hear the church is to be treated as a heathen. Matt. xvi. 19; xviii. 15–18.

5th. The church is commanded to discriminate between

truth and error, and must consequently be qualified and authorized to do so.—2 Thessalonians iii. 6; Romans xvi. 17; 2 John 10.

6th. From the necessity of the case, men need and crave an ever-living, visible, and cotemporaneous infallible Interpreter and Judge.

7th. From universal analogy every community among men has the living judge as well as the written law, and the one would be of no value without the other.

8th. This power is necessary to secure unity and universality, which all acknowledge to be essential attributes of the true church.

18. *By what arguments may this claim of the Romish church be shown to be utterly baseless?*

1st. A claim vesting in mortal men a power so momentous can be established only by the most clear and certain evidence, and the failure to produce such converts the claim into a treason at once against God and the human race.

2d. Her evidence fails, because the promises of Christ to preserve his church from extinction and from error do none of them go the length of pledging infallibility. The utmost promised is, that the true people of God shall never perish entirely from the earth, or be left to apostatize from the essentials of the faith.

3d. Her evidence fails, because these promises of Christ were addressed not to the officers of the church as such, but to the body of true believers. Compare John xx. 23 with Luke xxiv. 33, 47, 48, 49, and 1 John ii. 20, 27.

4th. Her evidence fails, because the church to which the precious promises of the Scriptures are pledged is not an external, visible society, the authority of which is vested in the hands of a perpetual line of apostles. For—(1.) the word church (ἐκκλησία) is a collective term, embracing the effectually called (κλητοὶ) or regenerated.—Rom. i. 7; viii. 28; 1 Cor. i. 2; Jude i.; Rev. xvii. 14; also Rom. ix. 24; 1 Cor. vii. 18–24; Gal. i. 15; 2 Tim. i. 9; Heb. ix. 15; 1 Pet. ii. 9; v. 10; Eph. i. 18; 2 Pet. i. 10. (2.) The attributes ascribed to the church prove it to consist alone of the true, spiritual people of God as such.—Eph. v. 27; 1 Pet. ii. 5; John x. 27; Col. i. 18, 24. (3.) The epistles are addressed to the church, and in their salutations explain that phrase as equivalent to "the called," "the saints," "all true worshippers of God;" witness the salutations of 1st and 2d Corinthians, Ephesians, Colossians, 1st and 2d Peter and Jude. The same attributes are ascribed to the members of the true church as such throughout the body of the Epistles.—1 Cor. i.

30; iii. 16; vi. 11, 19; Eph. ii. 3–8, and 19–22; 1 Thes. v. 4, 5; 2 Thes. ii. 13; Col. i. 21; ii. 10; 1 Pet. ii. 9.

5th. The inspired apostles have had no successors. (1.) There is no evidence that they had such in the New Testament. (2.) While provision was made for the regular perpetuation of the offices of presbyter and deacon (1 Tim. iii. 1–13), there are no directions given for the perpetuation of the apostolate. (3.) There is perfect silence concerning the continued existence of any apostles in the church in the writings of the early centuries. Both the name and the thing ceased. (4.) No one ever claiming to be one of their successors have possessed the "signs of an apostle."—2 Cor. xii. 12; 1 Cor. ix. 1; Gal. i. 1, 12; Acts i. 21, 22.

6th. This claim, as it rests upon the authority of the Pope, is utterly unscriptural, because the Pope is not known to Scripture. As it rests upon the authority of the whole body of the bishops, expressed in their general consent, it is unscriptural for the reasons above shown, and it is, moreover, impracticable, since their universal judgment never has been and never can be impartially collected and pronounced.

7th. There can be no infallibility where there is not self-consistency. But as a matter of fact the Papal church has not been self-consistent in her teaching. (1.) She has taught different doctrines in different sections and ages. (2.) She affirms the infallibility of the holy Scriptures, and at the same time teaches a system plainly and radically inconsistent with their manifest sense; witness the doctrines of the priesthood, the mass, penance, of works, and of Mary worship. Therefore the Church of Rome hides the Scriptures from the people.

8th. If this Romish system be true then genuine spiritual religion ought to flourish in her communion, and all the rest of the world ought to be a moral desert. The facts are notoriously the reverse. If, therefore, we admit that the Romish system is true, we subvert one of the principal evidences of Christianity itself, viz., the self-evidencing light and practical power of true religion, and the witness of the Holy Ghost.

19. *By what direct arguments may the doctrine that the Scriptures are the final judge of controversies be established?*

That all Christians are to study the Scriptures for themselves, and that in all questions as to God's revealed will the appeal is to the Scriptures alone, is proved by the following facts:

1st. Scripture is perspicuous, see above, questions 11–13.

2d. Scripture is addressed to all Christians as such, see above, question 13.

3d. All Christians are commanded to search the Scriptures, and by them to judge all doctrines and all professed teachers.— John v. 39; Acts xvii. 11; Gal. i. 8; 2 Cor. iv. 2; 1 Thess. v. 21; 1 John iv. 1, 2.

4th. The promise of the Holy Spirit, the author and interpreter of Scripture, is to all Christians as such. Compare John xx. 23 with Luke xxiv. 47–49; 1 John ii. 20, 27; Rom. viii. 9; 1 Cor. iii. 16, 17.

5th. Religion is essentially a personal matter. Each Christian must know and believe the truth explicitly for himself, on the direct ground of its own moral and spiritual evidence, and not on the mere ground of blind authority. Otherwise faith could not be a moral act, nor could it "purify the heart." Faith derives its sanctifying power from the truth which it immediately apprehends on its own experimental evidence.—John xvii. 17, 19; James i. 18; 1 Pet. i. 22.

20. *What is the objection which the Romanists make to this doctrine, on the ground that the church is our only authority for believing that the Scriptures are the word of God?*

Their objection is, that as we receive the Scriptures as the word of God only on the authoritative testimony of the church, our faith in the Scriptures is only another form of our faith in the church, and the authority of the church, being the foundation of that of Scripture, must of course be held paramount.

This is absurd, for two reasons—

1st. The assumed fact is false. The evidence upon which we receive Scripture as the word of God is not the authority of the church, but—(1.) God did speak by the apostles and prophets, as is evident (*a*) from the nature of their doctrine, (*b*) from their miracles, (*c*) their prophecies, (*d*) our personal experience and observation of the power of the truth. (2.) These very writings which we possess were written by the apostles, etc., as is evident, (*a*) from internal evidence, (*b*) from historical testimony rendered by all competent cotemporaneous witnesses in the church or out of it.

2d. Even if the fact assumed was true, viz., that we know the Scriptures to be from God, on the authority of the church's testimony alone, the conclusion they seek to deduce from it would be absurd. The witness who proves the identity or primogeniture of a prince does not thereby acquire a right to govern the kingdom, or even to interpret the will of the prince.

21. *How is the argument for the necessity of a visible judge, derived from the diversities of sects and doctrines among Protestants, to be answered?*

1st. We do not pretend that the private judgment of Protestants is infallible, but only that when exercised in an humble, believing spirit, it always leads to a competent knowledge of essential truth.

2d. The term Protestant is simply negative, and is assumed by many infidels who protest as much against the Scriptures as they do against Rome. But Bible Protestants, among all their circumstantial differences, are, to a wonderful degree, agreed upon the essentials of faith and practice. Witness their hymns and devotional literature.

3d. The diversity that does actually exist arises from failure in applying faithfully the Protestant principles for which we contend. Men do not simply and without prejudice take their creed from the Bible.

4th. The Catholic church, in her last and most authoritative utterance through the Council of Trent, has proved herself a most indefinite judge. Her doctrinal decisions need an infallible interpreter infinitely more than the Scriptures.

22. *How may it be shown that the Romanist theory, as well as the Protestant, necessarily throws upon the people the obligation of private judgment?*

Is there a God? Has he revealed himself? Has he established a church? Is that church an infallible teacher? Is private judgment a blind leader? Which of all pretended churches is the true one? Every one of these questions evidently must be settled in the private judgment of the inquirer, before he can, rationally or irrationally, give up his private judgment to the direction of the self-asserting church. Thus of necessity Romanists appeal to the Scriptures to prove that the Scriptures can not be understood, and address arguments to the private judgment of men to prove that private judgment is incompetent; thus basing an argument upon that which it is the object of the argument to prove is baseless.

23. *How may it be proved that the people are far more competent to discover what the Bible teaches than to decide, by the marks insisted upon by the Romanists, which is the true church?*

The Romanists, of necessity, set forth certain marks by which the true church is to be discriminated from all counterfeits. These are (1.) Unity (through subjection to one visible head, the Pope); (2.) Holiness; (3.) Catholicity; (4.) Apostolicity, (involving an uninterrupted succession from the apostles of canonically ordained bishops.)—"Cat. of Council of Trent," Part I., Cap. 10. Now, the comprehension and intelligent application of these marks involve a great amount of learning and intelligent capacity upon the part of the inquirer. He might as easily prove himself to be descended from Noah by an unbroken series of legitimate marriages, as establish the right of Rome to the last mark. Yet he can not rationally give up the right of studying the Bible for himself until that point is made clear.

Surely the Scriptures, with their self-evidencing spiritual power, make less exhaustive demands upon the resources of private judgment.

ROMAN CATHOLIC DOCTRINE AS TO THE PRIVATE INTERPRETATION OF SCRIPTURE, AND AS TO TRADITION, AND AS TO THE INFALLIBILITY OF THE POPE.

1st. AS TO THE INTERPRETATION OF SCRIPTURE.—"*Decrees of Council of Trent,*" Sess. iv.—"Moreover the same sacred and holy Synod . . . ordains and declares, that the said old and vulgate edition, which, by the lengthened usage of so many ages, has been approved of in the Church, be, in public lectures, disputations, sermons, and expositions, held as authentic; and that no one is to dare or presume to reject it under any pretext whatever.

"Furthermore, in order to restrain petulant spirits, it decrees that no one, relying on his own skill, shall, in matters of faith and of morals pertaining to the edification of Christian doctrine,—wresting the sacred Scripture to his own senses, presume to interpret the said sacred Scripture contrary to that sense which holy mother Church—whose it is to judge of the true sense and interpretation of the Holy Scriptures—hath held and doth hold; or even contrary to the unanimous consent of the Fathers; even though such interpretations were never (intended) to be at any time published."

"*Dogmatic Decrees of the Vatican Council,*" ch. ii.—"And as the things which the holy Synod of Trent decreed for the good of souls concerning the interpretation of Divine Scripture, in order to curb rebellious spirits, have been wrongly explained by some, we, renewing the said decree, declare this to be their sense, that, in matters of faith and morals, appertaining to the building up of Christian doctrine, that is to be held as the true sense of Holy Scripture which our holy mother Church hath held and holds, to whom it belongs to judge of the true sense of the Holy Scripture; and therefore that it is permitted to no one to interpret the sacred Scripture contrary to this sense, nor, likewise contrary to the unanimous consent of the Fathers."

2d. AS TO TRADITION.—"*Prof. Fidei Tridentinœ*" (A. D. 1564) ii. and iii. "I most steadfastly admit and embrace apostolic and ecclesiastic traditions, and all other observances and constitutions of the same Church. I also admit the Holy Scriptures, according to that sense which our holy mother Church has held and does hold, to which it belongs to judge of the true sense and interpretation of the Scriptures; neither will I ever take and interpret them otherwise than according to the unanimous consent of the Fathers."

"*Council of Trent,*" Sess. iv.—"And seeing clearly that this truth and discipline are contained in the written books, and the unwritten traditions which, received by the apostles from the mouth of Christ himself, or from the apostles themselves the Holy Ghost dictating, have come down even unto us transmitted as it were from hand to hand."

3d. AS TO THE ABSOLUTE AUTHORITY OF THE POPE.—"*Dogmatic Deci-*

sions of the Vatican Council," chap. iii.—"Hence we teach and declare that by the appointment of our Lord . . the power of jurisdiction of the Roman Pontiff is immediate, to which all, of whatever rite and dignity, both pastors and faithful, both individually and collectively, are bound, by their duty of hierarchical subordination and true obedience, to submit not only in matters which belong to faith and morals, but also in those that appertain to the discipline and government of the Church throughout the world. . . We further teach and declare that he is the supreme judge of the faithful, and that in all causes, the decision of which belongs to the Church, recourse may be had to his tribunal, and that none may reopen the judgment of the Apostolic See, than whose authority there is no greater, nor can any lawfully review his judgment. Wherefore they err from the right course who assert that it is lawful to appeal from the judgments of the Roman Pontiff to an œcumenical council, as to an authority higher than that of the Roman Pontiff."

4th. CONCERNING THE ABSOLUTE INFALLIBILITY OF THE POPE AS THE TEACHER OF THE UNIVERSAL CHURCH.—*"Dogmatic Decrees of the Vatican Council,"* Chap. iv.—"Therefore faithfully adhering to the tradition received from the beginning of the Christian faith, for the glory of God our Saviour, the exaltation of the Catholic religion, and the salvation of Christian people, the sacred Council approving, we teach and define that it is a dogma divinely revealed: That the Roman Pontiff when he speaks *ex cathedra,* that is, when in discharge of the office of pastor and doctor of all Christians, by virtue of his supreme Apostolic authority, he defines a doctrine regarding faith or morals to be held by the universal Church, by the divine assistance promised to him in blessed Peter, is possessed of the infallibility with which the divine Redeemer willed that his Church should be endowed for defining doctrine according to faith and morals; and that therefore such definitions of the Roman Pontiff are irreformable of themselves, and not from the consent of the Church. But if any one —which may God avert—presume to contradict this our definition: let him be anathema."

Cardinal Manning in his *"Vatican Council"* says, "In this definition there are six points to be noted:

"1st. It defines the meaning of the well-known phrase *loquens ex cathedra;* that is, speaking from the Seat, or place, or with the authority of the supreme teacher of all Christians, and binding the assent of the universal Church.

"2d. The subject matter of the infallible teaching, namely, the doctrine of faith and morals.

"3d. The efficient cause of infallibility, that is, the divine assistance promised to Peter, and in Peter to his successors.

"4th. The act to which this divine assistance is attached, the defining of doctrines of faith and morals.

"5th. The extension of this infallible authority to the limits of the doctrinal office of the Church.

"6th. The dogmatic value of the definitions *ex cathedra,* namely that they are in themselves irreformable, because in themselves infallible, and not because the Church, or any part or member of the Church, should assent to them."

"Dogmatic Decrees of Vatican Council," Ch. iv.—"For the Holy Spirit was not promised to the successors of Peter, that by his revelation they might make known new doctrine; but that by his assistance they might inviolably keep and faithfully expound the revelation or deposit of faith delivered through the Apostles."

CHAPTER VI.

A COMPARISON OF SYSTEMS.

In this chapter will be presented a brief sketch of the main contrasting positions of the three rival systems of Pelagianism, Semipelagianism, and Augustinianism, or as they are denominated in their more completely developed forms, Socinianism, Arminianism, and Calvinism—together with an outline of the history of their rise and dissemination.

1. *What, in general, was the state of Theological thought during the first three centuries?*

During the first three hundred years which elapsed after the death of the apostle John the speculative minds of the church were principally engaged in defending the truth of Christianity against unbelievers—in combating the Gnostic heresies generated by the leaven of Oriental philosophy—and in settling definitely the questions which were evolved in the controversies concerning the Persons of the Trinity. It does not appear that any definite and consistent statements were made in that age, as to the origin, nature, and consequences of human sin; nor as to the nature and effects of divine grace; nor of the nature of the redemptive work of Christ, or of the method of its application by the Holy Spirit, or of its appropriation by faith. As a general fact it may be stated, that, as a result of the great influence of Origen, the Fathers of the Greek Church pretty unanimously settled down upon a loose Semipelagianism, denying the *guilt* of original sin, and maintaining the ability of the sinner to predispose himself for, and to cooperate with divine grace. And this has continued the character of the Greek Anthropology to the present day. The same attributes characterized the speculations of the earliest writers of the Western Church also, but during the third and fourth centuries there appeared a marked tendency among the Latin Fathers to those more correct views afterwards triumphantly vindicated by the great Augustine. This tendency may be traced most clearly in the writings of Tertullian of Carthage, who died circum. 220, and Hilary of Poictiers (†368) and Ambrose of Milan (†397).

2. *By what means has the Church made advances in the clear discrimination of divine. truth? And in what ages, and among what branches of the Church, have the great doctrines of the Trinity and Person of Christ, of sin and grace, and of redemption and the application thereof been severally defined?*

The Church has always advanced toward clearer conceptions and more accurate definitions of divine truth through a process of active controversy. And it has pleased Providence that the several great departments of the system revealed in the inspired Scriptures should have been most thoroughly discussed, and clearly defined in different ages, and in the bosom of different nations.

Thus the profound questions involved in the departments of Theology proper and of Christology were investigated by men chiefly of Greek origin, and they were authoritatively defined in Synods held in the Eastern half of the General Church during the fourth and immediately following centuries. As concerns THEOLOGY the consubstantial divinity of Christ was defined in the Council of Nice, 325, and the Personality and divinity of the Holy Ghost in the first Council of Constantinople, 381; the Filioque clause being added by the Latins at the Council of Toledo, 589. As concerns *Christology.* The Council of Ephesus, 431, asserted the personal unity of the Theanthropos. The Council of Chalcedon, 451, asserted that the two natures remain distinct. The sixth Council of Constantinople, 680, asserted that the Lord possessed a human as well as a divine will. These decisions have been accepted by the whole Church, Greek and Roman, Lutheran and Reformed.

The questions concerning sin and grace embraced under the general head of *Anthropology* were in the first instance most thoroughly investigated by men of Latin origin, and definite conclusions were first reached in the controversy of Augustine with Pelagius in the first half of the fifth century.

Questions concerning redemption, and the method of its application, embraced under the grand division of Soteriology, were never thoroughly investigated until the time of the Reformation and subsequently by the great theologians of Germany and Switzerland.

Many questions falling under the grand division of Ecclesiology even yet await their complete solution in the future.

3. *What are the three great systems of theology which have always continued to prevail in the Church?*

Since the revelation given in the Scriptures embraces a complete system of truth, every single department must sustain many obvious relations, logical and otherwise, to every other as the several parts of one whole. The imperfect development, and the defective or exaggerated conception of any one doctrine, must inevitably lead to confusion and error throughout the entire system. For example, Pelagian views as to man's estate by nature always tend to coalesce with Socinian views as to the Person and work of Christ. And Semipelagian views as to sin and grace are also irresistibly attracted by, and in turn attract Arminian views as to the divine attributes, the nature of the Atonement, and the work of the Spirit.

There are, in fact, as we might have anticipated, but *two* complete self-consistent systems of Christian theology possible. 1st. On the right hand, Augustinianism completed in Calvinism. 2d. On the left hand, Pelagianism completed in Socinianism. And 3d. Arminianism comes between these as the system of compromises. and is developed Semipelagianism.

In the common usage of terms Socinianism is principally applied as the designation of those elements of the false system which relate to the Trinity of the Person of Christ; the terms Pelagianism and Semipelagianism are applied to the more extreme or the more moderate departures from the truth under the head of *Anthropology;* and the term Arminianism is used to designate the less extreme errors concerned with the Department of Soteriology.

4. *When and where and by whom were the fundamental principles of the two great antagonistic schools of theology first clearly discriminated ?*

The contrasted positions of the Augustinian and Pelagian systems were first taught out and defined through the controversies maintained by the eminent men whose name they bear, during the first third of the fifth century.

Augustine was bishop of Hippo in Northern Africa from A. D. 395 to A. D. 430. Pelagius, whose family name was Morgan, was a British monk. He was assisted in his controversies by his disciples Cœlestius and Julian of Eclanum in Italy.

The positions maintained by Pelagius were generally condemned by the representatives of the whole Church, and have ever since been held by all denominations, except professed Socinians, to be fatal heresy. They were condemned by the two councils held at Carthage A. D. 407 and A. D. 416, by the Council held at Milevum in Numidia A. D. 416; by the popes Innocent and Zosimus, and by the Œcumenical Council held at Ephesus A. D. 431. This speedy and universal repudiation of Pelagianism proves that while the views of the early Fathers upon this class of questions were very imperfect, nevertheless the system taught by Augustine must have been in all essentials the same with the faith of the Church as a whole from the beginning.

5. *State in contrast the main distinguishing positions of the Augustinian and Pelagian systems.*

"1st. As to ORIGINAL SIN.*

"*Augustinianism.* By the sin of Adam, in whom all men together sinned, sin and all the other positive punishments of Adam's sin came into the world. By it human nature has been both physically and morally corrupted. Every man brings into the world with him a nature already so corrupt, that it can do nothing but sin. The propagation of this quality of his nature is by concupiscence.

"*Pelagianism.* By his transgression, Adam injured only himself, not his posterity. In respect to his moral nature, every man is born in precisely the same condition in which Adam was created. There is therefore no original sin.

"2d. As to FREE WILL.

"*Augustinianism.* By Adam's transgression the freedom of the human will has been entirely lost. In his present corrupt state man can will and do only evil.

"*Pelagianism.* Man's will is free. Every man has the power to will and to do good as well as the opposite. Hence it depends upon himself whether he be good or evil.

"3d. As to GRACE.

"*Augustinianism.* If nevertheless man in his present state, wills and does good, it is merely the work of grace. It is an inward, secret, and wonderful operation of God upon man. It is a preceding as well as an accompanying work. By preceding grace, man attains faith, by which he comes to an insight of good, and by which power is given him to will the good. He needs co-operating grace for the performance of every individual good act. As man can do nothing without grace, so he can do nothing against it. It is irresistible. And as man by nature has no merit at all, no respect at all can be had to man's moral disposition, in imparting grace, but God acts according to his own free will.

"*Pelagianism.* Although by free will, which is a gift of God, man has the capacity of willing and doing good without God's special aid, yet for the *easier* performance of it, God revealed the law; for the easier performance, the instruction and example of Christ aid him; and for the easier performance, even the supernatural operations of grace are imparted to him. Grace, in the most limited sense (gracious influence) is given to those

*"Historical Presentation of Augustinianism and Pelagianism," by G. F. Wiggers, D.D., Translated by Rev. Ralph Emerson, pp. 268–270.

only who deserve it by the faithful employment of their own powers. But man can resist it.

"4th. As to PREDESTINATION AND REDEMPTION.

"*Augustinianism.* From eternity, God made a free and unconditional decree to save a few * from the mass that was corrupted and subjected to damnation. To those whom he predestinated to this salvation, he gives the requisite means for the purpose. But on the rest, who do not belong to this small * number of the elect, the merited ruin falls. Christ came into the world and died for the elect only.

"*Pelagianism.* God's decree of election and reprobation is founded on prescience. Those of whom God foresaw that they would keep his commands, he predestinated to salvation; the others to damnation. Christ's redemption is general. But those only need his atoning death who have actually sinned. *All*, however, by his instruction and example, may be led to higher perfection and virtue."

6. *What was the origin of the Middle or Semipelagian system?*

In the mean time, while the Pelagian controversy was at its height, John Cassian, of Syrian extraction and educated in the Eastern Church, having removed to Marseilles, in France, for the purpose of advancing the interests of monkery in that region, began to give publicity to a scheme of doctrine occupying a middle position between the systems of Augustine and Pelagius. This system, whose advocates were called Massilians from the residence of their chief, and afterward Semipelagians by the Schoolmen, is in its essential principles one with that system which is now denominated Arminianism, a statement of which will be given in a subsequent part of this chapter. Faustus, bishop of Riez, in France, from A. D. 427 to A. D. 480, was one of the most distinguished and successful advocates of this doctrine, which was permanently accepted by the Eastern Church, and for a time was widely disseminated throughout the western also, until it was condemned by the Synods of Orange and Valence, A. D. 529.

7. *What is the relation of Augustinianism to Calvinism and of Semipelagianism to Arminianism?*

After this time Augustinianism became the recognized orthodoxy of the Western Church, and the name of no other uninspired man exerts such universal influence among Papists and Protestants alike. If any human name ought to be used to designate a system of divinely revealed truth, the phrase

---

* The doctrine of Augustine does not by any means involve the conclusion that the elect are "few" or "a small number."

Augustinianism as opposed to *Pelagianism* properly designates all those elements of faith which the whole world of Evangelical Christians hold in common. On the other hand *Augustinianism* as opposed to *Semipelagianism* properly designates that system commonly called Calvinism—while *Cassianism* would be the proper historical designation of that Middle or Semipelagian Scheme now commonly styled Arminianism.

8. *How were parties divided with respect to these great systems among the Schoolmen, and how are they in the modern Papal Church?*

After the lapse of the dark ages, during which all active speculation slumbered, the great Thomas Aquinas, an Italian by birth, A. D. 1224, and a monk of the order of St. Dominic, Doctor Angelicus, advocated with consummate ability the Augustinian system of theology in that cumbrous and artificial manner which characterized the Schoolmen. John Duns Scotus, a native of Britain, A. D. 1265, a monk of the order of St. Francis, Doctor Subtilis, was in that age the ablest advocate of the system then styled Semipelagian. The controversies then revived were perpetuated for many ages, the Dominicans and the Thomists in general advocating unconditional election and efficacious grace, and the Franciscans and the Scotists in general advocating conditional election and the inalienable power of the human will to co-operate with or to resist divine grace. The same disputes under various party names continue to agitate the Romish Church since the Reformation, although the genius of her ritualistic system, and the predominance of the Jesuits in her councils, have secured within her bounds the almost universal prevalence of Semipelagianism.

The general Council, commenced at Trent, A. D. 1546, attempted to form a non-committal Creed that would satisfy the adherents of both systems. Accordingly the Dominicans and Franciscans have both claimed that their respective views were sanctioned by that Synod. The truth is that while the general and indefinite statements of doctrine to be found among its canons are often Augustinian in form, the more detailed and accurate explanations which follow these are uniformly Semipelagian.—Principal Cunningham's "Historical Theology," vol. 1, pp. 483–495.

The order of the Jesuits, founded by Ignatius Loyola, A. D. 1541, has always been identified with Semipelagian Theology. Lewis Molina, a Spanish Jesuit, A. D. 1588, the inventor of the distinction denoted by the term "Scientia Media," attained to such distinction as its advocate, that its adherents in the Papal Church have been for ages styled Molinists. In 1638 Jansenius, Bishop of Ypres in the Netherlands died leaving behind him his great work, Augustinus, wherein he clearly unfolded and established by copious extracts the true theological system of Augustine. This book occasioned very wide-spread contentions, was ferociously opposed by the Jesuits, and condemned by the Bulls of Popes Innocent X. and Alexander VII., A. D. 1653 and 1656—which last were followed in 1713 by the more celebrated Bull "*imigenitus*" of Clement XI., condemning the New Testament Commentary of Quesnel. The Augustinians in that Church were subsequently called Jansenists, and had their principal seat in Holland and Belgium and at Port Royal near Paris. They have numbered among them some very illustrious names, as Tillemont, Arnauld, Nicole, Pascal, and Quesnel. These controversies between the Dominicans and Molinists, the Jansenists and Jesuits, have continued even to our own time, although at present Semipelagianism shares with Jesuitism in its almost unlimited sway in the Papal Church, which has definitely triumphed in the Vatican Council, 1870.

9. *What is the position of the Lutheran Church with relation to these great systems?*

Luther, a monk of the order of Augustine, and an earnest disciple of that father, taught a system of faith agreeing in spirit and in all essential points with that afterwards more systematically developed by Calvin. The only important point in which he differed from the common consensus of the Calvinistic Churches related to the literal physical presence of the entire person of Christ *in*, *with*, and *under* the elements in the Eucharist. With these opinions of Luther Melanchthon appears to have agreed at the time he published the first edition of his " Loci Communes." His opinions however as to the freedom of man and the sovereignty of divine grace were subsequently gradually modified. After the death of Luther, at the Leipsic Conference in 1548, he explicitly declared his agreement with the *Synergists*, who maintain that in the regenerating act the human will co-operates with divine grace. Melanchthon, on the other hand, held a view of the relation of the sign to the grace signified thereby in the Sacraments, much more nearly conforming to opinions of the disciples of Zwingle and Calvin than generally prevailed in his own Church. His position on both these points gave great offence to the Old Lutherans, and occasioned protracted and bitter controversies. Finally, the Old or Strict Lutheran party prevailed over their antagonists, and their views received a complete scientific statement in the "Formula Concordiæ" published 1580. Although this remarkable document never attained a position by the side of the Augsburg Confession and Apology as the universally recognized Confession of the Lutheran Churches, it may justly be taken as the best available witness as to what strictly Lutheran theology when developed into a complete system really is.

The Characteristics of Lutheran theology as contrasted with that of the Reformed Churches may be briefly stated under the following heads:

1st. As to THEOLOGY proper and CHRISTOLOGY the only points in which it differs from Calvinism are the following:

(1.) As to the divine attributes of sovereign foreordination, they hold that as far as it is concerned with the actions of moral agents it is limited to those actions which are morally good, while it sustains no determining relation to those which are bad. God *foreknows* all events of whatever kind; he foreordains all the actions of necessary agents, and the good actions of free agents—but nothing else.

(2.) As to Christology, they hold that in virtue of the hypostatical union the human element of Christ's person partakes with the divine in at least some of its peculiar attributes. Thus his human soul shares in the omniscience and omnipotence of his divinity, and his body in its omnipresence, and together they have the power of giving life to the truly believing recipient of the sacrament.

2d. As to ANTHROPOLOGY, they hold views identical with those held by the staunchest advocates of the Reformed Theology—as for instance the antecedent and immediate imputation of Adam's public sin; the total moral depravity of all his descendants from birth and by nature, and their absolute inability to do aright in their own strength any thing which pertains to their relation to God.

3d. As to the great central elements of SOTERIOLOGY, they agree with the Reformed with great exactness as to the nature and necessity of the expiatory work of Christ; as to forensic justification through the imputation to the believer of both the active and passive obedience of Christ; as to the nature and office of justifying faith; as to the sole agency of divine grace in the regeneration of the sinner, with which, *in the first instance*, the dead soul is unable to co-operate; as to God's eternal and sovereign election of believers in Christ, not because of any thing foreseen in them, but because of his own gracious will—and consequently as to the fact that the salvation of every soul really saved is to be attributed purely and solely to the grace of God, and not in any degree to the co-operating will or merit of the man himself.

At the same time they teach, with obvious logical inconsistency, that the grace of the gospel is in divine intention absolutely universal. Christ died equally and in the same sense for all men. He gives grace alike to all men. Those who are lost are lost because they resist the grace. Those who are saved owe their salvation simply to the grace they have in common with the lost—to the very same grace—not to a greater degree of grace nor to a less degree of sin—not to their own improvement of grace, but simply to the grace itself. According to them God sovereignly elects all those who are saved, but he does not sovereignly pass over those who are lost. He gives the same grace to all men, and the difference is determined by the persistent resistance of those who are lost.

The grand distinction of Lutheranism however relates to their doctrine of the Eucharist. They hold to the real physical presence of the Lord in the Eucharist, in, with, and under the elements, and that the grace signified and conveyed by the sacraments is necessary to salvation, and conveyed ordinarily by no other means. Hence the theology and church life of the strict Lutherans centre in the sacraments. They differ from the high sacramental party in the Episcopal Church chiefly in the fact that they ignore the dogma of apostolical succession, and the traditions of the early church.

10. *Into what two great parties has the Protestant world always been divided?*

The whole Protestant world from the time of the Reformation has been divided into two great families of churches, classified severally as LUTHERAN, or those whose character was derived from Luther and Melanchthon; and as REFORMED, or those who have received the characteristic impress of Calvin. The LUTHERAN family of churches comprises all of those Protestants of Germany, of Hungary, and the Baltic provinces of Russia, who adhere to the Augsburg Confession, together with the national churches of Denmark and of Norway and Sweden, and the large denomination of the name in America. These are estimated as amounting to a population of about twenty-five millions of pure Lutherans, while the Evangelical Church of Prussia, which was formed of a political union of the adherents of the two Confessions, embraces probably eleven millions and a half. Their Symbolical Books are the Augsburg Confession and Apology, the Articles of Smalcald, Luther's Larger and Smaller Catechism, and, as received by the Stricter party, the Formula Concordiæ. The CALVINISTIC or REFORMED churches embrace, in the strict usage of the term, all those Protestant Churches which derive their Theology from Geneva; and among these, because of obvious qualifying conditions, the Episcopal Churches of England, Ireland, and America form a subdivision by themselves; and the Wesleyan Methodists, who are usually classed among the Reformed because they were historically developed from that stock, are even yet more distinctly than the parent church of England removed from the normal type of the general class. In a general sense, however, this class comprises all those churches of Germany which subscribe to the Heidelburg Catechism, the churches of Switzerland, France, Holland, England, and Scotland, the Independents and Baptists of England and America, and the various branches of the Presbyterian Church in England, Ireland, and America. These embrace about eight millions German Reformed; two millions in the Reformed church of Hungary; twelve millions and a half Episcopalians; Presbyterians, six millions; Methodists, three millions and a half; Baptists, four millions and a half; and Independents, one million and a half;—in all about thirty-eight millions.

The principal confessions of the Reformed Church are the Gallic, Belgic, 2d Helvetic, and Scotch Confessions; the Heidelburg Catechism; the Thirty-nine Articles of the Church of England; the Canons of the Synod of Dort, and the Confession and Catechisms of the Westminster Assembly.

11. *State the Origin of the Unitarian Heresy.*

In the early church the *Ebionites*, a Jewish-Gnostic Christian sect, were the only representatives of those in modern times called Socinians. A party among them were called Elkesaïtes. Their ideas, with special modifications, are found expressed in the "Clementine Homilies," written about A. D. 150 in Oriental Syria. The most distinguished humanitarians in the early church were the two Theodotuses of Rome, both laymen, Artemon (†180) and Paul of Samosata, bishop of Antioch (260–270), deposed by a Council held 269. Most of these admitted the supernatural birth of Christ, but maintained that he was a mere man, honored by a special divine influence. They admitted an apotheosis or relative deification of Christ consequent upon his earthly achievements. (Dr. E. De Pressensé, "Early Years of Christianity," Part 3, bk. 1, chs. 3 and 5).

Cerinthus, who lived during the last of the first and the first of the second century, held that Jesus was a mere man born of Mary and Joseph, that the Christ or Logos came down upon him in the shape of a dove at his baptism, when he was raised to the dignity of the son of God, and wrought miracles, etc. The Logos left the man Jesus to suffer alone at his crucifixion. The resurrection also was denied.

They were succeeded by the Arians in the fourth century. During the Middle Ages there remained no party within the church that openly denied the supreme divinity of our Lord. In modern times Unitarianism revived at the period of the Reformation through the agency of Lælius Socinus of Italy. It was carried by him into Switzerland and existed there as a doctrine professed by a few conspicuous heretics from 1525 to 1560. The most prominent of its professors were the Socini, Servetus, and Ochino. It existed as an organized church at Racow in Poland, where the exiled heretics found a refuge from 1539 to 1658, when the Socinians were driven out of Poland by the Jesuits, and passing into Holland became absorbed in the Remonstrant or Arminian Churches. In 1609 Schmetz drew up from materials afforded by the teaching of Faustus Socinus, the nephew of Lælius, and of J. Crellius, the Racovian Catechism, which is the standard of Socinianism (see Ree's translation, 1818.) After their dispersion, Andrew Wissowatius and others collected the most important writings of their leading theologians under the title "Bibliotheca Fratrum Polonorum." Socinianism was developed by these writers with consummate ability, and crystalized into its most perfect form, as a logical system. It is purely *Unitarian* in its theology— *Humanitarian* in its *Christology*, *Pelagian* in its *Anthropology*— and its *Soteriology* was developed in perfect logical and ethical consistency with those elements. A statement of its characteristic positions will be found below.

It reappeared again as a doctrine held by a few isolated men in England in the seventeenth century. During the eighteenth century a number of degenerate Presbyterian Churches in England lapsed into Socinianism, and towards the end of the same century a larger number of Congregational Churches in Eastern Massachusetts followed their example, and these together constitute the foundation of the modern Unitarian Denomination.

"Its last form is a modification of the old Socinianism formed under the pressure of evangelical religion on the one hand, and of rationalistic criticism on the other. Priestley, Channing, and J. Martineau are the examples of the successive phases of Modern Unitarianism. Priestley, of the old Socinianism, building itself upon a sensational philosophy; Channing, of an attempt to gain a large development of the spiritual element; Martineau, of the elevation of view induced by the philosophy of Cousin, and the introduction of the idea of historical progress in religious ideas."—"Farrar's Crit. Hist. of Free Thought," Bampton Lecture, 1862.

12. *At what date and under what circumstances did modern Arminianism arise?*

James Arminius, professor of theology in the university of

Leyden from 1602 until his death in 1609, although a minister of the Calvinistic Church of Holland, at first secretly, and afterwards more openly, advocated that scheme of theological opinion which has ever subsequently been designated by his name. These views were rapidly diffused, and at the same time strongly opposed by the principal men in the church. His disciples, consequently, about a year after his death formed themselves into an organized party, and in that capacity presented a *Remonstrance* to the States of Holland and West Friesland, praying to be allowed to hold their places in the church without being subjected by the ecclesiastical courts to vexatious examinations as to their orthodoxy. From the fact that the utterance of this Remonstrance was their first combined act as a party, they were afterwards known in history as *Remonstrants.*

Soon after this the Remonstrants, for the sake of defining their position, presented to the authorities five Articles expressing their belief on the subject of Predestination and Grace. This is the origin of the famous "Five Points" in the controversy between Calvinism and Arminianism. Very soon however the controversy took a much wider range, and the Arminians were forced by logical consistency to teach radically erroneous views with respect to the nature of sin, original sin, imputation, the nature of the Atonement, and Justification by faith. Some of their later writers carried the rationalistic spirit inherent in their system to its legitimate results in a hardly qualified Pelagianism, and some were even suspected of Socinianism.

As all other means had failed to silence the innovators, the States General called together a General Synod at Dort in Holland, which held its sessions in the year 1618–1619. It consisted of pastors, elders, and theological professors from the churches of Holland, and deputies from the churches of England, Scotland, Hesse, Bremen, the Palatinate and Switzerland: the promised attendance of delegates from the French churches being prevented by an interdict of their king. The foreign delegates present were nineteen Presbyterians from Reformed churches on the Continent, and one from Scotland, and four Episcopalians from the church of England headed by the bishop of Llandaff. This Synod unanimously condemned the doctrines of the Arminians, and in their Articles confirmed the common Calvinistic faith of the Reformed churches. The most distinguished Remonstrant Theologians who succeeded Arminius were Episcopius, Curcellæus, Limborch, Le Clerc, Wetstein, and the illustrious jurisconsult Grotius.

The denomination of Methodists in Great Britain and America is the only large Protestant body in the world with an avowedly Arminian Creed. Their Arminianism, however, as presented by their standard writer, Richard Watson, an incomparably more competent theologian than Wesley, is far less removed from the Calvinism of the Westminster Assembly than the system of the later Remonstrants, and should always be designated by the qualified phrase "Evangelical Arminianism." In the hands of Watson the Anthropology and Soteriology of Arminianism are in a general sense nearly assimilated to the corresponding provinces of Lutheranism, and of the Calvinism of Baxter, and of the French School of the seventeenth century.

13. *Give an outline of the main positions of the Socinian System.*

THEOLOGY AND CHRISTOLOGY.

1st. Divine Unity.

(*a.*) This unity inconsistent with any personal distinctions in the Godhead.

(*b.*) Christ is a mere man.

(*c.*) The Holy Ghost is an impersonal divine influence.

2d. Divine Attributes.

(*a.*) There is no principle of vindicatory justice in God. Nothing to prevent his acceptance of sinners on the simple ground of repentance.

(*b.*) Future contingent events are essentially unknowable. The foreknowledge of God does not extend to such events.

ANTHROPOLOGY.

(*a.*) Man was created without positive moral character. The "image of God" in which man was said to be created did not include holiness.

(*b.*) Adam in eating the forbidden fruit committed actual sin, and thereby incurred the divine displeasure, but he retained nevertheless the same moral nature and tendencies with which he was created, and he transmitted these intact to his posterity.

(*c.*) The guilt of Adam's sin is not imputed.

(*d.*) Man is now as able by nature to discharge all his obligations as he ever was. The circumstances under which man's character is now formed are more unfavorable than in Adam's case, and therefore man is weak. But God is infinitely merciful; and obligation is graded by ability. Man was created naturally mortal and would have died had he sinned or not.

SOTERIOLOGY.

The great object of Christ's mission was to teach and to give assurance with respect to those truths concerning which the conclusions of mere human reason are problematical. This he does both by doctrine and example.

1st. Christ did not execute the office of priest upon earth; but only in heaven, and there in a very indefinite sense.

2d. The main office of Christ was prophetical. He taught a new law. Gave an example of a holy life. Taught the personality of God. And illustrated the doctrine of a future life by his own resurrection.

3d. His death was necessary only as a condition unavoidably prerequisite to his resurrection. It was also designed to make a moral impression upon sinners, disposing them to repentance on account of sin, and assuring them of the clemency of God. No propitiation of divine justice was necessary, nor would it be possible by means of *vicarious* suffering.

ESCATOLOGY.

1st. In the intermediate period between death and the resurrection the soul remains unconscious.

2d. "For it is evident from the authorities cited, that they (the older Socinians), equally with others, constantly maintain that there will be a resurrection both of the just and of the unjust, and that the latter shall be consigned to everlasting punishment, but the former admitted to everlasting life."—B. Wissowatius.

"The doctrine of the proper eternity of hell torments is rejected by most Unitarians of the present day (1818), as in their opinion wholly irreconcilable with the divine goodness, and unwarranted by the Scriptures. In reference to the future fate of the wicked, some hold that after the resurrection they will be annihilated or consigned to 'everlasting destruction' in the literal sense of the words: but most have received the doctrine of universal restoration, which maintains that all men, however depraved their characters may have been in this life, will, by a corrective discipline, suited in the measure of its severity to the nature of each particular case, be brought ultimately to goodness and consequently to happiness."—Rees's "Racovian Catechism," pp. 367, 368.

ECCLESIOLOGY.

1st. The church is simply a voluntary society. Its object mutual improvement. Its common bond similarity of sentiments and pursuits. Its rule is human reason.

2d. The Sacraments are simply commemorative and teaching ordinances.

14. *Give an outline of the main features of the Arminian System.*

DIVINE ATTRIBUTES.

1st. They admit that vindicatory justice is a divine attribute, but hold that it is relaxable, rather optional than essential, rather belonging to administrative policy than to necessary principle.

2d. They admit that God foreknows all events without exception. They invented the distinction expressed by the term *Scientia Media* to explain God's certain foreknowledge of future events, the futurition of which remain undetermined by his will, or any other antecedent cause.

3d. They deny that God's foreordination extends to the volitions of free agents, and hold that the eternal election of men to salvation is not absolute, but conditioned upon foreseen faith and obedience.

ANTHROPOLOGY.

1st. Moral character can not be created but is determined only by previous self-decision.

2d. Both liberty and responsibility necessarily involve possession of power to the contrary.

3d. They usually deny the imputation of the guilt of Adam's first sin.

4th. The strict Arminians deny total depravity, and admit only the moral enfeeblement of nature. Arminius and Wesley were more orthodox but less self-consistent.

5th. They deny that man has ability to originate holy action or to carry it on in his own unassisted strength—but affirm that every man has power to co-operate with, or to resist "*common grace.*" That which alone distinguishes the saint from the sinner is his own use or abuse of grace.

6th. They regard gracious influence as rather moral and suasory than as a direct and effectual exertion of the new creative energy of God.

7th. They maintain the liability of the saint at every stage of his earthly career to fall from grace.

SOTERIOLOGY.

1st. They admit that Christ made a vicarious offering of himself in place of sinful men, and yet deny that he suffered either the literal penalty of the law, or a *full* equivalent for it, and maintain that his sufferings were graciously accepted as a substitute for the penalty.

2d. They hold that not only with respect to its sufficiency and adaptation, but also in the intention of the Father in giving the Son, and of the Son in dying, Christ died in the same sense for all men alike.

3d. That the acceptance of Christ's satisfaction in the place of the infliction of the penalty on sinners in person involves a relaxation of the divine law.

4th. That Christ's satisfaction enables God in consistency with his character, and the interests of his general government, to offer salvation on easier terms. The gospel hence is a new law, demanding faith and evangelical obedience in the stead of the original demand of perfect obedience.

5th. Hence Christ's work does not actually save any, but makes the salvation of all men possible—removes legal obstacles out of the way—does not secure faith but makes salvation available on the condition of faith.

6th. Sufficient influences of the Holy Spirit, and sufficient opportunities and means of grace are granted to all men.

7th. It is possible for and obligatory upon all men in this life to attain to evangelical perfection—which is explained as a being perfectly sincere—a being animated by perfect love —and a doing all that is required of us under the gospel dispensation.

8th. With respect to the heathen some have held that in some way or other the gospel is virtually, if not in form, preached to all men. Others have held that in the future world there are three conditions corresponding to the three great classes of men as they stand related to the gospel in this world—the *Status Credentium;* the *Status Incredulorum;* the *Status Ignorantium.*

15. *Give a brief outline of the main features of the Calvinistic System.*

THEOLOGY.

1st. God is an absolute sovereign, infinitely wise, righteous, benevolent, and powerful, determining from eternity the certain futurition of all events of every class according to the counsel of his own will.

2d. Vindicatory Justice is an essential and immutable perfection of the divine nature demanding the full punishment of all sin, the exercise of which can not be relaxed or denied by the divine will.

CHRISTOLOGY.

The Mediator is one single, eternal, divine person, at once very God, and very man. In the unity of the Theanthropic person the two natures remain pure and unmixed, and retain each its separate and incommunicable attributes distinct. The personality is that of the eternal and unchangeable Logos. The human nature is impersonal. All mediatorial actions involve the concurrent exercise of the energies of both natures according to their several properties in the unity of the single person.

ANTHROPOLOGY.

1st. God created man by an immediate fiat of omnipotence and in a condition of physical, intellectual, and moral faultlessness, with a positively formed moral character.

2d. The guilt of Adam's public sin is by a judicial act of God immediately charged to the account of each of his descendants from the moment he begins to exist antecedently to any act of his own.

3d. Hence men come into existence in a condition of condemnation deprived of those influences of the Holy Spirit upon which their moral and spiritual life depends.

4th. Hence they come into moral agency deprived of that original righteousness which belonged to human nature as created in Adam, and with an antecedent prevailing tendency in their nature to sin, which tendency in them is of the nature of sin, and worthy of punishment.

5th. Man's nature since the fall retains its constitutional faculties of reason, conscience, and free-will, and hence man continues a responsible moral agent, but he is nevertheless spiritually dead, and totally averse to spiritual good, and absolutely unable to change his own heart, or adequately to discharge any of those duties which spring out of his relation to God.

SOTERIOLOGY.

1st. The salvation of man is absolutely of grace. God was free in consistency with the infinite perfections of his nature to save none, few, many, or all, according to his sovereign good pleasure.

2d. Christ acted as Mediator in pursuance of an eternal covenant formed between the Father and the Son, according to which he was put in the law-place of his own elect people as their personal substitute, and as such by his obedience and suffering he discharged all the obligations growing out of their federal relations to law—by his sufferings vicariously enduring their penal debt—by his obedience vicariously discharging those covenant demands, upon which their eternal well-being was suspended—thus fulfilling the requirements of the law, satisfying the justice of God, and securing the eternal salvation of those for whom he died.

3d. Hence, by his death he purchased the saving influences of the Holy Spirit for all for whom he died. And the Holy Spirit infallibly applies the redemption purchased by Christ to all for whom he intended it, in the precise time and under the precise conditions predetermined in the eternal Covenant of Grace—and he does this by the immediate and intrinsically efficacious exercise of his power, operating directly within them, and in the exercises of their renewed nature bringing them to act faith and repentance and all gracious obedience.

4th. Justification is a judicial act of God, whereby imputing to us the perfect righteousness of Christ, including his active and passive obedience, he proceeds to regard and treat us accordingly, pronouncing all the penal claims of law to be satisfied, and us to be graciously entitled to all the immunities and rewards conditioned in the original Adamic covenant upon perfect obedience.

5th. Although absolute moral perfection is unattainable in this life, and assurance is not of the essence of faith, it is nevertheless possible and obligatory upon each believer to seek after and attain to a full assurance of his own personal salvation, and leaving the things that are behind to strive after perfection in all things.

6th. Although if left to himself every believer would fall in an instant, and although most believers do experience temporary seasons of backsliding, yet God by the exercise of his grace in their hearts, in pursuance of the provisions of the eternal Covenant of Grace and of the purpose of Christ in dying, infallibly prevents even the weakest believer from final apostasy.

CHAPTER VII.

As Creeds and Confessions, their uses and their history, form a distinct subject of study by themselves, they will be considered together in this chapter, while references will be found under the several chapters of this work to the particular Creed in which the particular doctrine is most clearly or authoritatively defined.

On this entire subject consult the admirable historical and critical work of Dr. Philip Schaff of Union Theological Seminary, New York—the "Creeds of Christendom." In the first volume he presents a history of the authorship and occasion of each Creed or Confession and a critical estimate of its contents and value. In volumes second and third he gives the text of all the principal creeds in two languages.

1. *Why are Creeds and Confessions necessary, and how have they been produced?*

The Scriptures of the Old and New Testament having been given by inspiration of God, are for man in his present state the only and the all-sufficient rule of faith and practice. This divine word, therefore, is the only standard of doctrine which has any intrinsic authority binding the consciences of men. All other standards are of value or authority only as they teach what the Scriptures teach.

But it is the inalienable duty and necessity of men to arrive at the meaning of the Scriptures in the use of their natural faculties, and by the ordinary instruments of interpretation. Since all truth is self-consistent in all its parts, and since the human reason always instinctively strives to reduce all the elements of knowledge with which it grapples to logical unity and consistency, it follows that men must more or less formally construct a system of faith out of the materials presented in the Scriptures. Every student of the Bible necessarily does this in the very process of understanding and digesting its teaching, and all such students make it manifest that they have found, in one way or another, a system of faith as complete as for him has been possible, by the very language he uses in prayer, praise, and ordinary religious discourse. If men refuse the assistance afforded by the statements of doctrine slowly elaborated and defined by the church, they must severally make out their own creed by their own unaided wisdom. The real question between the church and the impugners of human creeds, is not, as the latter often pretend, between the word of God and the creed of man, but between the tried and proved faith of the collective body of God's people, and the private judgment and the unassisted wisdom of the individual objector. As it would have been anticipated, it is a matter of fact that the church has advanced very gradually in this work of accurately interpreting Scripture, and defining the great doctrines which compose the system of truths it reveals. The attention of the church has been especially directed to the study of one doctrine in one age, and of another doctrine in a subsequent age. And as she has gradually advanced in the clear discrimination of gospel truth, she has at different periods set down an accurate statement of the results of her new attainments in a creed, or Confession of Faith, for the purpose of preservation and of popular instruction, of discriminating and defending the truth from the perversion of heretics and the attacks of infidels, and of affording a common bond of faith, and rule of teaching and discipline.

The ancient creeds of the universal Church were formed by the first four œcumenical or general councils, except the so-called Apostle's Creed, gradually formed from the baptismal confessions in use in the different churches of the West, and the so-called Athanasian Creed, which is of private and unknown authorship. The great authoritative Confession of the Papal Church was produced by the œcumenical council held at Trent, 1545. The mass of the principal Protestant Confessions were the production of single individuals or of small circles of individuals, e. g., the Augsburg Confession and Apology, the 2d Helvetic Confession, the Heidelburg Catechism, the Old Scotch Confession, the Thirty-nine Articles of the Church of England, etc. Two, however, of the most valuable and generally received Protestant Confessions were produced by large and venerable Assemblies of learned divines, namely: the Canons of the international Synod of Dort, and the Confession and Catechisms of the national Assembly of Westminster.

2. *What are their legitimate uses?*

They have been found in all ages of the church useful for the following purposes. (1.) To mark, preserve, and disseminate the attainments made in the knowledge of Christian truth by any branch of the church in any grand crisis of its development. (2.) To discriminate the truth from the glosses of false teachers, and accurately to define it in its integrity and due proportions. (3.) To act as the bond of ecclesiastical fellowship among those so nearly agreed as to be able to labor together in harmony. (4.) To be used as instruments in the great work of popular instruction.

3. *What is the ground and extent of their authority, or power to bind the conscience?*

The matter of all these Creeds and Confessions binds the consciences of men only so far as it is purely scriptural, and because it is so. The form in which that matter is stated, on the other hand, binds only those who have voluntarily subscribed the Confession and because of that subscription.

In all churches a distinction is made between the terms upon which private members are admitted to membership, and the terms upon which office-bearers are admitted to their sacred trusts of teaching and ruling. A church has no right to make any thing a condition of membership which Christ has not made a condition of salvation. The church is Christ's fold. The Sacraments are the seals of his covenant. All have a right to claim admittance who make a credible profession of the true religion, that is, who are presumptively the people of Christ. This credible profession of course involves a competent knowledge of the fundamental doctrines of Christianity, a declaration of personal faith in Christ and of devotion to his service, and a temper of mind and a habit of life consistent therewith. On the other hand, no man can be inducted into any office in any church who does not profess to believe in the truth and wisdom of the constitution and laws it will be his duty to conserve and administer. Otherwise all harmony of sentiment and all efficient co-operation in action would be impossible.

It is a universally admitted principle of morals that the *animus imponentis,* the sense in which the persons who impose an oath, or promise, or engagement, understand it, binds the conscience of the persons who bind themselves by oath or promise. All candidates for office in the Presbyterian Church, therefore, do either personally believe the "system of doctrine" taught in our Standards, in the sense in which it has been historically understood to be God's truth, or solemnly lie to ₁od and man.

4. *What were the Creeds of the ancient Church, which remain the common inheritance of all branches of the modern Church?*

I. THE APOSTLE'S CREED, so called. This Creed gradually grew out of the comparison and assimilation of the Baptismal Creeds of the principal Churches in the West or Latin half of the ancient Church. The most complete and popular forms of these baptismal creeds were those of Rome, Aquileja, Milan, Ravenna, Carthage, and Hippo, "of which the Roman form, enriching itself by additions from others, gradually gained the more general acceptance. While the several articles considered separately are all of Nicene or Anti-nicene origin, the creed as a whole in its present form, can not be traced beyond the sixth century."—Schaff's "Creeds of Christendom," vol. 1. p. 20.

It was subjoined by the Westminster divines to their Catechism, together with the Lord's Prayer and Ten Commandments. "Not as though it was composed by the apostles, or ought to be esteemed canonical Scripture, but because it is a brief sum of Christian faith, agreeable to the word of God, and anciently received in the Churches of Christ." It was retained by the framers of the Constitution of the Presbyterian Church in the United States as part of our Catechism. It is a part of the Catechism of the Methodist Episcopal Church also. "It is used in the baptismal Confession of the Roman, English, Reformed, Lutheran, Methodist Episcopal, and Protestant Episcopal Churches."

It is as follows:

"I believe in God the Father almighty, maker of heaven and earth; and in Jesus Christ his only Son, our Lord ; who was conceived by the Holy Ghost; born of the Virgin Mary; suffered under Pontius Pilate ; was crucified, dead and buried ; he descended into hell (Hades); the third day he rose again from the dead, he ascended into heaven, and sitteth on the right hand of God the Father almighty; from thence he shall come to judge the quick and the dead. I believe in the Holy Ghost, the holy catholic church, the communion of saints, the forgiveness of sins, the resurrection of the body, and the life everlasting. Amen."

II. THE NICENE CREED, in which the true Trinitarian faith of the church is accurately defined in opposition to Arian and Semiarian errors. It exists in three forms, and evidently was moulded upon pre-existing forms similar to those from which the Apostles' Creed grew.

1st. The original form in which it was composed and enacted by the Œcumenical Council of Nice, A. D. 325.

"We believe in one God, the Father Almighty, Maker of all things visible and invisible.

"And in one Lord Jesus Christ, the Son of God, begotten of the

Father, the only begotten; that is, of the essence of the Father, God of God, Light of Light, very God of very God, begotten, not made, being of one substance (ὁμοούσιον) with the Father; by whom all things were made, both in heaven and on earth; who for us men, and for our salvation, came down and was incarnate, and was made man; he suffered, and the third day he rose again, ascended into heaven; from thence he shall come to judge the quick and the dead.

"And in the Holy Ghost.

"But those who say: 'There was a time when he was not;' and, 'He was not before he was made;' and, 'He was made out of nothing,' or, 'He is of another substance' or 'essence,' or, 'The Son of God is created' or 'changeable,' or 'alterable'—they are condemned by the holy catholic and apostolic Church."

2d. The Nicæno-Constantinopolitan Creed. This consists of the Nicene Creed, above given, slightly changed in the first article, and with the clauses defining the Person and work of the Holy Ghost added, and the Anathema omittted. This new form of the Creed has been generally attributed to the Council of Constantinople, convened by the Emperor Theodosius, A. D. 381, to condemn the doctrine of the Macedonians, who denied the divinity of the Holy Ghost. These changes in the Nicene Creed were unquestionably made about that date, and the several "clauses" added existed previously in formularies proposed by individual theologians. But there is no evidence that the changes were made by the Council of Constantinople. They were, however, recognized by the Council of Chalcedon, A. D. 451.

It is in this latter form that the Creed of Nice is now used in the Greek Church.

3d. The third or Latin form of this creed, in which it is used in the Roman, Episcopal, and Lutheran Churches, differs from the *second* form above mentioned only in (*a.*) restoring the clause ("Deus de Deo") "God of God," to the first clause; it belonged to the original Creed of Nice, but had been dropped out of the Greek Nicæno-Constantinopolitan form. (*b.*) The famous "*Filioque*" term was added to the clause affirming the procession of the Spirit from the Father. This was added by the provincial Council of Toledo, Spain, A. D. 589, and gradually accepted by the whole Western Church, and thence by all Protestants, without any œcumenical ratification. That phrase is rejected by the Greek Church. The text of this Creed as received with reverence by all Catholics and Protestants is as follows (Schaff's "Creeds of Christendom," pp. 25–29):

"I believe in one God the Father almighty, maker of heaven and earth, and of all things visible and invisible; and in one Lord Jesus Christ, the only begotten son of God, begotten of his Father before all worlds; God of God, Light of Light, very God of very God, begotten not made, being of one substance with the Father; by whom all things were made; Who for us men and for our salvation came down from heaven, and was incarnate by the Holy Ghost of the Virgin Mary, and was made man; He was crucified, also for us, under Pontius Pilate. He suffered and was buried; and the third day he rose again according to the Scriptures; and ascended into heaven, and sitteth on the right hand of the Father. And he shall come again with glory to judge both the quick and the dead; whose kingdom shall have no end. And I believe in the Holy Ghost, the Lord and Giver of life, who proceedeth from the Father and the Son (this phrase "filioque" was added to the creed of Constantinople by the council of the western church held at Toledo, A. D. 589), who, with the Father and the Son together is worshipped and glorified, who spake by the prophets. And I believe one Catholic and Apostolic Church, I acknowledge one baptism for the remission of sins; and I look for the resurrection of the dead, and the life of the world to come."

III. THE ATHANASIAN CREED, so called, also styled, from its opening words, the symbol *Quicunque vult*, is vulgarly ascribed to the great Athanasius, bishop of Alexandria, from about A. D. 328 to A. D. 373, and the leader of the orthodox party in the church in opposition to the arch heretic, Arius. But modern scholars unanimously assign to it a later origin, and trace it to Northern Africa and the school of Augustine. Bigham refers it to Virgilius Tapsensis at the end of the fifth century. Schaff says its complete form does not appear before the end of the eighth century.

This Creed is received in the Greek, Roman, and English Churches, but it has been left out of the Prayer Book of the Episcopal Church of America. It presents a most admirably stated exposition of the faith of all Christians, and it is objected to only because of the "damnatory clauses," which ought never to be attached to any human composition, especially one making such nice distinctions upon so profound a subject.

It is as follows:

"1. Whosoever wishes to be saved, it is above all necessary for him to hold the Catholic faith. 2. Which, unless each one shall preserve perfect and inviolate, he shall certainly perish for ever. 3. But the Catholic faith is this, that we worship one God in trinity, and trinity in unity. 4. Neither confounding the persons, nor separating the substance. 5. For the person of the Father is one, of the Son another, and of the Holy Ghost another. 6. But of the Father, of the Son, and of the Holy Ghost there is one divinity, equal glory and co-eternal majesty. 7. What the Father is, the same is the Son, and the Holy Ghost. 8. The Father is uncreated, the Son uncreated, the Holy Ghost uncreated. 9. The Father is immense, the Son immense, the Holy Ghost immense. 10. The Father is eternal, the Son eternal, the Holy Ghost eternal. 11. And yet there are not three eternals, but one eternal. 12. So there are not three (beings) uncreated, nor three immense, but one uncreated, and one immense. 13. In like manner the Father is omnipotent, the Son is omnipotent, the Holy Ghost is omnipotent. 14. And yet there are not three omnipotents, but one omnipotent. 15. Thus the Father is God, the Son is God, the Holy Ghost is God.

16. And yet there are not three Gods, but one God. 17. Thus the Father is Lord, the Son is Lord, and the Holy Ghost is Lord. 18. And yet there are not three Lords, but one Lord. 19. Because as we are thus compelled by Christian verity to confess each person severally to be God and Lord; so we are prohibited by the Catholic religion from saying that there are three Gods or Lords. 20. The Father was made from none, nor created, nor begotten. 21. The Son is from the Father alone, neither made, nor created, but begotten. 22. The Holy Ghost is from the Father and the Son, neither made, nor created, nor begotten, but proceeding. 23. Therefore there is one Father, not three fathers, one Son, not three sons, one Holy Ghost, not three Holy Ghosts. 24. And in this trinity no one is first or last, no one is greater or less. 25. But all the three co-eternal persons are co-equal among themselves; so that through all, as is above said, both unity in trinity, and trinity in unity is to be worshipped. 26. Therefore, he who wishes to be saved must think thus concerning the trinity. 27. But it is necessary to eternal salvation that he should also faithfully believe the incarnation of our Lord Jesus Christ. 28. It is, therefore, true faith that we believe and confess that our Lord Jesus Christ is both God and man. 29. He is God, generated from eternity from the substance of the Father; man, born in time from the substance of his mother. 30. Perfect God, perfect man, subsisting of a rational soul and human flesh. 31. Equal to the Father in respect to his divinity, less than the Father in respect to his humanity. 32. Who, although he is God and man, is not two but one Christ. 33. But one, not from the conversion of his divinity into flesh, but from the assumption of his humanity into God. 34. One not at all from confusion of substance, but from unity of person. 35. For as a rational soul and flesh is one man, so God and man is one Christ. 36. Who suffered for our salvation, descended into hell, the third day rose from the dead. 37. Ascended to heaven, sitteth at the right hand of God the Father omnipotent, whence he shall come to judge the living and the dead. 38. At whose coming all men shall rise again with their bodies, and shall render an account for their own works. 39. And they who have done well shall go into life eternal; they who have done evil into eternal fire. 40. This is the Catholic faith, which, unless a man shall faithfully and firmly believe, he can not be saved."

IV. The Creed of Chalcedon. The Emperor Marcianus called the fourth oecumenical council to meet at Chalcedon in Bithynia, on the Bosphorus, opposite Constantinople, to put down the Eutychian and Nestorian heresies. The Council consisted of 630 bishops and sat from Oct. 8 to Oct. 31, A. D. 451.

The principal part of the "Definition of Faith" agreed upon by this Council is as follows:

"We, then, following the holy Fathers, all with one consent, teach men to confess, one and the same Son, our Lord Jesus Christ; the same perfect in Godhead and also perfect in Manhood; truly God, and truly Man, of a reasonable soul and body; consubstantial with the Father according to the Godhead, and consubstantial with us according to the Manhood ; in all things like unto us without sin ; begotten before all ages of the Father according to the Godhead, and in these latter days, for us and for our salvation, born of Mary the Virgin Mother of God according to the Manhood. He is one and the same Christ, Son, Lord,

Only-begotten, existing in two natures without mixture (ἀσυγχύτως), without change (ἀτρέπτως), without division (ἀδιαιρέτως), without separation (ἀχωρίστως); the diversity of the two natures not being at all destroyed by their union, but the peculiar properties of each nature being preserved, and concurring to one person and one subsistence, not parted or divided into two persons, but one and the same Son, and Only-begotten, God the Word, the Lord Jesus Christ; as the prophets from the beginning have declared concerning Him, and as the Lord Jesus Christ Himself hath taught us, and as the Creed of the holy fathers has delivered to us."

This completed the development of the orthodox Church doctrine of the Trinity of Persons in the one God, and of the duality of natures in the one Christ. It remains a universally respected statement of the common faith of the Church.

5. *What are the doctrinal Standards of the Church of Rome?*

Besides the above mentioned Creeds, all of which are of recognized authority in the Romish Church, their great Standards of Faith are—1st. The *"Canons and Decrees of the Council of Trent,"* which they regard as the twentieth œcumenical council, and was called by Pope Pius IV. to oppose the progress of the Reformation (A. D. 1545–1563). The decrees contain the positive statements of Papal doctrine. The canons explain the decrees, distribute the matter under brief heads, and condemn the opposing doctrine on each point. Although studiously ambiguous, the system of doctrine taught is evidently though not consistently Semipelagian.

2d. The *"Roman Catechism,"* which explains and enforces the canons of the Council of Trent, was prepared by order of Pius IV. and promulgated by the authority of Pope Pius V., A. D. 1566.

3d. The *"Creed of Pope Pius IV."* also called *"Professio Fidei Tridentinœ,"* or *"Forma Professionis Fidei Catholicœ,"* contains a summary of the doctrines taught in the Canons and Decrees of the Council of Trent, and was promulgated in a bull by Pope Pius IV., A. D. 1564. It is subscribed to by all grades of Papal teachers and ecclesiastics, and by all converts from Protestantism.

It is as follows:

"I, A. B., believe and profess with a firm faith all and every one of the things which are contained in the symbol of faith which is used in the holy Roman Church; namely, I believe in one God the Father Almighty, Maker of heaven and earth, and of all things visible and invisible; and in one Lord Jesus Christ, the only-begotten Son of God, begotten of the Father before all worlds; God of God, Light of Light, very God of very God, begotten, not made, consubstantial with the Father, by whom all things were made; who for us men and for our salvation came down from heaven, and was incarnate by the Holy Ghost of the Virgin Mary, and was made man; was crucified for us under Pontius Pilate, suffered and was buried, and rose again the third day according to the Scriptures, and ascended into heaven, sits at the right hand of the Father, and will come again with glory to judge the living and the dead, of whose kingdom there will be no end; and in the Holy Ghost, the Lord and Life-giver, who proceeds from the Father and the Son, who, together with the Father and the Son, is adored and glorified, who spake by the holy prophets; and one holy catholic and apostolic Church. I confess one baptism for the remission of sins, and I expect the resurrection of the dead, and the life of the world to come. Amen.

"I most firmly admit and embrace the apostolic and ecclesiastical traditions, and all other constitutions and observances of the same Church. I also admit the sacred Scriptures according to the sense which the holy mother Church has held and does hold, to whom it belongs to judge of the true sense and interpretation of the Scriptures; nor will I ever take or interpret them otherwise than according to the unanimous consent of the fathers.   I profess, also, that there are truly and properly seven sacraments of the new law, instituted by Jesus Christ our Lord, and necessary for the salvation of mankind, though all are not necessary for every one—namely baptism, confirmation, eucharist, penance, extreme unction, orders, and matrimony, and that they confer grace; and of these, baptism, confirmation, and order can not be reiterated without sacrilege.   I do also receive and admit the ceremonies of the Catholic Church, received and approved in the solemn administration of all the above-said sacraments.   I receive and embrace all and every one of the things which have been defined and declared in the holy Council of Trent concerning sin and justification.   I profess likewise that in the mass is offered to God a true, proper, and propitiatory sacrifice for the living and the dead; and that in the most holy sacrament of the eucharist there is truly, really, and substantially the body and blood, together with the soul and divinity of our Lord Jesus Christ, and that there is made a conversion of the whole substance of the bread into the body, and of the whole substance of the wine into the blood, which conversion the Catholic Church calls transubstantiation.   I confess, also, that under either kind alone, Christ whole and entire, and a true sacrament is received.   I constantly hold that there is a purgatory, and that the souls detained therein are helped by the suffrages of the faithful. Likewise that the saints reigning together with Christ are to be honored and invoked, that they offer prayers to God for us, and that their relics are to be venerated.   I most firmly assert that the images of Christ, and of the mother of God ever Virgin, and also of the other saints, are to be had and retained, and that due honor and veneration are to be given to them.   I also affirm that the power of indulgences was left by Christ in the Church, and that the use of them is most wholesome to Christian people.   I acknowledge the Holy Catholic and Apostolic Church, the mother and mistress of all churches; and I promise and swear true obedience to the Roman bishop, the successor of St. Peter, prince of the apostles, and vicar of Jesus Christ.   I also profess, and undoubtedly receive all other things delivered, defined, and declared by the sacred canons and general councils, and particularly by the holy Council of Trent [and by the Œcumenical Vatican Council delivered, defined, and declared, particularly concerning the primacy and infallible rule of the Roman Pontiff *]

_____

*Added by Decree of the "Sacred Congregation of the Council," Jan. 2, 1877.

"And likewise I also condemn, reject, and anathematize all things contrary thereto, and all heresies whatsoever condemned, rejected and anathematized by the Church. This true Catholic faith, out of which none can be saved, which I now freely profess and truly hold, I., A. B., promise, vow and swear most constantly to hold, and profess the same whole and entire, with God's assistance, to the end of my life; and to procure as far as lies in my power, that the same shall be held, taught and preached by all who are under me, or who are intrusted to my care, in virtue of my office, so help me God, and these holy gospels of God —Amen."

4th. The Holy Œcumenical Vatican Council assembled at the call of Pius IX. in the Basilica of the Vatican, Dec. 8, 1869, and continued its sessions until October 20, 1870, after which it was indefinitely postponed.

The Decrees of this Council embrace two sections.

I. "The Dogmatic Constitution on the Catholic Faith." This embraces four chapters. Chap. 1 treats of God as Creator; chap. 2, of revelation; chap. 3, of faith; chap. 4, of faith and reason. These are followed by eighteen canons, in which the errors of modern rationalism and infidelity are condemned.

II. "First Dogmatic Constitution on the Church of Christ." This also embraces four chapters. Chap. 1 is entitled "Of the Institution of the Apostolic Primacy in Blessed Peter;" chap. 2, "Of the Perpetuity of the Primacy of Blessed Peter in the Roman Pontiffs;" chap. 3, "On the Power and Nature of the Primacy of the Roman Pontiff;" chap. 4, "Concerning the Infallible Teaching of the Roman Pontiff." "The new features are contained in the last two chapters, which teach *Papal Absolutism, and Papal Infallibility.*" These definitions are presented to a sufficient extent under Chapter V. of these "Outlines."

In consequence of this principle of Papal Infallibility it necessarily follows, that the whole succession of Papal Bulls, and especially those directed against the Jansenists and the Decree of Pius IX. "On the Immaculate Conception of the Blessed Virgin Mary," Dec. 8, 1854; and his Syllabus of Errors, Dec. 8, 1864, are all infallible and irreformable and parts of the amazing Standards of Faith professed by the Roman Church.

6. *What are the Doctrinal Standards of the Greek Church?*

The ancient church divided, from causes primarily political and ecclesiastical, secondarily doctrinal and ritual, into two great sections—the Eastern or Greek Church, and the Western or Latin Church. This division began to culminate in the seventh, and was consummated in the eleventh century. The Greek Church embraces about eighty millions of people, the majority of the Christians inhabitants of the Turkish Empire, and the national churches of Greece and Russia. All the Protestant Churches have originated from the Western or Latin division of the church.

She arrogates to herself, pre-eminently, the title of "Orthodox," because the original œcumenical Creeds defining the doctrines of the Trinity and the Person of Christ were produced in the Eastern division of the ancient church and in the Greek language, and hence are in a special sense her inheritance, and because from the fact that her theology is absolutely unprogressive, she contents herself with the literal repetition of the old formulas.

She adheres to the ancient Creeds and doctrinal decisions of the first seven œcumenical councils, and possesses a few modern Confessions and Catechisms. The most important of these are—

1st. The "Orthodox Confession of the Catholic and Apostolic Greek Church," composed by Peter Mogilas, Metropolitan of Kieff in Russia, A. D. 1643, and approved by all the Eastern Patriarchs.

2d. The "Decrees of the Synod of Jerusalem," or the Confession of Dositheus, 1672.

3d. The Russian Catechisms which have the sanction of the Holy Synod, especially the Longer Catechism of Philaret, Metropolitan of Moscow, 1820–1867, unanimously approved by all the Eastern Patriarchs, and since 1839 generally used in the schools and churches of Russia.

The Decrees of the Synod of Jerusalem teach substantially though less definitely the same doctrine as those of the Council of Trent as to the Scriptures and Tradition, good works and faith, justification, the sacraments, the sacrifice of the mass, the worship of saints, and purgatory.

The Catechism of Philaret "approaches more nearly to the evangelical principle of the supremacy of the Bible in matters of Christian faith and life than any other deliverance of the Eastern Church."—Schaff's "Creeds of Christendom," Vol. I., pp. 45 and 71.

7. *What are the Doctrinal Standards of the Lutheran Church?*

Besides the great General Creeds which they receive in common with all Christians their Symbolical Books are—

1st. The *Augsburg Confession*, the joint authors of which were Luther and Melanchthon. Having been signed by the Protestant princes and leaders, it was presented to the emperor and imperial diet in Augsburg, A. D. 1530. It is the oldest Protestant Confession, the ultimate basis of Lutheran theology, and the only universally accepted standard of the Lutheran Churches. It consists of two grand divisions. The first embracing twenty-one articles, presents a positive statement of Christian doctrines as the Lutherans understand them; and the second, embracing seven articles, condemns the principal characteristic errors of the Papacy. It is evangelical in the Augustinian sense, although not as precise in statement as the more perfect Calvinistic Confessions, and it, of course, contains the germs of the peculiar Lutheran views as to the necessity of the Sacraments, and the relation of the sacramental signs to the grace they signify. Yet these peculiarities are so far from being explicitly stated, that Calvin found it consistent with his views of divine truth to subscribe this great Confession during his residence in Strasburg.

In 1540, ten years after it had been adopted as the public symbol of Protestant Germany, Melanchthon produced an edition in Latin which he altered in several particulars, and which was hence distinguished as the *Variata*, the original and only authentic form of the Confession being distinguished as the *Invariata*. The principal changes introduced in this edition incline towards Synergistic or Arminian views of divine grace on the one hand, and on the other to simple views as to the sacraments more nearly corresponding with those prevailing among the Reformed Churches.—See Shedd's "Hist. of Christ. Doctrine," Book vii., chap. 2. See also the accurate and learnedly illustrated edition of the Augsburg Confession by Rev. Charles Krauth, D.D.

2d. The *Apology* (Defence) *of the Augsburg Confession*, prepared by Melanchthon, A. D. 1530, and subscribed by the Protestant theologians, A. D. 1537, at Smalcald.

3d. The *Larger and Smaller Catechisms* prepared by Luther, A. D. 1529, "the first for the use of preachers and teachers, the last as a guide for youth."

4th. The *Articles of Smalcald*, drawn up by Luther, A. D. 1536, and inscribed by the evangelical theologians in February, A. D. 1537, at the place whose name they bear.

5th. The *Formula Concordiæ* (Form of Concord), prepared in A. D. 1577 by Jacob Andreæ and Martin Chemnitz and others for the purpose of settling certain controversies which had sprung up in the Lutheran Church, especially (*a*) concerning the relative action of divine grace and the human will in regeneration, (*b*) concerning the nature of the Lord's presence in the Eucharist. This Confession contains a more scientific and thoroughly developed statement of the Lutheran doctrine than can be found in any other of their public symbols. Its authority is, however, acknowledged only by the high Lutheran party, that is, by that party in the church which consistently carries the peculiarities of Lutheran theology out to the most complete logical development. All these Lutheran Symbols may be found in Latin accurately edited in "Libri Symbolici," by Dr. C. A. Hase, Leipsic, 1836, and in Schaff's "Creeds of Christendom."

8. *What are the principal Confessions of the Reformed or Calvinistic Churches?*

The Confessions of the Reformed Churches are very considerable in number, and vary somewhat in character, although they substantially agree in the system of doctrines they teach.

1st. "The oldest Confession of that branch of Protestantism which was not satisfied with the Lutheran tendency and symbol is the *Confessio Tetrapolitana*,—so-called, because the theologians of four cities of upper Germany, Strasburg, Constance, Memmingen, and Lindau, drew it up, and presented it to the emperor at the same diet of Augsburg, in 1530, at which the first Lutheran symbol was presented. The principal theologian concerned in its construction was Martin Bucer, of Strasburg. It consists of twenty-two articles, and agrees generally with the Augsburg Confession. The points of difference pertain to the doctrine of the sacraments. Upon this subject it is Zwinglian. These four cities, however, in 1532 adopted the Augsburg Confession, so that the *Confessio Tetrapolitana* ceased to be the formally adopted symbol of any branch of the church."—Shedd's "Hist. of Christ. Doctrine," Book vii., chap. 2.

2d. The Reformed Confessions of the highest authority among the churches are the following:

(1.) The *Second Helvetic Confession*, prepared by Bullinger, A. D. 1564, and published 1566, superseded the First Helvetic Confession of A. D. 1536. It was adopted by all the Reformed Churches in Switzerland with the exception of Basle (which was content with the old Confession) and by the Reformed Churches in Poland, Hungary, Scotland and France, and it has always been esteemed as of the highest authority by all the Reformed Churches.

(2.) The *Heidelberg Catechism*, prepared by Ursinus and Olevianus A. D. 1562. It was established by civil authority as the doctrinal standard as well as the instrument of religious instruction for the churches of the Palatinate, a German state at that time including both banks of the Rhine. It was indorsed by the Synod of Dort, and is a doctrinal standard of the Reformed Churches of Germany and Holland, and of the [German and Dutch] Reformed Churches in America. It was used for the instruction of children in Scotland, before the adoption of the Catechisms of the Westminster Assembly, and its use was sanctioned by an unanimous vote of the first General Assembly of the reunited Presbyterian Church in the United States A. D. 1870.—See Minutes.

(3.) *The Thirty-nine Articles of the Church of England.* In 1552, Cranmer, with the advice of other bishops, drew up the *Forty-two Articles of Religion*, and which were published by royal authority in 1553. These were revised and reduced to the number of thirty-nine by Archbishop Parker and other bishops, and ratified by both houses of Convocation, and published by royal authority in 1563. They constitute the doctrinal standard of the Protestant Episcopal Churches of England, Ireland, Scotland, the Colonies, and the United States of America. The question whether these Articles are Calvinistic or not has been very unwarrantably made a matter of debate. See Lawrence's "Bampton Lecture" for 1804 on the Arminian side, and Toplady's "Doctrinal Calvinism of the Church of England," Dr. Goode's "Doctrine of Church of England as to Effects of Infant Baptism," and Dr. William Cunningham's "Reformers and their Theology," on the Calvinistic side. The seventeenth Article on Predestination is perfectly decisive of the question, and is as follows:

"Predestination to life is the everlasting purpose of God, whereby (before the foundations of the world were laid) he hath constantly decreed by his counsel, secret to us, to deliver from curse and damnation those whom he hath chosen in Christ out of mankind, and to bring them by Christ to everlasting salvation, as vessels made to honor. Wherefore they which he endued with so excellent a benefit of God, he called according to God's purpose by his Spirit working in due season: they, through grace, obey the calling; they he justified freely; they he made sons of God by adoption; they he made like the image of his only begotten Son, Jesus Christ; they walk religiously in good works, and at length, by God's mercy, they attain to everlasting felicity.

"As the godly consideration of predestination and our election in Christ is full of sweet, pleasant, and unspeakable comfort to godly persons, and such as feel in themselves the working of the Spirit of Christ, mortifying the works of the flesh and their earthly members, and drawing up their mind to high and heavenly things, as well because it doth greatly establish and confirm their faith of eternal salvation to be enjoyed through Christ, as because it doth fervently kindle their love toward God. So, for curious and carnal persons, lacking the Spirit of Christ, to have continually before their eyes the sentence of God's predestination, is a most dangerous downfall, whereby the devil doth thrust them either into desperation, or into wretchedness of most unclean living, no less perilous than desperation.

"Furthermore, we must receive God's promises in such wise as they be generally set forth to us in Holy Scripture; and, in our doings, that will of God is to be followed which we have expressly declared unto us in the word of God."

These Articles purged of their Calvinism and reduced in number to twenty-five, including a new political Article (the twenty-third) adopting as an article of faith the political system of the United States Government, constitute the doctrinal Standard of the Methodist Episcopal Church in America.

(4.) The *Canons of the Synod of Dort*. This famous Synod was convened in Dort, Holland, by the authority of the States General, for the purpose of settling the questions brought into controversy by the disciples of Arminius. Its sessions continued from Nov. 13, A. D. 1618, to May 9, A. D. 1619. It consisted of pastors, elders, and theological professors from the churches of Holland, and deputies from the churches of England, Scotland, Hesse, Bremen, the Palatinate, and Switzerland. The Canons of this Synod were received by all the Reformed Churches as a true, accurate, and eminently authoritative exhibition of the Calvinistic system of theology. They constitute in connection with the Heidelberg Catechism the doctrinal Confession of the Reformed Church of Holland and of its daughter the [Dutch] Reformed Church in America.

(5.) The *Confession and Catechisms of the Westminster Assembly*. This Assembly of Divines was convened by an act of the Long Parliament passed June 12, 1643. The original call embraced ten lords and twenty commoners as lay members, and one hundred and twenty-one divines—twenty ministers being afterward added—all shades of opinion as to Church Government being represented. The body continued its sessions from 1st of July, 1643, to 22d of February, 1649. The Confession and Catechisms they produced were immediately adopted by the General Assembly of the Church of Scotland. The Congregational Convention, also, called by Cromwell to meet at Savoy, in London, A. D. 1658, declared their approval of the doctrinal part of the Confession and Catechisms of the Westminster Assembly, and conformed their own deliverance, the *Savoy Declaration*, very nearly to it. Indeed "the difference between these two Confessions is so very small, that the modern Independents have in a manner laid aside the use of it (Savoy Declaration) in their families, and agreed with the Presbyterians in the use of the Assembly's Catechisms."—Neal, "Puritans," II., 178. This Confession together with the Larger and Smaller Catechisms is the doctrinal standard of all the Presbyterian bodies in the world of English and Scotch derivation. It is also of all Creeds the one most highly approved by all bodies of Congregationalists in England and America.

All of the Assemblies convened in New England for the purpose of settling the doctrinal basis of their churches have either indorsed or explicitly adopted this Confession and these Catechisms as accurate expositions of their own faith. This was done by the Synod which met at Cambridge, Massachusetts, June, 1647, and again August, 1648, and prepared the *Cambridge Platform.* And it was done again by the Synod which sat in Boston, September, 1679, and May, 1680, and produced the *Boston Confession.* And again by the Synod which met at Saybrook, Connecticut, 1708, and produced the Saybrook Platform.

3d. There remain several other Reformed Confessions, which, although they are not the doctrinal standards of large denominations of Christians, are nevertheless of high classical interest and authority because of their authors, and the circumstances under which they originated.

(1.) The *"Consensus Tigurinus,"* or the *"Consensus of Zurich,"* or "The mutual consent with respect to the doctrine of the sacrament of the ministers of the Church of Zurich and John Calvin, minister of the Church of Geneva." It consisted of twenty-six Articles, and deals exclusively with the questions relating to the Lord's Supper, and it was drawn by Calvin, A. D. 1549, for the purpose of bringing about a mutual consent among all parties in the Reformed Church on the subject of which it treats. It was subscribed by the Churches of Zurich, Geneva, St. Gall, Schaffhausen, the Grisons, Neuchatel, and Basle, and was received with favor by all parts of the Reformed Church, and remains an eminent monument of the true mind of the Reformed Church upon this so much debated question; and especially it is of value as setting forth with eminent clearness and unquestionable authority the real opinions of Calvin on the subject, deliberately stated *after* he had ceased from the vain attempt to secure the unity of Protestantism by a compromise with the Lutheran views as to the Lord's presence in the Eucharist. An accurate translation of this important document will be found in the Appendix.

(2.) The *"Consensus Genevensis"* was drawn up by Calvin, A. D. 1552, in the name of the Pastors of Geneva, and is a complete statement of Calvin's views on the subject of *Predestination.* It was designed to unite all the Swiss Churches in their views of this great doctrine. It remains a pre-eminent monument of the fundamental principles of true Calvinism.

(3.) The *"Formula Consensus Helvetica,"* composed at Zurich, A. D. 1675, by John Henry Heidegger of Zurich, assisted by Francis Turretin of Geneva and Luke Gernler of Basle. Its title is "Form of agreement of the Helvetic Reformed Churches respecting the doctrine of universal grace, the doctrines connected therewith, and some other points." It was designed to unite the Swiss Churches in condemning and excluding that modified form of Calvinism, which in that century emanated from the Theological School of Saumur, represented by Amyraldus, Placæus, etc. This is the most scientific and thorough of all the Reformed Confessions. Its eminent authorship* and the fact that it distinctively represents the most thoroughly consistent school of old Calvinists gives it high classical interest. It was subscribed by nearly all the Swiss Churches, but ceased to have public authority as a Confession since A. D. 1722.† All the Confessions of the Reformed Churches may be found collected in one convenient volume in the "Collectio Confessionum in Ecclesiis Reformatis publicatarum," by Dr. H. A. Niemeyer, Leipsic, 1840, and in Dr. Schaff's "Creeds of Christendom."

* See Herzog's Real–Encyclopedia. Bomberger's translation. Article, "Helvetic Confessions."
† An accurate translation will be found in the Appendix.

CHAPTER VIII.

THE ATTRIBUTES OF GOD.

1. *What are the three methods of determining what attributes belong to the divine Being?*

1st. The method of analyzing the idea of infinite and absolute perfection. This method proceeds upon the assumption that *we* are, as intelligent and moral agents, created in the image of God. In this process we attribute to him every excellence that we have any experience or conception of, in an infinite degree, and in absolute perfection, and we deny of him every form of imperfection or limitation.

2d. The method of inferring his characteristics from our observation of his works around us and our experience of his dealings with ourselves.

3d. The didactic statements of Scripture, the illustration of his character therein given in his supernatural revelation and gracious dispensations, and above all in the personal revelation of God in his Son Jesus Christ.

All these methods agree and mutually supplement and limit each other. The idea of absolute and infinite perfection, which in some sense is native to us, aids us in interpreting Scripture —and the Scriptures correct the inferences of the natural reason, and set the seal of divine authority upon our opinions about the divine nature.

2. *How far can we have assurance that the objective reality corresponds with our subjective conceptions of the divine nature?*

There are upon this subject *two* opposite extreme positions which it is necessary to avoid. 1st. The extreme of supposing that our conceptions of God either in kind or degree are adequate to represent the objective reality of his perfections. God is incomprehensible to us in the sense (*a*) that there remains an immeasurably greater part of his being and excellence of which we have and can have no knowledge, and (*b*) in the sense that even what we know of him we know imperfectly, and at best conceive of very inadequately. In this respect the imperfection of the knowledge which men have of God is analogous in kind, though indefinitely greater in degree to the imperfection of the knowledge which a child may have of the life of a great philosopher or statesman dwelling in the same city. The child not only knows *that* the philosopher or statesman in question lives—but he knows also in some real degree *what* that life is—yet that knowledge is imperfect both in respect to the fact that it apprehends a very small proportion of that life, and that it very imperfectly comprehends even that small proportion. 2d. The second extreme to be avoided is that of supposing that our knowledge of God is purely illusory, that our conceptions of the divine perfections can not correspond in any degree to the objective reality. Sir Wm. Hamilton, Mr. Mansel, and others, having proved that we are forced to think of God as "first cause," as "infinite," and as "absolute," proceed to give definitions of these abstract terms, which they then show necessarily involve mutual contradictions, of which the human reason is intolerant. They then conclude that our conceptions of God can not correspond to the real objective existence of the divine being. "To think that God is as we can think him to be is blasphemy." The last and highest consecration of all true religion, must be an altar—Ἀγνώστῳ θεῷ—"To the unknown and unknowable God" (Sir William Hamilton's "Discussions," p. 22). They hold that all the representations of God conveyed in the Scriptures, and the best conceptions we are with the aid of Scripture able to form in our minds, do not at all correspond to the outward reality, but are designed simply to be accepted not as actual scientific knowledge, but as regulative assumptions "abundantly instructive in point of sentiment and action" and practically sufficient for our present needs; "sufficient to guide our practice, but not to satisfy our intellect—which tell *not what God is in himself, but how he wills that we should think of him*."—Mansel's "Limits of Religious Thought," p. 132.

This view, although not so intended, really leads to skeptical if not to dogmatic atheism. (1.) It is founded upon an artificial and inapplicable definition of certain abstract notions entertained by philosophers concerning the "absolute" and the "infinite." As shown below, Question 6, a true definition of the absolute and infinite, in the sense in which the Scriptures and the unsophisticated minds of men hold God to be absolute and infinite, involves no contradictions or absurdities whatsoever. (2.) It will be shown below, Questions 3 and 5, that there is adequate ground for the assumption that as intellectual and moral beings we are really and truly created in the image of

God, and therefore capable of knowing him as he really exists. (3.) If our consciousness and the Sacred Scriptures present us illusory conceptions as to *what* God is, we have no reason to trust to their assurance *that* God is. (4.) This principle leads to absolute skepticism. If our Creator wills that we should think of him as he does not really exist, we have no reason to trust our constitutional instincts or faculties in any department. (5.) This principle is immoral since it makes a false representation of the divine attributes the regulative principle of man's moral and religious life. (6.) The highest and most certain dictates of human reason necessitates the conviction that moral principles, and the essential nature of moral attributes, must be identically the same in all worlds and in all beings possessed of a moral character in any sense. Truth and justice and loving-kindness must be always and only the same in Creator and creature, in God and man.

3. *What is anthropomorphism, and in what different senses is the word used?*

Anthropomorphism (ἄνθρωπος, man; μορφή, form) is a phrase employed to designate any view of God's nature which conceives of him as possessing or exercising any attributes common to him with mankind.

The Anthropomorphites in ancient times held that God possessed bodily parts and organs like ours, and hence that all those passages of Scripture which speak of his eyes, hands, etc., are to be interpreted literally.

The Pantheists, Sir William Hamilton, and other philosophers designate all our conceptions of God as a personal Spirit, etc., as anthropomorphic—that is, as modes of conception not conformed to objective fact, but determined necessarily by the subjective conditions of our own human modes of thought.

It hence follows that this phrase is to be taken in two senses.

1st. A *good sense*, in which, since man as a free rational spirit was created in the image of God, it is both Scriptural, rational, and according to objective fact, for man to conceive of God as possessing all the essential attributes which belong to our spirits in absolute perfection of kind, and with no limit inconsistent with absolute perfection in degree. When we say that God knows, and wills, and feels, that he is just, true, and merciful, we mean to ascribe to him attributes of the same kind as the corresponding ones belonging to men, only in absolute perfection, and without limit.

2d. The word is used in a *bad sense* when it designates any mode of conceiving of God which involves the ascription to him of imperfection or limitation of any kind. Thus to conceive of God as possessing hands or feet, or as experiencing the perturbations of human passion, or the like, is a false and unworthy anthropomorphism.

4. *How are we to understand those passages of Scripture which attribute to God bodily parts and the infirmities of human passion?*

The passages referred to are such as speak of the *face* of God, Ex. xxxiii. 11, 20; his eyes, 2 Chron. xvi. 9; his nostrils, 2 Sam. xxii. 9, 16; his arms and feet, Isa. lii. 10, and Ps. xviii. 9; and such as speak of his repenting and grieving, Gen. vi. 6, 7; Jer. xv. 6; Ps. xcv. 10; of his being jealous, Deut. xxix. 20, etc. These are to be understood only as metaphors. They represent the truth with respect to God only analogically, and as seen from our point of view. That God can not be material is shown below, Question 20.

When he is said to repent, or to be grieved, or to be jealous, it is only meant that he acts towards us as a man would when agitated by such passions. These metaphors occur principally in the Old Testament, and in highly rhetorical passages of the poetical and prophetical books.

5. *State the proof that Anthropomorphic conceptions of God, in the good sense of the word, are both necessary and valid.*

The fundamental fact upon which all science, all theology, and all religion rests is that God made man a living soul in his own image. Otherwise man could have no understanding of God's works any more than of his nature, and all relations of thought or feeling between them would be impossible. That man has the right thus far to conceive of God as the original and all perfect fountain of the moral and rational qualities with which he is himself endowed is proved—

1st. It is determined by the necessary laws of our nature. (*a.*) This is a matter of consciousness. If we believe in God at all we *must* conceive of him as a rational and righteous personal spirit. (*b.*) Such a conception of God has universally prevailed even amidst the degrading adulterations of heathen mythology.

2d. We have no other possible mode of knowing God. The alternative ever must be the principle for which we contend, or absolute atheism.

3d. The same is determined by the necessities of our moral nature. The innate and indestructible moral nature of man includes a sense of subjection to a righteous will superior to ourselves, and accountability to a moral Governor. This is nonsense unless the moral Governor is in our sense of the word an intelligent and righteous personal spirit.

4th. The most enduring and satisfactory argument for establishing the facts of God's existence is the *à posteriori* argument from the evidences of "design" in the works of God. If this argument has any force to prove *that* God is, it has equal force to prove that he must possess and exercise intelligence, benevolent intention and choice, *i. e.*, that he must be in our sense of the terms an intelligent personal spirit.

5th. The Scriptures characteristically ascribe the same attributes to God, and everywhere assume their existence.

6th. God manifested in the person of Jesus Christ, who is the express image of his person, has in all situations exhibited these very attributes, yet in such a way as to prove himself to be God as truly as he was man.

6. *What is the meaning of the terms "infinite" and "absolute," and in what sense are they applied to the being of God, and to his attributes severally?*

Hamilton and Mansel define the *infinite* "that which is free from all possible limitation; that than which a greater is inconceivable, and which, consequently, can receive no additional attributes or mode of existence which it had not from eternity;" and the *absolute* as "that which exists by itself, having no necessary relations to any other being." Hence they argue (*a*) that that which is infinite and absolute must include the sum total of all things, evil and good, actual and possible; for if any thing actual or possible is excluded from it, it must be finite and relative; (*b*) that it can not be an object of knowledge, for to know is both to limit—to define—and to bring into relation to the one knowing; (*c*) that it can not be a person, for personal consciousness implies limitation and change; (*d*) that it can not know other things, because to know, implies relation as before said.—Hamilton's "Discussions," Art. 1; Mansel's "Limits of Religious Thought," Lectures 1, 2, 3.

All of this logical bewilderment results from these philosophers starting from the false premise of an abstract, notional "infinite" and "absolute," and substituting their definition of *that* in the place of the true infinite and absolute person revealed in Scripture and consciousness as the first cause of all things, the moral Governor and Redeemer of mankind.

"Infinite" means that which has no limits. When we say God is infinite in his being, or in his knowledge, or in his power, we mean that his essence and the active properties thereof, have no limitations which involve imperfections of any kind whatsoever. He transcends all the limitations of time and space, he knows all things in an absolutely perfect manner. He is able to effect whatsoever he wills to effect with or without

means, and with perfect facility and success. When men say
that God is infinite in his justice, or his goodness, or his truth,
they mean that his inexhaustible and unchangeable being possesses these properties in absolute perfection.

"Absolute" when applied to the being of God signifies that
he is an eternal self-existent person, who existed before all
other beings, and is the intelligent and voluntary cause of
whatsoever else has or will exist in the universe, etc., that he
*sustains, consequently, no necessary relation to any thing without
himself.* Whatever exists is conditioned upon God, as the circle is conditioned upon its centre, but God himself neither in
his existence, nor in any of the modes or states of it, is conditioned upon any of his creatures, nor upon his creation as a
whole. God is what he is because he is, and he wills whatsoever he does will because "it seemeth good in his sight." All
other things are what they are because God has willed them
to be as they are. Whatsoever relation he sustains to any
thing without himself is voluntarily assumed.

7. *In what different ways do the Scriptures reveal God?*

They reveal God—1st. By his names. 2d. By the works
which they ascribe to him. 3d. By the attributes which they
predicate of him. 4th. By the worship they direct to be paid
to him. 5th. By the manifestation of God in Christ.

8. *State the etymology and meaning of the several names appropriated to God in the Scriptures.*

1st. JEHOVAH, from the Hebrew verb הָיָה *to be.* It expresses
self-existence and unchangeableness; it is the incommunicable
name of God, which the Jews superstitiously refused to pronounce, always substituting in their reading the word Adonai,
Lord. Hence it is represented in our English version by the
word LORD, printed in capital letters.

JAH, probably an abbreviation of the name Jehovah, is used
principally in the Psalms.—Ps. lxviii. 4. It constitutes the
concluding syllable of hallelujah, *praise Jehovah.*

God gave to Moses his peculiar name, "I AM THAT I AM,"
Ex. iii. 14, from the same root, and bearing the same fundamental significance as Jehovah.

2d. EL, *might, power,* translated *God,* and applied alike to
the true and to the false gods.—Isa. xliv. 10.

3d. ELOHIM and ELOAH, the same name in its singular and
plural form, derived from אָלַה, *to fear,* reverence. "In its singular form it is used only in the latter books and in poetry."
In the plural form it is sometimes used with a plural sense for

gods, but more commonly as *a pluralis excellentiœ*, for God. It is applied to false gods, but pre-eminently to Jehovah as the great object of adoration.

4th. ADONAI, *the Lord, a pluralis excellentiœ,* applied exclusively to God, expressing possession and sovereign dominion, equivalent to κύριος, *Lord,* so frequently applied to Christ in the New Testament.

5th. SADDAI, *almighty, a pluralis excellentiœ.* Sometimes it stands by itself.—Job v. 17; and sometimes combined with a preceding El.—Gen xvii. 1.

6th. ELYŌN, *Most High,* a verbal adjective from עָלָה, *to go up, ascend.*—Ps. ix. 3; xxi. 8.

7th. The term TZEBAOTH, of hosts, is frequently used as an epithet qualifying one of the above-mentioned names of God. Thus, *Jehovah of Hosts, God of Hosts, Jehovah, God of Hosts.*— Amos iv. 13; Ps. xxiv. 10. Some have thought this equivalent to God of Battles. The true force of the epithet, however, is "sovereign of the stars, material hosts of heaven, and of the angels their inhabitants."—Dr. J. A. Alexander, "Com. on Ps. xxiv. 10," and Gesenius's "Heb. Lex."

8th. Many other epithets are applied to God metaphorically, to set forth the relation he sustains to us and the offices he fulfills, *e. g.,* King, Lawgiver, Judge.—Isa. xxxiii. 17; Ps. xxiv. 8; l. 6. Rock, Fortress, Tower, Deliverer.—2 Sam. xxii. 2, 3; Ps. lxii. 2. Shepherd, Husbandman.—Ps. xxiii. 1; John xv. 1. Father.—Matt. vi. 9; John xx. 17, etc.

9. *What are the divine attributes?*

The divine attributes are the perfections which are predicated of the divine essence in the Scriptures, or visibly exercised by God in his works of creation and providence and redemption. They are not properties or states of the divine essence separable in fact or idea from the divine essence, as the properties and modes of every created thing are separable from the essence of the creature. God's knowledge is his essence knowing, and his love is his essence loving, and his will is his essence willing, and all these are not latent capacities of action, nor changing states, but co-existent and eternally unchangeable states of the divine essence which in state and mode as well as in existence is "the same yesterday, today and forever" and "without variableness or shadow of turning."

Concerning the nature and operations of God, we can know only what he has vouchsafed to reveal to us, and with every conception, either of his being or his acts, there must always attend an element of incomprehensibility, which is inseparable from infinitude. His knowledge and power are as truly beyond all understanding as his eternity or immensity.—Job. xi. 7–9; xxvi. 14; Ps. cxxxix. 5, 6; Isa. xl. 28. The moral elements of his glorious nature are the norm or original type of our moral faculties; thus we are made capable of comprehending the ultimate principles of truth and justice upon which he acts. Truth and justice and goodness are of course the same in essence in God and in angel and in man. Yet his action upon those principles is often a trial of our faith, and an occasion of our adoring wonder.—Rom. xi. 33–36; Isa. lv. 8, 9.

10. *What do theologians mean by the phrase* SIMPLICITY, *when applied to God?*

The term simplicity is used, *first*, in opposition to material composition, whether mechanical, organic, or chemical; *second*, in a metaphysical sense in negation of the relation of substance and property, essence and mode. In the first sense of the word human souls are simple, because they are not composed of elements, parts, or organs. In the second sense of the word our souls are complex, since there is in them a distinction between their essence and their properties, and their successive modes or states of existence. As, however, God is infinite, eternal, self-existent from eternity, necessarily the same without succession, theologians have maintained that in him essence, and property, and mode are one. He always is what he is; and his various states of intellection, emotion, and volition are not successive and transient but co-existent and permanent; and he is what he is essentially, and by the same necessity that he exists. Whatever is in God, whether thought, emotion, volition, or act, is God.

Some men conceive of God as passing through various transient modes and states just as men do, and therefore they suppose the properties of the divine nature are related to the divine essence as the properties of created things are related to the essences which are endowed with them. Others press the idea of simplicity so far that they deny any distinction in the divine attributes in themselves, and suppose that the only difference between them is to be found in the mode of external manifestation, and in the effects produced. They illustrate their idea by the various effects produced on different objects by the same radiance of the sun.

In order to avoid both extremes theologians have been accustomed to say that the divine attributes differ from the divine essence and from one another, 1st, not *realiter* or as one thing differs from another, or in any such way as to imply composition in God. Nor 2d, merely *nominaliter*, as though there were nothing in God really corresponding to our conceptions of his perfections. But 3d, they are said to differ *virtualiter*, so that there is in him a foundation or adequate reason for all the representations which are made in Scripture with regard to the divine perfections, and for the consequent conceptions which we have of them.—Turretin's "Institutio Theologicæ," Locus iii., Ques. 5 and 7, and Dr. C. Hodge's "Lectures."

11. *State the different principles upon which the classification of the divine attributes has been attempted.*

From the vastness of the subject and the incommensurateness of our faculties, it is evident that no classification of the divine attributes we can form can be any thing more than approximately accurate and complete. The most common classifications rest upon the following principles:

1st. They are distinguished as *absolute* and *relative*. An absolute attribute is a property of the divine essence considered in itself: *e. g.*, self-existence, immensity, eternity, intelligence. A relative attribute is a property of the divine essence considered in relation to the creation: *e. g.*, omnipresence, omniscience, etc.

2d. They are also distinguished as *affirmative* and *negative*. An affirmative attribute is one which expresses some positive perfection of the divine essence: *e. g.*, omnipresence, omnipotence, etc. A negative attribute is one which denies all defect or limitation of any kind to God: *e. g.*, immutability, infinitude, incomprehensibility, etc.

3d. The attributes of God, distinguished as communicable and incommunicable. The communicable are those to which the attributes of the human spirit bear the nearest analogy: *e. g.*, his power, knowledge, will, goodness, and righteousness. The incommunicable are those to which there is in the creature nothing analogous, as eternity, immensity, etc. This distinction, however, must not be pressed too far. God is infinite in his relation to space and time; we are finite in our relation to both. But he is no less infinite as to his knowledge, will, goodness, and righteousness in all their modes, and we are finite in all these respects. All God's attributes known to us, or conceivable by us, are communicable, inasmuch as they have their analogy in us, but they are all alike incommunicable, inasmuch as they are all infinite.

4th. The attributes of God, distinguished as natural and moral. The natural are all those which pertain to his existence as an infinite, rational Spirit: *e. g.*, eternity, immensity, intelligence, will, power. The moral are those additional attributes which belong to him as an infinite, righteous Spirit: *e. g.*, justice, mercy, truth.

I would diffidently propose the following fourfold classification:

(1.) Those attributes which equally qualify all the rest— *Infinitude*, that which has no bounds; *absoluteness*, that which is determined either in its being, or modes of being or action, by nothing whatsoever without itself. This includes immutability.

(2.) Natural attributes. God is an infinite *Spirit, self-existent, eternal, immense, simple, free of will, intelligent, powerful.*

(3.) Moral attributes. God is a Spirit infinitely *righteous, good, true,* and *faithful.*

(4.) The consummate glory of all the divine perfections in union. The beauty of HOLINESS.

THE UNITY OF GOD.

12. *In what two senses of the word is* UNITY *predicated of God?*

1st. God is unique: there is only one God to the exclusion of all others.

2d. Notwithstanding the threefold personal distinction in the unity of the Godhead, yet these three Persons are numerically one substance or essence, and constitute one indivisible God.

13. *How may the proposition, that God is one and indivisible, be proved?*

1st. There appears to be a necessity in reason for conceiving of God as one. That which is absolute and infinite can not but be one and indivisible in essence. If God is not one, then it will necessarily follow that there are more gods than one.

2d. The uniform representation of Scripture.—John x. 30.

14. *Prove from Scripture that the proposition, there is but one God, is true.*

Deut. vi. 4; 1 Kings viii. 60; Isa. xliv. 6; Mark xii. 29, 32; 1 Cor. viii. 4; Eph. iv. 6.

15. *What is the argument from the harmony of creation in favor of the divine unity?*

The whole creation, between the outermost range of telescopic and of microscopic observation, is manifestly one indivisible system. But we have already (Chapter II.) proved the existence of God from the phenomena of the universe; and we now argue, upon the same principle, that if an effect proves the prior operation of a cause, and if traces of design prove a designer, then singleness of plan and operation in that design and its execution prove that the designer is ONE.

16. *What is the argument upon this point from necessary existence?*

The existence of God is said to be necessary, because it has its cause from eternity in itself. It is the same in all duration and in all space alike. It is absurd to conceive of God's not existing at any time or in any portion of space, while all other existence whatsoever, depending upon his mere will, is contingent. But the necessity which is uniform in all times and in every portion of space, is evidently only one and indivisible, and can be the ground of the existence only of one God.

This argument is logical, and has been prized highly by many distinguished theologians. It however appears to involve the error of presuming human logic to be the measure of existence.

17. *What is the argument from infinite perfection, in proof that there can be but one God?*

God is infinite in his being and in all of his perfections. But the infinite, by including all, excludes all others, of the same kind. If there were two infinite beings, each would necessarily include the other, and be included by it, and thus they would be the same, one and identical. It is certain that the idea of the co-existence of two infinitely perfect beings is as repugnant to human reason as to Scripture.

18. *What is polytheism? and what dualism?*

Polytheism, as the etymology of the word indicates, is a general term designating every system of religion which teaches the existence of a plurality of gods.

Dualism is the designation of that system which recognizes two original and independent principles in the universe, the one good and the other evil. At present these principles are in a relation of ceaseless antagonism, the good ever struggling to oppose the evil, and to deliver its province from its baneful intrusion.

THE SPIRITUALITY OF GOD.

19. *What is affirmed and what is denied in the proposition that God is a Spirit?*

We know nothing of substance except as it is manifested by its properties. Matter is that substance whose properties manifest themselves directly to our bodily senses. Spirit is that substance whose properties manifest themselves to us *directly* in self-consciousness, and only *inferentially* by words and other signs or modes of expression through our senses.

When we say God is a Spirit we mean—

1st. Negatively, that he does not possess bodily parts or passions; that he is composed of no material elements; that he is not subject to any of the limiting conditions of material existence; and, consequently, that he is not to be apprehended as the object of any of our bodily senses.

2d. Positively, that he is a rational being, who distinguishes with infinite precision between the true and the false; that he is a moral being, who distinguishes between the right and the wrong; that he is a free agent, whose action is self-determined by his own will; and, in fine, that all the essential properties of our spirits may truly be predicated of him in an infinite degree.

This great truth is inconsistent with the doctrine that God is the soul of the world (*anima mundi*) a plastic organizing force inseparable from matter; also with the Gnostic doctrine of emanation, and with all forms of modern Materialism and Pantheism.

20. *Exhibit the proof that God is a Spirit.*

1st. It is explicitly asserted in Scripture.—John iv. 24.

2d. It follows from our idea of infinite and absolute perfections. Matter is obviously inferior to Spirit, and inseparable from many kinds of imperfections and limitations. Matter consisting of separate and ceaselessly reacting atoms can not be "one," nor "infinite," nor "immutable," etc. The idea that matter may be united with spirit in God, as it is in man, is felt to degrade him, and bind him fast under the limitations of time and space.

3d. There is no trace anywhere of material properties in the Creator and Providential Governor of the universe—whereas all the evidence that a God exists conspires to prove also that he is a supremely wise, benevolent, righteous, and powerful person—that is, that he is a personal spirit.

God's Relation to Space.

21. *What is meant by the immensity of God?*

The immensity of God is the phrase used to express the fact that God is infinite in his relation to space, *i. e.*, that the entire indivisible essence of God is at every moment of time cotemporaneously present to every point of infinite space.

This is not in virtue of the infinite multiplication of his Spirit, since he is eternally one and individual; nor does it result from the infinite diffusion of his essence through infinite space, as air is diffused over the surface of the earth, since, being a Spirit he is not composed of parts, nor is he capable of extension, but the whole Godhead in the one indivisible essence is equally present in every moment of eternal duration to the whole of infinite space, and to every part of it.

22. *How does immensity differ from omnipresence?*

Immensity characterizes the relation of God to space viewed abstractly in itself. Omnipresence characterizes the relation of God to his creatures as they severally occupy their several positions in space. The divine essence is immense in its own being, absolutely. It is omnipresent relatively to all his creatures.

23. *What are the different modes of the divine presence, and how may it be proved that he is everywhere present as to his essence?*

God may be conceived of as present in any place, or with any creature, in several modes, first, as to his essence; second, as to his knowledge; third, as manifesting that presence to any intelligent creature; fourth, as exercising his power in any way in or upon the creature. As to essence and knowledge, his presence is the same everywhere and always. As to his self-manifestation and the exercise of his power, his presence differs endlessly in different cases in degree and mode. Thus God is present to the church as he is not to the world. Thus he is present in hell in the manifestation and execution of righteous wrath, while he is present in heaven in the manifestation and communication of gracious love and glory.

24. *Prove that God is omnipresent as to his essence.*

That God is everywhere present as to his essence is proved, first from Scripture (1 Kings viii. 27; Ps. cxxxix. 7–10; Isa. lxvi. 1; Acts xvii. 27, 28); second, from reason. (1.) It follows necessarily from his infinitude. (2.) From the fact that his knowledge is his essence knowing, and his actions are his essence acting. Yet his knowledge and his power reach to all things.

25. *State the different relations that bodies, created spirits, and God sustain to space.*

Turretin says: Bodies are conceived of as existing in space *circumscriptively*, because occupying a certain portion of space they are bounded by space upon every side. Created spirits do not occupy any portion of space, nor are they embraced by any, they are, however, in space *definitely*, as here and not there. God, on the other hand, is in space *repletively*, because in a transcendent manner his essence fills all space. He is included in no space; he is excluded from none. Wholly present to each point, he comprehends all space at once.

Time and Space are neither substances, nor qualities, nor mere relations. They constitute a genus by themselves, absolutely distinct from all other entities, and therefore defying classification. "We know that space and time exist; we know on sufficient evidence that God exists; but we have no means of knowing how space and time stand related to God. The view taken by Sir Isaac Newton,—'Deus durat semper et adest ubique, et, existendo semper et ubique, durationem et spatium constituit'—is certainly a grand one, but I doubt much whether human intelligence can dictatorially affirm that it is as true as it is sublime."—McCosh, "Intuitions of the Mind," p. 212.

THE RELATION OF GOD TO TIME.

26. *What is eternity?*

Eternity is infinite duration; duration discharged from all limits, without beginning, without succession, and without end. The schoolmen phrase it a *punctum stans*, an ever-abiding present.

We, however, can positively conceive of eternity only as duration indefinitely extended from the present moment in two directions, as to the past and as to the future, improperly expressed as eternity *a parte ante*, or past, and eternity *a parte post*, or future. The eternity of God, however, is one and indivisible. *Eternitas est una individua et tota simul.*

27. *What is time?*

Time is limited duration, measured by succession, either of thought or motion. It is distinguished in reference to our perceptions into past, present, and future.

28. *What relation does time bear to eternity?*

Eternity, the unchanging present, without beginning or end, comprehends all time, and co-exists as an undivided moment, with all the successions of time as they appear and pass in their order.

Thought is possible to us, however, only under the limitations of time and space. We can conceive of God only under the finite fashion of first purposing and then acting, of first promising or threatening and then fulfilling his word, etc. He that inhabiteth eternity infinitely transcends our understanding. Isa. lvii. 15.

29. *When we say that God is eternal, what do we affirm and what do we deny?*

We affirm, first, that as to his existence, he never had any beginning, and never will have any end; second, that as to the mode of his existence, his thoughts, emotions, purposes, and acts are, without succession, one and inseparable, the same forever; third, that he is immutable.

We deny, first, that he ever had a beginning or ever will have an end; second, that his states or modes of being occur in succession; third, that his essence, attributes, or purposes will ever change.

30. *In what sense are the acts of God spoken of as past, present, and future?*

The acts of God are never past, present, or future as respects God himself, but only in respect to the objects and effects of his acts in the creature. The efficient purpose comprehending the precise object, time, and circumstance was present to him always and changelessly; the event, however, taking place in the creature occurs in time, and is thus past, present, or future to our observation.

31. *In what sense are events past or future as it regards God?*

As God's knowledge is infinite, every event must, first, be ever equally present to his knowledge from eternity to eternity; second, these events must be known to him as they actually occur in themselves, *e. g.*, in their true nature, relations, and successions. This distinction, therefore, holds true—God's knowledge of all events is without beginning, end, or succession; but he knows them as in themselves occurring in the successions of time, past, present, or future, relatively to one another.

THE IMMUTABILITY OF GOD.

32. *What is meant by the immutability of God?*

By his immutability we mean that it follows from the infinite perfection of God; that he can not be changed by any thing from without himself; and that he will not change from any principle within himself. That as to his essence, his will, and his states of existence, he is the same from eternity to eternity. Thus he is absolutely immutable in himself. He is also immutable relatively to the creature, insomuch as his knowledge, purpose, and truth, as these are conceived by us and are revealed to us, can know neither variableness nor shadow of turning.—James i. 17.

33. *Prove from Scripture and reason that God is immutable.*

1st. Scripture: Mal. iii. 6; Ps. xxxiii. 11; Isa. xlvi. 10; James i. 17.

2d. Reason: (1.) God is self-existent. As he is caused by none, but causes all, so he can be changed by none, but changes all. (2.) He is the absolute being. Neither his existence, nor the manner of it, nor his will, are determined by any necessary relation which they sustain to any thing exterior to himself. As he preceded all and caused all, so his sovereign will freely determined the relations which all things are permitted to sustain to him. (3.) He is infinite in duration, and therefore he can not know succession or change. (4.) He is infinite in all perfection, knowledge, wisdom, righteousness, benevolence, will, power, and therefore can not change, for nothing can be added to the infinite nor taken from it. Any change would make him either less than infinite before, or less than infinite afterwards.

34. *How can the creation of the world and the incarnation of the Son be reconciled with the immutability of God?*

1st. As to the creation. The efficacious purpose, the will and power to create the world dwelleth in God from eternity without change, but this very efficacious purpose itself provided that the effect should take place in its proper time and order. This effect took place *from* God, but of course involved no shadow of change *in* God, as nothing was either taken from him or added to him.

2d. As to the incarnation. The divine Son assumed a created human nature into personal union with himself. His uncreated essence of course was not changed. His eternal person was not changed in itself, but only brought into a new relation. The change effected by that stupendous event occurred only in the created nature of the man Christ Jesus.

THE INFINITE INTELLIGENCE OF GOD.

35. *How does God's mode of knowing differ from ours?*

God's knowledge is, 1st, his essence knowing; 2d, it is one eternal, all-comprehensive, indivisible act.

(1.) It is not *discursive, i. e.,* proceeding logically from the known to the unknown; but *intuitive, i. e.,* discerning all things directly in its own light.

(2.) It is *independent, i. e.,* it does in no way depend upon his creatures or their actions, but solely upon his own infinite intuition of all things *possible* in the light of his own reason, and of all things *actual* and *future* in the light of his own eternal purpose.

(3.) It is *total* and *simultaneous*, not *successive.* It is one single, indivisible act of intuition, beholding all things in themselves, their relations and successions, as ever present.

(4.) It is *perfect* and *essential*, not *relative, i. e.*, he knows all things directly in their hidden essences, while we know them only by their properties, as they stand related to our senses.

(5.) We know the present imperfectly, the past we remember dimly, the future we know not at all. But God knows all things, past, present, and future, by one total, unsuccessive, all-comprehensive vision.

36. *How has this divine perfection been defined by theologians?*

Turretin, Locus iii., Q. 12.—"Concerning the knowledge of God, before all else, two things are to be considered, viz., its *mode* and its *object.* The *Mode* of the divine knowledge consists in this, that he perfectly, individually, distinctly, and immutably knows all things, and his knowledge is thus distinguished from the knowledge of men and angels. He knows all things *perfectly*, because he has known them through himself, or his own essence, and not by the phenomena of things, as the creatures know objects. . . . 2. He knows all things *individually* because he knows them intuitively, by a direct act of cognition, and not inferentially, by a process of discursive reasoning, or by comparing one thing with another. . . . 3. He knows all things *distinctly*, not that he unites by a different conception the various predicates of things, but that he sees through all things by one most distinct act of intuition, and nothing, even the least thing, escapes him. . . . 4. And he knows all *immutably*, because that with him there is no shadow of change, and he remaining himself unmoved, moves all things, and so perceives all the various changes of things, by one immutable act of cognition."

37. *How may the objects of divine knowledge be classified?*

1st. God himself in his own infinite being. It is evident that this, transcending the sum of all other objects, is the only adequate object of a knowledge really infinite.

2d. All possible objects, as such, whether they are or ever have been, or ever will be or not, seen in the light of his own infinite reason.

3d. All things actual, which have been, are, or will be, he comprehends in one eternal, simultaneous act of knowledge, as ever present actualities to him, and as known to be such in the light of his own sovereign and eternal purpose.

38. *What is the technical designation of the knowledge of things possible, and what is the foundation of that knowledge?*

Its technical designation is *scientia simplicis intelligentiæ, knowledge of simple intelligence,* so called, because it is conceived by us as an act simply of the divine intellect, without any concurrent act of the divine will. For the same reason it has been styled *scientia necessaria,* necessary knowledge, *i. e.,* not voluntary, or determined by will. The foundation of that knowledge is God's essential and infinitely perfect knowledge of his own omnipotence.

39. *What is the technical designation of the knowledge of things actual, whether past, present, or future, and what is the foundation of that knowledge?*

It is called *scientia visionis, knowledge of vision,* and *scientia libera, free knowledge,* because his intellect is in this case conceived of as being determined by a concurrent act of his will.

The foundation of this knowledge is God's infinite knowledge of his own all-comprehensive and unchangeable eternal purpose.

40. *Prove that the knowledge of God extends to future contingent events.*

The contingency of events in our view of them has a twofold ground: first, their immediate causes may be by us indeterminate, as in the case of the dice; second, their immediate cause may be the volition of a free agent. The first class are in no sense contingent in God's view. The second class are foreknown by him as contingent in their cause, but as none the less certain in their event.

That he does foreknow all such is certain—

1st. Scripture affirms it.—1 Sam. xxiii. 11, 12; Acts ii. 23; xv. 18; Isa. xlvi. 9, 10.

2d. He has often predicted contingent events future, at the time of the prophecy, which has been fulfilled in the event. Mark xiv. 30.

3d. God is infinite in all his perfections, his knowledge, therefore, must (1) be perfect, and comprehend all things future as well as past, (2) independent of the creature. He knows all things in themselves by his own light, and can not depend upon the will of the creature to make his knowledge either more certain or more complete.

41. *How can the certainty of the foreknowledge of God be reconciled with the freedom of moral agents in their acts?*

The difficulty here presented is of this nature. God's foreknowledge is certain; the event, therefore, must be certainly future; if certainly future, how can the agent be free in enacting it.

In order to avoid this difficulty some theologians, on the one hand, have denied the reality of man's moral freedom, while others, on the other hand, have maintained that, God's knowledge being free, he voluntarily abstains from knowing what his creatures endowed with free agency will do.

We remark—

1st. God's certain foreknowledge of all future events and man's free agency are both certain facts, impregnably established by independent evidence. We must believe both, whether we can reconcile them or not.

2d. Although necessity is inconsistent with liberty, moral certainty is not, as is abundantly shown in Chapter XV., Question 25.

42. *What is scientia media?*

This is the technical designation of God's knowledge of future contingent events, presumed, by the authors of this distinction, to depend not upon the eternal purpose of God making the event certain, but upon the free act of the creature as foreseen by a special intuition. It is called scientia media, *middle knowledge,* because it is supposed to occupy a middle ground between the knowledge of *simple intelligence* and the knowledge of *vision.* It differs from the former, since its *object* is not all possible things, but a special class of things actually future. It differs from the latter, since its *ground* is not the eternal purpose of God, but the free action of the creature as simply foreseen.

43. *By whom was this distinction introduced, and for what purpose?*

By *Luis Molina,* a Jesuit, born 1535 and died 1601, professor of theology in the University of Evora, Portugal, in his work entitled "Liberi arbitrii cum gratiæ donis, divina præscientia, prædestinatione et reprobatione concordia."—Hagenbach's "Hist. of Doc.," vol. 2, p. 280. It was excogitated for the purpose of explaining how God might certainly foreknow what his free creatures would do in the absence of any sovereign foreordination on his part, determining their action. Thus making his foreordination of men to happiness or misery to depend upon his foreknowledge of their faith and obedience, and denying that his foreknowledge depends upon his sovereign foreordination.

44. What are the arguments against the validity of this distinction?

1st. The arguments upon which it is based are untenable. Its advocates plead—(1.) Scripture.—1 Sam. xxiii. 9–12; Matt. xi. 22, 23. (2.) That this distinction is obviously necessary, in order to render the mode of the divine foreknowledge consistent with man's free agency.

To the first argument we answer, that the events mentioned in the above-cited passages of Scripture *were not future.* They simply teach that God, knowing all causes, free and necessary, knows how they would act under any proposed condition. Even we know that *if* we add fire to powder an explosion would ensue. This comes under the first class we cited above (Question 38), or the knowledge of all possible things. To the second argument we answer, that the certain foreknowledge of God involves the *certainty* of the future free act of his creature as much as his foreordination does; and that the sovereign foreordination of God, with respect to the free acts of men, only makes them *certainly future,* and does not in the least provide for causing those acts in any other way than by the free will of the creature himself acting freely.

2d. This middle knowledge is unnecessary, because all possible objects of knowledge, all *possible things,* and all *things actually to be,* have already been embraced under the two classes already cited (Questions 38, 39).

3d. If God certainly foreknows any future event, then it must be certainly future, and he must have foreknown it to be certainly future, either because it was antecedently certain, or because his foreknowing it made it certain. If his foreknowing it made it certain, then his foreknowledge involves foreordination. If it was antecedently certain, then we ask, what could have made it certain, except what we affirm, the decree of God, either to cause it himself immediately, or to cause it through some necessary second cause, or that some free agent should cause it freely? We can only choose between the foreordination of God and a blind fate.

4th. This view makes the knowledge of God to depend upon the acts of his creatures exterior to himself. This is both absurd and impious, if God is infinite, eternal, and absolute.

5th. The Scriptures teach that God does foreordain as well as foreknow the free acts of men.—Isa. x. 5–15; Acts ii. 23; iv. 27, 28.

45. How does wisdom differ from knowledge, and wherein does the wisdom of God consist?

Knowledge is a simple act of the understanding, apprehending *that* a thing is, and comprehending its nature and relations, or *how* it is.

Wisdom presupposes knowledge, and is the practical use which the understanding, determined by the will, makes of the material of knowledge. God's wisdom is infinite and eternal. It is conceived of by us as selecting the highest possible end, the manifestation of his own glory, and then in selecting and directing in every department of his operations the best possible means to secure that end. This wisdom is gloriously manifested to us in the great theatres of creation, providence, and grace.

The Infinite Power of God.

46. *What is meant by the omnipotence of God?*

Power is that efficiency which, by an essential law of thought, we recognize as inherent in a cause in relation to its effect. God is the uncaused first cause, and the causal efficiency of his will is absolutely unlimited by any thing outside of the divine perfections themselves.

47. *What distinction has been marked between the Potestas absoluta, and the Potestas ordinata of God?*

The Scriptures and right reason teach us that the causal efficiency of God is not confined to the universe of second-causes and their active properties and laws. The phrase *Potestas absoluta* expresses the omnipotence of God absolutely considered in himself—and specifically that infinite reserve of power which remains with him, as a free personal attribute, above and beyond all the powers of nature and his ordinary providential actings upon and through them. Creation, miracles, etc., are exercises of *this* power of God. The *Potestas ordinata* on the other hand is the power of God as it is now exercised in and through the established system of second causes, in the ordinary course of Providence. Rationalists and advocates of mere naturalism, who deny miracles, and any form of divine interference with the established order of nature, of course admit only the latter and deny the former mode of divine power.

48. *In what sense is the power of God limited and in what sense is it unlimited?*

We are conscious with respect to our own causal efficiency. 1st. That it is very limited. We have direct control only over the course of our thoughts, and the contractions of a few muscles. 2d. That we depend upon the use of means to pro-

duce the effects we design. 3d. We are dependent upon outward circumstances which limit and condition us continually.

The power inherent in the divine will on the other hand can
produce whatever effects he intends immediately, and when he
condescends to use means he freely endows them with whatever efficiency they possess. All outward circumstances of
every kind are his own creation, conditioned upon his will,
and therefore incapable of limiting him in any way. He is
absolutely unlimited in the exercise of his power. He *can not*
do wrong, nor work contradictions, because his power is the
causal efficiency of an infinitely rational and righteous essence.
His power therefore is limited only by his own perfections.

49. *Is the distinction in us between power and will a perfection
or a defect, and does it exist in God?*

It is objected that if our power was equal to our design, and
every volition resulted immediately in act, we would not be
conscious of the difference between power and will. We admit
that when a man's power fails to be commensurate with his will
it is a defect—and that this never is the case with God. But
on the other hand when a man is conscious that he possesses
powers which he might but does not will to exercise, he is
conscious that it is an excellence—and that his nature is the
more perfect for the possession of such reserves of power than
it would otherwise be. To hold that there is nothing in God
which is not in actual exercise, that his power extends no
further than his will, is to make him no greater than his finite
creation. The actions of a great man impress us chiefly as the
exponents of vastly greater power which remains in reserve.
So it is with God.

50. *How can absolute omnipotence be proved to belong to God?*

1st. It is asserted by Scripture.—Jer. xxxii. 17; Matt. xix.
26; Luke i. 37; Rev. xix. 6.

2d. It is necessarily involved in the very idea of God as an
infinite being.

3d. Although we have seen *but part of his ways* (Job xxvi.
14), yet our constantly extending experience is ever revealing
to us new and more astonishing evidences of his power, which
always indicate an inexhaustible reserve.

THE WILL OF GOD.

51. *What is meant by the will of God?*

The will of God is the infinitely and eternally wise, powerful,
and righteous essence of God willing. In our conception it is

that attribute of the Deity to which we refer his purposes and decrees as their principle.

52. *In what sense is the will of God said to be free, and in what sense necessary?*

The will of God is the wise, powerful, and righteous essence of God willing. His will, therefore, in every act is certainly and yet most freely both wise and righteous. The liberty of indifference is evidently foreign to his nature, because the perfection of wisdom is to choose the most wisely, and the perfection of righteousness is to choose the most righteously.

On the other hand, the will of God is from eternity absolutely independent of all his creatures and all their actions.

53. *What is intended by the distinction between the decretive and the preceptive will of God?*

The decretive will of God is God efficaciously purposing the certain futurition of events. The preceptive will of God is God, as moral governor, commanding his moral creatures to do that which he sees it right and wise that they in their circumstances should do.

These are not inconsistent. What he wills as our duty may very consistently be different from what he wills as his purpose. What it is right for him to permit may be wrong for him to approve, or for us to do.

54. *What is meant by the distinction between the secret and revealed will of God?*

The secret will of God is his decretive will, called secret, because although it is sometimes revealed to man in the prophecies and promises of the Bible, yet it is for the most part hidden in God.

The revealed will of God is his preceptive will, which is always clearly set forth as the rule of our duty.—Deut. xxix. 29.

55. *In what sense do the Arminians maintain the distinction between the antecedent and consequent will of God, and what are the objections to their view of the subject?*

This is a distinction invented by the schoolmen, and adopted by the Arminians, for reconciling the will of God with their theory of the free agency of man.

They call that an *antecedent* act of God's will which precedes the action of the creature, *e. g.*, before Adam sinned God willed him to be happy. They call that a *consequent* act of God's will which followed the act of the creature, and is consequent upon that act, e. g., after Adam sinned God willed him to suffer the penalty due to his sin.

It is very evident that this distinction does not truly represent the nature of God's will, and its relation to the acts of his creatures: *first*, God is eternal, and therefore there can be no distinction in his purposes as to time; *second*, God is eternally omniscient and omnipotent. If he wills any thing, therefore, he must from the beginning will the means to acomplish it, and thus secure the attainment of the end willed. Otherwise God must have, at the same time, two inconsistent wills with regard to the same object. The truth is that God, eternally and unchangeably, by one comprehensive act of will, willed all that happened to Adam from beginning to end in the precise order and succession in which each event occurred; *third*, God is infinitely independent. It is degrading to God to conceive of him as first willing that which he has no power to effect, and then changing his will consequently to the independent acts of his creatures.

It is true, indeed, that because of the natural limits of our capacities we necessarily conceive of the several intentions of God's one, eternal, indivisible purpose, as sustaining a certain logical (not temporal), relation to each other as principal and consequent. Thus we conceive of God's first (in logical order) decreeing to create man, then to permit him to fall, then to elect some to everlasting life, and then to provide a redemption.—Turretin.

56. *In what sense do Arminians hold the distinction between the absolute and conditional will of God, and what are the objections to that view?*

In their view that is the absolute will of God which is suspended upon no condition without himself, e. g., his decree to create man. That is the conditional will of God which is suspended upon a condition, e. g., his decree to save those that believe, i. e., on condition of their faith.

It is evident that this view is entirely inconsistent with the nature of God as an eternal, self-existent, independent being, infinite in all his perfections. It degrades him to the position of being simply a co-ordinate part of the creation, mutually limiting and being limited by the creature.

The mistake results from detaching a fragment of God's will from the one whole, all-comprehensive, eternal purpose. It is evident that, when properly viewed as eternal and one, God's purpose must comprehend all conditions, as well as their consequents. God's will is suspended upon no condition, but he eternally wills the event as suspended upon its condition, and its condition as determining the event.

It is admitted by all that God's preceptive will, as expressed in commands, promises, and threatenings, is often suspended upon condition. If we believe we shall certainly be saved. This is the relation which God has immutably established between faith as the condition, and salvation as the consequent, *i. e.*, faith is the condition of salvation. But this is something very different from saying that the faith of Paul was the condition of God's eternal purpose to save him, because the same purpose determined the faith as the condition, and the salvation as its consequent. See further, Chapter X., on the decrees.

57. *In what sense is the will of God said to be eternal?*

It is one eternal, unsuccessive, all-comprehensive act, absolutely determining either to effect or to permit all things, in all of their relations, conditions, and successions, which ever were, are, or ever will be.

58. *In what sense may the will of God be said to be the rule of righteousness?*

It is evident that in the highest sense, with respect to God willing, his mere will can not be regarded as the ultimate ground of all righteousness, any more than it can be as the ultimate ground of all wisdom. Because, in that case, it would follow, *first*, that there would be no essential difference between right and wrong in themselves, but only a difference arbitrarily constituted by God himself; and, *second*, that it would be senseless to ascribe righteousness to God, for then that would be merely to say that he wills as he wills. The truth is,.that his will acts as his infinitely righteous wisdom sees to be right.

On the other hand, God's revealed will is to us the absolute and ultimate rule of righteousness, alike when he commands things in themselves indifferent, and thus *makes* them right, as when he commands things in themselves essentially right, because they are right.

THE ABSOLUTE JUSTICE OF GOD.

59. *What is meant by the distinctions, absolute and relative, rectoral, distributive, and punitive or vindicatory justice of God?*

The absolute justice of God is the infinite moral perfection or universal righteousness of his own being.

The relative justice of God is his infinitely righteous nature, viewed as exercised in his relation to his moral creatures, as their moral governor.

This last is called rectoral, when viewed as exercised generally in administering the affairs of his universal government, in providing for and governing his creatures and their actions. It is called distributive, when viewed as exercised in giving unto each creature his exact proportionate due of rewards or punishment. It is called punitive or vindicatory, when viewed as demanding and inflicting the adequate and proportionate punishment of all sin, because of its intrinsic ill desert.

60. *What are the different opinions as to the nature of the punitive justice of God, i. e., what are the different reasons assigned why God punishes sin?*

The Socinians deny the punitive justice of God altogether, and maintain that he punishes sin simply for the good of the individual sinner, and of society, only so far as it may be interested in his restraint or improvement. Those theologians who maintain the governmental theory of the Atonement, hold that God punishes sin not because of a changeless principle in himself demanding its punishment, but for the good of the universe, on the basis of great and changeless principles of governmental policy. Thus resolving justice into a form of general benevolence. Leibnitz held that "justice is goodness conducted by wisdom." This principle assumes that happiness is the chief good. That the essence of virtue is the desire to promote happiness, and that consequently the end of justice can only be to prevent misery. This is the foundation of the Governmental theory of the Atonement. See Chapter XXV. See Park on the "Atonement."

Some hold that the necessity for the punishment of sin is only hypothetical, *i. e.*, results only from the eternal decree of God.

The true view is that God is immutably determined by his own eternal and essential righteousness to visit every sin with a proportionate punishment.

61. *Prove that disinterested benevolence is not the whole of virtue.*

1st. Some exercises of disinterested benevolence, for example, natural parental affection, are purely instinctive, and have no positive moral character.

2d. Some exercises of disinterested benevolence, such as the weak yielding of a judge to sympathy with a guilty man or his friends, are positively immoral.

3d. There are virtuous principles incapable of being resolved into disinterested benevolence, such as proper prudential regard for one's own highest good; aspiration and effort after personal excellence; holy abhorrence of sin for its own sake, and just punishment of sin in order to vindicate righteousness.

4th. The idea of oughtness is the essential constitutive idea of virtue. No possible analysis of the idea of benevolence will give the idea of moral obligation. This is simple, unresolvable, ultimate. Oughtness is the genus, and benevolence one of the species comprehended in it.

62. *State the evidence derived from the universal principles of human nature, that the justice of God must be an ultimate and unchangeable principle of his nature, determining him to punish sin because of its intrinsic ill desert.*

The *obligation* of a righteous ruler to punish sin, the intrinsic ill desert of sin, the principle that sin *ought to be punished*, are ultimate facts of moral consciousness. They can not be resolved into any other principle whatsoever. This is proved—

1st. Because they are involved in every awakened sinner's consciousness of his own demerit.—Ps. li. 4. "I have done this evil in thy sight; that thou mightest be just when thou speakest, and clear when thou judgest." In its higher degree this feeling rises into remorse, and can be allayed only by expiation. Thus many murderers have had no rest until they have given themselves up to the law, when they have experienced instant relief. And millions of souls have found peace in the application of the blood of Jesus to their wounded consciences.

2d. All men judge thus of the sins of others. The consciences of all good men are gratified when the just penalty of the law is executed upon the offender, and outraged when he escapes.

3d. This principle is witnessed to by all the sacrificial rites common to all ancient religions, by the penances in some form universal even in modern times, by all penal laws, and by the synonyms for guilt, punishment, justice, etc., common to all languages.

4th. It is self-evident, that to inflict an unjust punishment is itself a crime, no matter how benevolent the motive which prompts it, nor how good the effect which follows it. It is no less self-evident that it is the justice of the punishment so deserved which renders its effect on the community good, and not its effect on the community which renders it just. To hang a man for the good of the community is both a crime and a blunder, unless the hanging is justified by the ill desert of the man. In that case his ill desert is seen by all the community to be the real *reason* of the hanging.

63. *Prove the same from the nature of the divine law.*

Grotius in his great work, "*Defensio Fidei Catholicæ De Satisfactione Christi*," in which he originates the Governmental Theory of the Atonement, maintains that the divine law is a product of the divine will, and therefore at the option of God relaxable, alike in its preceptive and its penal elements. But the truth is (*a*) that the penalty is an essential part of the divine law; (*b*) that the law of God, as to all its essential principles of right and wrong, is *not* a product of the divine will, but an immutable transcript of the divine nature; (*c*) therefore the law is immutable and must needs be fulfilled in every iota of it.

This is proved—1st. Because fundamental principles must have their changeless ground in the divine nature, or (*a*) otherwise the distinction between right and wrong would be purely arbitrary—whereas they are discerned by our moral intuitions to be absolute and independent of all volition divine or human; (*b*) otherwise it would be meaningless to say that God is rightous if righteousness be an arbitrary creature of his own will; (*c*) because he declares that he "*can not* lie," that "he *can not* deny himself."

2d. The Scriptures declare that the law *can not* be relaxed, that it *must* be fulfilled.—John vii. 23, and x. 35; Luke xxiv. 44; Matt. v. 25, 26.

3d. The Scriptures declare that Christ came to *fulfil* the law not to relax it.—Matt. v. 17, 18; Rom. iii. 31; x. 4.

64. *How may it be argued from the independence and absolute self-sufficiency of God, that punitive justice is an essential attribute of his nature?*

It is inconsistent with these essential attributes to conceive of God as obliged to any course of action by the external exigencies of his creation. Both the motive and the end of his action must be in himself.—Col. i. 16; Rom. xi. 36; Eph. i. 5, 6; Rom. ix. 22, 23. If he punishes sin because determined so to do by the principles of his own nature, then he acts independently. But if he resorts to this merely as the necessary means of restraining and governing his creatures, then their actions control his.

65. *How may it be proved from God's love of holiness and hatred of sin?*

God's love for holiness and hatred of sin is represented in

Scripture as essential and intrinsic. He loves holiness for its own sake. He hates sin and is determined to punish it because of its intrinsic ill desert. He hates the wicked every day.—Ps. v. 5; vii. 11. "To me belongeth vengeance and recompense."—Deut. xxxii. 35. "According to their deeds accordingly he will repay."—Isa. lix. 18; 2 Thess. i. 6. "Seeing it is a *righteous* thing with God to *recompense* tribulation to them that trouble you."—Rom. i. 32. "Knowing the judgment of God that they which commit such things are *worthy* of death."—Deut. xvii. 6; xxi. 22.

66. *How can this truth be proved from what the Scriptures teach as to the nature and necessity of the atonement of Christ?*

As to its *nature* the Scriptures teach that Christ suffered the penalty of sin vicariously in the place and stead of his elect people, and that he thus expiated their guilt, and reconciled God and redeemed their souls by giving himself the ransom price demanded in their stead. The Scriptures everywhere, and in every way teach that the design of Christ's death was to produce a sin-expiating effect upon the Governor of the moral universe, and not a moral impression either upon the heart of the individual sinner, or upon the public conscience of the intelligent universe. All this will be proved at length under Chapters XXV and XXXIII.

As to the *necessity* of the Atonement the Scriptures teach that it was absolute. That Christ *must* die or sinners perish. Gal. ii. 21, and iii. 21. But the propriety of producing a moral impression upon each sinner personally, or upon the public mind of the universe generally, *can not* give rise to an *absolute* necessity on the part of God—since God who created the universe and all its members might, of course, if he so pleased, produce moral impressions upon them of whatever kind, either without means, or by whatsoever means he pleases. An *absolute* necessity *must* have its ground in the unchangeable nature of God, which lies back of and determines his will in all its acts. *Therefore* the eternal nature of God immutably determines him to punish all sin.

"*Political Science,*" President Theodore D. Woolsey, vol. I., pp. 330–335. "The theory that correction is the main end of punishment will not bear examination. (1.) The state is not a humane institution. (2.) The theory makes no distinction between crimes. If a murderer is apparently reformed in a week, the ends of detention are accomplished, and he should be set free; while the petty offender must stay for months or years until the inoculation of good principles becomes manifest. (3.) What kind of correction is to be aimed at? Is it such as will insure society itself against his repeating his crime? In that case it is society, and not the person himself who is to be benefited by the corrective process.   Or must a thorough cure, a recovery from selfishness and covetousness, an awakening of the highest principle of soul be aimed at; an established church, in short, be set up in the house of correction?

"The explanation that the state *protects its own existence*, or the innocent inhabitants of the country, by striking its subjects with awe and deterring them from evil-doing through punishment, is met by admitting that, while this effect is real and important, it is not as yet made out that the state has a right to do this.   Crime and desert of punishment must be pre-supposed before the moral sense can be satisfied with the infliction of evil.   And the measure of the amount of punishment, supplied by the public good for the time, is most fluctuating and tyrannical; moreover mere awe, unaccompanied by an awakening of the sense of justice, is as much a source of hatred as a motive to obedience."

"The theory that in punishing an evil-doer, the state renders to him *his deserts*, is the only one that seems to have a solid foundation.   It assumes that moral evil has been committed by disobedience to rightful commands, that according to a propriety which commends itself to our moral nature it is fit and right that evil, physical or mental, suffering or shame, should be incurred by the wrong-doer, and that in all forms of government over moral beings there ought to be a power able to decide how much evil ought to follow special kinds and instances of transgressions.   The state is in fact, as St. Paul calls it, the minister of God to execute wrath upon him that doeth evil.   But only in a very limited sphere and for special ends. . .   It punishes acts, not thoughts; intentions appearing in acts, not feelings; it punishes persons within a certain territory over which it has the jurisdiction, and perhaps its subjects who do wrong elsewhere, but none else; it punishes acts hurtful to its own existence and to the community of its subjects; it punishes not according to an exact scale of deserts, for it can not, without a revelation, find out what the deserts of individuals are, nor what is the relative guilt of different actions of different persons." *

The Absolute Goodness of God.

67. *What distinctions are signified by the terms benevolence, complacency, mercy, and grace?*

The infinite goodness of God is a glorious perfection which pre-eminently characterizes his nature, and which he, in an infinitely wise, righteous, and sovereign manner, exercises towards his creatures in various modes according to their relations and conditions.

Benevolence is the goodness of God viewed generically.   It embraces all his creatures, except the judicially condemned on account of sin, and provides for their welfare.

The love of *complacency* is that approving affection with which God regards his own infinite perfections, and every image and reflection of them in his creatures, especially in the sanctified subjects of the new creation.

God's *mercy*, of which the more passive forms are *pity* and

* This extract is slightly condensed.

compassion, is the divine goodness exercised with respect to the miseries of his creatures, feeling for them, and making provision for their relief, and in the case of impenitent sinners, leading to long-suffering *patience*.

The *grace* of God is his goodness seeking to communicate his favors, and, above all, the fellowship of his own life and blessedness to his moral creatures,—who, *as creatures*, must be destitute of all merit,—and pre-eminently his electing love, securing at infinite cost the blessedness of its objects, who, *as sinful* creatures, were positively ill deserving.

68. *State a false definition of divine benevolence often given, and state how it is rightly defined.*

The infinite Benevolence of God is often defined as that attribute in virtue of which he communicates to all his creatures the greatest possible amount of happiness, *i. e.*, as great as they are capable of receiving, or as great as is consistent with the attainment of the greatest amount of happiness on the aggregate in the moral universe.

But this supposes that God is limited by something out of himself, that he *could* not have secured more happiness for his creatures than he has actually done. It also makes happiness paramount in the view of God to excellence.

Benevolence should, on the other hand, be defined as that attribute in virtue of which God produces all the happiness in the universe, which is consistent with the end he had in view in its creation. These ends stand in this order. 1. The manifestation of his own glory. 2. The highest moral excellence of his creatures. 3. Their highest blessedness in himself.—Dr. Charles Hodge's Lectures.

69. *What are the sources of our knowledge of the fact that God is benevolent?*

1st. Reason. Benevolence is an essential element of moral perfection. God is infinitely perfect, and therefore infinitely benevolent.

2d. Experience and observation. The wisdom of God in designing, and the power of God in executing, in the several spheres of creation, providence, and revealed religion, have evidently been constantly determined by benevolent intentions.

3d. The direct assertions of Scripture.—Ps. clxv. 8, 9; 1 John iv. 8.

70. *How may it be proved that God is gracious and willing to forgive sin?*

Neither reason nor conscience can ever raise a presumption

on this subject. It is the evident duty of fellow-creatures mutually to forgive *injuries*, but we have nothing to do with forgiving *sin* as sin.

It appears plain that there can be no moral principle making it essential for a sovereign ruler to forgive sin as trangression of law. All that reason or conscience can assure us of in that regard is, that sin can not be forgiven without an atonement. The gracious affection which should prompt such a ruler to provide an atonement, must, from its essential nature, be perfectly free and sovereign, and therefore it can be known only so far as it is graciously revealed. The gospel is, therefore, *good news* confirmed by signs and wonders.—Ex. xxxiv. 6, 7; Eph. i. 7–9.

71. *What are the different theories or assumptions on which it has been attempted to reconcile the existence of sin with the goodness of God?*

1st. It has been argued by some that free agency is essential to a moral system, and that absolute independence of will is essential to free agency. That to control the wills of free agents is no more *an object of power* than the working of contradictions; and consequently God, although omnipotent, could not prevent sin in a moral system without violating its nature.—See Dr. N. W. Taylor's "Concio ad Clerum," 1828.

2d. Others have argued that sin was permitted by God in infinite wisdom as the necessary means to the largest possible measure of happiness in the universe as a whole.

On both of these we remark—

1st. That the first theory above cited is founded on a false view of the conditions of human liberty and responsibility (see below, Chapter XV.); and, further, that it grossly limits the power of God by representing him as desiring and attempting what he can not effect, and that it makes him dependent upon his creatures.

2d. With reference to the second theory it should be remembered that God's own glory, and not the greatest good of the universe, is the great end of God in creation and providence.

3d. The permission of sin, in its relation both to the righteousness and goodness of God, is an insolvable mystery, and all attempts to solve it only darken counsel with words without knowledge. It is, however, the privilege of our faith to know, though not of our philosophy to comprehend, that it is assuredly a most wise, righteous, and merciful permission; and that it shall redound to the glory of God and to the good of his chosen.

72. *How can the attributes of goodness and justice be shown to be consistent?*

Goodness and justice are the several aspects of one unchangeable, infinitely wise, and sovereign moral perfection. God is not sometimes merciful and sometimes just, nor so far merciful and so far just, but he is eternally infinitely merciful and just. Relatively to the creature this infinite perfection of nature presents different aspects, as is determined by the judgment which infinite wisdom delivers in each individual case.

Even in our experience these attributes of our moral nature are found not to be inconsistent in *principle*, though our want both of wisdom and knowledge, a sense of our own unworthiness, and a mere physical sympathy, often sadly distract our judgments as well as our hearts in adjusting these principles to the individual cases of life.

God's Absolute Truth.

73. *What is truth considered as a divine attribute?*

The truth of God in its widest sense is a perfection which qualifies all his intellectual and moral attributes. His knowledge is infinitely true in relation to its objects, and his wisdom unbiassed either by prejudice or passion. His justice and his goodness in all their exercises are infinitely true to the perfect standard of his own nature. In all outward manifestations of his perfections to his creatures, God is always true to his nature —always self-consistently divine. This attribute in its more special sense qualifies all God's intercourse with his rational creatures. He is true to us as well as to himself; and thus is laid the foundation of all faith, and therefore of all knowledge. It is the foundation of all confidence, first, in our senses; second, in our intellect and conscience; third, in any authenticated, supernatural revelation.

The two forms in which this perfection is exercised in relation to us are, first, his entire truth in all his communications; second, his perfect sincerity in undertaking and faithfulness in discharging all his engagements.

74. *How can the truth of God be reconciled with the apparent non-performance of some of his threatenings?*

The promises and threatenings of God are sometimes *absolute*, when they are always infallibly fulfilled in the precise sense in which he intended them. They are often also *conditional*, made to depend upon the obedience or repentance of the creature.—Jonah iii. 4, 10; Jer. xviii. 7, 8. This condition may be either expressed or implied, because the individual case is understood to be, of course, governed by the general principle that genuine repentance and faith delivers from every threatening and secures every promise.

75. *How can the invitations and exhortations of the Scriptures, addressed to those whom God does not propose to save, be reconciled with his sincerity?*

See above (Question 42), the distinction between God's preceptive and his decretive will. His invitations and exhortations are addressed to all men in good faith: first, because it is every man's duty to repent and believe, and it is God's preceptive will that every man should; second, because nothing ever prevents the obedience of any sinner, except his own unwillingness; third, because in every case .in which the condition is fulfilled the promise implied will be performed; fourth, God never has promised to enable every man to believe; fifth, these invitations and exhortations are not addressed to the reprobate as such, but to all sinners as such, with the avowed purpose of saving thereby the elect.

The Infinite Sovereignty of God.

76. *What is meant by the sovereignty of God?*

His absolute right to govern and dispose of all his creatures, simply according to his own good pleasure.

77. *Prove that this right is asserted in Scripture.*

Dan. iv. 25, 35; Rev. iv. 11; 1 Tim. vi. 15; Rom. ix. 15–23.

78. *On what does the absolute sovereignty of God rest?*

1st. His infinite superiority in being and in all his perfections to any and to all his creatures.

2d. As creatures they were created out of nothing, and are now sustained in being by his power, for his own glory and according to his own good pleasure.—Rom. xi. 36.

3d. His infinite benefits to us, and our dependence upon and blessedness in him, are reasons why we should not only recognize, but rejoice, in this glorious truth. The Lord reigneth, let the earth rejoice.

79. *Is there any sense in which there are limits to the sovereignty of God?*

The sovereignty of God, viewed abstractly as one attribute among many, must of course be conceived of as qualified by all the rest. It can not be otherwise than an infinitely wise, righteous, and merciful sovereignty.

But God, viewed concretely as an infinite sovereign, is absolutely unlimited by any thing without himself. "He doeth according to his will in the army of heaven, and among the inhabitants of the earth."—Dan. iv. 35.

THE INFINITE HOLINESS OF GOD.

80. What is meant by the holiness of God?

The holiness of God is not to be conceived of as one attribute among others; it is rather a general term representing the conception of his consummate perfection and total glory. It is his infinite moral perfection crowning his infinite intelligence and power. There is a glory of each attribute, viewed abstractly, and a glory of the whole together. The intellectual nature is the essential basis of the moral. Infinite moral perfection is the crown of the Godhead. Holiness is the total glory thus crowned.

Holiness in the Creator is the total perfection of an infinitely righteous intelligence. Holiness in the creature is not mere moral perfection, but perfection of the created nature of moral agents after their kind, in spiritual union and fellowship with the infinite Creator.—1 John i. 3.

The word holiness, as applied to God in Scripture, represents, first, moral purity—Lev. xi. 44; Ps. cxlv. 17; second, his transcendently august and venerable majesty.—Isa. vi. 3; Ps. xxii. 3; Rev. iv. 8.

To "sanctify the Lord," *i. e.*, to make him holy, is to declare and adore his holiness by venerating his august majesty wherever and whereinsoever his person or character is represented.—Isa. viii. 13; xxix. 23; Ezek. xxxviii. 23; Matt. vi. 9; 1 Pet. iii. 15.

CHAPTER IX.

THE HOLY TRINITY.

1. What is the etymology and meaning of the word Trinity, and when was it introduced into the language of the Church?

The word trinity (*Trinitas*) is derived either from *tres-unus, trinus,* or from τριάς, three in one, or the one which is three, and the three which are one; not triplex—*trinitas* not *triplicitas.* This word is not found in the Scriptures. Technical terms are however an absolute necessity in all sciences. In this case they have been made particularly essential because of the subtle perversions of the simple, untechnical Biblical statements by infidels and heretics. This term, as above defined, admirably expresses the central fact of the great doctrine of the one essence eternally subsisting as three Persons, all the elements of which are explicitly taught in the Scriptures. The Greek word τριάς was first used in this connection by Theophilus, bishop of Antioch, in Syria, from A. D. 168 to A. D. 183. The Latin term *Trinitas* was first used by Tertullian, circum. 220. Mosheim's "Eccle. Hist.," vol. I., p. 121, note 7; Hagenbach, "Hist. of Doc.," vol. I., 129.

2. What is the theological meaning of the term substantia (substance), and what change has occurred in its usage?

Substantia, as now used, is equivalent to essence, independent being. Thus, in the Godhead, the three persons are the same in substance, *i. e.,* of one and the same indivisible, numerical essence.

The word was at first used by one party in the church as equivalent to *subsistentia* (subsistence), or mode of existence. In which sense, while there is but one essence, there are three substantiæ or persons, in the Godhead.—See Turretin, Tom. I., locus iii., ques. 23.

3. What other terms have been used as the equivalents of substantia in the definitions of this doctrine?

The Greek οὐσία and φύσις. The Latin *essentia, natura.* The English *essence, substance, nature, being.*

4. What is the theological meaning of the word subsistentia (subsistence)?

It is used to signify that mode of existence which distinguishes one individual thing from every other individual thing, one person from every other person. As applied to the doctrine of the Trinity, subsistence is that mode of existence which is peculiar to each of the divine persons, and which in each constitutes the one essence a distinct person.

5. What is the New Testament sense of the word ὑπόστασις (hypostasis)?

This word, as to its etymology, is precisely equivalent to substance; it comes from ὑφίστημι, "to stand under."
In the New Testament it is used five times—
1st. Figuratively, for confidence, or that state of mind which is conscious of a firm foundation, 2 Cor. ix. 4; xi. 17; Heb. iii. 14, which faith realizes, Heb. xi. 1.
2d. Literally, for essential nature, Heb. i. 3.—See Sampson's "Com. on Heb."

6. In what sense is this word used by the ecclesiastical writers?

Until the middle of the fourth century this word, in connection with the doctrine of the Trinity, was generally used in its primary sense, as equivalent to substance. It is used in this sense in the creed published by the Council of Nice A. D. 325, and again in the decrees of the Council of Sardica, in Illyria, A. D. 347. These agreed in affirming that there is but one hypostasis in the Godhead. Some, however, at that time understanding the word in the sense of person, its usage was changed by general consent, chiefly through the influence of Athanasius, and ever since it has been established in theological language in the sense of *person*, in contradistinction to οὐσία, essence. It has been transferred into the English language in the form of an adjective, to designate the hypostatical or personal union of two natures in the God-man.

7. What is essential to personality, and how is the word person to be defined in connection with the doctrine of the Trinity?

The Latin word, "*suppositum*," signifies a distinct individual existence, e. g., a particular tree or horse. A person is "*suppositum intellectuale*," a distinct individual existence, to which belongs the properties of reason and free will. Throughout the entire range of our experience and observation of personal existence among creatures, personality rests upon and appears to be inseparable from distinction of essence. Every distinct person is a distinct soul, with or without a body.

That distinguishing mode of existence which constitutes the one divine essence co-ordinately three separate persons, is of course an infinite mystery which we can not understand, and therefore can not adequately define, and which we can know only so far as it is explicitly revealed. All that we know is, that this distinction, which is called personality, embraces all those incommunicable properties which eternally belong to Father, Son, or Holy Ghost separately, and not to all in common; that it lays the foundation for their concurrence in counsel, their mutual love and action one upon another, as the Father sending the Son, and the Father and Son sending the Spirit, and for use of the personal pronouns I, thou, he, in the revelation which one divine person gives of himself and of the others.

Person is defined by Gerhard—"Persona est substantia individua, intelligens, incommunicabilis, quæ non sustentatur in alio, vel ab alio." In relation to this great mystery of the divine trinity of persons in the unity of essence Calvin's definition of Person is better because more modest. "By *person*, then, I mean a subsistence in the divine essence—a subsistence which, while related to the other two, is distinguished from them by incommunicable properties."—"Institutes," Book I., Chap. 13, § 6.

8. *What other terms have been used by theologians as the equivalent of Person in this connection?*

Greek, ὑπόστασις, and πρόσωπον—aspect; Latin, *persona, hypostasis, subsistentia, aspectus;* English, *person, hypostasis.*—Shedd's "Hist. Christ Doc.," B. III., Ch. 3, § 5.

9. *What is meant by the terms ὁμοούσιον (of the same substance), and ὁμοιούσιον (of similar substance)?*

In the first general council of the church which, consisting of three hundred and eighteen bishops, was called together by the Emperor Constantine at Nice, in Bithynia, A. D. 325, there were found to be three great parties representing different opinions concerning the Trinity.

1st. The orthodox party, who maintained the opinion now held by all Christians, that the Lord Jesus is, as to his divine nature, of the same identical substance with the Father. These insisted upon applying to him the definite term ὁμοούσιον (homoousion), compounded of ὁμός, same, and οὐσία, substance, to teach the great truth that the three persons of the Godhead are one God, because they are of the same numerical essence.

2d. The Arians, who maintained that the Son of God is the greatest of all creatures, more like God than any other, the only-begotten Son of God, created before all worlds, through whom God created all other things, and in *that sense only* divine. They held that the Son was ἑτεροούσιον of different or generically unlike essence from the Father.

3d. The middle party, styled Semiarians, who confessed that the Son was not a creature, but denied that he was in the same sense God as the Father is. They held that the Father is the only absolute self-existent God; yet that from eternity he, by his own free will, caused to proceed from himself a divine person of *like nature and properties.* They denied, therefore, that the Son was of the same substance (homoousion) with the Father, but admitted that he was of an essence truly similar, and derived from the Father (homoiousion, ὁμοιόυσιον, from, ὅμοιος, *like*, and ὀυσία, *substance*), generically though not numerically one.

The opinions of the first, or orthodox party, prevailed at that council, and have ever since been represented by the technical phrase, *homoousian.*

For the creed promulgated by that council, see Chapter VII.

10. *What are the several propositions essentially involved in the doctrine of the Trinity?*

1st. There is but one God, and this God is one, *i. e.*, indivisible.

2d. That the one indivisible divine essence, as a whole, exists eternally as Father, and as Son, and as Holy Ghost; that each person possesses the whole essence, and is constituted a distinct person by certain incommunicable properties, not common to him with the others.

3d. The distinction between these three is a *personal* distinction, in the sense that it occasions (1) the use of the personal pronouns, I, thou, he, (2) a concurrence in counsel and a mutual love, (3) a distinct order of operation.

4th. Since there is but one divine essence, and since all attributes or active properties are inherent in and inseparable from the essence to which they pertain, it follows that all the divine attributes must be identically common to each of the three persons who subsist in common of the one essence. Among all creatures every distinct person is a distinct numerical substance, and possesses a distinct intelligence, a distinct will, etc. In the Godhead, however, there is but one substance, and one intelligence, one will, etc., and yet three persons eternally co-exist of that one essence, and exercise that one intelligence and one will, etc. In Christ on the contrary, there are two spirits, two intelligences, two wills, and yet all the while *one* indivisible person.

5th. These divine persons being one God, all the divine attributes being common to each in the same sense, nevertheless they are revealed in the Scriptures in a certain order of subsistence and of operation. (1.) *Of subsistence* insomuch as the Father is neither begotten nor proceedeth, while the Son is eternally begotten by the Father, and the Spirit eternally proceedeth from the Father and the Son; (2.) of operation, insomuch that the first person sends and operates through the second, and the first and second send and operate through the third.

Hence the Father is always set forth as *first*, the Son as *second*, the Spirit as *third*.

6th. While all the divine attributes are common equally to the three persons, and all divine works wrought *ad extra*, such as creation, providence, or redemption, are predicated alike of the one divine being—the one God considered absolutely—and of the Father, and of the Son, and of the Holy Ghost severally; nevertheless the Scriptures attribute some divine works wrought *ad intra*, exclusively to each divine person respectively, *e. g.*, generation to the Father, filiation to the Son, procession to the Holy Ghost; and there are likewise some divine works wrought *ad extra* which are attributed pre-eminently to each person respectively, *e. g.*, creation to the Father, redemption to the Son, and sanctification to the Holy Ghost.

In order, therefore, to establish this doctrine in all its parts by the testimony of Scripture, it will be necessary for us to prove the following propositions in their order:

1st. That God is one.

2d. That Jesus of Nazareth, as to his divine nature, was truly God, yet a distinct person from the Father.

3d. That the Holy Spirit is truly God, yet a distinct person.

4th. That the Scriptures directly teach a trinity of persons in one Godhead.

5th. It will remain to gather what the Scriptures reveal as to the eternal and necessary relations which these three divine persons sustain to each other. These are distributed under the following heads: (1) The relation which the second person sustains to the first, or the eternal generation of the Son; (2) the relation which the third person sustains to the first and second, or the eternal procession of the Holy Ghost; and, (3) their personal properties and order of operation, *ad extra.*

I. God is one, and there is but one God.

The proof of this proposition, from reason and Scripture,

has been fully set forth above, in Chap. VIII., on the Attributes of God, questions 12–18.

The answer to the question, How the co-ordinate existence of three distinct persons in the Trinity can be reconciled with this fundamental doctrine of the divine unity, is given below in question 94 of this chapter.

II. JESUS OF NAZARETH, AS TO HIS DIVINE NATURE, IS TRULY GOD, AND YET A DISTINCT PERSON FROM THE FATHER.

11. *What different views have been entertained with respect to the person of Christ?*

The orthodox doctrine as to the person of Christ, is that he from eternity has existed as the co-equal Son of the Father, constituted of the same infinite self-existent essence with the Father and the Holy Ghost.

The orthodox doctrine as to his person as at present constituted, since his incarnation, is set forth in chap. XXIII. An account of the different heretical opinions as to his person are given below, in questions 96–99, of this chapter.

12. *How far did the Jews at the time of Christ expect the Messiah to appear as a divine person?*

When Christ appeared, it is certain that the great mass of the Jewish people had ceased to entertain the Scriptural expectation of a divine Saviour, and only desired a temporal prince, in a pre-eminent sense, a favorite of heaven. It is said, however, that scattered hints in some of the rabbinical writings indicate that some of the more learned and spiritual still continued true to the ancient faith.

13. *How may the pre-existence of Jesus before his birth by the Virgin be proved from Scripture?*

1st. Those passages which say that he is the creator of the world.—John i. 3; Col. i. 15–18.

2d. Those passages which directly declare that he was with the Father before the world was; that he was rich, and possessed glory.—John i. 1, 15, 30; vi. 62; viii. 58; xvii. 5; 2 Cor. viii. 9.

3d. Those passages which declare that he "came into the world," "came down from heaven."—John iii. 13, 31; xiii. 3; xvi. 28; 1 Cor. xv. 47.

14. *How can it be proved that the Jehovah who manifested himself as the God of the Jews under the old economy was the second person of the Trinity, who became incarnate in Jesus of Nazareth?*

As this fact is not affirmed in any single statement of

Scripture, it can be established only by a careful comparison of many passages. The evidence, as compiled from Hill's Lects., Book III., ch. v., may be summed up as follows:

1st. All the divine appearances of the ancient economy are referred to *one person.*—Compare Gen. xviii. 2, 17; xxviii. 13; xxxii. 9, 31; Ex. iii. 14, 15; xiii. 21; xx. 1, 2; xxv. 21; Deut. iv. 33, 36, 39; Neh. ix. 7–28. This one person is called Jehovah, the incommunicable name of God, and at the same time *angel,* or *one sent.*—Compare Gen. xxxi. 11, 13; xlviii. 15, 16; Hosea xii. 2, 5. Compare Ex. iii. 14, 15, with Acts vii. 30–35; and Ex. xiii. 21, with Ex. xiv. 19; and Ex. xx. 1, 2, with Acts vii. 38; Isa. lxiii. 7, 9.

2d. But God the Father has been seen by no man (John i. 18; vi. 46): neither could he be an angel, or one sent by any other; yet God the Son has been seen (1 John i. 1, 2), and sent (John v. 36).

3d. This Jehovah, who was at the same time the angel, or one sent, of the old economy, was also set forth by the prophets as the Saviour of Israel, and the author of the new dispensation. In Zech. ii. 10, 11, one Jehovah is represented as sending another. See Micah v. 2. In Mal. iii. 1, it is declared that " the Lord," " the messenger of the covenant," shall come to his own temple. This applied to Jesus (Mark i. 2).—Compare Ps. xcvii. 7, with Heb. i. 6; and Isa. vi. 1–5, with John xii. 41.

4th. Certain references in the New Testament to passages in the Old appear directly to imply this fact. Compare Ps. lxxviii. 15, 16, 35, with 1 Cor. x. 9.

5th. The Church is one under all dispensations, and Jesus from the beginning is the Redeemer and Head of the Church; it is, therefore, most consistent with all that has been revealed to us as to the offices of the three divine persons in the scheme of redemption, to admit the view here presented. See also John viii. 56, 58; Matt. xxiii. 37; 1 Pet. i. 10, 11.

15. *In what form are the earliest disclosures made in the Old Testament of the existence and agency of a Person distinct from God and yet as divine?*

In the earlier books an Angel is spoken of, sent from God, often appearing to men, and yet himself God.—Gen. xvi. 7–13. The Angel of Jehovah appears to Hagar, claims divine power, and is called God.—Gen. xviii. 2–33. Three angels appeared to Abraham, one of whom is called Jehovah, v. 17. — Gen. xxxii. 25. An Angel wrestles with Jacob and blesses him as God, and in Hosea, xii. 3–5, that Angel is called God.—Ex. iii. 2. The Angel of Jehovah appeared to Moses in the burning bush, and in the following verses this angel is called Jehovah, and other divine titles are ascribed to him. This Angel led the Israelites in the wilderness.—Ch. xiv. 19; Isa. lxiii. 9. Jehovah is represented as saving his people by the *Angel of his Presence.* Thus Malachi iii. 1—"The Lord, the Angel of the covenant shall suddenly come to his temple." This applied to Christ.—Mark i. 2.

16. *What evidence of the divinity of the Messiah does the 2d Psalm present?*

It declares him to be the Son of God, and as such to receive universal power over the whole earth and its inhabitants. All are exhorted to submit to him, and to trust him, on pain of his anger. In Acts xiii. 33, Paul declares that Psalm refers to Christ.

17. *What evidence is furnished by the 45th Psalm?*

The ancient Jews considered this Psalm addressed to the Messiah, and the fact is established by Paul (Heb. i. 8, 9). Here, therefore, Jesus is called God, and his throne eternal.

18. *What evidence is furnished by Psalm 110?*

That this Psalm refers to the Messiah is proved by Christ (Matt. xxii. 43, 44), and by Paul (Heb. v. 6; vii. 17). He is here called David's Lord (Adonai), and invited to sit at the right hand of Jehovah until all his enemies be made his footstool.

19. *What evidence is furnished by Isaiah ix. 6?*

This passage self-evidently refers to the Messiah, as is confirmed by Matt. iv. 14–16. It declares explicitly that the child born "is also the mighty God, the everlasting Father, the Prince of Peace."

20. *What is the evidence furnished by Micah v. 2?*

This was understood by the Jews to refer to Christ, which is confirmed by Matt. ii. 6, and John vii. 42. The passage declares that his goings forth have been "from ever of old," *i. e.,* from eternity.

21. *What evidence is furnished by Malachi iii. 1, 2?*

This passage self-evidently refers to the Messiah, as is confirmed by Mark i. 2.

The Hebrew term (Adonai), here translated Lord, is never applied to any other than the supreme God. The temple, which was sacred to the presence and worship of Jehovah, is called his temple. And in verse 2d, a divine work of judgment is ascribed to him.

22. *What evidence is afforded by the way in which the writers of the New Testament apply the writings of the Old Testament to Christ?*

The apostles frequently apply the language of the Old Testament to Christ, when it is evident that the original writers intended to speak of Jehovah, and not of the Messiah as such.

Psalm 102 is evidently an address to the supreme Lord, ascribing to him eternity, creation, providential government, worship, and the hearing and answering of prayer. But Paul (Heb. i. 10–12) affirms Christ to be the subject of the address. In Isa. xlv. 20–25, Jehovah speaks and asserts his own supreme Lordship. But Paul, in Rom. xiv. 11, quotes a part of Jehovah's declaration with regard to himself, to prove that we must all stand before the judgment-seat of Christ.—Compare also Isa. vi. 3, with John xii. 41.

23. *What is the general character of the evidence upon this subject afforded by the New Testament?*

This fundamental doctrine is presented to us in every individual writing, and in every separate paragraph of the New Testament, either by direct assertion or by necessary implication, as may be ascertained by every honest reader for himself. The mass of this testimony is so great, and is so intimately interwoven with every other theme in every passage, that I have room here to present only a general sample of the evidence, classified under the usual heads.

24. *Prove that the New Testament ascribes divine titles to Christ.*

John i. 1; xx. 28; Acts xx. 28; Rom. ix. 5; 2 Thess. i. 12; 1 Tim. iii. 16; Titus ii. 13; Heb. i. 8; 1 John v. 20.

25. *Prove that the New Testament ascribes divine perfections to Christ.*

Eternity.—John i. 2; viii. 58; xvii. 5; Rev. i. 8, 17, 18; xxii. 13.

Immutability.—Heb. i. 11, 12, and xiii. 8.

Omnipresence.—John iii. 13; Matt. xviii. 20; xxviii. 20.

Omniscience.—Matt. xi. 27; John ii. 23–25; xxi. 17; Rev. ii. 23.

Omnipotence.—John v. 17; Heb. i. 3; Rev. i. 8; xi. 17.

26. *Prove that the New Testament ascribes divine works to Christ.*

Creation.—John i. 3, 10; Col. i. 16, 17.

Preservation and Providence.—Heb. i. 3; Col. i. 17; Matt. xxviii. 18.

Miracles.—John v. 21, 36.

Judgment.—2 Cor. v. 10; Matt. xxv. 31, 32; John v. 22.

A work of grace, including election.—John xiii. 18.

Sanctification, Eph. v. 26; sending the Holy Ghost, John xvi. 7, 14; giving eternal life, John x. 28; Turretin, Tom. I., L. 3, Q. 28.

27. *Prove that the New Testament teaches that supreme worship should be paid to Christ.*

Matt. xxviii. 19; John v. 22, 23; xiv. 1; Acts vii. 59, 60; 1 Cor. i. 2; 2 Cor. xiii. 14; Phil. ii. 9, 10; Heb. i. 6; Rev. i. 5, 6; v. 11, 12; vii. 10.

28. *Prove that the Son, although God, is a distinct person from the Father.*

This fact is so plainly taught in Scripture, and so universally implied, that the Sabellian system, which denies it, has never obtained any general currency.

Christ is sent by the Father, comes from him, returns to him, receives his commandment, does his will, loves him, is loved by him, addresses prayer to him, uses the pronouns thou and he when speaking to and of him. This is necessarily implied, also, in the relative titles, Father and Son. See the whole New Testament.

In establishing the doctrine of the Trinity, as far as the Second Person is involved, the stress lies altogether in proving the absolute Divinity of Christ, his distinct personality being so obvious as to be practically beyond dispute. While in vindicating the truth of the doctrine as it respects the Third Person the whole stress lies in proving His distinct personality, his absolute divinity being so clearly revealed as to be unquestionable.

III. The Holy Ghost is truly God, yet a distinct person.

29. *What sects have held that the Holy Ghost is a creature?*

The divinity of the Holy Ghost is so clearly revealed in Scripture that very few have dared to call it in question. The early controversies of the orthodox with the Arians precedent and consequent to the Council of Nice, A. D. 325, to such a degree absorbed the mind of both parties with the question of the divinity of the Son, that very little prominence was given in that age to questions concerning the Holy Ghost. Arius, however, is said to have taught that as the Son is the first and greatest creature of the Father, so the Holy Ghost is the first and greatest creature of the Son; a κτίσμα κτίσματος, a creature of a creature.—See Neander's "Ch. Hist.," Vol. I., pp. 416–420.

Some of the disciples of Macedonius, bishop of Constantinople, A. D. 341–360, are said to have held that the Holy Ghost was not Supreme God. These were condemned by the second General Council, which met at Constantinople, A. D. 381. This council defined and guarded the orthodox faith, by adding definite clauses to the simple reference which the ancient creed had made to the Holy Ghost.—See the Creed of the Council of Constantinople, Chapter 7.

30. *By whom has the Holy Spirit been regarded merely as an energy of God?*

Those early heretical sects, generally styled Monarchians and Patripassians, all with subordinate distinctions taught that there was but one person as well as one essence in the Godhead, who, in different relations, is called Father, Son, or Holy Ghost. In the sixteenth century Socinus, who taught that Jesus Christ was a mere man, maintained that the term Holy Ghost is in Scripture used as a designation of God's energy, when exercised in a particular way. This is now the opinion of all modern Unitarians and Rationalists.

31. *How can it be proved that all the attributes of personality are ascribed to the Holy Ghost in the Scriptures?*

The attributes of personality are such as intelligence, volition, separate agency. Christ uses the pronouns, I, thou, he, when speaking of the relation of the Holy Spirit to himself and the Father: "I will send him." "He will testify of me." "Whom the Father will send in my name." Thus he is sent; he testifies; he takes of the things of Christ, and shows them to us. He teaches and leads to all truth. He knows, because he searches the deep things of God. He works all supernatural gifts, dividing to every man as he wills.—John xiv. 17, 26; xv. 26; 1 Cor. ii. 10, 11; xii. 11. He reproves, glorifies, helps, intercedes.—John xvi. 7–13; Rom. viii. 26.

32. *How may his personality be argued from the offices which he is said in the Scriptures to execute?*

The New Testament throughout all its teachings discovers the plan of redemption as essentially involving the agency of the Holy Ghost in applying the salvation which it was the work of the Son to accomplish. He inspired the prophets and apostles; he teaches and sanctifies the church; he selects her officers, qualifying them by the communication of special gifts at his will. He is the advocate, every Christian is his client. He brings all the grace of the absent Christ to us, and gives it effect in our persons in every moment of our lives. His personal distinction is obviously involved in the very nature of these functions which he discharges.—Luke xii. 12; Acts v. 32; xv. 28; xvi. 6; xxviii. 25; Rom. xv. 16; 1 Cor. ii. 13; Heb. ii. 4; iii. 7; 2 Pet. i. 21.

33. *What argument for the personality of the Holy Ghost may be deduced from the formula of baptism?*

Christians are baptized "in the name of the Father, Son, and Holy Ghost." It would be inconsistent with every law of language and reason to speak of the "name" of an energy, or to associate an energy co-ordinately with two distinct persons.

34. *How may his personality be proved by what is said of the sin against the Holy Ghost?*

In Matt. xii. 31, 32; Mark iii. 28, 29; Luke xii. 10, this sin is called "blasphemy against the Holy Ghost." Now, blasphemy is a sin committed against a person, and it is here distinguished from the same act as committed against the other persons of the Trinity.

35. *How can such expressions as "giving," and "pouring out the Spirit," be reconciled with his personality?*

These and other similar expressions are used figuratively to set forth our participation in the gifts and influences of the Spirit. It is one of the most natural and common of all figures to designate the gift by the name of the giver. Thus we are said "to put on Christ," "to be baptized into Christ," etc.— Eph. v. 30; Rom. xiii. 14; Gal. iii. 27.

36. *Show that the names of God are applied to the Spirit.*

Compare Ex. xvii. 7, and Ps. xcv. 7, with Heb. iii. 7–11.— See Acts v. 3, 4.

37. *What divine attributes do the Scriptures ascribe to him?*

Omnipresence.—Ps. cxxxix. 7; 1 Cor. xii. 13.
Omniscience.—1 Cor. ii. 10, 11.
Omnipotence.—Luke i. 35; Rom. viii. 11.

38. *What agency in the external world do the Scriptures ascribe to him?*

Creation.—Gen. i. 2; Job xxvi. 13; Ps. civ. 30.
The power of working miracles.—Matt. xii. 28; 1 Cor. xii. 9–11.

39. *How is his supreme divinity established by what the Script-ures teach of his agency in redemption?*

He is declared to be the immediate agent in regeneration, John iii. 6; Titus iii. 5; and in the resurrection of our bodies, Rom. viii. 11. His agency in the generation of Christ's human nature, in his resurrection, and in the inspiration of the Script-ures, were exertions of his divine power in preparing the re-demption which he now applies.

40. *How can such expressions as, "he shall not speak of himself," be reconciled with his divinity?*

This and other similar expressions are to be understood as referring to the official work of the Spirit; just as the Son is said in his official character to be sent by and to be subordinate to the Father. The object of the Holy Ghost, in his official work in the hearts of men, is not to reveal the relations of his own person to the other persons of the Godhead, but simply to reveal the mediatorial character and work of Christ.

IV. The Scriptures directly teach a Trinity of Persons in One Godhead.

41. *How is this trinity of persons directly taught in the formula of baptism?*

Baptism in the name of God implies the recognition of God's divine authority, his covenant engagement to give us eternal life, and our engagement to render him divine worship and obedience. Christians are baptized thus into covenant relation with three persons distinctly named in order. The language necessarily implies that each name represents a person. The nature of the sacrament proves that each person must be divine.—See Matt. xxviii. 19.

42. *How is this doctrine directly taught in the formula of the apostolical benediction?*

See 2 Cor. xiii. 14. We have here distinctly named three persons, and each communicating a separate blessing, accord-ing to his own order and manner of operation. The benevo-lence of the Father in designing, the grace of the Son in the acquisition, the communion of the Holy Ghost in the applica-tion of salvation. These are three distinct personal names, three distinct modes of personal agency, and each equally divine.

43. *What evidence is afforded by the narrative of Christ's baptism?*

See Matt. iii. 13–17. Here also we have presented to us three persons distinctly named and described as severally acting, each after his own order. The Father speaking from heaven, the Spirit descending like a dove and lighting upon Christ, Christ acknowledged as the beloved Son of God ascending from the water.

44. *State the argument from* John xv. 26, *and the context.*

In this passage again we have three persons severally named at the same time, and their relative action affirmed. The Son is the person speaking of the Father and the Spirit, and claiming for himself the right of sending the Spirit. The Father is the person from whom the Spirit proceeds. Of the Spirit the Son says that " he will come," " he will be sent," " he proceedeth," " he will testify."

45. *What is the state of the evidence with regard to the genuineness of* 1 John v. 7 *?*

I have not room in which to present a synopsis of the argument for and against the genuineness of the disputed clause which could be of any value.—See " Horne's Intro.," Vol IV., Part II., chapter iv., section 5.

It will suffice to say—

1st. The disputed clause is as follows, including part of the eighth verse: " *in heaven, the Father, the Word, and the Holy Ghost; and these three are one. And there are three that bear witness in earth.*"

2d. Learned and pious men are divided in their opinions as to the preponderance of the evidence; the weight of opinion inclining against the genuineness of the clause.

3d. The doctrine taught is so scriptural, and the grammatical and logical connection of the clause with the rest of the passage is so intimate, that for *the purpose of edification*, in the present state of our knowledge, the clause ought to be retained, although for the purpose of *establishing doctrine*, it ought not to be relied upon.

4th. The rejection of this passage does in no degree lessen the irresistible weight of evidence of the truth of the orthodox doctrine of the Trinity which the Scriptures afford.

46. *What passages in the Old Testament imply the existence of more than one person in the Godhead?*

Mark the use of the plural in the following passages.—Gen. i. 26; iii. 22; xi. 7; Isa. vi. 8; Compare the three-fold repetition of the name Jehovah (Num. vi. 24–26) with the apostolical benediction—2 Cor. xiii. 14. Mark also in Isa. vi. 3, the threefold repetition of the ascription of holiness.

47. *What passages in the Old Testament speak of the Son as a distinct person from the Father, and yet as divine?*

In Ps. xlv. 6, 7, we have the Father addressing the Son as God, and anointing him.—See also Ps. cx. 1; Isa. xliv. 6, 7, 14.

The prophecies always set forth the Messiah as a person distinct from the Father, and yet he is called "Mighty God," etc.—Isa. ix. 6; Jer. xxiii. 6.

48. *What passages of the Old Testament speak of the Spirit as a distinct person from the Father, and yet as divine?*

Gen. i. 2; vi. 3; Ps. civ. 30; cxxxix. 7; Job xxvi. 13; Isa. xlviii. 16.

V. It remains for us to consider what the Scriptures teach concerning the Eternal and Necessary Relations which the Three Divine Persons sustain to each other.

(I.) The Relation which the Second Person sustains to the First, or the Eternal Generation of the Son.

49. *What is the idiomatic use of the Hebrew word בֵּן (son)?*

It is used in the sense—1st. Of son. 2d. Of descendant; hence in the plural "children of Israel," for Israelites. Also when joined to a name of place or nation to denote inhabitants or citizens thereof, as "sons of Zion," etc. 3d. Of pupil, disciple, worshipper; thus "sons of the prophets" (1 Kings xx. 35); and "sons of God," applied, (1) to kings, Ps. ii. 7; (2) to angels, Gen. vi. 2; (3) to worshippers of God, his own people, Deut. xiv. 1. 4th. In combination with substantives, expressing age or quality, etc.; thus, "sons of years," for aged, Lev. xii. 6; "son of Belial," for worthless fellow, Deut. xiii. 13; "son of death," for one deserving to die, 1 Sam. xx. 31; "a hill son of fatness," for a fruitful hill. The same idiom has been carried into the Greek of the New Testament.—See Gesenius' "Heb. Lex."

50. *In what sense are men called "sons of God" in Scripture?*

The general idea embraced in the relation of sonship includes—1st, similarity and derivation of nature; 2d, parental and filial love; and 3d, heirship.

In this general sense all God's holy, intelligent creatures are called his sons. The term is applied in an eminent sense to kings and magistrates who receive dominion from God (Ps. lxxxii. 6), and to Christians who are the subjects of spiritual regeneration and adoption (Gal. iii. 26), the special objects of divine favor (Matt. v. 9), and are like him (Matt. v. 45). When applied to creatures, whether men or angels (Job i. 6), this word is always used in the plural. In the singular it is applied only to the second person of the Trinity, with the single exception of its application once to Adam (Luke iii. 38), when the reason is obviously to mark the peculiarity of his derivation from God immediately without the intervention of a human father.

51. *What reasons do Socinians assign for the application of the term Son of God to Christ?*

1st. Some Socinians hold that he is called Son of God only as an official title, as it is applied in the plural to ordinary kings and magistrates.

2d. Other Socinians hold that he was called Son of God only because he was brought into being by God's supernatural agency, and not by ordinary generation. To maintain this they appeal to Luke i. 35.

52. *How can you answer the Socinian argument derived from Luke i. 35; to the effect that Christ was called "Son of God" because of his miraculous birth alone?*

We answer—1st. If that reason is the fundamental one why the phrase "Son of God" is generally applied to Christ it should render him the "Son of the Spirit," who overshadowed the Virgin, and not the "Son of the Father." But he is never once so called, nor is any such relation ever indicated in Scripture.

2d. Even if this was one reason for the application of the phrase it would not follow that there are not other and deeper reasons for its use revealed in Scripture—whieh will be proved below to be the fact.

3d. Probably the real design of the passage was simply to convey to Mary the knowledge that in consequence of his supernatural generation her son, that is the man child born of her, is to be called "the Son of God." It was not a common child—the thing born of her was to be regarded as peculiarly related to God, until the complete revelation of his eternal Sonship as a divine person.

53. *What reason do Arians assign for the ascription of this title to Christ?*

Arians hold that he is so called because he was created by God more in his own likeness than any other creature, and first in the order of time.

54. *What reason do some Trinitarians, who at this point depart from the orthodox faith, give for the application of this title to Christ, and to what passages do they appeal?*

They hold that the title "Son of God" applies to Christ not as Logos, the eternal Second Person of the Trinity, but as Theanthropos. They object to the orthodox doctrine of the eternal Sonship of Christ.

1st. That Sonship implies derivation and hence inferiority.

2d. That the term "Son" in many passages is applied to him interchangeably with the term "Christ" and other *official* titles, belonging to his Mediatorial office and not to his eternal relations within the Godhead. They refer to Matt. xvi. 16; John i. 49, etc.

3d. That in Ps. ii. 7 it is expressly declared that Christ is constituted "Son of God" in time, instead of his co-existing as such from eternity with the Father by necessity of nature.

4th. The same is argued from Rom. i. 4.

55. *Show that the orthodox doctrine is not open to the objection that it represents the Second Person as inferior to the First.*

This objection derives all its plausibility from unduly pressing the analogy between the human relations of Father and Son and the divine relations signalized by the same terms. The one may be so far the best existing analogy of the other known to us, as to lay the foundation for the proper application of the terms derived from the known relation to designate the unknown, while we must remember that the two things are necessarily as different as the material is from the spiritual, as the temporal is from the eternal, as the finite is from the infinite. Besides it rests upon a misapprehension of the orthodox doctrine as to the following particulars:

1st. The church doctrine is that the *Person* not the *essence* of the Son is generated by the Father. The self-existent essence of the Godhead belongs to the Son equally with the Father from eternity.

2d. That the Father begets the Son by an eternal and necessary constitutional (not voluntary) act. This prevents the

Son from being in any sense dependent upon or inferior to the Father, and distinguishes the church doctrine from Semi-arianism, see below, Question 97.

56. *Show that their objection to the church doctrine based upon* Matt. xvi. 16; John i. 49, *etc., does not hold good.*

In none of these passages is it affirmed that he is Son *as* the Christ, *i. e., as* Mediator, but that being the eternal Son of God he is the Christ, the King of Israel, etc.

57. *Prove that neither the* 2d Psalm *nor* Rom. i. 4, *teach that Christ was made Son of God.*

Dr. Alexander says (see "Com. on Psalms") with relation to Psalm ii. 7, that it means simply, "Thou art my Son, this day I am thy Father, now always eternally thy Father. Even if '*this day*' be referred to the inception of the filial relation, it is thrown indefinitely back by the form of reminiscence, or narration, in the first clause of the verse. 'Jehovah said to me,' but when? If understood to mean from everlasting the form of expression would be perfectly in keeping with the other figurative forms by which the Scriptures represent things really ineffable in human language."

Rom. i. 4—"And declared (ὁρισθέντος) to be the Son of God with power according to the spirit of holiness, by the resurrection from the dead." The word ὁρισθέντος everywhere else in the New Testament signifies to constitute, to appoint, but here it is insisted that it signifies to manifest. The word strictly means to *bound, to define,* and may naturally mean to set forth, to characterize. This sense is said (Dr. Charles Hodge, "Com. Rom.") to be adopted by the great majority of commentators, including some of the ancient Greek Fathers. Besides, even if our opponents' interpretation of this passage were allowed, the indubitable evidence afforded to our position by other passages would remain. The two reasons for calling Christ Son are not inconsistent.

It is very evident that Christ called himself Son of God, and was so recognized by his disciples before his resurrection, and, therefore, he might have been revealed or manifested to be the Son of God, but could not have been constituted such by that event.

58. *Show that Acts xiii. 32, 33, does not prove that Jesus was made Son of God.*

It is argued from this passage that Jesus was constituted Son of God by his resurrection, as the first stage of his official exaltation. This can not be—1st. Because he was sent into the world as Son of God. 2d. Because the word ἀναστήσας, *having raised up*, refers to the raising up Christ at his birth, and not to his resurrection (there is nothing in the Greek corresponding to the word *again* in the English). When this word is used to designate the resurrection it is usually qualified by the phrase *from the dead*, as in verse 34. Ὅτι δὲ ἀνέστησεν αὐτὸν ἐκ νεκρῶν. Verse 32 declares the fulfillment of the promise referred to in verse 23.—See Alexander's "Com. on Acts."

59. *State the orthodox answer to the question why Christ is called "Son of God."*

The orthodox doctrine is that Christ is called "Son of God" in Scripture to indicate his eternal and necessary personal relation as the Second Person of the Godhead to the First Person, who is called Father to indicate the reciprocal relation.

60. *How is the doctrine stated in the Nicene and Athanasian Creeds and in the Westminster Confession?*

Nicene Creed.—"Son of God, begotten of his Father before all worlds; God of God, Light of Light, very God of very God, begotten not made, being of one substance with the Father."

Athanasian Creed.—"The Son is from the Father alone, neither made, nor created, but begotten."

Westminster Confession.—"The Father is of none, neither begotten nor proceeding; the Son is eternally begotten of the Father; the Holy Ghost eternally proceeding from the Father and the Son."

61. *What is the common statement and explanation of this doctrine given by orthodox writers?*

The eternal generation of the Son is commonly defined to be an eternal personal act of the Father, wherein, by necessity of nature, not by choice of will, he generates the person (not the essence) of the Son, by communicating to him the whole indivisible substance of the Godhead, without division, alienation, or change, so that the Son is the express image of his Father's person, and eternally continues, not from the Father, but in the Father, and the Father in the Son.—See particularly Heb. i. 3; John x. 38; xiv. 11; xvii. 21. The principal Scriptural support of the doctrine of derivation is John v. 26.—Turretin, Tom. I., L. 3, Q. 29.

Those theologians who insist upon this definition believe that the idea of derivation is necessarily implied in generation; that it is indicated by both the reciprocal terms Father and Son, and by the entire representation given in the Scriptures as to the relation and order of the persons of the Godhead, the

Father always standing for the Godhead considered absolutely; and they hold that this theory is necessary to the vindication of the essential unity of the three persons. The older theo logians, therefore, styled the Father πηγή θεότητος, *fountain of Godhead,* and αἰτία υἱοῦ, *principle or cause* of the Son, while the Son and Holy Ghost were both called αἰτιατοι (those depend ing upon another as their principle or cause).

They at the same time guarded the essential equality of the Son and the Holy Ghost with the Father, by saying, 1st, that the whole divine essence, without division or change, and, therefore, all the divine attributes, were communicated to them ; and, 2d, that this communication was made by an eternal and necessary act of the Father, and not of his mere will. In all the early Creeds this identity as to essence, and subordination as to mode of subsistence and operation, is ex pressed by the phrases as above. Θεὸς ἐκ θεοῦ, φῶς ἐκ φωτός; ἐκ τοῦ πατρός; θεὸς ἀληθινός ἐκ θεοῦ ἀληθινοῦ; γεννηθείς ὸν ποιηθείς; ὁμοούσιον τῷ πατρί.

62. *State how they endeavored to guard their doctrine from all anthropomorphic grossness.*

In order to guard their doctrine of derivation and eternal generation from all gross anthropomorphic conceptions they carefully maintained that it was—(1) ἀχρόνως, *timeless, eternal;* (2) ἀσώματως, *not bodily, spiritual;* (3) ἀόρατος, *invisible;* (4) ἀχω ρίστως, *not a local transference, a communication not without but within the Godhead;* (5) ἀπαθῶς, *without passion or change;* (6) παντελῶς ἀκατάληπτος, *altogether incomprehensible.*

63. *What is essential to the Scriptural doctrine of the eternal generation of the Son?*

In the above rendered account of the orthodox doctrine there is nothing inconsistent with revealed truth. The idea of derivation, as involved in the generation of the Son by the Father, appears rather to be a rational explanation of revealed facts than a revealed fact itself. On such a subject, therefore, it should be held in suspense. All that is explicitly revealed is, 1st, the term Son is applied to Christ as the second person of the Godhead. 2d. This term, and the equivalent one, "only begotten," reveal some relation, within the Godhead, of the person of the Son to the person of the Father; the designa tion Father being reciprocal to that of Son. 3d. That this re lation is such that Father and Son are the same in substance, and are personally equal; that the Father is first and the Son second in the order of revelation and operation, that the Son is the express image of the Father's person, not the Father of the Son's, and that the Son is not from the Father, but in the Father, and the Father in the Son.

64. *How may it be shown that the common doctrine is not self-contradictory?*

There is evidently no inconsistency in the simple Scriptural statement given in the answer to the last question. Heterodox controversialists, however, have claimed that there is a manifest inconsistency in the orthodox theory that the Father communicates to the Son the whole divine essence without alienating it from himself, dividing or otherwise changing it. This subject does not fall within the legitimate sphere of human logic, yet it is evident that this theory involves no contradiction and no mystery greater than that involved in the whole essence of God being at the same time present, without division or diffusion, to every point of space.

65. *By what terms, besides that of "Son" is the personal character of the Second Person, and his relation to the First Person designated?*

Λόγος πρὸς τὸν θεόν᾽καὶ θεὸς ἦν ὁ λόγος. *The Word with God, and who is God*—John i. 1. Εἰκὼν τοῦ θεοῦ τοῦ ἀοράτου. *The Image of the invisible God*—2 Cor iv. 4; Col. i. 15. Χαρακτὴρ τῆς ὑποστάσεως αὐτοῦ. "*The image or impression of his being or substance*"—Heb. i. 3. Ἐν μορφῇ θεοῦ. *The form of God*—Phil. ii. 6; Ἀπαύγασμα τῆς δόξης αὐτοῦ. "*The shining forth of his glory*"—Heb. i. 3.

66. *What is the distinction which some of the fathers made between the eternal, the ante-mundane, and the mundane generation of the Son?*

1st. By his eternal generation they intended to mark his essential relation to the Father as his consubstantial and eternal Son.

2d. By his ante-mundane generation they meant to signify the commencement of the outgoings of his energy, and the manifestation of his person beyond the bosom of the Godhead, in the sphere of external creation, etc.—Col. i. 15.

3d. By his mundane generation they intended his supernatural birth in the flesh.—Luke i. 35.

67. *What is the distinction which some of the fathers made between the* λόγος ἐνδιάθετος (*ratio insita, reason*), *and the* λόγος προφορικός (*ratio prolata, reason brought forth, or expressed*)?

The orthodox fathers used the phrase *logos endiathetos* to designate the Word, whom they held to be a distinct person, dwelling from eternity with the Father. The ground of their use of this phrase was a fanciful analogy which they conceived existed between the relation which the eternal *logos* (word, or reason) (John i. 1) sustains to the Father, and the relation which the reason of a man sustains to his own rational soul. Thus the *logos endiathetos* was God's own reflective idea hypostatized. They were led to this vain attempt to philosophize upon an incomprehensible subject by the influence exerted upon them by the Platonic philosophers of that age, who taught a sort of metaphysical trinity, *e. g.*, that in the one God there were three constituent principles, τό ἀγαθόν, goodness, νοῦς, intelligence, ψυχή, vitality. Their immediate object was to illustrate the essential unity of the Trinity, and to prove, against the Arians, the essential divinity of the Son, from the application to him by John of the epithet λογος θεου.

By the phrase *logos prophoricos* they intended to designate him as the reason of God revealed, when he proceeded from the Father in the work of creation.—See Hill's "Lectures."

The Arians, taking advantage of the essential inadequacy of this language, confused the controversy by acknowledging that the phrase *logos prophoricos* did truly apply to Christ, since he came forth from God as the first and highest creation and image of his mind. But declaring, with some color of truth, that the phrase *logos endiathetos*, when applied to Christ, taught pure Sabellianism, since it marked no personal distinction, but signified nothing else than the mind of the Father itself.

68. *If God is "ens a se ipso," self-existent, how can the Son be really God, if he be "θεος εκ θεου," God from the Father?*

The objection presented in this question does not press against the Scriptural statement of the eternal generation of the Son presented above (Question 63), but solely against the theory of derivation as involved in the ordinary definition (see Question 61). Those who insist upon the validity of that view rebut the objection by saying that self-existence is an attribute of essence, not of person. The Father, as a person, generates the person, not the essence of the Son, whose person is constituted of the very same self-existent essence with the Father's. Thus the Son is αὐτοθεος, *i. e.*, *Deus a se ipso* as to his essence, but θεός εκ θεοῦ, God from God, as to his person.

69. *What argument for the eternal sonship of Christ may be derived from the designation of the persons of the Trinity as Father, Son, and Holy Ghost?*

In the apostolical benediction and the formula of baptism the one God is designated as Father, Son, and Holy Ghost. The term Son can not here be applied to Christ as an official title, or as a miraculously generated man, because, 1st, he is so called as one of the three divine persons constituting the Godhead. 2d. The term Son is reciprocal to the term Father, and therefore designates the relation of the second person to the first. Whatever this relation may involve besides, it evidently must be eternal and necessary, and includes paternity on the part of the first person, and filiation on the part of the second.

70. *What argument in support of this doctrine may be derived from the use of the word son in* Matt. xi. 27 *and* Luke x. 22 ?

In both of these passages the term Son is used to designate the divine nature of the second person of the Trinity in his relation to the first. The Son, as Son, knows and is known by the Father as Father. He is infinite in knowledge and therefore knows the Father. He is infinite in being and therefore can be known by none other than the Father.

71. *State the argument from* John i. 1–14.

Here the eternal Word, who was God, discovered himself as such to his disciples by the manifestation of his native divine glory, "the glory as of the only begotten of the Father." He was "only begotten Son," therefore as God, and not either as Mediator or as man.

72. *State the argument from the application in Scripture of the terms* μονογενής, *(only begotten) and* ἴδιος, *(own) to the Sonship of Christ.*

Although many of God's creatures are called his sons, the phrase, Son of God, in the singular, and when limited by the terms "own" and "only begotten," is applied only to Christ.

Christ is called "only begotten Son of God."—John i. 14, 18; iii. 16, 18; 1 John iv. 9.

In John v. 18, Christ calls God his *own* Father (see Greek). He is called the own Son of the Father.—Rom. viii. 32.

The use of these qualifying terms proves that Christ is called Son of God in a sense different from that in which any other is so called. Therefore it designates him as God and not as man, nor as the bearer of an office.

73. *What is the argument derived from* John v. 22, *and context, and from* John x. 33–37 ?

In the first passage the terms Father and Son are used to

designate two divine and equal persons. As Son, Christ does whatsoever the Father doeth, and is to receive equal honor.

In the second passage, Jesus assumes the title, "Son of God," as equivalent to asserting that he was God. The Jews charging it upon him as blasphemy.

74. *What is the evidence furnished by such passages as speak of the manifestation, giving or sending of the Son?*

See 1 John iii. 8; Rom. viii. 3; John iii. 16, etc.

To say that the Son was sent or manifested implies that he was Son before he was sent or manifested as such.

75. *State the argument from* Rom. i. 3, 4.

The argument from this passage is twofold: 1st. The Son of God is declared to have been made flesh, and therefore must have pre-existed as Son. 2d. By the resurrection he was powerfully manifested to be the Son of God as to his divine nature. The phrases, *according to the flesh*, and *according to the spirit of holiness*, are evidently anthithetical, designating severally the Lord's human and divine natures.

76. *State the argument from* Rom. viii. 3.

Here God's own Son was sent in the likeness of sinful flesh. Obviously he must have pre-existed as such before he assumed the likeness of sinful flesh, the assumption of which certainly could not have constituted him the *own* Son of God.

77. *State the argument from* Col. i. 15–21.

In this passage the apostle sets forth at length the nature and glory of him whom, in the thirteenth verse, he had called God's dear Son. Thus he proves that Christ as Son is the image of the invisible God, and that by him all things consist, etc.

78. *State the argument from* Heb. i. 5–8.

Paul is here setting forth the superiority of Christ as a divine person. As divine he calls him "the Son," "the first begotten." This Son is brought into the world, and therefore must have pre-existed as such. As Son he is declared to be God, and to reign upon an everlasting throne.

79. *How can those passages which speak of the Son as inferior and subject to the Father be reconciled with this doctrine?*

It is objected that such passages prove that Jesus, *as Son,* is inferior and subject to the Father.

We answer that in John iii. 13 the "Son of Man" is said to have come down from heaven, and to be in heaven. But surely

Jesus, *as Son of Man*, was not omnipresent. In Acts xx. 28 God is said to purchase his church with his own blood; but surely Christ, *as God*, did not shed his blood. The explanation of this is that it is the common usage of Scripture to designate the single person of the God-man by a title belonging to him as the possessor of one nature, while the condition, attribute, relation, or action predicated of him is true only of the other nature. Thus in the passages in question he is called "Son of God," because he is the eternal Word, while at the same time he is said to be inferior to the Father, because he is also man and mediator.

(II.) The relation which the third Person sustains to the first and second, or the eternal procession of the Holy Ghost.

80. *What is the etymology of the word Spirit, and the usage of its Hebrew and Greek equivalents?*

The English word spirit is from the Latin spiritus, *breath, wind, air, life, soul*, which in turn is from the verb spiro, *to breathe*. The equivalent Hebrew word, רוּחַ, has a perfectly analogous usage. 1st. Its primary sense is wind, air in motion, Gen. viii. 1; then, 2d, breath, the breath of life, Gen. vi. 17; Job xvii. 1; 3d, animal soul, vital principle in men and animals, 1 Sam. xxx. 12; 4th, rational soul of man, Gen. xli. 8, and hence, metaphorically, disposition, temperament, Num. v. 14; 5th, Spirit of Jehovah, Gen. i. 2; Ps. li. 11.—Gesenius' "Lex."

The equivalent Greek word, $\pi\nu\epsilon\tilde{v}\mu\alpha$, has also the same usage. It is derived from $\pi\nu\epsilon\omega$, *to breathe, to blow*. It signifies, 1st, breath, Rev. xi. 11; 2d, air in motion, John iii. 8; 3d, the vital principle, Matt. xxvii. 50; 4th, the rational soul, spoken (1) of the disembodied spirits of men, Heb. xii. 23; (2) of devils, Matt. x. 1; (3) of angels, Heb. i. 14; (4) the Spirit of God, spoken of God, *a*, absolutely as an attribute of his essence, John iv. 24; and *b* as the personal designation of the third person of the Trinity, who is called Spirit of God, or of the Lord, and the Holy Spirit, and the Spirit of Christ, or of Jesus, or of the Son of God, Acts xvi. 6, 7; Rom. viii. 9; 2 Cor. iii. 17; Gal. iv. 6; Phil. i. 19; 1 Pet. i. 11.

81. *Why is the third person of the Trinity called the Spirit?*

As the one indivisible divine essence which is common to each of the divine persons alike is spiritual, this term, as the personal designation of the third person, can not be intended to signify the fact that he is a spirit as to his essence, but rather to mark what is peculiar to his person, *i. e.*, his personal relation to the Father and the Son, and the peculiar mode of his operation *ad extra.* As the reciprocal epithets Father and Son are used to indicate, so far forth, the mutual relations of the first and second persons, so the epithets, Spirit, Spirit of God, Spirit of the Son, Spirit which proceedeth from the Father, are applied to the third person to indicate, so far forth, the relation of the third person to the first and second.

82. *Why is he called Holy Spirit?*

As holiness is an attribute of the divine essence, and the glory equally of Father, Son and Holy Ghost, it can not be applied in any pre-eminent sense as a personal characteristic to the third person. It indicates, therefore, the peculiar nature of his operation. He is called the *Holy* Spirit because he is the author of holiness throughout the universe. As the Son is also styled *Logos,* or God, the Revealer, so the Holy Spirit is God, the Operator, the end and glory of whose work in the moral world is holiness, as in the physical world beauty.

83. *Why is he called the Spirit of God?*

This phrase expresses his divinity, his relation to the Godhead as himself God, 1 Cor. ii. 11; his intimate personal relation to the Father as his consubstantial spirit proceeding from him, John xv. 26; and the fact that he is the divine Spirit, which proceeding from God operates upon the creature, Ps. civ. 30; 1 Pet. iv. 14.

84. *Why is the third person called the Spirit of Christ?*

See Gal. iv. 6; Rom. viii. 9; Phil. i. 19; 1 Peter i. 11. As the form of expression is identical in the several phrases, Spirit of God, and Spirit of the Son, and as the Scriptures, with one exception, John xv. 26, uniformly predicate every thing of the relation of the Spirit to the Son, that they predicate of the relation of the Spirit to the Father, it appears evident that he is called Spirit of the Son for the same reason that he is called Spirit of God.

This phrase also additionally sets forth the official relation which the Spirit in his agency in the work of redemption sustains to the God-man, in taking of his, and showing them to us, John xvi. 14.

85. *What is meant by the theological phrase, Procession of the Holy Ghost?*

Theologians intend by this phrase to designate the relation which the third person sustains to the first and second, wherein by an eternal and necessary, *i. e.,* not voluntary, act of the Father and the Son, their whole identical divine essence, without alienation, division, or change, is communicated to the Holy Ghost.

86. What distinction do theologians make between "procession" and "generation?"

As this entire subject infinitely transcends the measure of our faculties, we can do nothing further than classify and contrast those predicates which inspiration has applied to the relation of Father and Son with those which it has applied to the relation of the Spirit to the Father and Son.

Thus Turretin, Vol. I., L. 3., Q. 31. They differ, "1st. *As to source*, the Son emanates from the Father only, but the Spirit from the Father and the Son at the same time. 2d. *As to mode.* The Son emanates in the way of generation, which affects not only personality, but similitude, on account of which the Son is called the image of the Father, and in consequence of which he receives the property of communicating the same essence to another person; but the Spirit, by the way of spiration, which effects only personality, and in consequence of which the person who proceeds does not receive the property of communicating the same essence to another person. 3d. *As to order.* The Son is second person, and the Spirit third, and though both are eternal, without beginning or succession, yet, in our mode of conception, generation precedes procession." The technical terms used to express these two mysteries are Γέννησις, *generatio, generation.* Ἐκπόρευσις, ἔκπεμψις, *processio, missio, procession.*

"The schoolmen vainly attempted to found a distinction between generation and spiration upon the different operations of the divine intellect and the divine will. They say the Son was generated *per modum intellectus*, whence he is called the Word of God. The Spirit proceeds *per modum voluntatis*, whence he is called Love."

87. What is the Scripture ground for this doctrine?

What we remarked above (Question 53), concerning the common theological definition of the eternal generation of the Son, holds true also with reference to the common definition of the eternal procession of the Holy Ghost, viz., that in order to make the method of the divine unity in Trinity more apparent, theologians have pressed the idea of derivation and subordination in the order of personal subsistence too far. This ground is at once sacred and mysterious. The points given by Scripture are not to be pressed nor speculated upon, but received and confessed nakedly.

The data of inspiration are simply as follows: 1st. Father,

Son, and Holy Ghost, three divine persons, possess from eternity the one whole identical, indivisible, unchangeable essence. 2d. The Father from his characteristic personal name, and the order in which his name uniformly occurs in Scripture, and from the fact that the Son is called his and his only begotten, and that the Spirit is called his, the one proceeding from him, and from the order of his manifestation and operation ad extra, is evidently *in some way* first in order of personal subsistence relatively to the Son and Spirit. 3d. For the same reason (see below, Question 89) the Son, in the order of personal subsistence, is before the Spirit. 4th. What the real nature of these distinctions in the order of personal subsistence may be is made known to us only so far—(1.) That it involves no distinction as to time, since all are alike eternal. (2.) It does not depend upon any *voluntary* action, for that would make the second person dependent upon the first, and the third upon the first and second, while they are all "equal in power and glory." (3.) It is such a relation that the second person is eternally only begotten Son of the first, and the third is eternally the Spirit of the first and second.

88. *What was the difference between the Greek and Latin churches on this doctrine?*

The famous Council of Nice, A. D. 325, while so accurately defining the doctrine of the Godhead of the Son, left the testimony concerning the Holy Ghost in the vague form in which it stood in the ancient creed, "in the Holy Ghost." But the heresy of Macedonius, who denied the divinity of the Holy Ghost, having sprung up in the meantime, the Council of Constantinople, A. D. 381, completed the testimony of the Nicene Creed thus, "I believe in the Holy Ghost, the Lord, the Author of Life, who proceedeth from the Father."

There subsequently arose a controversy upon the question, whether the Scriptures do or do not represent the Holy Spirit as sustaining precisely the same relation to the Son that he does to the Father. This the Latins generally affirmed, and at the third ecclesiastical assembly at Toledo, A. D. 589, they added the word *filioque* (and the Son) to the Latin version of the Constantinopolitan Creed, making the clause read "Credimus in Spiritum Sanctum qui à Patre *Filioque* procedit." The Greek Church violently opposed this, and to this day reject it. For a short time they were satisfied with the compromise, "The Spirit proceeding from the Father *through* the Son," which was finally rejected by both parties. The Constantinopolitan Creed, as amended at the Council of Toledo, is the one now adopted by the Catholic Church, and recognized by all Protestants, currently bearing the title of "Nicene Creed."

89. *How may it be proved that, as far as revealed, the Spirit sustains precisely the same relation to the Son which he does to the Father?*

The epithet "Spirit" is the characteristic personal designation of the third Person. Whatever is revealed of his eternal and necessary personal relation to either the Father or the Son is indicated by this word. Yet he is called the Spirit of the Son, as well as the Spirit of the Father. He possesses the same identical essence of the Son as of the Father. The Son sends and operates through the Spirit as the Father does. Wherever their Spirit is there both Father and Son are revealed, and there they exercise their power.—John xiv. 16, 26; xv. 26; xvi. 7. With the single exception of the phrase, "which proceedeth from the Father" (John xv. 26), the Scriptures apply precisely the same predicates to the relation of the Spirit to the Son that they do to his relation to the Father.

90. *What office does the Spirit discharge in the economy of redemption?*

In the economy of redemption, as universally in all the actings of the Godhead upon the creature, God the Son is the revealed God, God as known, and God the Spirit is that divine person who exerts his energy immediately upon and in the creature. He is styled in this relation in the creed το Κύριον, καὶ τὸ ζωοποιόν. The Lord, and the Giver of life. For a more detailed answer see Chapter XXIV., on "The Mediatorial Office of Christ," Question 9.

(III.) THE PERSONAL PROPERTIES PECULIAR TO EACH OF THE THREE PERSONS OF THE GODHEAD, AND THEIR ORDER OF OPERATION AD EXTRA.

91. *What is the theological meaning of the word property as applied to the doctrine of the Trinity? and what are severally the personal properties of each Person of the Godhead.*

The *attributes* of God are the perfections of the divine essence, and therefore common to each of the three persons, who are "the same in substance," and therefore "equal in power and glory." These have been discussed under Chapter VIII. The *properties* of each divine person, on the other hand, are those peculiar modes of personal subsistence whereby each divine person is constituted as such, and that peculiar order of operation whereby each person is distinguished from the others. The peculiar distinguishing properties which belong to each Person severally is called technically his *charatêr hypostaticus—personal character.*

As far as these are revealed to us the personal properties of the Father are as follows: He is begotten by none, and proceeds from none; he is the Father of the Son, having begotten him from eternity; the Spirit proceeds from him and is his Spirit. Thus he is the first in order and in operation, sending and operating through the Son and Spirit.

The personal properties of the Son are as follows: He is the Son, from eternity the only begotten of the Father. The Spirit is the Spirit of the Son even as he is the Spirit of the Father, he is sent by the Father, whom he reveals: he, even as the Father, sends and operates through the Spirit.

The personal properties of the Spirit are as follows: He is the Spirit of the Father and the Son, from eternity proceeding from them: he is sent by the Father and the Son, they operating through him; he operates immediately upon the creature.

92. *What kind of subordination did the early writers attribute to the second and third persons in relation to the first?*

They held, as above shown, that the eternal generation of the Son by the Father, and the eternal procession of the Holy Ghost from the Father and the Son involved in both instances the derivation of essence. They illustrated their idea of this eternal and necessary act of communication by the example of a luminous body, which necessarily radiates light the whole period of its existence. Thus the Son is defined in the words of the Nicene Creed, "God of God, Light of Light." Thus as the radiance of the sun is coeval with its existence, and of the same essence as its source, by this illustration they designed to signify their belief in the identity and consequent equality of the divine persons as to essence, and the relative subordination of the second to the first, and of the third to the first and second, as to personal subsistence and consequent order of operation.

93. *What is expressed by the use of the terms first, second, and third in reference to the persons of the Trinity.*

These terms are severally applied to the persons of the Trinity because—1st. The Scriptures uniformly state their names in this order. 2d. The personal designations, Father and Son, and Spirit of the Father and of the Son, indicate this order of personal subsistence. 3d. Their respective modes of operation ad extra is always in this order. The Father sends and operates through the Son, and the Father and Son send and operate through the Spirit. The Scriptures never either directly or indirectly indicate the reverse order.

As to the outward bearing of the Godhead upon the creature it would appear, that the Father is revealed only as he is seen in the Son, who is the eternal Logos, or divine Word, the express image of the Father's person. "No man hath seen God at any time, the only begotten Son, who is in the bosom of the Father, he hath declared him."—John i. 18. And the Father and Son act *immediately* upon the creature only through the Spirit.

"The Father is all the fulness of the Godhead invisible, without form, whom no man hath seen or can see."

"The Son is all the fulness of the Godhead manifested."

"The Spirit is all the fulness of the Godhead acting immediately upon the creature, and thus making manifest the Father in the image of the Son, and through the power of the Spirit."—"Higher Christian Life," by Rev. W. E. Boardman, p. 105.

94. *How can the assumption of personal distinctions in the Godhead be reconciled with the divine unity?*

Although this tripersonal constitution of the Godhead is altogether beyond the capacity of reason, and is ascertained to us only through a supernatural revelation, there is evidently no contradiction in the twofold proposition, that God is one, and yet Father, Son, and Holy Ghost are that one God. They are one in one sense, and threefold in an entirely different sense. The eternal, self-existent, divine essence, constituting all those divine perfections called attributes of God is, in the same sense and degree, common to all the persons. In *this* sense they are one. But this divine essence exists eternally as Father, and as Son, and as Holy Ghost, distinguished by personal properties. In *this* sense they are three. We believe this, not because we understand it, but because thus God has revealed himself.

95. *How can the separate incarnation of the Son be reconciled with the divine unity?*

The Son is identical with the Father and Spirit as to essence, but distinct from them as to personal subsistence. In the incarnation, the divine essence of the Son was not made man, but as a divine person he entered into a personal relation with the human nature of the man Christ Jesus. This did not constitute a new person, but merely introduced a new element into his eternal person. It was the personal union of the Son with a human soul and body, and not any change either in the divine essence, or in the personal relation of the Son to the Father or the Spirit.

HERETICAL OPINIONS.

96. *What are the three great points which together embrace the mystery of the Trinity as revealed in Scripture, and the apparent irreconcilability of which, with each other, occasions the great objection to this doctrine in the minds of heretics of all classes?*

The three great points are as follows. 1st. There is absolutely but one God, but one self-existent, eternal, immutable, spiritual substance. 2d. Father, Son, and Holy Ghost are each equally this one God—are each in common constituted of the whole of this inalienable indivisible essence, having the same identical numerical essence, and the same identical attributes. 3d. Nevertheless Father, Son, and Holy Ghost are three distinct persons, distinguished each by his several personal properties. The difficulty is, that in the case of the only created spirits of which we know any thing, every person is a separate spiritual essence, and distinct personality is definitely discriminated by numerical difference of attribute. We can not conceive how three persons can have among them but one intelligence and one will.

Hence all heresies on this subject have sprung from one or other of three distinct tendencies, or efforts to disembarrass this doctrine of its apparent inconsistencies by the denial or abatement of one or other of its three constituent elements. Thus—1st. One tendency is to cut the knot of the difficulty by denying the divinity of the Lord Jesus Christ, and the personality of the Holy Ghost. This makes God the Father the only divine Person and the possessor of the only divine substance. 2d. A second heretical tendency is to deny the divine unity and to maintain the co-existence of three distinct Gods, distinct in essence as well as in person. 3d. The third heretical tendency is to press the divine unity so far as to make Father, Son, and Holy Ghost one and the same identical Person as well as the same divine essence, admitting them only to be different names, or different aspects or functions of the one divine Person.

97. *What different opinions have been held by those who deny the divinity of Christ, and either the divinity or personality of the Holy Ghost?*

1st. That of the Humanitarians, or those who maintain that Christ is a mere Man. These in the early Church were known

by the name of Ebionites, and Alogi—the deniers of the Logos,
while in the Modern Church they are known as Socinians.   For
a statement of the History and Doctrine of the Socinians, see
above, Chapter VI., Ques. 11 and 13.   Those who have held
that Christ is a mere man have differed among themselves as
to whether he was miraculously conceived in the womb of the
Virgin or not, and as to the question of his supernatural en-
dowments as a prophet, and as to the degree of honor and
obedience owed from us to him.   Some admit that he possessed
a supernatural divine commission and qualification beyond that
vouchsafed to any other prophet.   Others deny the supernatural element altogether, and regard him as a mere man naturally endowed with a very superior moral and religious genius.

All of this class, of course, hold that God is one Person as
well as one essence, and for the most part they regard the term
Holy Ghost as only a designation of the divine energy exercised in human affairs.   Some of the German Rationalists, who
for the most part agree with the Socinians, hold that the phrase
Holy Ghost properly designates the one divine person working
in the world of nature—Creation and Providence.   Others hold
it designates God in the church.

2d. The *Gnostics*, as a general class, held that the supreme
God is one alike in essence and in Person, and that from him
emanates different orders of spiritual beings, none of them in
any proper sense God, yet all divine, since they all proceeded
by way of emanation from him.   These are called Æons.   The
Old Testament Jehovah, or Creator, was one of these Æons, of
which class Christ was one of the greatest.   The entire sum
of these Æons constituted, in the view of the Gnostics, the
πᾶν τὸ πλήρωμα τῆς θεότητος, the entire sum of all the actual
or possible self-revelations, or self-communications, of the un-
approachable Godhead, which the Apostle Paul declared to be
alone and fully realized in Christ.—Col. ii. 9.

3d. The earlier *Nominal Trinitarians.* "In their construction of the doctrine of the trinity, the Son is not a *subsistence*
(ὑπόστασις) in the Essence, but only an *effluence* (δύναμις) or energy issuing from it, hence they could not logically assert the
union of the divine *nature*, or the very substance of the Godhead with the humanity of Jesus.   A merely effluent energy
proceeding from the deity, and entering the humanity of Christ,
would be nothing more than an indwelling inspiration kindred
to that of the prophets."—Shedd's "Hist. Christ. Doc.," Book
III., Ch. 5, § 1.

4th. The *Arians*, so called from Arius, a presbyter of Alexandria during the first part of the fourth century, the great
opponent of Athanasius.   He maintained that the Godhead

consists of one eternal person, who in the beginning, before all worlds, created in his own image a super-angelic being (ἑτεροούσιον—of a different essence), his only begotten Son, the beginning of the creation of God, by whom also he made the worlds. The first and greatest creature thus created, through the Son of God, was the Holy Ghost. In the fullness of time this Son became incarnate in the person of Jesus of Nazareth.

4th. The doctrine of the Semiarians. This party was so called as occupying middle ground between the Arians and the Orthodox. They held that the absolute, self-existent God was one person, but that the Son was a divine person of a glorious essence, like to (ὁμοιούσιον) but not identical with (ὁμοούσιον) that of the Father, and from eternity begotten by the Father by a free exercise of will and power, and therefore subordinate to and dependent upon him. This was the view first disseminated by Origen, and advocated with great power at the council of Nice by Eusebius bishop of Cæsarea, and Eusebius bishop of Nicomedia.

It appears that some of the Semiarians agreed with the Arians in regarding the Holy Spirit as the first and most glorious creature of the Son, but that the majority regarded the words "Holy Spirit," as significant of a divine energy, or as a synonym of the word God.—See Neander's "Ch. Hist.," Torrey's translation, Vol. II., pp. 419, 420.

98. *What was the position of those who sought to relieve the difficulty of the doctrine by denying the divine unity?*

These were the Tritheists, who admitted that there were three ὀυσίαι numerically considered, as well as three ὑπόστασεις in the Godhead. They held the idea of ὀυσία (essence) by which the essence was expressed, should be understood as the mere concept of a genus, and the ὑπόστασις as an individual (a species) falling under this generic conception. "That is there are three Gods, generically one, individually distinct." John Ascusnages of Constantinople, and John Philoponus of Alexandria (of the latter part of sixth century) were leaders of the Tritheists.—Smith's edition of Hagenbach's "Hist. of Doc.," Vol. I., pp. 267, 268.

99. *What was the position of those who pressed the divine unity in opposition to the Tritheists so far as to make Father, Son, and Holy Ghost one Person as well as one essence?*

The *Monarchians*, so called because they rejected the Triad and maintained the Monad, or absolute unity as to person as well as to essence in the Godhead, were of several kinds;

some, as the Alogi, were very much the same as the modern *Unitarian*, which term is intended to express the same idea. Others, as Praxeas of Asia Minor, circum. A. D. 200; Noetus of Smyrna, circum. A. D. 230, and Beryl of Bostra in Arabia, circum. A. D. 250, held that this one single divine Person became incarnate in the man Christ, and hence they were called Patripassians. "Sabellius, a presbyter of Ptolemais, who lived about the middle of the third century, adopted the notions of the earlier Monarchians, and maintained in opposition to the doctrine propounded by Origen and his followers, that the appellations Father, Son, and Holy Spirit were only so many different manifestations and names of one and the same divine being. He thus converted the objective and real distinction of persons (a Trinity of essence) into a merely subjective and modalistic view (the Trinity of manifestation)."—Smith's edition of Hagenbach's "Hist. of Doctrine," Vol. I., p. 246. "They affirmed that there is only one divine Person. This one only Person conceived of in his abstract simplicity and eternity was denominated God the Father; but in his incarnation, he was denominated God the Son. Sometimes a somewhat different mode of apprehension and statement was employed. God in his concealed, unrevealed nature and being was denominated God the Father, and when he comes forth from the depths of his essence, creating a universe, and revealing and communicating himself to it, he therein takes on a different relation, and assumes another denomination; namely, God the Son, or the Logos."—Shedd's "History of Christian Doctrine," Book III., Ch. 2, § 2.

100. *By what considerations may it be shown that the doctrine of the Trinity is a fundamental element of the Gospel?*

It is not claimed that the refinements of theological speculations upon this subject are essential points of faith, but simply that it is essential to salvation to believe in the three persons in one Godhead, as they are revealed to us in the Scriptures. 1st. The only true God is that God who has revealed himself to us in the Scriptures, and the very end of the gospel is to bring us to the knowledge of that God precisely in the aspect in which he has revealed himself. Every other conception of God presents a false god to the mind and conscience. There can be no mutual toleration without treason. Socinians, Arians, and Trinitarians worship different Gods.

2d. The Scriptures explicitly assert that the knowledge of this true God and of Jesus Christ whom he hath sent is eternal life, and that it is necessary to honor the Son even as we honor the Father.—John v. 23; xiv. 1; xvii. 3; 1 John ii. 23; v. 20.

3d. In the initiatory rite of the Christian church we are baptized into the name of every several person of the Trinity. Matt. xxviii. 19.

4th. The whole plan of redemption in all its parts is founded upon it. Justification, sanctification, adoption, and all else that makes the gospel the wisdom and power of God unto salvation, can be understood only in the light of this fundamental truth.

5th. As an historical fact it is beyond dispute that in whatever church the doctrine of the Trinity has been abandoned or obscured, every other characteristic doctrine of the gospel has gone with it.

CHAPTER X.

THE DECREES OF GOD IN GENERAL.

1. *What are the decrees of God?*

See "Con. of Faith," chap. iii. "Larger Cat.," Q. 12, and "Shorter Cat.," Q. 7.

The decree of God is his eternal, unchangeable, holy, wise, and sovereign purpose, comprehending at once all things that ever were or will be in their causes, conditions, successions, and relations, and determining their certain futurition. The several contents of this one eternal purpose are, because of the limitation of our faculties, necessarily conceived of by us in partial aspects, and in logical relations, and are therefore styled DECREES.

2. *How are the acts of God classified, and to which class do theologians refer the decrees?*

All conceivable divine actions may be classified as follows:

1st. Those actions which are *immanent and intrinsic*, belonging essentially to the perfection of the divine nature, and which bear no reference whatever to any existence without the Godhead. These are the acts of eternal and necessary generation, whereby the Son springs from the Father, and of eternal and necessary procession, whereby the Spirit proceeds from the Father and the Son, and all those actions whatsoever involved in the mutual society of the divine persons.

2d. Those actions which are *extrinsic and transient, i. e.,* those free actions proceeding from God and terminating upon the creature, occurring successively in time, as God's acts in creation, providence, and grace.

3d. The third class are like the first, inasmuch as they are intrinsic and immanent, essential to the perfection of the divine nature and permanent states of the divine mind, but they differ, on the other hand, from the first class, inasmuch as they have respect to the whole dependent creation exterior to the Godhead. These are the eternal and immutable decrees of God respecting all beings and events whatsoever exterior to himself.

3. *What is the essential nature and source of the difficulties which oppress the human reason when speculating on this subject?*

These difficulties all have their ground in the perfectly inscrutable relations of the eternal to the temporal, of the infinite to the finite, of God's absolute sovereignty to man's free agency, and of the unquestionable fact of the origination of sin to the holiness, goodness, wisdom, and power of God. They are peculiar to no system of theology, but press equally upon any system which acknowledges the existence and moral government of God, and the moral agency of man. They have perplexed heathen philosophers of old, and deists in modern times, and Socinians, Pelagians, and Arminians just as sorely as Calvinists.

4. *From what fixed point of view are we to start in the study of this subject?*

A self-existent, independent, all-perfect, and unchangeable God, existing alone from eternity, began to create the universe physical and moral in an absolute vacuum, moved to do so from motives and with reference to ends, and according to ideas and plans, wholly interior and self-prompted. Also, if God governs the universe, he must, as an intelligent being, govern it according to a plan; and this plan must be perfect in its comprehension, reaching to all details. If he has a plan now, he must have had the same plan unchanged from the beginning. The decree of God therefore is the act of an infinite, absolute, eternal, unchangeable, and sovereign person, comprehending a plan including all his works of all kinds, great and small, from the beginning of creation to an unending eternity. It *must* therefore be incomprehensible, and it *can not* be conditioned by any thing exterior to God himself—since it was matured before any thing exterior to him existed, and hence itself embraces and determines all these supposed exterior things and all the conditions of them forever.

5. *What is the distinction between foreknowledge and foreordination, and what is the general position of the Socinians on this point?*

Foreknowledge is an act of the infinite intelligence of God, knowing from all eternity, without change, the certain futurition of all events of every class whatsoever that ever will come to pass.

Foreordination is an act of the infinitely intelligent, foreknowing, righteous, and benevolent will of God from all eternity *determining* the certain futurition of all events of every class whatsoever that come to pass. Foreknowledge recognizes the certain futurition of events, while foreordination makes them certainly future.

Socinians admit that the foreknowledge and the foreordination of God are co-extensive, but they limit both to such events in creation and providence as God has determined to do by his own immediate agency, or to bring about through the agency of such second causes as act under the law of necessity. They deny that God has either foreordained or foreknown the voluntary actions of free agents, which from their very nature are contingent, and not objects of knowledge until after their occurrence.

6. *What is the position of the Arminians on this subject?*

The Arminians agree with the Socinians in denying that God foreordains the voluntary acts of free agents, or in any way whatever determines them beforehand to be certainly future. But they differ from the Socinians and agree with us in holding that the certain foreknowledge of God extends equally to all events, as well to those in their nature contingent, as to those produced by second causes acting under the law of necessity. They hold that he foresees with absolute certainty from all eternity the futurition of the free actions of moral agents, and that he embraces and adjusts them in his eternal plan—which plan embraces all things, the free actions of moral agents as simply foreseen, and the actions of necessary agents as absolutely foreordained.

7. *State under several heads the Calvinistic doctrine on this subject.*

1st. God foreknows all events as certainly future *because* he has decreed them and thus made them certainly future.

2d. God's decree relates equally to all future events of every kind, to the free actions of moral agents, as well as to action of necessary agents, to sinful as well as morally right actions.

3d. Some things God has eternally decreed to do himself immediately, *e. g.*, creation; other things to bring to pass through the action of second causes acting under a law of necessity, and again other things he has decreed to prompt or to permit free agents to do in the exercise of their free agency; yet the one class of events is rendered by the decree as certainly future as the other.

4th. God has decreed ends as well as means, causes as well as effects, conditions and instrumentalities as well as the events which depend upon them.

5th. God's decree determines only the certain futurition of

events, it directly effects or causes no event. But the decree itself provides in every case that the event shall be effected by causes acting in a manner perfectly consistent with the nature of the event in question. Thus in the case of every free act of a moral agent the decree itself provides at the same time—(*a.*) That the agent shall be a free agent. (*b.*) That his antecedents and all the antecedents of the act in question shall be what they are. (*c.*) That all the present *conditions* of the act shall be what they are. (*d.*) That the act shall be perfectly spontaneous and free on the part of the agent. (*e.*) That it shall be certainly future.

6th. God's purposes relating to all events of every kind constitute one single, all-comprehensive intention comprehending all events, the free as free, the necessary as necessary, together with all their causes, conditions, and relations, as one indivisible system of things, every link of which is essential to the integrity of the whole.

8. *Show that as respects the eternal plan of an omniscient and omnipotent Creator, foreknowledge is equivalent to foreordination.*

God possessing infinite foreknowledge and power, existed alone from eternity; and in time, self-prompted, began to create in an absolute vacuum. Whatever limiting causes or conditions afterwards exist were first intentionally brought into being by himself, with perfect foreknowledge of their nature, relations, and results. If God then foreseeing that if he created a certain free agent and placed him in certain relations he would freely act in a certain way, and yet with that knowledge proceeded to create that very free agent and put him in precisely those positions, God would, in so doing, obviously predetermine the certain futurition of the act foreseen. God can never in his work be reduced to a choice of evils, because the entire system, and each particular end and cause, and condition, was clearly foreseen and by deliberate choice admitted by himself.

9. *What reasons may be assigned for contemplating the decrees of God as one all-comprehensive intention?*

1st. Because as shown below it is an eternal act, and *æternitas est una, individua et tota simul.*

2d. Because every event that actually occurs in the system of things is interlaced with all other events in endless involution. No event is isolated. The color of the flower and the nest of the bird are related to the whole material universe. Even in our ignorance we can trace a chemical fact as related to myriad other facts, classified under the heads of mechanics, electricity, and light and life.

3d. God decrees events as they actually occur, *i. e.*, events produced by causes, and depending upon conditions. The decree that determines the event can not leave out the cause or the condition upon which it depends. But the cause of one event, is the effect of another, and every event in the universe is more immediately or remotely the condition of every other, so that an eternal purpose on the part of God must be one all-comprehensive act.

As our minds are finite, as it is impossible for us to embrace in one act of intelligent comprehension an infinite number of events in all their several relations and bearings, we necessarily contemplate events in partial groups, and we conceive of the purpose of God relating to them as distinct successive acts. Hence the Scriptures speak of the counsels, the purposes, and the judgments of God in the plural, and in order to indicate the intended relation of one event to another, they represent God as purposing one event, as the means or condition upon which another is suspended. This is all true because these events do have these relations to one another, but they all alike fall within, and none remain without, that one eternal design of God which comprehends equally all causes and all effects, all events and all conditions.

All the *speculative* errors of men on this subject, spring from the tendency of the human mind to confine attention to one fragment of God's eternal purpose, and to regard it as isolated from the rest. The Decree of God separates no event from its causes or conditions any more than we find them separated in nature. We are as much unable to take in by one comprehensive act of intelligence all the works of God in nature as we are to take in all his decrees. We are forced to study his works part by part. But no intelligent student of nature thinks that any event is isolated. So we are forced to study his decrees part by part, but no intelligent theologian should suppose that there are any broken links or imperfect connection either here or there.

10. *How may it be proved that the decrees of God are eternal?*

1st. As God is infinite, he is necessarily eternal and unchangeable, from eternity infinite in wisdom and knowledge, and absolutely independent in thought and purpose of every creature. There can never be any addition to his wisdom, nor surprise to his foreknowledge, nor resistance to his power, and therefore there never can be any occasion to reverse or modify that infinitely wise and righteous purpose which, from the perfection of his nature, he formed from eternity.

2d. It is asserted in Scripture.—(ἀπ᾽ αἰῶνος) Acts xv. 18;

(πρὸ καταβολῆς κόσμου) Eph. i. 4; 1 Pet. i. 20; (ἀπ' ἀρχῆς) 2 Thes. ii. 13; (πρὸ χρόνων αἰωνίων) 2 Tim. i. 9; (πρὸ τῶν αἰωνων) 1 Cor. ii. 7; Eph. iii. 11, etc.

11. *Prove that the decrees are immutable.*

1st. This is certain from the fact that they are eternal, as just shown.

2d. From the fact that God is eternal, absolute, immutable, and all-perfect in wisdom and power.

3d. It is taught in Scripture.—Ps. xxxiii. 11; Is. xlvi. 9, etc.

12. *Prove from reason that the decrees of God comprehend all events.*

As shown above no event is isolated. If one event is decreed absolutely all events must therefore be determined with it. If one event is left indeterminate all future events will be left in greater or less degrees indeterminate with it.

13. *Prove the same from Scripture.*

1st. They affirm that the whole system in general is embraced in the divine decrees.—Eph. i. 11; Acts xvii. 26; Dan. iv. 34, 35.

2d. They affirm the same of fortuitous events.—Prov. xvi. 33; Matt. x. 29, 30.

3d. Of the free actions of men.—Eph. ii. 10, 11; Phil. ii. 13.

4th. Even of the wicked actions of men. "Him, being delivered by the determinate counsel and foreknowledge of God, ye have taken and with wicked hands have crucified and slain." —Acts ii. 23. "For of a truth against thy Holy Child whom thou hast anointed, both Herod and Pontius Pilate, with the Gentiles and the people of Israel were gathered together, for to do whatsoever thy hand and thy counsel determined beforehand to be done."—Acts iv. 27, 28; Acts xiii. 29; 1 Peter ii. 8; Jude 4; Rev. xvii. 17. As to the history of Joseph, compare Gen. xxxvii. 28 with Gen. xlv. 7, 8, and l. 20: "So now it was not you that sent me hither but God." "But as for you, ye thought evil against me, but God meant it unto good."—See also Ps. xvii. 13, 14, and Is. x. 5 and 15, etc.

14. *Prove the universality of God's decrees from providence.*

It follows from the eternity, immutability, and infinite wisdom, foreknowledge, and power of God, that his temporal working in providence must in all things proceed according to his eternal purpose.—Eph. i. 11, and Acts xv. 18. But both Scripture and reason alike teach us that the providential government of God comprehends all things in heaven and on earth *as a whole,* and every event in detail.—Prov. xvi. 33; Dan. iv. 34, 35; Matt. x. 29, 30.

15. *Prove this doctrine from prophecy.*

God has in the Scriptures foretold the certain occurrence of many events, including the free actions of men, which have afterwards surely come to pass. Now the ground of prophecy is foreknowledge, and the foundation of the foreknowledge of an event as certainly future, is God's decree that made it future. The eternal immutability of the decree is the only foundation of the infallibility either of the foreknowledge or of the prophecy. But if God has decreed certain future events, he must also have included in that decree all of their causes, conditions, co-ordinates, and consequences. No event is isolated; to make one certainly future implies the determination of the whole concatenation of causes and effects which constitute the universe.

16. *In what sense are the decrees of God free?*

The decrees of God are free in the sense that in decreeing he was solely actuated by his own infinitely wise, righteous, and benevolent good pleasure. He has always chosen as he pleased, and he has always pleased consistently with the perfection of his nature.

17. *In what sense are the decrees of God sovereign?*

They are sovereign in the sense that while they determine absolutely whatever occurs without God, their whole reason and motive is within the divine nature, and they are neither suggested nor occasioned by, nor conditioned upon any thing whatsoever without him.

18. *What is the distinction between absolute and conditional decrees?*

An absolute decree is one which, while it may include conditions, is suspended upon no condition, *i. e.,* it makes the event decreed, of whatever kind, whether of mechanical necessity or of voluntary agency, certainly future, together with all the causes and conditions, of whatever nature, upon which the event depends.

A conditional decree is one which decrees that an event shall happen upon the condition that some other event, possible but uncertain (not decreed), shall actually occur.

The Socinians denied that the free actions of men, being intrinsically uncertain, are the objects of knowledge, and therefore affirmed that they are not foreknown by God. They held that God decreed absolutely to create the human race, and after Adam sinned he decreed absolutely to save all repenting and believing sinners, yet that he decreed nothing concerning the sinning nor the salvation of individual men.

The Arminians, admitting that God certainly foreknows the acts of free agents as well as all other events, maintain that he absolutely decreed to create man, and foreseeing that man would sin he absolutely decreed to provide a salvation for all, and actually to save all that repent and believe, but that he conditionally decreed to save individual men on the condition, foreseen but not foreordained, of their faith and obedience.

19. *What are the objections to attributing conditional decrees to God?*

Calvinists admit that the all-comprehensive decree of God determines all events according to their inherent nature, the actions of free agents as free, and the operation of necessary causes, necessarily. It also comprehends the whole system of causes and effects of every kind; of the motives and conditions of free actions, as well as the necessary causes of necessary events. God decreed salvation upon the condition of faith, yet in the very same act he decreed the faith of those persons whose salvation he has determined. "Whom he did *predestinate*, them he *also called*." Thus his decree from the beginning embraced and provided for the free agency of man, as well as the regular procedures of nature, according to established laws. Thus also his covenants, or conditional promises, which he makes in time, are in all their parts the execution of his eternal purpose, which comprehended the promise, and the condition in their several places as means to the end. But that the decree of God can be regarded as suspended upon conditions which are not themselves determined by the decree is evidently impossible.

1st. This decree has been shown above (Questions 3–7) to be eternal and all-comprehensive. A condition implies liability to change. The whole universe forming one system, if one part is contingent the whole must be contingent, for if one condition failed the whole concatenation of causes and effects would be deranged. If the Arminian should rejoin that although God did not foreordain the free acts of men, yet he infallibly foreknew and provided for them, and therefore his plans can not fail; then the Calvinist replies that if God foresaw that a given man, in given circumstances, would act at a given juncture in a certain way, then God in decreeing to create that very man and place him in those very circumstances, at that very juncture, did foreordain the certain futurition of that very event, and of all its consequences. That God's decree is immutable and does not depend upon uncertain conditions, is proved (1) from its eternity, (2) from the direct assertions of Scripture.—Isa. xiv. 24, 27; xlvi. 10; Ps. xxxiii. 11; Prov. xix. 21; Rom. ix. 11; Eph. iii. 11.

2d. The foreknowledge of God, as Arminians admit, is eternal and certain, and embraces all events, free as well as necessary. But, (1) as shown in the preceding paragraph, this foreknowledge involves foreordination, and (2) certainty in the foreknowledge implies certainty in the event; certainty implies determination; determination leaves us to choose between the decree of an infinitely wise, righteous, and benevolent God, and a blind fate.

3d. A conditional decree would subvert the sovereignty of God and make him, as to the administration of his whole government and the execution of all his plans, dependent upon the uncontrollable actions of his own creatures. But the decrees of God are sovereign.—Isa. xl. 13, 14; Dan. iv. 35; Rom. ix. 15–18.

4th. His decree is declared to depend upon his own "good pleasure," and the "counsel of his own will."—Eph. i. 5, 11; Rom. ix. 11; Matt. xi. 25, 26.

5th. The decree of God includes the means and conditions. 2 Thess. ii. 13; 1 Pet. i. 2; Eph. i. 4.

6th. His decree absolutely determines the free actions of men.—Acts iv. 27, 28; Eph. ii. 10.

7th. God himself works in his people that faith and obedience which are called the conditions of their salvation.—Phil. ii. 13; Eph. ii. 8; 2 Tim. ii. 25.

20. *How far are the decrees of God efficacious and how far permissive?*

All the decrees of God are equally efficacious in the sense that they all infallibly determine the certain futurition of the event decreed. Theologians, however, classify the decrees of God thus: 1st. As efficacious in as far as they respect those events which he has determined to effect through necessary causes, or in his own immediate agency. 2d. As permissive, as far as they respect those events which he has determined to allow dependent free agents to effect.

21. *How may it be proved that the decree of God renders the event certain?*

1st. From the nature of the decree itself as sovereign and unchangeable (see above).

2d. From the essential nature of God in his relation to his creation, as an infinitely wise and powerful sovereign.

3d. The foreknowledge of God regards future events as certain. The ground of this certainty must be either in God, or in the events themselves, which last is fatalism.

4th. The Scriptures ascribe a certainty of futurition to the events decreed. There is a needs-be that the event should happen "as it was determined."—Luke xviii. 31–33; xxiv. 46; Acts ii. 23; xiii. 29; 1 Cor. xi. 19; Matt. xvi. 21.

22. *How does this doctrine, that God's universal decree renders the occurrence of all future events certain, differ from the ancient doctrine of faith?*

The Calvinistic doctrine of Decrees agrees with Fatalism only at one point, *i. e.*, in maintaining that the events in question are certainly future. But the Arminian doctrine of divine foreknowledge does precisely the same thing. In every other point our doctrine differs from the heathen doctrine of Fate.

Fatalism supposes all events to be certainly determined by a universal law of necessary causation, acting blindly and by a simple unintelligent force effecting its end irresistibly and irrespective of the free wills of the free agents involved. There was no room left for final ends or purposes, no place for motive or choice, no means or conditions, but a simple evolution of necessity.

On the other hand the Calvinistic doctrine of Decrees postulates the infinite all-comprehensive plan of an infinitely wise, righteous, powerful, and benevolent Father, whose plan is determined not by mere will, but according to the "*counsel of his will,*" securing the best ends, and adopting the best means in order to attain those ends—and whose plan is not executed by mere force, but through the instrumentality of all classes of second causes, free as well as necessary, each pre-adapted to its place and function, and each acting without constraint according to its nature.

There is an infinite difference between a machine and a man, between the operation of motives, intelligence, free choice, and the mechanical forces which act upon matter. There is precisely the same difference between the system of divine decrees, and the heathen doctrine of fate.

23. *What objection to this doctrine of unconditional decrees is derived from the admitted fact of man's free agency?*

Objection.—Foreknowledge implies the certainty of the event. The decree of God implies that he has determined it to be certain. But that he has determined it to be certain implies, upon the part of God, an efficient agency in bringing about that event which is inconsistent with the free agency of man

We answer: It is evidently only the *execution* of the decree, and not the decree itself, which can interfere with the free agency of man. On the general subject of the method in which God executes his decrees, see below, the chapters on Providence, Effectual Calling, and Regeneration.

We have here room only for the following general statement:

1st. The Scriptures attribute all that is good in man to God; these "he works in us both to will and to do of his good pleasure." All the sins which men commit the Scriptures attribute wholly to the man himself. Yet God's permissive decree does truly determine the certain futurition of the act; because God knowing certainly that the man in question would in the given circumstances so act, did place that very man in precisely those circumstances that he should so act. But in neither case, whether in working the good in us, or in placing us where we will certainly do the wrong, does God in executing his purpose ever violate or restrict the perfect freedom of the agent.

2d. We have the fact distinctly revealed that God has decreed the free acts of men, and yet that the actors were none the less responsible, and consequently none the less free in their acts.—Acts ii. 23; iii. 18; iv. 27, 28; Gen. l. 20, etc. We never can understand *how* the infinite God acts upon the finite spirit of man, but it is none the less our duty to believe.

3d. According to that theory of the will which makes the freedom of man to consist in the *liberty of indifference*, *i. e.*, that the will acts in every case of choice in a state of perfect equilibrium equally independent of all motives for or against, and just as free to choose in opposition to all desires as in harmony with them, it is evident that the very essence of liberty consists in uncertainty. If this be the true theory of the will, God could not execute his decrees without violating the liberty of the agent, and certain foreknowledge would be impossible.

But as shown below, in Chapter XV., the true theory of the will is that the liberty of the agent consists in his acting in each case as, upon the whole, he pleases, *i. e.*, according to the dispositions and desires of his heart, under the immediate view which his reason takes of the case. These dispositions and desires are determined in their turn by the character of the agent in relation to his circumstances, which character and circumstances are surely not beyond the control of the infinite God.

24. *What is meant by those who teach that God is the author of sin?*

Many reasoners of a Pantheistic tendency, *e. g.*, Dr. Emmons, maintain that as God is infinite in sovereignty, and by his decree determines, so by his providence he effects every thing which comes to pass, so that he is actually the only real agent in the universe. Still they religiously hold that God is an infinitely holy agent in effecting that which, produced *from* God, is righteous, but, produced *in* us, is sin.

25. *How may it be shown that God is not the author of sin?*

The admission of sin into the creation of an infinitely wise, powerful, and holy God is a great mystery, of which no explanation can be given. But that God can not be the author of sin is proved—

1st. From the nature of sin, which is, as to its essence, ἀνομία, want of conformity to law, and disobedience to the Lawgiver.

2d. From the nature of God, who is as to essence holy, and in the administration of his kingdom always forbids and punishes sin.

3d. From the nature of man, who is a responsible free agent who originates his own acts. The Scriptures always attribute to divine grace the good actions, and to the evil heart the sinful actions of men.

26. *How may it be shown that the doctrine of unconditional decrees does not represent God as the author of sin?*

The whole difficulty lies in the awful fact that sin exists. If God foresaw it and yet created the agent, and placed him in the very circumstances under which he did foresee the sin would be committed, then he did predetermine it. If he did not foresee it, or, foreseeing it, could not prevent it, then he is not infinite in knowledge and in power, but is surprised and prevented by his creatures. The doctrine of unconditional decrees presents no special difficulty. It represents God as decreeing that the sin shall eventuate as the free act of the sinner, and not as by any form of co-action causing, nor by any form of temptation inducing, him to sin.

27. *What is the objection to this doctrine derived from the use of means?*

This is the most common form of objection in the mouths of ignorant and irreligious people. If an immutable decree makes all future events certain, "*if what is to be, will be,*" then it follows that no means upon our part can avoid the result, nor can any means be necessary to secure it.

Hence as the use of means is commanded by God, and instinctively natural to man, since many events have been effected by their use, and many more in the future evidently depend upon them, it follows that God has not rendered certain any of those events which depend upon the use of means on the part of men.

28. *What is the ground upon which the use of means is founded?*

This use is founded upon the command of God, and upon that fitness in the means to secure the end desired, which our instincts, our intelligence, and our experience disclose to us. But neither the fitness nor the efficiency of the means to secure the end, reside inherently and independently in the means themselves, but were originally established and are now sustained by God himself; and in the working of all means God always presides and directs providentially. This is necessarily involved in any Christian theory of Providence, although we can never explicate the relative action (*concursus*) of God on man, the infinite upon the finite.

29. *How may it be shown that the doctrine of decrees does not afford a rational ground of discouragement in the use of means?*

This difficulty (stated above, Question 27) rests entirely in a habit of isolating one part of God's eternal decree from the whole (see Question 7), and in confounding the Christian doctrine of decrees with the heathen doctrine of fate (see Ques. 22.) But when God decreed an event he made it certainly future, not as isolated from other events, or as independent of all means and agents, but as dependent upon means and upon agents freely using those means. The same decree which makes the event certain, also determines the mode by which it shall be effected, and comprehends the means with the ends. This eternal, all-comprehensive act embraces all existence through all duration, and all space as one system, and at once provides for the whole in all its parts, and for all the parts in all their relations to one another and to the whole. An event, therefore, may be certain in respect to God's decree and foreknowledge, and at the same time truly contingent in the apprehension of man, and in its relation to the means upon which it depends.

30. *What are the distinctions to be borne in mind between the objections to the proof of a doctrine, and objections to the doctrine when proved?*

Reasonable objections to the evidence, Scriptural or otherwise, upon which the claims of any doctrine is based, are evidently legitimate. These objections against the *proof* establishing the truth of the doctrine ought always to be allowed their full weight. But when once the doctrine has been proved to be taught in Scripture objections levelled against *it*, obviously have no weight at all until they amount to a sufficient force to prove that the Scriptures themselves are not the word of God. Before they reach *that* measure, objections levelled against the doctrine itself, which do not affect the evidence upon which it rests (and most of the objections to the Calvinistic doctrine of Decrees are of this order) only illustrate the obvious truth that the finite mind of man can not fully comprehend the matters partially revealed and partially concealed in the word of God.

31. *What are the proper practical effects of this doctrine?*

Humility, in view of the infinite greatness and sovereignty of God, and of the dependence of man. Confidence and implicit reliance upon the wisdom, righteousness, goodness, and immutability of God's purposes, and cheerful obedience to his commandments; always remembering that God's precepts, as distinctly revealed, and not his decrees, are the rule of our duty.

CHAPTER XI.

PREDESTINATION.

1. *What are the different senses in which the word predestination is used by theologians?*

1st. As equivalent to the generic word decree, as including all God's eternal purposes.

2d. As embracing only those purposes of God which specially respect his moral creatures.

3d. As designating only the counsel of God concerning fallen men, including the sovereign election of some and the most righteous reprobation of the rest.

4th. It is sometimes restricted in the range of its usage so far as to be applied only to the eternal election of God's people to everlasting life.

The sense marked as 3d, above, is the most proper usage.— See Acts iv. 27, 28.

2. *In what senses are the words προγινώσκω (to know beforehand), and πρόγνωσις (foreknowledge), used in the New Testament?*

Προγινώσκω is compounded of πρό, *before*, and γινώσκω, of which the primary sense is *to know*, and the secondary sense *to approve, e. g.*, 2 Tim. ii. 19; John x. 14, 15; Rom. vii. 15. This word occurs five times in the New Testament. Twice, *e. g.*, Acts xxvi. 5 and 2 Pet. iii. 17, it signifies previous knowledge, *apprehension*, simply. In the remaining three instances, Rom. viii. 29; xi. 2; 1 Pet. i. 20, it is used in the secondary sense of approve beforehand. This is made evident from the context, for it is used to designate the ground of God's predestination of individuals to salvation, which elsewhere is expressly said to be "not according to our works, but according to his own purpose and grace," and "to the good pleasure of his will," 2 Tim. i. 9; Rom. ix. 11; Eph. i. 5.

Πρόγνωσις occurs but twice in the New Testament, *e. g.*, Acts ii. 23 and 1 Pet. i. 2, in both of which instances it evidently signifies approbation, or choice from beforehand. It is explained by the equivalent phrase "determinate counsel."

3. *What is the New Testament usage of the words ἐκλέγω (to elect) and ἐκλογή (election)?*

Ἐκλέγω occurs twenty-one times in the New Testament. It is used to signify, 1st, Christ's choice of men to be apostles. Luke vi. 13; John vi. 70. 2d. God's choice of the Jewish nation as a peculiar people.—Acts xiii. 17. 3d. The choice of men by God, or by the church, for some special service.—Acts xv. 7, 22. 4th. The choice made by Mary of the better part. Luke x. 42. 5th. In the great majority of instances God's eternal election of individual men to everlasting life.—John xv. 16; 1 Cor. i. 27, 28; Eph. i. 4; James ii. 5.

Ἐκλογή occurs seven times in the New Testament. Once it signifies an election to the apostolic office.—Acts ix. 15. Once it signifies those chosen to eternal life.—Rom. xi. 7. In every other case it signifies the purpose or the act of God in choosing his own people to salvation.—Rom. ix. 11; xi. 5, 28; 1 Thess. i. 4; 2 Pet. i. 10.

4. *What other words are used by the Holy Ghost in the New Testament to set forth the truth on this subject?*

Προορίζειν occurs six times in the New Testament.—Acts iv. 28; Rom. viii. 29, 30; 1 Cor. ii. 7, and Eph. i. 5, 11. In every case it signifies the absolute predestination of God.

Προτίθημι occurs three times in the New Testament. In Rom. i. 13 it signifies a purpose of Paul, and in Rom. iii. 25 and Eph. i. 9, a purpose of God.

Προετοιμάζειν occurs twice, Rom. ix. 23 and Eph. ii. 10, prepare or appoint beforehand.

5. *To whom is election referred in the Scriptures?*

The eternal decree, as a whole, and in all its parts, is doubtless the concurrent act of all the three persons of the Trinity, in their perfect oneness of counsel and will.

But in the economy of salvation, as revealed to us, the act of sovereign election is specially attributed to the Father, as his personal part, even as redemption is attributed to the Son, and sanctification to the Spirit.—John xvii. 6, 9; vi. 64, 65; 1 Thess. v. 9.

6. *State that theory of Predestination designated by its advocates the "Theory of National Election."*

This is the theory that the only election spoken of in the Bible concerning the salvation of men consists of the divine predestination of communities and nations to the knowledge of the true religion and the external privileges of the gospel. This form of election, which undoubtedly represents a great gospel fact, is eminently illustrated in the case of the Jews. This is the view advocated by Archbishop Sumner in his work on "Apostolic Preaching," quoted by Dr. Cunningham.

7. *State the theory styled by its advocates the "Theory of Ecclesiastical Individualism."*

The view advocated by Mr. Stanley Faber in his "Primitive Doctrine of Election," and by Archbishop Whately in his "Essays on some of the Difficulties in the Writings of the Apostle Paul," and others, is styled the doctrine of "Ecclesiastical Individualism," and it involves the affirmation that God predetermines the relation of individual men to the outward church and the means of grace. Thus by birth and subsequent providences he casts the lot of some men in the most favorable, and of others in the least favorable circumstances.

8. *What is the Arminian doctrine of election?*

The Arminians admit the foreknowledge of God, but they deny his absolute foreordination as it relates to the salvation of individuals. Their distinguishing doctrine is that God did not eternally make choice of certain persons and ordain their salvation, but that he made choice of certain characters, as holiness and faith and perseverance; or of certain classes of men who possess those characters, *e. g.*, believers who persevere unto the end.

Since they admit that God foreknows from eternity with absolute certainty precisely what individuals will repent and believe and persevere therein to the end, it follows that their doctrine admits of the statement that God eternally predestinated certain persons, who he foresaw would repent and believe and persevere to life and salvation, on *the ground of that faith and perseverance* thus foreseen.

9. *Point out the several principles in which the above-mentioned views agree and wherein they differ.*

The theories of "National Election" and of "Ecclesiastical Individualism," both teach universally admitted facts, namely that God does predestinate individuals and communities and nations to the external privileges of the gospel and the use of the means of grace. This neither any Arminian nor any Calvinist will deny. But these theories are both vicious and both identical with the Arminian theory, in that they deny that God unconditionally predestinates either the free actions or the ultimate salvation of individuals. They admit that he gives certain men a better chance than others, but hold that each man's ultimate fate is not determined by God's decree, but left dependent upon the free wills of the men themselves. Nevertheless, while these theories are all consistently Arminian in fundamental principle, yet they differ in the manner in which they attempt to bring the Scriptures concerned into harmony with that system. These theories differ among themselves as to the *objects*, the *ends*, and the *grounds* of this election. As to the *objects* of the election spoken of in Scripture, the Arminian, the Calvinistic, and "Ecclesiastical Individualism" theories agree in making them individuals. The theory of "National Election" makes them nations or communities. As to the *end* of this election the Calvinistic and Arminian theories make it the eternal salvation of the individuals elected. The theories of "National Election" and of "Ecclesiastical Individualism" make it admission to the privilege of the means of grace. As to the *ground* of this election spoken of in the Scripture, advocates of the Calvinistic, the "National Election," and the "Ecclesiastical Individualism" theories agree in making it the sovereign good pleasure of God, while the Arminians hold it is conditioned upon the faith, repentance, and perseverance certainly foreseen in each individual case.

It is obvious that the Calvinistic Doctrine of Decrees includes the absolute election of both individuals and of communities and nations to the use of the means of grace and the external advantages of the Church. It is also obvious that the admission of the principle of absolute election, as far as this, must be made by all Arminians as well as Calvinists, and hence this admission alone does not discriminate between the two great contesting systems. The only question which touches the true matter in debate is, What is the ground of the eternal predestination of individuals to salvation? Is it the foreseen faith and repentance of the individuals themselves, or the sovereign good pleasure of God? Every Christian must take one side or the other of this question. If he takes the side which makes foreseen faith the ground, he is an Arminian no matter what else he holds. If he takes the side which makes the good pleasure of God the ground, he is a Calvinist.

This division among themselves, and this alternate agreement with and difference from the Calvinistic positions on this subject, is a very suggestive illustration of the extreme difficulty the advocates of Arminian principles have in accommodating the words of Scripture to their doctrine.

In a polemic point of view the Calvinists have the capital advantage of being able to divide their opponents, and to refute them in detail

10. *State the three points involved in the Calvinistic doctrine on this subject.*

Calvinists hold, as shown in the preceding chapter, that God's Decrees are absolute and relate to all classes of events whatsoever. They therefore maintain that while nations, communities, and individuals are predestined absolutely to all of every kind of good and bad that befalls them, nevertheless the Scriptures teach specifically an election (1) of individuals, (2) to grace and salvation, (3) founded not upon the foreseen faith of the persons elected, but upon the sovereign good pleasure of God alone.

11. *State the Presumption of the truth of the above arising from the fact that impartial infidel and rationalistic interpreters admit that the letter of the Scriptures can be interpreted only in a Calvinistic sense.*

Besides the presumption in favor of Calvinism arising from the fact above stated, that anti-Calvinistic interpreters of the Scripture are reduced to all kinds of various hypotheses in order to avoid the obvious force of the Scriptural testimony upon the subject, we now cite the additional presumption, arising from the fact that rationalists and infidels generally, who agree with Arminians in their intense opposition to Calvinistic Principles, yet not being restrained by faith in the inspiration of the Bible, are frank enough to confess that the Book can be fairly interpreted only in a Calvinistic sense. This is thus the impartial testimony of an enemy. Wegscheider in his "*Institutiones Theologiæ Christianæ Dogmaticæ,*" Pt. III., Ch. iii., § 145,* the highest authority as to the results of German Rationalists in Dogmatic theology, says that the passages in question do teach Calvinistic doctrine, but that Paul was misled by the crude and erroneous notions prevalent in that age, and especially by the narrow spirit of Jewish particularism. See also Gibbon's "Decline and Fall of the Roman Empire," Chapter xxxiii., Note 31.—"Perhaps a reasoner still more independent may smile in *his* turn, when he peruses an Arminian Commentary on the Epistle to the Romans."

12. *Prove from Scripture that the subjects of election are individuals and that the end of election is eternal life.*

1st. They are always spoken of as individuals, and the election of which they are the subjects is always set forth as having grace or glory as its end.—Acts xiii. 48; Eph. i. 4; 2 Thess. ii. 13.
2d. The elect are in Scripture explicitly distinguished from the

* Dr. Wm. Cunningham, "Hist. Theo.," Vol. II., p. 463.

mass of the visible Church, and hence their election could not have been merely to the external privileges of that Church.— Rom. xi. 7. 3d. The names of the elect are said "to be written in heaven" and to be in "the book of life."—Heb. xii. 23; Phil. iv. 3. 4th. The blessings which it is explicitly declared are secured by this election are gracious and saving, they are the elements and results of salvation, inseparable from it, and pertain not to nations but to individuals as their subjects, *e. g.*, "adoption of sons," "to be conformed to the image of his Son," etc.—Rom. viii. 29; Eph. i. 5; 2 Thess. ii. 13; 1 Thess. v. 9; Rom. ix. 15, 16.

13. *Show that this election is not founded on works whether foreseen or not.*

This follows—1st. From the general doctrine of Decrees which has been established in the last chapter. If God's decrees relate to and determine all events of every class, it follows that no undecreed events remain to condition his decree or any element thereof, and also that he has decreed faith and repentance as well as the salvation which is conditioned upon them.

2d. It is expressly declared in Scripture that this election is not conditioned upon works of any kind.—Rom. xi. 4–7; 2 Tim. i. 9; Rom. ix. 11.

14. *Show that in Scripture it is habitually declared to be founded on "the good pleasure of God," and "the counsel of his own will."*

Eph. i. 5–11; 2 Tim. i. 9; John xv. 16, 19; Matt. xi. 25, 26; Rom. ix. 10–18.

15. *State the argument derived from the fact that "faith," "repentance," and "evangelical obedience" are said to be the fruits of the Election.*

It is self-evident that the same actions *can not* be both the *grounds* upon which election rests, and the *fruits* in which that election is designed to result. Since the Bible teaches that "faith," "repentance," and "evangelical obedience" are the latter, they *can not* be the former. The Scriptures do so teach in Eph. i. 4. "According as he hath chosen us in him before the foundation of the world *that we should be holy, and without blame before him in love.*"—2 Thess. ii. 13; 1 Pet. i. 2; Eph. ii. 10.

16. *The same from the fact that faith and repentance are said to be the gifts of God.*

If faith and repentance are the "gifts of God," then a man's possessing them results from God's act. If it results from God's act it must result from his eternal purpose. If they be the results of his purpose, they can not be the conditions upon which that purpose is suspended. They are affirmed to be the "gifts of God" in Eph. ii. 8; Acts v. 31; 1 Cor. iv. 7.

17. *State the argument derived from what the Scriptures teach as to the nature and extent of innate depravity and inability.*

The teaching of Scripture on these heads will be found stated and established in Chapters XIX. and XX. Now if men are born into the world with an antecedent prevailing tendency in their nature to sin, and they are ever, until regenerated by the Spirit of God, totally and inalienably averse to and incapable of all good, it follows that unregenerate human nature is incapable either of tending to or of perfecting faith and repentance as the conditions required. If election is conditioned upon faith and repentance, then the man must produce his own faith and repentance, or help to produce them. But if human nature can neither produce nor help to produce them, it follows either that no man can be elected, or that faith and repentance *can not* be the condition of election.

18. *State the same from what the Scriptures teach of the nature and necessity of regeneration.*

In Chapter XXIX. it will be proved that the Scriptures teach (1) that regeneration is an act of God; (2) that with respect to that act the soul is passive; (3) that it is absolutely necessary in the case of every living man. Hence it follows that if it be in no sense man's work, but in every sense God's act alone, it can not be the condition upon which God's purpose is suspended, but an event determined by that purpose.

19. *Show that the Scriptures teach that* ALL *the elect believe, and that* ONLY *the elect believe.*

All the elect believe.—John x. 16, 27–29; John vi. 37–39; John xvii. 2, 9, 24. And *only the elect believe.*—John x. 26. And those who believe do so because they are elect.—Acts xiii. 48, and ii. 47.

20. *What argument is to be drawn from the fact that all evangelical Christians of every theological school express the sentiments proper to the Calvinistic doctrine of unconditional election in all their prayers and hymns?*

That form of doctrine must be false which can not be consistently embodied in personal religious experience and in devotion. That form of doctrine must be true which all Christians of all theoretical opinions always find themselves obliged to express when they come to commune with God. Now all the psalms and hymns and prayers, written and spontaneous, of all evangelical Christians, embody the principles and breathe the spirit of Calvinism. They all pray God to make men repent and believe, to come to and to receive the Saviour. If God gives all men common and sufficient grace, and if the reason why one man repents, is that he makes good use of that grace, and the reason another does not believe, is that he does not use that grace, if the only cause of difference is in the men, it follows that we ought to pray men to convert themselves, *i. e.,* to make themselves to differ. But all agree in asking God to save us, and in giving him all the thanks when it is done.

21. *Show that Paul must have held our position on this subject from the nature of the objections made against his doctrine, and from the answers he gave them.*

Paul's doctrine is identical with the Calvinistic view. 1st. Because he expressly teaches it. 2d. Because the objections he notices as brought against his doctrine are the same as those brought against ours. The design of the whole passage is to prove God's sovereign right to cast off the Jews as a peculiar people, and to call all men indiscriminately by the gospel.

This, he argues, 1st, that God's ancient promises embraced not the natural descendants of Abraham as such, but the spiritual seed. 2d. That " God is perfectly sovereign in the distribution of his favors."

But against this doctrine of divine sovereignty two objections are introduced and answered by Paul.

1st. It is unjust for God thus of his mere good pleasure to show mercy to one and to reject another, v. 14. This precise objection is made against our doctrine at the present time also. " It represents the most holy God as worse than the devil, as more false, more cruel, and more unjust."—" Methodist Doctrinal Tracts," pp. 170, 171. This Paul answers by two arguments. (1.) God claims the right, "I will have mercy on whom I will have mercy."—Rom. ix. 15, 16. (2.) God in his providence exercises the right, as in the case of Pharaoh, vs. 17, 18.

2d. The second objection is that this doctrine is inconsistent with the liberty and accountability of men. This would be an absurd objection to bring against Paul's doctrine if he were an Arminian, but it is brought every day by Arminians against our doctrine.

Paul answers this objection by condescending to no appeal to human reason, but simply (1) by asserting God's sovereignty as Creator, and man's dependence as creature, and (2) by asserting the just exposure of all men alike to wrath as sinners, vs. 20–24.—See Analysis of chap. ix. 6–24, in Hodge's "Com. on Romans."

22. *Discriminate accurately the two elements involved in the doctrine of Reprobation.*

Reprobation is the aspect which God's eternal decree presents in its relation to that portion of the human race which shall be finally condemned for their sins.

It is, 1st, negative, inasmuch as it consists in passing over these, and refusing to elect them to life; and, 2d, positive, inasmuch as they are condemned to eternal misery.

In respect to its negative element, reprobation is simply sovereign, since those passed over were no worse than those elected, and the simple reason both for the choosing and for the passing over was the sovereign good pleasure of God.

In respect to its positive element, reprobation is not sovereign, but simply judicial, because God inflicts misery in any case only as the righteous punishment of sin. "The rest of mankind God was pleased, according to the unsearchable counsel of his own will, to pass by, and to ordain them to dishonor and wrath *for their sins.*—" Con. Faith," Chap. iii., Sec. 7.

23. *Show that these positions are necessarily involved in the general doctrine of Decrees and in the special doctrine of the election of some men to eternal life.*

As above stated, this doctrine of reprobation is self-evidently an inseparable element of the doctrines of decrees and of election. If God unconditionally elects whom he pleases, he must unconditionally leave whom he pleases to themselves. He must foreordain the non-believing, as well as the believing, although the events themselves are brought to pass by very different causes.

24. *Prove that it is taught in Scripture.*

Rom. ix. 18, 21; 1 Pet. ii. 8; Jude 4; Rev. xiii. 8. "I thank thee, O Father, Lord of heaven and earth, because thou hast hid these things from the wise and prudent, and hast revealed them unto babes, even so, Father, for so it seemeth good in thy sight."—Matt. xi. 25. "Ye believe not, because ye are not my sheep."—John x. 26.

25. *Show that the same objection was made against Paul's doctrine that is made against ours.*

"Why doth he yet find fault?" If he has not given gracious ability to obey, how can he command?—See also "Methodist Doctrinal Tracts," p. 171.

The apostle answers by showing, 1st (verses 20, 21), that God is under no obligation to extend his grace to all or to any; and, 2d, that the "vessels of wrath" were condemned for their own sins, to manifest God's just wrath, while the "vessels of mercy" were chosen not for any good in them, but to manifest his glorious grace (verses 22, 23).

26. *Show the identity of Paul's doctrine with ours from the illustrations he uses in the ninth chapter of Romans.*

"Hath not the potter power (ἐξουσία) over the *clay of the same lump* to make one vessel to honor, and another to dishonor, v. 21. Here the whole point of the illustration lies in the fact that there is *no* difference in the clay—it is *clay of the same lump*—the sole difference is made by the will of the potter. In the case of Esau and Jacob, the very point is that one is just as good as the other—that there is no difference in the children—but that the whole difference is made by the "purpose of God according to election"—"for the children *being not yet born, neither having done any good or evil, that the purpose of God according to election might stand, not of works, but of him that calleth,*" v. 11.

27. *In what sense is God said to harden men?*

See Rom. ix. 18, and John xii. 40.

This is doubtless a judicial act wherein God withdraws from sinful men, whom he has not elected to life, for the just punishment of their sins, all gracious influences, and leaves them to the unrestrained tendencies of their own hearts, and to the uncounteracted influences of the world and the devil.

28. *State the objection brought against the Calvinistic doctrine of election on the ground that it is inconsistent with Justice.*

It is maintained that if God by a sovereign unconditional decree determines to pass by some men, and to withhold from them the grace necessary to enable them to repent and believe in Christ, it is unjust in God to hold them accountable, and to punish them for their want of faith.

29. *State the fundamental view which necessarily underlies all Arminianism as to the relation which the remedial work of Christ sustains to the justice of God, and as to the relation which the human race by nature sustains to the divine government.*

When the Arminian system is sifted to its fundamental principles, it is found to rest upon the postulate that the gift of Christ is a necessary compensation to the human race for the evils brought upon it for the sin of Adam. It is admitted that the sin of Adam was the cause of his whole race becoming sinners, and that every one of his descendants comes into the world with a nature so far depraved as to be morally incapable of loving God and disposed to evil. But they maintain that men are by nature in the first instance not responsible for their moral condition, since it comes upon them each at his birth, antecedent to all personal action They hold, therefore, that man can not be punished for original sin, nor could any man ever be held responsible for any act of disobedience springing as an inevitable consequence out of that original depravity, if God had not through Christ provided a remedy, giving to each man gracious ability to do all that is required of him as the condition of his salvation.   This redemption and gracious ability to believe and obey God owes to all men, and they are necessary to render any man responsible and punishable for his sins, since thus alone is he, as far as this class of exercises go, endowed with the power of contrary choice.

Dr. D. D. Whedon, in the "Bibliotheca Sacra," April, 1862, p. 257.—"It is not then until there is redemptively conferred upon man what we call a gracious ability for the right, that man can be strictly responsible for the wrong."   He says, p. 254, that after Adam sinned the only alternatives open to God in consistency with justice were either, 1st, to send Adam and Eve to perdition before they had children, or, 2d, to allow him to propagate his kind under the antecedent disabilities of sin, and provide a redemptive system for all.

He distinguishes between guilt or moral responsibility for character and moral corruption of nature.   Under the conditions of pure nature, he teaches that only Adam and Eve were responsible, as well as corrupt, because they, having been created morally free, voluntarily made themselves vile by their own act.   On the other hand their descendants are all morally polluted and spiritually dead, because they inherit corrupt natures from Adam; but they are not guilty, neither responsible for their birth sin nor for any of its consequences, because it was determined inevitably by an act not their own.   In the actual state of things consequent to the gift of Christ every man is responsible because every man has sufficient grace.

Hence it follows—1st. That the provision of redemption was not a work of infinite free grace, but a mere act of justice in compensation for evils brought upon our nature by Adam. 2d. That this is owed equally to each and every man without exception.   "I reject," says John Wesley, "Methodist Doc. Tracts," pp. 25, 26, "the assertion that God might justly have passed by me and all men, as a bold, precarious assertion, utterly unsupported by Holy Scripture."   3d. It follows also that the gracious help of the Holy Ghost is just as necessary to render men responsible sinners as to bring them to salvation. 4th. It follows that grace sends men to hell, as well as takes them to heaven, and that it has done far more of the former than of the latter work.

30. *Show that their position here is absolutely inconsistent with what the Scriptures and the entire Christian Church teach of the nature and necessity of the* SATISFACTION *made to divine justice by Christ.*

It will be shown under Chap. XXV., that the Scriptures teach, the entire Church being witness, that in order to the salvation of man, a full satisfaction to the inalienable principle of justice essential to the Divine nature was absolutely necessary. So that if God's justice is not satisfied, grace can not be shown to any man. This would be absurd if men were not antecedently responsible for the sins for which it is necessary that they should make satisfaction. What is the sense of a *"Redemptively* conferred *gracious* ability" respecting parties who have forfeited nothing because they are responsible for nothing? In their case is not both "redemption" and "grace" an impertinence?

31. *Prove from Scripture that salvation is of grace.*

Grace is free, undeserved favor showed to the undeserving. If redemption is a debt owed to all men, or if it be a compensation prerequisite to their accountability, then it can not be a gratuity, and the gift of Christ can not be an eminent expression of God's free favor and love. It can only be an expression of his rectitude.

But the Scriptures declare that the gift of Christ is an unparalleled expression of free love, and that salvation is of grace. Lam. iii. 22; John iii. 16; Rom. iii. 24; xi. 5, 6; 1 Cor. iv. 7; xv. 10; Eph. i. 5, 6; ii. 4–10, etc. And every true Christian recognizes the essential graciousness of salvation as an inseparable element of his experience. Hence the doxologies of heaven.—1 Cor. vi. 19, 20; 1 Pet. i. 18, 19; Rev. v. 8–14.

But if salvation is of grace, then it is obviously consistent with God's justice for him to save all, many, few, or none, just as he pleases.

32. *Show that the objection that unconditional election is inconsistent with the justice of God is absurd and antichristian.*

Justice necessarily holds all sinners alike destitute of all claims upon God's favor. It is *unjust* to justify the unjust. It would be inconsistent with righteousness for a sinful man to claim, or for God to grant, salvation to any one as his due.

Otherwise the condemning sentence of conscience is denied, and the cross of Christ made of none effect. On the very grounds of justice itself, therefore, salvation must be of grace, and it must rest upon the sovereign option of God himself whether he provides salvation for few, many, or for none. The salvation of none is consistent with justice, or the sacrifice of Christ was a payment of debt not a grace. And the salvation of one undeserving sinner obviously can lay no foundation upon which the salvation of another can be demanded as a right.

33. *State and refute the objection that our doctrine is inconsistent with the rectitude of God as an* IMPARTIAL RULER.

Arminians often argue that reason teaches us to expect the great omnipotent Creator and Sovereign of all men to be impartial in his treatment of individuals—to extend the same essential advantages and conditions of salvation to all alike. They argue also that this fair presumption of reason is reaffirmed in the Scriptures, which declare that God is "no respecter of persons."—Acts x. 34, and 1 Pet. i. 17. In the first-named passage this applies simply to the application of the gospel to Gentiles as well as Jews. In the second passage it is affirmed that in the judgment of human works God is absolutely impartial. The question as to election, however, is as to grace not as to judgment pronounced on works, and the Scriptures nowhere say that God is impartial in the communication of his grace.

On the other hand, the presumptions of reason and the texts of Scripture must be interpreted in a sense consistent with the palpable facts of human history and of God's daily providential dispensations. If it is unjust in principle for God to be partial in his distributions of spiritual good, it can be no less unjust for him to be partial in his distribution of temporal good. As a matter of fact, however, we find that God in the exercise of his absolute sovereignty makes the greatest possible distinctions among men from birth, and independently of their own merits in the allotments both of temporal good and of the essential means of salvation. One child is born to health, honor, wealth, to the possession of a susceptible heart and conscience, and to all the best means of grace as his secure inheritance. Many others are born to disease, shame, poverty, an obtuse conscience and hardened heart, and absolute heathenish darkness and ignorance of Christ. If God may not be partial to individuals, why may he be partial to nations, and how can his dealings with heathen nations and the children of the abandoned classes in the nominally Christian cities be accounted for?

Archbishop Whately gives this excellent word of warning to his Arminian friends: "I would suggest a caution relative to a class of objections frequently urged against Calvinists drawn from the moral attributes of God. We should be very cautious how we employ such weapons as may recoil upon ourselves. It is a frightful but undeniable truth that multitudes, even in Christian countries, are born and brought up in such circumstances as afford them no probable, even no possible, chance of obtaining a knowledge of religious truths, or a habit of moral conduct, but are even trained from infancy in superstitious error and gross depravity. Why this should be permitted neither Calvinist nor Arminian can explain; nay, why the Almighty does not cause to die in the cradle every infant whose future wickedness and misery, if suffered to grow up, he foresees, is what no system of religion, natural or revealed, will enable us satisfactorily to account for."—"Essays on some of the Difficulties of St. Paul." Essay 3d, on Election.

34. *Refute the objection drawn from such passages as* 1 Tim. ii. 4.

"Who will (θέλει) all men to be saved and to come unto the knowledge of the truth."

The word θέλειν has two senses—(*a*) to be *inclined* to, to *desire; (b)* to *purpose*, to *will*. In such connections as the above it is evident that it *can not* mean that God *purposes* the salvation of all, because (*a*) all are not saved, and none of God's purposes fail, and (*b*) because it is affirmed that he *wills* all to "come to the knowledge of the truth" in the same sense that he wills all to be saved—yet he has left the vast majority of men to be born and to live and to die, irrespective of their own agency, in heathenish darkness.

Such passages simply assert the essential benevolence of God. He takes no pleasure in the death of the wicked. He does take great pleasure in the salvation of men. Yet as a matter of fact, in perfect consistency with his benevolence, for reasons sufficient, though not revealed to us, he has provided no redemption for lost angels, and no efficacious grace for the non-elect among mankind. These passages simply assert that, if it were not for these reasons, it would be agreeable to his benevolent nature that all men should be saved.

35. *Show that our doctrine does not discourage the use of means.*

It is objected that if God from eternity has determined that one man is to be converted and saved and another is to be left to perish in his sins, there is no room left for the use of means. As John Wesley, in "Methodist Doc. Tracts," falsely represents

the doctrine of Toplady, "There are suppose twenty men, ten
are ordained to be saved do what they may, and ten are ordained to be damned do what they can." This is an absurd as
well as wicked caricature of the doctrine.

1st. The decree of election does not secure salvation without
faith and holiness, but salvation *through* faith and holiness, the
means being just as much decreed as the end. The Calvinist believes, as well as the Arminian, that every man who does
evil will be damned, elect or non-elect.

2d. The doctrine of election does not presume that God con-
strains men inconsistently with their freedom. The non-elect
are simply let alone, to do as their own evil hearts prompt.
The elect are made willing in the day of God's power. God
works in them to *will* as well as to *do* of his good pleasure.
To be *made willing* takes away no man's liberty.

3d. The decree of election only makes the repentance and
faith of the elect certain. But the antecedent certainty of a
free act is not inconsistent with its freedom, otherwise the
certain foreknowledge of a free act would be impossible. The
decree of election does not cause the faith, and it does not
interfere with the agent in acting, and certainly it does not
supersede the absolute necessity of it.

36. *How far is assurance of our election possible, and on what
grounds does such assurance rest?*

An unwavering and certain assurance of the fact of our election is possible in this life, for whom God predestinates them
he also calls, and whom he calls he justifies, and we know that
whom he justifies, he also sanctifies. Thus the fruits of the
Spirit prove sanctification, and sanctification proves effectual
calling, and effectual calling election.—See 2 Pet. i. 5–10; 1
John ii. 3.

Besides this evidence of our own gracious states and acts,
we have the Spirit of adoption, who witnesseth with our spirits
and seals us.—Rom. viii. 16, 17; Eph. iv. 30.

In confirmation of this we have the example of the apostles
(2 Tim. i. 12) and of many Christians.

37. *How does this doctrine consist with the general benevolence
of God?*

The only difficulty at this point is to reconcile the general
benevolence of God with the fact that he, being infinitely wise
and powerful, should have admitted a system involving the sin,
final impenitence, and consequent damnation of any. But this
difficulty presses equally upon both systems.

The *facts* prove that God's general benevolence is not inconsistent with his allowing some to be damned for their sins. This is all that reprobation means. Gratuitous election, or the positive choice of some does not rest upon God's general benevolence, but upon his special love to his own.—John xvii. 6, 23; Rom. ix. 11–13; 1 Thess. v. 9.

38. *How does this doctrine consist with the general gospel offer?*

In the general offers of the gospel God exhibits a salvation sufficient for and exactly adapted to all, and sincerely offered to every one without exception, and he unfolds all the motives of duty, hope, fear, etc., which ought to induce every one to accept it, solemnly promising that whosoever comes in no wise shall be cast out. Nothing but a sinful unwillingness can prevent any one who hears the gospel from receiving and enjoying it.

The gospel is for all, election is a special grace in addition to that offer. The non-elect may come if they will. The elect will come. The decree of election puts no barrier before men preventing them from accepting the gospel offer. Any man, elect or non-elect, will be saved if he accepts. The non-elect are left to act as they are freely determined by their own hearts.

There is just as great an apparent difficulty in reconciling God's *certain* foreknowledge of the final impenitence of the great majority of those to whom he offers and upon whom he presses, by every argument, his love with the fact of that offer; especially when we reflect that he foresees that his offers will certainly increase their guilt and misery.

39. *How can the doctrine of reprobation be reconciled with the holiness of God?*

Reprobation leaves men in sin, and thus leads to the increase of sin throughout eternity. How then can God, in consistency with his holiness, form a purpose the designed effect of which is to leave men in sin, and thus lead inevitably to the increase of sin.

But it is acknowledged by Arminians as well as Calvinists, that God did create the human race in spite of his certain foreknowledge that sin would be largely occasioned thereby, and he did create individual men in spite of his certain foreknowledge that these very men would continue eternally to sin. The real difficulty lies in the insoluble problem of the permission of evil. Why is the existence of evil tolerated in the universe of an infinitely wise, righteous, merciful, and powerful God?

The Arminians are as little able to answer that question as the Calvinist.

40. *What is the practical bearing of this doctrine on Christian experience and conduct?*

It must be remembered, 1st. That this truth is not inconsistent with, but is part of, the same gracious system with the equally certain principles of the moral liberty and responsibility of man, and the free offers of the gospel to all. 2d. That the sole rule of our duty is the commands, threatenings, and promises of God clearly expressed in the gospel, and not this decree of election, which he never reveals except in its consequents of effectual calling, faith, and holy living.

When thus held, the doctrine of predestination—

1st. Exalts the majesty and absolute sovereignty of God, while it illustrates the riches of his free grace and his just displeasure with sin.

2d. It enforces upon us the essential truth that salvation is entirely of grace. That no one can either complain, if passed over, or boast himself, if saved.

3d. It brings the inquirer to absolute self-despair, and the cordial embrace of the free offer of Christ.

4th. In the case of the believer, who has the witness in himself, this doctrine at once deepens his humility, and elevates his confidence to the full assurance of hope.

41. *State the true nature of the question discussed by theologians concerning the* ORDER OF THE DIVINE DECREES.

As we believe that the Decree of God is one single, eternal intention, there can not be an order of succession in his purposes either (*a*) in time, as if one purpose actually preceded the other, or (*b*) in distinct deliberation or option on the part of God. The whole is one choice. Yet in willing the entire system God, of course, comprehended all the parts of the system willed in their several successions and relations. In like manner as a man by one act of mind recognizes a complicated machine with which he is familiar, and in the same act discriminates accurately the several parts, and comprehends their unity and relation in the system, and the design of the whole.—Dr. Charles Hodge's "Lectures." The question, therefore, as to the Order of the Decrees is *not* a question as to the order of acts in God decreeing, but it *is* a question as to the true relation sustained by the several parts of the system which he decrees to one another. That is, What relation between Creation, Predestination, and Redemption did the one eternal purpose of God establish? What do the Scriptures teach as to the purpose of God in giving his Son, and as to the object and ground of election? The ground and object of election has been fully considered above. The design of God in the gift of Christ will be fully considered under Division IV. of Chapter XXV.

42. *What is the Arminian theory as to the order of the decrees relating to the human race?*

1st. The decree to create man. 2d. Man, as a moral agent, being fallible, and his will being essentially contingent, and his sin therefore being impreventible, God, foreseeing that man would certainly fall into the condemnation and pollution of sin, decreed to provide a free salvation through Christ for all men, and to provide sufficient means for the effectual application of that salvation to the case of all. 3d. He decreed absolutely that all believers in Christ should be saved, and all unbelievers reprobated for their sins. 4th. Foreseeing that certain individuals would repent and believe, and that certain other individuals would continue impenitent to the last, God from eternity elected to eternal life those whose faith he foresaw, on the condition of their faith, and reprobated those whom he foresaw would continue impenitent on the condition of that impenitence.

43. *What is the view of this subject entertained by the French Protestant theologians, Camero, Amyraut, and others?*

These theological professors at Saumur, during the second quarter of the seventeenth century, taught that God—1st. Decreed to create man. 2d. To permit man to fall. 3d. To provide, in the mediation of Christ, salvation for all men. 4th. But, foreseeing that if men were left to themselves none would repent and believe, therefore he sovereignly elected some to whom he decreed to give the necessary graces of repentance and faith.

44. *What is the infra-lapsarian view of predestination?*

The infra-lapsarian (*infra lapsum*) theory of predestination, or the decree of predestination, viewed as subsequent in purpose to the decree permitting man to fall, represents man as created and fallen as the object of election. The order of the decrees then stand thus: 1st. The decree to create man. 2d. To permit man to fall. 3d. The decree to elect certain men, out of the mass of the fallen and justly condemned race, to eternal life, and to pass others by, leaving them to the just consequences of their sins. 4th. The decree to provide salvation for the elect

THIS IS THE COMMON VIEW OF THE REFORMED CHURCHES, CONFIRMED ALIKE BY THE SYNOD OF DORT AND THE WESTMINSTER ASSEMBLY.

45. *What is the supra-lapsarian theory of predestination?*

The term supra-lapsarian (*supra lapsum*) designates that view of the various provisions of the divine decree in their logical relations which supposes that the ultimate end which God proposed to himself was his own glory in the salvation of some men and in the damnation of others, and that, as a means to that end, he decreed to create man, and to permit him to fall. According to this view, man simply as creatible, and fallible, and not as actually created or fallen, is the object of election and reprobation. The order of the decrees would then be— 1st. Of all possible men, God first decreed the salvation of some and the damnation of others, for the end of his own glory. 2d. He decreed, as a means to that end, to create those already elected or reprobated. 3d. He decreed to permit them to fall. 4th. He decreed to provide a salvation for the elect. This view was held by Beza, the successor of Calvin in Geneva, and by Gomarus, the great opponent of Arminius.

46. *State the respective points of agreement and of difference between these several schemes.*

1st. The Arminian as compared with the Calvinistic scheme. With the Arminian the decree of redemption precedes the decree of election, which is conditioned upon the foreseen faith of the individual.

With the Calvinist, on the other hand, the decree of election precedes the decree of redemption, and the decree of election is conditioned upon the simple good pleasure of God alone.

2d. The French or Salmurian as compared with the legitimate view of the Reformed Churches and with the Arminian view. The French view agrees with the Reformed and differs from the Arminian view in making the sovereign good pleasure of God the sole ground of election; while it differs from the Reformed and agrees with the Arminian in making the decree of redemption precede the decree of election.

3d. The supra-lapsarian scheme as compared with the infra-lapsarian view prevalent among the Reformed Churches. The supra-lapsarian scheme makes the decree to elect some and reprobate others, precede the decree to create and to permit to fall. The infra-lapsarian view makes the decree of election come after the decree to create and permit to fall. The supra-lapsarian view regards man not as created and fallen, but simply as creatible, the object of election and reprobation. The infra-lapsarian view makes man as already created and fallen the only object of those decrees.

47. *State the arguments against the supra-lapsarian scheme.*

This scheme is unquestionably the most logical of all. It is postulated upon the principle, that what is last in execution is first in intention, which undoubtedly holds true in all spheres comprehended in human experience. Hence it is argued that if the final result of the whole matter is the glorification of God in the salvation of the elect and the perdition of the non-elect, it must have been the deliberate purpose of God from the beginning. But the case is too high and too vast for the *à priori* application and enforcement of the ordinary rules of human judgment; we can here only know in virtue of and within the limits of a positive revelation.

The objections against this scheme are—

1st. Man creatible is a nonentity. He could not have been loved or chosen unless considered as created.

2d. The whole language of Scripture upon this subject implies that the "elect" are chosen as the objects of eternal love, not from the number of creatible, but from the mass of actually sinful men.—John xv. 19; Rom. xi. 5, 7.

3d. The Scriptures declare that the elect are chosen to sanctification, and to the sprinkling of the blood of Christ. They must therefore have been regarded when chosen as guilty and defiled by sin.—1 Pet. i. 2; Eph. i. 4–6.

4th. Predestination includes reprobation. This view represents God as reprobating the non-elect by a sovereign act, without any respect to their sins, simply for his own glory. This appears to be inconsistent with the divine righteousness, as well as with the teaching of Scripture. The non-elect are "ordained to dishonor and wrath *for their sins*, to the praise of his glorious *justice*.—"Conf. Faith," ch. 3, sec. 3–7, "L. Cat.," question 13; "S. Cat.," question 20.

48. *Show that a correct exegesis of Eph. iii. 9, 10, does not support the supra-lapsarian view.*

This passage is claimed as a direct affirmation of the supra-lapsarian theory. If the ἵνα, introducing the tenth verse, refers to the immediately preceding clause, then the passage teaches that God created all things *in order that* his manifold wisdom might be displayed by the church to the angels. It is evident, however, that ἵνα, refers to the preceding phrase, in which Paul declares that he was ordained to preach the gospel to the Gentiles, and to enlighten all men as to the mystery of redemption. All this he was commissioned to do, *in order that* God's glory might be displayed, etc.—See "Hodge on Ephesians."

49. *State the arguments against the French scheme.*

1st. It is not consistent with the fact that God's purposes are one. The scheme is that God in one eternal act determined to provide the objective conditions of salvation (redemption through the blood of Christ), for all, and to provide the subjective conditions of salvation (efficacious grace) only for some. This is in reality an attempt to weld together Arminianism and Calvinism. 2d. The Scriptures declare that the purpose of Christ's coming was to execute the purpose of election. He came to give eternal life to as many as the Father has given him. John xvii. 2, 9; x. 15. Redemption therefore can not precede election. 3d. The true doctrine of the Atonement (see Chapter XXV.) is that Christ did not come to make salvation possible, but to effect it for all for whom he died. The Atonement secures remission of sin, and faith, and repentance, and all the fruits of the Spirit. Therefore all who are redeemed repent and believe.

50. *In what sense do the Lutherans teach that Christ is the ground of election?*

They hold that God elected his own people to eternal life *for Christ's sake.* They appeal to Eph. i. 4, "According as he hath chosen us in him [Christ] before the foundation of the world." This view may evidently be construed either with the Arminian or the French theory of the decrees above stated, *i. e.,* we were chosen in Christ for his sake, either as we were foreseen to be in him through faith, or because God, having provided through Christ salvation for all men, would, by the election of certain individuals, secure at least in their case the successful effect of Christ's death.

This view, of course, is rebutted by the same arguments which we urge against the theories above mentioned. We are said to be chosen "in him," not *for Christ's sake,* but because the eternal covenant of grace includes all the elect under the headship of Christ. The love of God is everywhere represented as the ground of the gift of Christ, not the work of Christ the ground of the love of God.—John iii. 16; 1 John iv. 10.

DIFFERENT VIEWS OF THE CHURCHES.

THE LUTHERAN VIEW.—"That which first of all should be accurately observed, is the difference between foreknowledge and predestination or the eternal election of God. For the 'Foreknowledge of God' is nothing more than that God knew all things before they existed. . . . . This foreknowledge of God pertains alike to good and to bad men, but it is not consequently the cause of evil, nor the cause of sin, which impels man to crime. For sin originates from the devil and from the depraved and wicked will of man. Neither is this foreknowledge of God the cause that men perish; for that they ought to charge upon themselves; but the foreknowledge of God disposes evil, and sets bounds to it, determining whither it shall go, and how long it shall last, so that, although it be in itself evil, it conspires to the salvation of God's elect.

"On the other hand, 'Predestination,' or the eternal election of God, pertains only to the good and chosen sons of God, and it is the cause of their salvation. For it procures their salvation, and disposes to those things which pertain to it. Our salvation is so founded upon this predestination that the gates of hell shall never be able to overturn it. This predestination of God is not to be sought in the secret council of God, but in the word of God, in which it is revealed. For the word of God leads us to Christ, *that* is that book of life in which all are inscribed and elect who attain to eternal salvation. For so it is written (Eph. i. 4) he chose us *in Christ* before the foundation of the world. . . . The word of God, the 'book of life' offers Christ to us, and this is opened and developed to us through the preaching of the gospel, as it is written (Rom. viii. 30) whom he chose, them he called. *In Christ therefore* the eternal election of the Father is to be sought. He in his eternal counsel has decreed that, except those who know his Son Jesus Christ, and truly believe on him, none shall be saved."—"*Formula Concordiæ*," *Hase Collect.*, pp. 617–619.

John Gerhard (1582–1637), *Loci* II., 86 B.—"We say that all those, and those alone, are elected from eternity by God to salvation, whom he foresaw would believe in Christ the redeemer through the efficacy of the Holy Spirit, and the ministry of the gospel, and should persevere in faith until the end of life."

THE DOCTRINE OF THE REFORMED CHURCHES.—"*Thirty-Nine Articles of the Church of England.*" Article XVII.—See above, Chap. VII.

"*Westminster Confession of Faith*," Chap. iii.—"The rest of mankind, God was pleased, according to the unsearchable counsel of his own will, whereby he extendeth or withholdeth mercy as he pleaseth, for the glory of his sovereign power over his creatures, *to pass by*, and to ordain them to dishonor and wrath *for their* SINS, *and to the praise of his glorious* JUSTICE."—"Conf. Faith," ch. iii., § 7.

"*Canons of Synod of Dort,*" Cap. I., § 7.—"But election is the immutable purpose of God, by which, before the foundations of the world were laid, he chose, out of the whole human race, fallen by their own fault from their primeval integrity into sin and destruction, according to the most free good pleasure of his own will, and of mere grace, a certain number of men, neither better nor worthier than others, but lying in the same misery with the rest, to salvation in Christ, whom he had ever from eternity constituted Mediator and Head of all the elect, and the foundation of salvation. . . . . § 9. This same election is not made from any foreseen faith, obedience of faith, holiness, or any other good quality or disposition, as a prerequisite cause or condition in the man who should be elected, but *unto* faith, and *unto* obedience of faith, and holiness. And truly election is the fountain of every saving benefit; whence faith, holiness, and other salutary gifts, and, finally, eternal life itself, flow as its fruit and effect. § 15. Moreover, holy Scripture doth illustrate and commend to us this eternal and free grace of our election, in this more especially, that it doth also testify all men not to be elected, but that some are non-elect, or passed by in the eternal election of God, whom truly God, from most free, just, irreprehensible and immutable good pleasure, decreed to live in the *common misery*, into which they had, by *their own fault*, cast themselves, and not to bestow upon them living faith and the grace of conversion."

REMONSTRANTS.—" *Remonstrantia*," etc., five articles prepared by the Dutch advocates of universal redemption (1610), Art. I.—" God by an immutable decree, before he laid the foundations of the world, ordained in Jesus Christ his Son, to save out of the fallen human race, exposed to punishment on account of sin, those in Christ, on account of Christ, and through Christ, who by the grace of the Holy Spirit believe his Son, and who through the same grace persevere in the obedience of faith to the end. And on the other hand (he decreed) to leave in sin and exposed to wrath those who are not converted, and are unbelieving, and to condemn them as aliens from Christ, according to John iii. 36."

CHAPTER XII.

THE CREATION OF THE WORLD.

1. *What is the origin of the Doctrine of Creation ex nihilo?*

The prevalency, if not the conception, of the idea of absolute creation, or of creation *ex nihilo*, is to be referred to the influence of the inspired word of God. Anterior to revelation there were two prevalent causes which prevented the acceptance of this idea. (*a.*) The universally assumed truth of the axiom that *ex nihilo nihil fit*. Hence all theists and atheists alike failed to conceive of, or conceiving repudiated, the idea of absolute creation as absurd. (*b.*) The second cause influencing theists was the presumed interest of natural theology, in the impossibility, on that hypothesis, of reconciling the existence of evil with the perfections of God.

2. *What views were respectively held by the great theists Plato and Aristotle?*

Plato held that there are two eternal, self-existent principles, God and matter, ὕλη; which exist co-ordinately in an indivisible, unsuccessive eternity; that time and the actual phenomenal world which exists in time, are the work of God, who freely moulds matter into forms which image his own infinitely perfect and eternal ideas. Aristotle also held that God and matter are co-ordinately self-existent and eternal; but he differed from Plato in regarding God as eternally self-active in organizing the world out of matter, and consequently in regarding the universe thus organized as eternal as well as the mere matter of which it is formed.—"Ancient Phil.," W. Archer Butler, Series 3, Lectures 1 and 2.

3. *What views on this point prevailed among the Gnostics?*

Some of the Gnostics taught that the universe proceeds from God by way of emanation, which was explained as "a necessary and gradual unfolding *ad extra* of the germ of existence that lay in God," as radiance proceeds from the sun, etc. Most of the Gnostics united with this theory of emanation the doctrine of dualism, *i. e.*, of the co-ordinate self-existence of two independent principles, God and matter (ὕλη). From God by successive emanations proceeded the Æons, the Demimgos, Creator of the world, the Jehovah of the Old Testament, and finally Christ. The material universe springs from self-existent matter, intrinsically evil, organized by the Demimgos. All souls have emanated from the world of light, but have become entangled in matter, hence the historical contest between good and evil, which Christ came to settle by giving power to souls ultimately to escape from the toils of matter.

4. *What is the view on this subject common to all schemes of Pantheism?*

Pantheists identify God and the universe. God is the absolute being of which things are the special and transient modes. God is the self-existent and persistent principle of all things, which by an inherent self-acting law of development is eternally running through ceaseless cycles of change.

5. *State the true doctrine as to creation.*

The Christian doctrine as to Creation involves the following points: 1st. "In the beginning," at some unknown point of definite commencement in time. 2d. God called all things (that is the original principles and causes of all things) into being out of nothing. Thus every thing which has or will or can exist, exterior to the Godhead, owes its being and substance as well as its form to God. 3d. This creative act is an act of free, self-determined will. It was not a necessary constitutional act analogous to the immanent and eternal acts of the Generation of the Son or the Procession of the Holy Spirit. 4th. It was not necessary to complete the divine excellence or blessedness, which were eternal and complete and inseparable from the divine essence. But it was done in the exercise of absolute discretion for infinitely wise reasons.—Dr. Charles Hodge.

This doctrine is essential to Theism. All opposing theories of the origin of the world are essentially Pantheistic or Atheistic.

6. *What distinction is signalized by the terms* Creatio prima seu immediata, *and* Creatio secunda seu mediata, *and by whom was it introduced?*

The phrase *Creatio prima seu immediata* signifies the originating act of the divine will whereby he brings, or has brought, into being, out of nothing, the principles and elementary essences of all things. The phrase *Creatio secunda seu mediata* signifies the subsequent act of God in originating different forms of things, and especially different species of living beings out of the already created essences of things. The Christian Church holds both. These phrases originated in the writings of certain Lutheran theologians of the seventeenth century, *e. g.*, Gerhard, Quenstedt, etc.

7. *What is the primary signification, and what the biblical usage of the word* בָּרָא?

"1st. Strictly, *To hew, cut out.* 2d. *To form, make, produce* (whether out of nothing or not).—Gen. i. 1, 21, 27; ii. 3, 4; Isa. xliii. 1, 7; xlv. 7; lxv. 18; Ps. li. 12; Jer. xxxi. 22; Amos iv. 13. Niphal, 1st. *To be created.*—Gen. ii. 4; v. 2. 2d. *To be born.*—Ps. cii. 19; Ezek. xxi. 35. Piel, 1st. *To hew, cut down, e. g.*, a wood. Josh. xvii. 15, 18. 2d. *To cut down* (with the sword), *to kill.* Ezek. xxiii. 47. 3d. *To form, engrave, mark out.*—Ezek. xxi. 24." Gesenius' "Lex."

8. *State the direct proof of the truth of this doctrine afforded in Scripture.*

1st. Since the idea itself is new, and foreign to all precedent modes of thought, it could be conveyed in Scripture only through the use of old terms, previously bearing a different sense, but so employed as to suggest a new meaning. The word "bārā," however, is the best one the Hebrew language afforded to express the idea of absolute making.

2d. This new idea is inevitably suggested by the way in which the term is first used by Moses, when giving account from the very commencement of the genesis of the heavens and the earth. As a general introduction to the history of the formation of the world and its inhabitants, it is declared that "In the beginning—in the absolute beginning, God made the heavens and the earth." There is not the slightest hint given of any previously existing material. In the *beginning* God made the heavens and the earth, *after that* Chaos existed, for then it is said "the earth was without form and void," and the Spirit of God brooded over the abyss.

3d. The same truth is also inevitably suggested in all the various modes of expression by which the agency of God in originating the world is set forth in Scripture. In no case is there the faintest trace of any reference to any pre-existing materials or precedent conditions of creation. In every case the whole causal agency to which the creation is referred is the "Word," the bare "fiat" of Jehovah.—Ps. xxxiii. 6 and cxlviii. 5. "By faith we understand that the worlds were framed by the word of God, so that things which are seen (τα βλεπόμενα) were not made of things which do appear (μη εκ φαινομένων).—Heb. xi. 3. See Rom. iv. 17; 2 Cor. iv. 6.

9. *In what manner is this doctrine of the absolute creation of the world by God* implied *in Scripture?*

1st. In all those passages that teach that God is an absolute Sovereign, and that the creature is *absolutely* dependent on him, "in whom we live and move and have our being."—Acts xvii. 28; Neh. ix. 6; Col. i. 16; Rev. iv. 11; Rom. xi. 36; 1 Cor. viii. 6.

Now it is evident that if the essences and primordial principles of all things are not immediately created by God out of nothing, but are eternally self-existent independently of him, then he, in his offices of Creator and Providential governor of all things, must be conditioned and limited by the pre-existing essential properties and powers of those primordial elements. In which case God would not be absolute Sovereign, nor the things made absolutely dependent upon his will.

2d. In all those passages which teach that the kosmos, the "all things" had a beginning.—Ps. xc. 2; John xvii. 5, 24.

10. *What arguments derived from reason and consciousness, and from the elementary constitution of matter, may be adduced in proof of absolute creation?*

1st. This doctrine alone is consistent with the feeling of absolute dependence of the creature upon the Creator, which is inherent in every heart, and which is inculcated in all the teachings of the Scriptures. It could not be said that "he upholds all things by the word of his power," nor that "we live and move and have our being in him," unless he be absolutely the Creator as well as the Former of all things.

2d. It is manifest from the testimony of consciousness: (1.) That our souls are distinct individual entities, and not parts or particles of God; (2.) that they are not eternal. It follows consequently that they were created. And if the creation of the spirits of men *ex nihilo* be once admitted, there remains no special difficulty with respect to the absolute creation of matter.

3d. Although the absolute origination of any new existence out of nothing is to us confessedly inconceivable, it is not one whit more so than the relation of the infinite foreknowledge, or foreordination, or providential control of God to the free agency of men, nor than many other truths which we are all forced to believe.

4th. After having admitted the necessary self-existence of an infinitely wise and powerful personal Spirit, whose existence, upon the hypothesis of his possessing the power of absolute creation, is sufficient to account for all the phenomena of the universe, it is unphilosophical gratuitously to multiply causes by supposing the independent, eternal self-existence of matter also.

5th. When the physical philosopher has analyzed matter to its ultimate atoms, and determined their essential primary properties, he finds in them as strong evidence of a powerful antecedent cause, and of a wisely designing mind, as he does in the most complex organizations of nature; for what are the ultimate properties of matter but the elementary constituents of the universal laws of nature, and the ultimate conditions of all phenomena. If design discovered in the constitution of the universe *as finished* proves a divine Former, by equal right must the same design discovered in the *elementary* constitution of matter prove a divine Creator.

Atoms were asserted by Sir John Herschell to have all the appearance of "a manufactured article," on account of their uniformity.

"Whether or not the conception of a multitude of beings existing from all eternity is in itself self-contradictory, the conception becomes palpably absurd when we attribute a relation of quantitive equality to all those beings. We are then forced to look beyond them to some common cause, or common origin, to explain why this singular relation of equality exists . . . We have reached the utmost limit of our thinking faculties when we have admitted that because matter can not be eternal and self-existent it must have been created."—Prof. J. Clerk-Maxwell in Art. Atom, "Encyclo. Britannica," 9th ed.

11. *State and refute the objection to this doctrine based upon the axiom,* "Ex nihilo nihil fit."

It is objected that it is an original and self-evident principle of reason, that only nothing can come from nothing. We answer that this statement is indefinite. If it is meant that no new thing, nor any change in a previously existing thing, can begin to be without an adequate cause, we answer that it is true, but does not apply to the case in hand. Our doctrine is not that the universe came into being without an adequate cause, but that the essences as well as the forms of all things had a beginning in time, and their cause exists only in the will of God. The infinite power inherent in a self-existent Spirit is precisely the Cause to which we refer the absolute origination of all things. But if it is meant by the above objection that this infinite God has not power to create new entities, then the principle is simply false and not self-evident; it bears not one of the marks of a valid intuition—neither self-evidence, necessity, nor universality.

12. *State and refute the position of some who maintain on moral grounds the self-existence of matter.*

Those among theistic thinkers who have been tempted to regard matter as eternal and self-existent, have been influenced by the vain hope of explaining thereby the existence of moral evil in consistency with the holiness of God. They would refer all the phenomena of sin to an essentially evil principle inherent in matter, and would justify God by maintaining that he has done all that in him lay to limit that evil. Now, besides the inconsistency of this theory's attempt to vindicate the holiness of God at the expense of his independence, it proceeds upon absurd principles, as appears from the following considerations: (1.) Moral evil is in its essence an attribute of spirit. To refer it to a material origin must logically lead to the grossest materialism. (2.) The entire Christian system of religion, and the example of Christ, is in opposition to that asceticism and "neglecting of the body" (Col. ii. 23), which necessarily springs from the view that matter is the ground of sin. (3.) When God created the material universe he pronounced his works "very good." (4.) The second Person of the holy Trinity assumed a real material body into personal union with himself. (5.) The material creation, now "made subject to vanity" through man's sin, is to be renovated and made the temple in which the God-man shall dwell forever.—See below, Chap. XXXIX., Question 17. (6.) The work of Christ in delivering his people from their sin does not contemplate the renunciation of the material part of our natures, but our bodies, which are now "the members of Christ," and the "temples of the Holy Ghost," are at the resurrection to be transformed into the likeness of his glorified body. Yet nothing could be more absurd than to argue that the σῶμα πνευματικόν is not as literally material as the present σῶμα ψυχικόν. (7.) If the cause of evil is essentially inherent in matter, and if its past developments have occurred in spite of God's efforts to limit it, what certain ground of confidence can any of us have for the future.

13. *Prove that the work of creation is in Scripture attributed to God absolutely, i. e., to each of the three persons of the Trinity co-ordinately, and not to either as his special personal function.*

1st. To the Godhead absolutely.—Gen. i. 1, 26. 2d. To the Father, 1 Cor. viii. 6. 3d. To the Son.—John i. 3; Col. i. 16, 17. 4th. To the Holy Spirit.—Gen. i. 2; Job xxvi. 13; Ps. civ. 30.

14. *How can it be proved that no creature can create?*

1st. From the nature of the work. It appears to us that

the work of absolute creation *ex nihilo* is an infinite exercise of power. It is to us inconceivable because infinite, and it can belong, therefore, only to that Being who, for the same reason, is incomprehensible. 2d. The Scriptures distinguish Jehovah from all creatures, and from false gods, and establish his sovereignty and rights as the true God by the fact that he is the *Creator*, Is. xxxvii. 16; xl. 12, 13; liv. 5; Ps. xcvi. 5; Jer. x. 11, 12. 3d. If it were admitted that a creature could create, then the works of creation would never avail to lead the creature to an infallible knowledge that his creator was the eternal and self-existent God.

15. *Why is it important for us to know, if such knowledge be possible, what God's chief end in creation was?*

This is not a question of vain curiosity. It is evident, since God is eternal, immutable, and of absolutely perfect intelligence, that the great end or ultimate purpose for which he at the beginning created all things must have been kept in view unchangeably in all his works, and so all his works must be more directly or remotely a means to that end. Now our minds are so constituted that we can understand a system only when we understand its ultimate purpose or end. Thus we can comprehend the parts of a watch or steam engine, and their relations and functions, only *after* we understand the end or purpose which the entire watch or engine was intended to serve. And although God has hid from us many of his subordinate purposes, we believe that he has revealed to us that great ultimate design, without a glimpse of which the true character of his general administration never could be in any degree comprehended. None can deny that *if* he has revealed his ultimate purpose in creation, that it must be a matter to us of the very highest importance.

It is self-evident that *we* can not rise to so high a generalization as this by any process of induction from what we know or can know of his works. Our conclusion on this subject must therefore be drawn, in the first instance at least, entirely from what we know of God's attributes and from the explicit teachings of his word.

16. *What is the meaning of the term* THEODICY, *and by whom was this department of speculative theology in the first instance formally explored?*

The term *Theodicy* (θεός δίκη) signifies a speculative justification of the ways of God towards the human race, especially as respects the origin of evil, and the moral government of the world. It was first exalted into a department of theological science by the great German philosopher Leibnitz, in his great work entitled "Theodicy, or the Goodness of God, the Liberty of Man, and the Origin of Evil," A. D. 1710.

17. *What view as to the end of God in creation did Leibnitz advocate, and by whom has he been followed?*

Leibnitz held that all moral excellence can be resolved into benevolence, and that the grand, all-comprehending purpose of God in the creation of the universe, and in his preservation and government thereof, is the promotion of the happiness of his creatures. Hence he concludes that God has chosen the best possible system to attain that end in the largest possible degree. This is the system of Optimism.

This view has prevailed largely among the New England theologians, in connection with the prevalent theory which regards all virtue as consisting in disinterested benevolence.

The objections to this view are—1st. All virtue does not consist in disinterested benevolence.—See above, Chapter VIII., Ques. 61. And happiness is not the highest good. 2d. It subordinates the Creator to the creature, the greater to the less, as the means to an end. When God from eternity formed the purpose to create, no creatures existed to be made happy or miserable. The motive to create therefore could not have originated in the non-existent, and could have its origin and object only in the divine being himself. 3d. The Scriptures (see next question) never either directly or indirectly intimate that any thing in the creature is the chief end of God, nor do they ever propose any personal or public good of the creature as the chief end of the creature himself.

18. *State the true view and quote the statements of the Confession of Faith?*

The true view is that the great end of God in creation was his own glory. Glory is manifested excellence. The excellence of his attributes are manifested by their exercise. This end therefore was not the increase either of his excellence or blessedness, but their manifestation *ad extra.*

"It pleased God, the Father, Son, and Holy Ghost, *for the manifestation of the glory of his eternal power, wisdom, and goodness,* in the beginning to create or make of nothing the world, and all things therein, whether visible or invisible, in the space of six days, and all very good."—"Conf. Faith," Ch. iv., § 1. The same is affirmed to be the chief end of God in all his purposes and works of Providence and Redemption.—Ch. iii. § 3,

5, 7, and Ch. v. § 1; Ch. vi. § 1; Ch. xxxiii. § 2; "Larger Cat.," Qs. 12 and 18; "S. Cat.," Qs. 7.

19. *State from reason and Scripture the arguments which sustain this view.*

1st. Since God formed the purpose to create before any creature existed, it is evident that the motive to create must have its source and object in the pre-existing Creator and not in the non-existing creature. The absolute Creator can not be subordinated to nor conditioned upon the finite and dependent creature.

2d. Since God himself is infinitely worthier than the sum of all creatures, it follows that the manifestation of his own excellence is infinitely a higher and worthier end than the happiness of the creatures, indeed the highest and worthiest end conceivable.

3d. Nothing can so exalt and bless the creature as his being made thus the instrument and the witness of the infinite Creator's glory, hence the proposing that glory as the "chief end" of the creation is the best security for the creature's advance in excellence and blessedness.

4th. The Scriptures explicitly assert that this is the chief end of God in creation (Col. i. 16; Prov. xvi. 4), and of things as created.—Rev. iv. 11; Rom. xi. 36.

5th. They teach that the same is the chief end of God in his eternal decrees.—Eph. i. 5, 6, 12.

6th. Also of God's providential and gracious governing and disposing of his creatures.—Rom. ix. 17, 22, 23; Eph. iii. 10.

7th. It is made the duty of all moral agents to adopt the same as their personal end in all things.—1 Cor. x. 31; 1 Pet. iv. 11.

20. *What is the present attitude of Geological science in relation to the Mosaic Record of creation?*

The results of modern geological science clearly establish the conclusions—(*a.*) That the elementary materials of which the world is composed existed an indefinitely great number of ages ago. (*b.*) That the world has been providentially brought to its present state by a gradual progression, through many widely contrasted physical conditions, and through long intervals of time. (*c.*) That it has successively been inhabited by many different orders of organized beings, each in turn adapted to the physical conditions of the globe in its successive stages, and generally marked in each stage by an advancing scale of organization, from the more elementary to the more complex and more perfect forms. (*d.*) That man completes the pyramid of creation, the most perfect, and the last formed of all the inhabitants of the world. The only difficulty in adjusting these results with the Mosaic Record of creation is found in matters of detail, in which the true sense of the inspired record is obscure, and the conclusions of the science are immature. Therefore all such detailed adjustments as that attempted by Hugh Miller in his "Testimony of the Rocks" have failed. As to the relation of the findings of science with respect to the antiquity of man to Biblical Chronology see below, Chapter XVI. In general, however, there is a most remarkable agreement between the Mosaic Record and the results of Geology as to the following principal points. The Record agrees with the science in teaching—(*a.*) The creation of the elements in the remote past. (*b.*) The intermediate existence of chaos. (*c.*) The advance of the earth through various changes to its present physical condition. (*d.*) The successive creations of different genera and species of organized beings—the vegetable before the animal—the lower forms before the higher forms—in adaptation to the improving condition of the earth—and man last of all.

If we remember when and where and for what purpose this Record was produced, and compare it with all other ancient or mediæval cosmogonies, this wonderful agreement with the last results of modern science will be felt to contribute essentially to the evidences of its divine origin. It is certainly, even when read subject to the most searching modern criticism, seen to be amply sufficient for the end intended, as a general introduction to the history of Redemption, which although rooted in creation is henceforward carried on as a system of supernatural revelations and influences.

21. *State the several principles which should always be borne in mind in considering questions involving an apparent conflict of science and revelation.*

1st. God's works and God's word are equally revelations from him. They are consequently both alike true, and both alike sacred, and to be treated with reverence. It is absolutely impossible that when they are both adequately interpreted they can come into conflict. Jealousy on either part, is treason to the Author and Lord of both.

2d. Science, or the interpretation of God's works, is therefore a legitimate and obligatory department of human study. It has its rights which must be respected, and its duties which it must observe. It is the right of every science to pursue the investigation of its own branch according to its own legitimate methods. We can not require of the chemist that he should pursue the methods of the philologist, nor of the geologist that he should go to history, either profane or sacred, for his facts. It is the duty of the students of every science to keep within its province, to recognize the fact that it is only one department of the vast empire of truth, and to respect alike all orders of truth, historical and inspired as well as scientific; mental and spiritual, as well as material.

3d. It follows as a practical consequence from the narrowness of the human faculties, that men confined to particular branches of inquiry acquire special habits of thought, and associations of ideas peculiar to their line, by which they are apt to measure and judge the whole world of truth. Thus the man of science misinterprets and then becomes jealous of the theologian, and the theologian misinterprets and becomes jealous of the man of science. This is narrowness, not superior knowledge; weakness, not strength.

4th. Science is only the human interpretation of God's works, it is always imperfect and makes many mistakes. Biblical interpreters are also liable to mistakes and should never assert the absolute identity of their interpretations of the Bible with the mind of God.

5th. All sciences in their crude condition have been thought to be in conflict with Scripture. But as they have approached perfection, they have been all found to be perfectly consistent with it. Sometimes it is the science which is amended into harmony with the views of the theologian. Sometimes it is the views of the theologian which are amended into harmony with perfected and demonstrated science, e. g., the instance of the universal and now grateful acceptance by the church of the once abhorred Copernican system.

6th. In the case of many sciences, as eminently of Geology, the time has not yet come to attempt an adjustment between their conclusions and revelation. Like contemporaneous history in its relation to prophecy, Geology in its relation to the Mosaic Record of creation is *in transitu.* Its conclusions are not yet mature. When geologists are all agreed among themselves, when all the accessible facts of the science are observed, analyzed, and classified, and when Generalization has done its perfect work, and when all of its results are finished and finally fixed as part of the intellectual heritage of man forever, then the adjustment between science and revelation will stand self-revealed, and science will be seen to support and illustrate, instead of oppose, the written word of God.

7. There are hence two opposite tendencies which equally damage the cause of religion, and manifest the weakness of the faith of its professed friends. *The first* is the weak accept-

ance of every hostile conclusion of scientific speculators as certainly true; the constant confession of the inferiority of the light of revelation to the light of nature, and of the certainty of the conclusions of Biblical exegesis and Christian theology to that of the results of modern science; the constant attempt to accommodate the interpretation of the Bible, like a nose of wax, to every new phase assumed by the current interpretations of nature. *The second and opposite* extreme is that of jealously suspecting all the findings of science as probable offences against the dignity of revelation, and of impatiently attacking even those passing phases of imperfect science which for the time appear to be inconsistent with our own opinions. Standing upon the rock of divine truth, Christians need not fear, and can well afford to await the result. PERFECT FAITH, as well as perfect love, CASTETH OUT ALL FEAR. All things are ours, whether the natural or the supernatural, whether science or revelation.—See Isaac Taylor's "Restoration of Belief," pp. 9, 10.

CHAPTER XIII.

ANGELS.

1. *What are the different senses in which the word ἄγγελος, angel, or messenger, is used in Scripture?*

"Ordinary messengers, Job i. 14; Luke vii. 24; ix. 52; prophets, Is. xlii. 19; Mal. iii. 1; priests, Mal. ii. 7; ministers of the New Testament, Rev. i. 20; also impersonal agents, as pillar of cloud, Ex. xiv. 19; pestilence, 2 Sam. xxiv. 16, 17; winds, Ps. civ. 4; plagues, called 'evil angels,' lxxviii. 49; Paul's thorn in the flesh, 'angel of Satan,' 2 Cor. xii. 7." Also the second person of the Trinity, "Angel of his presence;" "Angel of the Covenant," Isa. lxiii. 9; Mal. iii. 1. But the term is chiefly applied to the heavenly intelligences, Matt. xxv. 31.— See Kitto's "Bib. Ency."

2. *What are the Scriptural designations of angels, and how far are those designations expressive of their nature and offices?*

Good angels (for evil spirits, see Question 15) are designated in Scripture as to their nature, dignity, and power, as "spirits," Heb. i. 14; "thrones, dominions, principalities, powers, mights," Eph. i. 21, and Col. i. 16; "sons of God," Luke xx. 36; Job i. 6; "mighty angels," and "powerful in strength," 2 Thess. i. 7; Ps. ciii. 20; "holy angels," "elect angels," Luke ix. 26; 1 Tim. v. 21; and as to the offices they sustain in relation to God and man, they are designated as "angels or messengers," and as "ministering spirits," Heb. i. 13, 14.

3. *What were the cherubim?*

"They were ideal creatures, compounded of four parts, those namely, of a man, an ox, a lion, and an eagle." "The predominant appearance was that of a man, but the number of faces, feet, and hands differed according to circumstances."—Ezek. i. 6, compare with Ezek. xli. 18, 19, and Ex. xxv. 20.

To the same ideal beings is applied the designation "living

creatures" (Ezek. i. 5–22; x. 15, 17; Rev. iv. 6–9; v. 6–14; vi. 1–7; vii. 11; xiv. 3; xv. 7; xix. 4), rendered in our version "beasts."

"They were *symbolical* of the highest properties of creature life, and of these as the outgoings and manifestation of the divine life; but they were *typical* of redeemed and glorified manhood, or prophetical representations of it, as that in which these properties were to be combined and exhibited.

"They were appointed immediately after the fall to man's original place in the garden, and to his office in connection with the tree of life."—Gen iii. 24.

"The other and more common connection in which the cherub appears is with the throne or peculiar dwelling-place of God. In the holy of holies in the tabernacle, Ex. xxv. 22, he was called the God who dwelleth between and sitteth upon the cherubim, 1 Sam. iv. 4; Ps. lxxx. 1; Ezek. i. 26, 28; whose glory is above the cherubim. In Rev. iv. 6, we read of the living creatures who were in the midst of the throne and around about it."

"What does this bespeak but the wonderful fact brought out in the history of redemption, that man's nature is to be exalted to the dwelling-place of the Godhead? In Christ it is taken, so to speak, into the very bosom of the Deity; and because it is so highly honored in him, it shall attain to more than angelic glory in his members."—Fairbairn's "Typology," Pt. II., Chapter i., Section 3. See also "Imperial Bible Dictionary," Art. Cherubim.

4. *What is the etymology of the word seraphim, and what is taught in Scripture concerning them?*

The word signifies *burning, bright, dazzling*. It occurs in the Bible only once.—Isa. vi. 2, 6. It probably presents, under a different aspect, the ideal beings commonly designated cherubim and living creatures.

5. *Is there any evidence that angels are of various orders and ranks?*

That such distinctions certainly exist appears evident—1st. From the language of Scripture. Gabriel is distinguished as one that stands in the presence of God (Luke i. 19), evidently in some pre-eminent sense; and Michael as one of the chief princes.—Dan. x. 13. Observe also the epithets archangel, thrones, dominions, principalities, powers.—Jude 9; Eph. i. 21. 2d. From the analogy of the fallen angels.—See Eph. ii. 2; Matt. ix. 34. 3d. From the analogy of human society and of the universal creation. Throughout all God's works gradation of rank prevails.

6. *Do the Scriptures speak of more than one archangel, and is he to be considered a creature?*

This term occurs but twice in the New Testament, and in both instances it is used in the singular number, and preceded by the definite article ὁ.—1 Thes. iv. 16; Jude 9. Thus the term is evidently restricted to one person, called, Jude 9, Michael, who, in Dan. x. 13, and xii. 1, is called "one of the chief princes," and "the great prince," and in Rev. xii. 7, is said to have fought with his angels against the dragon and his angels.

Many suppose that the archangel is the Son of God. Others suppose that he is one of the highest class of creatures, since he is called "*one of the chief princes*," Dan. x. 13; and since divine attributes are never ascribed to him.

7. *What do the Scriptures teach concerning the number and power of angels?*

1st. Concerning their number, revelation determines only that it is very great. "Thousand thousands, and ten thousand times ten thousand."—Dan. vii. 10. "More than twelve legions of angels."—Matt. xxvi. 53. "Multitude of the heavenly host." Luke ii. 13. "Myriads of angels."—Heb. xii. 22.

2d. Concerning their power, the Scriptures teach that it is very great when exercised both in the material and in the spiritual worlds. They are called "mighty angels," and are said to "excel in strength."—2 Thess. i. 7; Ps. ciii. 20; 2 Kings xix. 35. Their power, however, is not creative, but, like that of man, it can be exercised only co-ordinately with the general laws of nature, in the absolute sense of that word.

8. *What are their employments?*

1st. They behold the face of God in heaven, adore the divine perfections, study every revelation he makes of himself in providence and redemption, and are perfectly blessed in his presence and service.—Matt. xviii. 10; Rev. v. 11; 1 Pet. i. 12.

2d. God employs them as his instruments in administering the affairs of his providence.—Gen. xxviii. 12; Dan. x. 13. (1.) The law "was ordained by angels."—Gal. iii. 19; Acts vii. 53; Heb. ii. 2. (2.) They are instruments of good to God's people.—Heb. i. 14; Acts xii. 7; Ps. xci. 10–12. (3.) They execute judgment upon God's enemies.—Acts xii. 23; 2 Kings xix. 35; 1 Chron. xxi. 16. (4.) They will officiate in the final judgment, in separating the good from the bad, in gathering the elect, and in bearing them up to meet the Lord in the air. Matt. xiii. 30, 39; xxiv. 31; 1 Thess. iv. 17.

9. *Have angels bodies, and how are the apparitions of angels to be accounted for?*

Angels are called in the Scriptures "spirits" ($\pi\nu\varepsilon\acute{\nu}\mu\alpha\tau\alpha$), Heb. i. 14, a word which is also used to designate the souls of men when separate from the body.—1 Pet. iii. 19. There is however nothing in that word, nor in the opinions of the Jews at the time of Christ, nor in any thing which is told us of the nature or the employments of angels in the Scriptures, which prove that angels are absolutely destitute of proper material bodies of *any kind.* Indeed as the Son of God is to have "a glorious body," "a spiritual body" forever, and since all the redeemed are to have bodies like his, and since the angels are associated with redeemed men as members of the same infinitely exalted kingdom, it may appear probable that angels may have been created with physical organizations not altogether dissimilar to the "spiritual bodies" of the redeemed. They always appeared and spoke to men in Bible times in the bodily form of men, and as such they ate food and lodged in houses like common men.—Gen. xviii. 8 and xix. 3.

It has hence been supposed by some that angels have bodies like the present "natural" or animal bodies of men ($\sigma\tilde{\omega}\mu\alpha$ $\psi\nu\chi\iota\kappa\grave{o}\nu$), 1 Cor. xv. 44, of flesh, bones, and blood, of head and features, hands and feet, and that the apparition of an angel involved no change in him, but only a coming within the sphere of the sense perception of the observer, when the angel appeared just as he habitually is.

Now this is inconsistent with the facts of the inspired record. In certain situations the angels "appeared" precisely like common men, and in other situations they acted very differently (Acts xii. 7–10; Num. xxii. 31), in passing through stone walls, appearing and disappearing at will, etc. Besides, one of the three men who appeared to Abraham at Mamre, and whose feet he washed, and who ate the meat he had prepared, was Jehovah, the second Person of the Trinity, who had no body till he acquired it many centuries afterwards in the womb of the Virgin. If the apparent human body of the one angel was not a real, permanent human body, there is not ground to argue from the recorded phenomena that the others were.—Gen. xviii. 1–33.

Besides this, the theory in question indicates absurd confusion of thought. The animal human body, as we know it, is a physical organization in equilibrium with certain definite and nicely adjusted physical conditions, and it can exist only under those conditions. The vertebrate type, of which the human body is the highest form, has been continually changed as the physical conditions of the globe have changed, and it ceases always to exist whenever those conditions are changed in any decided degree. If it would be absurd to conceive of a human body existing in water, or in fire, how much more absurd is it to conceive of a warm-blooded, food-consuming animal existing indifferently on earth and in heaven; traversing at will the interstellar spaces, and as a true cosmopolite inhabiting alternately and indifferently all worlds, and all elements, ether, air and water, and all temperatures, from the molten sun to the absolue zero of the starless void.

The bodily appearance of angels, therefore, must have been something new assumed, or something pre-existent and permanent greatly modified for the purpose of enabling them to hold, upon occasion, profitable intercourse with men.

10. *What is the Romish doctrine and practice with regard to the worship of angels?*

"Catechismus Romanus," iii. 2, 9, 10.—"For the Holy Spirit who says, *Honor and glory unto the only God* (1 Tim. i. 17), commands us also to honor our parents and elders (Lev. xix. 32, etc.); and the holy men who worshipped one God only are also said in the sacred Scriptures to have *adored* (Gen. xxiii. 7, 12, etc.), that is, to have suppliantly venerated, kings. If then kings, by whose agency God governs the world, are treated with so high an honor, shall we not give to the angelic spirits an honor greater in proportion as these blessed minds exceed kings in dignity; [to those angelic spirits] whom God has been pleased to constitute his ministers; whose services he makes use of, not only in the government of the Church, but also of the rest of the universe; by whose aid, although we see them not, we are daily delivered from the greatest dangers both of soul and body? Add to this the charity with which they love us, through which, as Scripture informs us, they pour out their prayers for those countries (Dan. ii. 13) over which they are placed by Providence, and for those too, no doubt, whose guardians they are, for they present our prayers and tears before the throne of God (Job iii. 25; xii. 12; Rev. viii. 3). Hence our Lord has taught us in the gospel not to scandalize the little ones, because *in heaven their angels do always behold the face of his Father which is in heaven.*

"Their intercession, therefore, we must invoke, because they always behold God, and receive from him the most willing advocacy of our salvation. To this, their invocation, the sacred Scriptures bear testimony.—Gen. xlviii. 15, 16."

11. *What views have been entertained with respect to "Guardian Angels"?*

"It was a favorite opinion of the Christian Fathers that every individual is under the care of a particular angel, who is assigned to him as a guardian. They spoke also of two angels,—the one good, the other evil,—whom they conceived to be attendant on each individual: the good angel prompting to all good, and averting ill; and the evil angel prompting to all ill, and averting good (Hermas xi. 6). The Jews (excepting the Sadducees) entertained this belief, as do the Moslems. The heathen held it in a modified form—the Greeks having their tutelary dæmon, and the Romans their genius. There is however nothing to support this notion in the Bible. The passages usually referred to for its support (Ps. xxxiv. 7; Matt. xviii. 10), have assuredly no such meaning. The former simply denotes that God employs the ministry of angels to deliver his people from affliction and danger; and the celebrated passage in Matthew means that the infant children of believers, or the least among the disciples of Christ, whom the ministers of the church might be disposed to neglect, are in such estimation elsewhere, that angels do not think it below their dignity to minister unto them." Nothing is said of the personal assignment of angels to individual men.—Kitto's "Bib. Encyclo."

12. *What are the names by which Satan is distinguished, and what is their import?*

Satan, which signifies adversary, Luke x. 18. The Devil ($\delta\iota\acute{\alpha}\beta o\lambda os$ always occurs in the singular) signifying slanderer, Rev. xx. 2; Apollyon, which means destroyer, and Abbadon, Rev. ix. 11; Beelzebub, the prince of devils, from the god of the Ekronites, chief among the heathen divinities, all of which the Jews regarded as devils, 2 Kings i. 2; Matt xii. 24; Angel of the Bottomless Pit, Rev. ix. 11; Prince of the World, John xii. 31; Prince of Darkness, Eph. vi. 12; A Roaring Lion, 1 Pet. v. 8; a Sinner from the Beginning, 1 John iii. 8; Accuser, Rev. xii. 10; Belial, 2 Cor. vi. 15; Deceiver, Rev. xx. 10; Dragon, Rev. xii. 7; Liar and Murderer, John viii. 44; Leviathan, Is. xxvii. 1; Lucifer, Is. xiv. 12; Serpent, Is. xxvii. 1; Tormentor, Matt. xviii. 34; God of this World, 2 Cor. iv. 4; he that hath the Power of Death, Heb. ii. 14.—See Cruden's "Concordance."

13. *How may it be proved that Satan is a personal being, and not a mere personification of evil?*

Throughout all the various books of Scripture Satan is

always consistently spoken of as a person, and personal attributes are predicated of him. Such passages as Matt. iv. 1–11, and John viii. 44, are decisive.

14. *What do the Scriptures teach concerning the relation of Satan to other evil spirits and to our world?*

Other evil spirits are called "his angels," Matt. xxv. 41; and he is called "Prince of Devils," Matt. ix. 34; and "Prince of the powers of the Air," and "Prince of Darkness," Eph. vi. 12. This indicates that he is the master spirit of evil.

His relation to this world is indicated by the history of the Fall, 2 Cor. xi. 3; Rev. xii. 9, and by such expressions as "God of this World," 2 Cor. iv. 4; and "Spirit that worketh in the children of disobedience," Eph. ii. 2; wicked men are said to be his children, 1 John iii. 10; he blinds the minds of those that believe not and leads them captive at his will, 2 Tim. ii. 26; he also pains, harasses, and tempts God's true people as far as is permitted for their ultimate good.—Luke xxii. 31; 2 Cor. xii. 7; 1 Thess. ii. 18.

15. *What are the terms by which fallen spirits are designated?*

The Greek word ὁ διάβολος, the devil, is in the original applied only to Beelzebub. Other evil spirits are called δαίμονες, dæmons, Mark v. 12 (translated devils); unclean spirits, Mark v. 13; angels of the devil, Matt. xxv. 41; principalities, powers, rulers of the darkness of this world, Eph. vi. 12; angels that sinned, 2 Pet. ii. 4; angels that kept not their first estate, but left their own habitation, Jude vi.; lying spirits, 2 Chron. xviii. 22.

16. *What power or agency over the bodies and souls of men is ascribed to them?*

Satan, like all other finite beings, can only be in one place at a time; yet all that is done by his agents being attributed to him, he appears to be practically ubiquitous.

It is certain that at times at least they have exercised an inexplicable influence over the bodies of men, yet that influence is entirely subject to God's control.—Job ii. 7; Luke xiii. 16; Acts x. 38. They have caused and aggravated diseases, and excited appetites and passions.—1 Cor. v. 5. Satan, in some sense, has the power of death.—Heb. ii. 14.

With respect to the souls of men, Satan and his angels are utterly destitute of any power either to change the heart or to coerce the will, their influence being simply moral, and exercised in the way of deception, suggestion, and persuasion. The descriptive phrases applied by the Scriptures to their working are such as—"the deceivableness of unrighteousness," "power, signs, lying wonders," 2 Thess. ii. 9, 10; he "transforms himself into an angel of light."—2 Cor. xi. 14. If he can deceive or persuade he uses "wiles," Eph. vi. 11; "snares," 1 Tim. iii. 7; "depths," Rev. ii. 24; he "blinds the mind," 2 Cor. iv. 4; "leads captive the will," 2 Tim. ii. 26; and so "deceives the whole world."—Rev. xii. 9. If he can not persuade he uses "fiery darts," Eph. vi. 16; and "buffetings."—2 Cor. xii. 7.

As examples of his influence in tempting men to sin the Scriptures cite the case of Adam, Gen iii.; of David, 1 Chron. xxi. 1; of Judas, Luke xxii. 3; Ananias and Sapphira, Acts v. 3, and the temptation of our blessed Lord, Matt. iv.

17. *What evidence is there that the heathen worship devils?*

"The δαίμων is the object of their worship, δεισιδαιμωνία describes their worship itself, and δεισιδαίμων the worshipper." Paul (Acts xvii. 22) declared that the men of Athens were δεισιδαιμονεστέρους, i. e., too much addicted to demon-worship. David says (Ps. cvi. 37), "The gods of the heathen are demons," and Paul (1 Cor. x. 20), "The things which the Gentiles sacrifice, they sacrifice to demons and not to God." Moses said of apostate Israelites (Deut. xxxii. 17), "They sacrificed to demons and not to God, to gods whom they knew not; to new gods that came newly up; whom your fathers feared not."—"The Imperial Bible Dictionary."

18. *Where do they reside, and what is the true interpretation of* Eph. ii. 2, and vi. 12?

These passages simply declare that evil spirits belong to the unseen spiritual world, and not to our mundane system. Nothing is taught us in Scripture as to the place of their residence, further than that they originally dwelt in and fell from heaven, that they now have access to men on earth, and that they will be finally sealed up in the lake of fire prepared for them.—Rev. xx. 10; Matt. xxv. 41.

19. *By what terms were those possessed by evil spirits designated?*

They are called "demoniacs," translated *possessed with devils,* Matt. iv. 24; "having the spirit of an unclean devil," Luke iv. 33; "oppressed of the devil," Acts x. 38; "lunatics," Matt. xvii. 15.

20. *What arguments are urged by those who regard the demoniacs mentioned in the New Testament as simply diseased or deranged?*

That we can not discriminate between the effects of demoniacal possession and disease. That precisely the same symptoms have, in other cases, been treated as disease and cured.

That, like witchcraft, the experience of such possessions has been confined to the most ignorant ages of the world.

They argue further that this doctrine is inconsistent with clearly revealed principles. 1st. That the souls of dead men go immediately either to heaven or hell. 2d. That fallen angels are already shut up in chains and darkness in expectation of the final judgment:—2 Pet. ii. 4; Jude 6.

They attempt to explain away the language of Christ and his apostles upon this subject by affirming, that as it was no part of their design to instruct men in the true science of nature or disease, they conformed their language on such subjects to the prevalent opinions of the people they addressed, calling diseases by the popular name, without intending thereby to countenance the theory of the nature of the disease, out of which the name originated. Just as we now call crazed people "lunatics," without believing in the influence of the moon upon them.—"Kitto's Bib. Ency."

21. *How may it be proved that the demoniacs of the New Testament were really possessed of evil spirits?*

The simple narratives of all the evangelists put it beyond peradventure that Christ and his apostles did believe, and wished others to believe, that the demoniacs were really possessed with devils.

They distinguish between possession and disease.—Mark i. 32; Luke vi. 17, 18.

The "dæmons," as distinct from the "possessed," spoke (Mark. v. 12), were addressed, commanded, and rebuked by Christ.—Mark i. 25, 34; ix. 25; Matt. viii. 32; xvii. 18. Their desires, requests, and passions are distinguished from those of the possessed.—Matt. viii. 31; Mark ix. 26, etc. The number of dæmons in one person is mentioned.—Mark xvi. 9. They went out of the "possessed" into the swine.—Luke viii. 32. We never speak of the moon entering into, and sore vexing a man, or being cast out of a lunatic, or of the moon crying aloud, etc. The argument of those who would explain away the force of Christ's language on this subject, therefore fails.

CHAPTER XIV.

PROVIDENCE.

1. *What is the etymology and technical usage of the term* PROVIDENCE, *and what is the relation which Providence sustains to God's eternal Decree?*

Providence, from *pro* and *video*, literally means foresight, and then a careful arrangement prepared beforehand for the accomplishment of predetermined ends. Turretin defines this term as in its widest sense including (*a*) foreknowledge, (*b*) foreordination, and (*c*) the efficacious administration of the thing decreed. In the technical theological as well as in the common usage of the word, however, it is restricted to the last sense, namely the execution by God of his eternal decree in time, by means of the second causes he has originated in creation. Foreordination gives the plan and is eternal, all-comprehensive, and unchangeable. Creation gives the absolute commencement of things in time. Providence includes the two great departments (*a*) of the continued *Preservation* of all things as created, and (*b*) of the continued *Government* of all things thus preserved, so that *all* the ends for which they were created, are infallibly accomplished.—See "Conf. Faith," chap. v., and "L. Cat.," Q. 18, and "S. Cat.," Q. 11.

2. *State the true doctrine of* PRESERVATION.

Turretin says, L. 6, Ques. 4.—"Conservatio est, quâ Deus creaturas omnes in statu suo conservat, quod fit conservatione *essentiæ* in speciebus, *existentiæ* in individuis, et *virtutis* in operationes."

Preservation is that continued exercise of the divine energy whereby the Creator upholds all his creatures in being, and in the possession of all those inherent properties and qualities with which he endowed them at their creation, and of those also which they may subsequently have acquired by habit or development. That is, both the being, the attributes of every species, and the form and faculties of every individual are constantly preserved in being by God.

3. *State the arguments which establish the conclusion that a constant exercise of divine energy is essential for the preservation of all creatures.*

1st. This truth appears to be involved in the very conception of a creature in his dependent relation to his Creator. The creature is one who has the whole ground of his being in the will of his Creator. Being thus absolutely dependent, he can no more continue than he can originate his own being.

2d. This is implied in the sense of *absolute* dependence, which is an essential element of the religious sentiment which is an invariable characteristic of human nature.

3d. It is taught in Scripture. "In him we live and move and have our being."—Acts xvii. 28. "By him all things consist."—Col. i. 17. "Upholding all things by the word of his power."—Heb. i. 3; Neh. ix. 6; Ps. lxiii. 8; lxix. 8, 9.

4. *State the Deistic and Rationalistic view as to the nature of Preservation.*

They regard the action of God in the matter of the continued preservation of the creature as merely negative—a not willing to destroy. This view represents the Creator as exterior to his creation in the same manner in which a mechanician is exterior to the machine he has made and set in motion. It regards the system of second causes as dependent upon the great First Cause only *at the beginning of* the long line, in the indefinitely remote past. They maintain that in the beginning God created all things and endowed them severally with their active powers as second causes, and adjusted them in a balanced system, but then left them to act, independently of all support or direction from without, according to their nature, in their relations, as a man may leave a wound up-clock.

5. *State the objections to that view.*

1st. This view, as above shown, is inconsistent with the essential relation of the creature as an effect to the Creator as a cause. God is the only *ens a seipso*. The only cause of the creature's being is the will of the Creator. As long as he so wills that cause exists. If he should cease so to will the cause would be vacated and the effect consequently cease.

2d. This view is to an unworthy degree anthropomorphic. It involves a deplorably unintellectual failure to apprehend the essential difference between the relation to the creation sustained by God, and that sustained by man to the work of his hand. A man is necessarily *exterior* to his work, and even when present capable of directing his attention only to one point at a time. But God is omnipresent, not as to his essence only, but as to his infinite knowledge, wisdom, love, righteousness, and power, with every atom of creation for every instant of duration. The creature is always interpenetrated as well as embraced in the divine thought and will, and ever is what it is and as it is because of God.

3d. This view obviously removes God so far from the creation as to be irreligious in its practical effect. This also has been uniformly its influence as historically ascertained.

4th. It is obviously opposed to the entire spirit of the Scriptures, and to those special texts above quoted.

6. *State the view as to the nature of the divine agency involved in* PRESERVATION, *which stands at the opposite extreme to the above.*

The extreme position opposite to the Deistical one above stated is that Preservation is a continued creation. That creatures or second causes have no real continuous existence, but are reproduced every successive moment out of nothing, in their respective successive states, conditions, and actions by the perpetual efflux of the "vis creatrix" of God. Thus the state or action of any created thing in one moment of time has no causal relation to its state or action in another moment, but the sole, perpetual, and immediate cause of all that exists is God himself.

The foundations of this doctrine were first laid by Des Cartes in his views of the relation of the creation to the Creator, viewing the former as sustained by the latter by a continued creation. These views were pushed to the furthest extreme consistent with Theism by Malebranche, in the doctrine of "Occasional Causes," and of "our seeing all things in God," and were carried to their legitimate, logical conclusion, in absolute pantheism by Spinoza.—Morell's "Hist. of Modern Philosophy," Part I., ch. 2, § 1.

President Edwards teaches the same doctrine incidentally in his great work on "Original Sin," Part IV., ch. 3. He says that the existence either of the substance, or of the mode, or of the action of any created thing in any one moment of time has no causal connection with its existence, state, or action the next moment. He says that what we call "course of nature is nothing separate from the agency of God." He illustrates his doctrine thus: "The images of things in a glass, as we keep our eye upon them, seem to remain precisely the same, with a continuing perfect identity. But it is known to be otherwise. Philosophers well know that these images are constantly renewed, by the impression and reflection of new rays of light; so that the image impressed by former rays is constantly vanishing, and a new image impressed by new rays every moment, both on the glass and on the eye . . . . The image that exists this moment is not at all derived from the image which existed the last preceding moment . . . . the past existence of the image has no influence to uphold it so much as for one moment . . . So it is with bodies as well as images . . . . their present existence is not, strictly speaking, the effect of their past existence, but it is wholly, every instant, the effect of a new agency, or exertion of the powerful cause of their existence."

7. *Show that this doctrine is false and dangerous.*

1st. If God is continually creating anew every creature in every moment of time in its successive states and actions, and if the state or act of the creature in one moment has no causal relation to its state or act in the next moment, it is evident that second causes are only modifications of the First Cause, and that God is the only real Agent in the universe, and the immediate and sole cause of whatever comes to pass. This obviously logically involves Pantheism, and as a historical fact leads to its adoption.

2d. It is inconsistent with our original and necessary intuitions of truth of all kinds, physical, intellectual, and moral. Our original intuitions assure us of the real and permanent existence of spiritual and material substances exercising powers, and of our own spirits as real, self-determining causes of action, and consequently as responsible moral agents. But if this doctrine is true these primary, constitutional intuitions of our nature deceive us, and if these deceive us, the whole universe is an illusion, our own natures a delusion, and absolute skepticism inevitable.

3d. It immediately cuts up by the roots the foundations of free agency, moral accountability, moral government, and hence of religion.

8. *State the several points in the true doctrine of Providential Preservation.*

The true view stands intermediate between the two extremes above stated. It involves the following propositions:

1st. Created substances, both spiritual and material, possess real and permanent existence, *i. e.*, they are real entities.

2d. They possess all such active or passive properties as they have been severally endowed with by God.

3d. The properties or active powers have a real, and not

merely apparent, efficiency as second causes in producing the effects proper to them; and the phenomena alike of consciousness and of the outward world are really produced by the efficient agency of second causes, as we are informed by our native and necessary intuitions.

4th. But these created substances are not self-existent, *i. e.*, the ground of their continued existence is in God and not in themselves.

5th. They continue to exist not merely in virtue of a negative act of God, whereby he merely does not will their destruction, but in virtue of a positive, continued exercise of divine power, whereby they are sustained in being, and in the possession of all their properties and powers with which God has endowed them.

6th. The precise nature of the divine action concerned in upholding all things in being and action is, like every mode of the intercourse of the infinite with the finite, inscrutable—but not more mysterious in this case than in every other.—Dr. Charles Hodge's "Lectures."

9. *How may the Scriptural doctrine of Providential* GOVERNMENT *be stated?*

God having from eternity absolutely decreed whatsoever comes to pass, and having in the beginning created all things out of nothing by the word of his power, and continuing subsequently constantly present to every atom of his creation, upholding all things in being and in the possession and exercise of all their properties, he ALSO continually controls and directs the actions of all his creatures thus preserved, so that while he never violates the law of their several natures, he yet infallibly causes all actions and events singular and universal to occur according to the eternal and immutable plan embraced in his decree. There is a design in providence. God has chosen his great end, the manifestation of his own glory, but in order to that end he has chosen innumerable subordinate ends; these are fixed; and he has appointed all actions and events in their several relations as means to those ends; and he continually so directs the actions of all creatures that all these general and special ends are brought to pass precisely at the time, by the means, and in the mode and under the conditions, which he from eternity proposed.

Turretin, L. 6, Quæs. 1, says, "The term Providence embraces three things πρόγνωσιν, πρόθεσιν et διοίκησιν—the cognition of the mind, the decree of the will, and the efficacious administration of the things decreed—knowledge directing, will commanding, and power executing. . . . Hence Providence may be regarded either in the antecedent decree, or in the subsequent execution; the *first* is the eternal destination of all things to their appointed ends; the *second* is the temporal government of all things according to that decree; the *first* is an act immanent *within* God; the second is an act transient *out of* God. We here treat for the most part of Providence in the *second* sense of the term."

"Conf. of Faith," Chap. v.; "L. Cat.," Q. 18; "S. Cat.," Q. 11.

10. *State the proof of the fact of such a universal Government derived from a consideration of the divine perfections.*

1st. The stupendous fact that God is infinite in his being, in his relation to time and space, and in his wisdom and power, makes it evident that a universal providence is possible to him, and that all the difficulties and apparent contradictions involved therein to the eye of man are to be referred to our very limited capacity of understanding.

2d. God's infinite wisdom makes it certain that he had a definite object in view in the creation of the universe, and that he will not fail in the use of the best means to secure that object in all its parts.

3d. His infinite goodness makes it certain that he would not leave his sensitive and intelligent creatures to the toils of a mechanical, soulless fate; nor his religious creatures to be divorced from himself, in whose communion their highest life consists.

4th. His infinite righteousness makes it certain that he will continue to govern and reward and punish those creatures which he has made subject to moral obligations.

11. *State the argument derived from the innate religious constitution of mankind.*

The religious sentiment when analyzed is found to embrace (*a*) a sense of absolute dependence, and (*b*) a sense of immediate moral accountability. The *sense of absolute* dependence naturally and actually leads all men of all nations and conditions to cling to the conviction of the immediate presence and providential control of God throughout the universe and in every event. To be without God in the world is to be in a condition in which the elementary demands of human nature are denied. The sense of moral accountability leads all men to believe in a universal and supreme moral government present in the world, protecting the good, and restraining and punishing the wicked. If God is not actually and immediately present in nature and in human history, then we can not know him, and he neither controls nor protects us, and hence obedience is neither due nor possible, and morality, religion, and prayer are all alike vain delusions.

12. *State the argument from the intelligence evinced in the operations of nature.*

The great inductive argument for the being of God is based upon the evident traces of design in the universe. Now, just as the traces of design in the *constitution* of nature proves the existence of a designing mind in the relation of creator, so the traces of design in the *operations* of nature prove the existence of a designing mind in the relation of providential ruler.

The material elements, with their active properties, are all incapable of design, yet we find all these elements so adjusted in all their proportions and relations as to work harmoniously in the order of certain general laws, and we find these general laws so adjusted in all their intricate coincidences and interferences, as, by movements simple and complex, fortuitous and regular, to work out harmoniously everywhere the most wisely and beneficently contrived results. The mechanical and chemical properties of material atoms; the laws of vegetable and animal life; the movements of the sun, moon, and stars in the heavens; the luminous, calorific, and chemical radiance of the sun; and the instinctive and voluntary movement of every living thing upon the face of the earth, are all mutually acting and reacting without concert or possible design of their own; yet everywhere bringing forth the most wise and beneficent results. As the designing mind can not be found in any of the elements it, of course, can not be found in the resultant of the whole together. It can be looked for only in a present personal God, all-wise and all-powerful, who directs all things by the present exercise of his intelligent power in and through the creature.

13. *How may this doctrine be established by the evidence afforded by the general history of the world?*

If the *constitution* of human nature (soul and body), in its elemental relations to human society, proves a designing mind in the relation of creator, exactly so must the wisely contrived *results* of human association, in general and in individual instances, prove the exercise of a designing mind in the relation of providential ruler.

Individual men and communities, it is true, differ in their action from the elements of the external world, inasmuch as they act, 1st, freely, self-moved; and 2d, from design. Yet so narrow is the sphere both of the foresight and the design of every individual agent, so great is the multiplicity of agents, and the complications of interacting influences upon each community from within, from every other community, and from the powers of external nature, that the designs of either individuals or communities are never carried beyond a short distance, when they are lost in the general current, the result of which lies equally beyond the foreknowledge and the control of all. But the student of history, with the key of revelation, clearly discerns the traces of a general design running through all the grand procedures of human history, and at points even visibly linking itself with the actions of individual agents. God's providence, as a whole, therefore, comprehends and controls the little providences of men.

14. *State the Scriptural argument from the prophecies, promises, and threatenings of God.*

In innumerable instances has God in the Scriptures prophesied with great particularity the certain occurrence of an event absolutely, and he has promised or threatened the occurrence of other events contingently upon certain conditions. This would be a mockery, if God did not use the means to fulfil his word.

It is not reasonable to object that God simply foresaw the event, and so prophesied, promised, or threatened it, because the event is frequently promised or threatened contingently, upon a condition which does not stand in the relation of a cause to that event. God could not foresee one event as contingent upon another which sustains no causal relation to it. The truth of the promise or threatening in such a case can not depend upon the natural connection between the two events, but upon God's determination to cause one to follow the other.

15. *Prove from Scripture that the providence of God extends over the natural world.*

Ps. civ. 14; cxxxv. 5–7; cxlvii. 8–18; cxlviii. 7, 8; Job ix. 5, 6; xxi. 9–11; xxxvii. 6–13; Acts xiv. 17.

16. *Prove from Scripture that it includes the brute creation.*

Ps. civ. 21–29; cxlvii. 9; Matt. vi. 26; x. 29.

17. *Prove from Scripture that it extends to the general affairs of men.*

1 Chron. xvi. 31; Ps. xlvii. 7; lxvi. 7; Prov. xxi. 1; Job xii. 23; Isa. x. 12–15; Dan. ii. 21; iv. 25.

18. *Show from Scripture that the circumstances of individuals are controlled by God.*

1 Sam. ii. 6; Ps. xviii. 30; Prov. xvi. 9; Isa. xlv. 5; Luke i. 53; James iv. 13–15.

19. *Prove that events considered by us fortuitous are subject to the control of God.*

1st. A fortuitous event is one whose proximate causes, because either of their complexity or their subtlety, escape our observation. Every such event, however, as the falling of a leaf, is linked with the general system of things, both by its antecedents and its consequences.

2d. Scripture affirms the fact.—Ex. xxi. 13; Ps. lxxv. 6, 7; Job v. 6; Prov. xvi. 33.

20. *What distinction has been made between a general and a special providence, and what is the true view of the subject?*

Many men admit that God exercises a general superintending Providence over affairs, controlling the general current, and determining great and important events, while they regard it superstitious and derogatory to the sublime dignity and greatness of God to conceive of him as interesting himself in every trivial detail. Many who do not clearly understand themselves feel and practically judge of all events in their relation to divine Providence in like manner.

But this whole mode of conception and feeling springs from a very low anthropomorphic view of God's attributes and manner of action, as if there could be with the absolute Cause and the infinite Ruler the same difference between little things and great things as there is with us; as if to him, as to us, a multitude of details were more burdensome, or less worthy of attention, than some grand result. A general and a special Providence can not be two different modes of divine operation. The same providential administration is necessarily at the same time general and special for the same reason, because it reaches without exception equally to every event and creature in the world. A General Providence is special because it secures general results by the control of every event, great and small, leading to that result. A Special Providence is general because it specially controls all individual beings and actions in the universe. All events are so related together as a concatenated system of causes, and effects, and conditions, that a general Providence that is not at the same time special is as inconceivable as a whole which has no parts, or as a chain which has no links.

21. *Prove that the providential government of God extends to the free acts of men.*

1st. The free actions of men are potent causes influencing the general system of things precisely as all other classes of causes in the world, and consequently, on the principle indicated in the answer to the preceding question, they also must be subject to God, or every form of providence whatever would be impossible for him.

2d. It is affirmed in Scripture.—Ex. xii. 36; 1 Sam. xxiv. 9–15; Ps. xxxiii. 14, 15; Prov. xvi. 1; xix. 21; xx. 24; xxi. 1; Jer. x. 23; Phil. ii. 13.

22. *Show from Scripture that God's providence is exercised over the sinful acts of men.*

2 Sam. xvi. 10; xxiv. 1; Ps. lxxvi. 10; Rom. xi. 32; Acts iv. 27, 28.

23. *What do the Scriptures teach as to God's providential agency in the good acts of men.*

The Scriptures attribute all that is good in man to the free grace of God, operating both providentially and spiritually, and influencing alike the body and the soul, and the outward relations of the individual.—Phil. ii. 13, iv. 13; 2 Cor. xii. 9, 10; Eph. ii. 10; Gal. v. 22–25.

It is to be remembered, however, that while a material cause may be analyzed into the mutual interaction of two or more bodies, a human soul acts spontaneously, *i. e.*, originates action. The soul also, in all its voluntary acts, is determined by its own prevailing dispositions and desires.

When all the good actions of men, therefore, are attributed to God, it is not meant, 1st, that he causes them, or, 2d, that he determines man to cause them, irrespectively of man's free will; but it is meant that God so acts upon man from within spiritually, and from without by moral influences, as to induce the free disposition. He works in us first to will, and then to do his good pleasure.

24. *What do the Scriptures teach as to the relation of Providence to the sinful acts of men?*

The Scriptures teach—

1st. The sinful acts of men are in such a sense under the divine control that they occur only by his permission and according to his purpose.—I Chron. i. 4–14; Gen. xlv. 5 and l. 20. Compare 1 Sam. vi. 6 and Ex. vii. 13 and xiv. 17; Is. lxvi. 4; 2 Thess. ii. 11; Acts iv. 27, 28; ii. 23; iii. 18.

2d. He restrains and controls sin.—Ps. lxxvi. 10; Gen. l. 20; Is. x. 15.

3d. He overrules it for good.—Gen. l. 20; Acts iii. 13.

4th. God neither causes sin, nor approves it, he only permits, directs, restrains, limits, and overrules it. Man, the free agent, is the sole responsible and guilty cause of his own sin. Turretin sets forth the testimony of Scripture upon this subject thus—

1st. *As to the beginning of the sin,* (1.) God freely permits it. But this permission is neither *moral, i. e.,* while permitting it physically, he never approves it; nor merely *negative, i. e.,* he does not simply concur in the result, but he positively determines that bad men shall be permitted for wise and holy ends to act according to their bad natures.—Acts xiv. 16; Ps. lxxxi. 12. (2.) He deserts those who sin, either by withdrawing grace abused, or by withholding additional grace. This desertion may be either (*a*) partial, to prove man's heart (2 Chron. xxxii. 31), or (*b*) for correction, or (*c*) penal (Jer. vii. 29; Rom. i. 24–26). (3) God so orders providential circumstances that the inherent wickedness of men takes the particular course of action he has determined to permit (Acts ii. 23; iii. 18). (4.) God delivers men to Satan, (*a*) as a tempter (2 Thess. ii. 9–11), (*b*) as a torturer (1 Cor. v. 5).

2d. *As to the progress of the sin,* God restrains it as to its intensity and its duration, and as to its influence upon others. This he effects both by internal influences upon the heart, and by the control of external circumstances.—Ps. lxxvi. 10.

3d. *As to the end or result of the sin,* God uniformly overrules it and directs it for good.—Gen. l. 20; Job i. 12; ii. 6–10; Acts iii. 13; iv. 27, 28.

25. *What are the* THREE *general classes in which all theories as to God's Providential Government may be embraced?*

1st. Those views which remove God from all present active agency in the creation, and assert the entire independence of *second causes.* 2d. Those theories which more or less explicitly deny the real agency of second causes and make God the only real agent in the universe. 3d. The middle or Christian view, which maintains *all* the principles on this subject taught in the Scriptures as: The real efficiency of second causes, especially the moral freedom and accountability of man in his acts, and at the same time the universal, efficient control of God, whereby in perfect consistency with the attributes of his own nature, and with the several properties of his creatures, he determines and disposes of all actions and events according to his sovereign purpose.

26. *State the Mechanical Theory of Providence.*

This view supposes that when God created the universe he

endowed all the various material and spiritual elements with their respective properties and powers, that he then grouped them in certain combinations and proportions, and so made them subject to certain general laws. The world is thus a machine, which the maker has so calculated that it works out of itself all his purposes. Having wound it up he leaves it to itself. God is the *first* cause in the sense of his being the first member in an endless series of causes always flowing on further and further from their source. Some of these philosophers confine this rigid mechanism to the physical world, and regard the free wills of men as an absolutely indeterminate element embraced in the general mechanism of the world. The majority however deny free agency, and regard man as one of the cosmical elements not essentially different from the rest.

All providential interferences and all miracles therefore would be impossible. To suppose any necessity for such interferences would be to suppose some radical defect in God's work—that either he must have been incapable of precalculating all necessary combinations, or that he was unable to execute a machine that would run of itself. Prof. Baden Powel says, "It is derogatory to the idea of infinite power and wisdom to suppose an order of things so imperfectly established that it must be occasionally interrupted and violated." And Theodore Parker says, "Men have their precarious make-shifts; the Infinite has no tricks, no subterfuges—not a whim in God, and so not a miracle in nature."

27. *Expose the fallacy of that view.*

1st. It is opposed to the plain teaching of God's word as set forth under Questions 15–24. 2d. It is essentially irreligious, and materialistic. It fails to recognize the education and discipline of free intelligent agents as the great end to which the universe as a system of means is adapted. It separates the souls of men from God, it makes prayer a mockery, revelation impossible, moral accountability a prejudice, and religion a delusion. 3d. It is based on a miserably shallow anthropomorphic idea of God. It conceives of the universe simply as a mechanical system of causes, and as sustaining the same relation to God that a human work does to its maker, who is necessarily exterior to his work. It utterly fails—1st. To apprehend the real indwelling of the Creator in the creation as an omnipresent, ever-active, and controlling spirit, a personal agent making law by working through law for the purpose of accomplishing elected ends. 2d. To apprehend the true nature of the universe in relation to its highest ends as a moral system designed for the instruction and development of free, personal, moral agents, created in the image of God.

A system involving an established order of nature, and proceeding in wise adaptation of means to ends, is necessary as a means of communication between the Creator and the intelligent creation, and to accomplish the intellectual and moral education of the latter. Thus only can the divine attributes of wisdom, righteousness, or goodness be exercised or manifested, and thus only can angel or man understand the character, anticipate the will, or intelligently and voluntarily co-operate with the plan of God.

Occasional direct exercises of power, moreover, in connection with a general system of means and laws, appears to be necessary not only "in the beginning," to create second causes and inaugurate their agency, but also subsequently, in order to make to the subjects of his moral government the revelation of his free personality, and of his immediate interest in their affairs. At any rate, such occasional direct action and revelation is necessary for the education of man in his present state. A miracle, although effected by divine power without means, is itself a means to an end and part of a plan. All natural law has its birth in the divine reason, and is an expression of will to effect a purpose.—"Reign of Law," by Duke of Argyle. The "order of nature" is only an instrument of the divine will, and an instrument used subserviently to that higher moral government in the interests of which miracles are wrought. Thus the "order of nature," the ordinary providence of God, and miracles, instead of being in conflict, are the intimately correlated elements of one comprehensive system.

28. *What classes of philosophers have actually or virtually denied the real efficiency of second causes?*

All Pantheists, of course, regard all second causes as modifications of the First Cause, and God the only real agent in the universe. Des Cartes, although a believer in God, and in the real objective existence of material as well as spiritual agents, nevertheless held that they were created anew every moment in all their successive states and actions, and so virtually made second causes only a modification of the First Cause. His disciples deduced therefrom the theory of occasional causes, making changes in the second cause merely the occasion upon which the First Cause exercises its efficient agency and accomplishes the effect. This led to the Pantheism of Spinoza. Dr. Emmons, of New England, held in connection with the "exercise scheme" the doctrine of divine efficiency. That we know nothing in the human soul but a series of exercises connected with an obscure thread of consciousness. God is the real cause creating each moment each of these exercises in their successions, the good and the bad alike, just as a musician blows the successive notes on a pipe at his will.

To this class of speculations belongs the theory of "Concursus," which prevailed so long in the Church.

29. *What doctrine was represented by the phrase* "general and indifferent concursus," *and who were its advocates?*

Theologians were occupied during many centuries with debating the question as to the nature of the "concursus," or inflowing and co-working of God in second causes.

The Jesuits, and with them the Socinians and Remonstrants, maintain that this "concursus" is only "general" and "indifferent"; that is, that it is common alike to all causes, quickening them to action, but indifferently, *i. e.*, the first cause is, as it were, a mere general stimulant to the second cause, leaving each one to determine its own particular mode of action. This they illustrate by the general quickening power of the sun, which sheds the same radiance universally and indifferently upon all earthly objects, which radiance is the common principle of all life and all movement. Where this radiance is absent there is no life. Yet it is indifferent to any particular form of life or movement—and every particular germ germinates after its own kind under the quickening power of the same sun.

This theory obviously admits the preservation of the essences and active powers of all things by God, but it virtually denies by omission all real providential *government*. According to *this* view, God created and preserves all things, and they in turn act spontaneously according to their nature and tendencies without his control.

30. *What doctrine was expressed by the phrase* "concursus simultaneous and immediate"?

This phrase expresses an act of God whereby he co-operates with the creature in his act, as a concause, in the production of the act as an entity. In support of this view, and in opposition to the bare admission of the above-explained "concursus general and indifferent," the disciples of Thomas Aquinas in the Roman Church and all the Lutheran and Reformed theologians agreed. The question however remained a point of difficulty and of difference as to which is the *determining* factor in this dual causality. Does God determine the creature in every case to act, and to act as he does and not otherwise, or does the creature determine himself?

31. *What doctrine was expressed by the phrase "*concursus, previous and determining," *and who were its advocates?*

Hence the Reformed or Calvinistic theologians maintained in addition the doctrine of *"Precursus,"* or of a *"*Concursus, previous and• determining." This signified a divine energy acting upon the creature, and in every case determining it to act, and to act precisely as it does. Some applied this to such human actions as are good, others more logically applied it to all actions of every kind whatsoever.

32. *How did the Reformed theologians attempt to reconcile this doctrine with the freedom of man and with the holiness of God?*

As to the freedom of man, they—1st. Pleaded mystery. 2d. They pleaded that the two facts, (*a*) that human action is free, and (*b*) that God efficiently governs that action, are both certainly revealed in Scripture and therefore must be mutually consistent whether we can reconcile them or not. 3d. They argued that the *modus operandi* of this divine concursus in every case varied with the nature of the creature upon which it is exerted, and that it is always perfectly consistent with the nature of that creature, and its modes of action. "Therefore since Providence does not concur with the human will, either by the way of co-action, forcing an unwilling will, nor by the way of a physical determination, as though it were a thing brutish and blind, devoid of all judgment, but rationally by turning the will in a manner congruous to itself that it may determine itself, it follows, that the proximate cause of each man's action being in the judgment of his own understanding, and spontaneous election of his own will, it exerts no constraining force upon our liberty, but rather sustains it."—Turretin, L. 6, Q. 6.

"Moveri voluntarie est moveri ex se, *i. e.,* a principio intrinsico. Sed illud principium intrinsicum potest esse ab alio principio extrinsico. Et sic moveri ex se non repugnat si, quod movetur ex alio. Illud quod movetur ab alio dicitur cogi, si moveatur contra inclinationem propriam; sed si moveatur ab alio quod sibi dat propriam inclinationem, non dicitur cogi. Sic igitur Deus movendo voluntatem non cogit ipsam, quia dat ei ejus propriam inclinationem."—Thomas, Vol. I., 105, 4, quoted by Dr. Charles Hodge.

As to the holiness of God in relation to the sinful acts of his creatures they held: 1st. That sin originates in a defect or privative cause. 2d. That there is a difference between the mere matter of the act as an entity and its moral quality. God is an efficient concause of the former, but not of the latter, if it be evil. They illustrated this by the use of an illy-tuned instrument in the hands of a skilful player. The player is the cause of each of the sounds in their order, but the derangement of the instrument alone is the cause of the discord. 3d. Hence the relation of God's providence to the evil actions of man, is very different from its relation to their good actions. In the case of the latter he gives the grace which communicates the moral quality, as well as co-operates in the production of the action. In the case of the former his concursus is confined to the matter of the act, the sinful quality is derived from the creature only.

33. *State the several objections which lie against this theory of concursus.*

1st. It is an unsuccessful attempt to go beyond the mere facts taught by Scripture in the search of an explanation of the manner in which God acts upon the creature in effecting his ends.

2d. This theory tends to the denial of the real efficiency of second causes, and therefore tends to Pantheism. This was a danger less appreciated by the Great Reformers and their successors of the sixteenth and seventeenth centuries than it has of necessity come to be in our day. It is of the highest importance that we hold both the correlated truths of the real efficiency of second causes, and of the controlling providence of God, of human freedom and of divine sovereignty, and then leave the question of their reconciliation to the future.

34. *How far do the Scriptures teach any thing as to the nature of God's providential government?*

The mode in which the divine agency is exerted is left entirely unexplained, but the fact that God does govern all his creatures and all their actions is expressly stated and everywhere assumed, and many of the characteristics of that government are set forth.

It is declared—

1st. To be universal.—Ps. ciii. 17–19; Dan. iv. 34, 35; Ps. xxii. 28–29.

2d. Particular.—Matt. x. 29–31.

3d. It embraces the thoughts and volitions of men and events apparently contingent.—Prov. xxi. 1; xvi. 9, 33; xix. 21; 2 Chron. xvi. 9.

4th. It is efficacious.—Lam. ii. 17; Ps. xxxiii. 11; Job xxiii. 13.

5th. It is the execution of his eternal purpose, embracing all his works from the beginning in one entire system.—Acts xv. 18; Eph. i. 11; Ps. civ. 24; Isa. xxviii. 29.

6th. Its chief end is his own glory, and subordinately thereto, the highest good of his redeemed church.—Rom. ix. 17; xi. 36; viii. 28.

7th. The Scriptures teach that the manner in which God executes his providential government *must* be consistent with his own perfections, since "God can not deny himself," 2 Tim. ii. 13.

8th. Also congruous with the nature of every creature effected thereby, since all free agents remain free and responsible.

9th. Also that God in the case of the good actions of men gives the grace and the motive, and co-operates in the act from first to last.—Phil. ii. 13. But in the case of the sinful actions of men he simply permits the sinful action, restrains it, and then overrules it for his own glory and the highest good of his creation.

35. *How can the existence of moral and physical evil be reconciled with the doctrine of God's providential government?*

The mystery of the origin and permission of moral evil we can not solve.

As to physical evil, we answer—

1st. That it is never provided for as an end in itself, but always a means to an overbalancing good.

2d. That in its existing relations to moral evil as corrective and punitive, it is justified alike by reason and conscience as perfectly worthy of a wise, righteous, and merciful God.

36. *Show that the apparently anomalous distribution of happiness and misery in this world is not inconsistent with the doctrine of providence.*

1st. Every moral agent in this world has more of good and less of evil than he deserves.

2d. Happiness and misery are much more equally distributed in this world than appears upon the surface.

3d. As a general rule, virtue is rewarded and vice punished even here.

4th. The present dispensation is a season of education, preparation, and trial, and not one of rewards and punishments.— See Ps. lxxiii.

Extraordinary Providences and Miracles.

37. *How do Extraordinary Providences differ from ordinary events in their relation to God's providential control?*

Events like that of the flight of quails, and the draught of fishes, mentioned in Num. xi. 31, 32, and Luke v. 6, *as far as we know*, differ from events occurring under the ordinary providential control of God only in respect to the divinely prearranged conjunction of circumstances. The events are not supernatural, only unusual, and their peculiarity is only that they occur in eminently felicitous conjunction with other events, such as the need of the Israelites, and of the apostles, with which they have no natural connection.

38. *How are miracles designated in the New Testament?*

They are called—(1) τέρατα, wonders, Acts ii. 19; (2) δύνα-μεις, works of superhuman power, and (3) σημεῖα, signs, John ii. 18, Matt. xii. 38. The last designation expresses their true office. They are designed to be "signs" incapable of being counterfeited, of God's commission and authentication of a religious teacher and of his doctrine.

39. *How then is a miracle, in the Scriptural sense of that word, to be defined, so as to signalize its specific distinction from supernatural events in general, and from extraordinary Providences, as above explained?*

A miracle is (1) an event occurring in the physical world, capable of being discerned and discriminated by the bodily senses of human witnesses, (2) of such a character that it can be rationally referred to no other cause than the immediate volition of God, (3) accompanying a religious teacher, and designed to authenticate his divine commission and the truth of his message.

40. *State and answer the à priori objection to the possibility of miracles, that they essentially involve the violation of the laws of nature.*

It is maintained that all experience, and the integrity of human reason, unite in guaranteeing the absolute inviolability of the law of continuity—that every possible event finds its full explanation in adequate causes which precede it, and that every event in its turn causes endless consequences to succeed it. No event can be isolated from its antecedents and consequences, nor from its conditions, and every cause acts according to an intelligible law of its nature.

This is all true, and as true of miracles as of any other events.

If by "law of nature" we mean the physical forces which produce effects, then no miracle involves any suspension or violation of such law. It is a common experience that forces modify each other, and each added force combines with others in producing effects otherwise impossible. If by "law of nature" we mean the ordinary course of events observed in nature, then a miracle is, by definition, a signal suspension of that order. But the same thing is brought about every day by the intervention in nature of the intelligent wills of men.

In every physical event there are a combination of concauses combining to effect it. The human will in acting violates no law, and annihilates no force, it simply combines natural forces under special conditions, and interpolates into the sum of concauses a new concause—the human volition.

When the sons of the prophets "cut down a stick and cast it into the water and the iron of the axe-head did swim" (2 Kings vi. 6), neither the specific gravities of the iron nor of the water were altered, nor was the law of gravitation suspended. The miracle consisted only in a divine volition interpolating a new transient force, equal to the excess of the specific gravity of the iron over that of the water, and acting in a direction opposite to that of gravity. This is precisely analogous to the action of the human will upon physical objects—with this exception—man's will acts upon outward objects only indirectly through the mechanism of his body, and directly only upon his voluntary muscles; while God's will acts directly upon every element of the world he has created. And what is true in this simple miracle could be shown to be true in the most complex ones, such as the raising of Lazarus, if we knew enough of the chemistry and physiology of human life.

John Stuart Mill ("Essay on Theism," Pt. iv.) says, "It may be argued that 'the power of volition over phenomena is itself a law, and one of the earliest known and acknowledged laws of nature. . . . The interference of human will with the course of nature is only not an exception to law, when we include among laws the relation of motive to volition; and by the same rule interference by the divine will would not be an exception either; since we can not but suppose Deity, in every one of his acts, to be determined by motives.' The alleged analogy holds good: but what it proves is only what I have from the first maintained—that divine interference with nature could be proved if we had the same sort of evidence for it which we have for human interferences."

That is, this greatest of all the philosophical rationalists maintains that there is no *à priori* ground to judge miracles impossible. It is purely a question as to the sufficiency of the evidence. Every Christian is perfectly satisfied that the evidence (historical, moral, and spiritual) for the resurrection of

Christ, and the miracles historically associated with that event, is abundantly sufficient.

41. *State and answer the objection to the occurrence of a miracle drawn from the balance of the physical universe.*

It is a fact that the whole physical universe forms one system, and that as at present adjusted it is in a state of such delicate equilibrium that the addition or subtraction of a single atom in any one portion of it would disturb that equilibrium throughout the entire system. A disturbance, however slight, *ab extra*—the intrusion of an agent not belonging to the system of things, would be destructive of the whole.

It is obvious that this objection would have weight if the material universe were an exclusive whole by itself, and if it sustained no constitutional relation to God. But if God and the created world together constitute a whole—a complete universe of things—the objection is absurd. The sum of his activities of every kind is the necessary complement of the sum of the activities of all his creatures, and only thus the equilibrium is maintained.

It is plain that the will of God is no more outside the sum of things constituting the universe than is the will of man. And man is constantly modifying nature over wide areas, and every moment bringing his will as a new concause to act upon the physical laws of the universe *ab extra*, and giving them new directions and conditions.

The equilibrium of the physical universe, moreover, is not a permanent one, but one constantly changing, especially through the diffusion of heat and the massing of matter at the centres of attraction.

42. *State and answer the objection that the assumption of the necessity of miraculous interference is derogatory to the wisdom and power of the Creator.*

It is argued that the skill of a human workman is always exhibited in proportion to the ability of his work to perform its designed function independently of his repair, or correction, or guidance. That the necessity of interference for any purpose *ab extra* is a proof of defect or at least of limitation in the skill or power of the maker. Any occasion for a miracle therefore could only arise, they argue, from a change of purpose on the part of God, or a radical defect upon the part of his creation. Theodore Parker said, "There is no whim in God, and therefore no miracle in nature."

This would have force if miracles were designed to correct

the defective working of the physical universe. But this no Christian has ever dreamed.

The design of a miracle is simply to signify to God's intelligent creatures his active intervention in the moral universe for the purpose of restoring the order disturbed by sin. The *moral* system is essentially different from the physical one. The one is mechanical, the other embraces the reason, conscience, FREE WILL, and the law of motive. Free will makes sin possible, and sin makes direct divine intervention necessary, either to redeem or to damn.

All the miracles of Scripture are grouped around the great crises in the work of Redemption, or the restoration of the original natural law disturbed by sin. Hence the miracles of Scripture, unlike all the miracles of the heathen, or of the Papal Church, or of modern spiritualism, instead of being mere wonders, exhibitions of power, wanton violations of natural order, are pre-eminently works of healing, acts the whole bearing and spirit of which imply the restoration and confirmation, not the violation, of law.

The highest meaning of the word LAW is order, arrangement, assignment of function, to the *end of effecting a purpose.*

The supreme essence of all law, therefore, is the eternal purpose of God. Not a single miraculous intervention was an after-thought. One eternal act of absolutely intelligent volition embraced the whole scheme of being and events in all space and all duration, appointing all ends and all means and all methods at once, the necessary and the free, the physical and the moral, the acts of the creature obeying law, and the interventions of the Creator imposing law.

43. *How can an event actually occurring be certainly recognized as coming under the category of miracles as above defined?*

I. A miracle, according to the foregoing definition, is "an event occurring in the physical world capable of being discerned and certainly discriminated by the bodily senses." The miracles of Scripture fulfil this condition, especially the most important of them. They were exhibited (1) in the clear light of day, (2) on several occasions, (3) under varying circumstances (4) to a number of witnesses, and (5) to the scrutiny of several senses, as of sight, hearing, and touch, mutually corroborating one another.

II. A miracle, by the same definition, must "accompany a religious teacher, and is designed to authenticate his divine commission and the truth of his message." It hence follows that every such event, in order to be credible, must (1) be itself of a character, rationally and morally, congruous with its professedly divine origin. (2.) The character of the religious teacher whose commission it authenticates, and the character of his doctrine, must be such that it is credible that they represent the mind and will of God: (3.) The messenger and his message must be found to be consistent, historically and doctrinally, with the entire organism of preceding revelations and divine interventions.

III. The miracle, in the third place, must be "of such a character that it can be rationally referred to no other cause than the immediate volition of God."

It has been objected at this point that a miracle could not be certainly determined to be such, even if it occur, because— 1st. No man knows all the laws of nature, nor what is the true line between the natural and the supernatural. What is new or inexplicable is relatively supernatural, *i. e.*, by us incapable of being reduced to the categories of nature. 2d. Because evil spirits often have wrought supernatural works—and it is impossible for us, therefore, to determine in any case that the cause of the event can be only a direct volition of God.

WE ANSWER—1st. As far as evil spirits are concerned, the kingdom of Satan can easily be recognized by its character. No isolated event is ever to be recognized as a miracle. The man, and the doctrine, and their relation to the whole system of past revelations and miraculous interventions, will in every case be sufficient to discriminate the identity of the supernatural cause of an event. 2d. As far as the question of determining with certainty what effects transcend the powers of nature, we answer—(1.) There are some classes of effects about which no man can possibly doubt, *e. g.*, the raising of Lazarus, and the multiplying of the loaves and fishes; we may doubt about the exact boundaries of the supernatural—but no man can mistake that which so far transcends the boundaries. (2.) These effects were accomplished two thousand years ago, in an unscientific age, by an unlearned people. (3.) These effects were produced over and over again *at the mere word of command, without the use of any sort of means, or fixed physical conditions.* (4.) The works were divine in character, and the occasions were worthy, the religious teachers and doctrines carried their own corroborative spiritual evidence, and the events fell into their place in the entire system of revelation.

CHAPTER XV.

THE MORAL CONSTITUTION OF THE SOUL, WILL, LIBERTY, ETC.

1. *What general department of theology are we now entering, and what are the principal topics embraced in it?*

The general department of ANTHROPOLOGY, and the principal topics embraced in this department, are the moral constitution of man psychologically considered, the moral condition of man when created, and the providential relations into which man was introduced at his creation,—the nature of sin, the sin of Adam, the effects of his sin upon himself and upon his posterity, and the consequent moral condition and legal relations into which his descendants are introduced at birth.

It is obvious that an accurate understanding of the nature of sin, original or actual, of the influence of divine grace, and of the change wrought in the soul in regeneration, of course involves some previous knowledge of the constitutional faculties of the soul, and especially of those faculties which particularly distinguish man as a moral agent. Hence there are certain psychological and metaphysical questions inseparable from theological discussions.

2. *What is the general principle which it is always necessary to bear in mind while treating of the various faculties of the human soul?*

The soul of man is one single indivisible agent, not an organized whole consisting of several parts; and, therefore, what we call its several faculties are rather the capacity of the one agent, for discharging successively or concurrently the several functions involved, and are never to be conceived of as separately existing parts or organs. These several functions exercised by the one soul are so various and complex, that a minute analysis is absolutely necessary, in order to lay open to us a definite view of their nature. Yet we must carefully remember that a large part of the errors into which philosophers have fallen in their interpretation of man's moral constitution, has resulted from the abuse of this very process of analysis. This is especially true with respect to the interpretation of the voluntary acts of the human soul. In prosecution of his analysis the philosopher comes to recognize *separately* the differences and the likenesses of these various functions of the soul, and too frequently forgets that these functions themselves are, in fact, never exercised in that isolated manner, but concurrently by the one soul, as an indivisible agent, and that thus they always qualify one another. Thus, it is not true, in fact, that the understanding reasons, and the heart feels, and the conscience approves or condemns, and the will decides, as different members of the body work together, or as the different persons constituting a council deliberate and decide in mutual parts; but it is true that the one indivisible, rational, feeling, moral, self-determining soul reasons, feels, approves, or condemns and decides.

The self-determining power of the *will* as an *abstract* faculty is absurd as a doctrine, and would be disastrous as an experience; but the self-determining power of the human soul as a *concrete*, rational, feeling agent, is a fact of universal consciousness, and a fundamental doctrine of moral philosophy and of Christian theology. The real question is not as to the *liberty of the will*, but as to the *liberty of the man in willing*. It is obvious that we are free if we have liberty to will as *we* please, i. e., as upon the whole we judge best, and all things considered desire.

3. How may the leading faculties of the human soul be classified? and which are the seat of our moral nature?

1st. The intellectual. This class includes all those faculties in different ways concerned in the general function of knowing; as the reason, the imagination, the bodily senses, and the moral sense (when considered as a mere source of knowledge informing the understanding).

2d. The emotional. This class includes all those feelings which attend, in any manner, the exercise of the other faculties.

3d. The will.

It will be observed that the functions of the conscience involve faculties belonging to both the first and second classes (see below, Question 5).

It is often asked, Which of our faculties is the seat of our moral nature? Now while there is a sense in which all moral questions concern the relation of the states or acts of the will to the law of God revealed in the conscience, and therefore in which the will and the conscience are pre-eminently the foundation of man's moral nature, it is true, nevertheless, that every one of the faculties of the human soul, as above classified, is exercised in relation to all moral distinctions, e. g., the intellectual in the perception and judgment; the emotional in pleasant feeling or the reverse; the will, in choosing or refusing, and in acting. Every state or act of any one of the faculties of the human soul, therefore, which involves the judging, choosing, refusing, or desiring, upon a purely moral question, or the feeling corresponding thereto, is a moral state or act, and all the faculties, viewed in their relations to the distinction between good and evil, are moral faculties.

4. *What is the Will?*

The term "will" is often used to express the mere faculty of volition, whereby the soul chooses, or refuses, or determines to act, and the exercise of that faculty. It is also used in a wider sense, and in this sense I use it here, to include the faculty of volition, together with all of the spontaneous states of the soul (designated by Sir William Hamilton, "Lectures on Metaphysics," Lect. XI., the faculties of conation, the excitive, striving faculties, possessing, as their common characteristic, "a tendency toward the realization of their end"), the dispositions, affections, desires, which determine a man in the exercise of his free power of volition. It must be remembered, however, that these two senses of the word "will" are essentially distinct. The will, as including all the faculties of conation (the dispositions and desires), is to be essentially distinguished from the single faculty of soul exercised in the resulting volition, i. e., the choosing or the acting according to its prevailing desire.

The term "will" is used in the wider sense in this chapter. A man in willing is perfectly free, i. e., he always exercises volition according to the prevailing disposition or desire of his will at the time. This is the highest freedom, and the only one consistent with rationality or moral responsibility.

5. *Define the term Volition.*

By the term "faculty of volition" we mean the executive faculty of the soul, the faculty of choice or self-decision; and by the term "volition" we mean the exercise of that faculty in any act of choice or self-decision.

6. *What is Conscience?*

Conscience, as a faculty, includes (a) a moral sense or intuition, a power of discerning right and wrong, which, combining with the understanding, or faculty of comparing and judging, judges of the right or wrong of our own moral dispositions and voluntary actions, and of the dispositions and voluntary actions of other free agents. (*b.*) This faculty judges according to a divine law of right and wrong, included within itself (it is a law to itself, the original law written upon the heart, Rom. ii. 14), and (*c*) it is accompanied with vivid emotions, pleasurable in view of that which is right, and painful in view of that which is wrong, especially when our conscience is engaged in reviewing the states or the actions of our own souls. This faculty in its own province is sovereign, and can have no other superior than the revealed word of God.—See M'Cosh, "Divine Government," Book III., chap. i. sec. 4.

7. *What is the true test for determining the moral quality of any mental act or state?*

The only true tests of the moral quality of any state or act are—1st. The inspired word of God, and 2d. The spontaneous, practical, and universal judgments of men.

The moral judgments of men, like all our intuitive judgments, are certainly reliable only when they respect concrete and individual judgments. The generalized and abstract propositions which being supposed to be formed by abstraction and generalization from these individual judgments may be true or not, but they can not be received as a reliable foundation upon which to erect a system of evidence. Very absurd attempts have been often made to demonstrate the moral or non-moral character of any principle, by means of general formularies representing partial truths imperfectly stated, and by means of other,—either false, senseless, or irrelevant,—*à priori* considerations.

8. *Into what classes are the spontaneous affections of the soul to be distributed, and what are the distinguishing characteristics of each class?*

The spontaneous desires and affections of the soul are of two distinct classes. 1st. The *animal*, or those which arise blindly without intelligence, *e. g.*, the appetites and instinctive affections, these have no intrinsic moral quality in themselves, and become the occasion of moral action only when they are restrained or inordinately indulged. 2d. The rational affections and desires called out by objects apprehended by the intellect.

9. *What rational spontaneous affections possess a moral quality, and in what does that quality inherently attach?*

Such rational spontaneous affections are intrinsically and essentially either good or bad or morally indifferent, and their quality is discriminated by the quality of the objects by which they are attracted. They are good when their objects are good, evil when their objects are evil, and morally indifferent when their objects are indifferent. Their moral quality, whatever it be, is intrinsic to them. When they are good, all men consider them worthy of approbation, and when they are evil, all men consider them worthy of condemnation and righteous indignation, because of their essential nature as good or as evil, and without any consideration of their origin. When good these spontaneous affections determine the volitions to good, when they are evil they determine the volitions to evil.

10. *To what do we apply the designation "permanent principles, or dispositions" of soul? and when do they possess a moral character, and what is the source of that character?*

There are in the soul, underlying its passing states and affections, certain permanent habits or dispositions involving a tendency to or facility for certain kinds of exercises. Some of these habits or dispositions are innate and some are acquired. These constitute the character of the man, and lay the foundation for all his successive exercises of feeling, affection, desire, volition, or action. As far as these are morally good, the man and his action are good; as far as these are evil, the man and his action are evil; as far as these are morally indifferent, *i. e.*, concern objects morally indifferent, the actions which spring from them are morally indifferent. The moral character of these inherent moral tendencies of the soul is intrinsic and essential. They are the ultimate tendencies of the soul itself, and their goodness or badness is an ultimate fact of consciousness.

11. *Show that the state and action of the intellect may possess a moral character.*

The intellect is so implicated in its exercises with the moral affections and emotions, that its views and judgments on all moral subjects have a moral character also. A man is hence responsible for his moral judgments—and hence for his beliefs as well as for his moral feelings, because the one is as immediately as the other determined by the general moral state or character of the soul. A man who is blind to moral excellence, or to the deformity of sin, is condemned by every enlightened conscience. The Scriptures pronounce a woe upon those "who call evil good and good evil, who put light for darkness and darkness for light."—Isa. v. 20. Sin is called in Scripture "blindness" and "folly."—1 John ii. 11; Eph. iv. 18; Rev. iii. 17; Matt. xxiii. 17; Luke xxiv. 25.

12. What are the essential conditions of moral responsibility?

To be morally responsible a man must be a free, rational, moral agent (see answer to preceding question). 1st. He must be in present possession of his reason to distinguish truth from falsehood. 2d. He must also have in exercise a moral sense to distinguish right from wrong. 3d. His will, in its volitions or executive acts, must be self-decided, i. e., determined by its own spontaneous affections and desires. If any of these are wanting, the man is insane, and neither free nor responsible.

13. Is the conscience indestructible and infallible?

The conscience, the organ of God's law in the soul, may virtually, i. e., as to its effects and phenomena, be both rendered latent and perverted for a time, and in this phenomenal sense, therefore, it is neither indestructible nor infallible. But if the moral sense be regarded simply in itself it is infallible, and if the total history of even the worst man is taken into the account, conscience is truly indestructible.

1st. As to its *indestructibility*. Conscience, like every other faculty of the soul, is undeveloped in the infant, and very imperfectly developed in the savage; and, moreover, after a long habit of inattention to its voice and violation of its law, the individual sinner is often judicially given up to carnal indifference; his conscience for a time lying latent. Yet it is certain that it is never destroyed—(1.) From the fact that it is often aroused to the most fearful energy in the hearts of long-hardened reprobates in the agonies of remorse. (2.) From the fact that this remorse or accusing conscience constitutes the essential torment of lost souls and devils. This is the worm that never dieth. Otherwise their punishment would lose its moral character.

2d. As to its *infallibility*. Conscience, in the act of judging of moral states or actions, involves the concurrent action of the understanding and the moral sense. This understanding is always fallible, especially when it is prejudiced in its action by depraved affections and desires. Thus, in fact, conscience constantly delivers false decisions from a misjudgment of the facts and relations of the case; it may be through a selfish or sensual or a malignant bias. Hence we have virtually a deceiving as well as a latent conscience. Notwithstanding this, however, the normal sense of the distinction between right and wrong, as an eternal law to itself, lies indestructible even in the most depraved breasts, as it can not be destroyed, so it can not be changed; when aroused to action, and when not deceived as to the true state of the case, its language is eternally the same.—See M'Cosh, "Divine Government," Book III., chapter ii., section 6, and Dr. A. Alexander, "Moral Science," chapters iv. and v.

14. *What is the essential nature of virtue?*

"Virtue is a peculiar quality of" certain states of the will, *i. e.*, either permanent dispositions or temporary affections of the will, and "of certain voluntary actions of a moral agent, which quality is perceived by the moral faculty with which every man is endowed, and the perception of which is accompanied by an emotion which is distinct from all other emotions, and is called moral."—Dr. Alexander, "Moral Science," ch. xxvi.

The essence of virtue is, that it *obliges* the will. If a thing is morally right it *ought* to be done. The essence of moral evil is, that it intrinsically deserves disapprobation, and the agent punishment.

This point is of great importance, because the truth here is often perverted by a false philosophy, and because this view of moral good is the only one consistent with the Scriptural doctrine of sins, rewards, and punishments, and, above all, of Christ's atonement.

The idea of virtue is a simple and ultimate intuition; attempted analysis destroys it. Right is right because it is. It is its own highest reason. It has its norm in the immutable nature of God.

15. *What constitutes a virtuous and what a vicious character?*

Virtue, as defined in the answer to the last question, attaches only to the will of man (including all the conative faculties), 1st, to its permanent disposition; 2d, to its temporary affections; and 3d, to its volitions. Some of these states and actions of the will are not moral, *i. e.*, they are neither approved nor condemned by the conscience as virtuous or vicious. But virtue or vice belong only to moral states of the soul, and to voluntary acts. A virtuous character, therefore, is one in which the permanent dispositions, the temporary affections and desires, and the volitions of the soul, are *conformable to the divine law.*

A vicious character, on the other hand, is one in which these states and acts of the will are not conformable to the divine law.

The acts of volition are virtuous or vicious as the affections or desires by which they are determined are the one or the other. The affections and desires are as the permanent dispositions or the character. This last is the nature of the will itself, and its character is an ultimate unresolvable fact. Whether that character be innate or acquired by habit, the fact of its moral quality as virtuous or vicious remains the same, and the consequent moral accountability of the agent for his character is unchanged.

It must be remembered that the mere possession of a conscience which approves the right and condemns the wrong, and which is accompanied with more or less lively emotion, painful or pleasurable as it condemns or approves, does not make a character virtuous, or else the devils and lost souls would be eminently virtuous. But the virtuous man is he whose *heart and actions*, in biblical language, or whose *dispositions, affections, and volitions*, in philosophical language, are conformed to the law of God.

16. *State both branches of the Utilitarian theory of virtue.*

The *first* and lowest form is that which maintains that virtue consists in the intelligent desire for happiness. Dr. N. W. Taylor says—"Nothing is good but happiness and the means of happiness, and nothing evil but misery and the means of misery."

The *second* and higher form of the Utilitarian theory of virtue is that it consists in disinterested benevolence, and that all sin is a form of selfishness. This is shown, Chapters VIII., XII., and XVIII., to be a defective and therefore a false view.

17. *What do we mean when we say that a man is a free agent?*

1st. That, being a spirit, he originates action. Matter acts only as it is acted upon. A man acts from the spring of his own active power.

2d. That, although a man may be forced by fear to will and to do many things which he would neither will nor do if it were not for the fear, yet he never can be made to will what he does not himself desire to will, in full view of all the circumstances of the case.

3d. That he is furnished with a reason to distinguish between the true and the false, and with a conscience, the organ of an innate moral law, to distinguish between right and wrong, in order that his desires may be both rational and righteous. And yet his desires are not *necessarily* either rational or righteous, but are formed under the light of reason and conscience, either conformable to or contrary to them, according to the permanent, habitual dispositions of the man; *i. e.*, according to his own character.

18. *Show that this attribute of human nature is inalienable.*

A man is said to be free in willing when he wills in conformity with his own prevailing dispositions and desires at the time. A man's judgment may be deceived, or his actions may be coerced, but his will *must be free*, because, if it be truly his *will*, it must be as he desires it to be, in his present state of mind and under all the circumstances of the case at the time.

It hence follows that volition is of its very essence free, whether the agent willing or the act willed be wise or foolish, good or bad.

19. *Do not the Scriptures, however, speak of man's being under the bondage of corruption, and his liberty as lost?*

As above shown, a man is always free in every responsible volition, as much when he chooses, in violation of the law of God and conscience, as in conformity to it. In the case of unfallen creatures, and of perfectly sanctified men, however, the permanent state of the will, the voluntary affections and desires (in Scripture language, the heart), are conformed to the light of reason and the law of conscience within, and to the law of God, in its objective revelation. There are no conflicting principles then within the soul, and the law of God, instead of coercing the will by its commands and threatenings, is spontaneously obeyed. This is "the liberty of the sons of God;" and the law becomes the "royal law of liberty" when the law in the heart of the subject perfectly corresponds with the law of the moral Governor.

In the case of fallen men and angels, on the other hand, the reason and conscience, and God's law, are opposed by the governing dispositions of the will; and the agent, although free, because he wills as he chooses, is said to be in bondage to an evil nature, and "the servant of sin," because he is impelled by his corrupt dispositions to choose that which he sees and feels to be wrong and injurious, and because the threatenings of God's law tend to coerce his will through fear.

The Scriptures do not teach that the unregenerate is not free in his sin, for then he would not be responsible. But the contrast between the liberty of the regenerate and the bondage of the unregenerate arises from the fact that in the regenerate the habitually controlling desires and tendencies are not in conflict with the voice of conscience and the law of God. The unregenerate, viewed psychologically, is free when he sins, because he wills as upon the whole he desires; but viewed theologically, in his relation to God's law as enforced by reason and conscience and Scripture, he may be said to be in bondage to the evil dispositions and desires of his own heart, which he sees to be both wrong and foolish, but which, nevertheless, he is impotent to change.

20. *What is the distinction between liberty and ability?*

Liberty consists in the power of the agent to will as he pleases, from the fact that the volition is determined only by the character of the agent willing. Ability consists in the power of the agent to change his own subjective state, to make himself prefer what he does not prefer, and to act in a given case in opposition to the coexistent desires and preferences of the agent's own heart.

Thus man is as truly free since the fall as before it, because he wills as his evil heart pleases. But he has lost all ability to obey the law of God, because his evil heart is not subject to that law, neither can he change it.

21. *Give Turretin's and President Edwards' definitions of Liberty.*

Turretin, L. 10, Quæs. 1.—"As only three things are found in the soul besides its essence, namely, *faculties*, *habits* (habitus), *acts*, so will (arbitrium) in the common opinion is regarded as an act of the mind; but here it properly signifies neither an act nor a *habit* which may be separated from an individual man, and which also determines him to one at least of two contraries; but it signifies a faculty, not one which is vegetative nor sensuous, common to us and the brutes, in which there can be no place for either virtue or vice, but a rational faculty, the possession of which does not indeed constitute us either good or bad, but through the states of which, and actions, we are capable of becoming either good or bad."

Quæs. 3.—"Since, therefore, the essential nature of liberty does not consist in indifference, it can not be found in any other principle than in (*lubentia rationali*) a rational willingness or desire, whereby a man does what he prefers or chooses from a previous judgment of the reason (*facit quod lubet prævio rationis judicio*). Hence two elements united are necessary to constitute this liberty. (1.) τὸ προαιρετικὸν (the purpose), so that what is done is not determined by a blind, and certain brutish impulse, but ἐκ προαιρέσεως, and from a previous illumination by the reason, and from a practical judgment of the intellect. (2.) τὸ ἑκούσιον (the spontaneous), so that what is done is determined spontaneously and freely and without coaction."

President Edwards "On the Will," Section 5, defines Liberty as being "the power, opportunity, or advantage, that any one has to do as he pleases."

19

22. *What are the two senses in which the word motive, as influencing the will, is used? and in which sense is it true that the volition is always as the strongest motive?*

1st. A motive to act may be something *outside the soul itself*, as the value of money, the wishes of a friend, the wisdom or folly, the right or the wrong, of any act in itself considered, or the appetites and impulses of the body. In this sense it is evident that the man does not always act according to the motive. What may attract one man may repel another, or a man may repel the attraction of an outward motive by the superior force of some consideration drawn from within the soul itself. So that the dictum is true, "The man makes the motive, and not the motive the man."

2d. A motive to act may be the state of the man's own mind, as desire or aversion in view of the outward object, or motive in the first sense. This internal motive evidently must sway the volition, and as clearly it can not in the least interfere with the perfect freedom of the man in willing, since the internal motive is only the man himself desiring, or the reverse, according to his own disposition or character.

23. *May there not be several conflicting desires, or internal motives, in the mind at the same time, and in such a case how is the will decided?*

There are often several conflicting desires, or impelling affections, in the mind at the same time, in which case the strongest desire, or the strongest group of desires, drawing in one way, determine the volition. That which is strongest proves itself to be such only by the result, and not by the intensity of the feeling it excites. Some of these internal motives are very vivid, like a thirst for vengeance, and others calm, as a sense of duty, yet often the calm motive proves itself the strongest, and draws the will its own way. This, of course, must depend upon the character of the agent. It is this inward contest of opposite principles which constitutes the warfare of the Christian life. It is the same experience which occasions a great part of that confusion of consciousness which prevails among men with respect to the problem of the will and the conditions of free agency. Man often acts against motives, but never without motive. And the motive which actually determines the choice in a given case may often be the least clearly defined in the intellect, and the least vividly experienced in the feelings. Especially in sudden surprises, and in cases of trivial concernment, the volition is constantly determined by vague impulses, or by force of habit almost automatically. Yet in every case, if the whole contents of the mind, at the time of the volition, be brought up into distinct consciousness, it will be found that the man chose, as upon the whole view of the case presented by the understanding at the instant he desired to choose.

24. *If the immediately preceding state of the man's mind certainly determines the act of his will, how can that act be truly free if certainly determined?*

This objection rests solely upon the confusion of the two distinct ideas of liberty of the will as an abstract faculty, and liberty of the man who wills. The man is never determined to will by any thing without himself. He always himself freely gives, according to his own character, all the weight to the external influences which bear upon him that they ever possess. But, on the other hand, the mere act of volition, abstractly considered, is determined by the present mental, moral, and emotional state of the man at the moment he acts. His rational freedom, indeed, consists, not in the uncertainty of his act, but in the very fact that his whole soul, as an indivisible, knowing, feeling, moral agent, determines his own action as it pleases.

25. *Prove that the certainty of a volition is in no degree inconsistent with the liberty of the agent in that act.*

1st. God, Christ, and saints in glory, are all eminently free in their holy choices and actions, yet nothing can be more certain than that, to all eternity, they shall always will according to righteousness.

2d. Man is a free agent, yet of every infant, from his birth, it is absolutely certain that if he lives he will sin.

3d. God, from eternity, foreknows all the free actions of men as certain, and he has foreordained them, or made them to be certain. In prophecy he has infallibly foretold many of them as certain. And in regeneration his people are made "his workmanship created unto good works, which God has before ordained that we should walk in them."

4th. Even we, if we thoroughly understand a friend's character, and all the present circumstances under which he acts, are often absolutely certain how he will freely act, though absent from us. This is the foundation of all human faith, and hence of all human society.

26. *What is that theory of moral liberty, styled "Liberty of Indifference," "Self-determining Power of the Will," "Power of Contrary Choice," "Liberty of Contingency," etc., held by Arminians and others?*

This theory maintains that it is essentially involved in the idea of free agency—1st. That the will of man in every volition may decide in opposition, not only to all outward inducements, but equally to all the inward judgments, desires, and to the whole coexistent inward state of the man himself. 2d. That man is conscious in every free volition, that he might have willed precisely the opposite, his outward circumstances and his entire inward state remaining the same. 3d. That every free volition is contingent, *i. e.*, uncertain, until the event, since it is determined by nothing but the bare faculty of volition on the part of the agent.—Hamilton's "Reid," pp. 599–624.

The true theory of moral certainty, on the other hand, is that the soul is a unit; that the will is not self-determined, but that man, when he wills, is self-determined; and that his volition is certainly determined by his own internal, rational, moral, emotional state at the time, viewed as a whole.

In opposition to the former theory, and in favor of the latter, we argue—1st. That the character of the agent does certainly determine the character of his free acts, and that the certainty of an act is not inconsistent with the liberty of the agent in his act.—See above, Question 12.

2d. The Christian doctrines of divine foreknowledge, foreordination, providence, and regeneration. For the Scriptural evidence of these, see their respective chapters. They all show that the volitions of men are neither uncertain nor indeterminate.

3d. We agree with the advocates of the opposite theory in maintaining that in every free act we are conscious that we had power to perform it, or not to perform it, as we chose. "But we maintain that we are none the less conscious that this intimate conviction that we had power not to perform an act is conditional. That is, we are conscious that the act might have been otherwise, had other views or feelings been present to our minds, or been allowed their due weight. A man can not prefer against his preference, or choose against his choice. A man may have one preference at one time, and another at another. He may have various conflicting feelings or principles in action at the same time, but he can not have coexisting opposite preferences."

4th. The theory of the "self-determining power of the will" regards the will, or the mere faculty of volition, as isolated from the other faculties of the soul, as an independent agent within an agent. Now, the soul is a unit. Consciousness and Scripture alike teach us that the *man* is the free, responsible agent. By this dissociation of the volitional faculty from the moral dispositions and desires, the volitions can have no moral character. By its dissociation from the reason, the volitions can have no rational character. If they are not determined by the inward state of the man himself, they must be fortuitous, and beyond his control. He can not be free if his will is independent alike of his head and his heart, and he ought not to be held responsible.—See "Bib. Rep.," January, 1857, Article V.

27. *Why is a man responsible for his outward actions; why for his volitions; why for his affections and desires; and prove that he is responsible for his affections?*

"A man is responsible for his outward acts, because they are determined by the will; he is responsible for his volitions, because they are determined by his own principles and feelings (desires); he is responsible for his principles and feelings, because of their inherent nature as good or bad, and because they are his own and constitute his character."—"Bib. Rep.," January, 1857, p. 130.

It is the teaching of Scripture and the universal judgment of men, that "a good man out of the good treasures of his heart bringeth forth that which is good," and that a "wicked man out of the evil treasures of his heart bringeth forth that which is evil." The act derives its moral character from the state of the heart from which it springs, and a man is responsible for the moral state of his heart, whether that state be innate, formed by regenerating grace, or acquired by himself, because—1st. Of the obliging nature of moral right, and the ill desert of sin; 2d. Because a man's affections and desires are himself loving or refusing that which is right. It is the judgment of all, that a profane or malignant man is to be reprobated, no matter how he became so.

28. *How does Dr. D. D. Whedon state and contrast the position of Arminian and Calvinistic philosophy?*

Dr. Whedon, in the "Bibliotheca Sacra," April, 1862, says, "To this maxim, that it is no matter how we come by our evil volitions, dispositions, or nature in order to responsibility, provided that we really possess them, we (the Methodists) oppose the counter maxim that *in order to responsibility for a given act or state, power in the agent for a contrary act or state is requisite.* In other words *power underlies responsibility.*" The only limit which he admits to this principle is the case of an inability induced by the *free act of the agent himself.* This, he says, is a fundamental maxim by which all the issues between Arminianism and Calvinism are determined.

29. *Show that the Arminian view leads to consequences inconsistent with the gospel, and that the Calvinistic view is true.*

Dr. Whedon admits that Adam after his fall lost all ability to obey the law of God, and was responsible for that inability and all its consequences, because, having been created with full ability, he lost it by his own free act. He also admits that every child of Adam is born into the world with a corrupt nature, and without any ability to obey the law of God. But no infant is responsible nor punishable for *this* want of ability nor for any sinful action which results from it, because it was entailed upon him, without any fault of his own, by the sin of another. In the way of just compensation, however, for this their great misfortune of being innocent sinners, God gives to all men in Christ sufficient grace, and hence gracious ability to obey the gospel law. If a man uses this gracious ability he is saved, and faith and evangelical obedience is accounted for perfect righteousness; *if he does not use this gracious ability* he is condemned as responsible for that abuse of ability, and consequently responsible for all the sinful feelings, actions, and subsequent inability which result from that abuse of power.

We argue that it follows from this Arminian view—1st. That salvation by Christ is not of free grace, but a tardy and incomplete compensation granted men for undeserved evils brought upon them at their birth in consequence of Adam's sin. 2d. The "grace" given to all men is as necessary to render them punishable sinners, as it is to save their souls. In fact, according to this principle, grace sends more souls to hell by making them responsible through the possession of ability, than it sends to heaven through faith in Christ. 3d. Those who die in infancy, not being punishable, because not responsible, for original sin, go to heaven as a matter of natural right.

On the contrary we maintain that the responsibility of a man for his moral dispositions, affections, and desires, no matter how they may have originated, if he be a sane man, is an ultimate fact of consciousness, confirmed by Scripture, conscience, and the universal judgments of men. An act derives its moral character from the state of the heart from which it springs, but the state of the heart does not acquire its moral character from the action. But the moral quality of the state of the heart itself is inherent, and moral responsibility is inseparable from moral quality.

This is so—1st. Because of the essential nature of right and wrong. The essence of right is that it *ought* to be—that it *obliges* the will. The essence of wrong is that it *ought not* to be —that the will is under obligation to the contrary, and that the doing of it involves *ill desert.* 2d. Because a man's moral affections or desires are nothing other than the man himself loving or abhorring goodness. It is the judgment of all men that a profane and malignant man is to be reprobated no matter how he became so. It is the character, not the origin, of the moral disposition of the heart which is the real question. Christ says, "A good man out of the good treasure of his heart bringeth forth that which is good, and a wicked man out of the evil treasure of his heart bringeth forth that which is evil."—Luke vi. 45

CHAPTER XVI.

CREATION AND ORIGINAL STATE OF MAN.

1. *State the evidence that the human race was originated by an immediate creation by God.*

1st. This is explicitly taught in the Bible.—Gen. i. 26, 27; ii. 7

2d. It is implied by the immeasurable gulf which separates man in his lowest savage condition from the very nearest order of the lower creation; indicating an amazing superiority in respect to qualities in which the two are comparable, and an absolute difference of kind in respect to man's intellectual, moral, and religious nature, and capacity for indefinite progress. Even Prof. Huxley, who rashly maintains an extreme position with regard to the anatomical relations of man to the inferior animals, admits that when man's higher nature is taken into the account there exists between him and the nearest beast "an enormous gulf, a divergence immeasurable and practically infinite."—" Primeval Man," by the Duke of Argyle.

3d. It is implied by the fact revealed in the Scriptures and realized in history, that man was destined to exercise universal dominion over all other creatures and over the system of nature. Therefore he could not be a mere product of nature. One of a series of co-ordinate beings.

4th. It is implied by the fact that men are called "sons of God," and in the whole scheme of Providence and Redemption are treated as such. It is universally testified to by man's moral and religious nature, all the more strongly the more these elements of his nature are enlightened and developed. And the fact is pre-eminently signalized by the assumption of our nature into personal union with the Godhead.

It is obvious that as the intellectual, moral, religious, and social natures and habits of men are transmitted by natural descent just as much as their anatomical structure, it is not only arbitrary but absurd to leave out of view the one set of elements, while retaining the other, in any scientific investigation of the question of his origin, or of his place and relations in the order of nature.

2. *Give the present state of the question as to the antiquity of the human race.*

1st. The Scriptures and the entire body of the results of modern science agree in teaching that man came into being on this earth the last of all its organized inhabitants. There has been no new species introduced since the advent of man.

2d. From the *prima facie* indications afforded in the incomplete historical and genealogical records of the pre-Abrahamic period found in the first chapters of Genesis, the generally received systems of biblical chronology have been constructed. The shorter system, constructed by Usher from the Hebrew Text, fixes the date of the creation of man about 4,000 years before the birth of Christ, or about 6,000 years ago. The longer system, constructed by Hales and others from the Septuagint and Josephus, makes the date of the creation of man about 5,500 years before Christ, or about 7,500 years ago.

Of these biblical systems of chronology, Prof. W. H. Green, D.D., of Princeton, says, ("Pentateuch Vindicated," n. p. 128)— "It must not be forgotten that there is an element of uncertainty in a computation of time which rests upon genealogies as the sacred chronology so largely does. Who is to certify us that the antediluvian and ante-Abrahamic genealogies have not been condensed in the same manner as the post-Abrahamic. If Matthew omitted names from the ancestry of our Lord in order to equalize the three great periods over which he passes, may not Moses have done the same in order to bring out seven generations from Adam to Enoch, and ten from Adam to Noah? Our current chronology is based upon the *prima facie* impression of these genealogies. This we shall adhere to until we shall see good reason for giving it up. But if these recently discovered indications of the antiquity of man, over which scientific circles are now so excited, shall, when carefully inspected and thoroughly weighed, demonstrate all that any have imagined they might demonstrate, what then? They will simply show that the popular chronology is based upon a wrong interpretation, and that a select and partial register of ante-Abrahamic names has been mistaken for a complete one."

3d. Modern research has developed a vast and constantly increasing amount of evidence that the human race has existed upon the earth many centuries longer than is allowed for even by the chronology of the Septuagint. The principal classes of evidence upon this point are as follows.

(1.) Ethnological Pictures, showing that all the divergent peculiarities of the Caucasian and African types were fully developed as they now exist, nineteen hundred years before Christ, are found on the Egyptian Monuments. In all historic time no changes of climate or habit have produced appreciable changes in any variety of the race, therefore, we must conclude that many centuries as well as great changes were requisite to make such great permanent variations in the descendants of the same pair. The Duke of Argyle well says, "And precisely in proportion as we value our belief in the Unity of the Human Race ought we to be ready and willing to accept any evidence on the question of Man's Antiquity. The older the human family can be proved to be, the more possible and probable it is that it has descended from a single pair."—"Primeval Man," p. 128.

(2.) The science of Language, which proves that in very remote ages all the nations which speak cognate languages must have lived together, speaking the same language and branching from a common stock. And that unknown ages must have been consumed in the development of so many and so various dialects.

(3.) The science of Geology. The remains of human bodies and of human works of art have been found embedded in alluvial deposits in gravel pits, and in caves at such depth and in such association with the remains of extinct species of animals, as to prove conclusively that since man existed on the earth whole groups of great quadrupeds have become totally extinct; the climate of the Northern Temperate Zone has been revolutionized, and very radical changes have been wrought in the physical Geography of the countries which have been examined.

3. *How can the Unity of the Human Race as descended from a single pair be proved?*

Agassiz is the only naturalist of the highest rank who teaches that all species and varieties of organized beings must have had an independent origin, and been propagated from different parents. He holds consequently that mankind is a genus, originally created in several specific varieties. The same view is ably advocated in a recent work which has attracted attention in England, viz., "The Genesis of the Earth and of Man."

That man, although generically different from all other creatures, is nevertheless one single species is proved—

1st. From Scripture.—Acts xvii. 26; Rom. v. 12; 1 Cor. xv. 21, 22.

2d. Because the absolute unity of the race by descent from one pair is essentially implied in the propagation by imputation and by descent of guilt and corruption from Adam, and of the representative Headship and vicarious obedience and suffering of Jesus Christ.

3d. The higher moral and religious natures of all varieties of mankind are specifically identical.

4th. The same is generally indicated by history and the science of comparative philology.

5th. Greater differences have been generated in the processes of domestication between different branches of the same species of lower animals, as among pigeons or dogs for instance, than exists between the different varieties of mankind.

6th. It is a fact universally admitted by naturalists, that the union of different species are never freely fertile, and that the offspring of such union are seldom if ever fertile. But all the varieties of mankind freely intermix, and the offspring of all such unions propagate themselves indefinitely with perfect facility.

4. *Show that the Scriptures teach that human nature is composed of two and only two distinct substances.*

The Scriptures teach that man is composed of two elements, בָּשָׂר, σῶμα, *corpus, body,* and רוּחַ, πνεῦμα, ψυχή, πνοή, ζωή, *animus, soul, spirit.* This is clearly revealed—

1st. In the account of creation.—Gen. ii. 7. The body was formed of the earth, and *then* God breathed into man the breath of life and he became thenceforth a living soul.

2d. In the account given of death, Eccle. xii. 7, and of the state of soul immediately after death, while the bodies are decaying in the ground.—2 Cor. v. 1–8; Phil. i. 23, 24; Acts vii. 59.

3d. In all the current language of Scripture these two elements are always assumed, and none other are mentioned.

5. *State the view of those who maintain that our nature embraces three distinct elements, and its supposed Biblical basis.*

Pythagoras, and after him Plato, and subsequently the mass of Greek and Roman philosophers, maintained that man consists of three constituent elements: the *rational spirit,* νοῦς, πνεῦμα, *mens;* the *animal soul,* ψυχή, *anima;* the *body,* σῶμα, *corpus.* Hence this usage of the words became stamped upon the Greek popular speech. And consequently the apostle uses all three when intending to express exhaustively in popular language the totality of man and his belongings. "I pray God that your whole spirit, soul, and body be preserved blameless." 1 Thess. v. 23; Heb. iv. 12; 1 Cor. xv. 44. Hence some theologians conclude that it is a doctrine given by divine inspiration that human nature is constituted of three distinct elements.

6. *Refute this position and show that the words* ψυχή *and* πνεῦμα *are used in the New Testament interchangeably.*

The use made of these terms by the apostles proves nothing more than that they used words in their current popular sense to express divine ideas.   The word πνεῦμα designates the one soul emphasizing its quality as rational.   The word ψυχή designates the same soul emphasizing its quality as the vital and animating principle of the body.   The two are used together to express popularly the entire man.

That the πνεῦμα and ψυχή are distinct entities can not be the doctrine of the New Testament, because they are habitually used interchangeably and often indifferently.   Thus ψυχή as well as πνεῦμα is used to designate the soul as the seat of the higher intellectual faculties.—Matt. xvi. 26; 1 Pet. i. 22; Matt. x. 28.   Thus also πνεῦμα as well as ψυχή is used to designate the soul as the animating principle of the body.—James ii. 26. Deceased persons are indifferently called ψυχαι, Acts ii. 27, 31; Rev. vi. 9; xx. 4; and πνεύματα, Luke xxiv. 37, 39; Heb. xii. 23.

7. *What do our standards teach as to the state of man at his creation?*

The "Conf. Faith," Ch. iv., § 2, "L. Cat.," Q. 17, and "S. Cat.," Q. 10, teach the following points—1st. God created man in his own image.   2d. A reasonable and immortal soul endued with knowledge, righteousness, and true holiness, and placed in dominion over the creatures.   3d. Having God's law written on his heart and power to fulfil it, and yet under possibility of transgressing, being left to the freedom of his own will, which was subject to change.

The likeness of man to God respected—1st. The kind of his nature; man was created like God a free, rational, personal Spirit.   2d. He was created like God as to the perfection of his nature; in knowledge, Col. iii. 10; and righteousness and true holiness, Eph. iv. 24; and 3d. In his dominion over nature. Gen. i. 28.

8. *Give in psychological terms the true state of the question.*

In the preceding chapter it was shown that the volition is determined and derives its character from the desires and affections which prompt to it; and that the temporary affections and desires, which prompt the volitions in any given case, themselves spring from the permanent habit, disposition, or tendency of will which constitute the moral character of the man. It was also shown that the moral character of these permanent dispositions of will, and the responsibility of the man for them, is an ultimate fact, incapable of being referred back to any principle more fundamental or essential and confirmed by the unanimous judgment of the human race.

It hence follows that the original righteousness and holiness in which Adam was created consisted in the perfect conformity of all the moral dispositions and affections of his will (in Bible language, heart) to the law of God—of which his unclouded and faithful conscience was the organ.

As a consequence there was no schism in man's nature. The will, moving freely in conformity to the lights of reason and of conscience, held in harmonious subjection all the lower principles of body and soul. In perfect equilibrium a perfect soul dwelt in a perfect body.

This original righteousness *is natural* in the sense (1) that it was the moral perfection of man's nature as it came from the hands of the Creator. It belonged to that nature originally, and (2) is always essential to its perfection as to quality. (3) It would also have been propagated, if man had not fallen, just as native depravity is now propagated by natural descent. On the other hand, it *is not natural* in the sense that reason or conscience or free agency are essential constituents of human nature, necessary to constitute any one a real man. As a quality it is essential to the perfection, but as a constituent it is not necessary to the reality of human nature.

9. *Prove that Adam was created holy in the above sense.*

It belongs to the essence of man's nature that he is a moral responsible agent.

But, 1st. As a moral creature man was created in the image of God.—Gen. i. 27.

2d. God pronounced all his works, man included, to be "very good."—Gen i. 31. The goodness of a mechanical provision is essentially its fitness to attain its end. The "goodness" of a moral agent can be nothing other than his conformity of will to the moral law. Moral indifference in a moral agent is itself of the nature of sin.

3d. This truth is asserted.—Eccle. vii. 29.

4th. In regeneration, man is renewed in the image of God; in creation, man was made in the image of God; the image, in both cases, must be the same, and includes holiness.—Eph. iv. 24.

5th. Christ is called, 1 Cor. xv. 45, ὁ ἔσχατος Ἀδάμ, and in v. 47, δεύτερος ἄνθρωπος. He is recognized by friend and foe as the only perfect man in all history, the exemplar of normal humanity. Yet his human nature was formed by the Holy Ghost, antecedently to all action of its own, absolutely holy. He was called in his mother's womb, "That Holy Thing." Luke i. 35.

10. *What is the Pelagian doctrine with regard to the original state of man?*

The Pelagians hold—1st. That a man can rightly be held responsible only for his unbiassed volitions; and 2d. Consequently moral character as antecedent to moral action is an absurdity, since only that disposition is moral which has been formed as a habit by means of preceding unbiassed action of the free will, *i. e.*, man must choose his own character, or he can not be responsible for it.

They hold, therefore, that man's will at his creation was not only free, but, moreover, in a state of moral equilibrium, equally disposed to virtue or vice.

11. *State and contrast the positions of the Pelagians, of Dr. D. D. Whedon (Arminian), and of the Calvinists, as to innate righteousness and sin.*

The Pelagian holds—1st. That Adam was created a moral agent, but with no positive moral character; that he was at first indifferent either to good or evil, and left free to form his own character by his own free, unbiassed choice. 2d. That all men are born into the world in all essential particulars in the same moral state in which Adam was created. 3d. That man is naturally mortal, and that the mortality of the race is not in consequence of sin.

Dr. D. D. Whedon (Arminian), in "Bib. Sacra," April, 1862, p. 257, while agreeing with the Pelagian in the main as to the original moral state into which Adam was introduced by creation, differs from him as to the moral condition into which the descendants of Adam are introduced by birth. He admits that a "created" inclination may be either good and hence lovable, or bad and hence hateful—but he denies that the agent can be in the first case rewardable, or in the second case punishable for his disposition, the character of which he did not determine for himself by previously unbiassed volitions. If Adam had formed for himself a holy character he would have been both good and rewardable. Since he formed for himself a sinful character he was both bad and punishable. His descendants are propagated with corrupt natures without any fault of their own, therefore they are bad and corrupt, but not deserving of punishment.

In opposition to these positions the orthodox hold—1st. There are permanent dispositions and inclinations which determine the volitions. 2d. Many of these inclinations are good, many are bad, and many others are morally indifferent in their essential nature. 3d. These moral dispositions may be innate as well as acquired, in which case the agent is as responsible for them as he is for any other state or act of his will. 4th. Adam was created with holy dispositions prompting to holy action. He did not make himself holy, but was made so by God.

12. *Why do we judge that men are morally responsible for innate and concreated dispositions?*

1st. Children are born with moral dispositions and tendencies very various. Yet it is the spontaneous and universal judgment of men, that men *naturally* malicious and cruel and false are both to be abhorred and held morally responsible for their tempers and actions. 2d. The Scriptures, as will be shown under Ch. XIX., on "Original Sin," teach that all men come into the world with an inherent tendency in their nature to sin, which tendency is itself sin and worthy of punishment. 3d. President Edwards "On Will," Pt. 4, § 1, says, "The essence of the virtue and vice of dispositions of the heart and acts of the will lie *not in their cause but in their nature.*" And even the Arminian, John Wesley, says, as quoted by Richard Watson, "Holiness is not the right use of our powers, it is the right state of our powers. It is the right disposition of our soul, the right temper of our mind. Take that with you and you will no more dream that God could not create man in righteousness and true holiness." "What is holiness? Is it not essentially love? And can not God shed abroad this love in any soul without his concurrence, and antecedent to his knowledge or consent? And supposing this to be done, will love change its nature? will it be no longer holiness? This argument can never be sustained."

13. *Prove that a state of moral indifferency is itself sin, and that if it were not so no exercise of a volitional faculty so conditioned could possibly originate a moral act or character.*

That moral indifferency on the part of a moral agent in view of a moral obligation is itself sin is self-evident. The essence of morality is that it obliges the will of a moral agent. A *non*-moral agent may be indifferent to moral things. A moral agent may be indifferent to indifferent things. But from the very nature of the case it is absurd to pretend that a moral agent can be indifferent with respect to a known moral obligation resting on himself, and yet that that indifference is non-moral, but the prerequisite condition of all morality.

Besides a morally indifferent disposition can not originate a holy act or habit. The goodness or badness of an act depends upon the goodness or badness of the disposition or affection which prompted it. It is the moral state of the will (or *heart*, see Matt. vii. 17–20 and xii. 33) which makes the act of the will right or wrong, and not the act which makes the state wrong. A man's motives may be right, and yet his choice may be wrong through his mistake of its nature, because of ignorance or insanity; yet if all the prevalent dispositions and desires of the heart in any given case be *right*, the volition must be morally right; if wrong, the volition must be morally wrong; if indifferent, or neither right or wrong, the volition must be morally indifferent also. Hence appears the absurdity of their position. If Adam had been created, as they feign, with a will equally disposed either to good or evil, his first act could have had no moral character whatever. And yet Pelagians assume that Adam's first act, which had no moral character itself, determined the moral character of the man himself, and of all his acts and destinies for all future time. This, if true, would have been unjust on God's part, since it involves the infliction of the most awful punishment upon an act in itself neither good nor bad. As a theory it is absurd, since it evolves all morality out of that which is morally indifferent.

Richard Watson, Vol. II., p. 16, well says: "In Adam that rectitude of principle from which a right choice and right acts flowed, was either created with him, or flowed from his own volitions. If the latter be affirmed, then he must have willed right before he had a principle of rectitude, which is absurd; if the former then his creation in a state of moral rectitude, with an aptitude and disposition to good, is established."

14. *Show that the Pelagian theory can not be based upon experience.*

This whole theory is built upon certain *à priori* notions, and is contrary to universal experience. If Adam was created without positive moral character, and if infants are so born, then the conditions of free agency in these supposed cases must be different from the conditions of free agency in the case of every adult man or woman, from whose consciousness alone we can gather the facts from which to deduce any certain knowledge on the subject. Every man who ever thought or wrote upon this subject, was conscious of freedom only under the conditions of an already formed moral character. Even if the Pelagian view were true, we never could be assured of it, since we never have *consciously* experienced such a condition of indifferency. It is nothing more than an hypothesis, contrived to solve a difficulty; a difficulty resulting from the limits of our finite powers of thought.—See Sir William Hamilton's "Discussions," p. 587, etc.

15. *What distinction did the Fathers make between the εἰκών and the ὁμοίωσις of God in which man was created?—Gen. i. 26.*

By the εἰκών or "image" of God the Fathers understood the natural constitutional powers of man, intellectual and moral, as reason, conscience, and free will. By the ὁμοίωσις or "likeness" of God they understood the matured and developed moral perfection of human nature consequent upon man's holy exercise of his faculties.

Neander, "Hist. Christ. Dogmas," p. 180, says that this was the germ of the subsequent mediæval and Roman doctrine as to the original state of man.

Bellarmin, "De Gratia," et Lib. Arbitrio I., c. 6.—"We are forced, by these many testimonies of the Fathers, to conclude that the image and likeness are not in all respects the same, but that the image pertains to the nature and the likeness to the virtues (moral perfections); whence it follows that Adam by sinning lost not the image but the likeness of God."

16. *What does the Catechism of the Council of Trent teach as to the state in which Adam was created?*

See below the doctrines of the various churches at the end of this chapter.

17. *What is the Romish doctrine with respect to the* dona naturalia, *and the* dona supernaturalia *?*

1st. They hold that God endowed man at his creation with the *dona naturalia*, that is, with all the natural constitutional powers and faculties of body and soul without sin, in perfect innocency. There was no vice or defect in either body or soul.

2d. God duly attempered all these powers to one another, placing the lower in due subordination to the higher. *This* harmony of powers was called *Justicia*—natural righteousness.

3d. There was, however, in the very nature of things, a natural tendency in the lower appetites and passions to rebel against the authority of the higher powers of reason and conscience. This tendency is not sin in itself, but becomes sin only when it is consented to by the will, and passes into voluntary action. *This* is *concupiscence;* not sin, but the fuel and occasion of sin.

4th. To prevent this natural tendency to disorder from the rebellion of the lower elements of the human constitution against the higher, God granted man the additional gift of the *dona supernaturalia*, or gifts extra constitutional. *This* is *original righteousness*, which was a foreign gift superadded to his constitution, by means of which his natural powers duly attempered are kept in due subjection and order. Some of their theologians held that these supernatural gifts were bestowed upon man immediately upon his creation, at the same time with his natural powers. The more prevalent and consistent view, however, is that it was given subsequently as a reward for the proper use of his natural powers. See Moehler's "Symbolism," pp. 117, 118.

5th. Both the "*justicia*" and the "*dona supernaturalia*" were accidental or superadded properties of human nature, and were lost by the fall.

18. *How does this doctrine modify their view as to original sin and the moral character of that concupiscence which remains in the regenerate?*

They hold that man lost at the fall only the superadded gifts of "original righteousness" (*dona supernaturalia*), while the proper nature of man itself, the *dona naturalia*, comprising all his constitutional faculties of reason, conscience, free-will (in which they include "moral ability"), remain intact. Thus they make the effect of the fall upon man's moral nature purely negative. The Reformers defined it "the want of original righteousness, *and* the corruption of the whole nature."

Hence, also, they hold that concupiscence, or the tendency to rebellion of the lower against the higher powers remaining in the regenerate, being natural and incidental to the very constitution of human nature, is not of the nature of sin. See below.

AUTHORITATIVE PUBLIC STATEMENTS OF THE VARIOUS CHURCHES.

ROMISH DOCTRINE.—"*Cat. Council of Trent*," Pt. 2, ch. ii., Q. 19.— " Lastly, He formed man from the slime of the earth, so created and qualified in body as to be immortal and impassable, not, however, in virtue of the strength of nature, but of the divine gift. But as regards the soul of man, he created it in his own image and likeness ; gifted him with free-will, and so tempered all his motions and appetites that they should at all times be subject to the control of the reason. He then added the admirable gift of original righteousness ; and next gave him dominion over all other animals."—Ib. Pt. 2, ch. ii., Q. 42, and Pt. 4, ch. xii., Q. 3.

BELLARMIN.—"*Gratia Primi Hominis*," 5.—"It is to be understood, *in the first place*, that man naturally consists of flesh and spirit, and therefore his nature partly assimilates with the beasts and partly with the angels ; and because of his flesh and his fellowship with the beasts he has a certain propensity to corporeal and sensible good, to which he is induced through the senses and appetites ; and because of his spirit and his fellowship with the angels he has a propensity to spiritual and rational good, to which he is induced by his reason and will. But from these different and contrary propensities there exists in one and the same man a certain contest, and from these contests a great difficulty of acting, while the one propensity antagonizes the other. It is to be understood *in the second place*, that divine providence at the beginning of creation, that it might administer a remedy to this disease or languor of human nature arising from the condition of its "matter," added the excellent gift of original righteousness, by which as by a golden bridle the inferior part might be held in subjection to the superior part, and the superior part subject to God ; although the flesh was so subject to the spirit, that it could not be moved the spirit forbidding, nor rebel against the spirit unless the spirit rebel against God; nevertheless it was in the power of the spirit to rebel or not to rebel."

For the statement of Bellarmin's doctrine as to the present moral condition into which the descendants of Adam are born, see below, Ch. XIX., on "Original Sin."

LUTHERAN DOCTRINE.—"*Formula Concordiæ*" (Hase), p. 640. [Original Sin] "is the privation of that righteousness concreated in human nature in Paradise, or of that image of God in which man was in the beginning created in truth, holiness, and righteousness."

REFORMED DOCTRINE.—"*Canon. Dordt,*" iii. 1.—"Man, from the beginning, was created in the image of God, adorned in his mind, with the true and saving knowledge of his Creator, and of spiritual things, with righteousness in his will and heart, and purity in all his affections, and thus was altogether holy."

"*Conf. Faith,*" ch. iv.; "*L. Cat.,*" Ques. 17; "*S. Cat.,*" Ques. 10.

REMONSTRANT DOCTRINE.—Limborch, "*Theol. Christ.,*" ii. 24, 5.— "They are wont to locate original righteousness in illumination and rectitude of the mind, in holiness and righteousness of the will, in harmony of the senses and affections, and in a promptitude for good. It is, indeed, most evident that the first of mankind were, in their primeval state, of a far more perfect condition than we are when we are born. For their mind was not like a blank paper, and void of all knowledge; but had been endowed by God with actual knowledge, and instructed in the wisdom necessary for that state ; and they possessed also the capacity for acquiring further knowledge by reasoning, experience, and revelation. . . Their will was not neutral equally indifferent in respect to good and evil, but before that the Law was imposed upon it by God, it had a natural rectitude, so that it could neither desire nor act inordinately. For where there is no law, there the most free use of the will is clear of blame.—ii. 24, 10. That the first man would not have died if he had not sinned, is beyond doubt, for death was the penalty of sin. But thence the immortality [natural] of man is not correctly inferred. . . . Nevertheless God would have preserved this mortality in perpetual immunity of actual death, if man had not sinned."

SOCINIAN DOCTRINE.—F. Socinus, "*Prælectiones Theol.,*" c. 3.—"We therefore conclude that Adam, even before he had transgressed that command of God, was not truly righteous, since he was neither impeccable, nor had he hitherto been subjected to any occasion of sinning; at least it is not possible ·to affirm that he was certainly righteous, since it in no manner appears that he for any consideration had abstained from sinning.   But there are those who say that the original righteousness of the first man consisted in this, that he possessed a reason dominating over his appetite and senses and covering them, and that there was no variance between them.   But they say this without reason, since it clearly appears from the sin Adam committed that his appetite and senses dominated over his reason, neither had these previously agreed well together."

"*Cat. Racov.*," p. 18.—"From the beginning man was created mortal, *i. e.*, such an one as not only might consistently with his nature die, but also if left to his nature could not but die, although it was possible that he might be preserved always in life by a special divine blessing."

CHAPTER XVII.

COVENANT OF WORKS.

1. *In what different senses is the term covenant used in Scripture?*

1st. For a natural ordinance.—Jer. xxxiii. 20.
2d. For an unconditional promise.—Gen. ix. 11, 12.
3d. For a conditional promise.—Is. i. 19, 20.
4th. A dispensation or mode of administration.—Heb. viii. 6–9.
For the usage with respect to the Greek term διαθήκη, usually translated in our version *testament* and *covenant*.—See Chapter XXII., on "Covenant of Grace," Question 1.

In the theological phrases "covenant of works," and "covenant of grace," this term is used in the third sense of a promise suspended on conditions.

2. *What are the several elements essential to a covenant?*

1st. Contracting parties. 2d. Conditions. These conditions in a covenant between equals are mutually imposed and mutually binding, but in a sovereign constitution, imposed by the Creator upon the creature, these "conditions" are better expressed as (1) promises on the part of the Creator suspended upon (2) conditions to be fulfilled by the creature. And (3) an alternative penalty to be inflicted in case the condition fails.

3. *Show that the constitution under which Adam was placed by God at his creation may be rightly called a covenant.*

The inspired record of God's transactions with Adam presents definitely all the essential elements of a covenant as co-existing in that constitution.

1st. The "contracting parties."—(1.) God, the moral Governor, by necessity of nature and relation demanding perfect conformity to moral law. (2.) Adam, the free moral agent, by necessity of nature and relation under the inalienable obligation of moral law.

2d. The "promises," life and favor.—Matt. xix. 16, 17; Gal. iii. 12.

3d. The "conditions" upon which the promises were suspended, perfect obedience, in this instance subjected to a special test, that of abstaining from the fruit of the "tree of knowledge."

4th. The "alternative penalty." "In the day thou eatest thereof thou shalt surely die."—Gen. ii. 16, 17.

This constitution is called a covenant.—Hosea vi. 7.

4. *How is it defined in our standards?*

"Con. Faith," Chap. iv., Sec. 2; Chap. vii., Sec. 1 and 2; Chap. xix., Sec. 1; "L. Cat.," Q. 20; "S. Cat.," Q. 12.

5. *Why is it not absurd to apply the term " Covenant" to a sovereign constitution imposed by the Creator upon the creature without consulting his will?*

1st. Although it was a sovereign constitution imposed by God, there is no reason to suppose that Adam did not enter upon it voluntarily. He was a holy being, and the arrangement was pre-eminently to his advantage. 2d. We call it a Covenant because that is the proper word to express a conditional promise made to a free agent. 3d. The term "Covenant" is constantly applied in Scripture to other sovereign constitutions of like character which the Creator has imposed upon men. If God could make covenants with fallen and guilty Noah, Gen. ix. 11, 12, and with Abraham, Gen. xvii. 1–21, why could he not make a covenant with unfallen Adam.

6. *By what titles has this covenant been designated and why?*

1st. It has been called the Covenant of Nature, because it expresses the relations which man in his natural state as newly created and unfallen sustained to the Creator and Moral Governor of the universe. It is adjusted to the natural or unfallen man, just as the Covenant of Grace is adjusted to unnatural or fallen man. 2d. It has been called a legal covenant, because its "condition" is perfect conformity to the law of absolute moral perfection. 3d. It has been called the Covenant of Works, because its demands terminate upon man's own being and doing. 4th. It has been called a Covenant of Life, because the promise attached to well-doing was life.

It was also essentially a gracious covenant, because although every creature is, as such, bound to serve the Creator to the full extent of his powers, the Creator can not be bound as a mere matter of justice to grant the creature fellowship with himself, or to raise him to an infallible standard of moral power, or to crown him with eternal and inalienable felicity.

7. *Who were the parties to this covenant, and how may it be proved that Adam therein represented all his natural descendants?*

The "parties" were God and Adam, and in him representatively all his natural posterity. That he did thus represent his descendants is evident—

1st. From the parallel which is drawn in Scripture between Adam in his relation to his descendants, and Christ in his relation to his elect.—Rom. v. 12–19, and 1 Cor. xv. 22, 47.

2d. From the matter of fact that the very penalty denounced upon Adam, in case of his disobedience, has taken effect in each individual descendant.—Gen. ii. 17; iii. 17, 18.

3d. From the Biblical declaration that sin, death, and all penal evil came into the world through Adam.—Rom. v. 12; 1 Cor. xv. 22. See Chapter XXI., on "Imputation of Adam's Sin."

8. *What was the promise attached to the Covenant?*

The promise was "life"—1st. Because it is necessarily implied in the penalty of "death," which is expressly denounced. If disobedience is linked to death, obedience is linked to life. 2d. It is clearly taught in other passages of Scripture.—Lev. xviii. 5; Neh. ix. 29; Matt. xix. 16, 17; Gal. iii. 12; Rom. x. 5.

This life was not a mere continuation of the existence with which man was endowed by creation as a fallible, moral agent, but it was an additional gift of infallible, moral excellence, and inalienable blessedness, conditioned upon obedience during a probationary period. 1st. This is evident because the reward suspended on "conditions" must involve something more than had been already granted. 2d. Because man was as created liable to sin, and there could be no permanent and secure bliss nor high excellence in that condition. 3d. Because the granting of the reward necessarily closes the probation, supersedes the conditions, and secures inalienable blessedness. 4th. Because the angels who had *not* left their first estate had been rewarded with such a life. 5th. Because the life promised must correspond to the death threatened, and the death threatened involved eternal separation from God and irretrievable destruction. 6th. Because the life secured to us by the "Second Adam" is of this nature.

9. *What is a "probation"? and when and where had the human race its probation under the Covenant of Works?*

A probation is a trial. The word is variously used to express the state, or the time, or the act of trial. The time of probation under such a constitution as the covenant of works *must* be a definitely limited one, because it is self-evident that either the infliction of the penalty or the granting of the reward would, *ipso facto*, close the probation forever, and the reward could not accrue until the period of probation was completed.

The probation of the human race took place once for all in the trial of Adam in the garden of Eden. That trial resulted in loss, and since then the conditions of the covenant being impossible, and its penalty having been incurred, any probation is of course impossible. Men are now by *nature* children of wrath.

10. *What was the condition of that covenant? and why was the command not to eat of the tree of knowledge of good and evil selected as a test?*

Perfect conformity of heart, and perfect obedience in act to the whole will of God as far as revealed.—Deut. xxvii. 26; Gal. iii. 10; James ii. 10. The command to abstain from eating the forbidden fruit was only made a special and decisive test of that general obedience. As the matter forbidden was morally indifferent in itself, the command was admirably adapted to be a clear and naked test of submission to God's absolute will as such. The forbidden tree was doubtless called the tree of the knowledge of good and evil, because through the disobedient eating of it mankind came to the thorough experience of the value of goodness and of the infinite evil of sin.

The obedience required by the law as a rule of duty is of course perpetual. But the demand of the law for obedience as a covenant condition of life must be limited to the period of probation. The term "perpetual" in "Conf. F.," Ch. xix., § 1, and "L. Cat.," Q. 20, was admitted doubtless by inadvertence.

11. *What was the nature of the death threatened in case of disobedience?*

This word, "dying thou shalt die," in this connection evidently includes all the penal consequences of sin. These are— 1st, death, natural, Eccle. xii. 7; 2d, death, moral and spiritual, Matt. viii. 22; Eph. ii. 1; 1 Tim. v. 6; Rev. iii. 1; 3d, death, eternal, Rev. xx. 6–14.

The instant the law was violated its penalty began to operate, although on account of the intervention of the dispensation of grace the full effect of the sentence is suspended during the present life. The Spirit of God was withdrawn the instant man fell, and he at once became spiritually dead, physically mortal, and under sentence of death eternal.

This appears—1st. From the nature of man as a spiritual

being. "This is life eternal to know the only true God," etc.—John xvii. 3. The instant the soul is cut off from God it dies, and his wrath and curse is incurred, and the entire person, body, and soul, involved in an endless series of evil conditions. 2d. The Scriptures everywhere declare that the wages of sin is death.—Rom. vi. 23; Ezek. xviii. 4.

The nature of this death is to be determined. (1.) By the narrative of the effects produced in our first parents, *e. g.*, shame of nakedness, fear, alienation from God, unbelief, and after a time dissolution of body, etc. (2.) By the experience of its effects in their descendants, *e. g.*, corruption of nature, mortality of body, miseries in this life, the second death.

12. *What does C. F. Hudson and others hold to be the penalty of the Covenant of Works?*

The annihilationists, of whom C. F. Hudson is one of the ablest, hold that the precise thing God said to Adam was "THOU, *thyself, thine entire person* art dust, and to dust thou shalt return." They quote Num. xxiii. 10; Judges xvi. 30, etc. They hold that death means precisely and only cessation of being. They say Adam could have had no other idea associated with the word. Death in this sense had pre-existed in the world for innumerable ages among the lower orders of creatures, and this was all Adam knew on the subject.

It is idle for us to speculate as to what the original language God spoke to Adam was, or what the word he used, corresponding to our word death, precisely signified and suggested. Adam probably simply understood God to say that if he sinned he should be utterly and irretrievably cut off from the divine favor. That is precisely what happened. But the facts are clear. 1st. The word death in Scripture is used to express not cessation of being but a certain godless condition of being.—Rev. iii. 1; Eph. ii. 1–5, and v. 14; 1 Tim. v. 6; Rom. vi. 13; xi. 15; John v. 24; vi. 47. 2d. It will be shown below, Chapters XXXVII. and XL., that the Scriptures do not allow the notion either of the sleep of the soul during the intermediate state, or of the annihilation of the wicked after the judgment.

13. *What is meant by the seal of a covenant, and what was the seal of the Covenant of Works?*

A seal of a covenant is an outward visible sign, appointed by God as a pledge of his faithfulness, and as an earnest of the blessings promised in the covenant.

Thus the rainbow is the seal of the covenant made with Noah.—Gen. ix. 12, 13. Circumcision was the original seal of the covenant made with Abraham (Gen. xvii. 9–11; Rom. iv. 11), in the place of which baptism is now instituted.—Col. ii. 11, 12; Gal. iii. 26, 27.　The tree of life was the seal of the covenant of works, because it was the outward sign and seal of that life which was promised in the covenant, and from which man was excluded on account of sin, and to which he is restored through the second Adam in the Paradise regained.—Compare Gen. ii. 9; iii. 22, 24, with Rev. ii. 7; xxii. 2–14.

14. *What according to Witsius, in his great work "on the Covenants," are the seals or sacraments of the Covenant of Works?*

In Vol. I., Ch. vi., Witsius enumerates four—1st. Paradise. 2d. The tree of life.　3d. The tree of knowledge of good and evil.　4th. The Sabbath.

These were all doubtless symbolical institutions connected with the original divine dispensation of which the Covenant of Works was the foundation.　But there appears to be no reason for designating them as belonging to that particular class of symbolical institutions called sacraments under the New Testament.　The tree of the knowledge of good and evil sealed death, and therefore could not have been a seal of the Covenant of Works which offered life.

15. *In what sense is the Covenant of Works abrogated, and in what sense is it in force?*

This Covenant having been broken by Adam, not one of his natural descendants is ever able to fulfil its conditions, and Christ having fulfilled all of its conditions in behalf of all his own people, salvation is offered now on the condition of faith. In *this* sense the Covenant of Works having been fulfilled by the second Adam is henceforth abrogated under the gospel.

Nevertheless, since it is founded upon the principles of immutable justice, it still binds all men who have not fled to the refuge offered in the righteousness of Christ.　It is still true that "he that doeth these things shall live by them," and "the soul that sinneth it shall die."　This law in *this* sense remains, and in consequence of the unrighteousness of men condemns them, and in consequence of their absolute inability to fulfil it, it acts as a schoolmaster to bring them to Christ.　For he having fulfilled alike its condition wherein Adam failed, and its penalty which Adam incurred, he has become the end of this covenant for righteousness to every one that believeth, who in him is regarded and treated as one who has fulfilled the covenant, and merited its promised reward.

CHAPTER XVIII.

THE NATURE OF SIN AND THE SIN OF ADAM.

1. *What are the only tests by which the answer to the question "What is sin?" can be determined?*

1st. The word of God. 2d. The intuitive judgments of men. The tests of the validity of these intuitions are (*a*) self-evidence, (*b*) universality, (*c*) necessity. The intuitive judgments of men are immediately passed not upon abstract notions nor upon general propositions, but upon concrete and individual instances. General maxims are generalized by the understanding from many individual intuitive convictions, and are true or false as this process of generalization has been well or badly done. The vast amount of confusion and error which prevails as to the nature of sin, and as to what comes under the category of sin, is due to crude generalization of general principles from individual intuitions, and the indiscriminate application of the maxim thus generated beyond the range to which they are guaranteed by the intuitions themselves. The maxims that all sin consists in voluntary action, and that ability is the measure of responsibility, are instances of this abuse. It is as absurd to attempt to make the bare understanding settle a question belonging only to the moral sense as it would be to make the nose decide a question of sound.—See M'Cosh, "Intuitions of the Mind," Book I., ch. ii., §§ 4 and 5, and Book IV., ch. ii. §§ 1–3.

2. *What must a true definition of the nature of sin embrace?*

A definition of sin must—1st. Include *all* that either the Word of God or an enlightened conscience decides to be sin. 2d. It must include nothing else. Otherwise in either case it is false.

3. *State the definitions of sin given by Turretin, and by our Standards, and by Vitringa.*

Turretin, Locus 9, Quæs. 1.—"Inclinatio, actio, vel omissio pugnans cum lege Dei, vel carens rectitudine legáli debitâ in esse."

"Conf. Faith," Ch. vi., § 6; "L. Cat.," Q. 24; "S. Cat.," Q. 14.
"Sin is any want of conformity unto, or transgression of the
law of God."

Campejus Vitringa, Prof. Theo. in Franeker, died 1722.—
"Forma peccati est disconvenientia, actus, habitus, ant status
hominis cum divina lege."

This last excellent definition embraces two constitutent propositions.—1st. Sin is any and every want of conformity with
the moral law of God, whether of excess or defect, whether of
omission or commission.   2d. Sin is any want of conformity of
the moral states and habits as well of the actions of the human
soul with the law of God?

4. *What is Law? And what is the Law of God?*

The word law is used in a great many and in very different
senses.   It is used by natural philosophers often to express—
1st. A general fact, *e. g.*, the general fact that all matter at-
tracts all matter inversely as the square of the distance.   2d. An
established order of sequence in which certain events occur, as
the order of the seasons, and any established order of nature.
3d. The mode of acting of a specific force, as the law of electri-
cal induction, etc.   4th. A spontaneous order of development,
as the internal self-acting law of the growth of animals and
plants from the seed.

The moral law of God, however, is not an internal, self-reg-
ulating principle of man's moral nature, like the feigned inner
light of the Quakers, but an imperial standard of moral excellence imposed upon mankind from without and from above
them by the supreme authority of a personal moral Governor
over personal moral subjects.   It involves (*a*) a certain degree
of enlightenment as to truth and duty, (*b*) a rule of action regulating the will and binding the conscience, (*c*) armed with
sanctions, or imperative motives constraining to obedience.

5. *Prove that sin is any want of conformity to "Law."*

1st. Whenever we sin conscience condemns us for not coming up to a standard which we intuitively recognize as morally
obligatory upon us.   Conscience implies (*a*) moral accountability, and hence subjection to a moral Governor, and (*b*) a
standard to which we ought to be conformed.   The conscience
itself, as the organ of God's law, contains the law written on the
heart.

2d. It is implied in all the language used by the Holy Ghost
in Scripture to express the idea of sin שָׂטִים שָׂט from שָׂטָה *to devi-*

ate from the way. חָטָא *to miss the mark,* ἁμαρτάνω *to err, to miss the mark,* παράβάσις (Gal. iii. 19), *a going aside from, a transgresssion.*

3d. It is explicitly asserted in Scripture, "Every one that doeth sin, also doeth τὴν ἀνομίαν, and sin is ἀνομία."—1 John iii. 4. "For where no law is there is no transgression."—Rom. iv. 15.

6. *Prove that sin is any want of conformity to the moral Law of God.*

As above shown this is implied in the action of conscience. It testifies to a law imposed upon us by an authority external to us, the supreme authority of God. In the absence of all supernatural revelation it has led all heathen nations to the recognition of the authority of God, or of gods exercising government, to a belief in rewards and punishments administered by God, and hence to expiatory and propitiatory rites.

It is also asserted by David that sin of any kind is disobedience and dishonor done to God.—See fifty-first Psalm.

Hence sin is not a mere violation of the law of our own constitution, nor of the system of things, but an offence against a personal Lawgiver and moral Governor, who vindicates his law with penalties. The soul that sins is always conscious that his sin is (*a*) intrinsically vile and polluting, and (*b*) that it justly deserves punishment and calls down the righteous wrath of God. Hence sin carries with it two inalienable characters— (*a*) ill desert, guilt, *reatus,* (*b*) pollution, *macula.*

7. *Show that this Law, any want of conformity to which is sin, demands absolute moral perfection.**

This is necessarily involved in the very essence of moral obligation. *The very essence of right is that it ought to be.* The very essence of wrong is that it ought not to be. If any thing be indifferent it is not moral, and if it be moral it is a matter of obligation. This being of the essence of right it is, of course, true of each consistent part as well as of the whole. Any degree short of full conformity with the highest right is therefore of the nature of sin. "For whosoever shall keep the whole law and yet offend in one point is guilty of all."—James ii. 10. The old maxim is true, *Omne minus bonum habet rationem mali.*

It evidently follows from this principle that the Romish doctrine of works of Supererogation is absurd as well as wicked, since if these works are obligatory they are not supererogatory, and if they are not obligatory they are not moral, and if not moral they can have no moral value. Hence also all those Perfectionists who admit that men are not now able to keep

* Dr. C. Hodge's Unpublished Lectures.

perfectly the law of absolute moral perfection, while they maintain that Christians may in this life live without sin, obviously use incorrect and misleading language.

8. *Prove that any want of conformity with this Law in the states and* permanent habit *of soul, as well as in its acts, is sin.*

1st. This is proved by the common judgments of all men. All judge that the moral state of the heart determines the moral character of the actions, and that the moral character of the actions discloses the moral state of the heart, and that a man whose acts are habitually profane, or malignant, or impure, is himself in the permanent state of his heart profane, or malignant, or impure.

2d. The same is proved by the common religious experience of all Christians. This experience always involves conviction of sin, and conviction of sin involves as its most uniform and prominent element not merely a conviction that our actions fail to come up to the proper standard of excellence, but a sense that in the depths of our nature, below and beyond the reach of volition, we are spiritually dead and polluted, and impotent and insensible to divine things, and worthy of condemnation therefore. Every Christian has been brought with Paul to cry out, "O wretched man that I am: who shall deliver me from the body of this death."—Rom. vii. 24. This finds expression, and this principle for which we are contending finds proof in all the prayers, supplications, confessions, and in all the hymns and devotional literature of Christians of all ages and denominations.

3d. The Scriptures explicitly call the permanent states of the soul "sin" when they are not conformed to the law of God. Sin and its lusts are said to reign in the mortal body; the members are the instruments of sin; the unregenerate are the servants of sin.—Rom. vi. 12–17. The disposition or permanent "tendency" to sin is called "flesh" as opposed to "spirit," Gal. v. 17; also "lust," James i. 14, 15; "old Adam," and "body of sin," "ignorance," "blindness of heart," "alienation from the life of God," and "a condition of being past feeling," Eph. iv. 18, 19.

9. *Show that the very first spontaneous motions of concupiscence are sin?*

1st. The heart of the Christian often for the moment spontaneously lusts for evil when the conscience promptly condemns and the will forbids and restrains and diverts the attention. Although the man does not consent to the sin that is present in him, nevertheless the Christian feels that such movements of concupiscence are unholy, and worthy of condemnation, and he not only resists them but condemns and loathes himself because of them, and seeks to be purged from them at once by the atoning blood, and the sanctifying spirit of Jesus.

2d. Concupiscence is called "sin" in Scripture. "I had not known sin, but by the law, for I had not known ἐπιθυμίαν (concupiscence) except the law had said thou shalt not ἐπιθυμήσεις." Also τὰ παθήματα τῶν ἁμαρτιῶν, "the motions of sin," and "the law in the members," and "sin that dwelleth in me," that worketh without "my consent," which "works all manner of concupiscence," etc.—Rom. vii. 5–24.

10. *What is the* FIRST *great mystery connected with the origin of sin?*

How or why was the existence of sin tolerated in the creation of a God at once eternal, self-existent, and infinite in wisdom, power, holiness, and benevolence?

All the attempted solutions of this enigma which have been entertained in our day have been summed up by Prof. Haven of Chicago as follows:

"Either God can not prevent sin, *i. e.*, either (*a*) in any system, (*b*) in a moral system involving free agency.

"Or for some reason God does not choose to prevent sin, *i. e.*, either because (*a*) its existence is of itself desirable, (*b*) or though not in itself desirable it is the necessary means of the greatest good, or (*c*) though not in itself tending to good it may be overruled to that result, or (*d*) because, in general terms, its permission will involve less evil than its absolute prevention.

It is obvious (*a*) that God has permitted sin, and (*b*) hence it was right for him to do so. But why it was right must ever remain a mystery demanding submission and defying solution.

11. *What was the Manichœan doctrine as to the origin of sin?*

They held the opinion that sin had its ground in some eternal, self-existent principle independent of God, either matter or self-existent devil. This doctrine is inconsistent (*a*) with the independence, infinitude, and sovereignty of God; (*b*) with the nature of sin as essentially the revolt of a created free-will from God. Sin is an element of perverted moral agency. To consider it an attribute of matter is to deny it. All the Christian fathers united in opposing Manichæism and in maintaining that sin is the product of the free-will of man alone.

12. *State the doctrine of St. Augustine with respect to the privative nature of sin.*

St. Augustine held — 1st. That God is the creator of all

entities and the absolutely sovereign Governor of all moral agents and of all their actions; and 2d. That nevertheless God is in no sense either the author or the cause of sin. In order to reconcile these he held, 3d. That sin is not an entity, but is in its essence simply a defect. His dictum, which hence has passed into general currency with all classes of theologians, was *Nihil est malum nisi privatio boni.* They have properly distinguished between "negation" and "privation." Negation is the absence of that which does not belong to the nature of the subject, as sight to a stone. Privation is the absence of that which belonging to the nature of the subject is necessary to its perfection, as sight to a man.

Sin therefore is privative because it originates in the absence of those moral qualities which *ought* to be present in the states and actions of a free, responsible, moral agent.

It is to be remembered, however, that the inherent depravity which "comes from a defective or privative cause" instantly assumes a positive form, from the essentially active nature of the human soul. In a passive condition of being, a defect might remain purely negative. But in a ceaselessly active being, and one acting under ceaseless moral obligations, a moral defect must instantly become a positive vice. Not to love God is to hate him. Not to be in all things conformed to his will is to rebel against him, and to break his law at all points.—See Edwards, "Original Sin," pt. 4. sec. 2.

13. *What is the Pelagian doctrine as to the nature of sin?*

The Pelagian view of sin, which has been rejected by all branches of the Christian Church, is—1st. That law can command only volitions. 2d. That states of the soul can be commanded only in so far as they are the direct effect of previous volitions. 3d. Hence that sin consists simply in acts of volition. 4th. That whatever a man has not plenary ability to do he is under no obligation to do. 5th. That there is no such thing, therefore, as innate depravity. 6th. That since a volition to be moral or the subject of approbation or of condemnation, must be a pure self-decision of the will, it follows that sin is beyond the absolute control of God.

14. *In what sense is the dictum that "all sin is voluntary" true, and in what sense false?*

It all turns upon the sense of the phrase "Voluntary." If it be in the Pelagian sense restricted to "acts of volition;" then the dictum that "all sin is voluntary" is false. If, however, it is used so as to include the spontaneous dispositions, tendencies, and affections which constitute the permanent character of the soul, and which prompt to and decide the nature of the volitions, then all sin is voluntary, because all sin has its ground and spring in these spontaneous tendencies and dispositions, *i. e.*, in the permanent moral states of the soul.

15. *State the peculiarities of the Romish position upon this subject, and also that of the Arminian Perfectionists.*

The Roman Church agrees with all Protestants in holding that all the habits and permanent dispositions as well as the actions of the soul which are not conformed to the law of God are sinful. But it is a prominent characteristic of their doctrine that they hold that moral condition of soul which remains in the regenerate as the consequence of original sin, and the *fomes* or fuel of actual sin, is not properly of the nature of sin. They maintain that the first spontaneous movement of this concupiscence is not sin in itself, and not to be treated as such —but that it becomes the cause of sin as soon as its solicitations are entertained and translated into action by the will.— "Cat. of Council of Trent," Pt. II., ch. ii., Q. 42.

The Arminians avail themselves of the same positions when defending their doctrine of Christian Perfection. Wesley (in "Meth. Doc. Tracts," pp. 294–312) distinguishes between "sin properly so called, *i. e.*, voluntary transgression of known law, and sin improperly so called, *i. e.*, involuntary transgression of law, known or unknown," and declares, "I believe there is no such perfection in this life as excludes these involuntary transgressions, which I apprehend to be naturally consequent upon the ignorance and mistakes inseparable from mortality."

The Sin of Adam.

16. *What is the* second *great mystery connected with the origin of sin?*

How could sin originate in the will of a creature created with a positively holy disposition?

The difficulty is to reconcile understandingly the fact that sin did so originate—

1st. With the known constitution of the human will. If the volitions are as the prevalent affections and desires, and if the affections and desires excited by outward occasions are good or evil, according to the permanent moral state of the will, how could a sinful volition originate in a holy will? or how could the permanent state of his soul become spontaneously unholy?

2d. With universal experience. As it is impossible that a sinful desire or volition should originate in the holy will of

God, or in the holy will of saints and angels, or that a truly holy affection or volition should originate in the depraved wills of fallen men without supernatural regeneration (Luke vi. 43-45), how could a sinful volition originate in the holy will of Adam?

That Adam was created with a holy yet fallible will, and that he did fall, are facts established by divine testimony. We must believe them, although we can not rationally explain them. This is for us impossible—1st. Because there remains an inscrutable element in the human will, adopt whichever theory of it we may.

2d. Because all our reasoning must be based upon consciousness, and no other man ever had in his consciousness the experience of Adam. The origin of our sinful volitions is plain enough. But we lack some of the data necessary to explain his case.

In the way of approximation, however, we may observe— 1st. It is unsound to reason from the independent will of the infinite God to the dependent will of the creature.

2d. The infallibility of saints and angels is not inherent, but is a superinduced *confirming grace* of God. They are not in a state of probation. Adam was—his will was free, but not *confirmed*.

3d. The depraved will of man can not originate holy affections and volitions, because the presence of a positively holy principle is necessary to constitute them holy. But, on the other hand, there were already in the holy will of Adam many principles morally indifferent, in themselves neither good nor bad, and becoming sinful only when, in default of the control of reason and conscience, they prompt to their indulgence in ways forbidden by God; *e. g.*, admiration and appetite for the fruit, and desire for knowledge. The sin commenced the moment that, under the powerful persuasion of Satan, these two motives were dwelt upon in spite of the prohibition, and thus allowed to become so prevalent in the soul as temporarily to neutralize reverence for God's authority, and fear of his threatening.

4th. Adam, although endowed with a holy disposition, was inexperienced in the assaults of temptation.

5th. He was assailed through the morally indifferent principles of his nature by a vastly superior intelligence and character, to whom, in the highest sense, the origin of all sin must be referred.

17. *What appears from the history of the Fall to have been the precise nature of the first sin of Adam?*

It appears from the record (Gen. iii. 1–6) that the initial influences inducing our first parents, in their first transgression, were in themselves considered morally indifferent. These were —1st. Natural appetite for the attractive fruit. 2d. Natural desire for knowledge. 3d. The persuasive power of Satan upon Eve, including the known influence of a superior mind and will. 4th. The persuasive power of both Satan and Eve upon Adam. Their dreadful sin appears to have been essentially— 1st. Unbelief, they virtually made God a liar. 2d. Deliberate disobedience, they set up their will as a law in place of his.

18. *What relation did God sustain to Adam's sin?*

Concerning the relation sustained by God to the sin of Adam all we know is—1st. God created Adam holy, with all natural powers necessary for accountable agency. 2d. He rightfully withheld from him, during his probation, any higher supernatural influence necessary to render him infallible. 3d. He neither caused nor approved Adam's sin. 4th. He sovereignly decreed to permit him to sin, thus determining that he should sin as he did.

19. *What was the effect of Adam's sin upon himself?*

1st. In the natural relation which Adam sustained to God as the subject of his moral government, his sin must have instantly had the effect of (1) displeasing and alienating God, and (2) of depraving his own soul.

2d. In the covenant relation which Adam sustained to God the penalty of the covenant of works was incurred, *i. e.*, death, including, (1) mortality of body, (2) corruption of soul, (3) sentence of eternal death.

20. *In what sense did he become totally depraved, and how could total depravity result from one sin?*

By the affirmation that total depravity was the immediate result of Adam's first sin, it is not meant that he became as bad as he could be, or even as corrupt as the best of his unregenerate descendants; but it is meant—1st. His apostasy from God was complete. God demands perfect obedience. Adam was now a rebel in arms.

2d. That the favor and communion of God, the sole condition of his spiritual life, was withdrawn.

3d. A schism was introduced into the soul itself. The painful reproaches of conscience were excited, and could never be allayed without an atonement. This led to fear of God, distrust, prevarication, and, by necessary consequence, to innumerable other sins.

4th. Thus the whole nature became depraved. The will being at war with the conscience, the understanding became darkened; the conscience, in consequence of constant outrage and neglect, became seared; the appetites of the body inordinate, and its members instruments of unrighteousness.

5th. There remained in man's nature no recuperative principle; he must go on from worse to worse, unless God interpose.

Thus the soul of man being essentially active, although one sin did not establish a confirmed habit, it did alienate God and work confusion in the soul, and thus lead to an endless course of sin.

THE CONSEQUENCES OF ADAM'S SIN TO HIS POSTERITY are—1st. The judicial charging of the legal responsibility of that sin upon all at their creation whom he represented in the Covenant of Works.   2d. The consequent birth of each of his descendants in a state of exclusion from the life-giving communion of the divine Spirit.   3d. The consequent loss of original righteousness, and the inherent and prevailing tendency to sin which is the invariable moral condition of each of his descendants from birth.   4th. The absolute moral inability of men to change their natures or to fulfil their obligations.

For reasons which will appear subsequently, the subjects connected with man's natural moral corruption and impotency, are discussed before the subject of Imputation, or the reason and method of the passing over of the consequences of Adam's sin from him to his descendants.

CHAPTER XIX.

ORIGINAL SIN.—(*Peccatum Habituale.*)

1. *How is original sin to be defined?*

See "Confession of Faith," Chapter vi.; "L. Cat.," Questions 25, 26; "S. Cat.," Question 18.

The phrase, *original sin,* is used sometimes to include the judicial imputation of the guilt of Adam's sin, as well as the hereditary moral corruption, common to all his descendants, which is one of the consequences of that imputation. More strictly, however, the phrase original sin designates only the hereditary moral corruption common to all men from birth.

In the definition of this doctrine WE DENY—

1st. That this corruption is in any sense physical, that it inheres in the essence of the soul, or in any of its natural faculties as such.

2d. That it consists primarily in the mere supremacy of the sensual part of our nature. It is a depraved habit or bias of will.

3d. That it consists solely in the absence of holy dispositions, because, from the inherent activity of the soul, sin exhibits itself from the beginning in the way of a positive proneness to evil.

On the other hand, WE AFFIRM—

1st. That original sin is purely moral, being the innate proneness of the will to evil.

2d. That having its seat in the will averse to the holy law of God, it biasses the understanding, and thus deceives the conscience, leads to erroneous moral judgments, to blindness of mind, to deficient and perverted sensibility in relation to moral objects, to the inordinate action of the sensuous nature, and thus to corruption of the entire soul.

3d. Thus it presents two aspects: (1.) The loss of the original righteous habit of will. (2.) The presence of a positively unrighteous habit.

4th. Yet from the fact that this innate depravity does embrace a positive disposition to evil, it does not follow that a positive evil quality has been infused into the soul. Because, from the essentially active nature of the soul, and from the essential nature of virtue, as that which obliges the will, it evidently follows that moral indifference is impossible; and so that depravity, which President Edwards says "comes from a defective or privative cause," instantly assumes a positive form. Not to love God is to rebel against him, not to obey virtue is to trample it under foot. Self-love soon brings us to fear, then to hate the vindicator of righteousness.—Edwards on "Original Sin," Part IV., sec. 2.

2. *Why is this sin called original?*

Not because it belongs to the original constitution of our nature as it came forth from the hand of God, but because, 1st, it is derived by ordinary generation from Adam, the original root of the human race; and 2d, it is the inward root or origin of all the actual sins that defile our lives.

This sin is also technically styled *Peccatum Habituale*, or the sin which consists in a morally corrupt habit or state of soul, in distinction from imputed sin and actual sin.

3. *How may it be proved that the doctrine of original sin does not involve the corruption of the substance of the soul?*

It is the universal judgment of men that there are in the soul, besides its essence and its natural faculties, certain habits, innate or acquired, which qualify the action of those faculties, and constitute the character of the man. Those habits, or inherent dispositions which determine the affections and desires of the will, govern a man's actions, and, when good, are the subjects of moral approbation, and, when evil, the subjects of moral disapprobation on the part of all men. An innate moral habit of soul, *e. g.*, original sin, is no more a physical corruption than any acquired habit, intellectual or moral, is a physical change.

Besides this, the Scriptures distinguish between the sin and the agent in a way which proves that the sinful habit is not something consubstantial with the sinner, Rom. vii. 17; "sin that dwelleth in me," Heb. xii. 1, etc.

4. *How can it be shown that original sin does not consist in disease, or merely in the supremacy of the sensuous part of our nature?*

While it is true that many sins have their occasions in the inordinate appetites of the body, yet it is evident the original or root of sin can not be in them—

1st. From the very nature of sin it must have its seat in the moral state of the voluntary principle. Disease, or any form of physical disorder, is not voluntary, and therefore not an element of moral responsibility. It is, moreover, the obligation of the will to regulate the lower sensuous nature, and sin must originate in the failure of those moral affections which would have been supreme if they still continued to reign in the will.

2d. From the fact that the most heinous sins are destitute of any sensuous element, e. g., pride, anger, malice, and AVERSION FROM GOD.

5. *How can it be proved that this innate disposition or habit of soul, which leads to sinful action, is itself sin?*

1st. This innate habit of soul is a state of the will, and it is an ultimate principle that all the states as well as acts of the will *related to the law of conscience* are moral, i. e., either virtuous or vicious.—See above, Chapter XV., Questions 9 and 10.

2d. These permanent habits or states of the will constitute the moral character of the agent, which all men regard as the proper subject of praise or blame.

3d. This inherent disposition to sinful action is called "sin" in Scripture.—Rom. vi. 12, 14, 17; vii. 5–17. It is called "flesh" as opposed to "spiritual," Gal. v. 17, 24; also "lust," James i. 14, 15; and "old Adam" and "body of sin," Rom. vi. 6; also "ignorance," "blindness of heart," "alienation from the life of God," and a condition of "being past feeling," Eph. iv. 18, 19.

6. *How can it be shown that original sin does not consist simply in the want of original righteousness?*

1st. It follows from the inherent activity of the human soul, and from the inherently obliging power of moral right, that the absence of right dispositions immediately leads to the formation of positively sinful dispositions. Not to love God is to hate him, not to obey him is to disobey. Disobedience leads to fear, to falsehood, and to every form of sin.—See above, Question 1.

2d. As a matter of fact, innate depravity exhibits its positive character by giving birth to sins, involving positive viciousness in the earliest stages of accountable agency, as pride, malice, etc.

3d. The Scriptures assign it a positive character, when they apply to it such terms as "flesh," "concupiscence," "old man," "law in the members," "body of sin," "body of death," "sin taking occasion," "deceived me," and "wrought all manner of concupiscence."—Rom. vii.

7. *How may it be shown that it affects the entire man?*

Original sin has its seat in the will, and primarily consists in that proneness to unlawful dispositions and affections which is the innate habit of the human soul. But the several faculties of the human soul are not separate agents. The one soul acts in each function as an indivisible agent, its several faculties or powers after their kind mutually qualifying one another. When the soul is engaged in understanding an object, or an aspect of any object, *e. g.*, mathematics, with which its affections are not concerned, then its action has no moral element. But when it is engaged in understanding an object with respect to which its depraved affections are perversely interested, its action must be biassed. The consequence, therefore, of the sinful bias of the will in its controlling influence over the exercises of the soul, in all its functions, will be—

1st. The understanding, biassed by the perverted affections, acting concurrently with the moral sense in forming moral judgments, will lead to erroneous judgments, to a deceiving conscience, and to general "blindness of mind" as to moral subjects.

2d. The emotions and sensibilities which accompany the judgments of conscience in approving the good and in condemning the wrong, by repeated outrage and neglect, will be rendered less lively, and thus lead to a seared conscience, and general moral insensibility.

3d. In a continued course of sinful action the memory will become defiled with its stores of corrupt experiences, from which the imagination also must draw its materials.

4th. The body in its turn will be corrupted. (1.) Its natural appetites will become inordinate in the absence of proper control. (2.) Its active powers will be used as "instruments of unrighteousness unto sin."

5th. The Scriptures teach—(1.) That the understanding of the "natural man" is depraved as well as his affections.— 1 Cor. ii. 14; 2 Cor. iv. 4; Eph. iv. 18; Col. i. 21. (2.) That regeneration involves illumination as well as renewal of the heart.—Acts xxvi. 18; Eph. i. 18; v. 8; 1 Pet. ii. 9. (3.) That truth addressed to the understanding is the great instrument of the Spirit in regeneration and sanctification.—John xvii. 17; James i. 18.

8. *What is meant by the affirmation that man by nature is totally depraved?*

By this orthodox phrase IT IS NOT TO BE UNDERSTOOD, 1st, that the depraved man has not a conscience. The virtuousness of an agent does not consist in his having a conscience, but in the conformity of the dispositions and affections of his will to the law of which conscience is the organ. Even the devils and lost souls retain their sense of right and wrong, and those vindicatory emotions with which conscience is armed.

Or, 2d, that unregenerate men, possessing a natural conscience, do not often admire virtuous character and actions in others.

Or, 3d, that they are incapable of disinterested affections and actions in their various relations with their fellow-men.

Or, 4th, that any man is as thoroughly depraved as it is possible for him to become, or that each man has a disposition inclined to every form of sin.

But IT IS MEANT—1st. That virtue consisting in the conformity of the dispositions of the will with the law of God, and the very soul of virtue consisting in the allegiance of the soul to God, every man by nature is totally alienated in his governing disposition from God, and consequently his every act, whether morally indifferent, or conformed to subordinate principles of right, is vitiated by the condition of the agent as a rebel.

2d. That this state of will leads to a schism in the soul, and to the moral perversion of all the faculties of soul and body (see preceding question.)

3d. The tendency of this condition is to further corruption in endless progression in every department of our nature, and this deterioration would, in every case, be incalculably more rapid than it is, if it were not for the supernatural restraints of the Holy Ghost.

4th. There remains no recuperative element in the soul. Man can only and forever become worse without a miraculous recreation.

9. *What proof of the doctrine of original sin may be derived from the history of the Fall?*

God created man in his own image, and pronounced him as a moral agent to be very good. He threatened him with death in the very day that he should eat the forbidden fruit, and only in the sense of spiritual death was that threat literally fulfilled. The spiritual life of man depends upon communion with God; but God drove him at once forth in anger from his presence. Consequently the present spiritual state of man is declared to be "death," the very penalty threatened.—Eph. ii. 1; 1 John iii., 14.

10. *What is the account which the Scriptures give of human nature, and how can the existence of an innate hereditary depravity be thence inferred?*

The Scriptures represent all men as totally alienated from God, and morally depraved in their understandings, hearts, wills, consciences, bodies, and actions.—Rom. iii. 10–23; viii. 7;

Job xiv. 4; xv. 14; Gen. vi. 5; viii. 21; Matt. xv. 19; Jer. xvii. 9; Is. i. 5, 6. This depravity of man is declared to be, 1st, of the act, 2d, of the heart, 3d, from birth and by nature, 4th, of all men without exception.—Ps. li. 5; John iii. 6; Eph. ii. 3; Ps. lviii. 3.

11. *State the evidence for the truth of this doctrine afforded by* Rom. v. 12–21.

Paul here proves that the guilt,—legal obligation to suffer the penalty,—of Adam's sin is imputed to us, by the unquestionable fact that the penalty of the law which Adam broke has been inflicted upon all. But that penalty was all penal evil, death physical, spiritual, eternal. Original sin, therefore, together with natural death, is in this passage assumed as an undeniable fact, upon which the apostle constructs his argument for the imputation of Adam's sin.

12. *How is the truth of this doctrine established by the fact of the general prevalence of sin?*

All men, under all circumstances, in every age of the world, and under whatever educational influences they may be brought up, begin to sin uniformly as soon as they enter upon moral agency. A universal effect must have a universal cause. Just as we judge that a man is by nature an intelligence, because the actions of all men involve an element of intelligence, so we as certainly judge that man is by nature depraved, because all men act sinfully.

13. *If Adam sinned, though free from any corruption of nature, how does the fact that his posterity sin prove that their nature is corrupt?*

The fact that Adam sinned proves that a moral agent may be at once sinless and fallible, and that such a being, left to himself, *may* sin, but with respect to his posterity the question is, what is the universal and uniform cause that every individual always certainly begins to sin as soon as he begins to act as a moral agent? The question in the one case is, *How could such an one sin?* but in the other, *Why do all certainly sin from the beginning?*

14. *By what other objections do Pelagians and others attempt to avoid the force of the argument from the universality of sin?*

1st. Those who maintain that the liberty of indifference is essential to responsible agency, and that volitions are not determined by the precedent moral state of the mind, attribute all sinful actions to the fact that the will of man is unconditioned, and insist that his acting as he acts is an ultimate fact.

In answer, we acknowledge that a man always wills as he pleases, but the question is, *Why does he always certainly please to will wrong?* An indifferent cause can not account for a uniform fact. The doctrine of original sin merely assigns the depraved character of the will itself as the uniform cause of the uniform fact.

2d. Others attempt to explain the facts by the universal influence of sinful example.

We answer: (1.) Children uniformly manifest depraved dispositions at too early a period to admit of that sin being rationally attributed to the influence of example. (2.) Children manifest depraved dispositions who have been brought up from birth in contact with such influences only as would incline them to holiness.

3d. Others, again, attempt to explain the facts by referring to the natural order in the development of our faculties, *e. g.*, first the animal, then the intellectual, then the moral: thus the lower, by anticipating, subverts the higher.

For answer, see above, Question 4. Besides, while this is an imperfect explanation, it is yet a virtual admission of the fact of innate hereditary depravity. Such an order of development, leading to such uniform consequences, is itself a total corruption of nature.

15. *What argument for the doctrine of original sin may be derived from the universality of death?*

The penalty of the law was death, including death spiritual, physical, and moral. Physical death is universal; eternal death, temporarily suspended for Christ's sake, is denounced upon all the impenitent. As one part of the penalty has taken effect, even upon infants, who have never been guilty of actual transgression, we must believe the other part to have taken effect likewise. Brutes, who also suffer and die, are not moral agents, nor were they ever embraced in a covenant of life, and therefore their case, although it has its own peculiar difficulties, is not analogous to that of man. Geology affirms that brutes suffered and died in successive generations before the creation and apostasy of man. This is at present one of the unsolved questions of God's providence.—See Hugh Miller's "Testimonies of the Rocks."

16. *How may it be proved by what the Scriptures say concerning regeneration?*

The Scriptures declare—

1st. That regeneration is a radical change of the moral character, wrought by the Holy Ghost in the exercise of supernatural power. It is called "a new creation"; the regenerated are called "God's workmanship, created unto good works," etc. Ezek. xxxvi. 26; Eph. i. 19; ii. 5, 10; iv. 24; 1 Pet. i. 23; James i. 18.

2d. Regeneration is declared to be necessary absolutely and universally.—John iii. 3; 2 Cor. v. 17.

17. *How may it be proved from what the Scriptures say of redemption?*

The Scriptures assert of redemption—

1st. *As to its nature*, that the design and effect of Christ's sacrifice is to deliver, by means of an atonement, all his people from the *power* as well as from the *guilt* of sin.—Eph. v. 25–27; Titus ii. 14; Heb. ix. 12–14; xiii. 12.

2d. *As to its necessity*, that it was absolutely necessary for all—for infants who never have committed actual sin, as well as for adults.—Acts iv. 12; Rom. iii. 25, 26; Gal. ii. 21 and iii. 21, 22; Matt. xix. 14; Rev. i. 5; v. 9.

Some have essayed to answer, that Christ only redeemed infants from the "liability to sin." But redemption being an atonement by blood, the "just for the unjust," if infants be not sinners they can not be redeemed. A sinless liability to sin is only a misfortune, and can admit of no redemption.—See Dr. Taylor's "Concio ad Clerum" (New Haven, 1828), pp. 24, 25; also Harvey's Review of the same (Hartford, 1829), p. 19.

18. *State the evidence afforded by infant baptism.*

Baptism, as circumcision, is an outward rite, signifying the inward grace of spiritual regeneration and purification.—Mark i. 4; John iii. 5; Titus iii. 5; Deut. x. 16; Rom. ii. 28, 29. Both of these rites were designed to be applied to infants. The application of the sign would be both senseless and profane if infants did not need, and were not capable of the thing signified.

19. *If God is the author of our nature, and our nature is sinful, how can we avoid the conclusion that God is the author of sin?*

That conclusion would be unavoidable if, 1st, sin was an essential element of our nature, or if, 2d, it inhered in that nature originally, as it came from God.

But we know, 1st, that sin originated in the free act of man, created holy, yet fallible; 2d, that entire corruption of nature sprang from that sin; and, 3d, that in consequence of sin God has justly withdrawn the conservative influences of his Holy

Spirit, and left men to the natural and penal consequences of their sin.—See Calvin's "Instit.," Lib. II., Chap. I., secs. 6 and 11.

20. *How can this doctrine be reconciled with the liberty of man and his responsibility for his acts?*

1st. Consciousness affirms that a man is always responsible for his free actions, and that his act is always free when he wills as, upon the whole, he prefers to will. 2d. Original sin consists in corrupt dispositions, and, therefore, in every sin a man acts freely, because he acts precisely as he is disposed to act. 3d. Consciousness affirms that inability is not inconsistent with responsibility. The inherent habit or disposition of the will determines his action, but no man, by a mere choice or volition, can change his disposition.—See Chap. XVIII., Questions 4 and 25.

21. *How is this corruption of nature propagated?*

See below, under Chapter XXI.

22. *In what sense may sin be the punishment of sin?*

1st. In the way of natural consequence (1) in the interior working of the soul itself, in the derangement of its powers; (2) in the entangled relations of the sinner with God and his fellowmen.

2d. In the way of judicial abandonment. Because of sin God withdraws his Holy Spirit, and further sin is the consequence.—Rom. i. 24–28.

23. *What do the Scriptures teach concerning the sin against the Holy Ghost?*

See Matt. xii. 31, 32; Mark iii. 29, 30; Heb. vi. 4–6; x. 26, 27; 1 John v. 16.

These passages appear to teach that this sin consists in the malicious rejection of the blood of Christ, and of the testimony of the Holy Ghost against evidence and conviction. It is called the sin against the Holy Ghost because he is immediately present in the heart of the sinner, and his testimony and influence is directly rejected and contemptuously resisted. It is unpardonable, not because its guilt transcends the merit of Christ, or the state of the sinner transcends the renewing power of the Holy Ghost, but because it consists in the final rejection of these, and because at this limit God has sovereignly staid his grace.

24. *What are the main positions involved in the Pelagian doctrine of original sin?*

The system called Pelagian originated with Pelagius in his controversies with St. Augustine in the beginning of the fifth century, and was afterwards completely developed by the disciples of Faustus and Lælius Socinus in the sixteenth century, is embodied in the Racovian Catechism, and prevails among the English and American Unitarians of the eighteenth and nineteenth centuries.

It embraces the following points : 1st. Adam's sin affected himself alone. 2d. Infants are born in the same moral state in which Adam was created. 3d. Every man possesses plenary ability to sin or to repent and obey whenever he will. 4th. Responsibility is in exact proportion to ability; and God's demands are adjusted to the various capacities (moral as well as constitutional) and circumstances of men.

25. *What are the main positions involved in the Semipelagian doctrine?*

According to the critical estimate of Wiggers in his "Hist. Present. of Augustinianism and Pelagianism," Pelagianism regards man as morally and spiritually well. Semipelagianism regards him as sick. Augustinianism regards him as dead.

The current positions of Semipelagianism during the middle ages were—1st. Denial of the imputation of the guilt of Adam's sin. 2d. Acknowledgment of a morbid condition of man's moral nature from birth by inheritance from Adam. 3d. Which morbid condition is not itself sin but the certain cause of sin. 4th. It involves the moral powers of the soul to such an extent that no man can fulfil the requirements either of the law or of the gospel without divine assistance. Man, however, has the power to *begin* to act aright, when God seeing his effort, and knowing that otherwise it would be fruitless, gives him the gracious help he needs.

The doctrine of the Arminians, and the "Synergism" of Melanchthon amount practically to very much the same thing with the statements just made. The main difference is that the Semipelagians held that man can and must *begin* the work of repentance and obedience when God instantly co-operates with him. While the Arminians and Synergists held that man is so far depraved that he needs grace to dispose and enable him to begin as well as to continue and to succeed in the work, but that all men as a matter of fact have the same common grace acting upon them, which grace effects nothing until the man voluntarily co-operates with it, when it becomes efficacious through that co-operation.

The Greek Church, which occupies the same general position as to original sin and grace, holds—1st. Original sin is not voluntary and therefore not true sin. 2d. The influence of Adam extends only to the sensuous, and not to the rational nor moral nature of his descendants, and hence it extends to their will only through the sensuous nature. 3d. Infants are guiltless because they possess only a physical propagated nature. 4th. The human will takes the initiative in regeneration but needs divine assistance. This is Semipelagianism. While the corresponding Arminian position is that grace takes the initiative in regeneration but depends for its effect upon human c -operation.

26. *What is the New Haven view on this subject?*

Dr. Nathaniel W. Taylor, of New Haven, the prince of American new school theology, taught that sin consists solely in acts of the will. That "original sin is man's own act, consisting in a free choice of some object rather than God as his chief good." He includes in this definition the permanent governing preference of the will, which determines special and transient acts of choice; which preference is formed by each human being as soon as he becomes a moral agent, and is uniformly a preference of some lesser good in place of God. He maintains also that the nature of man, in the condition in which it comes into being, in consequence of Adam's fall, is the *occasion*, not the *cause*, of all men invariably making a wrong moral preference, and consequently original sin is *by nature* in the sense that the will enacts it freely though uniformly as occasioned by nature, yet that the nature itself, or its inherent tendency to occasion sin, is not itself sin, or ill-deserving.—See "Concio ad Clerum," New Haven, 1828, and Harvey's Review thereof.

27. *What is the Romish doctrine as to the change effected in the moral nature of man by the fall?*

See below the public statements of the various churches.

28. *What distinction do the Romanists make between mortal and venial sins?*

By mortal sins they mean those that turn away the soul from God, and forfeit baptismal grace. By venial sins they mean those which only impede the course of the soul to God. See below Bellarmin, quoted under "Authoritative Statement of Church Doctrine," etc.

The objections are—1st. This distinction is never made in the Scriptures. 2d. Except for the sacrifice of Christ, every sin is mortal.—James ii. 10; Gal. iii. 10.

The Authoritative Statements of Church Doctrine.

Romish Doctrine.—*"Council of Trent,"* Sess. v. Can. 2.—"If any one shall assert that the apostasy of Adam injured himself alone and not his posterity; and that he lost the sanctity and righteousness received from God, for himself alone and not also for us, his posterity; or that the stain which results from the sin of disobedience, death, and physical evils only have overflowed over the whole human race, and not also sin which is the disease of the soul—*anathema sit.*" *Ib.*, Sess. vi. Cap. 1. "The Holy Synod declares that in order properly to understand the doctrine of justification it is necessary that every one should acknowledge and confess that since all men lost their innocency in the apostasy of Adam, so that . . . . they are servants of sin, under the power of the devil and of death . . . nevertheless in them free will is by no means extinct, although it is weakened as to its strength and biassed." *Ib.*, Sess. vi. Can. 5.—"If any one shall say that the free-will of man has been lost and extinguished in consequence of the sin of Adam . . . . . *anathema sit.*" Can. 7.—"If any one shall say that all works performed by a man anterior to justification (regeneration), from whatever reason performed, are true sins which merit the hatred of God, or that the more vehemently one may strive to dispose himself to grace, only the more grievously he sins—*anathema sit.*"

Bellarmin, *"Amiss. Gratia,"* iii. 1.—"The penalty which properly stands over against the first sin, is the loss of original righteousness and of the supernatural gifts with which God had furnished our nature. *"De Gratia primi hom.,"* 1.—"They (the Catholics) teach that, through the sin of Adam the whole man was truly deteriorated, but that he has not lost free will nor any other of the *dona naturalia*, but only the *dona supernaturalia.*" *Ib.*, c. 5.—"Wherefore the state of man since the fall of Adam does not differ more from his state in *puris naturalibus* (*i. e.*, as created and antecedent to his endowment with the *dona supernaturalia*, see Statement of Romish Doctrine end of Ch. XVI.) than a man robbed of his clothes differs from one originally naked, neither is human nature any worse (if you subtract original guilt) nor does it labor under greater ignorance and infirmity, than it was and did as created in *puris naturalibus*. Whence it follows that corruption of nature does not result from the loss of any gift, nor from the accession of any evil quality, but only from the loss of the supernatural gift because of the sin of Adam."

"Amiss. Gra.," v. 5.—"The question between us and our adversaries is not whether human nature has been grievously depraved through the sin of Adam. For that we freely confess. Neither is the question whether this depravity pertains in any manner to original sin, so that it may be spoken of as the material of that sin. But the whole controversy is whether that corruption of nature and especially concupiscence *per se* and of its own nature, as it is found in the baptized and justified, is properly original sin. This the Catholics deny."

Lutheran Doctrine.—*"Formula Concordiæ,"* p. 640.—"(It is to be believed)—1st. That this hereditary evil is fault or guilt (ill-desert) by which on account of the disobedience of Adam and Eve, we all are made subject to the wrath of God, and are by nature children of wrath, as the Apostle testified (Rom. v. 12, sqq., Eph. ii. 3). 2d. That there is through all a total want, defect, and privation of that original righteousness concreated in Paradise, or of that image of God in which man in the beginning was created in truth, holiness, and righteousness; and there is at the same time that impotency and incapacity, that weakness and stupidity, by which man is rendered utterly incapable of all things divine or spiritual. . . . 3d. Moreover that original sin in human nature does not only involve the total loss and absence of all good in matters spiritual and pertaining to God; but that also in the place of the lost likeness to God there is in man an inward, most evil, profound (like an abyss), inscrutable, and ineffable corruption of the whole nature and of all the powers, and primarily in the principle and superior faculties of the soul, in the mind, intellect, heart, and will.

Ib., p. 645.—"But although this original sin infects and corrupts the whole nature of man, as a kind of spiritual poison and leprosy (as Dr. Luther says), so that now in our corrupted nature it is not possible to show to the eye these two apart, the nature alone, or the original sin alone; nevertheless that corrupt nature, or substance of the corrupt man, the body and soul, or the man himself as created by God in whom the original sin dwells, is not one and the same with that original sin which dwells in the nature or essence of man and corrupts it; just as in the body of a leper, the leprous body and the leprosy itself, which is in the body, is not one and the same.

REFORMED DOCTRINE. —*"Belgic Confession,"* Art. 15. — "(Peccatum originis) is that corruption of the whole nature and that hereditary vice, by which even themselves in their mothers' wombs are polluted, and which, as a root, produces every kind of sin in man, and is therefore so base and execrable in the sight of God, that it suffices to the condemnation of the human race."

"Gallic Conf.," Art. 11.—"We believe that this vice (originis) is true sin, which makes all and every man, not even excepting little infants, hitherto hiding in the womb of their mothers, deserving (reos) before God of eternal death."

"Thirty-nine Articles of Ch. of Eng.," Art. 9.—"(Original or birth sin) is the fault and corruption of the nature of every man, that naturally is engendered of the offspring of Adam; whereby man is very far gone from original righteousness, and is of his own nature inclined to evil, so that the flesh lusteth always contrary to the spirit; and therefore in every person born into this world, it deserveth God's wrath and damnation."

REMONSTRANT DOCTRINE.—*"Apol. Conf. Remonstrant.*, p. 84.—"They (the Remonstrants) do not regard original sin as sin properly so called, nor as an evil which as a penalty, in the strict sense of that word, passes over from Adam upon his posterity, but as an evil, infirmity, or vice, or whatever name it may be designated by, which is propagated from Adam, deprived of original righteousness, to his posterity.

Limborch "Theol. Christ.," iii. 3, 4.—"We confess also that infants are born less pure than Adam was created, and with a certain propensity to sinning, but this they receive not so much from Adam, as from their immediate parents, since if it were from Adam, it ought to be equal in all men. But now it is in the highest degree unequal, and ordinarily children are inclined to the sins of their parents.

SOCINIAN DOCTRINE.—*"Racovian Catechism,"* p. 294.—"And the fall of Adam, since it was one act, could not have had the power of corrupting the nature of Adam himself, much less that of his posterity. We do not deny, however, that from the constant habit of sinning, the nature of man has become infected with a certain fall and excessive proclivity to sinning. But we deny that this is *per se* sin, or of that nature."

CHAPTER XX.

INABILITY.

1. *State the* three *main elements involved in the consequences entailed by the sin of Adam upon his posterity.*

These are—1st. The guilt, or just penal responsibility of Adam's first sin or apostatizing act, which is imputed or judicially charged upon his descendants, whereby every child is born into the world in a state of antenatal forfeiture or condemnation. 2d. The entire depravity of our nature, involving a sinful innate disposition inevitably leading to actual transgression. 3d. The entire inability of the soul to change its own nature, or to do any thing spiritually good in obedience to the divine law.

2. *What* three *great types of doctrine on the subject of human ability to fulfil the law of God have always coexisted in the church?*

1st. *Pelagian.*—(*a.*) Moral character can be predicated only of volitions. (*b.*) Ability is always the measure of responsibility. (*c.*) Hence every man has always plenary power to do all that it is his duty to do. (*d.*) Hence the human will alone, to the exclusion of the interference of any internal influence from God, must decide human character and destiny. The only divine influence needed by man or consistent with his character as a self-determined agent is an external, providential, and educational one.

2d. *Semipelagian.*—(*a.*) Man's nature has been so far weakened by the fall that it can not act aright in spiritual matters without divine assistance. (*b.*) This weakened moral state which infants inherit from their parents is the cause of sin, but not itself sin in the sense of deserving the wrath of God. (*c.*) Man must strive to do his whole duty, when God meets him with co-operative grace, and renders his efforts successful. (*d.*) Man is not responsible for the sins he commits until after he has enjoyed and abused the influences of grace.

3d. *Augustinian.*—Which was adopted by all the original Protestant Churches, Lutheran and Reformed. (*a.*) Man is by nature so entirely depraved in his moral nature as to be totally unable to do any thing spiritually good, or in any degree to begin or to dispose himself thereto. (*b.*) That even under the exciting and suasory influences of divine grace the will of man is totally unable to act aright in co-operation with grace, until after the will itself is by the energy of grace radically and permanently renewed. (*c.*) Even after the renewal of the will it ever continues dependent upon divine grace, to prompt, direct, and enable it in the performance of every good work.

3. *How does the* usus loquendi *of the words " Liberty " and "Ability " in this connection, among the early differ from that of the later Protestant writers?*

The early writers often use the term "liberty" in the sense in which we now use the term "ability," and deny that man since the fall possesses any "liberty" of will with respect to divine things.

While modern theologians hold precisely the same doctrine entertained by these early writers, they now think it more judicious to distinguish between the two terms in their constant use. By "liberty" is meant the inalienable property of a free agent, good or bad, to exercise volitions as he pleases; that is, according to the prevailing dispositions and tendencies of his soul. By "ability," on the other hand, is meant the power of a depraved human soul, naturally indisposed to spiritual good, to change its governing tendencies or dispositions by means of any volition, however strenuous, or to obey the requirements of the law in the absence of all holy dispositions. The permanent affections of the soul govern the volitions, but the volitions can not alter the affections. And when we say that no man since the fall has any ability to render that spiritual obedience which the law demands, we mean (*a*) that the radical moral dispositions of every man is opposed to that obedience, and (*b*) man has absolutely no ability to change them or (*c*) to exercise volitions contrary to them.

4. *State the orthodox doctrine both negatively and positively.*

The orthodox doctrine does *not* teach—1st. That man by the fall has lost any of his constitutional faculties necessary to constitute him a responsible moral agent. These are (*a*) reason, (*b*) conscience, (*c*) free will. Man possesses all of these in exercise. He has power to know the truth; he recognizes and feels moral distinctions and obligations; his affections and tendencies and habits of action are spontaneous; in all his volitions he chooses and refuses freely as he pleases. Therefore he is responsible. Nor, 2d, that man has not power to feel and to do many things which are good and amiable, benevolent and just, in the relations he sustains to his fellow-men. This is often admitted in the Protestant confessions and Theological Classics, where it is conceded that man since the fall has a capacity for *humana justicia,* and "*civil good,*" etc.

But the Orthodox doctrine *does* teach—1st. That the inability of man since the fall concerns things which involve our relation as spiritual beings to God—the apprehension and love of spiritual excellence and action in conformity therewith. These matters are designated in the Confessions "things of God," "things of the Spirit," "things which pertain to salvation." 2d. That man since the fall is utterly unable to know, or to feel, or to act in correspondence with these things. A natural man may be *intellectually* illuminated but he is *spiritually* blind. He may possess *natural* affections, but his heart is *dead* toward God, and invinceably averse to his person and law. He may obey the letter, but he can not obey in spirit and in truth.

5. *In what sense is this inability* absolute, *and in what sense* natural, *and in what sense* moral *?*

1st. It is *absolute* in the proper sense of that term. No unregenerate man has power either directly or indirectly to do what is required of him in this respect; nor to change his own nature so as to increase his power; nor to *prepare* himself for grace, nor in *the first instance* to co-operate with grace, until in the act of regeneration God changes his nature and gives him through grace gracious ability to act graciously in constant dependence upon grace.

2d. It is *natural* in the sense that it is not accidental or adventitious but innate, and that it belongs to our fallen nature as propagated by natural law from parent to child since the fall.

3d. It is *not* natural in *one* sense, because it does not belong to the nature of man as created. Man was created with plenary ability to do all that was in any way required of him, and the possession of such ability is always requisite to the moral perfection of his nature. He may be a real man without it, but can be a perfect man only with it. The ability graciously bestowed upon man in regeneration is not an endowment extra-natural, but consists in the restoration of his nature, in part, to its condition of primitive integrity.

4th. *It* is *not* natural in another sense, because it does not result in the least from any constitutional deficiency in human nature as it now exists as to its rational and moral faculties of soul.

5th. This inability is purely *moral*, because while every responsible man possesses all moral as well as intellectual faculties requisite for right action, the moral *state* of his faculties is such that right action is impossible. Its *essence* is in the inability of the soul to know, love, or choose spiritual good, and its *ground* exists in that moral corruption of soul whereby it is blind, insensible, and totally averse to all that is spiritually good.

6. *What is the history and value of the famous distinction between* natural *and* moral *ability?*

This distinction was first explicitly presented in this form by John Cameron, born in Glasgow, 1580, Prof. in the Theological School in Saumur, France, 1618, died 1625.

President Edwards in his great work "On the Will," Pt. I., Sec. 4, adopts the same terms, affirming that men since the fall have *natural* ability to do all that is required of them, but are destitute of *moral* ability to do so. By *natural* ability he meant the possession by every responsible free agent, as the condition of his responsibility, of all the constitutional faculties necessary to enable him to obey God's law. By *moral* ability he meant that inherent moral state of those faculties, that righteous *disposition* of heart, requisite to the performance of those duties.

As thus stated, and as President Edwards held and used it, there is no question as to the validity and importance of this distinction. The same principle is explicitly recognized in the statement of the orthodox doctrine given above, Questions 4 and 5. Nevertheless we seriously object to the phraseology used, for the following reasons:

1st. This phraseology has no warrant in the analogy of Scripture. They never say that man has one kind of ability but has not another. They everywhere consistently teach that man is not able to do what is required of him. They never teach that he is able in any sense.

2d. It has never been adopted in the Creed Statements of any one of the Reformed Churches.

3d. It is essentially ambiguous. It has been often used to express, sometimes to cover, Semipelagian error. It is naturally misleading and confusing when addressed to the struggling sinner. This language assures him that he is able in a certain sense, when it is only true that he possesses *some* of the essential prerequisites of ability. Ability *begins* only after *all* its essential conditions are present. To say that a dead bird has muscular ability to fly, and only lacks vital ability, is trifling with words. The truth is, the sinner is absolutely unable because of a moral deficiency. It is right enough to say that his inability is purely and simply moral. But it is simply untrue and misleading to tell him he has natural *ability*, when the fact is precisely that he is unable. The work of the Holy Spirit in regeneration is not a mere moral suasion but a new moral creation.

4th. Natural is not the proper antithesis of moral. A thing may be at the same time natural and moral. This inability of man as shown above, is certainly wholly moral, and it is yet in an important sense natural, *i. e.*, incident to his nature in its present state as naturally propagated.

5th. The language does not accurately express the important distinction intended. The inability is moral and is not either physical or constitutional. It has its ground not in the want of any faculty, but in the corrupt moral state of the faculties, in the inveterate disinclination of the affections and dispositions of the voluntary nature.

7. *Prove the fact of this inability from Scripture.*

Jer. xiii. 23; John vi. 44, 65; xv. 5; Rom. ix. 16; 1 Cor. ii. 14.

8. *Prove the same from what the Scriptures teach of the moral condition of man by nature.*

It is a state of spiritual blindness and darkness, Eph. iv. 18, of spiritual death.—Col. ii. 13. The unregenerate are the "*servants* of sin."—Rom. vi. 20. They are "without strength."—Rom. v. 6. Men are said to be subjects of Satan and led about by him at his will.—2 Tim. ii. 26. The only way to change the character of our actions is declared to be to change the character of our hearts.—Matt. xii. 33–35.

9. *Prove the same from what the Scriptures teach as to the nature and necessity of regeneration.*

As to its *nature* it is taught that regeneration is a "new birth," a "new creation," a "begetting anew," a "giving a new heart"—the subjects of it are "new creatures," "God's workmanship," etc. It is accomplished by the "exceeding greatness of the mighty power of God."—Eph. i. 18–20. All Christian graces, as love, joy, faith, peace, etc., are declared to be "fruits of the Spirit."—Gal. v. 22, 23. God "worketh in you to *will* and *to do* of his good pleasure."—Phil. ii. 13.

As to its *necessity* this radical change of the governing states and proclivities of the will itself is declared to be absolutely necessary in the case of every child of Adam, without exception, in order to salvation.

It is plain, therefore, that man must be absolutely spiritually impotent antecedent to this change wrought in him by divine power, and that all ability he may ever have even to co-operate with the grace that saves him, must be consequent upon that change.

10. *Prove the same from experience.*

1st. From the experience of every convinced sinner. All genuine conviction of sin embraces these two elements: (*a.*) A thorough conviction of responsibility and guilt, justifying God and prostrating self before him in confession and absolute self-emptying. (*b.*) A thorough conviction of our own moral impotence and dependence as much upon divine grace to enable us, as upon Christ's merits to justify us. A sinner must in both senses, *i. e.*, as to guilt and as to helplessness, be brought into a state of utter self-despair, or he can not be brought to Christ.

2d. From the experience of every true Christian. His most intimate conviction is (*a.*) that he was absolutely helpless and that he was saved by a divine intervention, *ab extra.* (*b.*) That his present degree of spiritual strength is sustained solely by the constant communications of the Holy Ghost, and that he lives spiritually only as he clings close to Christ.

3d. From the universal experience of the human family. We argue that man is absolutely destitute of spiritual ability, because there has never been discovered a single example of a mere man who has exercised it since the foundation of the earth.

11. *State and refute the objection brought against our doctrine on the alleged ground that "ability is the measure of responsibility."*

The maxim that "ability is the measure of responsibility" is undoubtedly true under some conditions and false under others. The mistake which utterly vitiates the above cited objection to the Scriptural doctrine of inability, consists in a failure to discriminate between the conditions under which the maxim is true, and the conditions under which it is false.

It is a self-evident truth, and one not denied by any party, that an inability which consists either (*a*) in the absence of the faculties absolutely necessary for the performance of a duty, or (*b*) in the absence of an opportunity to use them, is entirely inconsistent with moral responsibility in the case. If a man has not eyes, or if having them he is unavoidably destitute of light, he can not be morally bound to see. So, likewise, if a man is destitute of intellect, or of natural conscience, or of any of the constitutional faculties essential to moral agency, he can not be responsible for acting as a moral agent.

And it is further evident that this irresponsibility arises

solely from the bare fact of the inability. It matters not at all in *this respect* whether the inability be self-induced or not, if only it be a real incapacity. A man, for instance, who has put out his own eyes in order to avoid the draft, may be justly held responsible for *that act*, but he can never more be held responsible for seeing, *i. e.*, for using eyes that he does not possess.

On the other hand it is no less evident that when the inability consists solely in the want of the proper dispositions and affections, instead of being inconsistent with responsibility it is the very ground and reason of just condemnation. Nothing is more certain nor more universally confessed, than that the affections and dispositions are (1.) not under the control of the will. They can no more be changed than our stature by a mere volition. (2.) Yet we are responsible for them.

Those who maintain that responsibility is necessarily limited by ability must consequently hold either (1) that every man, however degraded, is able by a volition at once to conform himself to the highest standard of virtue, which is absurd; or (2) that the standard of moral obligation is lowered more and more in proportion as a man sins, and by sin loses the capacity for obedience, *i. e.*, that moral obligation decreases as guilt increases, or in other words that God's rights decrease as our rebellion against him increases. Which is also absurd. For the principle obviously vacates law altogether, making both its precept and penalty void, since the sinner carries the law down with himself. It takes the law out of God's hands, and puts it in the hands of the sinner, who always determines the extent of its requirements by the extent of his own apostasy.

12. *Prove that men are responsible for their affections.**

1st. The whole volume of Scripture testifies to the fact that God requires men to possess right affections, and that he judges and treats men according to their affections. Christ declares (Matt. xxii. 37–40) that the whole moral law is summarily comprehended in these two commandments, *to love* God with the whole heart, and our neighbor as ourselves. "On these two commandments hang all the law and the prophets." But "love" is an affection not a volition, nor is it under the immediate control of the volitions.

2d. It is the instinctive judgment of all men that moral dispositions and affections are intrinsically either good or evil, and worthy in every case according to their character, and irrespective of their origin of praise or blame. Some affections

* Dr. Charles Hodge's "Lectures."

indeed are in themselves morally indifferent and become right or wrong only when adopted by the will as a principle of action in preference to other competing principles, *e. g.*, the affection of self-love. But there are other affections which are intrinsically good, like love to God and disinterested benevolence towards our fellow-creatures, and others which are intrinsically evil, like malice or distrust of God, without any consideration of their origin.—Rom. vii. 14–23. Every volition derives all its moral quality from the quality of the affection that prompts it; while, on the other hand, the moral quality of the affection is original, and independent, and absolute.

3d. The Scriptures and universal Christian experience teach that the common condition of man is one at once morally impotent and responsible. Hence the two can not be inconsistent.

13. *How can man's inability be reconciled with the commands, promises, and threatenings of God?*

God righteously deals with the sinner according to the measure of his responsibility, and not according to the measure of his sinful inability. It would have been a compromise altogether unworthy of God to have lowered his demands in proportion to man's sin. Besides, under the gospel dispensation, God makes use of his commands, promises, and threatenings, as gracious means, under the influence of his Spirit, to enlighten the minds, quicken the consciences, and to sanctify the hearts of men.

14. *How can man's inability be shown to be consistent with the rational use of means?*

The efficiency of all means lies in the power of God, and not in the ability of man. God has established a connection between certain means and the ends desired; he has commanded us to use them, and has promised to bless them; and human experience has proved God's faithfulness to his engagements, and the instrumental connection between the means and the end.

15. *Show that the legitimate practical effect of this doctrine is not to lead sinners to procrastinate.*

It obviously and rightly tends to extinguish the *false* hopes of every sinner, and to paralyze their efforts to extricate themselves in the exercise of their own strength, or in reliance upon their own resources. But both reason and experience assure us that the natural and actual effect of this great truth is—
1st. To humble the soul and fill it with self-despair. 2d. To

shut it up to immediate and unreserved reliance upon the sovereign grace of God in Christ, the only ground of possible hope remaining. 3d. Subsequent to conversion this truth leads the soul of the Christian to habitual self-distrust, diligence, and watchfulness, and to habitual confidence in and gratitude towards God.

THE AUTHORITATIVE STATEMENTS OF THE VARIOUS CHURCHES.

ROMISH DOCTRINE.—" *Council of Trent,*" *Sess.* 6, *can.* 7.—"If any one shall say, that all the works performed before justification, on whatsoever principle they are done, are truly sins, and merit the wrath of God . . . . anathema sit." See further under the heads of "Original Sin" and "Effectual Calling."

LUTHERAN DOCTRINE.—"*Aug. Conf.,*" p. 15.—"Human will possesses a certain ability (libertatem) for effecting civil righteousness, and for choosing things apparent to the senses. But, without the Holy Spirit, it has not the power of effecting the righteousness of God, or spiritual righteousness, because the animal man does not perceive those things which are of the Spirit of God."

"*Formula Concordiœ,*" p. 579.—"Therefore we believe that as much as the power is wanting to a corpse to revive itself, and restore to itself corporeal life, by so much is all and every faculty wanting to a man, who by reason of sin is spiritually dead, of recalling himself to spiritual life." *Ib.*, p. 656.—"We believe that the intellect, heart, and will of an unrenewed man are altogether unable, in spiritual and divine things, and of their own proper natural vigor, to understand, to believe, to embrace, to think, to will, to commence, to perfect, to transact, to operate, or to co-operate any thing."

REFORMED DOCTRINE.—"*Thirty-nine Articles of the Church of England,*" Art. 10.—"The condition of man after the fall of Adam, is such, that he can not turn and prepare himself, by his own natural strength and good works, to faith and calling upon God : wherefore we have no power to do good works pleasant and acceptable to God, without the grace of God by Christ preventing us, that we may have a good-will, and working with us when we have that good-will."

"*Conf. Helvetica Posterior.*"—"In the unrenewed man there is no free-will for good, and no strength for performing that which is good. . . . . No one denies that in external things the renewed and the unrenewed alike have free-will; for man has this constitution in common with the other animals, that some things he wills, and some things he wills not. . . . We condemn on this subject the Manicheans, who deny that evil originated in the exercise of a free-will by a good man. We also condemn the Pelagians, who say that even the bad man possesses sufficient free-will for performing the good commanded."

"*Formula Consensus Helvetica,*" Can. 22.—"We hold therefore that they speak with too little accuracy and not without danger, who call this inability to believe *moral* inability, and do not hold it to be *natural*, adding that man in whatever condition he may be placed is able to believe if he will, and that faith in some way or other, indeed, is self-originated; and yet the Apostle most distinctly calls it the gift of God " (Eph. ii. 8).

"*Articles of Synod of Dort,*" Chap. iii. Art. 3.—"All men are conceived in sin, and born children of wrath, indisposed to all saving good, prepense to evil, dead in sins and the slaves of sin, and without the grace of the regenerating Holy Spirit they are neither willing nor able to return to God, to correct their depraved nature, or to dispose themselves to the correction of it."

"Confession of Faith," Chap. ix. § 3. —"Man, by his fall and state of sin, hath wholly lost all ability of will to any spiritual good accompanying salvation ; so as a natural man, being altogether averse from that good, and dead in sin, is not able, by his own strength, to convert himself, or to prepare himself thereunto."

REMONSTRANT DOCTRINE.—*Limborch,* *"Theol. Christ.,"* Lib. 4, ch. 14. § 21.—"The grace of God is the primary cause of faith, without which a man is not able rightly to use his free-will. . . . Therefore free-will co-operates with grace, otherwise the obedience or the disobedience of man would have no place. . . . Grace is not the sole cause, although it is the primary cause of salvation, . . for the co-operation itself of the free-will with grace is of grace as a primary cause : for unless the free-will had been excited by prevenient grace it would not have been able to co-operate with grace."

SOCINIAN DOCTRINE.—*"Racovian Catechism,"* Ques. 422.—"Is not free-will placed in our power so that we may obey God ? Surely, because it is certain that the first man was so constituted by God that he was endowed with free-will. Nor truly has any cause supervened why God should have deprived man of that free-will subsequently to his fall."

CHAPTER XXI.

1. *Give a summary statement of the facts already proved from Scripture, consciousness, and observation, and generally acknowledged in all Creeds of the Protestant Churches, as to man's moral and spiritual condition from birth and by nature.*

1st. All men, without exception, begin to sin as soon as they enter upon moral agency. 2d. They are all born with an antecedent and prevailing *tendency* in their nature to sin. 3d. This innate tendency is itself *sin* in the strictest sense. It is inherently ill-deserving as well as polluting and destructive, and without any reference to its origin in Adam, it fully deserves God's wrath and curse, and except when expiated by the blood of Christ is always visited with that curse. President Edwards, "Freedom of the Will," pt. 4, sec. 1, says, "The essence of the virtue and vice of dispositions of the heart lies not in their cause but their nature." 4th. Men are, therefore, by nature, totally averse to all good and unable of themselves to reverse the evil tendency inherent in their nature and to choose good in preference to evil. 5th. Consequently they are by nature children of wrath, their character formed and their evil destiny fixed antecedent to any personal action of their own.

2. *Show that the real difficulty in reconciling the ways of God to man lies in these unquestionable* FACTS; *and further, that recognition of these facts in their integrity is of far more doctrinal importance than any account of their origin can possibly be.*

That we begin to exist, antecedent to possible personal agency, with a nature which justly condemns us and infallibly predisposes us to actual sin, is an amazing mystery, an ineffable curse, and yet a certain and universal fact. No possible theory as to its origin can aggravate its mystery or its terrible significance. We do not claim that the doctrine of our responsibility for Adam's apostatizing act is without grave difficulties. But we do maintain (*a*) that it is taught in Scripture, and (*b*) that it is more satisfactory to reason and to our moral feelings than any other solution ever given.

It is no less evident that the full recognition of these facts is of far more doctrinal and practical importance than any explanation of their origin or occasion can be. Our views as to these facts must at once determine our relation to God, the entire character of our religious experience, and our views as to the nature of sin and grace, the necessity and nature of redemption, regeneration, and sanctification, while any rationale of these facts will only clear and enlarge our views as to the consistency of God's dealings with the human race with his own perfections, and as to the relations of the several parts of the divine plan with each other.

Hence we find—(1.) That these facts as to man's innate sinfulness are much more prominently and frequently set forth in the Scriptures than is the assertion of our responsibility for Adam's act of apostasy. (2.) That these have been clearly defined and uniformly agreed upon by all parties and in all ages of the Christian Church, while with respect to our connection with Adam there has prevailed a great deal of vagueness and contrariety of view.—Principal Cunningham's "Theo. of the Ref.," Essay vii., 1.

3. *State the self-evident moral principles which must be certainly presupposed in every inquiry into the dealings of God with his responsible creatures.*

(1.) God can not be the author of sin. (2.) We must not believe that he could consistently with his own perfections create a creature *de novo* with a sinful nature. (3.) The perfection of righteousness, not bare sovereignty, is the grand distinction of all God's dealings. The error that the volition of God determines moral distinctions, was for opposite reasons maintained by the Supralapsarians Twisse, Gomar, etc., and by such Arminians as Grotius, the one to show that God might condemn whom he pleased irrespective of real guilt, and the other to show that he could save whom he pleased irrespective of a real atonement. The fundamental truth, however, now admitted by all Christians, is that the immutable moral perfections of God's nature constitute the absolute standard of right, and in every action determine his will, and are manifested in all his works. (4.) It is a heathen notion, adopted by naturalistic rationalists, that the "order of nature," or the "nature of things," or "natural law," is a real agent independent of God, limiting his freedom, or acting with him as an independent

concause in producing effects. "Nature" is simply God's creature and instrument. What is generated by nature is made by
God. (5.) We can not believe that God would inflict either
moral or physical evil upon any creature whose natural rights
had not been previously justly forfeited. (6.) Every moral
agent must in justice enjoy a fair probation, *i. e.*, a trial so
conditioned as to afford at least as much opportunity of success
as liability to failure.

4. *State the two distinct questions thence arising, which though
frequently confused, it is essential to keep separate.*

1st. How does an innate sinful nature originate in each human being at the commencement of his existence, so that the
Maker of the man is not the cause of his sin. If this corruption of nature originated in Adam, How is it transmitted to us?

2d. WHY, on what ground of justice, does God inflict this
terrible evil, the root and ground of all other evils, at the very
commencement of personal existence? WHAT fair probation
have infants born in sin enjoyed? WHEN, and WHY, were their
rights as new created beings forfeited?

It is self-evident that these questions are distinct, and should
be treated as such. The first may possibly be answered on
physiological grounds. The second question however concerns
the moral government of God, and inquires concerning the
justice of his dispensations. In the history of theology of all
ages and in all schools very much confusion has resulted from
the failure to emphasize and preserve prominent this distinction.

I. HOW DOES IT COME TO PASS THAT HUMAN SOULS ARE CORRUPT FROM
   BIRTH? IF THIS CORRUPTION IS TRANSMITTED FROM ADAM,
   HOW IS IT TRANSMITTED?

5. *What answers have been given to this question which deny
or ignore the Adamic origin of sin?*

1st. The Manichæan theory, adopted by Manes, A. D. 240,
from the dualism of Zoroaster, of the eternal self-existence of
two principles, the one good identified with the absolute God,
the other evil identified with matter, or that principle of which
matter is one of the manifestations. Our spirits have their pri-
mal origin with God, while sin necessarily results from their
entanglement with matter. This system obviously destroys the
moral character of sin, and was earnestly opposed by all the
early fathers of the Christian church.

2d. The Pantheistic theory that sin is the necessary incident
of a finite nature (limitation). Some writers, not absolute Pan-

theists, regard it as incident to a certain stage of development and the appointed means of higher perfection.

3d. Pelagians and Rationalists, denying innate corruption, refer the general fact that actual sin occurs as soon as man emerges into free agency to the freedom of the will, or to the influence of example, etc.

4th. Others refer this guilty corruption of nature, which inheres in every human soul from birth, to an actual apostasy of each soul committed before birth, either in a state of individual pre-existence, as Origen and Dr. Edward Beecher in his " Conflict of Ages " teach; or as transcendental and timeless, as Dr. Julius Müller teaches in his " Christian Doctrine of Sin," Vol. II., p. 157. This is evidently a pure speculation, unsupported by any facts of consciousness or of observation, contradicted by the testimony of Scripture, Rom. v. 12, and Gen. iii., and one which has never been accepted by the Church.

6. *What different views have been held by Christian theologians who admit the Adamic origin of human sin, as to the mode of its propagation from Adam to his descendants?*

This is obviously a question of very inferior importance to the moral question which remains to be discussed, as to the grounds in right and justice upon which God directly or indirectly brings this curse upon all men at birth. Hence it is a point neither explicitly explained in Scripture, nor answered in any uniform way even by a majority of theologians.

From the beginning, orthodox theologians have been distinguished as Traducianists and Creationists. Tertullian advocated the doctrine that the souls of children are derived from the souls of their parents by natural generation. Jerome held that each soul is independently created by God at birth. Augustine hesitated between the two views. The majority of Romish theologians have been Creationists, the majority of Lutheran theologians, and New England theologians since Dr. Hopkins, have been Traducianists. Nearly all the theologians of the Reformed church have been Creationists.

1st. The common view of the Traducianists is not "that soul is begotten from soul, nor body from body, but the whole man from the whole man."—D. Pareus, Heidelberg (1548–1622), on Rom. v. 12. In this view it is plain that the corrupted moral nature of our first parents would be inevitably transmitted to all their descendants by natural generation.

2d. The doctrine of pure Realism is that humanity is a single generic spiritual substance which corrupted itself by its own voluntary apostatising act in Adam. The souls of individual men are not separate substances, but manifestations of this single generic substance through their several bodily organizations. The universal soul being corrupt, its several manifestations from birth are corrupt also.

3d. Those who hold that God creates each soul separately, have generally held that he withholds from them from the first those influences of the Holy Spirit upon which all spiritual life in the creature depends, as the just punishment of Adam's sin, as he restores this life-giving influence in consideration of the righteousness of Christ, to the elect in the act of regeneration. Dr. T. Ridgely, London (1667–1734), says Vol. I., pp. 413, 414, "God creates the souls of men destitute of heavenly gifts, and supernatural light, and that justly, because Adam lost those gifts for himself and his posterity."

A few Creationists have, like Lampé, Utrecht (1683–1729), Tom. I., p. 572, taught that the body derived from the parents "is corrupted by inordinate and perverse emotions through sin," which thus communicates like inordinate affections to the soul placed in it by God. This latter view has never prevailed, since sin is not an affection of matter, and can belong to the body only as an organ of the soul. Many Creationists, however, refer the propagation of habitual sin to natural generation, in a general sense, as a law whereby God ordains that children shall be like their parents, without inquiring at all as to the method. So De Moor, Cap. XV., § 33, and "Canons of Synod of Dort."

II. Why, on what Ground of Justice and Right, has God entailed this Curse of Antenatal Forfeiture upon all Human Beings antecedent to Personal Agency?

7. *What is the Arminian explanation of this fact?*

1st. They admit that all men inherit from Adam a corrupt nature predisposing them to sin, but they deny that this innate condition is itself properly sin, or involves guilt or desert of punishment.

2d. They affirm that it was consistent with the justice of God to allow this great evil to come upon all men at birth, only in view of the fact that he had determined to introduce an adequate compensation in the redemption of Christ, impartially intended for all men, and the sufficient influences of his grace which all men experience, and which restores to all ability to do right, and therefore full personal responsibility. Hence, infants are not under condemnation. Condemnation attaches to no man until he has abused his gracious ability. In the gift of Christ, God redresses the wrong done us by allowing Adam to use his fallen nature as the medium for the propagation of sinful children.—Dr. D. D. Whedon, "Bibliotheca Sacra," April, 1862, "Conf. Rem.," vii. 3, Limborch, "Theol. Christ," iii., 3, 4, 5, 67.

WE OBJECT to this doctrine.—(1.) That our condemnation in Adam is of *justice*, and our redemption in Christ of GRACE. (2.) The remedy of the compensatory system is not applied to many heathen, etc. (3.) The view is inconsistent with Scriptural doctrines as to sin, inability, regeneration, etc., etc.

8. *What has been the prevalent answer given by New England Theologians since the days of Dr. Hopkins?*

Dr. Hopkins taught the doctrine of divine efficiency in the production of sin. This, of course, dissolves the question as to the justice of God in bringing Adam's descendants into the world as sinners, since he is the ultimate cause of all sin. Later New England divines discard the doctrine of divine efficiency, but they agree with Hopkins in denying imputation, and in referring the law which entails the corruption of Adam upon each of his descendants to a sovereign divine constitution.

If this view, while acknowledging that this divine constitution is infinitely just and righteous, simply disclaims clear knowledge of its grounds and reasons, we have only to answer, that while in part we sympathize with it, we dare not refuse the partial light thrown upon the problem in Scripture, and exhibited below. But if the design of these theologians be to assert, either (1) that this constitution is not just, or (2) that God's bare will makes it to be just, and that its being sovereign is the ground of its being righteous, we protest against it as a grievous heresy.

9. *What is the orthodox answer to the above question in which the Romish Lutheran and Reformed Theologians as a body concur?*

It is certain that while there has been difference of opinion and looseness of statement as to the grounds of our just accountability for Adam's first sin, the whole Church has always regarded our loss of original righteousness and innate moral corruption to be a just and righteous, not sovereign, penal consequence of Adam's apostatizing act. This is the DOCTRINE, agreement with which is alike accordant with Scripture, honoring to the moral attributes of God and the equity of his moral government, and conformable to historical orthodoxy. In the explanation of this doctrine the orthodox have often differed. It is a simple fact that God as a just judge condemned the whole race on account of Adam's sin, and condemnation by God, the source of life, involves and is justly followed by spiritual and moral death.

10. *Where is the fact asserted in Scripture that God condemned the whole race because of Adam's apostasy?*

Rom. v. 17–19.—"For if by one man's offence death reigned by one;" "Therefore, as by the offence of one judgment came upon all men to condemnation;" "For as by one man's disobedience many were made sinners."

11. *Show that in this doctrine the whole Church has concurred?*

The sin of Adam was an act of apostasy. The spiritual desertion and consequent spiritual corruption which immediately occurred in his personal experience (the very penalty threatened) was, of course, a just penal consequence of that act. Augustine said ("De Nupt. et Concup." II. xxxiv.)—"Nothing remains but to conclude that in that first man all are understood to have sinned, because all were in him when he sinned; whereby sin is brought in with birth, and not removed save by the new birth."

Dr. G. F. Wiggers, the learned expounder of "Augustinianism and Pelagianism, from the Original Sources," says in his statement of Augustine's view of original sin, ch. 5, division 2, § 2. "The propagation of Adam's sin among his posterity is a punishment of the same sin. The corruption of human nature, in the whole race, was the righteous punishment of the transgression of the first man, in whom all men already existed."

The "Council of Trent," Sess. v., 1 and 2, says that "sin which is the death of the soul" was part of that penalty which Adam incurred by his transgression, and which is therefore transmitted to his descendants as well as inflicted on himself."

Bellarmin, "*Amiss. Grat.*," iii. 1, says, "The penalty which properly corresponds with the first sin is the forfeiture of original righteousness and of those supernatural gifts with which God had furnished our nature."

Luther (in Genes. 1, p. 98, cap. 5,) says, that the image of Adam in which Seth was begotten "included original sin, and the penalty of eternal death inflicted because of the sin of Adam."

Melanchthon ("Explicatio Symboli Niceni. Corp. Refor.," xxiii. 403 and 583) says, "Adam and Eve merited guilt and depravity for their descendants."

"Formula Concordiæ," p. 639 and p. 643, Hase ed.—"Especially since by the seduction of Satan, through the fall, by the just judgment of God in the punishment of men, concreated or original righteousness was lost . . . and human nature corrupted."

"Apol. Aug. Conf.," p. 58.—"In Genesis the penalty imposed for original sin is described. For there was human nature subjected not only to death and corporeal evils, but also to the reign of the devil. . . . Defect and concupiscence are both penal evils and sins."

Quenstedt (†1688), "Ques. Theo. Did.," Pol. I., 994.—"It was not simply of the good pleasure or the absolute sovereignty of God, but of the highest justice and equity, that the sin, which Adam as the root and origin of the whole human race committed, should be imputed to us, and propagated in us so as to constitute us guilty."

Both the Second Helvetic, Ch. 8, and the Gallic Confessions, Art. 9, say that Adam, "by his own fault (*culpa*) became subject to sin, and such as he became after the fall, such are all who were propagated by him, they being subject to sin, death, and various calamities."

Peter Martyr, Professor at Zurich (1500–1561), as quoted by Turretin (Loco ix., 2, 9, § 43), says, "Assuredly there is no one who can doubt that original sin (inherent) is inflicted upon us in revenge and punishment of the first fall."

Calvin.—"God by a just judgment condemned us to wrath in Adam, and willed us to be born corrupt on account of his sin."

Ursinus (1534–1583), friend of Melanchthon, professor at Heidelberg and author of the "Heidelberg Catechism," says (Quæst. 7, pp. 40, 41), "original sin" (inherent) "passes over" to their descendants, "not through the body, nor through the soul, but through the impure generation of the whole man, on account of (*propter*) the guilt of our first parents, on account of which, God, by a just judgment, while he creates our souls, at the same time, deprives them of the original rectitude and gifts which he had conferred upon the parents."

L. Danæus (1530–1596).—"There are three things which constitute a man guilty before God: 1. The sin flowing from this that we have all sinned in the first man. 2. Corruption, which is the punishment of this sin, which fell upon Adam and upon all his posterity. 3. Actual sins."

Theodore Beza (1519–1605), on Romans xii., etc.—"As Adam, by the commission of sin, first was made guilty of the wrath of God, then, as being guilty, underwent as the punishment of his sin the corruption of soul and body, so also he transmitted to posterity a nature in the first place guilty, next, corrupted."

J. Arminius, of Leyden (1560–1609).—"Whatever punishment, therefore, was inflicted on our first parents, has gone down through and now rests on all their posterity; so that

all are children of wrath by nature, being obnoxious to condemnation . . . and to a destitution of righteousness and
true holiness," "are destitute of original righteousness, which
penalty is usually called a loss of the divine image, and original sin."

G. J. Vossius, Leyden (1577–1649), "Hist. Pelag.," Lb. ii.,
1.—1. "The Catholic Church has always thus decided, that the
first sin is imputed to all; that is, that its effects are, according
to the just judgment of God, transmitted to all the children
of Adam . . . on account whereof we are born without
original righteousness."

Synod of Dort (1618).—"Such as man was after the fall,
such children also he begat, . . . by the propagation of a
vicious nature, by the just judgment of God."

Francis Turretin, Geneva (1623–1687), Locus 9, Q. 9, §§ 6, 14.

Amesius, "Medulla Theolog.," Lib. prim., cap. 17.—"2. This
propagation of sin consists in two parts, in *imputation* and in
real communication. 3. By *imputation* that single act of disobedience which Adam committed is made also ours. 4. By *real
communication*, not indeed the single sin. 5. Original sin, since
it essentially consists in deprivation of original righteousness,
and this deprivation follows the first sin as a penalty, this has
in the first instance the nature of a penalty rather than of a
sin. Inasmuch as that original righteousness is denied by the
justice of God, so far forth it is penalty; inasmuch as it ought
to be present and is absent by human fault, so far forth it is
sin. 6. Therefore this privation is handed down from Adam
after the manner of ill-desert in so far as it is penalty, and after
the manner of real efficiency in so far as it has adjoined to it
the nature of sin."

H. Witsius (1636–1708), "Economy," Bk. I., ch. 8, §§ 33
and 34.—"It is therefore necessary that the sin of Adam in
virtue of the covenant of works, be so laid to the charge of his
posterity, who were comprised with him in the same covenant,
that, on account of the demerit of his sin, they are born destitute of original righteousness," etc.

"Formula Consensus Helvetica" (1675), canon x.—"But
there appears no way in which hereditary corruption could
fall, as spiritual death, upon the whole human race by the
just judgment of God, unless some sin of that race preceded,
incurring the penalty of that death. For God, the supremely
just Judge of all the earth, punishes none but the guilty."

Westminster "Conf. and Cat"; "Conf. Faith," ch. vii., § 2
and ch. vi., § 3; "L. Cat.," 22 and 25; "S. Cat.," 18.

President Witherspoon, "Works," Vol. IV., p. 96. — "It
seems very plain that the state of corruption and wicked-

ness which men are now in, is stated in Scripture as being the effect and punishment of Adam's first sin."

See also the truth of this position affirmed by Dr. Tho. Chalmers, "Institutes of Theology," part 1, ch. 6; and by Dr. William Cunningham; "Theology of the Reformation," Essay vii., § 2; Dr. James Thornwell, "Collected Writings," Vol. I., pp. 479, 559, 561, etc.; and a learned article by Prof. Geo. P. Fisher, of New Haven, Theo. Sem., in the "New Englander," July, 1868.

Thus we have the consensus of Catholic and Protestant, Lutheran and Reformed, of Supralapsarian and Infralapsarian, of Gomar and Arminius, of the Synod of Dort and the Westminster Assembly, of Scotland and of New England.

12. *Why was this doctrine expressed technically as the imputation of the guilt of Adam's apostatizing act? and state the meaning of the terms.*

At the Council of Trent Albertus Pighius and Ambrosius Catherinus (F. Paul's "Hist. Con. Trent," Lib. ii., s., 65) maintained that the imputed guilt of Adam's first sin constituted the only ground of the condemnation which rests upon men at birth. The Council did not allow this heresy, but nevertheless maintained a rather negative than positive view of man's inherent guilty corruption. Consequently Calvin and all the first Reformers and Creeds were principally concerned in emphasizing the fact that original sin *inherent*, as distinguished from original sin *imputed*, is intrinsically and justly, as moral corruption, worthy of God's wrath and curse. It is the reason why the salvation of infants is referred to the sovereign grace of God, and the expiatory merits of Christ, and it continues in adults the source of all actual sin and the main ground of condemnation to eternal death. Infants and adults suffer, and adults are damned on account of the guilt of inherent sin, but never on account of Adam's sin imputed.

But when the question is asked why God, either directly or indirectly, brings us into existence thus corrupt, the whole church answered as above shown, *because God has thereby justly punished us for Adam's apostasy.*

This is technically expressed as the "imputation to us of the guilt of Adam's act."

"Guilt" is just liability to punishment. The recognition of guilt is a judicial and not sovereign act of God.

"Imputation" (the Hebrew חָשַׁב and the Greek λογίζομαι frequently occurring and translated "to count," "to reckon," "to impute," etc.) is simply to lay to one's charge as a just ground of legal procedure, whether the thing imputed antecedently belonged to the person to whom it is charged, or for any other adequate reason he is justly responsible for it. Thus not to impute sin to the doer of it, is of course graciously to refrain from charging the guilt of his own act or state upon him as a ground of punishment; while to impute righteousness without works is graciously to credit the believer with a righteousness which is not personally his own.—Rom. iv. 6, 8; 2 Cor. v. 19; see Num. xxx. 15; xviii. 22–27, 30; Lev. v. 17, 18; vii. 18; xvi. 22; Rom. ii. 26; 2 Tim. iv. 16, etc.

The imputation, *i. e.*, judicial charging of Adam's sin to us, is rather to be considered as contemplating the race as a whole, as one moral body, than as a series of individuals. The race was condemned as a whole, and hence each individual comes into existence in a state of just antenatal forfeiture. Turretin calls it "*commune peccatum, communis culpa*," L. 9, Q. 9. This and this alone is what the church has meant by this doctrine. Afterwards in our own persons God condemns us only and most justly because of our inherent moral corruption and our actual transgressions. The imputation of the guilt of Adam's apostatizing act to us in common leads judicially to spiritual desertion in particular, and spiritual desertion leads by necessary consequence to inherent depravity. The imputation of our sins in common to Christ leads to his desertion (Matt. xxvii. 46), but his temporary desertion leads to no tendency to inherent sin, because he was the God-man. The imputation of Christ's righteousness to us is the condition of the restoration of the Holy Ghost, and that restoration leads by necessary consequence to regeneration and sanctification. "It is only when *justificatio forensis* maintains its Reformation position at the head of the process of salvation, that it has any firm or secure standing at all."—Dr. J. A. Dorner's "Hist. Prot. Theo.," Vol. II., p. 160.

13. *What is the origin of the Distinction between the Mediate and the Immediate Imputation of Adam's sin, and what has been the usage with respect to those terms among theologians?*

As above shown, from the beginning, the universal Church has agreed in holding that the guilt of Adam's first sin was directly charged to the account of the human race in mass, just as it was charged to himself, and punished in the race by desertion and consequent depravity, just as it was punished in him. This was uniformly expressed by the technical phrase, the imputation of the guilt of his first sin to his descendants.

In the first half of the seventeenth century, Joshua Placæus, professor at Saumur, was universally understood to deny any imputation of Adam's sin to his posterity, and to admit only inherent innate corruption as derived from Adam by natural generation. This was explicitly condemned by the French National Synod at Charenton, 1645; and repudiated by all orthodox theologians, Lutheran and Reformed. Placæus subsequently originated the distinction between Immediate and Mediate Imputation. By the former he meant the direct charging of the guilt of Adam's sin antecedent to their own sinful state. By the latter he meant that we are found guilty with Adam of his apostasy because in virtue of inherent depravity we are apostates also. He denied the former and admitted the latter.

It is obvious—1st. That this doctrine of mediate imputation alone is virtually the "New England Root Theory," above discussed, which refers the abandoning of the human race to the operation of the natural law of inheritance to the sovereign will, instead of to the just judgment, of God.

2d. It is a denial of the universal doctrine of the Church that Adam's sin is justly charged to his descendants as to himself, and punished in them by depravity as it was punished in himself. That imputation was obviously, whatever its *ground*, purely immediate and antecedent.

3d. It is evident that Adam's sin can not at the same time be both immediately and mediately imputed to the same effect. It would be absurd to think that mankind are judicially punished with inherent corruption as a just punishment for Adam's sin, and at the same time counted guilty of Adam's sin because they are afflicted with that punishment. It is for this reason that so many advocates of the church doctrine of immediate imputation deny that imputation can in any sense be mediate.

4th. But the penalty of Adam's sin was "Death"; that is, all penal evils, temporal, and eternal. The strongest advocates of immediate imputation, in order to account for the infliction of innate inherent sin, admit that *all the other* elements of the penalty denounced upon Adam come upon *us* because of *our own inherent and actual sins.*—See Turretin, L. 9, Quæs. 9, § 14, and "Princeton Essays."

5th. The immediate imputation of the guilt of Adam's sin is to the race as a whole, and respects each individual antecedently to his existence as a judicial cause of his commencing that existence in a depraved condition. When each single man is considered in himself personally and subsequent to birth, all agree that he is condemned with Adam because of a common inherent depravity and life.

6th. Many found difficulty in conceiving how inherited inherent corruption can be guilt as well as pollution. Their idea was that a sinful state must originate in the free choice of the person concerned, in order to invoke the moral responsibility implied by guilt. Yet all acknowledge that inherent corruption is guilt. Some tacitly accounted for this on the principle of Edwards, that "the essence of the virtue or vice of dispositions of the heart lies not in their cause, but in their nature." Others, however, held that the guilt inherent in innate sin is due to the fact that this sin is connected as an effect with the apostasy of Adam. If the question then be, Why the race is under ban, and we are allowed to commence our moral agency in a depraved condition? all the orthodox answer in terms or in effect, "Because of the most just immediate imputation of Adam's first sin."

If the question be, Why are we severally, after birth, judged guilty as well as corrupt, and why are we punished with all the temporal and eternal penal evils denounced upon Adam? many of the orthodox say, "Because of our own inherent sin mediating the full imputation of his sin."

Andrew Quenstedt, Wittenberg (†1688), "Theo. Did. Pol.," I., 998.—"The first sin of Adam is imputed to us immediately inasmuch as we exist hitherto in Adam. But the sin of Adam is imputed to us mediately in so far as we are regarded individually and in our own proper persons."

F. Turretin, Geneva (†1687), Locus 9, Quæst. 9, § 14.—"The penalty which sin brings upon us is either privative or positive. The former is the want or privation of original righteousness. The latter is death both temporal and eternal, and in general all evils which are sent upon sinners. . . . With respect to the former we say that the sin of Adam is imputed to us immediately to the effect of the privative penalty, because it is the cause of the privation of original righteousness, and so ought to go before privation, at least in the order of nature; but as to the latter, the positive penalty may be said to be mediately imputed, because we are not obnoxious to that, unless after we are born and corrupt."

Hence—(1.) All in effect admit immediate imputation, and deny mediate imputation alone. (2.) Many ignore the distinction, which never emerged till the time of Placæus. (3.) A number, in the senses above shown, assert both.

14. *How is this Doctrine proved by the analogy which Paul (Rom. v. 12–21) asserts between our condemnation in Adam and our justification in Christ?*

"Therefore as by the offence of one, judgment came upon all men to condemnation; EVEN so by the righteousness of one the free gift came upon all men unto justification of life."

The analogy here asserted is as to the fact and nature of the imputation in both cases, not at all as to the ground of it.

Christ is one with his elect because of the gracious appointment of the Father and his voluntary assumption of their nature. Adam is one with his descendants because he is their natural head, and because of the gracious appointment of God. In these respects the cases differ. But the cases are identical in so far as in view of the oneness in both cases subsisting, we are justly charged with the guilt of Adam's first sin and punished therefor, and Christ is justly charged with the guilt of our "many offences" and punished therefor, and we are justly credited with the merit of his righteousness and accepted, regenerated, and saved therefor.—See above Ques. 12.

If the imputation of Christ's righteousness is immediate the imputation of Adam's sin must be the same, though the basis of the one is grace it is no less just, and though the basis of the other be justice, the original constitution from which it originated is no less gracious.

15. *How have orthodox theologians explained the* GROUND *for this universally assumed judicial charging of the guilt of Adam's apostatising act to his descendants?*

They are generally agreed that the race is justly responsible for the judicial consequences of that act. Beyond this the accounts rendered of the matter have been different, and often vague.

1st. Augustine conceived of the race as essentially one. As far as Adam is considered as a person his sin was his own, but as far as the entire race in its essential undistributed, unindividualized form of existence was in him, his act was the apostasy of that whole race, and the common nature being both guilty and depraved is justly distributed to each individual in that condition and under that condemnation. The whole race was not personally nor individually, but virtually or potentially, coexistent and coactive in him.—Dr. Philip Schaff in "Lange on Rom.," pp. 191–196; Dr. Geo. P. Fisher, "New Englander," July, 1860. This is a mode of thought which at least presupposes Realism, and language to the same effect became traditional in the church, and has been used in a general sense by many, who were in no degree philosophical realists, when treating of our relation to Adam. Forms of expression originating in this view have lingered among theologians who have explicitly rejected realism, and have definitely substituted for it a different explanation of the facts. The whole race has been considered one organically, and we have been said to have been in Adam as branches in a tree, etc. Such renderings of the matter have continued to late times, and been commingled with others essentially different, as that of representation, etc.

It is, however unsatisfactory as an explanation of guilt, in the highest degree orthodox, both because of the number and high authority of the writers who have used it, and because it implies the highest conceivable ground of immediate imputation. The apostatising act is imputed to us, as it is imputed to Adam, "because we were guilty coagents with him in that act."—Shedd's "Essays."

2d. The Federal View presupposes the natural relation. Adam stands before God in Eden a free, responsible, fallible moral agent, with an animal body and a generative nature. Without a miracle his children must be carried along with him in his destinies. His own status was and must ever continue according to bare law contingent upon free-will. God, therefore, as the benevolent and righteous guardian of the interests of all moral creatures, graciously constituted him the federal head and representative of his race as a whole, and promised him for himself and for all eternal life, or confirmed holiness and happiness, on condition of temporary obedience under favorable conditions, with the penalty for him and for them of death, or condemnation and desertion, on condition of disobedience. This was an act of grace to him, as it substituted a temporal for an eternal probation. It was no less an act of grace for the race, for reasons stated below.

This "Federal Theology" was developed and introduced in all its fulness of detail and bearings by Coccejus (1602–1669), Prof. at Franecker and Leyden. It was regarded as eminently a Scriptural system, supplanting the prevailing scholasticism, and destroying forever the influence of supralapsarian speculations, and it gradually found acceptance, under appropriate modifications, with Lutherans and Arminians as well as Calvinists.

Two things however are historically certain—1st. That the idea of a covenant with Adam including his descendants had long before been clearly conceived and prominently advanced. This was done by Catherinus before the "Council of Trent" (Father Paul's "Hist. Council Trent," pp. 175, 177), and by such men among Protestants as Hyperius (†1567), Olevianus (circum. 1563), and Raphael Eglin (Dorner's "Hist. Prot. Theo.," Vol. II., pp. 31–45).

2d. That the essential ideas of federal representation were long and very generally prevalent among Protestant theologians from the beginning. Dr. Charles P. Krauth says, with respect to Lutheran theology as a whole, "The reasons assigned for the imputation and transmission centre in the representative character of Adam (and Eve). The technicalities of the federal idea are late in appearing, but the essential idea itself comes in from the beginning in our theology." Melanchthon said, "Adam and Eve merited guilt and depravity for their posterity, because integrity had been bestowed on our first parents, that they might preserve them for their entire posterity, and in this trial they *represented* the whole human race."—"Explicatio Symboli Niceni, Corp. Refor.," xxiii. 403 and 583.

Chemnitz (1522–1586), "Loci. Theo.," fol. 213, 214, says, "God deposited those gifts with which he willed to adorn human nature with Adam, on this condition, that if he kept them for himself he should keep them for his posterity; but if he lost them and depraved himself, he should beget children after his own likeness."—Hutter, Wittenberg (†1616), Lb. "Chr. Con. Expli.," 90. "Adam *represented* the whole human race." Thus also James Arminius (†1609) (Disp. 31, Thes. ix); John Owen (1616–1683) ("Justification," p. 286), and West "Conf. Faith," Ch. vii. § 2, and "L. Cat.," 22 (1646 and 1647).

Hence it appears that when theological writers, subsequent to the prevalence of the realistic philosophy, explain our moral oneness with Adam by the uninterpreted general phrases "that we sinned in him being in his loins," or "he being our Root," they are not to be understood as excluding all reference to representation, or to covenant responsibility. The language holds true under either theory, or when both are combined in one notion. And from the interchange of terms it is certain that very often both theories were latent under a common general notion.

16. *What can be fairly adduced in support of the Augustinian mode of explaining our moral oneness with Adam?*

This view explains our moral oneness entirely on the ground of his being the natural head and root of the race, and the consequent physical or organic oneness of the whole race in him.

It may be fairly argued in behalf of this view—1st. That if it can be proved that we were "guilty coagents with Adam in his sin," the highest and most satisfactory reason possible is assigned for the righteous immediate imputation of the guilt of that sin to us.

2d. The analogy, as far as it goes, of all God's providential dealings, both general and special, with mankind. God's covenants with Noah, Abraham, and David embrace the children with the parents, and rest upon the natural relations of generator and generated. The constitutions alike of the Jewish and Christian Churches provide that the rights of infants are predetermined by the status of their parents. This is, of course, determined by a gracious covenant, yet that covenant presupposes the more fundamental and general natural relation of generation and education. All human condition and character, aside from any supernatural intervention, is determined by historical conditions. Hugh Miller ("Testimony of the Rocks") says, as a Christian scientist: "It is a fact broad and palpable as the economy of nature, that . . . lapsed progenitors, when cut off from civilization and all external interference of a missionary character, become founders of a lapsed race. The iniquities of the parents are visited upon their children." "It is one of the inevitable consequences of that nature of man which the Creator 'bound fast in fate,' while he left free his will, that the free-will of the parent should become the destiny of the child."

17. *What can be fairly argued against the sufficiency of this explanation of the ground of the immediate imputation of the guilt of Adam's first sin?*

1st. Observe (1) that the Jewish and Christian Churches, to whom the second commandment (Ex. xx. 5) was given, and the children of Noah, Abraham, and David were embraced under special gracious covenants. (2.) Observe that in cases in which God visits the iniquities of parents upon their children in natural providence, irrespective of any special covenant obligations, God is acting with a most just though sovereign discretion in dealing with rebels *already* under *previous* righteous condemnation.

2d. When the Natural Headship of Adam is referred to in general terms, and we are said to have been in him as a "Root," or as "branches in a tree," the notion is unsatisfactory, because (1) utterly indefinite. (2.) Because it is, as far as it goes, material and mechanical, and therefore utterly fails to explain moral responsibility, which is essentially spiritual and personal. (3.) Besides this notion at least latently assumes the fallacy that the laws of natural development are either necessary limits of divine agency, or agents independent of him, or independent concauses with him. The truth simply being that the constitution of nature is the creature and instrument of God. (4.) This theory assigns no reason, either on the ground of principle or analogy, why only the *first* sin of Adam, and not all the subsequent sins of all ancestors, is imputed to posterity as the ground of parental forfeiture.

3d. The idea of a non-personal but virtual or potential co-existence and coagency (see Dr. W. G. T. Shedd's "Essays" and "Hist. Christ. Doc.," and Dr. Philip Schaff's "Lange. Rom.," pp. 192–194) as the sole basis of just moral responsibility has no support in that testimony of CONSCIOUSNESS, which is our only citadel of defence from materialism, naturalism, and pantheism. Consciousness gives us no conception of sin but as a state or an act of a free personal agent. Even if impersonal, virtual, potential, moral coagency be a fact, it transcends both consciousness and understanding, and being dark itself can throw no light upon the mysterious facts it is adduced to explain and to justify.

4th. When the attempt is made to expound this theory in the full sense of realistic philosophy the case does not appear to be improved.

(1.) In pure realism humanity is a single, generic, spiritual substance which voluntarily apostatized and corrupted itself in Adam. Human persons are the individual manifestations of this common spirit in connection with separate bodily organizations. But — (*a.*) If we so far leave consciousness behind how can we defend ourselves from pantheism? (*b.*) How are individual spirits justified and sanctified while the general spirit remains corrupt and guilty? (*c.*) How did the Logos become incarnate? (*d.*) How, finally, will part of this spiritual substance be eternally glorified, while another part is eternally damned.

(2.) Dr. Shedd explains that the generic spiritual substance which sinned has since, through the agency of Adam, been distributed and explicated into a series of individuals. But can a spirit be divided and its parts distributed, each part an agent as the whole was from which it was separated? Is not this to confound the attributes of spirit and matter, and to explain spirit as material, and is not SIN pre-eminently spiritual and personal?

18. *State the reasons which establish the superior satisfactory character of the Federal Theory of our oneness with Adam?*

1st. The federal headship of Adam presupposes and rests upon his natural headship. He was our natural head before he was our federal head. He was doubtless made our federal representative because he was our natural progenitor, and was so conditioned that his agency must affect our destinies, and because our very nature was on trial (typically if not essentially) in him. Whatever, therefore, of virtue in this explanation the natural headship of Adam may be supposed to contain the federal theory retains.

2d. The Covenant as shown above was an act of supreme divine grace to Adam himself. It was still more so as it respects his descendants. All God's moral creatures are introduced into existence in a condition of real, though instable, moral integrity. This is obviously true of men and angels, and certainly equitable. They must, therefore, pass through a probation either limited or unlimited. Adam was under conditions to stand that graciously limited probation with every conceivable advantage. But, apparently, his descendants could have no fair probation except in his person. "Three plans exhaust the possible. (1.) The whole race might have been left under their natural relation to God forever. (2.) Each might have been left to stand for himself under a gracious covenant of works. (3.) That the race as a whole should stand for a limited period represented in its natural head. The *first* would have certainly led to universal sin. The *second* is the one Pelagians suppose actual. The *third* is incomparably the most advantageous for the whole." Dr. Robert L. Dabney's "Syllabus." The separate probation of nascent souls in infant bodies was certainly not to be preferred.

3d. God certainly did as a matter of fact condition Adam with a promise of "Life," and the alternative of "Death," upon a special and temporally limited probationary test. The precise penalty threatened upon him, has been in its general sense and special terms (Gen. ii. 17 and iii. 16–19) inflicted upon all his posterity.

4th. This view also is confirmed by the analogy which the Scriptures assert existed between the imputation of Adam's first sin to us, and the imputation of our sins to Christ, and of his righteousness to us. This, of course, implies necessarily that the race is one with Adam, and the elect one with Christ. And the analogy certainly is the more complete on the federal view of Adam's union with the race, than on that view which ignores it. Both the Covenant of Grace including the elect, and the Covenant of Works including the race, were gracious. Christ voluntarily assumed his headship out of love. Adam obediently assumed his out of interest and duty. God graciously chose the elect out of love, and graciously included the descendants of Adam in his representation out of benevolence.

Does not the remaining mystery lose itself in that abyss which is opened by the *fact of the permission of sin*, before which all schools of Theists on this side the veil must bow in silence.

CHAPTER XXII.

All questions concerned with the general subject of Redemption will fall under the heads of—

1st. The Plan of Redemption, including the Covenant of Grace and eternal Election, considered above, Ch. XI.

2d. The Person and Work of Christ in the Accomplishment of Redemption.

3d. The Application and Consummation of Redemption by the agency of the Holy Ghost, together with the Means of Grace divinely appointed to that end.

THE COVENANT OF GRACE.

It is evident.—1st. That as God is an infinite, eternal, and immutable intelligence he must have formed, from the beginning, an all-comprehensive and unchangeable Plan of all his works in time, including Creation, Providence, and Redemption.

2d. A Plan formed by and intended to be executed in its several reciprocal distributed parts by Three Persons, as Sender, and Sent, as Principal and Mediator, as Executor and Applier, must necessarily possess all the essential attributes of an eternal Covenant between those Persons.

3d. Since God in all departments of his moral government treats man as an intelligent, voluntary, and responsible moral agent, it follows that the execution of the eternal Plan of Redemption must be in its general character ethical and not magical, must proceed by the revelation of truth, and the influences of motives, and must be voluntarily appropriated by the subject as an offered grace, and obeyed as an enjoined duty upon pain of reprobation. Hence its application must possess all the essential attributes of a Covenant in time between God and his people.

1. *What is the usage of the word* בְּרִית *in the Hebrew Scriptures?*

This word occurs more than two hundred and eighty times in the Old Testament, and is in our translation in the vast majority of instances represented by the English word "Covenant," in a number of instances by the word "League," Jos. ix. 15, etc., and once each by the words "Confederate," Gen. xiv. 13, and "Confederacy," Obad. 7.

It is used to express.—1st. A natural ordinance. "God's covenant with the day, the night," etc.—Jer. xxxiii. 20.

2d. A covenant of one man with another. Jonathan and David.—1 Sam. xviii. 3 and ch. xx. David and Abner.—2 Sam. iii. 13.

3d. The covenant of God with Noah, Gen. vi. 18, 19, as to his family; and with the human race in him, Gen. ix. 9. The bow was "a token of a covenant."—Gen. ix. 13.

4th. The "Covenant of Grace" with Abraham, Gen. xvii. 2–7, which Paul calls the "gospel," Gal. iii. 17. Circumcision was the "token of this covenant."—Gen. xvii. 11; comp. Acts vii. 8.

5th. The same covenant as formed generally with Abraham, Isaac, and Jacob.—Ex. ii. 24, etc.

6th. The same covenant, with special and temporary modifications of form, constituting the National-Ecclesiastical Covenant of God with the people of Israel. The law of this Covenant on its legal side was written by Moses first in a book ("the book of the covenant," Ex. xxiv. 7), and then upon tables of stone ("the words of the covenant, the ten commandments, Ex. xxxiv. 27, 28), which were afterwards deposited in a golden chest, "the ark of the covenant."—Num. x. 33.

7th. The covenant with Aaron of an everlasting priesthood. Num. xxv. 12, 13.

8th. The covenant with David.—Jer. xxxiii. 21, 22; Ps. lxxxix. 3, 4.

2. *What is the New Testament usage of the term διαθήκη?*

This word occurs thirty-three times in the New Testament, and is almost uniformly translated *covenant* when it refers to the dealings of God with his ancient church, and *testament* when it refers to his dealings with his church under the gospel dispensation. Its fundamental sense is that of disposition, arrangement; in the classics generally that specific form of arrangement or disposition called a *testament*, which sense, however, it properly bears in but one passage in the New Testament, viz., Heb. ix. 16, 17. Although it is never used to designate that eternal Covenant of Grace which the Father made with the Son as the second Adam, in behalf of his people, yet it always designates either the old or the new dispensation, *i. e.*, mode of administration of that changeless covenant, or some special covenant which Christ has formed with his people in the way of administering the Covenant of Grace, *e. g.*, the covenants with Abraham and with David.

Thus the disposition made by God with the ancient church through Moses, the *Old* contrasted in the New Testament with the *New* διαθήκη (Gal. iv. 24), was really a covenant, both civil and religious, formed between Jehovah and the Israelites, yet alike in its legal element, "which was added because of transgressions, till the seed should come to whom the promise was made," and in its symbolical and typical element teaching of Christ, it was in a higher view a dispensation, or mode of administration of the Covenant of Grace. So also the present gospel dispensation introduced by Christ assumes the form of a covenant between him and his people, including many gracious promises, suspended on conditions, yet it is evidently in its highest aspect that mode of administering the changeless Covenant of Grace, which is called the "new and better dispensation," in contrast with the comparatively imperfect "old and first dispensation" of that same covenant.—See 2 Cor. iii. 14; Heb. viii. 6, 8, 9, 10; ix. 15; Gal. iv. 24.

The present dispensation of the Covenant of Grace by our Saviour, in one respect, evidently bears a near analogy to a will or testamentary disposition, since it dispenses blessings which could be fully enjoyed only after, and by means of his death. Consequently Paul uses the word διαθήκη in one single passage, to designate the present dispensation of the Covenant of Grace in this interesting aspect of it.—Heb. ix. 16, 17. Yet since the various dispensations of that eternal covenant are always elsewhere in Scripture represented under the form of special administrative covenants, and not under the form of testaments, it is to be regretted that our translators have so frequently rendered this term διαθήκη, by the specific word testament, instead of the word covenant, or by the more general word dispensation.—See 1 Cor. iii. 6, 14; Gal. iii. 15; Heb. vii. 22; xii. 24; xiii. 20.

3. *What are the three views as to the parties in the covenant of grace held by Calvinists?*

These differences do not in the least involve the truth of any doctrine taught in the Scriptures, but concern only the form in which that truth may be more or less clearly presented.

1st. The first view regards the Covenant of Grace as made by God with elect sinners. God promising to save sinners as such on the condition of faith, they, when converted, promising faith and obedience. Christ in this view is not one of the parties to the covenant, but its Mediator in behalf of his elect, and their surety; *i. e.*, he guarantees that all the conditions demanded of them shall be fulfilled by them through his grace.

2d. The second view supposes two covenants, the *first*, called the Covenant of Redemption, formed from eternity between the Father and the Son as parties. The Son promising to obey and suffer, the Father promising to give him a people and to grant them in him all spiritual blessings and eternal life. The *second*, called the Covenant of Grace, formed by God with the elect as parties, Christ being mediator and surety in behalf of his people.

3d. As there are two Adams set forth in the Scripture, the one representing the entire race in an economy of nature, and the other representing the whole body of the elect in an economy of grace, it appears more simple to regard as the foundation of all God's dealings with mankind, of whatever class, only the two great contrasted Covenants of works and of grace. The *former* made by God at the creation of the world with Adam, as the federal head and representative of all his posterity. Of the promises, conditions, penalty, and issue of that Covenant I have spoken under a former head, see Chapter XVII. The *latter*, or Covenant of Grace, formed in the counsels of eternity between the Father and the Son as contracting parties, the Son therein contracting as the Second Adam, representing all his people as their mediator and surety, assuming their place and undertaking all their obligations, under the unsatisfied Covenant of Works, and undertaking to apply to them all the benefits secured by this eternal Covenant of Grace, and to secure the performance upon their part of all those duties which are involved therein. Thus in one aspect this Covenant may be viewed as contracted with the head for the salvation of the members, and in another as contracted with the members in their head and sponsor. For that which is a grace from God is a duty upon our part, as St. Augustine prayed, "Da quod jubes, et jubes quod vis;" and hence results this complex view of the Covenant.

As embraced under one or other of these two great Covenants of works or of grace, every man in the world stands in God's sight. It is to be remembered, however, that in the several dispensations, or modes of administration of the eternal Covenant of Grace, Christ has contracted various special covenants with his people, as administrative provisions for carrying out the engagements, and for applying to them the benefits of his covenant with the Father. Thus, the covenant of Jehovah (the Second Person, see above, Chapter IX., Question 14) with Noah, the second natural head of the human family, Gen. ix. 11, 15. The covenant with Abraham, the typical believer, bearing the visible sign and seal of circumcision, and thus founding the visible church as an aggregate of families. This covenant continues to be the charter of the visible church to this day, the sacraments of baptism and the Lord's supper now attached to it, signifying and sealing the benefits of the Covenant of Grace, to wit, eternal life, faith, repentance, obedience, etc., on God's part, as matters of promise; on ours as matters of duty, *i. e.*, so far as they are to be performed by ourselves.—Compare Gen. xvii. 9–13, with Gal. iii. 15–17. The national covenant with the Jews, then constituting the visible church, Ex. xxxiv. 27. The covenant with David, the type of Christ as Mediatorial King, 2 Sam. vii. 15, 16; 2 Chron. vii. 18. The universal offers of the gospel during the present dispensation, also, are presented in the form of a covenant. Salvation is offered to all on the condition of faith, but faith is God's gift secured for and promised to the elect, and when given exercised by them. Every believer, when brought to the knowledge of the truth, enters into a covenant with his Lord, which he renews in all acts of faith and prayer. But these special covenants all and several are provisions for the administration of the eternal Covenant of Grace, and are designed solely to convey the benefits therein secured to those to whom they belong.

For the statements of our standards upon this subject, compare " Confession of Faith," chapter vii., section 3, with " L. Cat.," Questions 30–36.

4. *Prove from the Scriptures that a " Covenant of Grace" was actually formed in eternity between the Divine Persons, in which the "Son" represented this elect.*

1st. As shown at the opening of this chapter such a Covenant is virtually implied in the existence of an eternal Plan of salvation mutually formed by and to be executed by three Persons.

2d. That Christ represented his elect in that Covenant is necessarily implied in the doctrine of sovereign personal election to grace and salvation. Christ says of his sheep, " Thine they were, and thou gavest them me," and " Those whom thou gavest me I have kept," etc.—John xvii. 6, 12.

3d. The Scriptures declare the existence of the promise and conditions of such a Covenant, and present them in connection.—Isa. liii. 10, 11.

4th. The Scriptures expressly affirm the existence of such a Covenant.—Isa. xlii. 6; Ps. lxxxix. 3.

5th. Christ makes constant reference to a previous commission he had received of his Father.—John x. 18; Luke xxii. 29.

6th. Christ claims a reward which had been conditioned upon the fulfillment of that commission.—John xvii. 4.

7th. Christ constantly asserts that his people and his expected glory are given to him as a reward by his Father.—John xvii. 6, 9, 24; Phil. ii. 6–11.

5. *Who were the parties to this Covenant of Grace; what were its promises or conditions on the part of the Father; and what its conditions on the part of the Son?*

1st. The contracting parties were the Father representing the entire Godhead in its indivisible sovereignty; and, on the other hand, God the Son, as Mediator, representing all his elect people, and as administrator of the Covenant, standing their surety for their performance of all those duties which were involved on their part.

2d. The conditions upon the part of the Father were, (1) all needful preparation, Heb. x. 5; Isa. xlii. 1–7; (2) support in his work, Luke xxii. 43; (3) a glorious reward, *first* in the exaltation of his theanthropic person "above every name that is named," Phil. ii. 6–11, and the universal dominion committed to him as Mediator, John v. 22; Ps. cx. 1; and in committing to his hand the administration of all the provisions of the Covenant of Grace in behalf of all his people, Matt. xxviii. 18; John i. 12; xvii. 2; vii. 39; Acts ii. 33; and, *secondly*, in the salvation of all those for whom he acted, including the provisions of regeneration, justification, sanctification, perseverance, and glory—Titus i. 2; Jer. xxxi. 33; xxxii. 40; Isa. xxxv. 10; liii. 10, 11; Dicks' "Theo. Lect.," Vol. I., pp. 506–509.

3d. The conditions upon the part of the Son were—(1.) That he should become incarnate, made of a woman, made under the law.—Gal. iv. 4, 5. (2.) That he should assume and fully discharge, in behalf of his elect, all violated conditions and incurred liabilities of the covenant of works, Matt. v. 17, 18, which he was to accomplish, *first*, by rendering to the precept of the law a perfect obedience, Ps. xl. 8; Isa. xlii. 21; John ix. 4, 5; viii. 29; Matt. xix. 17; and, *secondly*, in suffering the full penalty incurred by the sins of his people.—Isa. liii.; 2 Cor. v. 21; Gal. iii. 13; Eph. v. 2.

6. *In what sense is Christ said to be the mediator of the Covenant of Grace?*

Christ is the mediator of the eternal Covenant of Grace because—1st. As the one mediator between God and man, he contracted it. 2d. As mediator, he fulfils all its conditions in behalf of his people. 3d. As mediator he administers it and dispenses all its blessings. 4th. In all this, Christ was not a mere mediatorial internuntius, as Moses is called (Gal. iii. 19), but he was mediator (1) plenipotentiary (Matt. xxviii. 18), and (2) as high priest actually effecting reconciliation by sacrifice (Rom. iii. 25). 5th. The phrase μεσίτης διαθήκης mediator *of the covenant*, is applied to Christ three times in the New Testament (Heb. viii. 6; ix. 15; xii. 24); but as in each case the term for covenant is qualified by either the adjective "new" or "better," it evidently here is used to designate not the Covenant of Grace properly, but that new dispensation of that eternal cove-

nant which Christ introduced in person in contrast to the less perfect administration of it which was instrumentally introduced by Moses. In the general administration of the Covenant of Grace, Christ has acted as sacerdotal mediator from the foundation of the world (Rev. xiii. 8). On the other hand, the first or "old dispensation," or special mode of administering that Covenant visibly among men, was instrumentally, and as to visible form, "ordained by angels in the hand of a mediator," *i. e.*, Moses (Gal. iii. 19). It is precisely in contradistinction to this relation which Moses sustained to the outward revelation of those symbolical and typical institutions, through which the Covenant of Grace was then administered, that the superior excellence of the "new" and "better" dispensation is declared to consist in this, that now Christ the "Son in his own house" visibly discloses himself as the true mediator in the spiritual and personal administration of his covenant. Hence he who from the beginning was the "one mediator between God and man" (1 Tim. ii. 5) now *is revealed* as in way of eminence, the mediator and surety of that eternal Covenant under the "new" and "better" dispensation of it, since now he is rendered visible in the fulness of his spiritual graces, as the immediate administrator thereof, whereas under the "first" and "old" dispensation he was hidden.—See Sampson's Com. on Hebrews."
5th. As Mediator also Christ undertakes to give His people faith and repentance and every grace, and guarantees for them that they shall on their part exercise faith and repentance and every duty.

7. *In what sense is Christ said to be Surety of the Covenant of Grace?*

In the only instance in which the term surety is applied to Christ in the New Testament (Heb. vii. 22), "surety of a better testament," the word translated *testament* evidently is designed to designate the new dispensation of the Covenant of Grace, as contrasted with the old. Paul is contrasting the priesthood of Christ with the Levitical. He is priest or surety after a higher order, under a clearer revelation, and a more real and direct administration of grace, than were the typical priests descended from Aaron. Christ is our surety at once as priest and as king. As priest because, as such, he assumes and discharges all our obligations under the broken covenant of works. As king (the two in him are inseparable, he is always a royal priest), because, as such, he administers the blessings of his covenant to his people, and to this end entering into covenants with them, offering them grace upon the condition of faith and obedience, and then, as their surety, giving them the graces of faith and obedience, that they may fulfil their part.

8. *What general method has characterized Christ's administration of his covenant under all dispensations?*

The purchased benefits of the covenant are placed in Christ's hand, to be bestowed upon his people as free and sovereign gifts. From Christ to us they are all *gifts*, but from us to Christ many of them are *duties*. Thus, in the administration of the Covenant of Grace, many of these purchased blessings, which are to take effect in our acts, *e. g.*, faith, etc., he demands of us as duties, and promises other benefits as a reward conditioned on our obedience. Thus, so to speak, he rewards grace with grace, and conditions grace upon grace. Promising faith to his elect, then working faith in them, then rewarding them for its exercise with peace of conscience, joy in the Holy Ghost, and eternal life, etc., etc.

9. *What is the Arminian view of the Covenant of Grace?*

They hold, 1st, as to the parties of the Covenant of Grace, that God offers it to all men, and that he actually contracts it with all believers. 2d. As to its promises, that they include all the temporal and eternal benefits of Christ's redemption. 3d. As to its conditions, that God now graciously accepts faith and evangelical obedience for righteousness, in the place of that perfect legal obedience he demanded of man under the covenant of works, the meritorious work of Christ making it consistent with the principles of divine justice for him so to do. They regard all men as rendered by sufficient grace capable of fulfilling such conditions, if they will.

10. *In what sense can faith be called a condition of salvation?*

Faith is a condition sine qua non of salvation, *i. e.*, no adult man can be saved if he does not believe, and every man that does believe shall be saved. It is, however, a gift of God and the first part or stage of salvation. Viewed on God's side it is the beginning and index of his saving work in us. Viewed on our side it is our duty, and must be our own act. It is, therefore, as our act, the instrument of our union with Christ, and thus the necessary antecedent, though never the meritorious cause, of the gracious salvation which follows. Faith as the condition is of course living faith, which necessarily brings forth "confession" and obedience.

11. *What are the promises which Christ, as the administrator of the covenant of grace, makes to all those who believe?*

The promise to Abraham to be a "God to him and to his seed after him" (Gen xvii. 7) embraces all others. All things alike, physical and moral, in providence and grace, for time and eternity, are to work together for our good. "All are yours, and ye are Christ's, and Christ is God's."—1 Cor. iii. 22, 23.

This gospel covenant is often called the "Covenant of Grace" as distinguished from the "Covenant of Redemption." See above, Q. 3, § 2. "He that believeth and is baptized shall be saved, but he that believeth not shall be damned." Mark xvi. 16.

12. *Prove that Christ was mediator of men before as well as after his advent in the flesh.*

1st. As mediator he is both priest and sacrifice, and as such it is affirmed that he is the "Lamb slain from the foundation of the world," and a "propitiation for the sins that are past." Rev. xiii. 8; Rom. iii. 25; Heb. ix. 15.

2d. He was promised to Adam.—Gen. iii. 15.

3d. In the 3d chapter of Gal. Paul proves that the promise made to Abraham (Gen. xvii. 7; xxii. 18) is the very same gospel that the apostle himself preached. Thus Abraham became the father of those that believe.

4th. Acts x. 43.—"To him give all the prophets witness, that through his name, whosoever believeth on him shall receive remission of sin."—See 53d chap. of Is., also chap. xlii. 6.

5th. The ceremonial institutions of Moses were symbolical and typical of Christ's work; as symbols they signified Christ's merit and grace to the ancient worshipper for his present salvation, while as types they prophesied the substance which was to come.—Heb. x. 1–10; Col. ii. 17.

6th. Christ was the Jehovah of the old dispensation.—See above, Chap. IX., Question 14.

13. *Prove that faith was the condition of salvation before the advent of Christ, in the same sense that it is now.*

1st. This is affirmed in the Old Testament.—Hab. ii. 4; Ps. ii. 12.

2d. The New Testament writers illustrate their doctrine of justification by faith by the examples of Old Testament believers.—See Rom. iv., and Heb. xi.

14. *Show that Christ, as administrator of the Covenant of Grace, gave to the members of the Old Testament Church precisely the same promises that he does to us.*

1st. The promises given to Christ's ancient people clearly embrace all spiritual and eternal blessings, *e. g.*, the promise given to Abraham, Gen. xvii. 7, as expounded by Christ, Matt. xxii. 32, and the promise given to Abraham, Gen. xxii. 18; xii. 3, as expounded by Paul, Gal. iii. 16; see also Is. xliii. 25; Ezek. xxxvi. 27; Dan. xii. 2, 3.

2d. This is plain also from the expectation and prayers of God's people.—51st Ps. and 16th Ps.; Job xix. 24-27; Ps. lxxiii. 24-26.

15. *How was the covenant of grace administered from Adam to Abraham?*

1st. By promise.—Gen. iii. 15.

2d. By means of typical sacrifices instituted in the family of Adam.

3d. By means of immediate revelations and appearances of the Jehovah, or divine mediator to his people. Thus "the Lord" is represented throughout the first eleven chapters of Genesis as "speaking" to men. That these promises and sacrifices were then understood in their true spiritual intent is proved by Paul.—Heb. xi. 4-7. And that this administration of the covenant of grace reached many of the people of the earth, during this era, is proved by the history of Job in Arabia, of Abraham in Mesopotamia, and of Melchisedec in Canaan.

16. *How was it administered from Abraham to Moses?*

1st. The promise given during the preceding period (Gen. iii. 15), is now renewed in the form of a more definite covenant, revealing the coming Saviour as in the line of Abraham's posterity through Isaac, and the interest of the whole world in his salvation is more fully set forth.—Gen. xvii. 7; xxii. 18. This was the gospel preached beforehand.—Gal. iii. 8.

2d. Sacrifices were continued as before.

3d. The church, or company of believers, which existed from the beginning in its individual members, was now formed into a general body as an aggregate of families, by the institution of circumcision, as a visible symbol of the benefits of the covenant of grace, and as a badge of church membership.

17. *What was the true nature of the covenant made by God with the Israelites through Moses?*

It may be regarded in three aspects—

1st. As a national and political covenant, whereby, in a political sense, they became his people, under his theocratical government, and in this peculiar sense he became their God. The church and the state were identical. In one aspect the whole system had reference to this relation.

2d. It was in one aspect a legal covenant, because the moral law, obedience to which was the condition of the covenant of works, was prominently set forth, and conformity to this law was made the condition of God's favor, and of all national blessings. Even the ceremonial system in its merely literal, and apart from its symbolical aspect, was also a rule of works, for cursed was he that confirmeth not all the words of this law to do them.—Deut. xxvii. 26.

3d. But in the symbolical and typical significance of all the Mosaic institutions, they were a clearer and fuller revelation of the provisions of the Covenant of Grace than had ever before been made. This Paul abundantly proves throughout the Epistle to the Hebrews.—Hodge on Romans.

18. *What are the characteristic differences between the dispensation of the Covenant of Grace under the law of Moses and after the advent of Christ?*

These differences, of course, relate only to the mode of administration, and not to the matter of the truth revealed, nor of the grace administered. 1st. The truth was then signified by symbols, which, at the same time, were types of the real atonement for sin afterwards to be made. Now the truth is revealed in the plain gospel history. 2d. That revelation was less full as well as less clear. 3d. It was so encumbered with ceremonies as to be comparatively a carnal dispensation. The present dispensation is spiritual. 4th. It was confined to one people. The present dispensation, disembarrassed from all national organizations, embraces the whole earth. 5th. The former method of administration was evidently preparatory to the present, which is final.

For the Calvinistic view of the "Covenant of Grace," see Turretin, "Inst. Theo. Elench.," Loc. 12.; Witsius, "Æcon. of the Covs." For Arminian view see Fletcher's works and Richard Watson's "Inst. of Theo."

CHAPTER XXIII.

THE PERSON OF CHRIST.

1. *How can it be proved that the promised Messiah of the Jewish Scriptures has already come, and that Jesus Christ is that person?*

We prove that he must have already come by showing that the conditions of time and circumstances, which the prophets declare should mark his advent, are no longer possible. We prove, secondly, that Jesus of Nazareth was that person by showing that every one of those conditions was fulfilled in him.

2. *Prove that Gen. xlix. 10, refers to the Messiah, and show how it proves that the Messiah must have already come.*

The original word translated *shiloh*, signifies *peace*, and is applied to the Messiah.—Compare Micah v. 2, 5, with Matt. ii. 6. Besides, it is only to the Messiah that the gathering of the nations is to be.—See Isa. lv. 5; lx. 3; Hag. ii. 7. The Jews, moreover, have always understood this passage as referring to the Messiah.

Up to the time of the birth of Jesus Christ the sceptre and the lawgiver did remain with Judah; but seventy years after his birth, at the destruction of Jerusalem, they finally departed. If the advent of the Messiah had not occurred previously this prophecy is false.

3. *Do the same with reference to the prophecy of Dan. ix. 24–27.*

This prophecy refers expressly to the Messiah, and to his peculiar and exclusive work. That the seventy weeks here mentioned are to be interpreted weeks of years is certain, 1st, from the fact that it was the Jewish custom so to divide time; 2d, from the fact that this was precisely the common usage of the prophetical books, see Ezek. iv. 6; Rev. xii. 6; xiii. 5; 3d, from the fact that the literal application of the language as seventy common weeks is impracticable.

The prophecy is, that seven weeks of years, or forty-nine years from the end of the captivity, the city would be rebuilt.

That sixty-two weeks of years, or four hundred and thirty-four years after the rebuilding of the city, the Messiah should appear, and that during the period of one week of years he should confirm the covenant, and in the midst of the week be cut off.

There is some doubt as to the precise date from which the calculation ought to commence. The greatest difference, however, is only ten years, and the most probable date causes the prophecy to coincide precisely with the history of Jesus Christ.

4. *What prophecies, relating to the time, place, and circumstances of the birth of the Messiah, have been fulfilled in Jesus of Nazareth?*

As to time, it was predicted that he should come before the sceptre departed from Judah (Gen. xlix. 10), at the end of four hundred and ninety years after the going forth of the command to rebuild Jerusalem, and while the second temple was still standing.—Hag. ii. 9; Mal. iii. 1.

As to place and circumstances, he was to be born in Bethlehem (Micah v. 2), of the tribe of Judah, of the family of David. Jer. xxiii. 5, 6. He was to be born of a virgin, Isa. vii. 14; and to be preceded by a forerunner.—Mal. iii. 1. All these met in Jesus Christ, and can never again be fulfilled in another, since the genealogies of tribes and families have been lost.

5. *What remarkable characteristics of the Messiah, as described in the Old Testament, were verified in our Saviour?*

He was to be a king and conqueror of universal empire, Ps. ii. 6 and Ps. xlv.; Isa. ix. 6, 7; and yet despised and rejected, a man of sorrow, a prisoner, pouring forth his soul unto death. Isa. liii. He was to be a light to lighten the Gentiles, and under his administration the moral condition of the whole earth was to be changed.—Isa. xlii. 6; xlix. 6; lx. 1-7. His death was to be vicarious.—Isa. liii. 5, 9, 12. He was to enter the city riding upon an ass.—Zech. ix. 9. He was to be sold for thirty pieces of silver, and his price purchase a potter's field. Zech. xi. 12, 13. His garments were to be parted by lot.—Ps. xxii. 18. They were to give him vinegar to drink.—Ps. lxix. 21. The very words he was to utter on the cross are predicted, Ps. xxii. 1; also that he should be pierced, Zech. xii. 10; and make his grave with the wicked and with the rich, Isa. liii. 9.—See Dr. Alexander's "Evidences of Christianity."

6. *What peculiar work was the Messiah to accomplish, which has been performed by Christ?*

All his mediatorial offices were predicted in substance. He was to do the work of a prophet (Is. xlii. 6; lx. 3), and that of a priest (Is. liii. 10), to make reconciliation for sin (Dan. ix. 24). As king, he was to administer the several dispensations of his kingdom, closing one and introducing another, sealing up the vision and prophecy, causing the sacrifice and oblation to cease (Dan. ix. 24), and setting up a kingdom that should never cease (Dan. ii. 44).

7. *State the five points involved in the church doctrine as to the Person of Christ.*

1st. Jesus of Nazareth was very God, possessing the divine nature and all its essential attributes.   2d. He is also true man, his human nature derived by generation from the stock of Adam.   3d. These natures continue united in his Person, yet ever remain true divinity and true humanity, unmixed and as to essence unchanged.   So that Christ possesses at once in the unity of his Person two spirits with all their essential attributes, a human consciousness, mind, heart, and will, and a divine consciousness, mind, feeling, and will.   "*Gemina substantia, gemina mens, gemina sapientia robur et virtus.*"—"*Admonitio Neostadtiensis,*" 1581, of which Ursinus was the principal author.   Yet it does not become us to attempt to explain the manner in which the two spirits mutually affect each other, or how far they meet in one consciousness, nor how the two wills co-operate in one activity, in the union of the one person. 4th. Nevertheless they constitute as thus united one single Person, and the attributes of both natures belong to the one Person.   5th. This Personality is not a new one constituted by the union of the two natures in the womb of the Virgin, but it is the eternal and immutable Person of the λογος, which in time assumed into itself a nascent human nature, and ever subsequently embraces the human nature with the divine in the Personality which eternally belongs to the latter.

8. *How may it be proved that Christ is really a man?*

He is called man.—1 Tim. ii. 5.   His most common title is Son of Man, Matt. xiii. 37, also seed of the woman, Gen. iii. 15; the seed of Abraham, Acts iii. 25; Son of David, and fruit of his loins, Luke i. 32; made of a woman.—Gal. iv. 4. He had a *body*, ate, drank, slept, and increased in stature, Luke ii. 52; and through a life of thirty-three years was recognized by all men as a true man.   He died in agony on the cross, was buried, rose, and proved his identity by physical signs.—Luke xxiv. 36–44.   He had a *reasonable soul*, for he increased in wisdom.   He exercised the common feelings of our nature, he groaned in spirit and was troubled, he wept.—John xi. 33, 35.

He loved Martha and Mary, and the disciple that Jesus loved leaned upon his bosom.—John xiii. 23.

The absolute divinity of Christ has been proved above, Chap. IX.

9. *How may it be proved that both these natures constituted but one person?*

In many passages both natures are referred to, when it is evident that only one person was intended.—Phil. ii. 6–11. In many passages both natures are set forth as united. It is never affirmed that divinity abstractly, or a divine power, was united to, or manifested in a human nature, but of the divine nature concretely, that a divine person was united to a human nature.—Heb. ii. 11–14; 1 Tim. iii. 16; Gal. iv. 4; Rom. viii. 3 and i. 3, 4; ix. 5; John i. 14; 1 John iv. 3.

The union of two natures in one person is also clearly taught by those passages in which the attributes of one nature are predicated of the person, while that person is designated by a title derived from the other nature. Thus human attributes and actions are predicated of Christ in certain passages, while the person of whom these attributes or actions are predicated, is designated by a divine title.—Acts xx. 28; Rom. viii. 32; 1 Cor. ii. 8; Matt. i. 23; Luke i. 31, 32; Col. i. 13, 14.

On the other hand, in other passages, divine attributes and actions are predicated of Christ, while his person, of whom those attributes are predicated, is designated by a human title. John iii. 13; vi. 62; Rom. ix. 5; Rev. v. 12.

10. *What is the general principle upon which those passages are to be explained which designate the person of Christ from one nature, and predicate attributes to it belonging to the other?*

The person of Christ, constituted of two natures, is one person. He may, therefore, indifferently be designated by divine or human titles, and both divine and human attributes may be truly predicated of him. He is still God when he dies, and still man when he raises his people from their graves.

Mediatorial actions pertain to both natures. It must be remembered, however, that while the person is one, the natures are distinct, as such. What belongs to either nature is attributed to the one person to which both belong, but what is peculiar to one nature is never attributed to the other. God, *i. e.*, the divine person who is at once God and man, gave his blood for his church, *i. e.*, died as to his human nature (Acts xx. 28). But human attributes or actions are never asserted of Christ's divine *nature*, nor are divine attributes or actions ever asserted of his human *nature*.

11. *How have theologians defined the ideas of "nature" and "person" as they are involved in this doctrine?*

In the doctrine of the Trinity the difficulty is that one Spirit exists as three Persons.   In the doctrine of the Incarnation the difficulty is that two spirits exist in union as one Person.

"Nature" in this connection has been defined by the terms, "essence," "being," "substance."

"Person" in this connection has been defined as "an individual substance, which is neither part of, nor is sustained by some other thing," or as "an intelligent individual subsistence, *per se subsistens.*"   The human nature in Christ never was "per se subsistens," but since it began to be as a germ generated into personal union with the eternal Second Person of the Godhead, so from the beginning "*in altero sustentatur.*"

12. *What were the effects of this personal union upon the Divine nature of Christ?*

His divine nature being eternal and immutable, and, of course, incapable of addition, remained essentially unchanged by this union.   The whole immutable divine essence continued to subsist as the eternal Personal Word, now embracing a perfect human nature in the unity of his person, and as the organ of his will.   Yet thereby is the relation of the divine nature changed to the whole creation, since he has become Emmanuel, "God with us," "God manifest in the flesh."

13. *What were the effects of that union upon his human nature?*

The human nature, being perfect after its kind, began to exist in union with the divine nature, and as one constituent of the divine Person, and as such it ever continues unmixed and essentially unchanged human nature.

The effect of this union upon Christ's human nature, therefore, was—

1st. Exaltation of all human excellencies above the standard of human and of creaturely nature.—John i. 14; iii. 34; Is. xii. 2.

2d. Unparalleled exaltation to dignity and glory, above every name that is named, and a community of honor and worship with the divinity in virtue of its union therewith in the one divine Person.

3d. As in the union of soul and body in the natural person, the soul although absolutely destitute of extension in itself, is in virtue of its union with the body present at once from the crown of the head to the sole of the foot,—that is virtually, if not essentially, present in conscious perception and active volition,—so through its personal union with the eternal Word is the human nature of Christ, (*a*) virtually present (although locally in heaven) with his people in the most distant parts of the earth at the same time, sympathizing with each severally as one who has himself also been tempted, (*b*) rendered practically inexhaustible in all those draughts made upon its energies by the constant exercise of those mediatorial functions which involve both natures.

Hence the church doctrine concerning the "communicatio idiomatum vel proprietatum" of the two natures of Christ. It is affirmed in the *concrete* in respect to the person, but denied in the *abstract* in respect to the natures; it is affirmed *utrius naturæ ad personam*, but denied *utrius naturæ ad naturam*.

14. *How far is the human nature of Christ included in the worship due to him?*

We must distinguish between the *object* and the *grounds* of worship. There can be no proper ground of worship, except the possession of divine attributes. The object of worship is not the divine excellence in the abstract, but the divine person of whom that excellence is an attribute. The God-man, consisting of two natures, is to be worshipped in the perfection of his entire person, because only of his divine attributes.

15. *State the analogy presented in the union of two natures in the persons of men.*

1st. Every human person comprehends two distinct natures, (*a*) a conscious, self-acting, self-determined spirit absolutely without extension in space, and (*b*) an extended highly organized body composed of passive matter.

2d. These constitute but one person. The body is part of the person.

3d. These natures remain distinct, the attributes of the spirit never being made common to the material body, nor the attributes of the body to the spirit, but the attributes of both body and spirit are common to the one person. The person is often designated by a title proper to one nature while the predicate is proper to the other nature.

4th. The spirit is the person. When the spirit leaves the body the latter is buried as a corpse, while the former goes to judgment. At the resurrection the spirit will resume the corpse into the person.

5th. While in union the person possesses and exercises the attributes of both natures. And in virtue of the union the unextended spirit is present virtually wherever the extended body is, and the inert insensible matter of the nerve tissues thrill with feeling and throb with will as organs of the feeling and willing soul.

16. *What is the peculiar view as to the "communicatio idiomatum" introduced into theology by the Lutherans? and state the reasons for not accepting it.*

In connection with, and in the process of maintaining, his peculiar view as to the presence of the very substance of Christ's body and blood in, with, and under the bread and the wine in the Eucharist, Luther and his followers introduced and elaborated a doctrine that, in consequence of the hypostatical union of the divine natures in the one person of Christ, each nature shares in the essential attributes of the other nature.

When they came to explain the matter more fully, they did not affirm that any distinctive attribute of humanity was shared by the divinity, nor that the human nature shared all the attributes of the divine; they affirmed in detail simply that the humanity shared with the divine in its omniscience, omnipresence, and power of giving life.

The advocates of this doctrine were divided into two schools:

1st. The most extreme and logically consistent, represented by John Brentz and the theologians of Tübingen. These maintained that the every act of incarnation effected, as the essence of the personal union, the participation of each nature in the properties of the other. From his conception in the womb of the Virgin the human nature of Christ was inalienably endowed with all the divine majesty, and all those properties which constitute it. These were necessarily exercised from the first, but not manifested during his earthly life, their exercise being hidden. The facts of Christ's life during his estate of humiliation are therefore explained by a voluntary Krypsis, or hiding of the divine properties of his humanity.

2d. The other less extreme view was represented by Martin Chemnitz, and the theologians of Giessen. They held also, that, by the very act of incarnation the humanity of Christ was endowed with divine perfections. That as to his relation to space, "*Logos non extra carnem, et caro non extra Logon.*" Yet they taught that the exercise of these perfections was not necessary, but subject to the will of the divine person, who causes his human nature to be present wherever and whensoever he wills, and who during the period of his humiliation on earth voluntarily emptied (Kenosis) his human nature of its use and exercise of its divine attributes. Prof. A. B. Bruce, D.D., "Humiliation of Christ," Lecture iii.—"The Lutherans held the exaltation of the humanity to meet the divinity, and (while on earth) the Kenosis of the humanity. The Reformed insisted on the reality of the human life of Christ, and the self-emptying (Kenosis) of the divinity to meet the humanity. The Lutherans held the double life of the glorified humanity (the local presence and the illocal omnipresence). The Reformed tendency was to recognize a double life of the Logos—*totus extra Jesum,* and *totus in Jesu.*"

We reject the Lutheran view because—1st. It is not taught in the Bible. It really rests upon their mistaken interpretation of the words of Christ—"This is my body."

2d. It is impossible to reconcile it with the phenomena of Christ's earthly life. It increases the difficulties of the problem it was invented to explain.

3d. It virtually destroys the incarnation by assimilating the human nature to the divine in the co-partnership of properties, whereby it is virtually abrogated, and in effect only the divine remains.

4th. It involves the fallacy of conceiving of properties as separable from the substances of which they are the active powers, and thus is open to the same criticisms as the doctrine of transubstantiation.

17. *How can it be shown that the doctrine of the incarnation is a fundamental doctrine of the Gospel?*

1st. This doctrine, and all the elements thereof, is set forth in the Scriptures with *pre-eminent* clearness and prominence.

2d. Its truth is essentially involved in every other doctrine of the entire system of faith; in every mediatorial act of Christ, as prophet, priest and king; in the whole history of his estate of humiliation, and in every aspect of his estate of exaltation; and, above all, in the significance and value of that vicarious sacrifice which is the heart of the gospel. If Christ is not in the same person both God and man, he either could not die, or his death could not avail. If he be not man, his whole history is a myth; if he be not God, to worship him is idolatry, yet not to worship him is to disobey the Father.—John v. 23.

3d. Scripture expressly declares that this doctrine is essential.—1 John iv. 2, 3.

18. *In what Creeds and by what Councils has this doctrine been most accurately defined?*

1st. The Creed of the Council of Nice, amended by the Council of Constantinople, and the Athanasian Creed, and the Creed of the Council of Chalcedon, are accurate and authoritative statements of the whole church as to this doctrine. They are all to be found above, Ch. VII.

2d. The decision of the Council of Ephesus, A. D. 431, condemning the Nestorians, and affirming the unity of the Person; the decision of the Council of Chalcedon (451) against Eutyches, affirming the distinction of natures; and the decision of the Council of Constantinople (681) against the Monothelites, affirming that Christ's human nature retains in its unimpaired integrity a separate will as well as intelligence, closed the gradually perfected definition of the church doctrine as to the Person of Christ, and have been accepted by all Protestants.

19. *How may all Heresies on this subject be classified?*

As they seek relief from the impossibility which reason experiences in the effort fully to comprehend the mutual consistency of all the elements of this doctrine (1) in the denial of the divine element, (2) or in the denial of the human element in its reality and integrity, or (3) in the denial of the unity of the person embracing both natures.

20. *What parties have held that Jesus was a mere man?*

In the early church the Ebionites, and the Alogi. At the time of the Reformation the Socinians. In latter times Rationalists and Unitarians. For an account of their history and doctrines, see above, Ch. VI., Q. 11, and Q. 13, and below, at the close of this chapter.

21. *What parties denied Christ's true humanity and on what grounds?*

These speculations were all of Gnostic origin. Hence came the conviction that matter was inherently evil, and that innumerable Æons, or great spiritual emanations from the absolute God, mediate between him and the actual world. $Πνεύματα$ come from God, but matter is self-existent, and the animal souls of men come from some being less than God. Hence the Docetæ (from $δοκέω$ to *think*, to *appear*) held that the human nature (body and soul) of Christ was a mere $φάντασμα$, or appearance, having no real substantial existence. It was a mere vision or phantom through which the Logos chose to manifest himself to mankind for a time.

22. *State the Apollinarian Heresy.*

Apollinaris, bishop of Laodicea, circum. 370, of general repute for orthodoxy and learning, taught that as man naturally consists of a body, $σῶμα$, and an animal soul, $ψυχή$, and a rational soul, $πνεῦμα$, all comprehended in one person, so in Christ the divine logos takes the place of the human $πνεῦμα$, and his one person consists of the divine $πνεῦμα$, or reasonable soul, and the human animal soul and body. He thus gets rid of the difficulty attending the coexistence of two rational, self-conscious, self-determining spirits in one person, and at the same time destroys the revealed fact that Christ is at once very man and very God. This was condemned by the Council of Constantinople, A. D. 381.

23. *What was the Nestorian Heresy ?*

This term rather expresses an exaggerated, one-sided tendency of speculation on this subject than a positive definable false doctrine. It is the tendency to so emphasize the distinction of the two complete, unmodified natures in Christ, as to throw into the shade the equally revealed fact of the unity of his Person.

This tendency was most conspicuous in the writings of Theodore of Mopsuestia, the leader of the Antiochian school, and from him it became the general character of that school. The theology of the Eastern Church of the fourth and fifth centuries was divided between the two great rival schools of Alexandria and Antioch. "In the Alexandrian school, an intuitive mode of thought inclining to the mystical; in the Antiochian, a logical reflective bent of the understanding predominated.—Neander, "Hist.," Torrey's Trans., Vol. II., p. 352.

Nestorius, who had been a monk at Antioch, became patriarch of Constantinople. He disapproved of the phrase, "Mother of God" ($\theta\varepsilon\acute{o}\tau o\kappa o\varsigma$), as applied to the Virgin, maintaining that Mary had given birth to Christ but not to God. Cyril, patriarch of Alexandria, opposed him, and both pronounced anathemas against each other. Nestorius supposed, in accordance with the Antiochian mode of thought, that the divine and the human natures of Christ ought to be distinctly separated, and admitted only a $\sigma v v \acute{\alpha} \varphi \varepsilon \iota \alpha$ (junction) of the one and the other, an $\grave{\varepsilon} v o \acute{\iota} \varkappa \eta \sigma \iota \varsigma$ (indwelling) of the Deity. Cyril, on the contrary, was led by the tendencies of the Egyptian (Alexandrian) school, to maintain the perfect union of the two natures ($\varphi v \sigma \iota \varkappa \acute{\eta} \, \ddot{\varepsilon} v \omega \sigma \iota \varsigma$). Nestorius, as the representative of his party, was condemned by the Council of Ephesus, A. D. 431.—Hagenbach's "Hist. of Doct.," Vol. I., § 100.

24. *What was the Eutychian or Monophysite Heresy ?*

Eutyches was an abbot at Constantinople, and an extreme disciple of Dioscuros, the successor of Cyril. He pressed the opposition to the Nestorians to the length of confounding the two natures of Christ, and hence holding that Christ possessed but one nature, resulting from the union of Divinity with humanity. They were styled Monophysites. They were condemned by the Council of Chalcedon (A. D. 451), which adopted the statement communicated by Leo the Great, bishop of Rome, to Flavian, patriarch of Constantinople. "*Totus in suis, totus in nostris.*"

25. *What was the doctrine of the Monothelites?*

The Emperor Heraclius attempted to reunite the Monophysites with the orthodox Church by adopting, as a compromise, the decision of the Council of Chalcedon as the coexistence of two distinct natures in the one Person of Christ, with the amendment that there was in consequence of the personal union but one divine-human energy (*ἐνέργεια*) and but one will in Christ. In opposition to this the sixth Œcumenical Council of Constantinople (A. D. 681), with the co-operation of the bishop of Rome, adopted the doctrine of *two* wills in Christ, and *two* energies, as the orthodox doctrine, but decided that the human will must always be conceived as subordinate to the divine."—Hagenbach's "Hist. of Doct.," § 104. With this decision the definition of this doctrine, as received by the whole church, Greek, Roman, and Protestant, was closed.

26. *What is the modern doctrine of Kenosis?*

The old Socinian doctrine teaches that Jesus, a true man after his ascension, becomes the subject of an apotheosis, whereby he is exalted into a condition and rank between that of God and the universe. The Eutychians taught that the human nature was absorbed by and assimilated to the divine. The Lutherans taught that the human nature was endowed with the properties of the divine. The modern doctrine of Kenosis is that instead of man becoming God, or being personally united to divinity, God literally became man. It is taught with various modifications by Drs. Thomasius, Hofmann, Ebrard, Martensen, and others, and very clearly by Dr. W. F. Gess in a work translated admirably by Dr. J. A. Reubelt, of Indiana.

The term signifies a voluntary emptying of himself, of his divinity, by the Logos. It is derived from Phil. ii. 7, *ἑαυτὸν ἐκένωσε*, "he emptied himself," and is supported by such declarations as John i. 14. "And the Word *was made* flesh, and dwelt among us."

I. The Father alone is from himself. He eternally communicates the fulness of his divine essence and perfections to the Son, thus giving to him to have life in himself. The Son thus eternally flowing from the Father unites with the Father in communicating their fulness to the Spirit, and is himself the life of the world.

II. "But the Logos is God; he has life in himself even as the Father; his volition to receive life from the Father is the source of his life; his self-consciousness is his own act. Hence it follows that he can suspend his self-consciousness."

III. In condescending to be conceived of the Virgin, the Logos laid aside his self-consciousness, and with it the communication of the Father's life to the Son, by which the Son has life in himself even as the Father, and hence his omniscience, omnipresence, and omnipotent government of the world was suspended.

IV. When the substance of the Logos awoke to self-consciousness as the infant Jesus, it was as a true human infant, and he grew and developed in knowledge and powers, as a true man without sin, endowed with pre-eminent grace and the fulness of the indwelling Spirit of God.

V. When glorified the ante-mundane eternal communication of the fulness of divine life from the Father to the Logos recommenced, and though continuing truly human, he is no less truly God. He is again eternal, omniscient, omnipotent, and omnipresent. "Thus a man is received into the trinitarian life of the Deity, from and by the glorification of the Son."—"Script. Doc. Pers. Christ. Gess.," by Reubelt.

This doctrine.—1st. Does violence to the infinite perfections and immutability of the divine nature. 2d. It is not consistent with the Scriptural fact that Christ, while on earth, was real and absolute God. 3d. It is not consistent with the fact that the humanity of Christ was real humanity generated of the seed of Abraham. 4th. It is confessedly different from the immemorial and universal faith of the Church.

For a thorough discussion, see Dr. A. B. Bruce's "Humiliation of Christ."

AUTHORITATIVE STATEMENTS.

The GREEK, ROMAN, and PROTESTANT Churches all agree in accepting the definitions of the Creeds, those of Nice and of Chalcedon and the Athanasian (so called).—See above Chap. VII.

The LUTHERAN DOCTRINE as to the Relations of the two Natures.

"*Formula Concordiæ*," Pars. I., Epitome, ch. 8, §§ 11 and 12.— "Therefore not only as God, but also as man, he knows all things, and had power to do all things, is present to all creatures, and has all things which are in heaven, on earth, and under the earth, under his feet, and in his hands. 'All things are given to me in heaven and on earth,' and 'he ascended above all heavens, and fills all things.' Being everywhere present, he is able to 'exercise this his power, neither is any thing to him either impossible or unknown. Hence, moreover, and most easily, is he being present, able to distribute his true body and blood in the sacred Supper. But this is done not according to the mode and property of human nature, but according to the mode and property of the right hand of God. . . . And this presence of Christ in the sacred Supper is neither physical nor earthly, nor capernaitish (see John vi. 52–59), nevertheless, it is most true and substantial."

Pars. 2 ("Solida Declaratio"), ch. 8, § 4.—"For that communion of natures, and of properties, is not the result of an essential, or natural effusion of the properties of the divine nature upon the human: as if the humanity of Christ had them subsisting independently and separate from divinity; or as, if by that communion, the human nature of Christ had laid aside its natural properties, and was either converted into the divine nature, or was made equal in itself, and *per se* to the divine nature by those properties thus communicated, or that the natural properties and operations were identical or even equal. For these and like errors have justly been rejected, etc."

Luther says, "Where you put God, there you must put the humanity (of Christ), they can not be sundered or riven; it is one person, and the humanity is more closely united with God than is our skin with our flesh, yea, more intimately than body with soul."

DOCTRINE OF THE REFORMED CHURCHES.

"*Confessio Helvetica Posterior*," ch. xi.—"We acknowledge, therefore, that in one and the same Lord Jesus Christ, there are two natures, and we say that these are so conjoined and united that they are not absorbed, nor confused nor mixed; but are rather united and conjoined in one person, being preserved with their permanent properties; so that we worship one Lord the Christ, and not two; one we say, true God and man, according to his divine nature consubstantial with the Father, and according to his human nature consubstantial with us men, and in all things like us, sin excepted. Therefore, as we abominate the Nestorian dogma making two out of one Christ, and dissolving the union of the Person; so, also, we heartily execrate the madness of Eutyches and of the Monophysites and the Monothelites, expunging the property of the human nature. Therefore, we in no wise teach that the divine nature in Christ suffered, or that Christ according to his human nature has hitherto been in this world, and so is everywhere."

"*West. Conf.*," Ch. 8, § 2.—"The Son of God, the second person in the Trinity, being very and eternal God, of one substance, and equal with the Father, did, when the fulness of time was come, take upon him man's nature, and all the essential properties and common infirmities thereof, yet without sin: being conceived by the power of the Holy Ghost in the womb of the Virgin Mary, of her substance. So that two whole, perfect, and distinct natures, the Godhead and the manhood, were inseparably joined together in one person, without conversion, composition, or confusion. Which person is very God and very man, yet one Christ, the only mediator between God and man."

CHAPTER XXIV.

MEDIATORIAL OFFICE OF CHRIST.

1. *What are the different senses of the word Mediator, and in which of these senses is it used when applied to Christ?*

1st. In the sense of internuntius or messenger, to explain the will and to perform the commands of one or both the contracting parties, *e. g.*, Moses, Gal. iii. 19.

2d. In the sense of simple advocate or intercessor, pleading the cause of the offending in the presence of the offended party.

3d. In the sense of efficient peace-maker. Christ, as Mediator, 1st, has all power and judgment committed to his hands, Matt. xxviii. 18, and ix. 6; John v. 22, 25, 26, 27; and, 2d, he efficiently makes reconciliation between God and man by an all-satisfactory expiation and meritorious obedience.

2. *Why was it necessary that the Mediator should be possessed both of a divine and human nature?*

1st. It was clearly necessary that the Mediator should be God. (1.) That he might be independent, and not the mere creature of either party, or otherwise he could not be the efficient maker of peace. (2.) That he might reveal God and his salvation to men, "For no man knoweth the Father save the Son, and he to whom the Son will reveal him."—Matt. xi. 27; John i. 18. (3.) That being, *as to person*, above all law, and *as to dignity of nature*, infinite, he might render to the law in behalf of his people a free obedience, which he did not otherwise owe for himself, and that his obedience and suffering might possess an infinite value. (4.) That he might possess the infinite wisdom, knowledge, and power requisite to administer the infinite realms of providence and grace, which are committed to his hands as mediatorial prince.

2d. It is clearly necessary that he should be man. (1.) That he might truly represent man as the second Adam. (2.) That he might be made under the law, in order to render obedience, suffering, and temptation possible.—Gal. iv. 4, 5; Luke iv. 1–13 (3.) "In all things it behoved him to be made like unto his brethren, that he might be a merciful and faithful high priest." Heb. ii. 17, 18, and iv. 15, 16. (4.) That in his glorified humanity he might be the head of the glorified church, the example and pattern to whom his people are "predestined to be conformed, that he might be the first-born among many brethren."—Rom. viii. 29.

3. *What diversity of opinion exists as to whether Christ acts as Mediator in one or both natures?*

The Romanists hold that Christ was Mediator only in his human nature, arguing that it is impossible that God could mediate between man and himself.

The very opposite has been maintained, viz., that Christ was Mediator only in his divine nature.

The doctrine of the Bible is, that Christ was Mediator as the God-man, in both natures.

4. *How may the acts of Christ be classified with reference to his two natures?*

Theologians have properly distinguished (vide Turretin, *in loco*) between the person who acts and the nature or inward energy whereby he acts.

Thus we affirm of the one man, that he thinks and that he walks. The same person performs these two classes of action so radically distinct, in virtue of the two natures embraced in his single person. So the single person of the God-man performs all actions involving the attributes of a divine nature in virtue of his divine nature, and all actions involving the attributes of a human nature in virtue of his human nature.

5. *How can it be proved that he was Mediator, and acted as such both in his divine and human natures?*

1st. From the fact that the discharge of each of the three great functions of the mediatorial office, the prophetical, priestly, and kingly, involves the attributes of both natures, as has been fully proved under Question 2.

2d. From the fact that the Bible attributes all his acts as Mediator to the one person, viewed as embracing both natures. The person is often designated by a term derived from the attributes of one nature, while the mediatorial action attributed to that person is plainly performed in virtue of the other nature embraced within it.—See Acts xx. 28; 1 Cor. ii. 8; Heb. ix. 14.

3d. From the fact that he was Mediator from the foundation of the earth (see Chapter XXII., Question 11), it is clear that he was not Mediator in his human nature alone; and from the fact that the Eternal Word became incarnate, in order to prepare himself for the full discharge of his mediatorial work (Heb. ii. 17, 18), it is equally plain that he was not Mediator in his divine nature alone.

6. *In what sense do the Romanists regard saints and angels as mediators?*

They do not attribute either to saints or angels the work of propitiation proper. Yet they hold that the merits of the saint are the ground and measure of the efficiency of his intercession, as in the case of Christ.

7. *How far do they ascribe a mediatorial character to their priests?*

The Protestant holds that the church is composed of a company of men united to one another in virtue of the immediate union of each with Christ the head. The Romanist holds, on the contrary, that each individual member is united immediately to the church, and through the church to Christ. Their priests, therefore, of the true apostolic succession, subject to apostolic bishops, being the only authorized dispensers of the sacraments, and through them of Christ's grace, are mediators—

1st. Between the individual and Christ, the necessary link of union with him.

2d. In their offering the sacrifice of the Mass, and making therein a true propitiation for the venial sins of the people. Christ's great sacrifice having atoned for original sin, and laid the foundation for the propitiatory virtue which belongs to the Mass.

3d. In their being eminent intercessors.

8. *How can it be proved that Christ is our only Mediator in the proper sense of the term?*

1st. Direct testimony of Scripture.—1 Tim. ii. 5.

2d. Because the Scriptures show forth Christ as fulfilling in our behalf every mediatorial function that is necessary, alike propitiation and advocacy, 1 John ii. 1; on earth and in heaven, —Heb. ix. 12, 24, and vii. 25.

3d. Because in virtue of the infinite dignity of his person and perfection of his nature, all these functions were discharged by him exhaustively.—Heb. x. 14; Col. ii. 10.

4th. Because there is "complete" salvation in him, and no salvation in any other, and no man can come to the Father except through him.—John xiv. 6; Acts iv. 12.

5th. There is no room for any mediator between the individual and Christ—(1) because he is our "brother" and "sympathizing high priest," who invites every man immediately to himself, Matt. xi. 28; (2) because the work of drawing men to Christ belongs to the Holy Ghost.—John vi. 44, and xvi. 14.

9. *What relation do the Scriptures represent the Holy Ghost as sustaining to the mediatorial work of Christ?*

1st. Begetting and replenishing his human nature.—Luke i. 35; ii. 40; John iii. 34; Ps. xlv. 7.

2d. All Christ's mediatorial functions were fulfilled in the Spirit; his prophetical teachings, his priestly sacrifice, and his kingly administrations. The Spirit descended upon him at his baptism, Luke iii. 22; and led him into the wilderness to be tempted, Matt. iv. 1; he returned in the power of the Spirit into Galilee, Luke iv. 14; through the eternal Spirit he offered himself without spot to God.—Heb. ix. 14.

3d. The dispensation of the Spirit, as "the Spirit of truth," "the Sanctifier," and "the Comforter," vests in Christ as Mediator, as part of the condition of the covenant of grace.—John xv. 26, and xvi. 7; and vii. 39; Acts ii. 33.

4th. The Holy Spirit thus dispensed by Christ as Mediator *acts for him*, and *leads to him* in teaching, quickening, sanctifying, preserving, and acting all grace in his people. As Christ when on earth led only to the Father, so the Holy Ghost now leads only to Christ.—John xv. 26, and xvi. 13, 14; Acts v. 32; 1 Cor. xii. 3.

5th. While Christ as Mediator is said to be our "παράκλητος," "advocate," *with the Father* (1 John ii. 1), the Holy Ghost is said to be our "παράκλητος," "advocate," translated "Comforter" *on earth*, to abide with us forever, to teach us the things of Christ, and to hold a controversy with the world.—John xiv. 16, 26, and xv. 26, and xvi. 7–9.

6th. While Christ is said to be our Mediator to make intercession for us in heaven, Heb. vii. 25; Rom. viii. 34, the Holy Ghost, by forming thoughts and desires within us according to the will of God, is said to make intercession for us with unutterable groanings.—Rom. viii. 26, 27.

7th. The sum of the whole is, "We have introduction *to* the Father *through* the Son *by* the Spirit."—Eph. ii. 18.

10. *On what ground are the threefold offices of prophet, priest, and king applied to Christ?*

1st. Because these three functions are all equally necessary, and together exhaust the whole mediatorial work.

2d. Because the Bible ascribes all of these functions to Christ. Prophetical, Deut. xviii. 15, 18; compare Acts iii. 22, and vii. 37;

Heb. i. 2; priestly, Ps. cx. 4, and the whole Epistle to the Hebrews; kingly, Acts v. 31; 1 Tim. vi. 15; Rev. xvii. 14.

It is always to be remembered that these are not three offices, but three functions of the one indivisible' office of mediator. These functions are abstractly most distinguishable, but in the concrete and in their exercise they qualify one another in every act. Thus, when he teaches, he is essentially a royal and priestly teacher, and when he rules he is a priestly and prophetical king, and when he either atones or intercedes he is a prophetical and kingly priest.

These were first grouped together as belonging to Christ by Eusebius (261–340), Bk. I, ch. iii.—"So that all these have a reference to the true Christ, the divine and heavenly Word, the only high priest of all men, the only king of all creation, and the Father's only supreme Prophet of prophets."

11. *What is the Scriptural sense of the word prophet?*

Its general sense is one who speaks for another with authority as interpreter. Thus Moses was prophet for his brother Aaron.—Ex. vii. 1.

A prophet of God is one qualified and authorized to speak for God to men. Foretelling future events is only incidental.

12. *How does Christ execute the office of a prophet?*

I. Immediately in his own person, as when (1) on earth with his disciples, and (2) the light of the new Jerusalem in the midst of the throne.—Rev. xxi. 23.

II. Mediately, 1st, through his Spirit, (1) by inspiration, (2) by spiritual illumination. 2d. Through the officers of his church, (1) those inspired as apostles and prophets, and (2) those naturally endowed, as the stated ministry.—Eph. iv. 11.

III. Both externally, as through his word and works addressed to the understanding, and,

IV. Internally, by the spiritual illumination of the heart.— 1 John ii. 20, and v. 20.

V. In three grand successive stages of development. (*a.*) Before his incarnation; (*b*) since his incarnation; (*c*) throughout eternity in glory.—Rev. vii. 17, and xxi. 23.

13. *How can it be proved that he acted as such before his incarnation?*

1st. His divine title of Logos, "Word," as by nature as well as office the eternal Revealer.

2d. It has been before proved (Chap. XXII., Question 11, and Chap. IX., Question 14) that he was the Jehovah of the Old

Testament economy. Called Counsellor.—Is. ix. 6. Angel of the Covenant.—Mal. iii. 1. Interpreter.—Job xxxiii. 23.

3d. The fact is directly affirmed in the New Testament.—1 Pet. i. 11.

14. *What is essential to the priestly office, or what is a priest in the Scriptural sense of that term?*

As the general idea of a prophet is, one qualified and authorized to speak for God to men, so the general idea of a priest is, one qualified and authorized to treat in behalf of men with God.

A priest, therefore, must—

1st. Be taken from among men to represent them.—Heb. v. 1, 2; Ex. xxviii. 9,*12, 21, 29.

2d. Chosen by God as his special election and property.— Num. xvi. 5; Heb. v. 4.

3d. Holy, morally pure and consecrated to the Lord.—Lev. xxi. 6, 8; Ps. cvi. 16; Ex. xxxix. 30, 31.

4th. They have a right to draw near to Jehovah, and to bring near, or offer sacrifice, and to make intercession.—Num. xvi. 5; Ex. xix. 22; Lev. xvi. 3, 7, 12, 15.

The priest, therefore, was essentially a mediator, admitted from among men to stand before God, for the purpose, 1st, of propitiation by sacrifice, Heb. v. 1, 2, 3; and, 2d, of intercession, Luke i. 10; Ex. xxx. 8; Rev. v. 8, and viii. 3, 4. Taken from Fairbairn's "Typology," Vol. II., Part III., Chap. iii.

15. *Prove from the Old Testament that Christ was truly a priest.*

1st. It is expressly declared.—Compare Ps. cx. 4, with Heb. v. 6, and vi. 20; Zech. vi. 13.

2d. Priestly functions are ascribed to him.—Is. liii. 10, 12; Dan. ix. 24, 25.

3d. The whole meaning and virtue of the temple, of its services, and of the Levitical priesthood, lay in the fact that they were all typical of Christ and his work as priest. This Paul clearly proves in the Epistle to the Hebrews.

16. *Show from the New Testament that all the requisites of a priest were found in him.*

1st. Christ was a man taken from among men to represent them before God.—Heb. ii. 16, and iv. 15.

2d. He was chosen by God.—Heb. v. 5, 6.

3d. He was perfectly holy.—Luke i. 35; Heb. vii. 26.

4th. He had the right of the nearest access, and the greatest influence with the Father.—John xvi. 28, and xi. 42; Heb. i. 3, and ix. 11, 12, 13, 14, 24.

17. *Show that he actually performed all the duties of the office.*

The duty of the priest is to mediate by (1) propitiation, (2) intercession.

1st. He mediated in the general sense of the word.—John xiv. 6; 1 Tim. ii. 5; Heb. viii. 6, and xii. 24.

2d. He offered propitiation.—Eph. v. 2; Heb. ix. 26, and x. 12; 1 John ii. 2.

3d. He offered intercession.—Rom. viii. 34; Heb. vii. 25; 1 John ii. 1.

That this propitiatory work of Christ was real, and not metaphorical, is evident from the fact that it superseded the temple services, which were only typical of it. A type and shadow necessarily presupposes a literal substance.—Heb. ix. 10–12, and x. 1; Col. ii. 17.

18. *What part of his priestly work did Christ execute on earth, and what part in heaven?*

On earth he rendered obedience, propitiation, intercession. Heb. v. 7–9, and ix. 26, 28; Rom. v. 19.

In heaven he has presented his sacrifice in the most holy place, and ever liveth to make intercession for us.—Heb. vii. 24, 25, and ix. 12, 24.

19. *In what respects did the priesthood of Christ excel the Aaronic?*

1st. In the dignity of his person. They were mere men. He was the eternal Son. They were sinners who had first to make atonement for their own sin, and afterwards for the sin of the people. He was holy, harmless and undefiled.—Heb. vii. 26, 27. He was perfect man, and yet his access to God was infinitely nearer than that of any other being.—John x. 30; Zech. xiii. 7.

2d. In the infinite value of his sacrifice. Theirs could not cleanse from sin, Heb. x. 4, and were repeated continually.— Heb. x. 1–3. His sacrifice was perfectly efficacious, and once for all.—Heb. x. 10–14. Thus theirs were only the shadow of his.—Heb. x. 1.

3d. In the manner of their consecration. They without, he with an oath.—Heb. vii. 20–22.

4th. They, being many, succeeded each other by generation. He continueth forever.—Heb. vii. 24.

5th. Christ's priesthood is connected with a "greater and

more perfect tabernacle," earth the outer court, heaven the true sanctuary.—Heb. ix. 11–24.

6th. Christ's intercession is offered from a *throne.*—Rom. viii. 34, and Heb. viii. 1, 2.

7th. While several of the Old Testament servants of God were at once both prophet and king, as David; and others both prophet and priest, as Ezra; Christ alone, and that in divine perfection, was at once prophet, priest, and king. Thus his divine, prophetical, and kingly perfections qualified and enhanced the transcendent virtue of every priestly act.—Zech. vi. 13.

20. *In what sense was Christ a priest after the order of Melchizedec?*

The Aaronic priesthood was typical of Christ, but in two principal respects it failed in representing the great antitype.

1st. It consisted of succeeding generations of mortal men.

2d. It consisted of priests not royal.

The Holy Ghost, on the other hand, suddenly brings Melchizedec before us in the patriarchal history, a royal priest, with the significant names "King of Righteousness" and "King of Peace," Gen. xiv. 18–20, and as suddenly withdraws him. Whence he comes and whither he goes we know not. As a private man he had an unwritten history, like others. But as a royal priest he ever remains without father, without mother, without origin, *succession,* or end; and *therefore,* as Paul says, Heb. vii. 3, made beforehand of God, an exact type of the eternity of the priesthood of Christ, Ps. cx. 4. The prophecy was, "Thou shalt be a priest *forever,*" or an eternal priest "after the order of Melchizedec."

The similitude of this type, therefore, included two things: 1st, an everlasting priesthood; 2d, the union of the kingly and priestly functions in one person.—Fairbairn's "Typology," Vol. II., Part III., Chap. iii.

21. *How can it be proved that the Christian ministry is not a priesthood?*

1st. Human priests were ever possible only as types, but types are possible only before the revelation of the antitype. The purpose of the Aaronic priesthood was fulfilled in Christ, and therefore the institution was forever abolished by Christ. Heb. x. 1, 9, 18.

2d. Christ exhaustively discharges all the duties and purposes of the priestly office, so that any human priest (so-called) is an antichrist.—Heb. x. 14; Col. ii. 10.

3d. There can be no need of any priest to open the way for us to Christ. Because, while the Scriptures teach us that we can only go to God by Christ, John xiv. 6, they teach us no less emphatically that we must come immediately to Christ, Matt. xi. 28; John v. 40, and vii. 37; Rev. iii. 20, and xxii. 17.

4th. No priestly function is ever attributed to any New Testament officer, inspired or uninspired, extraordinary or ordinary. The whole duty of all these officers of every kind is comprised in the functions of teaching and ruling.—1 Cor. xii. 28; Eph. iv. 11, 12; 1 Tim. iii. 1–13; 1 Pet. v. 2.

5th. They are constantly called by different designations, expressive of an entirely different class of functions, as "messengers, watchmen, heralds of salvation, teachers, rulers, overseers, shepherds, and elders."—See "Bib. Repertory," Jan., 1845.

22. *In what sense are all believers priests?*

Although there can not be in the Christian church any class of priests standing between their brethren and Christ, yet in consequence of the union, both federal and vital, which every Christian sustains to Christ, which involves fellowship with him in all of his human graces, and in all of his mediatorial functions and prerogatives, every believer has part in the priesthood of his head in such a sense that he has immediate access to God through Christ, even into the holiest of all, Heb. x. 19–22; and that being sanctified and spiritually qualified, he may there offer up, as a "holy priest," a "royal priest," spiritual sacrifices, not expiatory, but the oblation of praise, supplication, and thanksgiving, through Jesus Christ, and intercession for living friends, Heb. xiii. 15; 1 Tim. ii. 1, 2; 1 Pet. ii. 5, 9.

They are by equal reason also prophets and kings in fellowship with Christ.—1 John ii. 20; John xvi. 13; Rev. i. 6, and v. 10.

AUTHORITATIVE STATEMENTS.

Catholic Doctrine of the Christian Priesthood.—"*Council of Trent,*" Sess. 23, ch. 1.—"Sacrifice and priesthood are, by the ordinance of God, in such wise conjoined, as that both have existed in every law. Whereas, therefore, in the New Testament, the Catholic Church has received, from the institution of Christ, the holy visible sacrifice of the Eucharist; it must needs also be confessed, that there is, in that church, a new, visible, and external priesthood, into which the old has been translated. And the sacred Scriptures show, and the traditions of the Catholic Church have always taught, that this priesthood was instituted by the same Lord our Saviour, and that to the apostles, and their successors in the priesthood, was the power delivered of consecrating, offering, and administering his body and blood, as also of forgiving and of retaining sins."

Protestant Doctrine.—"*Conf. Helv.,*" ii. cap. 18.—"The priestly office and the ministerial office differ exceedingly from each other. The former is common to all Christians, the latter is not. . . . . In the

New Testament of Christ there is no more such a priesthood as that which existed among the ancient people, which had an external unction, sacred vestments, and numerous ceremonies, which were types of Christ, who by coming and fulfilling them has abrogated all these things. But he remains eternally the only priest, and lest we should derogate aught from him, we give the name of priest to none of the class of ministers. For our Lord himself has not ordained in the church of the New Testament any priests to offer daily the sacrifice of his body and blood . . . but only ministers to preach and to administer the sacraments."

Socinian Doctrine as to the Mediatorial Offices of Christ.—The *Racovian Catechism* teaches that Christ is both Prophet, Priest, and King. But it occupies one hundred and eighty pages (Section v.) in discussing his Prophetical office, and only eleven pages (Section vi.) in discussing his Priestly, and nine pages (Section vii.) his Kingly office. His death and the manner in which it contributes to our salvation is discussed (Sec. v. ch. 8.) under the head of his Prophetical office, while his Priestly work, though vaguely stated, is made to consist chiefly in his appearing in heaven as our advocate, his intercession being rendered prevalent with God by his virtues and sufferings as a martyr.

CHAPTER XXV.

THE ATONEMENT: ITS NATURE, NECESSITY, PERFECTION, AND EXTENT.

I. THE NATURE OF THE ATONEMENT.

1. Define the usage and true meaning of the different terms used in the discussion of this topic.

1st. The present word used to designate the precise nature of Christ's work of self-sacrifice on the cross is "ATONEMENT."

In the Old Testament, it is used frequently to translate the Hebrew word כָּפַר, *to cover by an expiatory sacrifice.* In the English New Testament it occurs but once, Rom. v. 11, and there translates the Greek word καταλλαγή, *reconciliation.* Its proper meaning is to make moral or legal reparation for a fault, or injury. In its Old Testament and proper theological usage, it expresses not the reconciliation effected by Christ, but that legal satisfaction which is the ground of that reconciliation.

Its sense is too limited to express adequately the full nature of Christ's work as our Substitute, because while it properly denotes the expiation of guilt effected by suffering the penalty of sin, it fails entirely to express the fact that Christ also merited for us the positive reward of eternal life by his active obedience.

2d. The old word used by the divines of the seventeenth century was "SATISFACTION." This accurately and adequately expresses what Christ did. As the Second Adam he satisfied all the conditions of the broken covenant of works, as left by the first Adam. (*a.*) He suffered the penalty of transgression. (*b.*) He rendered that obedience which was the condition of "life."

3d. The distinction between a PENAL AND A PECUNIARY SATISFACTION. The first concerns crime and person, the other concerns debt and things. They differ. (1.) In crime the demand terminates upon the person of the criminal; in debt upon the thing due. (2.) In crime the demand is for that kind, degree, and duration of suffering that enlightened reason discerns to be demanded by justice; in debt the demand is precisely and only for the thing due, an exact *quid pro quo.* (3.) In crime a vicarious suffering of the penalty is admissable only at the absolute discretion of the sovereign; and the consequent release of the criminal is a matter of grace; in debt the payment of the thing due, by whomsoever made, *ipso facto* liberates, and its acceptance and the release of the debtor is no matter of grace. (Turretin L. xiv. Qs. 10).

4th. The significance of the term PENALTY and the distinction between CALAMITIES, CHASTISEMENTS, and PENAL EVILS. Calamities are sufferings considered without any reference to the purpose with which they are inflicted or permitted. Chastisements are sufferings designed for the moral improvement of the sufferer. Penal evils are sufferings inflicted with the design of satisfying the claims of justice and law. "Penalty" is that kind and degree of suffering which the supreme legislator and judge determines to be legally and justly due in the case of any specific criminal. If these sufferings are endured by a substitute, they are no less the penalty of the law if they in fact satisfy the law. The nature and degree of the sufferings may be changed justly with the change of the person suffering, but the character of the sufferings as penalty remains, or the substitution fails.

5th. The meaning of the terms SUBSTITUTION and VICARIOUS. Substitution is the gracious act of a sovereign in allowing a person not bound to discharge a service, or to suffer a punishment in the stead of a person who is bound. The discharge of that service, and the suffering of that penalty by the substitute, and therefore the services and sufferings themselves, are strictly *vicarious*, that is in the stead of (*vice*) as well as in the behalf of the person originally bound.

6th. EXPIATION AND PROPITIATION. Both these words represent the Greek word ἱλάσκεσθαι. When construed, as it constantly is in the classics, with τὸν θεόν and τοὺς θεούς it means to propitiate for sin, by sacrificial atonement. In the New Testament it is construed with τάς ἁμαρτίας (Heb. ii. 17), and signifies to expiate the guilt of sin. Expiation has respect to the bearing which satisfaction has upon sin or the sinner. Propitiation has respect to the effect of satisfaction in thus removing the judicial displeasure of God.

7th. IMPETRATION and APPLICATION. Impetration signifies the purchase, or meritorious procurement by sacrifice, of that salvation which God provides for his own people, and Application signifies its subsequent application to them in the process commencing with Justification and Regeneration, and ending in Glorification.

8th. The usage as to ATONEMENT and REDEMPTION. (1.) During the sixteenth and seventeenth centuries, the words Redemption and Atonement were used by all parties, Calvinist and Arminian, as equivalent, as in Baxter's and Dr. Isaac Barrow's treatises on "Universal Redemption" (See Dr. Cunningham's "Hist. Theo.," Vol. 2, p. 327, and Dr. H. B. Smith in Hagenbach, "Hist. Doc.," Vol. 2, pp. 356 and 357). Also "Conf. of Faith," ch. 8, § 1, and "L. Cat.," Q. 59. (2.) In modern times some Calvinistic advocates of an indefinite atonement distinguish between the terms thus. Atonement, or the sacrificial impetration of salvation, they claim to be made indefinitely for all men. Redemption, which they understand to include the intended application as well as the impetration of salvation, they hold to be confined to the elect (Dr. W. B. Weeks, in "Park's Atonement," p. 579).

(3.) In the Scriptures Atonement (כִּפֻּרִים—ἰλασμός) signifies the expiation of guilt by means of a *pœna vicaria* in order to propitiate God. But the Scriptural usage of Redemption (ἀπολύτρωσις) is less definite and more comprehensive. It signifies deliverance from loss or from ruin by the payment for us of a ransom by our substitute. Hence it may signify either (a) the act of one substitute in paying that ransom, when it is precisely equivalent to Atonement (Gal. iii. 13); or, (b) it may mean our consequent deliverance from some particular element of our lost condition, as "death," or the "devil" (Col. ii. 15; Hosea xiii. 14); or, our complete investiture with the full salvation thereby secured (Eph. i. 14; and iv. 30; Rom. viii. 23, etc.)

9th. MERITUM and SATISFACTIO. This distinction was first signalized by Thomas Aquinas (†1274), "Summa Theologiæ," Pars. iii., Q. 48, 49. Christ as the Second Adam fulfils in our behalf all the conditions of the broken Covenant of Works. "Satisfactio" expresses the quality and effect of his entire earthly work of suffering obedience even unto death regarded as a suffering of the penalty, in order to the release therefrom of his people. "Meritum" expresses the quality and effect of the same work regarded as the rendering of that obedience which was for them the condition of life. In Protestant theology this distinction is expressed by the terms active and passive obedience, or the one vicarious work of Christ, viewed (a) as a suffering of penal evils, (b) viewed as obedience to covenant requirements.

2. *State the difference between the "natural," the "federal," and the "penal" relations which men sustain to the divine law.*

1st. Every moral agent is brought at the moment of creation, in consequence of his nature, necessarily under obligation to be conformed in state and act to the divine law of absolute moral perfection, any want of conformity to which is sin. This relation is "natural," perpetual, inalienable, and incapable of being assumed by one person in place of another, or representatively sustained.

2d. It pleased God graciously to place man at his creation under a special covenant, in which, upon condition of perfect obedience under a special test, and favorable conditions, for a limited period, he promised to endow the race with "eternal life," including establishment in an indefectable, holy character, and a heavenly inheritance forever. The penalty of instant "death" being the alternative. This is the "federal" relation to law, in which originally the whole race fell, represented by Adam, and in which subsequently the elect are made to stand, represented by Christ.

3d. By the fall of Adam all men are brought into "penal" relation to the law, from which the elect are relieved, since it has been voluntarily assumed in their behalf by Christ.

3. *What is Antinomianism? And show that this abominable heresy is in no degree involved in the common doctrine of the Protestant Reformers and their followers.*

"Antinomianism," as the word imports, is the doctrine that Christ has in such a sense fulfilled all the claims of the moral law in behalf of all the elect, or of all believers, that they are released from all obligations to fulfil its precepts as a standard of character and action. This horrible doctrine, slanderously charged against Paul, is repudiated by him.—Rom. iii. 8, and vi. 1.

In their natural reaction from the Papal doctrine of work-righteousness, Luther and Melanchthon at first used some unguarded expressions which seem to suggest this heresy. But their entire theological system, the spirit of their lives, and the body of their writings, are as far as possible removed from it. When real Antinomianism was consistently taught by John Agricola (†1566), he was strenuously opposed and successfully refuted by Luther, and caused to retreat. Some hyper-Calvinists in the 17th century, in England, *e. g.*, Dr. Crisp, rector of Brinkworth (†1642), are charged with it, though they denied the inferences put by others upon their doctrine. It has often been ignorantly or maliciously charged upon Calvinism as a necessary inference by Arminians. As a tendency it naturally besets the human heart when religious enthusiasm is unqualified by Scriptural knowledge and real sanctification, and is one to which ignorant fanatics and all classes of perfectionists are liable to be betrayed.

It is evident that the doctrines of satisfaction by Christ, and of justification by the imputation of his righteousness, as held by the Lutheran and Reformed Churches, have nothing in common with Antinomianism. Because they teach—(1.) That Christ discharges for his people only the federal and penal obligations of the law, and that his obedience and suffering *in that relation* constitute his righteousness, which is imputed. (2.) That the very end of his satisfaction is to "redeem us from all iniquity and purify unto himself a peculiar people, zealous of good works."—Titus ii. 14. (3.) Believers remain under the "natural" relation to the law, which is personally untransferable, in which they will be gradually perfected by that sanctification which the righteousness of Christ impetrates for them.—See "Vindication of Luther," by Julius C. Hare.

4. *Show how the perfect satisfaction of Christ embraces both his "active" and his "passive" obedience, and the relation which each of these elements sustains to our justification.*

Christ, although a man, was a divine person. As such he voluntarily "was made under the law," and all his earthly obedience to the law under human conditions was as vicarious as his sufferings. His "active" obedience embraces his entire life and death viewed as vicarious obedience. His "passive" obedience embraces his entire life, and especially his sacrificial death, viewed as vicarious suffering.

Adam represented the race under the original gracious covenant of works. He fell, forfeiting the "eternal life" conditioned on obedience, and incurring the penalty of death conditioned upon disobedience. Christ, the second Adam, assumes the covenant in behalf of his elect just as Adam left it. He (*a*) discharges the penalty—"the soul that sinneth it shall die," and (*b*) earns the reward—"he that doeth these things shall live by them." His whole vicarious suffering obedience, or obedient suffering is one righteousness. As "passive" obedience it "satisfies" the penal demand of the law. As "active" obedience it merits for us eternal life from regeneration to glorification. The imputation of this righteousness to us is our justification.

5. *State the true doctrine of Christ's Satisfaction.*

1st. *Negatively.* (1.) The sufferings of Christ were not a substitute for the infliction of the penalty of the law upon sinners in person, but they are the penalty itself executed on their Substitute. (2.) It was not of the nature of a pecuniary payment, an exact *quid pro quo.* But it was a strict penal satisfaction, the person suffering being a substitute. (3.) It was not a mere example of a punishment. (4.) It was not a mere exhibition of love, or of heroic consecration.

2d. *Positively.* (1.) Its MOTIVE was the ineffable love of God for the elect.—John x. 15; Gal. ii. 20.

(2.) As to its NATURE. (*a.*) Being a divine Person he assumed the legal responsibilities of his people under the conditions of a human being. (*b.*) He obeyed and suffered as their Substitute. His obedience and suffering were vicarious. (*c.*) The guilt, or just legal responsibility of our sins, were imputed to him, *i. e.*, charged upon and punished in him. (*d.*) He did not suffer the same sufferings either in kind, degree, or duration, which would have been inflicted on them, but he did suffer precisely that suffering which divine justice demanded of his person standing in their stead. (*e.*) His sufferings were those of a divine Person in a human nature.

(3.) As to its EFFECTS. (*a.*) It was the effect not the cause of God's love. It satisfied his justice and rendered the exercise of his love consistent with his righteousness. (*b.*) It expiated the guilt of sin, and reconciled God to us as a righteous Ruler. (*c.*) It secured the salvation of those for whom he died, purchasing the gift of the Holy Spirit, the means of grace, and the application and consummation of salvation. (*d.*) It did not *ipso facto* liberate, as a pecuniary satisfaction, but as a vicarious penal satisfaction its benefits accrue to the persons, at the times, and under the conditions, prescribed by the covenant between the Father and the Son. Its application is a matter of right to Christ, but of grace to us. (*e.*) Being an execution in strict justice of vicarious punishment it is a most effective and real example of punishment to the moral universe. (*f.*) Being an exercise of amazing love it produces legitimately the most profound moral impression, melting the heart, subduing the rebellion, and dissipating the fears of convinced sinners.

BIBLICAL PROOF OF THE DOCTRINE.

6. *State the argument in support of this doctrine derived from the nature of divine justice.*

It is obvious that God punishes sin, either (1) because of its intrinsic ill-desert, which is opposed to the essential and immutable rectitude of his nature; or, (2) because of the injury it does his creatures, from a principle of wise benevolence prompting him to restrain it by furnishing deterring motives; or, (3) from pure sovereignty.

But we have before proven (See above, Ch. VIII., Q. 59–66)— (1.) That the moral perfection of God is essential and fundamental, and not a product of his self-determination. (2.) That his essential moral perfection includes a principle of justice which makes the punishment of sin an end in itself. (3). That virtue, and especially justice, can not be resolved into disinterested benevolence.

The essential attributes of benevolence and justice do not conflict. Justice is free but not optional. Benevolence to the undeserving is grace, which is essentially optional.

7. *State the proof derived from the immutability of the divine law, and from the absolute truth of God.*

The will of God is freely determined by his nature. His law including precept and penalty is the expression and revelation at once of his nature and his will. As far as the law represents his nature and purpose it must be immutable. As far as it is a revelation of that purpose, its immutability is pledged by his inviolable truth.

But—1st. God has declared that his law is immutable, Luke xvi. 17, *i. e.*, his revealed law in all its elements, if the ceremonial, *a fortiori* the moral law. 2d. It is declared that Christ came to fulfil and not to suspend or abate the law.—Matt. v. 17, 18; Rom. x. 4, and iii. 31. 3d. It is affirmed that God will punish sin.—Gen. ii. 17; Ezek. xviii. 4; Rom. iii. 26.

8. *Show that the Scriptures teach that Christ suffered as our Substitute in the definite sense of that term.*

A substitute is one appointed or accepted to act or to suffer in the stead of another, and his actions or sufferings are vicarious. That Christ obeyed and suffered as the substitute of his people is proved—1st. The preposition ὑπέρ with the genitive signifies "instead of" (John xi. 50; 2 Cor. v. 20; Philem. 13), and this construction is used to set forth the relation of Christ's work to us.—2 Cor. v. 14 and 21; Gal. iii. 13; 1 Pet. iii. 18. 2d. The preposition ἀντί definitely and always expresses substitution (Winer, "N. T. Gram.," Pt. 3, § 47).—Matt. ii. 22; v. 38. This is rendered more emphatic by being associated with λύτρον, ransom, redemption price. Christ came as a ransom in the stead of many.—Matt. xx. 28; Mark x. 45; 1 Tim. ii. 6. Christ is called ἀντίλυτρον, *i. e.*, substitutionary ransom. 3d. The same is proved by what the Scriptures teach as to our sins being "laid upon" Christ.—See below, Q. 9. 4th. And by what the Scriptures teach as to the nature of sacrifices, and the sacrificial character of Christ's work.—See below, Qs. 10 and 11.

9. *Do the same with regard to those passages which speak of our sins being "laid upon" Christ, and of his "bearing" sin or iniquity.*

Sin may be considered (1) in its formal nature as "transgression of law," 1 John iii. 4; or, (2) as a moral quality inherent in the agent (*macula*), Rom. vi. 11–13; or, (3) in respect to its legal obligation to punishment (*reatus*). In this last sense alone is it ever said that the sin of one is laid upon or borne by another.

1st. To impute sin is simply to charge it to one's account as the ground of punishment. (1.) The Hebrew word חָשַׁב means to estimate, count, credit, impute as belonging to.—Gen. xxxi. 15; Lev. vii. 18; Num. xviii. 27; Ps. cvi. 31. (2.) The same is true with regard to the Greek word λογίζομαι.—Is. liii. 12; Rom. ii. 26; iv. 3–9; 2 Cor. v. 19. (3) The Scriptures assert that our sins are imputed to Christ.—Mark xv. 28; Is. liii. 6 and 12; 2 Cor. v. 21; Gal. iii. 13.

2d. (1.) The Hebrew word סָבַל has the precise sense of *bearing*, not bearing *away*, or *removing*, but in the sense of *carrying*. Lam. v. 7. This is applied to Christ's *bearing* our sins.—Is. liii. 11. (2.) Also נָשָׂא has the sense, when construed with "sin," of bearing sin in the sense of being "penally responsible" for it.—Num. xxx. 15; Lev. v. 17, 18; xvi. 22. (3.) The Septuagint translates these words sometimes by ἄιρω, to *bear*, and sometimes by φέρω and ἀναφέρω, which always means in this connection to *bear on one's self* in order to *bear away*.—Robinson, "Lex." Compare Matt. viii. 17 with Is. liii. 4.

10. *Show that the Jewish Sacrifices were vicarious sufferers of the penalties to which the offerers were exposed, and that they were in the strict sense typical of the Sacrifice of Christ.*

It is admitted by all that sacrifices prevailed among all heathen nations from the earliest times, and that they were designed to propitiate offended justice.

I. That victims of the Jewish bloody sacrifices vicariously suffered the penalty due the sins of the offenders is proved—
1st. From their *occasion.*—Lev. iv. 1—vi. 13. This was some sin, including moral as well as ceremonial transgressions.

2d. From the *qualifications of the victims.* They must be the highest class of clean animals intimately associated with man, *e. g.*, sheep, bullocks, goats, pigeons, the individuals selected to be the most perfect of their kind, as to age, sex, and physical condition.—Lev. xxii. 20–27; Ex. xxii. 30, and xxix. 1.

3d. From the *ritual of the sacrifice* itself. This included—
(1.) *The laying on of hands*, with confession of sins.—Lev. i. 4; iii. 2; iv. 4; xvi. 21; 2 Chron. xxix. 23. This act always in Scripture expresses transfer from the person imposing to the person or thing upon whom the hands are imposed; *e. g.*, of

official authority, Deut. xxxiv. 9; Acts vi. 6; or of healing virtue, Matt. ix. 18; Acts ix. 12, 17; or of sin, Lev. xvi. 7-22.
Rabbi Aaron Ben. Chajim says, "Where there is no confession
of sins there is no imposition of hands."—Outram, "De Sacrificiis," D. 1., C. xv., §§ 8, 10, 11. Hence the victim, although
perfect in itself, was always called חַטָּאת *sin*, Lev. iv. 3, and
אָשָׁם *guilt*, Lev. v. 6. (2.) The slaying of the victim. It was
offered by the sinner, and "accepted for him to make atonement for him," Lev. iv., and then executed, "for it is the blood
that maketh an atonement for the soul."—Lev. xvii. 11. (3.)
The sprinkling of blood, in the case of ordinary sacrifices on the
horns of the altar, but on the Day of Atonement the blood of
the victim offered for the whole people was carried within the
veil and sprinkled on the mercy-seat.—Lev. iv. 5, etc. This
signified its application to the *covering of sin*, and its acceptance by God.

4th. From their *effect* which was always *forgiveness*. "And
it shall be forgiven him" was the constant promise.—Lev. iv.
20-31; vi. 30, etc. It is expressed everywhere by the Hebrew
word כָּפַר, to *cover* sin, and by the Greek word ἱλάσκεσθαι, to expiate or propitiate.—See Lev. iv. and v. chs.; Heb. ii. 17. The
"mercy-seat" was called the כַּפֹּרֶת, ἱλάστηριον, *propitiatorium, or
seat of expiation.*

5th. This is the interpretation of these rites given by all
learned Jews of subsequent ages.—See Outram, "De. Sac.," D. 1.,
Chs. xx–xxii.

II. That they were in the strict sense typical of the sacrifice
of Christ is proved—

1st. They are expressly called "shadows" of which Christ
is the "body" and "patterns."—Heb. ix. 13-24; x. 1, 13; xi. 12.

2d. Christ affirms that the *law* as well as the prophets spoke
of him and his work.—John i. 45; v. 39; Luke xxiv. 27.

3d. He is declared to be "our Passover sacrificed for us."
1 Cor. v. 7 and Luke xxiv. 44. Compare Exodus xii. 46 and
Num. ix. 12.

4th. He is declared to be "sacrificed" for his people, by his
"blood" being made a *sin-offering*, etc.—John i. 29; Heb. ix. 26,
28; x. 12, 14; 1 Pet. i. 19; Eph. v. 2; 2 Cor. v. 21.

5th. He is everywhere declared to accomplish for the man
who comes to God through him precisely what the ancient
sacrifices did on a lower sphere.—Gal. iii. 13; Matt. xx. 28;
1 John ii. 2, and iv. 10; Rom. iii. 24, 25, and v. 9, 10; Eph. i. 7,
and ii. 13; Col. i. 14–20.

11. *Exhibit the argument derived from the fact that Christ made
satisfaction for his people as their High Priest.*

I. The priest was—1st. A man taken from among men to represent them in things pertaining to God.—Heb. v. 1. This was especially true of the high priest. "He represented the whole people, all Israel were reckoned as being in him." Vitringa, "Obs. Sac.," p. 292; Ex. xxviii. 9–29. If he sinned it was regarded as the sin of the whole people.—Lev. iv. 3. He wore the names of all the tribes on his breastplate. He placed his hands upon the scape-goat and confessed the sin of the whole people.—Lev. xvi. 15–21.

2d. He had a right to "bring near" to God, and all the people had access to God only through the priest, especially the High Priest.—Num. xvi. 5.

3d. This the priest effected by propitiary sacrifices and intercession.—See above, Ques. 10. Heb. v. 1–3; Num. vi. 22–27.

II. Christ is declared to save his people in the character of a High Priest. 1st. He is expressly asserted both in the Old Testament and in the New to be a Priest.—Ps. cx. 4; Zech. vi. 13; Heb. v. 6.

2d. He possessed all the qualifications for the office. (1.) He was chosen from among men to represent them.— Compare Heb. v. 1, 2 with Heb. ii. 14–18 and iv. 15. (2.) He was chosen of God.— Heb. v. 4–6. (3.) He was holy.—Heb. vii. 26. (4.) He possessed right of access to God.—Heb. i. 3; ix. 11–14.

3d. He discharged all the functions of a priest.— Daniel ix. 24–26; Eph. v. 2; Heb. ix. 26; x. 12; 1 John ii. 1.

4th. The instant Christ's work was accomplished the veil of the temple was rent in twain, and the whole typical sacrificial system was discharged as *functus officio*.—Matt. xxvii. 50, 51.

12. *Prove the truth of the doctrine as to the nature of the satisfaction of Christ above stated from the effects which are attributed to it in Scripture.*

1st. As these effects respect God they are declared to be *propitiation* and *reconciliation*. (1.) ἱλάσκεσθαι signifies to propitiate an offended Deity by means of expiatory sacrifice.—Heb. ii. 17; 1 John ii. 2, and iv. 10; Rom. iii. 25. (2.) כָּפַר in respect to sin a covering, and in respect to God propitiation. It is properly translated in our version to *make atonement*, to *appease*, to *pacify*, to *reconcile*, to *purge*, to *purge away*, Ezek. xvi. 63; Gen. xxxii. 20, 21; Ps. lxv. 3, 4; lxxviii. 38; 1 Sam. iii. 14; Num. xxxv. 33; to *ransom*, Ps. xlix. 7; to make *satisfaction*, Num. xxxv. 31, 32. (3.) Καταλλάσσειν, to reconcile—by the death of Christ, not imputing transgressions, justifying by blood, etc., Rom. v. 9, 10; 2 Cor. v. 18–20.

2d. As these effects respect sin they are declared to be *expiation*.—Heb. ii. 17; 1 John ii. 2, and iv. 10; Lev. xvi. 6–16.

3d. As they respect the sinner himself they are declared to be *redemption*, that is, *deliverance* by *ransom.*—1 Cor. vii. 23; Rev. v. 9; Gal. iii. 13; 1 Pet. i. 18, 19; 1 Tim. ii. 6; Is. li. 11, and lxii. 12.

Christ's work is set forth in the same sentences as (*a*) an expiatory offering, (*b*) a ransom price, (*c*) a satisfaction to the law. Thus we are *redeemed with the precious blood of Christ as of a lamb without blemish* and without spot." Christ "*gave his life a ransom* for many." He "*redeemed us from the curse of the law being made a curse for us.*" God "*hath made him, who knew no sin, to be a sin-offering for us that we might be made the righteousness of God in him.*" Thus Christ is not said to be a sacrifice *and* a ransom *and* a bearer of the curse of the law, but that he is that particular species of sacrifice which is a ransom—that his redemption is of that nature which is effected by his bearing the curse of the law in our stead, and that he redeems us by offering himself as a bleeding sacrifice to God.

13. *In what sense and on what grounds was the satisfaction rendered by Christ necessary? and how does the true answer to this question confirm the orthodox doctrine as to its nature?*

Since the salvation of men is a matter of sovereign grace, there could have been no necessity on the part of God for the provision of means to secure it, but on *condition* of God's determining to save sinners, *then* in what sense was the satisfaction rendered by Christ *necessary?*

1st. The advocates of the Socinian or Moral Influence Theory say that it was necessary only contingently and relatively, as the best means conceivable of proving the love of God and of subduing the opposition of sinners.

2d. The advocates of the Governmental Atonement Theory hold that it was only relatively necessary as the best sin deterring example of God's determination to punish sin.

3d. Some Supralapsarians, as Dr. Twisse, prolocutor of the Westminster Assembly, in order to exalt the sovereignty of God, held that it was only *hypothetically necessary, i. e.*, because God had sovereignly determined to forgive sin on no other condition.

4th. The true view is that it was *absolutely necessary* as the *only* means possible of satisfying the justice of God in view of the pardon of sin. The grounds of an absolute necessity on the part of God, can, of course, only be found in the immutable righteousness of his nature, lying behind and determining his will.

That it is *absolutely* necessary is proved—(1.) If salvation could have been secured otherwise Christ would be dead in vain.—Gal. ii. 21; iii. 21. (2.) God has declared that his gift of Christ is the amazing measure of his love for his people. If so, of course, he could have had no alternative, otherwise his love would not be the cause of the sacrifice.—Rom. v. 8; John iii. 16; iv. 9. (3.) Paul says it was necessary as a vindication of God's righteousness in view of the forgiveness of sins that were past.—Rom. iii. 25, 26.

It is plain that if the necessity for the satisfaction was absolute, it must have had its ground in the *nature* of God. If so, it must have been in its essence a satisfaction of the justice or essential righteousness of that nature. But a *satisfaction* of outraged justice is penal suffering.

14. *Prove that Christ's satisfaction includes his "active" as well as his "passive" obedience.*

See above, Ques. 1, § 8. Christ as the second Adam takes up the covenant obligations of his people as these were left by the fall of the first Adam. The sanctions of that covenant were—(1.) "The man that doeth these things shall live by them."—Lev. xviii. 5, comp., and Rom. x. 5, and Gal. iii. 12, and Matt. xix. 17. (2.) The penalty of death. If Christ should only suffer the penalty of death, and not render the federal obedience required of Adam, it would necessarily follow, either (1) God would alter the conditions of law and give "eternal life" in the absence of the condition demanded; or, (2) we must continue forever destitute of it; or, (3) we must start where Adam did before his apostasy, and work out the conditions of the covenant of works in our own persons. This last would have been impossible, and therefore Christ by his obedience fulfilled them for us.

This is proven—1st. The Scriptures explicitly declare that he not only suffered the penalty but also meritoriously secured for us "eternal life, the "adoption of sons," and an "eternal inheritance."—Gal. iii. 13, 14, and iv. 4, 5; Eph. i. 3–13, and v. 25–27; Rom. viii. 15–17.

2d. It is expressly said that he saves us by his obedience as well as by his suffering.—Rom. v. 18, 19.

15. *What is the Church doctrine as to the Perfection of Christ's Satisfaction?*

I. As to its *intrinsic justice-satisfying value* it has been held— 1st. By Duns Scotus (†1308), who referred the necessity of the Atonement to the will and not to the nature, that "every created oblation avails for just as much as God pleases to accept it." He graciously pleases to accept the sufferings of the human nature of Christ as sufficient, on the principle of *accepti latio,* " the optional taking of something for nothing, or of a part for the whole."

2d. Grotius (†1645) in his great work, *"De Satisfactione,"* etc., held that as the law was a product of the divine will, God had the inalienable prerogative of relaxing it (*relaxatio*), and that he did graciously relax it in accepting in the sufferings of Christ something different and less than the demands of the law, an *aliud pro quo,* not a *quid pro quo.*

3d. Limborch and Curcellæus (†1712 and †1659)—"Apol. Theo.," iii. 21, 6, and "Institutio Rel. Christ," vol. v., chap. xix., § 5—held that Christ did *not* suffer the penalty of the law, but saves us as a *sacrifice,* which was not a payment of a debt, but a condition graciously *estimated* as sufficient by God, upon which he *graciously* remitted the penalty.

4th. The Catholic, Lutheran, and Reformed Churches have always held that the satisfaction of Christ was that of a divine Person, and hence (1) was *superogatory,* not due from himself, and free to be credited to others, (2) was of infinite value. From the time of Thomas Aquinas the Catholic Church has held that it is of *superabundant* value. Hence they satisfy the claims of the law in strict rigor of justice.

II. As to its *intention and effect*—1st. The Reformed Churches all agree in opposition to the Romanists, Arminians, and advocates of an indefinite atonement, that the satisfaction of Christ is perfect in the sense of not only making the salvation of those for whom it was offered possible, but of meritoriously securing its own application to them and their certain and complete salvation.

2d. The Romanists hold that through the instrumentality of baptism the merits of Christ (1) cancel the guilt of all sins original and actual preceding baptism, and (2) transmute the penalty of all post-baptismal sins from eternal death to temporal pains. Nevertheless persons guilty of post-baptismal sins must expiate them by penances or works of charity in this world, or in the next by the pains of purgatory.—"Counc. Trident," Sess. 14, ch. viii., and Sess. 6, can. 29 and 30.

3. Arminians hold that the satisfaction of Christ makes the salvation of all men possible, and secures for them sufficient grace, but that its full effect is suspended on the condition of their free choice.

The truth of the Reformed doctrine is proved (1) from the fact that the Scriptures refer the removal of condemnation solely to the death of Christ, and represent all sufferings of believers as *disciplinary.*—Rom. viii. 1–34 and Heb. xii. 5–11. (2.) They declare that the blood of Christ "cleanses from *all* sin," and that we are "complete in him" who "by one sacrifice" perfects us.—Col. ii. 10; Heb. x. 12–14; 1 John. i. 7. (3.) Salvation is *conditioned* only upon trust in Christ's work, and this very trust (faith) is itself *given* to us as a result of Christ's merits.—Eph. ii. 7–10. (4.) We have above proved (Ques. 14) that the satisfaction of Christ meritoriously secures actual and complete salvation for its beneficiaries, and not merely the possibility of salvation upon conditions. See also below, Ques. 21.

16. *State and answer the objections which have been urged against the truth of the orthodox doctrine.*

1st. It is objected by Socinians and others that while it is an imperative duty and Christian virtue in man to forgive offences freely, that our doctrine ascribes the vice of vindictiveness to God.

We ANSWER.—(1.) That *we* forgive *injuries* and have nothing to do with the punishment of *sins*, while God punishes sin, and is incapable of suffering injury. (2.) We have proved above, Ch. VIII., Q. 53–58, that all virtue can not be resolved into benevolence, and that justice is an essential attribute of God, and that sin is intrinsic ill-desert.

2d. Socinus and others maintained that if sin is punished it can not be forgiven, and that if it is forgiven it can not be punished, and hence our doctrine excludes the exercise of free grace on the part of God in man's salvation.

We ANSWER.—(1.) Free grace is shown in the sovereign admission and acceptance by God of Christ's substitution. (2.) In the sovereign imputation of his merits to the individual sinner. (3.) That the infinite freeness of the love of God and the self-sacrificing grace of Christ is a thousand times more conspicuous in view of the facts that men were righteously condemned, and that justice inexorably demanded satisfaction in the self-humiliation of our Substitute, than it could have been in any merely sovereign relaxation of law, or by any simple forgiveness upon repentance.

3d. That Christ did not suffer the penalty of the law, because that included essentially (a) remorse, (b) eternal death.

We ANSWER that the penalty of the law is essentially simple divine displeasure involving the withdrawal of the life-giving communion of the Holy Ghost. This in the case of every creature (a) leads to spiritual death, (b) hence is naturally everlasting. Christ suffered this displeasure and desertion, Matt. xxvii. 46, but being a divine person spiritual death was impossible. He suffered precisely that kind and degree and duration of pain which divine wisdom, interpreting divine justice, required in a divine person suffering vicariously the penalty of human sin, for the same reason the temporal suffering of one divine Person, is a full legal equivalent for the ill-desert of all mankind.

4th. The objection urged by Piscator (Prof. at Herborn 1584–1625) and others against the recognition of the active obedience of Christ as an element of his satisfaction. (1.) That the law made obedience and penal suffering alternatives. If the precept is obeyed the penalty should not be inflicted. (2.) That Christ, as a man, needed his active righteousness for himself, as the essential qualification of his personal character.

We ANSWER.—(1.) As shown above, Ques. 2 and 14. Christ stood as our Representative in our *federal* and not in our *natural* relation to law. His active and his passive obedience have different purposes, the former merits the positive rewards conditioned on obedience, the latter merits the negative blessing of remission of penalty. (2.) Christ, although a man, was a divine person, and therefore never personally subject to the Adamic covenant of works. He was essentially righteous, but he was *made under the law* only as our representative, and his obedience under the *voluntarily assumed conditions of his earthly life* was purely vicarious.

5th. It is objected by Arminians and others that the doctrine that Christ satisfies in our behalf the preceptive demands of the law by his active obedience, as well as the penal demands by his passive obedience, leads to Antinomianism.

This is ANSWERED above, under Ques. 3.

6th. It is objected by Socinus (1539–1604) and by all the adversaries of the orthodox doctrine, that the demands of justice for penal satisfaction are essentially personal. The demand of outraged justice is specifically for the punishment of the person sinning. How then can the demands of the divine *nature* be satisfied by pains inflicted upon a person arbitrarily substituted in the place of the criminal by the divine *will?* How can the sufferings of an innocent man take the place in the eye of *justice* of those of the guilty man.

ANSWER.—The substitution of Christ in the stead of elect sinners was not arbitrary. He made satisfaction for them as the truly responsible Head of a community, constituting one moral person or corporate body. This responsible union with his people was constituted (*a*) by his own voluntary assumption of their legal responsibilities, (*b*) by the recognition of his sponsorship by God, the source of all law in the universe, (*c*) by his assumption of our nature. This, at least, is the testimony of revelation, if it can not be explained, it can not be disproved.

THE DESIGN OF THE ATONEMENT.

17. *State first negatively, and then positively, the true doctrine as to the design of the Father and the Son in providing satisfaction.*

I. *Negatively* — 1st. There is no debate among Christians as to the *sufficiency* of that satisfaction to accomplish the salvation of all men, however vast the number. This is absolutely limitless. 2d. Nor as to its *applicability* to the case of any and every possible human sinner who will ever exist. The relations of all to the demands of the law are identical. What would save one would save another. 3d. Nor to the *bona fide* character of the offer which God has made to "whomsoever wills" in the gospel. It is applicable to every one, it will infallibly be applied to every believer. 4th. Nor as to its *actual application.* Arminians agree with Calvinists that of adults only those who believe are saved, while Calvinists agree with Arminians that all dying in infancy are redeemed and saved. 5th. Nor is there any debate as to the universal reference of *some* of the benefits purchased by Christ. Calvinists believe that the entire dispensation of forbearance under which the human family rest since the fall, including for the unjust as well as the just temporal mercies -and means of grace, is part of the purchase of Christ's blood. They admit also that Christ did in such a sense die for all men, that he thereby removed all legal obstacles from the salvation of any and every man, and that his satisfaction may be applied to one man as well as to another *if God so wills it.*

II. But *positively* the question is what was the design of the Father and Son in the vicarious death of Christ. Did they purpose to make the salvation of the elect certain, or merely to make the salvation of all men possible? Did his satisfaction have reference indifferently as much to one man as to another? Did the satisfaction purchase and secure its own application, and all the means thereof, to all for whom it was specifically rendered? Has the impetration and the application of this atonement the same range of objects? Was it, in the order of the divine purpose, a means to accomplish the purpose of election, or is the election of individuals a means to carry into effect the satisfaction of Christ otherwise inoperative?

Our Confession answers—

Ch. viii., ? 5.—"The Lord Jesus, by his perfect obedience and sacrifice of himself, . . . purchased not only reconciliation, but an everlasting inheritance in the kingdom of heaven for all those whom the Father hath given unto him."—Chapter iii., ? 6. "As God hath appointed the elect unto glory, so hath he, by the eternal and most free purpose of his will, foreordained all the means thereunto. Wherefore they that are elected, being fallen in Adam, are redeemed in Christ. . . . Neither are any other redeemed by Christ . . . . but the elect only."

Ch. viii., § 8.—"To ALL those for whom Christ hath purchased redemption, he doth certainly and effectually apply and communicate the same."—"Articles of Synod of Dort," Ch. II., §§ 1, 2, 8.

The design of Christ in dying was to effect what he actually does effect in the result. 1st. *Incidentally* to remove the legal impediments out of the way of all men, and render the salvation of every hearer of the gospel objectively possible, so that each one has a right to appropriate it at will, to impetrate temporal blessings for all, and the means of grace for all to whom they are providentially supplied. But, 2d, *Specifically* his design was to impetrate the actual salvation of his own people, in all the means, conditions, and stages of it, and render it infallibly certain. This last, from the nature of the case, must have been his real motive. After the manner of the Augustinian Schoolmen Calvin, on 1 John ii. 2, says, "Christ died sufficiently for all, but efficiently only for the elect."—So Archbishop Ussher, Numbers 22 and 23 of Letters published by his Chaplain, Richard Parr, D.D.

18. *State the Arminian doctrine on this subject.*

That the design of Christ was to render a sacrificial oblation in behalf of all men indiscriminately, by which "sufficient grace" is meritoriously secured for each, and their sins rendered remissible upon the terms of the Evangelical Covenant; *i. e.*, upon condition of faith.—Watson's "Theo. Institutes," Pt. II., Ch. xxv.

19. *What was the doctrine of the "Marrow Men" in Scotland?*

The "Marrow of Modern Divinity" was published in England, 1646, and republished in Scotland by James Hog of Carnock, 1726. The "Marrow Men" were Hog, Thomas Boston, and Ralph and Ebenezer Erskine, and their followers in the Secession Church. They were perfectly orthodox with respect to the reference of the atonement to the elect. Their peculiarity was that they emphasized the general reference of the atonement to all men. They said Christ did not die for all, but he is dead for all, *i. e.*, available. "God made a deed of gift and grant of Christ unto all men." They distinguished between his "giving love," which was universal, and his "electing love," which was special ("Marrow of Mod. Divinity"). Dr. John Brown said before the Synod of the United Secession Church, 1845, "In the sense of the Universalist, that Christ died so as to secure salvation, I hold that he died only for the elect. In the sense of the Arminian, that Christ died so as to purchase easier terms of salvation, and common grace to enable men to comply with those terms, I hold that he died for no man. In the sense of the great body of Calvinists, that Christ died to remove legal obstacles in the way of human salvation by making perfect satisfaction for sin, I hold that he died for all men " ("Hist. of Atonement Controversy in Secess. Church," by Rev. And. Robertson).

20. *State the doctrine of Amyraldus of the French School of Saumur, and of Baxter in England.*

This scheme of Hypothetical or Conditional Universalism holds that God gave his Son to die in order to provide redemption for all men indiscriminately, suspending its actual enjoyment upon their free appropriation of it. At the same time he sovereignly wills to give the effectual grace which determines that free self-appropriation only to the elect.

The ordinary Calvinistic doctrine logically makes the decree to provide redemption the means to carry into effect the decree of election. The French and Baxterian view makes the decree of election the means of carrying into effect so far forth the general purpose of redemption (See "Universal Redemption of Mankind by the Lord Jesus Christ," by Richard Baxter. Answered by John Owen in his "Death of Christ," etc.). These "Novelties" were explained away before the French Synod, 1637, and virtually condemned.

21. *Exhibit the Biblical evidence upon which the Calvinistic doctrine as to the " Design" of the Atonement rests.*

1st. It is proved by the fact that this doctrine alone is consistent with the Scriptural doctrine that God has from eternity sovereignly elected certain persons to eternal life, and to all the means thereof. It is evident that the rendering of satisfaction specially for the elect is a rational means for carrying the decree of election into execution. But, on the other hand, the election of some to faith and repentance is no rational provision for executing the purpose to redeem all men. R. Watson ("Institutes," Vol. II., p. 411) says that the view of Baxter, etc., "is the most inconsistent theory to which the attempts to modify Calvinism have given rise." It is plain that if God purposed that the elect should certainly be saved, and others left to the just consequences of their sins, Christ *could not* have designed the benefits of his death indifferently for all men.

2d. Its design is shown from the very *nature* of the atonement as above proved. (1.) Christ expiated our sins as our substitute in the strict sense. But a substitute represents definite persons, and his service, when accepted, actually discharges the obligation of those for whom it was rendered. (2.) Christ being our substitute under the "covenant of works" actually and perfectly *satisfied* all the demands of the covenant. In that case the terms of the covenant itself provide that those for whom it is satisfied must enjoy the reward. It is not the possibility of life, but life itself that is *promised.*

3d. The Scriptures declare everywhere that the design and legal effect of Christ's work is not to render salvation possible but actually to save, to reconcile God and not to render him only reconcilable.—Matt. xviii. 11; Rom. v. 10; 2 Cor. v. 21; Gal. i. 4; iii. 13; Eph. i. 7, and ii. 16.

4th. The Scriptures everywhere teach that Christ purchased faith, repentance, and the Holy Spirit's influences by his death and obedience. Hence he must have purchased them for those for whom he suffered and obeyed, and they can not, therefore, be the conditions upon which the enjoyment of the benefits of his death are suspended. "We are blessed with *all spiritual blessings* in heavenly things *in Christ.*"—Eph. i. 3, 4. The Holy Ghost is "shed on us *through Jesus Christ our Saviour.*" Titus iii. 5, 6; Gal. iii. 13, 14; Phil. i. 29; Titus ii. 14; Eph. v. 25–27; 1 Cor. i. 30.

5th. Christ died in execution of the terms of an eternal covenant between the Father and himself. This is certain— (1.) Because three intelligent eternal Persons must have always had a mutual plan comprehending all their works, prescribing their several parts therein. (2.) The Scriptures often refer to this covenant.—Ps. lxxxix. 3, 4; Is. xlii. 6, 7, and liii. 10, 12. (3.) Christ made constant reference to it while executing it. Luke xxii. 29; John vi. 38, and x. 18. (4.) Christ claims its reward.—John xvii. 4–9. (5.) And speaks of those who had been previously given him by his Father.—John x. 15–26. Then he must have died specially for those "whom the Father had given him."

6th. The motive for his self-sacrifice is always declared to be the highest form of *personal love.*—John xv. 13; Rom. v. 8, and viii. 32; Gal. ii. 20; Eph. iii. 18, 19; 1 John iii. 16; iv. 9, 10.

7th. The doctrine that Christ died specifically for the elect is everywhere stated in Scripture.—John x. 11, 15; Acts xx. 28; Rom. viii. 32–35; Eph. v. 25–27.

22. *If Christ died only for his own people, on what ground does the general offer of the gospel rest?*

"The Lord Jesus, in order to secure the salvation of his people, and with a specific view to that end, fulfilled the condition of the law or covenant under which they and all mankind were placed. These conditions were—(1) perfect obedience; (2) satisfaction to divine justice. Christ's righteousness, therefore, consists of his obedience and death. That righteous ness is precisely what the law demands of every sinner in order to justification before God. It is, therefore, in its nature adapted to all sinners who were under that law. Its nature is not altered by the fact that it was wrought out for a portion only of such sinners, or that it is secured to them by the covenant between the Father and the Son. What is necessary for the salvation of one man is necessary for the salvation of another and of all. It is also of infinite value, being the righteousness of the eternal Son of God, and therefore sufficient for all."—Hodge's " Essays," pp. 181, 182.

A *bona fide* offer of the gospel, therefore, is to be made to all men—1st. Because the satisfaction rendered to the law is sufficient for all men. 2d. Because it is exactly adapted to the redemption of all. 3d. Because God designs that whosoever exercises faith in Christ shall be saved by him. Thus the atonement makes the salvation of every man to whom it is offered objectively possible. The design of Christ's death being to secure the salvation of his own people, incidentally to the accomplishment of that end, it comprehends the offer of that salvation freely and honestly to all men on the condition of their faith. No man is lost for the want of an atonement, or because there is any other barrier in the way of his salvation than his own most free and wicked will.

23. *How can the condemnation of men for the rejection of Christ be reconciled with the doctrine that Christ died for the elect only?*

A salvation all-sufficient and exactly adapted to his necessities is honestly offered to every man to whom the gospel comes; and in every case it is his, if he believes; and in no case does any thing prevent his believing other than his own evil disposition. Evidently he is in no way concerned with the design of God in providing that salvation beyond the assurance that God intends to give it to him if he believes. If a man is responsible for a bad heart, and the exercises thereof, he must be above all worthy of condemnation for rejecting such a Saviour.

24. *On what principles are those texts to be explained which speak of Christ's bearing the sins of the* WORLD, *and of his dying for* ALL?

These are such passages as Heb. ii. 9; 1 Cor. xv. 22; 1 John ii. 2; 1 Tim. ii. 6; John i. 29; iii. 16, 17; vi. 51. These terms, "world" and "all," are unquestionably used in very various degrees of latitude in the Scriptures. In many passages that latitude is evidently limited by the context, e. g., 1 Cor. xv. 22; Rom. v. 18; viii. 32; John xii. 32; Eph. i. 10; Col. i. 20; 2 Cor.

v. 14, 15. In others the word "world" is opposed to the Jewish nation as a people of exclusive privileges.—Rom. xi. 12, 15; 1 John ii. 2. It is evident that statements as to the design of Christ's death, involving such general terms, must be defined by the more definite ones above exhibited. Sometimes this general form of statement is used to give prominence to the fact that Christ, being a single victim, by one sacrifice atoned for so many.—Compare Matt. xx. 28, with 1 Tim. ii. 6, and Heb. ix. 28. And although Christ did not die with the design of saving all, yet he did suffer the penalty of that law under which all were placed, and he does offer the righteousness thus wrought out to all.

25. *How are we to understand those passages which speak of the possibility of those perishing for whom Christ died?*

Such passages are hypothetical, and truly indicate the nature and tendency of the action against which they warn us, and are the means which God uses under the administration of his Spirit to fulfil his purposes. God always deals with men by addressing motives to their understandings and wills, thus fulfilling his own design through their agency. In the case of Paul's shipwreck, it was certain that none should perish, and yet all would perish except they abode in the ship.—Acts xxvii. 24–31. On the same principle must be explained all such passages as Heb. x. 26–30; 1 Cor. viii. 11, etc.

History of the Various Views held in the Church.

26. *State the general character of the Soteriology of the Early Fathers.*

1st. From the very first the representative Christian Fathers taught in a crude, unscientific manner that Christ suffered as a substitute for his people, to expiate sin and to propitiate God. They freely applied to Christ's work the sacrificial language of the Scriptures. Outram, Dis. 1, ch. 17.—"As it regards the work of Christ as the Redeemer of mankind, we find already in the language used by the Church Fathers on this point, in the period under consideration, all the elements that lay at the basis of the doctrine as it afterwards came to be defined by the Church."—Neander's "Ch. Hist.," Vol. I., p. 640, see testimonies below. 2d. Together with this view there was combined during the whole earlier age until the time of Anselm a view especially emphasized by Origen (185–254) and Irenæus (†200), to the effect that Christ was offered by God as a ransom for his people to Satan, who held them by the power of conquest. This view was founded on such passages as Col. ii. 15, and Heb. ii. 14.

27. *State generally the four theories under one or other of which all views ever entertained as to the nature of the reconciliation effected by Christ may be grouped.*

1st. The MYSTICAL, which, although it has assumed various forms, may be generally stated thus: The reconciliation effected by Christ was brought about by the mysterious union of· God and man accomplished by the incarnation, rather than by his sacrificial death. This view was entertained by some of the Platonizing Fathers, by the disciples of Scotus Erigena during the Middle Ages, by Osiander and Schwenkfeld at the Reformation, and by the school of Schleiermacher among modern German theologians.

2d. The *Moral Influence* THEORY first distinctively elaborated by Abelard (†1142) and held by the Socinians, and such Trinitarians as Maurice, Young, Jowett, Bushnell, etc. The points involved are—(1.) There is no such principle as vindicatory justice in God. (2.) Benevolence is the single ultimate principle determining God in his provisions for human redemption. (3.) The sole object of the life and death of Christ is to produce a moral effect upon the individual sinner, subduing his obdurate aversion to God and his sullen distrust of his willingness to forgive. Thus reconciling man to God instead of God to man. (4.) The Socinians held in addition that Christ's death was the necessary precondition of his resurrection, by which he brought immortality to light.

3d. The *Governmental Theory*, which, presupposing all the positive truth contained in the "Moral Influence Theory," maintains—(1.) That justice in God is not vindicatory, but is to be referred to a general Governmental rectitude, based upon a BENEVOLENT regard for the highest ultimate and most general well-being of the subjects of his moral government. (2.) Law is a product of the divine will and therefore relaxable. (3.) God's sovereign prerogative includes the right of pardon. (4.) But the governmental rectitude above explained, in view of the fact that indiscriminate pardon would encourage the violation of law, determines God to condition the pardon of human sinners upon an imposing *example of suffering* in a victim so related to mankind and to himself, as effectually to demonstrate his determination that sin should not be indulged with impunity. Therefore—(*a.*) Christ's sufferings were not punishment, but an example of a determination to punish hereafter. (*b.*) They were designed not to satisfy divine justice, but to impress the public mind of the moral universe with a sin-deterring motive. This theory was first elaborated by Hugo Grotius (†1645) in his great work, "*Defensio Fidei Catholicæ de Satisfactione Christi*," in which he abandoned the faith he assumed to defend. It has never been embodied in the creed of any historical church, but has been held by several schools of theologians, *e. g.*, the Supernaturalists of the last age in Germany, as Staudlin, Flatt, and Storr, and in America by Jonathan Edwards, Jr., Smalley, Maxey, Dwight, Emmons, and Park.

REMARKS.—While this theory embraces much precious truth, it fails in the essential point on which the *integrity* of the whole depends. For—(1.) Only a real *bona fide* punishment can be an example of a punishment, or a proof of God's determination to punish sin. (2.) It ignores the essential justice of God, and (3) the fact that sin is an essential evil in itself, and (4) the fact that Christ suffered as the HEAD in whom all his members were UNITED.

4th. The SATISFACTION THEORY consistently embraces the positive elements of the "Moral Influence" and "Governmental" theories above stated. It was first analyzed and set forth in a scientific form by Anselm, archbishop of Canterbury (†1093–†1109), in his epoch-making book, "*Cur Deus Homo*," and it has formed the basis of the Soteriological doctrines of all the creeds and classical theological literature of all the historical churches since his time. It has been sufficiently stated and proved in the former part of this chapter.

LITERATURE.—Hase, "*Libri Symbolici Eccle. Evangelicæ*"; Niemeyer, "*Collectio Confessionum*," etc.; Streitwolf, "*Libri Symbolici Eccle. Catholicæ*." "*De Sacrificiis, Gulielmo Outramo Auctore*"; Neander's and Shaff's "*Church Histories*"; Archb. Magee, "*The Atonement*"; Shedd's "*History of Christian Doctrine*"; Owen's "*Works*," vol. 10, "*Redemption*"; Ritschl, "*Crit. Hist. of the Christ. Doctrine of Reconciliation*"; Candlish, "*The Atonement*"; Watson's "*Institutes*."

CLASSICAL AND CONFESSIONAL AUTHORITIES.

Origen, "*Homil. ad Levit.*," 1, speaking of Christ says, "He laid his hand upon the head of the calf, *i. e.*, he laid the sins of mankind upon his own head, for he is the head of the body, the Church."

Athanasius (†373), *contra Arianos*, 1, 45–†60.—"The death of the incarnate Logos is a ransom for the sins of men and a death of death." . . . "Laden with guilt the world was condemned by law, but the Logos assumed the condemnation, and suffering in the flesh gave salvation to all."

Gregory the Great (†604), "*Moralia in Jobum*," 17, 46.—"Guilt can be extinguished only by penal offering to justice. . . Hence a sinless man must be offered. . . . Hence the Son of God must be born of a virgin, and become man for us. He assumed our nature without our corruption (*culpa*). He made himself a sacrifice for us, and set forth for sinners his own body, a victim without sin, and able both to die by virtue of its humanity, and to cleanse the guilty, upon grounds of justice."

Bernard of Clairvaux (†1153), "*Tract. contr. Err. Abœlardi,*" cap. 6, 15.—"If One has died for all, then all are dead (2 Cor. v. 14), that is, the satisfaction of one is imputed to all, as that One bore the sins of all, neither is it found that he who offended is one, and he that satisfied another, for the head and the body is one Christ. Therefore the Head made satisfaction for his members."

Wycliffe (1324–1384), "*De Incarn. et Mort. Christi.*"—"And since according to the third supposition, it is necessary that satisfaction should be made for sin, so it was necessary that that same race of man should make the satisfaction as great, as it had, in the first parent, made the offence, which no man could do, unless he were at the same time God and man."

The Valenses of Piedmont, in 1542, presented a Confession to Francis I. of France through Cardinal Sadolet. In it they say, "This Confession is that which we have received from our ancestors, even from hand to hand, according as their predecessors in all times, and in every age, have taught and delivered. . . We believe and confess that the gratuitous remission of sins proceeds from the mercy and mere goodness of our Lord Jesus Christ, who died once for our sins, the just for the unjust; who bore our sins in his own body on the cross; who is our advocate with God, himself the price of our reconciliation; who alone has made satisfaction for believers, to whom sins are not imputed as they are to the unbelieving and the reprobates."

John Wessel (1419–1489), "*De Causis Incarnationis.*"—"Truly himself God, himself priest, himself victim, he made satisfaction for himself, of himself, to himself." "*Exempla Scalœ Meditationis,*" Ex. 1, p. 544.—"Our loving Father willed thee his own loving Son to be a surety, sponsor, guaranty with respect to sufficient doing and sufficient suffering, upon just pledge, for my universal failure and miscarriage."

"Orthodox Confession of the Catholic and Apostolic Eastern Church, composed by Petrus Mogilas, Metropolitan of Kiew, 1642, and sanctioned by the Synod of Jerusalem 1672, p. 85. "The death of Christ was of a very different kind from that of all other men in these respects; *first,* because of the weight of our sins; *secondly,* because he wholly fulfilled the priesthood even to the cross; he offered himself to God and the Father for the ransoming of the human race. Therefore even to the cross he fulfilled the mediation between God and men."

Roman Doctrine.—"*Council of Trent,*" Sess. 6, chap. 7.—"Christ, who when we were enemies, on account of the great love wherewith he loved us, merited justification by his most holy passion on the wood of the cross, and made satisfaction to God the Father for us." "*Catechism of Council of Trent,*" Pt. II., ch. 5, Q. 60.—"The first and most excellent satisfaction is that by which whatever is due by us to God, on account of our sins, has been paid abundantly, although he should deal with us according to the strictest rigor of his justice. This is said to be that satisfaction, which we say has appeased God and rendered him propitious to us, and for it we are indebted to Christ the Lord alone, who having paid the price of our sins on the cross, most fully satisfied God."

Lutheran Confessions, Hase's "*Collection,*" p. 684, "*Formula Concordiœ.*"—"That righteousness which before God is of mere grace imputed to faith, or to the believer, is the obedience, suffering, and resurrection of Christ, by which he for our sakes satisfied the law, and expiated our sins. For since Christ was not only man, but God and man in one undivided person, so he was not subject to the law, nor obnoxious to suffering and death on his own account, because he was Lord of the law. On which account his obedience (not merely in respect that he obeyed the Father in his sufferings and death, but also that he for our sakes willingly made himself subject to the law and fulfilled it by his obedience) is imputed to us, so that God on account of that whole obedience (which Christ by his acting and by his suffering, in his life and in his death, for our sakes rendered to his Father who is in heaven) remits our sins, reputes us as good and just, and gives us eternal salvation."

REFORMED DOCTRINE.—"*Thirty-nine Articles,*" Arts. 11 and 31.— "The offering of Christ once made is that perfect redemption, propitiation, and satisfaction for the sins of the whole world both original and actual; and there is none other satisfaction for sin but that alone." *Homily 3d.* "*On Salvation.*"—"God sent his only Son our Saviour Christ into this world, to fulfil the law for us, and by shedding his most precious blood, to make a sacrifice and satisfaction to his Father for our sins." "Heidelberg Cat.," Ques. 12–18 and 40. "West Conf. Faith," ch. viii., § 5, and ch. xi., § 3. "Form. Cons. Helvetica," cans. 13–15. Cocceius ("De Fæd. et Testam. Dei," cap. 5, 92). "Thus that greatest mystery (the eternal covenant between the Father and the Son) is revealed in what manner we are justified and saved by God, in what manner God may both be the one who judges, and who acts as surety, and who thus is himself judged, who absolves and who intercedes, who sends and is sent. That is in what manner God himself satisfied himself by his own blood."

REMONSTRANT DOCTRINE.—*Limborch,* "*Apol. Thes.,*" 3, 22, 5.—"It may here be questioned in what way the sacrifice of one man is able to suffice and in fact did suffice for expiating the innumerable sins of so many myriads of men. *Answer.* It sufficed on two accounts. *First* with respect to the divine will, which required nothing more for the liberation of the human race, but was satisfied with this one sacrifice alone. *Secondly* with respect to the dignity of the person, Jesus Christ . . . 21, 6. The satisfaction of Christ is so-called inasmuch as it releases from all the penalties due our sins, and by bearing and exhausting them, satisfies divine justice. But this sentiment has no foundation in Scripture. The death of Christ is called a sacrifice for sin; but sacrifices are not payments of debts, nor are they full satisfactions for sins; but a gratuitous remission is granted when they are offered."

Remonstrantia, etc., five articles prepared by the Dutch advocates of universal redemption (1610), Art 2.—"Therefore Jesus Christ, the Saviour of the world, died for all and every man, so that he impetrated for all through his death reconciliation and remission of sins, nevertheless on this condition, that no one should have actual fruition of that reconciliation, unless he is a believer, and that also according to the gospel."

SOCINIAN DOCTRINE.—"*Rac. Cat.,*" Sec. 5, ch. viii.—"What was the purpose of the divine will that Christ should suffer for our sins? *Ans. First,* that a most certain right to, and consequently a sure hope of, the remission of their sins, and of eternal life, might by this means be creted for all sinners (Rom. viii. 32 and v. 8–10). *Secondly,* that all sinners might be incited and drawn to Christ, seeking salvation in and by him alone who died for them. *Thirdly,* that God might in this manner testify his boundless love to the human race, and might wholly reconcile them to himself (John iii. 16)."

CHAPTER XXVI.

THE INTERCESSION OF CHRIST.

1. *In what sense is Christ to continue a priest forever?*

This is asserted by Paul, Heb. vii. 3, 24, to contrast the priesthood of Christ with that of Aaron, which consisted of a succession of mortal men in their generations. His priesthood is perpetual, because, 1st, by one sacrifice for sin he hath forever perfected them that are sanctified; 2d, he ever liveth to make intercession for us; 3d, his person and work as mediator will continue for all eternity the ground of our acceptance, and the medium of our communion with the Father.

2. *Did he intercede for his people on earth?*

He did exercise this function of his priesthood on earth, Luke xxiii. 34; John xvii. 20; Heb. v. 7; the principal scene of its exercise, however, is his estate of exaltation in heaven.

3. *What is the view which the Scriptures present of the intercession of Christ?*

1st. He appears in the presence of God for us, as the priestly advocate of his people, and presents his sacrifice.—Heb. ix. 12, 24; Rev. v. 6.

2d. He acts as our advocate with the Father, and on the basis of his own perfect work under the terms of the covenant of grace, claims as his own right, though as infinitely free grace to usward, the fulfillment of all the promises of his covenant. 1 John ii. 1; John xvii. 24; xiv. 16; Acts ii. 33; Heb. vii. 25.

3d. Because of his community of nature with his people, and his personal experience of the same sorrows and temptations which now afflict them, he sympathizes with them, and watches and succors them in all their varying circumstances, and adapts his ceaseless intercessions to the entire current of their experiences.—Heb. ii. 17, 18; iv. 15, 16; Matt. xxviii. 20; xviii. 20.

4th. He presents, and through his merits gains acceptance for the persons and services of his people.—1 Pet. ii. 5; Eph. i. 6; Rev. viii. 3, 4; Heb. iv. 14–16.

4. *For whom does he intercede?*

Not for the world, but for his own people of every fold, and of all times.—John x. 16; xvii. 9, 20.

5. *Show that his intercession is an essential part of his priestly work.*

It is absolutely essential, Heb. vii. 25, because it is necessary for him as mediator not merely to open up a way of possible salvation, but actually to accomplish the salvation of each of those given to him by the Father, and to furnish each with an "*introduction*" (προσαγωγή) to the Father.—John xvii. 12; Eph. ii. 18; iii. 12. The communion of his people with the Father will ever be sustained through him as mediatorial priest.—Ps. cx. 4; Rev. vii. 17.

6. *What relation does the work of the Holy Ghost sustain to the intercession of Christ?*

Christ is a royal priest.—Zech. vi. 13. From the same throne, as king, he dispenses his Spirit to all the objects of his care, while as priest he intercedes for them. The Spirit acts for him, taking only of his things. They both act with one consent, Christ as principal, the Spirit as his agent. Christ intercedes for us, without us, as our advocate in heaven, according to the provisions of the eternal covenant. The Holy Ghost works upon our minds and hearts, enlightening and quickening, and thus determining our desires "according to the will of God," as our advocate within us. The work of the one is complementary to that of the other, and together they form a complete whole.—Rom. viii. 26, 27; John xiv. 26.

CHAPTER XXVII.

MEDIATORIAL KINGSHIP OF CHRIST.

1. How does the sovereignty of Christ as Mediator differ from his sovereignty as God?

His sovereignty as God is essential to his nature, underived, absolute, eternal, and unchangeable.

His sovereignty as mediatorial King is derived, given to him by his Father as the reward of his obedience and suffering; it is special, having respect to the salvation of his own people and the administration of the provisions of the covenant of grace; and it attaches, not to his divine nature as such, but to his person as God-man, occupying the office of Mediator.

His kingdom is a very prominent subject in Scripture.—Dan. ii. 44; Matt. xiii. 1–58, and xx. 20–29; Luke xiii. 23–30, and xvii. 20 and 21; Rom. xiv. 17; 1 Pet. iii. 22; Eph. i. 10, 21, and 22.

2. What is the extent of Christ's mediatorial kingdom, and what are the different aspects which it presents?

Christ's mediatorial authority embraces the universe.—Matt. xxviii. 18; Phil. ii. 9–11; Eph. i. 17–23. It presents two great aspects. 1st. In its general administration as embracing the universe as a whole. 2d. In its special administration as embracing the church.

It has been distinguished as—(1.) His kingdom of *power*, which embraces the entire universe in his providential and judicial administration. The end of this is the subjection of his enemies (Heb. x. 12, 13; 1 Cor. xv. 25), the vindication of divine righteousness (John v. 22–27; ix. 39), and the perfecting of his church. (2.) His kingdom of *grace* which is spiritual alike as to its subjects, laws, modes of administration, and instrumentalities. (3.) His kingdom of *glory* is the consummation of his providential and gracious administration, and will continue forever.

3. *What are the objects of his mediatorial authority over the universe, and how is it administered?*

Its object is to accomplish the salvation of his church in the execution of all the provisions of the covenant of grace, which devolves upon him as Mediator. — Eph. i. 23. As the universe constitutes one physical and moral system, it was necessary that his headship as Mediator should extend to the whole, in order to cause all things to work together for good to his people, Rom. viii. 28; to establish a kingdom for them, Luke xxii. 29; John xiv. 2; to reduce to subjection all his enemies, 1 Cor. xv. 25; Heb. x. 13; and in order that all should worship him.—Heb. i. 6; Rev. v. 9–13. His general mediatorial government of the universe is administered, 1st, providentially; 2d, judicially.—John v. 22, 27; ix. 39; 2 Cor. v. 10.

Eph. i. 10, and Col. i. 20, seem to indicate that Christ's mediatorial headship sustains very comprehensive relations to the moral universe in general, which otherwise are entirely unrevealed.

4. *When did Christ formally assume his mediatorial kingdom?*

1st. The advocates of the premillennial advent, and personal reign of Christ on earth, admit that Christ now reigns at his Father's right hand, on his Father's throne, and in his Father's right, but maintain that he will not enter properly upon his own kingdom and sit upon his own throne as Mediator, until his second advent, when he will assume the literal throne of David, and constitute the kingdom from Jerusalem its capital.

2d. The truth as held by all branches of the historical church is, that while Christ has been virtually mediatorial King as well as Prophet and Priest from the fall of Adam, yet his public and formal assumption of his throne and inauguration of his spiritual kingdom dates from his ascension and session at the right hand of his Father. This is proved because the Old Testament predictions of his kingdom (Ps. ii. 6; Jer. xxiii. 5; Is. ix. 6; Dan. ii. 44) are in the New Testament applied to the *first* advent. John the Baptist declared that the kingdom of heaven was at hand. Christ declared "the kingdom of God is come unto you," and likens it to the field with wheat and tares growing together, etc.—Matt. iv. 23; Acts ii. 29–36.

5. *What are the different titles applied in Scripture to this kingdom, and what are the senses in which these titles of the kingdom are used?*

It is called—(1.) The "kingdom of God," Luke iv. 43, be-

cause it is pre-eminently of divine origin, and the authority of
God is with peculiar directness and fulness exercised in its
administration.   (2.) "The kingdom of Christ" and of "God's
dear Son," Matt. xvi. 28; Col. i. 13, because he is in person the
immediate sovereign.   (3.) "The kingdom of heaven," Matt.
xi. 12, because its origin and characteristics are from heaven,
and its consummation is to be in heaven.

These phrases are sometimes used to express—(1.) Christ's
mediatorial authority, or its administration, and the power and
and glory which belong to it, as when we ascribe to him the
"kingdom and the power and the glory," or affirm that of
"his kingdom there shall be no end."   (2.) The blessings and
advantages of all kinds, inward and outward, which are characteristic of this administration, as when we say the "kingdom is righteousness and peace and joy in the Holy Ghost."
Thus Napoleon III. said, "The Empire is peace."   (3.) The
subjects of the kingdom collectively, as when we are said to
"enter the kingdom," and speak of "the keys of the kingdom,"
which admit to or exclude from this community.   In this latter
sense the phrase "kingdom of God," or "of heaven," is synonymous with the word "Church."

The word βασιλεία, in this connection, occurs one hundred
and thirty-seven times in the entire New Testament, and one
hundred and ten times in the gospels, fifty-three times in Matthew alone, the gospel most nearly related to the Old Testament, and only twenty times in the epistles, while ἐκκλησία,
when referring to the Church of Christ, occurs but once in the
gospels and eighty-eight in the epistles and revelations.

6. *What is the nature of Christ's kingly administration of the
affairs of his own people, i. e., of his kingdom as distinct from the
universe?*

1st. It is providential. He administers his providential government over the universe with the design of accomplishing
thereby the support, defence, enrichment, and glorification of
his people.   2d. It is accomplished by the dispensation of his
Spirit effectually calling, sanctifying, comforting, preserving,
raising, and glorifying his people.—John xv. 26; Acts ii. 33–36.
3d. It is accomplished by his prescribing the form, and order,
and functions of his church, the officers who are to act as the
organs of those functions, and the laws which they are to administer.—Matt. xxviii. 18, 19, 20; Eph. iv. 8, 11.   4th. By designating the persons who are successively to assume those
offices, by means of a spiritual call, expressed in the witness
of the Spirit, the leadings of providence, and the call of the

brethren.—Acts i. 23, 24; vi. 5; xiii. 2, 3; xx. 28; 1 Tim. i. 12; iv. 14.

Under this administration this kingdom presents two aspects, 1st, as militant, Eph. vi. 11–16; 2d, as glorified.—Rev. iii. 21. And accordingly Christ presents himself as fulfilling, in his administration of the affairs of his kingdom, the functions of a great Captain, Rev. xix. 11, 16, and of a sovereign Prince reigning from a throne.—Rev. xxi. 5, 22, 23.

The throne upon which he sits and from which he reigns is presented in three different aspects, corresponding to the different relations he sustains to his people and the world; as a throne of grace, Heb. iv. 16; a throne of judgment, Rev. xx. 11–15; and a throne of glory. — Compare Rev. iv. 2–5 with Rev. v. 6.

7. *In what sense is Christ's kingdom spiritual?*

1st. The King is a spiritual and not an earthly sovereign. Matt. xx. 28; John xviii. 36. 2d. His throne is at the right hand of God.—Acts ii. 33. 3d. His sceptre is spiritual.—Is. liii. 1; Ps. cx. 2. 4th. The citizens of his kingdom are spiritual men.—Phil. iii. 20; Eph. ii. 19. 5th. The mode in which he administers his government is spiritual.—Zech. iv. 6, 7. 6th. His laws are spiritual.—John iv. 24. 7th. The blessings and the penalties of his kingdom are spiritual.—1 Cor. v. 4–11; 2 Cor. x. 4; Eph. i. 3–8; 2 Tim. iv. 2; Tit. ii. 15.

8. *What is the extent of the powers which Christ has vested in his visible church?*

In respect to the civil magistrate the church is absolutely independent. In subjection to the supreme authority of Christ her head the powers of the church are solely, 1st, declarative, *i. e.*, to expound the Scriptures, which are the perfect rule of faith and practice, and thus to witness to and promulgate the truth in creeds and confessions, by the pulpit and the press. And, 2d, ministerial, *i. e.*, to organize herself according to the pattern furnished in the Word, and then to administer, through the proper officers, the sacraments, and those laws and that discipline prescribed by the Master, and to make provision for the proclamation of the gospel of the kingdom to every creature.—Is. viii. 20; Deut. iv. 2; Matt. xxviii. 18–20; Heb. xiii. 17; 1 Pet. ii. 4.

9. *What are the conditions of admission into Christ's kingdom?*

Simply practical recognition of the authority of the sovereign. As the sovereign and the entire method of his administration are spiritual, it is plain that his authority must be

understood and embraced practically, according to its spiritual
nature. This is that spiritual faith which involves spiritual
illumination.—John iii. 3, 5; i. 12; 1 Cor. xii. 3.

10. *What is the Romish doctrine of the relation of the church to
the state?*

According to the strictly logical Romish doctrine, the state
is only one phase of the church. The whole nation being in
all its members a portion of the church universal, the civil organization is comprehended within the church for special subordinate ends, and is responsible to the church for the exercise
of all the authority delegated to it.

*First Dogmatic Constitution on the Church, Council of the Vat-
ican,* 1870, Ch. iv., declares that the judgments of the Pope,
pronounced *ex cathedra,* as pastor and doctor of all Christians,
upon any question *of faith or morals* is infallible and irreformable. This infallibility is personal, independent, separate, and
absolute. This comprehends all matter of fact and doctrine
revealed, and all such further matters of fact or truth unrevealed yet involved in the defence of that which is revealed.
In the third chapter the supreme authority of the infallible
Pope is extended "to the supreme and full power of jurisdiction over the universal church, *not only* in things which belong
to faith and morals, *but also* in those which relate to the discipline and government thereof."

In the "Papal Syllabus of Errors," 1864, sent to all the
bishops by the authority of the Pope, the right of religious
liberty is condemned, the right to enforce the decrees of the
church by force is asserted, and the marriage of those who refuse to accept the Romish Sacrament of matrimony declared
void (see the affirmative propositions published by Von P.
Clemens Schrader, with the approbation of the Pope).

Pope Pius himself, in his reply to the Address from the
Academia of the Catholic Religion (July 21, 1873), declares
that the Pope possesses the right, which he properly uses, under favorable circumstances, "to pass judgment even in civil
affairs, on the acts of princes and of nations."

Archbishop Manning, in "Cæsarism and Ultramontanism,"
p. 35, says, "If, then, the civil power be not competent to decide the limits of the spiritual power, and if the spiritual power
can define, with a divine certainty, its own limits, it is evidently supreme. Or in other words, the spiritual power knows
with divine certainty the limits of its own jurisdiction; and it
knows therefore the limits and competence of the civil power."
"Any power which is independent, and can alone fix the limits

of its own jurisdiction, and can thereby fix the limits of all other jurisdiction, is *ipso facto* supreme."—See Hon. Wm. E. Gladstone, "The Vatican Decrees in their bearing on Civil Allegiance," and his "Answer to Reproofs and Replies."

11. *What is the Erastian doctrine as to the relation of the church to the state?*

This doctrine, named from Erastus, a physician resident in Heidelberg in the sixteenth century, is precisely contrary to that of the Romanists, *i. e.*, it regards the church as only one phase of the state. The state, being a divine institution, designed to provide for all the wants of men, spiritual as well as temporal, is consequently charged with the duty of providing for the dissemination of pure doctrine, and for the proper administration of the sacraments, and of discipline. It is the duty of the state, therefore, to support the church, to appoint its officers, to define its laws, and to superintend its administration.

12. *What is the common doctrine of the Reformed Church on this point?*

That the church and the state are both divine institutions, having different objects, and in every respect independent of each other. The members and officers of the Church are, as men, members of the state, and ought to be good citizens; and the members and officers of the state, if Christians, are members of the church, and as such subject to her laws. But neither the officers nor the laws of either have any authority within the sphere of the other.

13. *What is the idea and design of the State?*

Civil government is a divine institution, designed to protect men in the enjoyment of their civil rights. It has, therefore, derived from God authority to define those rights touching all questions of person and property, and to provide for their vindication, to regulate intercourse, and to provide all means necessary for its own preservation.

14. *What is the design of the visible Church?*

It is a divine institution designed to secure instrumentally the salvation of men. To that end it is specially designed—
1st. To bring men to a knowledge of the truth.
2d. To secure their obedience to the truth, and to exercise their graces by the public confession of Christ, the fellowship of the brethren, and the administration of the ordinances and discipline.

3d. To constitute the visible witness and prophetic type of the church invisible and spiritual.

15. *What are the duties of the officers of the State with regard to the Church?*

The state is a divine institution, and the officers thereof are God's ministers, Rom. xiii. 1–4, Christ the Mediator is, as a revealed fact, "Ruler among the Nations," King of kings, and Lord of lords, Rev. xix. 16; Matt. xxviii. 18; Phil. ii. 9–11; Eph. i. 17–23, and the Sacred Scriptures are an infallible rule of faith and practice to all men under all conditions.

It follows therefore—1st. That every nation should explicitly acknowledge the Christ of God to be the Supreme Governor, and his revealed will the supreme fundamental law of the land, to the general principles of which all special legislation should be conformed. 2d. That all civil officers should make the glory of God their end, and his revealed will their guide. 3d. That, while no distinction should be made between the various Christian denominations, and perfect liberty of conscience and worship be allowed to all men, nevertheless the Christian magistrate should seek to promote piety as well as civil order ("Conf. Faith," ch. 23, § 2). This they are to do, not by assuming ecclesiastical functions, nor by attempting to patronize or control the church, but by their personal example, by giving impartial protection to church property and facility to church work, by the enactment and enforcement of laws conceived in the true spirit of the Gospel, and especially in maintaining inviolate the Christian Sabbath, and Christian marriage, and in providing for Christian instruction in the public schools.

16. *What relation does the civil law in the United States sustain to Church polity, discipline, and property?*

I. HISTORY.—1st. In England the established Church is a corporation created and controlled by the State.

2d. In most of the American Colonies, the State, at first undertook the absolute control of ecclesiastical affairs, and limited rights of citizenship by religious tests.

II. PRESENT FACTS.—1st. The Constitution of the United States provides that "No religious test shall ever be required as a qualification to any office or public trust under the United States, and that Congress shall make no law respecting an establishment of religion or prohibiting the free exercise thereof." The constitutions of the several states provide to the same effect.

2d. Christianity in a general sense is, as an historical fact, an essential element of the common law of England, and therefore that of the United States (except Louisiana, Texas, New Mexico, California, etc.), incorporated in our customs, principles, precedents, etc.*

3d. It is recognized by the civil law as the historical and actual religion of the vast majority of the citizens of the United States. The Christian faith and the institutions in which it finds expression, are, therefore, to be reverenced and protected by the civil law.

4th. The civil law, therefore, recognizes the church, as having an historic character, and as being an important element of society. It recognizes and protects its right to exist and enjoy the possession of its legitimate privileges and powers. Thus the civil law recognizes and protects (1) the autonomy of the church as to (*a*) its general polity and (*b*) its discipline of persons. (2.) The rights of each church as an organized whole to its property.

5th. The civil courts recognize as final the decisions of church courts as to (1) who are members of the church, and (2) who are the spiritual officers of the church. The civil court will not presume to go back of the decision of the church court in order to determine (1) whether it was rightly constituted (*i. e.*, if the church court in question be recognized by the highest authority in the church), or (2) whether subsequently to its constitution the church court has acted consistently with its own rules.

Judge Rogers, of the Supreme Court of Penna., in the case of the German Reformed Church of Lebanon Co., Pa., said, " The decisions of ecclesiastical courts, like every other judicial tribunal, are final, as they are the best judges of what constitutes an offence against the word of God and the constitution of the church."

The Supreme Court of the United States, in the case of the Walnut Street Church, Louisville, Ky., 1872, decided—

(1.) Where the subject matter of dispute is strictly and purely ecclesiastical in its character, a matter which concerns theological controversy, church discipline, ecclesiastical government, or the conformity of the members of the church to the standard of morals required of them, and the ecclesiastical courts claim jurisdiction—they will not even inquire into the right of the jurisdiction of the ecclesiastical court.

(2.) A spiritual court is the exclusive judge of its own ju-

* Case of Updegraff *v*. The Commonwealth of Penna., 11 S. and R. 400, before Supreme Court, Justices Duncan, Tilghman, and Gibson, 1824.

risdiction: its decision of that question is binding on the secular courts (see "Presbyterian Digest," Dr. Wm. E. Moore, p. 251).

6th. The civil law recognizes the right of the church to discipline its members. Even the public declaration made pursuant of the rules of order of a church from which a member has been excommunicated, because of his commission of an offence regarded as infamous by the law, is justified, and no action of slander can be maintained for such a publication.

7th. The church proper, or "ecclesiastical society," is distinguished from the incorporated "religious society" created to hold property for the use of the former. These incorporated religious societies are governed by their charters, and by the by-laws made in pursuance thereof; they hold property by means of trustees, and are virtually civil societies as much as any bank or railroad company. It is governed by the law precisely as other corporations are. It is subject to visitation. Intrusion into its offices may be remedied, and it will be restrained from a maladministration, or a misappropriation of the property. Its articles of association, and by-laws under its charter, providing for meetings, elections, and conduct of temporal affairs, may be changed according to the terms provided by the charter, but are binding while they exist. Substantial conformity to them is essential to the valid transaction of business, and may be reviewed by the civil court.

8th. When the "Will" or "Deed of Gift" or "Terms of Subscription" of the original donors of the property, or the charter of the church, prescribes neither (1) any specific doctrine, nor (2) any particular form of church government, nor connection with any definite religious denomination, then the majority of the members of the church in question control the property, and in case of change of doctrines, or discipline, or of denominational relation, may carry the property with them.

But whenever either the doctrine or the form of government or ecclesiastical connection is defined, either by the original donors or by the charter of the church, the civil courts will protect and enforce the trust. In such case, if any change is made by the majority in either of these essential points, the majority, however large, forfeits the property, and the minority, however small, will be maintained in possession. And the civil court will in all such cases receive and act on the decisions of the superior ecclesiastical courts as final (see Lectures by Hon. Wm. Strong, LL.D., Justice of Supreme Court of U. S., 1875).

17. *What is the relative jurisdictions of the "Boards of Trustees," and of the "Sessions" of our Presbyterian Churches, over the houses of worship pertaining to their respective Congregations?*

The "Session" is the only body of congregational officers known to our ecclesiastical constitution. The "Board of Trustees" is a creature of the civil courts for the purpose of holding the congregational property in trust.

As to their respective jurisdictions the decisions of the courts and of the general assembly are in harmony with each other The legal title to the property is vested in the trustees, and they have the custody of it "for the uses and purposes for which they hold it in trust," namely, the worship of God, etc., according to the order of the church to which it appertains, including business meetings relating to the congregation. The session is charged with the supervision of the spiritual interests of the congregation, including the right to direct and control the use of the building for such purposes. In the Supreme Court of the United States, in the Louisville Walnut Street case, the following principles were enunciated: "1. By the act of the legislature creating the trustees of a church, a body corporate, and by the acknowledged rules of the Presbyterian Church, the trustees are the mere nominal title-holders and custodians of the church property. 2. That in the use of the property for all religious services, or ecclesiastical purposes, the trustees are under the control of the church session." In a difference between trustees and the session of a church in Philadelphia respecting an organist, the question was carried to the Supreme Court of that state, who decided that the worship of the congregation was under the charge of the session, and that the service of song was a part of the worship, and hence the appointment of the organist was in the session. The civil courts are very firm in maintaining the rights and privileges of religious worship, and of churches, and in requiring the observance of the trust.

18. What are the duties of the Church with regard to the State?

1st. The church owes obedience to the state in the exercise of her lawful authority over the public property of the church. 2d. She is bound to use all the lawful means in her possession for carrying the gospel to all the members of the state. Beyond this the church owes no duty to the state whatever.

19. In what sense is Christ to return his kingdom to his Father, and in what sense will his mediatorial headship continue forever?

The sum of what is revealed to us upon this subject appears to be, that after the complete glorification of his people, and the destruction of his enemies, Christ will demit his mediatorial authority over the universe, which he has administered as God-man, in order that the Godhead absolute may be immediately all in all to the creature.—1 Cor. xv. 24–28. But his mediatorial headship over his own people, including the offices of prophet, priest, and king, shall continue forever. This is certain—1st. Because he is a priest forever, and of his kingdom there is no end.—Ps. cx. 4; Dan. vii. 14; Luke i. 33. 2d. The personal union between his divine and human nature is to continue forever. 3d. As Mediator he is the head of the church, which is his fulness, and the consummation of the marriage of the Lamb is the beginning of heaven.—Rev. xix. 7; xxi. 2, 9. 4th. As "a Lamb that had been slain," he is represented in heaven on the throne as ever more the temple and the light of the city, and as feeding his people, and leading them to fountains of living waters.—Rev. v. 6; vii. 17; xxi. 22, 23.

CHRIST EXECUTED HIS OFFICE OF MEDIATOR BOTH IN HIS ESTATE OF HUMILIATION AND EXALTATION.

20. *Wherein does Christ's humiliation consist?*

See "Larger Catechism," Questions 46–50; "Shorter Catechism," Question 27.

21. *In what sense was Christ made under the law, and how was that subjection an act of humiliation?*

In his incarnation Christ was born precisely into the law place of his people, and sustained to the law precisely that relation which they did.   He was born under the law, then, 1st, as a rule of duty; 2d, as a covenant of life; 3d, as a broken covenant, whose curse was already incurred.   His voluntary assumption of such a position was pre-eminently an act of humiliation: 1st. His assumption of a human nature was voluntary.   2d. After his incarnation his person remained divine, and the claims of law terminating upon persons, and not upon natures, his submission to those claims was purely gratuitous.   3d. This condescension is immeasurably heightened by the fact that he accepted the curse of the law as of a covenant of life already broken—Gal. iii. 10–13; iv. 4, 5.

22. *In what sense did Christ undergo the curse of the law, and how was that possible for God's well-beloved Son?*

In his own person, absolutely considered, Christ is often declared by the Father to be his "beloved Son, with whom he was well pleased," Matt. iii. 17; 2 Pet. i. 17; and he always did that which pleased God.—John viii. 29.   But in his office as mediator he had assumed our place, and undertaken to bear the guilt of our sin. The wrath of God, then, which Christ bore, was the infinite displeasure of God against our sins, which displeasure terminated upon Christ's person vicariously, because of the iniquity of us all which was laid upon him.— Matt. xxvi. 38; xxvii. 46; Luke xxii. 44.

23. *What are the different interpretations of the phrase in the apostles' creed, " he descended into hell," or Hades?*

The phrase, καταβασις εις ἅδου, *desensus ad inferos*, was one of the last incorporated into the ancient Creed. It is supposed to be derived from Ps. xvi. 10; Acts ii. 27; 1 Pet. iv. 18–20.

1st. The Catholic Church, on the basis of ancient tradition, interpret this phrase to mean that Christ after his death went in his entire person as God-man, to the *Limbus Patrum*, that department of Hades in which the Old Testament saints remained waiting for the revelation and application to them of his salvation. Here he preached the gospel, and brought them out to heaven. See below the "Cat. Council of Trent."

2d. The Lutherans hold that Christ's death was the last stage in his humiliation, and his descent to Hades the first stage of his exaltation, since he went to reveal and consummate his victory over Satan and the powers of darkness, and to pronounce their sentence of condemnation.

3d. The Church of England affirms in the 3d Article—"As Christ died for us and was buried, so also it is to be believed that he went down into hell." In the first book of Edward VI. it is stated more fully—"The body of Christ lay in the sepulchre until his resurrection, but his ghost departing from him, was with the ghosts which were in prison, or in hell, and did preach to the same, as the place of St. Peter doth testify." Bishop Pearson, in his *"Exposition of the Creed,"* teaches that Christ really went to the place of the damned to consummate the expiation of human sin, and to destroy the power of hell over his redeemed.

4th. Calvin ("Institutes," Bk. 2, ch. xvi., § 10) interprets this phrase metaphorically, as expressing the penal sufferings of Christ on the cross. Our "Conf. Faith" affixes to the Creed the explanatory clause, "continued in the state of the dead," and the American Episcopal Church affixes the equivalent clause, "he went into the place of departed spirits." That is, Christ was a real man, consisting of soul and body, and his death was a real death, his soul leaving the body and going into the invisible world of spirits, where it continued a separate conscious existence until his resurrection.

24. *What is the true meaning of* 1 Pet. iii. 19–21 *?*

This passage is very obscure. The Romish interpretation is shown in the answer to the preceding question, *i. e.*, that Christ went to the *Limbus Patrum* and preached the gospel to those imprisoned spirits that were awaiting his advent.

The common Protestant interpretation is that Ch ist was put to death in the body, but quickened, or restored to life by the Spirit, by which Spirit, inspiring Noah as a preacher of righteousness, Christ many centuries previously had descended from heaven, and preached to the men of that generation, who in their sin and unbelief were the "spirits in prison." Only eight persons believed and were saved; therefore, Christian professors and teachers ought not to faint because of the unbelief of mankind now.

Another interpretation, suggested by Archbishop Leighton in a note, as his last opinion, and expounded at large by the late Dr. John Brown, of Edinburgh, is, that Christ dying in the body as a vicarious sacrifice is quickened in the spirit, *i. e.*, spiritually quickened, manifested as a complete Saviour in a higher degree than was possible before, as a grain of wheat dying he began to bear much fruit; and thus quickened, he now, through the inspiration of his Spirit, preached to "spirits in prison," *i. e.*, prisoners of sin and Satan, just as he had before done, though with less power, through Noah and all the prophets, when the spirits were disobedient; under the ministry of Noah only eight souls being saved; but since Christ was quickened in spirit, *i. e.*, manifested as a complete Saviour, multitudes believed.

25. *Wherein does Christ's exaltation consist?*

"Shorter Cat.," Question 28, "Larger Cat.," Questions 51–54.

26. *In what sense was it possible for the co-equal Son of God to be exalted?*

As the co-equal Son of God this was impossible, yet his person as God-man was capable of exaltation in several respects.

1st. Through the union of the divine and human natures, the outward manifestations of the glory of his person had been veiled from the eyes of creatures. 2d. As Mediator he occupied officially a position inferior to the Father, condescending to occupy the place of sinners. He had been inconceivably humbled, and, as a reward consequent upon his voluntary self-humiliation, the Father highly exalted him.—Phil. ii. 8, 9; Heb. xii. 2; Rev. v. 6. 3d. His human soul and body were inconceivably exalted.—Matt. xvii. 2; Rev. i. 12–16; xx. 11.

27. *What are the various sources of proof by which the resurrection of Christ is established?*

1st. The Old Testament predicted it. Compare Ps. xvi. 10, and Acts ii. 24–31. All the other predictions concerning the Messiah were fulfilled in Christ, therefore this.

2d. Christ predicted it, and therefore, if he was a true prophet, he must have risen.—Matt. xx. 19; John x. 18.

3d. The event, his extraordinary origin and character considered, is not antecedently improbable.

4th. The testimony of the eleven apostles. These men are proved by their writings to have been good, intelligent, and serious, and they each had every opportunity of ascertaining the fact, and they sealed their sincerity with their blood.—Acts i. 3.

5th. The separate testimony of Paul, who, as one born out of due time, saw his risen Lord, and derived his revelation and commission from him in person.—1 Cor. xv. 8; Gal. i. 12; Acts ix. 3–8.

6th. He was seen by five hundred brethren at once, to whom Paul appeals.—Cor. xv. 6.

7th. The change of the Sabbath, from the last to the first day of the week, is a monument of the concurrent testimony of the whole of the first generation of Christians, to the fact that they believed that Christ rose from the dead.

8th. The miracles wrought by the apostles were God's seals to their testimony that he had raised Christ.—Heb ii. 4.

9th. The accompanying witness of the Holy Ghost, honoring the apostles' doctrine and ministry not merely by miraculous gifts, but by his sanctifying, elevating, and consoling power.—Acts v. 32. Dr. Hodge.

28. *By whose power did Christ rise from the dead?*

The Scriptures ascribe his resurrection—
1st. To himself.—John ii. 19; x. 17.
2d. To the Father.—Acts xiii. 33; Rom. x. 9; Eph. i. 20.
This is reconciled upon the principle that all acts of divine power, terminating upon objects external to the Godhead, may be attributed to either of the divine persons, or to the Godhead absolutely.—John v. 17–19.

29. *On what ground does the apostle declare that our faith is vain if Christ be not risen (1 Cor. xv. 14)?*

1st. If Christ be risen indeed, then he is the true Messiah, and all the prophecies of both dispensations have in that fact a pledge of their fulfilment.   If he has not risen, then are they all false.

2d. The resurrection proved him to be the Son of God, Rom. i. 4, for (1) he rose by his own power, (2) it authenticated all his claims with respect to himself.

3d. In the resurrection of Christ the Father publicly declared his approbation and acceptance of Christ's work as surety of his people.—Rom. iv. 25.

4th. If Christ has risen, we have an advocate with the Father.—Rom. viii. 34; Heb. 9, 11, 12, 24.

5th. If Christ be raised, we have assurance of eternal life; if he lives, we shall live also.—John xiv. 19; 1 Pet. i. 3–5.

6th. Owing to the union between Christ and his members, which is both federal and spiritual, his resurrection secures ours, (1) because, as we died in Adam, so we must live in Christ, 1 Cor. xv. 21, 22; (2) because of his Spirit, that dwelleth in us.—Rom. viii. 11; 1 Cor. vi. 15.; 1 Thess. iv. 14.

7th. Christ's resurrection illustrates and determines the nature of our resurrection as well as secures it.—1 Cor. xv. 49; Phil. iii. 21; 1 John iii. 2.   Dr. Hodge.

30. *When, at what place, and in whose presence did Christ ascend?*

He ascended forty days after his resurrection, from a portion of the Mount of Olives, near to the village of Bethany, in the presence of the eleven apostles, and possibly of other disciples, while he was in the act of blessing them, and while they beheld him, and were looking steadfastly.   Luke says, moreover, that there were two glorified men present, who are conjectured by Professor J. A. Alexander to have been Moses and Elijah.   He was attended also with angels celebrating his victory over sin, and his exaltation to his mediatorial throne.—Luke xxiv. 50, 51; Mark xvi. 19; Acts i. 9–11; Eph. iv. 8; Col. ii. 13–15; Ps. xxiv. 7–10; lxviii. 18.

31. *What are the different opinions as to the nature of Christ's ascension?*

Those who, as the Lutherans, believe that Christ's body is omnipresent to his church, of course, maintain that his ascension consisted not in any local change, but in the withdrawal of his former sensible intercourse with his disciples.

It is certain, however, that his human soul and body did actually pass up from earth to the abode of the blessed, and that his entire person, as the God-man, was gloriously exalted. He ascended as Mediator, triumphing over his enemies, and giving gifts to his friends, Eph. iv. 8–12; to complete his mediatorial work, John xiv. 2, 3; as the Forerunner of his people, Heb. vi. 20; and to fill the universe with the manifestations of his glory and power.—Eph. iv. 10.

32. *What is included in Christ's sitting at the right hand of the Father?*

See Ps. cx. 1; Mark xvi. 19; Rom. viii. 34; Eph. i. 20, 22; Col. iii. 1; Heb. i. 3, 4; x. 12; 1 Pet. iii. 22.

This language is evidently figurative, yet it very expressively sets forth the supreme glorification of Christ in heaven. It presents him as the God-man, and in his office as Mediator exalted to supreme and universal glory, felicity, and power over all principalities and powers, and every name that is named.—Heb. ii. 9; Ps. xvi. 11; Matt. xxvi. 64; Dan. vii. 13, 14; Phil. ii. 9, 11; John v. 22; Rev. v. 6. Thus publicly assuming his throne as mediatorial Priest and King over the universe for the benefit of his church.

Seated upon that throne he, during the present dispensation, as Mediator, effectually applies to his people, through his Spirit, that salvation which he had previously achieved for them in his estate of humiliation.

Authoritative Statements of Doctrines.

Roman Doctrine.—*"Cat. Conc. Trent,"* Pt. 1, ch. 6.—"Therefore we profess that, immediately Christ was dead, his soul descended into hell. . . But in these words we at the same time confess, that the same person of Christ was at the same time, in hell and in the sepulchre, for . . although his soul departed from his body, his divinity was never separated either from soul or body. . . The word "hell" signifies those hidden abodes in which are detained souls that have not attained heavenly bliss. . . These abodes were not all of the same kind. . . A third sort of receptacle is that in which were received the souls of the saints who died before the coming of Christ our Lord; and where, without any sense of pain, sustained by the blessed hope of redemption, they enjoyed a tranquil abode. The souls, then, of these pious men, who in the *bosom of Abraham* were expecting the Saviour; Christ the Lord liberated, descending into hell. . . . He descended not to suffer aught but to liberate from the miserable weariness of that captivity the holy and the just, and to impart to them the fruit of his passion."

Lutheran Doctrine. *"Formula Concordiæ"* (Hase), p. 788.—"Therefore we believe simply, that the entire person, God and man, after burial descended to the lower regions, overcame Satan, overthrew the infernal powers, and took away from the devil all force and authority." Pp. 767, 768.—"By virtue of this personal union and communion, he produced all his miracles, and manifested his divine majesty, according to a most free will, when and in what manner seemed good to him, not only after his resurrection and ascension to heaven, but even in his state of humiliation. Indeed he had this majesty immediately upon his conception, even in the womb of his mother; but as the apostle speaks (Phil. ii. 8), he emptied himself; and as Dr. Luther teaches, he had this majesty secretly in the state of his humiliation, nor did he use it always, but as often as seemed to him good. But now, after he has, not in a common manner like any other holy person, ascended into the heavens; but, as the Apostle testifies (Eph. iv. 10), has ascended above all heavens, and truly fills all things, and everywhere present, not only as God, but also as man, rules and reigns from sea to sea, and even to the ends of the earth. . . . These things, however, were not done in an earthly manner, but, as Dr. Luther was accustomed to say, in the way and manner of the right hand of God (*pro modo et ratione dexteræ Dei*), which is not any fixed and limited place in heaven, but signifies nothing else than the omnipotent power of God which fills heaven and earth—into possession of which Christ really and truly comes as to his humanity without any confusion or equalizing of his natures (divine and human), either as to their essences or essential attributes."

CHAPTER XXVIII.

The Application of Redemption accomplished by Christ as Mediatorial King through the Personal Agency of the Holy Ghost.

EFFECTUAL CALLING.

1. What is the New Testament usage of the words καλέιν (to call), κλῆσις (calling), and κλητός (the called)?

καλέιν is used in the sense, 1st, of calling with the voice, John x. 3; Mark i. 20; 2d, of calling forth, to summon authoritatively, Acts iv. 18; xxiv. 2; 3d, of inviting, Matt. xxii. 3; ix. 13; 1 Tim. vi. 12. Many are called, but few chosen. 4th. Of the effectual call of the Spirit.—Rom. viii. 28–30; 1 Pet. ii. 9; v. 10. 5th. Of an appointment to office.—Heb. v. 4. 6th. In the sense of naming, Matt. i. 21; κλῆσις occurs eleven times in the New Testament, in each instance it signifies the effectual call of the Holy Spirit, with the exception of 1 Cor. vii. 20, where it is used as synonymous with business or trade. See Rom. xi. 29; 1 Cor. i. 26, etc.—Robinson's "Lex."

κλητός occurs ten times in the New Testament. It is used to signify—1st. Those appointed to any office.—Rom. i. 1. 2d. Those who receive the external call of the word.—Matt. xx. 16. 3d. The effectually called.—Rom. i. 7; viii. 28; 1 Cor. i. 2, 24; Jude i.; Rev. xvii. 14.

The very word ἐκκλησία (church) designating the company of the faithful, the heirs of all the promises, signifies, etymologically, the company called forth, the body constituted by "the calling."

2. What is included in the external call?

1st. A declaration of the plan of salvation. 2d. A declaration of duty on the part of the sinner to repent and believe. 3d. A declaration of the motives which ought to influence the sinner's mind, such as fear or hope, remorse or gratitude.

4th. A promise of acceptance in the case of all those who comply with the conditions.—Dr. Hodge.

3. *How can it be proved that the external call to salvation is made only through the word of God?*

The law of God, as impressed upon the moral constitution of man, is natural, and inseparable from man as a moral responsible agent.—Rom. i. 19, 20; ii. 14, 15. But the gospel is no part of that natural law. It is of grace, not of nature, and it can be made known to us only by a special and supernatural revelation.

This is further evident, 1st, because the Scriptures declare that a knowledge of the word is essential to salvation, Rom. x. 14–17; and, 2d, because they also declare that those who neglect the word, either written or preached, are guilty of the eminent sin of rejecting all possibility of salvation.—Matt. xi. 21, 22; Heb. ii. 3.

4. *On what principle is this external call addressed equally to the non-elect as well as to the elect?*

That it is addressed indiscriminately to both classes is proved—1st. From the express declaration of Scripture.—Matt. xxii. 14. 2d. The command to preach the gospel to every creature.—Mark xvi. 15. 3d. The promise to every one who accepts it.—Rev. xxii. 17. 4th. The awful judgment pronounced upon those who reject it.—John iii. 19; xvi. 9.

It is addressed to the non-elect equally with the elect, because it is equally their duty and interest to accept the gospel, because the provisions of salvation are equally suited to their case, and abundantly sufficient for all, and because God intends that its benefits shall actually accrue to every one who accepts it.

5. *How can it be proved that there is an internal spiritual call distinct from an external one?*

1st. From those passages which distinguish the Spirit's influence from that of the word.—John vi. 45, 64, 65; 1 Thess. i. 5, 6. 2d. Those passages which teach that the Spirit's influence is necessary to the reception of the truth.—Eph. i. 17. 3d. Those that refer all good in man to God.—Phil. ii. 13; Eph. ii. 8; 2 Tim. ii. 25, *e. g.*, faith and repentance. 4th. The Scripture distinguishes between the two calls; of the subjects of the one it is said, "many are called and few are chosen," of the subjects of the other it is said, "whom he called, them he also justified." Of the one he says, "Because I have called, and ye have refused."—Prov. i. 24. Of the other he says, "Every man therefore who hath heard and hath learned of the Father cometh unto me."—John vi. 45. 5th. There is an absolute necessity for such an internal, spiritual call, man by nature is "blind" and "dead" in trespasses and sins.—1 Cor. ii. 14; 2 Cor. iv. 4; Eph. ii. 1.

6. *What is the Pelagian view of the internal call?*

Pelagians deny original sin, and maintain that right and wrong are qualities attaching only to executive acts of the will. They therefore assert—1st. The full ability of the free-will of man as much to cease from sin at any time as to continue in its practice. 2d. That the Holy Spirit produces no inward change in the heart of the subject, except as he is the author of the Scriptures, and as the Scriptures present moral truths and motives, which of their own nature exert a moral influence upon the soul. They deny "grace" altogether in the Scriptural sense.

7. *What is the Semipelagian view?*

These maintain that grace is necessary to enable a man successfully to return unto God and live. Yet that from the very nature of the human will man must first of himself desire to be free from sin, and to choose God as his chief good, when he may expect God's aid in carrying his desires into effect. They deny *prevenient* grace, but admit co-operative grace.

8. *What is the Arminian view?*

The Arminians admit the doctrine of man's total depravity, and that in consequence thereof man is utterly unable to do any thing aright in the unaided exercise of his natural faculties. Nevertheless, as Christ died equally for every man, sufficient grace, enabling its subject to do all that is required of him, is granted to all. Which sufficient grace becomes efficient only when it is co-operated with and improved by the sinner.— "Apol. Conf. Remonstr.," p. 162, b.; Limborch, "Theo. Christ.," 4, 12, 8.

9. *What is the doctrine on this subject taught by the Symbols of the Lutheran Church?*

They agree absolutely with the Reformed or Calvinists— 1st. That all men are by nature spiritually dead, utterly unable either to commence to turn to God, or to co-operate with his grace to that end prior to regeneration. 2d. That the gracious operation of the Holy Spirit on the human soul is the sole

efficient cause which quickens the dead soul to life. Hence—
3d. The foundation upon which the salvation of believers rests
is the eternal, gracious election of God to salvation. They refuse however to take the next step, and acknowledge that the
reason unbelievers are not quickened is due to the equally sovereign withholding of regenerating grace. They insist upon
attributing it solely to the criminal resistance to the grace, of
the initial stages of which all are the subjects.—"Formula Concordiæ," Hase, pp. 579–583, 662–666, 817–821.

A and B are alike sinners, A believes and B remains a reprobate. The Pelagian says, because A willed to believe and B
to reject. The Semipelagian says, because A commenced to
strive and was helped, and B made no effort. The Arminian
says, because A co-operated with common grace, and B did not
The Lutheran says, both were utterly unable to co-operate, but
B persistently resisted grace, and A ultimately yielded. The
Calvinist says, because A was regenerated by the new creative
power of God's Spirit, and B was not.

10. *What is the Synergistic view of this point?*

At the call of Maurice, the new elector of Saxony, the
divines of Wittemburg and Leipsic assembled at Leipsic, A. D.
1548, in conference, and on that occasion the Synergistic controversy arose. The term signifies *co-operation.* The Synergists were Lutheran theologians, who departed from their own
system on this one subject, and adopted the position of the
Arminians. Melanchthon taught that "there concur three
causes of a good action, the word of God, the Holy Spirit, and
the human will assenting, not resisting, the word of God."
"Loci Communes," p. 90.

11. *What is the common doctrine of the Reformed Churches as to the internal call?*

That it is an exercise of the divine power upon the soul,
immediate, spiritual, and supernatural, communicating a new
spiritual life, and thus making a new mode of spiritual activity
possible. That repentance, faith, trust, hope, love, etc., are
purely and simply the sinner's own acts; but as such are possible to him only in virtue of the change wrought in the moral
condition of his faculties by the recreative power of God.—See
"Conf. of Faith," Chap. x., Sections 1 and 2.

Common grace preceding regeneration makes a superficial
moral impression upon character and action but is generally
resisted. The act of grace which regenerates, operating within
the spontaneous energies of the soul and changing their char-

acter, can neither be co-operated with nor resisted. But the instant the soul is regenerated it begins to co-operate with and sometimes, alas! also to resist subsequent gracious influences prevenient and co-operative. But upon the whole and in the end grace preserves, overcomes, and saves. Regeneration is styled by the Reformed Theologians *Conversio habitualis seu passiva, i. e.,* the change of character in effecting which the soul is the subject, and not the agent of action. Conversion they style *Conversio actualis seu activa, i. e.,* the instantly consequent change of action in which the soul still prompted and aided by grace is the only agent.

12. *What diversity of opinion prevails among the Romanists upon this subject?*

The disciples of Augustine in that church, of whom the Jansenists were the most prominent, are orthodox, but these have been almost universally overthrown, and supplanted by their enemies the Jesuits, who are Semipelagians. The Council of Trent attempted to satisfy both parties.—"Council of Trent," Sess. 6, Can. 3 and 4. The doctrines of Quesnel, who advocated the truth on this subject, were condemned in the Bull "Unigenitus," A. D. 1713. Bellarmin taught that the same grace is given to every man, which, by the event only, is proved practically congruous to the nature of one man, and therefore in his case efficacious, and incongruous to the nature of another, and therefore in his case ineffectual.

13. *What is meant by "common grace," and how may it be shown that the Spirit does operate upon the minds of those who are not renewed in heart?*

"Common grace" is the restraining and persuading influences of the Holy Spirit acting only through the truth revealed in the gospel, or through the natural light of reason and of conscience, heightening the natural moral effect of such truth upon the understanding, conscience, and heart. It involves no change of heart, but simply an enhancement of the natural powers of the truth, a restraint of the evil passions, and an increase of the natural emotions in view of sin, duty, and self-interest.

That God does so operate upon the hearts of the unregenerate is proved, 1st, from Scripture, Gen. vi. 3; Acts vii. 51; Heb. x. 29; 2d, from universal experience and observation.

14. *How does common differ from efficacious grace?*

1st. As to its subjects. All men are more or less the subjects of the one; only the elect are subjects of the other.—Rom. viii. 30; xi. 7; 2 Thess. ii. 13.

2d. As to its nature. Common grace is only mediate, through the truth, and it is merely moral, heightening the moral influence natural to the truth, and exciting only the natural powers of the soul, both rational and moral. But efficacious grace is immediate and supernatural, since it is wrought directly in the soul by the immediate energy of the Holy Ghost, and since it implants a new spiritual life, and a capacity for a new mode of exercising the natural faculties.

3d. As to its effects. The effects of common grace are superficial and transient, modifying the action, but not changing the nature, and its influence is always more or less consciously resisted, as opposed to the prevailing dispositions of the soul. But efficacious grace, since it acts not *upon* but *in* the will itself, changing the governing desires, and giving a new direction to the active powers of the soul, is neither resistible nor irresistible, but most free, spontaneous, and yet most certainly effectual.

15. *How can it be proved that this efficacious grace is confined to the elect?*

1st. The Scriptures represent the elect as the called, and the called as the elect.—Rom. viii. 28, 30; Rev. xvii. 14. 2d. This effectual calling is said to be based upon the decree of election, 2 Thes. ii. 13, 14; 2 Tim. i. 9, 10. 3d. Sanctification, justification, and all the temporal and eternal benefits of union with Christ are declared to be the effects of effectual calling.—1 Cor. i. 2; Eph. ii. 5; Rom. viii. 30.

16. *Prove that it is given on account of Christ?*

1st. All spiritual blessings are given on account of Christ. Eph. i. 3; Titus iii. 5, 6. 2d. The Scriptures specifically declare that we are called in Christ.—Rom. viii. 2; Eph. ii. 4–6; 2 Tim. i. 9.

17. *What is meant by saying that this divine influence is immediate and supernatural?*

It is meant, 1st, to deny, (1) that it consists simply in the moral influence of the truth; (2) that it consists simply in the moral influence of the Spirit, heightening the moral influence of the truth as objectively presented; (3) that it excites the mere natural powers of the soul. It is meant, 2d, to affirm, (1) that the Holy Spirit acts immediately upon the soul from within; (2) that the Holy Spirit, by an exercise of recreative power, implants a new moral nature or principle of action.

18. *What arguments go to show that there is an immediate influence of the Spirit on the soul, besides that which is exerted through the truth?*

1st. The influence of the Spirit is distinguished from that of the word.—John vi. 45, 64, 65; Rom. xv. 13; 1 Cor. ii. 12–15; 1 Thess. i. 5, 6.

2d. A divine influence is declared to be necessary to the reception of the truth.—Ps. cxix. 18; Acts xvi. 14; Eph. i. 17.

3d. Such an internal operation on the heart is attributed to God.—Phil. ii. 13; 2 Thess. i. 11; Heb. xiii. 21.

4th. The gift of the Spirit is distinguished from the gift of the word.—John xiv. 16; 1 Cor. iii. 16; vi. 19; Eph. iv. 30.

5th. The nature of this influence is evidently different from that effected by the truth.—Eph. i. 19; iii. 7. And the effect is called a "new creation," "new birth," etc., etc.

6th. Man by nature is dead in sin, and needs such a direct intervention of supernatural power.—Turretin, "Theo. Instits.," L. XV., Quæstio 4.

19. *What are the different reasons assigned for calling this grace* EFFICACIOUS?

1st. The Jesuits and the Arminians, holding that all men receive sufficient grace to enable them to obey the gospel if they will, maintain that this grace becomes efficacious when it is co-operated with by the will of the individual, and in any case is proved to be such only by the event.

2d. Bellarmin, and others, maintain that the same grace given to all is congruous to the moral nature of one man, and in that case efficacious, and incongruous to the nature of another, and in his case ineffectual.

3d. Some Romanists have maintained what is called the doctrine of cumulative influence. The consent of the soul is secured by the suasive influence of the spirit, rendered effectual by constant repetition and long continuance.

4th. The orthodox doctrine is that the efficacy of this grace is inherent in its very nature, because it is the exercise of the mighty power of God in the execution of his eternal and unchangeable purpose.

20. *In what sense is grace irresistible?*

It must be remembered that the true Christian is the subject at the same time of those moral and mediate influences of grace *upon the will,* common to him and to the unconverted, and also of those special influences of grace *within the will,* which are certainly efficacious. The first class of influences Christians may, and constantly do resist, through the law of sin remaining in their members. The second class of influences are certainly efficacious, but are neither resistible nor irresistible, because they act from within and carry the will spontaneously with them. It is to be lamented that the term irresistible grace has ever been used, since it suggests the idea of a mechanical and coercive influence upon an unwilling subject, while, in truth, it is the transcendent act of the infinite Creator, making the creature spontaneously willing.

21. *How can this grace be proved to be certainly efficacious?*

1st. By the evidence we have given above, as to its nature, as the immediate operation of the mighty power of God.

2d. By the description of the work of grace. Men by nature are "blind," "dead," "slaves," etc. The change effected is a "new creation," etc.

3d. From the promises of God, which are certain. The means which he uses to vindicate his own faithfulness must be efficacious.—Ezek. xxxvi. 26; xi. 19; John vi. 45.

4th. From the connection asserted by Scripture between calling and election. The called are the elect. As God's decrees are certain, the call must be efficacious.—See above, Ques. 15.

5th. Faith and repentance are the gifts of God, and he who truly repents and believes is saved. Therefore, the grace which communicates those gifts is effectual.—Eph. ii. 8; Acts xi. 18; 2 Tim. ii. 25.

22. *How may it be proved that this influence is congruous with our nature?*

While discarding utterly the distinction made by Bellarmin (for which see above, Question 19), we say that efficacious grace is congruous to human nature as such, in the sense that the Spirit of God, while exerting an immediate and recreative influence upon the soul, nevertheless acts in perfect consistency with the integrity of those laws of our free, rational, and moral nature, which he has himself constituted. Even in the miraculous recreation of the new birth, he acts upon our reasons and upon our wills in perfect accordance with the constitution of each. This is certain. 1st. The same God creates and recreates; his object is not to destroy, but to restore his own work. 2d. The Scriptures and our own experience teach that the immediately consequent acts of the soul in the exercise of implanted grace, are pre-eminently rational and free. In fact, the soul never acted normally before.—Ps. cx. 3; 2 Cor. iii. 17; Phil. ii. 13. 3d. This divine influence is·described by such terms as " drawing," " teaching," "enlightening."—John vi. 44, 45; Eph. i. 18.

23. *What do the Scriptures teach as to the connection of this influence with the truth?*

In the case of the regeneration of infants the truth, of course, is not used. In the regeneration of adults the truth is always present. In the act of regeneration the Spirit acts immediately upon the soul, and changes its subjective state, while the truth is the object consciously apprehended, upon which the new faculties of spiritual discernment and the new affections are exercised. The Spirit gives sight, the truth is the light discerned. The Spirit gives feeling, the truth presents the object beloved.—Rom. x. 14, 17; James i. 18; John xvii. 17.

24. *What reason may be assigned for the belief that the Spirit does not renew those adults to whom the truth is not known?*

Negatively. The Bible never leads us to expect such an extension of grace, and neither the Scriptures nor our own experience among the modern heathen ever present us with any examples of such a work.

Positively. The Scriptures always associate all spiritual influence with the truth, and declare the necessity of preaching the truth to the end of saving souls.—Rom. x. 14.

25. *What are the objections to the Arminian doctrine of sufficient grace?*

They hold that God has willed the salvation of all men, and therefore has called all alike, giving to all a grace sufficient, if they will improve it.

We object—1st. The external call of the gospel has been extended to comparatively few. The heathen are responsible with the light of nature, and under the law of works, yet they have no means of grace.—Rom. i. 18–20; ii. 12–15.

2d. This doctrine is inconsistent with God's purpose of election.—See above, Chapter XI.

3d. According to the Arminian system it depends upon the free-will of the man to make the sufficient grace of God common to all men efficient in his case. But the Scriptures declare that salvation is altogether of grace, and a gift of God.—Eph. ii. 8; 2 Tim. ii. 25; Rom. ix. 15, 16.

4th. The Scriptures expressly declare that not even all who receive the external call have sufficient grace.—Rom. ix. 16–24; xi. 8.

Authoritative Statements of Doctrine.

Roman Doctrine.—" *Conc. Trent,*" Sess. 6, c. 1.—" If any one saith that a man can be justified (by justification they mean the removal of sin and infusion of a gracious habit of soul) by his own works, whether done through the teaching of human nature, or that of the law, without the grace of God through Jesus Christ; let him be anathema. C. 2.—If any one saith, that the grace of God, through Jesus Christ, is given only for this, that man may be able more easily to live justly, and to merit eternal life, as if, by free-will without grace, he were able to do both, though hardly indeed and with difficulty, let him be anathema. C. 3.—If any one saith, that without prevenient inspiration of the Holy Ghost, and without his help, man can believe, hope, love, or be penitent as he ought, so as that the grace of justification may be bestowed upon him; let him be anathema. C. 4.—If any one says that man's free-will moved and excited by God, by assenting to God exciting and calling, nowise co-operates towards disposing and preparing itself for obtaining the grace of justification; that it can not refuse its consent, if it would, but that as something inanimate it does nothing whatever, and is merely passive; let him be anathema. Can. 5.—If any one saith that since Adam's sin, the free-will of man is lost and extinguished; or that it is a thing with only a name, yea a name without a reality, a figment in fine introduced into the world by Satan; let him be anathema."

Doctrine of the Greek Church.—" *Jerem. in Act. Witem.*"—" Even after the fall nothing hinders man from turning away from the bad, and superinduced upon this, doing good and choosing the right, as one who has *free-will.* . . . From all these it is plain, that it is our part to awake and to obey, and we have ability to choose the good as well as the bad. We need only one thing, *i. e.,* God's help, in order to succeed in the good and be saved, and without this help we have no strength to finish the work."

Lutheran Doctrine.—" *Form. Concordiœ,*" p. 662.—" But before man is enlightened, converted, regenerated, and drawn by the Holy Spirit, he is not able of himself, and by his own natural powers, in things spiritual and (tending) to his own conversion and regeneration, to begin, to produce, or to co-operate in any thing, any more than is a stone a stock or a clod." *Ib.* p. 589.—" What Doctor Luther wrote—'That the will of man holds itself purely passive in conversion,' must be received rightly and fittingly, to wit, with respect to divine grace enkindling the new movements, that is, it ought to be understood concerning that, when the Spirit of God acts upon the will of man by the word heard, or by the use of the sacraments, and produces in man conversion and regeneration. For after the Holy Spirit has wrought this very thing, and has by his own divine energy alone changed and renewed the will of man; then, indeed, this new will is an instrument of the Holy Spirit of God, so that it may not only lay hold of grace, but also co-operate with the Holy Spirit in the works following."

Reformed Doctrine.—" *Conf. Faith,*" ch. x., § 1.—" All those whom God hath predestinated unto life, and those only, he is pleased, in his appointed and accepted time, effectually to call, by his word and Spirit, out of that state of sin and death, in which they are by nature, to grace and salvation by Jesus Christ; enlightening their minds, spiritually and savingly to understand the things of God, taking away their heart of stone, and giving unto them a heart of flesh; renewing their wills, and by his almighty power determining them to that which is good ; and effectually drawing them to Jesus Christ; yet so as they come most freely, being made willing by his grace." § 2.—"This effectual call is of God's free and special grace alone, not from any thing at all foreseen in man, who is altogether passive therein, until, being quickened and renewed by the Holy Spirit, he is thereby enabled to answer this call, and to embrace the grace offered and conveyed in it." "L. Cat.," Q. 67; "S. Cat.," Q. 31.—"*Canons of Synod of Dort,*" chs. iii. and iv., "Rejec. Er.," Error 4.—"(They are renounced) who teach that an unregenerate man is not strictly and totally dead in sins, nor void of all power as to spiritual good; but that he is able to hunger and thirst after righteousness, and to offer the sacrifice of a broken and contrite spirit, which is accepted of God." Art. 12.—"(Regeneration) is plainly supernatural, a most powerful and at the same time most gentle operation, wonderful, secret, and inexpressible, not inferior to a creation, nor less than a reviving of the dead; so that all those, in whose hearts God works in this wonderful manner, are surely regenerated infallibly and effectually, and act faith. And then the will, now renewed, is not only acted on and moved by God, but being so moved, also itself acts. Wherefore also man himself is rightly said, through this received grace, to believe and repent."

REMONSTRANT DOCTRINE.—"*Conf. Remonstr.,*" 17, 6.—"Therefore we decide that the grace of God is the beginning, progress, and completion of all good, so that the regenerate person himself, is not able to think, will, or do any saving good, without this previous prevenient, exciting, following, and co-operating grace."

"*Apol. Conf. Remonstr.,*" p. 162, b.—"Grace is called efficacious from the result, which, however can be taken in a twofold sense: *First,* so that grace may be judged to have, of itself, no power to produce consent in the will, but its entire efficacy may depend upon the human will: or, *Secondly,* so that grace may be judged to have of itself sufficient power to produce consent in the will, but because this power is partial, it can not go out in act without the co-operation of the free human will, and hence, that it may have effect, it depends on free-will. The Remonstrants wish the "second" to be taken as their meaning."

CHAPTER XXIX.

REGENERATION.

1. What are the various Scripture terms by which this work of God is designated?

1st. "Creating anew."—Eph. iv. 24. 2d. "Begetting."—James i. 18. 3d. "Quickening."—John v. 21; Eph. ii. 5. 4th. "Calling out of darkness into marvellous light."—1 Pet. ii. 9. The subjects of it are said, 1st, to be "alive from the dead." Rom. vi. 13. 2d. To be "new creatures."—2 Cor. v. 17. 3d. To be "born again."—John iii. 3, 7. 4th. To be "God's workmanship."—Eph. ii. 10.

2. What is the Pelagian view of regeneration?

They hold that sin can be predicated only of volitions, and that it is essential to the liberty and responsibility of man that he is always as able to cease from as to continue in sin. Regeneration is therefore a mere reformation of life and habit. The man who has chosen to transgress the law, now chooses to obey it.

3. What is the doctrine of the Romish church on this subject?

The Romanists, 1st, confound together justification and sanctification, making these one act of God, whereby, for his own glory, for Christ's merits' sake, by the efficient powers of the Holy Ghost, and through the instrumentality of baptism, he at once cancels the guilt of our sins, and delivers us from the inherent power and defilement of original sin.—"Council of Trent," Sess. 6, Chap. vii.

2d. They hold the doctrine that regeneration is accomplished only through the instrumentality of baptism. This is effectual in every instance of its application to an infant. In the case of adults its virtue may be either resisted and nullified, or received and improved. In baptism (1) sins are forgiven; (2) the moral nature of the subject is renewed, (3) he is made a son and heir of God.—"Cat. Rom.," Part II., Chap. ii.

4. *What are the different views as to baptismal regeneration entertained in the Church of England?*

1st. The theory of the party styled Puseyite, which is essentially the same with that of the Romish church. They hold in general that the Holy Spirit, through the instrumentality of baptism, implants a germ of spiritual life in the soul, which may long remain latent, and may be subsequently developed, or blasted.

2d. That of a large party most ably represented by the late Bishop H. U. Underdonk, in his "Essay on Regeneration," Phila., 1835. He maintained that there are two distinct regenerations; one a change of *state* or *relation*, and the other a change of *nature*. The first is baptismal, the second moral, though both are spiritual in so far as both are wrought by the Holy Ghost. The first or baptismal regeneration is a new birth, since it constitutes us sons of God, as the Jews were made his peculiar people by that covenant, the seal of which was circumcision. The second is a new birth, or creation in a higher sense, being a gradual sanctifying change wrought in the whole moral character by the Holy Ghost, and not necessarily connected with baptism.

5. *What view of regeneration is held by those in America who maintain the "Exercise Scheme"?*

These theologians deny the existence in the soul of any permanent moral habits or dispositions, and admit the existence only of the soul or agent and his acts or "exercises." In the natural man the series of acts are wholly depraved. In the regenerated man a new series of holy acts are created by the Holy Ghost, and continued by his power.—Emmons, Sermon LXIV., on the "New Birth."

6. *What is the New Haven view, advocated by Dr. N. W. Taylor, on this subject?*

Dr. Taylor agreed with the advocates of the "Exercise Scheme," that there is nothing in the soul but the agent and his actions; but he differed from them by holding that man and not God is the independent author of human actions. He held that when God and the world is held up before the mind, regeneration consists in an act of the sinner in choosing God as his chief good, thus confounding regeneration and conversion. The Holy Spirit, in some unknown way, assists in restraining the active operation of the natural, selfish principle which prefers the world as its chief good. "A mind thus detached from the world as its supreme good instantly chooses

God for its portion, under the impulse of that inherent desire for happiness, without which no object could ever be regarded as *good*, as either desirable or lovely." This original motive to that choice of God which is regeneration is merely natural, and neither morally good nor bad. Thus—1st. Regeneration is man's own act. 2d. The Holy Spirit helps man, (1) by suspending the controlling power of his sinful, selfish disposition; (2) by presenting to his mind in the clear light of truth the superiority of God as an object of choice. 3d. Then the sinner chooses God as his chief good under the conviction of his understanding, and from a motive of natural, though not sinful, self-love, which is to be distinguished from selfishness, which is of the essence of sin.—See "Christian Spectator," December, 1829, pp. 693, 694, etc.

7. *What is the common doctrine held by evangelical Christians?*

1st. That there are in the soul, besides its several faculties, habits, or dispositions, of which some are innate and others are acquired, which lay the foundation for the soul's exercising its faculties in some particular way. Thus we intuitively judge a man's moral disposition to be permanently evil when we see him habitually acting sinfully, or to be permanently good when we see him habitually acting righteously.

2d. These dispositions are anterior to moral action, and determine its character as good or evil.

3d. In creation God made the disposition of Adam's heart holy.

4th. In the new creation God recreates the governing disposition of the regenerated man's heart holy.

It is, therefore, properly called a "regeneration," a "new creation," a "new birth."

8. *When it is said that regeneration consists in giving a new heart, or in implanting a new principle or disposition, what is meant by the terms "heart," "principle," or "disposition"?*

President Edwards says, "By a principle of nature in this place, I mean that foundation which is laid in nature, either old or new, for any particular kind or manner of exercise of the faculties of the soul. So this new 'spiritual sense' is not a new faculty of understanding, but it is a new foundation laid in the nature of the soul for a new kind of exercise of the same faculty of understanding. So that new holy disposition of heart that attends this new sense is not a new faculty of will, but a foundation laid in the nature of the soul for a new kind of exercise of the same faculty of will."—Edwards on "Religious Affections," Pt. III., sec. 1.

The term "heart," signifying that prevailing moral disposition that determines the volitions and actions, is the phrase most commonly used in Scripture.—Matt. xii. 33, 35; xv. 19; Luke vi. 43, 45.

9. *How may it be shown that this view of regeneration does not represent it as involving any change in the essence of the soul?*

This charge is brought against the orthodox doctrine by all those who deny that there is any thing in the soul but its constitutional faculties and their exercises. They hence argue that if any thing be changed except the mere exercises of the soul, its fundamental constitution would be physically altered. In opposition to this, we argue that we have precisely the same evidence for the existence of a permanent moral quality or disposition inherent in the will, as the reason why a good man acts habitually righteously, or a bad man viciously, that we have for the existence of the invisible soul itself, or of any of its faculties, as the reason why a man acts at all, or why his actions are such as thought, emotion, volition. It is not possible for us to conceive of the choice being produced in us by the Holy Spirit in more than three ways: "*First*, by his direct agency in producing the choice, in which case it would be no act of ours. *Second*, by addressing such motives to our constitutional and natural principles of self-love as would induce us to make the choice, in which case there would be no morality in the act. Or, *thirdly*, by producing such a relish for the divine character, that the soul as spontaneously and immediately rejoices in God as its portion as it rejoices in the perception of beauty."

"If our Maker can endow us, not only with the general susceptibility of love, but also with a specific disposition to love our children; if he can give us a discernment and susceptibility of natural beauty, he may give us a taste for spiritual loveliness. And if that taste, by reason of sin, is vitiated and perverted, he may restore it by means of his spirit in regeneration."—Hodge's Essays.

10. *In what sense may the soul be said to be passive in regeneration?*

Dr. Taylor maintains that regeneration is that act of the soul in which man chooses God as his portion. Thus, the man himself, and not God, is the agent.

But the Christian church, on the contrary, holds that in regeneration the Holy Ghost is the agent, and man the subject. The act of the Holy Spirit, in implanting a new principle, does not interfere with the essential activity of the soul itself, but simply gives to that activity a new direction, for the soul, though active, is nevertheless capable of being acted upon. And although the soul is necessarily active at the very time it is regenerated, yet it is rightly said to be passive with respect to that act of the Holy Spirit whereby it is regenerated. 1st. The soul, under the conviction of the Holy Ghost, and in the exercise of merely natural feelings, regards some aspect of saving truth, and strives to embrace it. 2d. The Holy Ghost, by an exertion of creative power, changes the governing disposition of the heart in a manner inscrutable, and by an influence not apprehended by the consciousness of the subject. 3d. Simultaneously the soul exercises new affections and experimentally embraces the truth.

11. *What is the difference between regeneration and conversion?*

The term conversion is often used in a wide sense as including both the change of nature and the exercise of that nature as changed. When distinguished from regeneration, however, conversion signifies the first exercise of the new disposition implanted in regeneration, *i. e.*, in freely turning unto God.

Regeneration is God's act; conversion is ours. Regeneration is the implantation of a gracious principle; conversion is the exercise of that principle. Regeneration is never a matter of direct consciousness to the subject of it; conversion always is such to the agent of it. Regeneration is a single act, complete in itself, and never repeated; conversion, as the beginning of holy living, is the commencement of a series, constant, endless, and progressive. "Draw me, and I will run after thee." Cant. i. 4. This distinction is signalized by the divines of the seventeenth century (Turretin, L. 15, Ques. 4, § 13) by the phrases "*conversio habitualis seu passiva,*" *i. e.*, the infusion of a gracious habit of soul by God, in respect to which the subject is passive; and "*conversio actualis seu activa,*" *i. e.*, the consequent acts of faith and repentance elicited by co-operative grace and acted by the subject.

12. *How can it be proved that there is any such thing as that commonly called regeneration?*

1st. By those Scriptures that declare such a change to be necessary.—John iii. 3; 2 Cor. v. 17; Gal. vi. 15.

2d. By those passages which describe the change.—Eph. ii. 5; iv. 24; James i. 18; 1 Pet. i. 23.

3d. From the fact that it was necessary for the most moral as well as for the most profligate.—1 Cor. xv. 10; Gal. i. 13–16.

4th. That this inward change is not a mere reformation is

proved by its being referred to the Holy Spirit.—Eph. i. 19, 20; Titus iii. 5.

5th. From the comparison of man's state in grace with his state by nature.—Rom. vi. 13; viii. 6–10; Eph. v. 8.

6th. From the experience of all Christians, and from the testimony of their lives.

13. *What is the nature of supernatural illumination?*

The soul of man is a unit. A radically defective or perverted condition of any faculty will injuriously affect the exercise of all the other faculties. The essence of sin consists in the perverted moral dispositions and affections of the will. But a perverted condition of these affections must affect the exercises of the intellect, concerning all moral objects, as much as the volitions themselves. We can not love or desire any object unless we perceive its loveliness, neither can we intellectually perceive its loveliness unless its qualities are congenial to our inherent taste or dispositions. Sin, therefore, is essentially deceitful, and man as a sinner is spiritually blind. This does not consist in any physical defect. He possesses all the faculties requisite to enable him to see the beauty, and to experience the power of the truth, but his whole nature is morally perverted through his evil dispositions. As soon as these are changed he will see, and, seeing, love and obey the truth, although no constitutional change is wrought in his nature, *i. e.*, no new faculty given, but only his perverted faculties morally rectified. This illumination is called supernatural, 1st, because, having been lost, it can be restored only by the immediate power of God. 2d. In contradistinction to the maimed condition of man's present depraved nature. It, however, conveys no new truths to the mind, nor does it relieve the Christian, in any degree, from the diligent and prayerful study of the Word, nor does it lead to any fanciful interpretations of Scripture foreign to the plain sense of the letter; it only leads to the perception and appreciation of the native spiritual beauty and power of the inspired word, and the truths therein revealed.

14. *How may it be proved that believers are the subjects of such illumination?*

1st. It is necessary.—1 Cor. ii. 14; 2 Cor. iii. 14; iv. 3; John xvi. 3. From the constitution of our nature we must apprehend an object as lovely before we can love it for its own sake.

2d. The Scriptures expressly affirm it. "To know God is eternal life."—John xvii. 3; 1 Cor. ii. 12, 13; 2 Cor. iv. 6; Eph.

i. 18; Phil. i. 9; Col. iii. 10; 1 John iv. 7; v. 20; Ps. xix. 7, 8; xliii. 3, 4.

As the soul is a unit, a change in its radical moral dispositions must simultaneously modify the exercise of all its faculties in relation to moral and spiritual objects. The soul can not love that the loveliness of which it does not perceive, neither can it perceive the loveliness of an object which is totally uncongenial to its own nature. The first effect of regeneration, or a radical change of moral disposition, in the order of nature, therefore, is to open the eyes of our understandings to the excellency of divine truth, and the second effect is the going forth of•the renewed affections toward that excellency so perceived. This is what Pres. Edwards ("Religious Affections," Pt. III., sec. 4) calls "*the sense of the heart.*"

15. *What is the nature of that conviction of sin which is the attendant of regeneration?*

Spiritual illumination immediately leads to the perception of the righteousness, goodness, and exceeding breadth and exactness of God's law, and by contrast of the exceeding sinfulness of sin in the abstract, Rom. vii. 7, 13; and above all of his own sin—thus revealing, in contrast to the divine purity and righteousness, the pollution of his own heart, his total ill-desert, and his entire helplessness in all his relations to God. Job xlii. 5, 6. This is a practical experimental knowledge,— produced by the wrestling ἔλεγχος, of the Holy Ghost (John xvi. 8)—of guilt, of pollution, and of helplessness.

16. *What is the nature of that conviction of sin which often occurs before or without regeneration, and how may it be distinguished from the genuine?*

Natural conscience is an essential and indestructible element of human nature, including a sense of right and wrong, and painful emotions associated with a sense of the latter. Although this faculty may be for a time perverted, and the sensibility associated with it hardened, yet it may be, and often is, in the case of the unregenerate, quickened to a painful activity, leading to a sense of ill-desert, pollution, helplessness, and danger. In eternity this will constitute a large measure of the sufferings of the lost.

On the other hand, that conviction of sin which is peculiar to the regenerate is distinguished by being accompanied by a sense of the positive beauty of holiness, and an earnest desire to escape not merely the pangs of remorse, but chiefly the pollution and the dominion of sin.

17. *What is the nature of those new affections which flow from the renewal of the heart, and how are they distinguished from the exercises of unrenewed men?*

Spiritual illumination gives the perception of that loveliness which the renewed affections of the heart embrace and delight in. These are spiritual because they are formed in us, and preserved in healthy exercise by the Spirit of God. They are holy because their objects are holy, and because they delight in their objects as holy. The affections of unrenewed men, on the other hand, however pure or even religious they may be, are merely natural in their source, and attach merely to natural objects. They may be grateful to God for his benefits, but they never love him simply for the perfections of his own nature.

18. *What is·the nature of that new obedience which results from regeneration, and how does it differ from mere morality?*

The perfect law is spiritual, and consequently requires perfect conformity of being as well as of action; the central and governing principles of life must be in harmony with it. The regenerate man, therefore, thinks, and feels, and wills, and acts in conformity with the spirit of the whole word of God as far as revealed to him, because it is God's word, from a motive of love to God, and with an eye single to his glory. The sanctified affections are the spring, the heart-searching law the rule, and the glory of God the end, and the Holy Ghost the co-worker in every act of Christian obedience.

Morality, on the other hand, has its spring in the merely natural affections; it aims only at the conformity of the outward actions to the letter of the law, while self, in some form of self-righteousness, reputation, safety, or happiness, is the determining end.

19. *How may the absolute necessity of regeneration be proved?*

1st. The Scriptures assert it.—John iii. 3; Rom. viii. 6; Eph. ii. 10; iv. 21–24. 2d. It is proved from the nature of man as a sinner.—Rom. vii. 18; viii. 7–9; 1 Cor. ii. 14; Eph. ii. 1. 3d. From the nature of heaven.—Isa. xxxv. 8; lii. 1; Matt. v. 8; xiii. 41; Heb. xii. 14; Rev. xxi. 27. The restoration of holiness is the grand end of the whole plan of salvation.—Eph. i. 4; v. 5, 26, 27.

20. *Are infants susceptible of regeneration; and, if so, what is the nature of regeneration in them?*

Infants, as well as adults, are rational and moral agents, and by nature totally depraved. The difference is, that the faculties of infants are in the germ, while those of adults are developed. As regeneration is a change wrought by creative power in the inherent moral condition of the soul, infants may plainly be the subjects of it in precisely the same sense as adults; in both cases the operation is miraculous, and therefore inscrutable.

The fact is established by what the Scriptures teach of innate depravity, of infant salvation, of infant circumcision and baptism.—Luke i. 15; xviii. 15, 16; Acts ii. 39. See below, Chapter XLII.

AUTHORITATIVE STATEMENTS.

ROMAN DOCTRINE.—" *Conc. Trent,*" Sess. vi. Ch. 7.—"Justification (Regeneration) is not only a remission of sins, but also a renewal of the inner man through the voluntary reception of the grace and gifts whereby a man born unjust becomes just, and from an enemy becomes a friend, that so he may be an heir according to the hope of eternal life. The causes of this justification are—the *final* cause, the glory of God and of Christ, and eternal life; the *efficient* cause, the merciful God who gratuitously washes and sanctifies, sealing and anointing with the Holy Spirit of promise, who is the earnest of our inheritance; the *meritorious* cause, his own most beloved and only begotten Son, our Lord Jesus Christ, who, when we were enemies, did, on account of the great love wherewith he loved us, merit justification for us by his most holy passion on the wood of the cross; and did for us, make satisfaction to God the Father; also the *instrumental* cause, the sacrament of baptism, which is the sacrament of faith, without which (faith) justification has never come to any one; and finally the *formal* cause, is the righteousness of God, not that whereby he is himself righteous, but that whereby he makes us righteous, namely that with which we, being by him endowed, are renewed in the spirit of our mind, and are not only reputed, but are truly called, and are righteous."

LUTHERAN DOCTRINE.—"*Formula Concordiæ*" (Hase), page 679.— "For conversion is such a change of the man through the operation of the Holy Spirit in the understanding, will, and heart of man, that he is able (*i. e.,* by the operation of the Holy Spirit) to embrace the offered grace. *Ib.* p. 681.—But the understanding and will of the man not as yet renewed are only the subject to be converted, because they are the understanding and will of a man spiritually dead, in whom the Holy Ghost works conversion and renewal; in which work the man to be converted contributes nothing, but is acted upon, until he is regenerated. But afterwards in other good works enduring, he co-operates with the Holy Spirit, doing those things which are well pleasing to God, in that manner which has now been declared by us fully enough in this treatise."

REFORMED DOCTRINE AND REMONSTRANT DOCTRINE.—See under Chapter XXVIII.

CHAPTER XXX.

FAITH.

1. *What, according to its etymology and New Testament usage, is the meaning of the word πίστις, "faith," "belief?"*

It is derived from the verb πείθω, *to persuade, convince.* In the New Testament it is used—1st. To express that state of mind which is induced by persuasion.—Rom. xiv. 22. 2d. It often signifies good faith, fidelity, sincerity.—Rom. iii. 3; Titus ii. 10. 3d. Assent to the truth.—Phil. i. 27; 2 Thes. ii. 13. 4th. Faith towards, on, or in God (ἐπί, εἰς, πρός).—Heb. vi. 1; 1 Thes. i. 8; 1 Pet. i. 21; Mark xi. 22. In Christ, Acts xxiv. 24; Gal. iii. 26; and in his blood, Rom. iii. 22, 25; Gal. ii. 16, 20. 5th. It is used for the object of faith, viz., the revelation of the gospel.—Rom. i. 5; x. 8; 1 Tim. iv. 1. Robinson's "Lex. of New Testament."

2. *State the different meanings of the verb πιστεύειν (to believe), and of the phrases πιστεύειν εἰς, or ἐπί (to believe in or upon).*

πιστεύειν signifies—
1st. To assent to, to be persuaded of the truth.—Luke i. 20; John iii. 12.
2d. To credit the truth of a person.—John v. 46.
3d. To trust, to have confidence in.—Acts xxvii. 25.

The phrases πιστεύειν εἰς, or ἐπί, are always used to express trust and confidence terminating upon God, or upon Christ as Mediator. We are often said to believe or credit Moses or other teachers of the truth, but we can believe in or on God or Christ alone. Upon God, John xiv. 1; Rom. iv. 24; 1 Pet. i. 21; upon Christ.—Acts xvi. 31; John iii. 15–18.

3. *How may faith be defined?*

Faith is a complex act of the soul, involving the concurrent action of the understanding and the will, and modified in different instances of its exercise by the nature of its object, and of the evidence upon which it rests. The most general definition, embracing all its modifications, affirms faith to be "assent to truth upon the exhibition of the appropriate evidence. But it is evident that its nature must vary with the nature of the truth believed, and especially with the nature of the evidence upon which our assent is founded. Assent to a speculative or abstract truth is a speculative act; assent to a moral truth is a moral act; assent to a promise made to ourselves is an act of trust. Our belief that the earth moves round its axis is a mere assent; our belief in the excellence of virtue is of the nature of a moral judgment; our belief in a promise is an act of trust." So likewise with respect to the evidence upon which our faith is founded. "The same man may believe the same truth on different grounds. One may believe the Christian system simply because others around him believe it, and he has been brought up to receive it without question; this is the faith of credulity. Another may believe it on the ground of its external evidence, *e. g.*, of miracle, prophecy, history, its logical consistency as a system, or its plausibility as a theory in accounting for the phenomena of creation and providence. This is speculative faith. Another may believe, because the truths of the Bible recommend themselves to his reason and conscience, and accord with his inward experience. This faith is founded on moral evidence. There is another faith founded on the intrinsic excellence, beauty, and suitableness of the truth from a sense and love of its moral excellence. This is spiritual faith, which is the gift of God."—"Way of Life."

Religious faith is *belief of the truth on the testimony of God.* It includes, (1) *Notitia,* knowledge; (2) *Assensus,* assent; (3) *Fiducia,* trust.

4. *How far is faith an act of the understanding, and how far an act of the will?*

The one indivisible soul knows and loves, desires and decides, and these several acts of the soul meet on the same object. The soul can neither love, desire, nor choose that which it does not know, nor can it know an object as true or good without some affection of will towards it. Assent to a purely speculative truth may be simply an act of understanding, but belief in a moral truth, in testimony, in promises, must be a complex act, embracing both the understanding and the will. The understanding apprehends the truth to be believed, and decides upon the validity of the evidence, but the disposition to believe testimony, or moral evidence, has its foundation in the will. Actual trust in a promise is an act of the will, and not a simple judgment as to its trustworthiness. There is an exact relation between the moral judgment and the affections, and the will, as the seat of the moral affections, determines the moral judgments. Therefore, as a man is responsible for his will, he is responsible for his faith.

As far as faith includes an act of "cognition" it is, of course, purely an act of the understanding. But as far as it includes "Assent" and "Trust," it involves also the spontaneous and active powers of the soul, that is, "the will," and in its higher exercise it often involves deliberate volition itself.

5. *What is the difference between knowledge and faith?*

Generally, knowledge is the apprehension of an object as true, and faith is an assent to its truth. It is obvious, therefore, that in this general sense of the term every exercise of faith includes the knowledge of the object assented to. It is impossible to distinguish between the apprehension of the truthfulness of a purely speculative truth and an assent to it as true. In such a case faith and knowledge appear identical. But while the apprehension of the trustworthiness of a promise is knowledge, the actual reliance upon it is faith. The apprehension of the moral truthfulness of an object is knowledge, the assent to it, as good and desirable, is faith.

Sometimes the Scriptures use the word knowledge as equivalent to faith.—John x. 38; 1 John ii. 3.

Generally, however, the Scriptures restrict the term knowledge to the apprehension of those ideas which we derive through the natural sources of sensation and reason and human testimony, while the term faith is restricted to the assent to those truths which rest upon the direct testimony of God alone, objectively revealed in the Scriptures, as discerned through spiritual illumination. Thus, faith is the "evidence of things not seen." Heb. xi. 1. We are commanded "to walk by faith, and not by sight."—2 Cor. v. 7. Here the distinction between faith and knowledge has reference particularly to the mode of knowing. The one is natural and discursive, the other supernatural and intuitive.

6. *What distinction do the Romanists make between implicit and explicit faith?*

Romanists and Protestants agree that it is not essential to faith that its object should be comprehended by the understanding. But, on the other hand, Protestants affirm, and Romanists deny, that it is essential that the object believed should be apprehended by the mind; that is, that knowledge of what we believe is essential to faith. The Romanists, therefore, have invented the distinction between explicit faith, which terminates upon an object distinctly apprehended by the mind, and implicit faith, which a man exercises in the truth of propositions of which he knows nothing. They hold that if a man exercises explicit faith in a general proposition, he therein exercises implicit faith in every thing embraced in it, whether he knows what they are or not. If a man, for instance, has explicit faith that the church is an infallible teacher, he thereby exercises virtual or implicit faith in every doctrine taught by the church, although he may be ignorant as to what those doctrines are. They distinguish, moreover, between those truths which it is necessary to regard with explicit faith, and those which may be held implicitly. They commonly teach that it is necessary for the people to hold only three doctrines explicitly, 1st, that God is; 2d, that he is a rewarder, including future rewards and punishments; 3d, that he is a redeemer.

"This doctrine has been recently revived by the Puseyites, under the title of reserve. The distinguishing truths of the gospel, instead of being clearly presented, should, it is said, be concealed or kept in reserve. The people may gaze upon the cross as the symbol of redemption, but need not know whether it is the form, or the material, or the great sacrifice once enacted on it, to which the efficacy is due. 'Religious light is intellectual darkness,' says Dr. Newman. This theory rests upon the same false assumption that faith can exist without knowledge."—Dr. Hodge.

7. *What is the difference between knowing and understanding a thing, and how far is knowledge essential to faith?*

We know a thing when we simply apprehend it as true. We understand it only when we fully comprehend its nature, and the perfect consistency of all its properties with each other and with the entire system of things of which it forms a part. We know the doctrine of the trinity when its several parts are stated to us, but no creature can ever understand it.

That knowledge, or simple apprehension of the object believed and confided in, is essential to faith, is evident from the nature of faith itself. It is that state of mind which bears the relation of assent to a certain object, involving that action of understanding and of will which is appropriate to that object. If a man loves, fears, or believes, he must love, fear, or believe some object, for it is evident that these states of mind can exist only in relation to their appropriate objects. If a real object is not present the imagination may present an ideal one, but that very fiction of the imagination must first be apprehended as true (or known) before it can be assented to as true (or believed). Just as it is impossible for a man to enjoy beauty without perceiving it in some object of the mind, or to exercise complacent love in a virtuous act without perceiving it, so it is, for the same reason, impossible for a man to exercise faith without knowing what he believes. " Implicit faith " is a perfectly unmeaning formula.

8. *How can the fact that knowledge is essential to faith be proved from Scripture?*

1st. From the etymology of the word πίστις, from πείθω, to *persuade, instruct.* Faith is that state of mind which is the result of teaching. 2d. From the use of the word knowledge in Scripture as equivalent to faith.—John x. 38; 1 John ii. 3. 3d. From what the Bible teaches as to the source of faith. It comes by teaching.—Rom. x. 14–17. 4th. The Scriptures declare that the regenerate are enlightened, have received the unction, and know all things.—Acts xxvi. 18; 1 Cor. ii. 12–15; Col. iii. 10. 5th. The means of salvation consist in the dissemination of the truth. Christ is the great teacher. Ministers are teachers.—1 Cor. iv. 1; 1 Tim. iii. 2; iv. 13. Christians are begotten by the truth, sanctified by the truth.—John xvii. 19; James i. 18. Dr. Hodge.

9. *How are those passages to be explained which speak of knowledge as distinguished from faith?*

Although every act of faith presupposes an act of knowledge, yet both the faith and the knowledge vary very much, both with the nature of the object known and believed, and with the manner in which the knowledge is received, and with the evidence upon which the faith rests. The faith which the Scriptures distinguish from knowledge is the strong persuasion of things not seen. It is the conviction of the truth of things which do not fall within the compass of our own observation which may entirely transcend the powers of our understanding, and which rest upon the simple testimony of God. This testimony faith relies upon in spite of whatever to human reason appears inconsistent or impossible.

Knowledge though essential to faith may be distinguished from it—1st. As faith includes also an act of the will assenting, in addition to the act of the understanding apprehending. 2d. As knowledge derived through a natural is distinguished from knowledge derived through a divine source. 3d. As present imperfect apprehension of divine things (*i. e.*, faith) differs from that perfect knowledge of divine things we shall have in heaven.—1 Cor. xiii. 12.

10. *If faith necessarily includes knowledge, how can men be commanded to believe?*

1st. No man is ever commanded to believe that which is

not revealed to him, either in the light of nature or by the inspired word. 2d. No man is ever commanded to believe a purely speculative truth. The truths of religion rest on the testimony of God. They are enforced by moral evidence, and faith in them involves a moral and spiritual knowledge of them, and delight in them. Moral evidence can be appreciated only by a mind possessed of moral sensibility. And such moral insensibility as leads to blindness to the distinction between right and wrong is itself a very aggravated state of depravity.

The Scriptures, therefore, luminous with their own self-evidencing light, present the truth to all to whom they come, and demand its instant reception upon the testimony of God. If that evidence is not felt to be conclusive by any one, it must be because of the sinful blindness of his mind. Therefore Christ says, "ye *will* not come unto me that ye may have life." And unbelief is uniformly charged to the "evil heart."

11. *What are the ultimate grounds of that assent to the truth which is of the essence of faith?*

In general, the ultimate ground upon which our assent to the truth of any object of knowledge rests is the veracity of God. The testimony of our senses, the integrity of our consciences, the intuitions of our reasons, all rest upon his veracity as Creator. Practically the mind is moved to this assent through our universal and instinctive confidence in the constitution of our own natures.

Religious faith rests, 1st, upon the faithfulness of God as pledged in his supernatural revelation, John iii. 33; 2d, upon the evidence of spiritual illumination, personal experience of the power of the truth, and the witness of the Holy Ghost, the Sanctifier, and thus "not in the wisdom of man, but in the power of God."—1 Cor. ii. 5–12.

12. *What are the two kinds of evidence by which we know that God has revealed certain truths as objects of faith?*

1st. The evidence which resides in the truth itself. Moral, spiritual, experimental, rational.—John vi. 63; xiv. 17, 26; Jer. xxiii. 29. 2d. The accrediting evidence of the presence and power of God accompanying the promulgation of the truth, and proving that it is from him. These are miracles, providential dispensations, the fulfilment of prophecy, etc.—John v. 36; Heb. ii. 4.

13. *How can it be shown that the authority of the Church is not a ground of faith?*

See above, Chapter V., Question 18.

14. *What is the nature of historical faith, and upon what evidence does it rest?*

That mode of purely rational faith called historical is that apprehension of and assent to the truth which regards it in its purely rational aspects as mere facts of history, or as mere parts of a logical system of opinion. Its appropriate evidence is purely rational, *e. g.*, the solution afforded by the Scriptures of the facts of history and experience, and the evidence of history, prophecy, miracles, etc.

15. *What is the nature of temporary faith, and of the evidence upon which it is founded?*

Temporary faith is that state of mind often experienced in this world by impenitent hearers of the gospel, induced by the moral evidence of the truth, the common influences of the Holy Ghost, and the power of religious sympathy. Sometimes the excited imagination joyfully appropriates the promises of the gospel. — Matt. xiii. 20. Sometimes, like Felix, the man believes and trembles. Oftentimes it is at first impossible to distinguish this state of mind from genuine saving faith. But not springing from a divine work of recreation it has no root in the permanent principles of the heart. It is always, therefore, 1st, inefficient, neither purifying the heart nor overcoming the world; 2d, temporary.

16. *What is the specific evidence upon which saving faith is founded?*

This is the light let into the soul by the Holy Ghost in his work of spiritual illumination. Thus is the beauty, and excellence, and the suitableness of the truth to the practical wants of the subject apprehended. With this the witness of the Holy Ghost with and by the truth co-operates.—1 Cor. ii. 4, 5; Rom. viii. 16; 2 Cor. iv. 6; Eph. ii. 8.

17. *How may it be proved from Scripture and experience that spiritual illumination is the ground of saving faith?*

1st. The Scriptures, wherever they come, make a demand unconditional, immediate, and universal upon the most intelligent and the most ignorant alike, that they should be received and believed, and unbelief is always charged as sin, and not as mere ignorance or mental incapacity. The faith which they demand must, therefore, be a moral act, and must depend upon the spiritual congeniality of the believer with the truth.

2d. By nature men are spiritually blind, and subjects of an "evil heart of unbelief."—2 Cor. iii. 14; iv. 4.

3d. Believers are said to be enlightened, and to discern the things of the Spirit.—Acts xiii. 48; 2 Cor. iv. 6; Eph. i. 17, 18; 1 John ii. 20, 27; v. 9, 10.

4th. Men believe because they are taught of God.—John vi. 44, 45.

5th. Every Christian is conscious of believing, because he sees the truth believed to be true, lovely, powerful, and satisfying.

6th. This is proved by the effects of faith. "We are said to live by faith, to be sanctified by faith, to overcome by faith, to be saved by faith. Blind consent to authority, or rational conviction, produce no such effects; if the effects are spiritual, the source must be also spiritual."

18. *What are the different opinions as to the relation between faith and trust?*

In consequence of their doctrine of implicit faith, that nothing is required beyond blind assent to the teachings of the church, Romanists necessarily deny that trust enters into the essence of saving faith.

The Sandemanians, as the Campbellites, holding that faith is a mere affirmative judgment of the understanding passed upon the truth on the ground of evidence, also deny that trust is an element of saving faith.

Some orthodox theologians have held that trust is rather to be regarded as an immediate and invariable consequent of saving faith, than an element of that faith itself.

Religious faith, resulting from spiritual illumination, respects the entire word of God and his testimony, and, as such, is a complex state of mind, varying with the nature of the particular portion of revealed truth regarded in any particular act. Many of the propositions of Scripture are not the proper objects of trust, and then the faith which embraces them is only a reverent and complacent assent to them as true and good. But the specific act of saving faith which unites to Christ, and is the commencement, root, and organ of our whole spiritual life, terminates upon Christ's person and work as Mediator, as presented in the offers and promises of the gospel. This assuredly includes trust in its very essence, and this is called "saving faith" by way of eminence, since it is the faith that saves, and since only through this as their principle, are any other more general exercises of saving faith possible.

19. *How may the fact that saving faith includes trust be proved from the language of Scripture?*

The uniform and single condition of salvation presented in

the Scriptures is expressed in the words believe *in* or *on* Christ, εἰς or ἐπί τὸν χριστόν.—John vii. 38; Acts ix. 42; xvi. 31; Gal. ii. 16. To believe in or on a person necessarily implies trust as well as credit.

The same is abundantly proved by the usage with respect to the phrases "by faith *in* or *on* Christ."—2 Tim. iii. 15; Acts xxvi. 18; Gal. iii. 26; Heb. xi. 1. Faith is the substance of things hoped for, but the foundation of hope is trust.

20. *How may the same be proved from those expressions which are used in Scripture as equivalent to the phrase "believing in Christ"?*

"Receiving Christ."—John i. 12; Col. ii. 6. "Looking to Christ."—Is. xlv. 22; compare Num. xxi. 9 with John iii. 14, 15. "Flying to Christ for refuge."—Heb. vi. 18. "Coming to Christ."—John vi. 35; Matt. xi. 28. "Committing."—2 Tim. i. 12. All these illustrate as well as designate the act of saving faith, and all equally imply trust as an essential element, for we can "receive," or "come to," or "look to," Christ only in that character of a propitiation, an advocate and a deliverer, in which he offers himself to us.

21. *How may the same be proved from the effects which the Scriptures ascribe to faith?*

The Scriptures declare that by faith the Christian "embraces the promises," "is persuaded of the promises," "out of weakness is made strong," "waxes valiant in fight," "confesses himself a stranger and pilgrim seeking a better country." As faith in a threatening necessarily involves fear, so faith in a promise necessarily involves trust.

Besides, faith rests upon the trustworthiness of God, and therefore necessarily involves trust.—Heb. x. 23, and the whole of the 11th chapter.

22. *How may it be shown that this view of faith does not confound faith and hope?*

To our doctrine that saving faith involves trust, the Romanist objects that this confounds faith and hope, which the Scriptures distinguish (1 Cor. xiii. 13), since hope is only strong trust. But hope is not merely strong trust. Trust rests upon the *grounds* of assurance, while hope reaches forward to the *object* of which assurance is given. Trust is the foundation of hope. Hope is the fruit of trust. The more confiding the trust, the more assured the hope.

23. *What are the different opinions as to the relation between faith and love, and the Romish distinction between* "fides informis" *and* "fides formata"?

1st. The Romanists, in order to maintain their doctrine that faith alone is not saving, distinguish between a formed, or perfect, and an unformed faith. They acknowledge that faith is distinct from love, but maintain that love is essential to render faith meritorious and effectual as the instrument of our salvation. *Fides informis* is mere assent, explicit or implicit, to the teachings of the Church. It necessarily precedes "justificatio" as its condition. *Fides formata* is the fruit of the first justification, and the condition of those good works which merit further grace.

2d. Some have regarded love as the root out of which faith springs.

3d. The true view is that love is the immediate and necessary effect of faith. Faith includes the spiritual apprehension of the beauty and excellence of the truth, and an act of the will embracing it and relying upon it. Yet these graces can not be analytically separated, since they mutually involve one another. There can be no love without faith, nor any faith without love. Faith apprehends the loveliness of the object, the heart spontaneously loves it. Thus "faith works by love," since these affections are the source of those motives that control the will.

The Romish doctrine is inconsistent with the essential principles of the gospel. Faith is not a work, nor can it have, when formed or unformed, any merit; it is essentially a self-emptying act, which saves by laying hold of the merits of Christ. It leads to works, and proves itself by its fruits, but in its relation to justification it is in its very nature a strong protest against the merits of all human works.—Gal. iii. 10, 11; Eph. ii. 8, 9.

The Protestant doctrine that love is the fruit of faith, is established by what the Scriptures declare concerning faith, that it "sanctifies," "works by love," " overcomes the world." Gal. v. 6; Acts xxvi. 18; 1 John v. 4. This is accomplished thus—by faith we are united to Christ, Eph. iii. 17, and so become partakers of his Spirit, 1 John iii. 24, one of the fruits of the Spirit is love, Gal. v. 22, and love is the principle of all obedience.—Rom. xiii. 10.

24. *What is the object of saving faith?*

The spiritual illumination of the understanding and renewal of the affections, which lays the foundation for the soul's acting faith in any one portion of the testimony of God, lays the foundation for its acting faith in all that testimony. The whole revealed word of God, then, as far as known to the individual, to the exclusion of all traditions, doctrines of men, and pretended private revelations, is the object of saving faith. That particular act of faith, however, which unites to Christ, called, by way of distinction, justifying faith, has for its object the person and work of Christ as Mediator.—John vii. 38; Acts xvi. 31.

25. *What is meant by an article of faith as distinguished from a matter of opinion?*

The Romanists hold that every dogma decided by the church to be true, whether derived from Scripture or tradition, is, upon pain of damnation, to be believed by every Christian as an article of faith, if known to him by an explicit, if not known by an implicit faith. On the other hand, with respect to all subjects not decided by the church, every man is left free to believe or not as a matter of opinion.

26. *What is the Anglican or Puseyite criterion for distinguishing those doctrines which must be known and believed in order to salvation?*

They agree with the Romanists (see above, Question 6) that knowledge is not essential to faith. As to the rule of faith, however, they differ. The Romanist makes that rule the teaching of the Papal Church. The Puseyites, on the other hand, make it the uniform testimony of tradition running in the line of the succession of apostolic bishops.

27. *What is the common Protestant doctrine as to fundamentals in religion, and by what evidence can such fundamentals be ascertained?*

Every doctrine taught in the Bible is the object of an enlightened spiritual faith. No revealed principle, however comparatively subordinate, can be regarded as indifferent, to be adopted or rejected at will. Every man is bound to credit the whole testimony of God. Yet the gospel is a logically consistent system of truth, some of whose principles are essential to its integrity, while others are essential only to its symmetry and perfection; and ignorance, feebleness of logical comprehension, and prejudice may, and constantly do, lead good men to apprehend this system of truth imperfectly.

A fundamental doctrine, then, is either one which every soul must apprehend more or less clearly in order to be saved, or one which, when known, is so clearly involved with those the knowledge and belief of which is essential to salvation, that the one can not be rejected while the other is really believed.

A fundamental doctrine is ascertained—1st. In the same way that the essential principles of any other system are determined, by their bearing upon the system as a whole.

2d. Every fundamental doctrine is clearly revealed.

3d. These doctrines are in Scripture itself declared to be essential.—John iii. 18; Acts xvi. 31; 2 Cor. v. 17; Gal. ii. 21; 1 John i. 8.

28. *What is the object of* "fides specialis," *or that specific act of faith whereby we are justified?*

The person and work of the Lord Jesus Christ as Mediator. This is proved—

1st. The Scriptures expressly declare that we are justified by that faith of which Christ is the object.—Rom. iii. 22, 25; Gal. ii. 16; Phil. iii. 9.

2d. We are said to be saved by faith in Christ.—John iii. 16, 36; Acts x. 43; xvi. 31.

3d. Justifying faith is designated as a "looking to Christ," a "coming to Christ," etc.—John i. 12; vi. 35, 37; Isa. xlv. 22.

4th. Rejection of Christ; a refusal to submit to the righteousness of God is declared to be the ground of reprobation. John viii. 24; iii. 18, 19.

29. *How is the Romish doctrine on this point opposed to the Protestant?*

The Romanists, confounding justification and sanctification, hold that faith justifies through the sanctifying power of the truth. As all revealed truth has this sanctifying virtue, it follows that the whole revelation of God as ascertained by the decisions of the church, is the object of justifying faith. This is refuted by all we have established from Scripture concerning justification, sanctification, and faith.

30. *Is Christ in all his offices, or only as priest, the immediate object of justifying faith?*

In this act the believer appropriates and rests upon Christ as Mediator, which includes at once all his functions as such. These may be analytically distinguished, but in fact they are always inseparably united in him. When he acts as prophet he teaches as king and priest. When he reigns he sits as prophet and priest upon his throne. Besides this, his prophetical and kingly work are consciously needed by the awakened soul, and are necessarily apprehended as inseparable from his priestly work in the one act of faith.

It is true, however, that as the substitutionary work which Christ accomplished as priest is the meritorious ground of our salvation, so his priestly character is made the more prominent, both in the teachings of Scripture and in the experience of his people.

31. *How far is peace of conscience and peace with God a necessary consequence of faith?*

Peace with God is reconciliation with him.   Peace of conscience may either mean consciousness of that reconciliation, or the appeasement of our own consciences which condemn us. Faith in every instance secures our peace with God, since it unites us to Christ, Rom. v. 1; and in the proportion in which faith in the merits of Christ is clear and constant will be our consciousness of reconciliation with God, and the satisfaction of our own moral sense that righteousness is fulfilled, while we are forgiven.   Yet as faith may be obscured by sin, so the true believer may temporarily fall under his Father's displeasure, and lose his sense of forgiveness and his moral satisfaction in the perfection of the atonement.

32. *What are the three views entertained as to the relation between faith and assurance?*

1st. The Reformers generally maintained that justifying faith consisted in appropriating the promise of salvation through Christ made in the gospel, *i. e.*, in regarding God as propitious to us for Christ's sake.   Thus the very act of faith involves assurance.

2d. Some have held that assurance in this life is unattainable.   The Romanists, holding that Christian faith is chiefly implicit assent and obedient conformity to the teachings of an infallible, visible society, called the Church, strenuously denied that private individuals have any Scriptural authority to entertain an assured persuasion that they are specially objects of divine favor.   They were accustomed to assert that it is neither "obligatory," nor "possible," nor "desirable" that any one should attain such assurance without a special supernatural revelation. See Bellarmin, etc., quoted below.

3d. The true view is that "although this infallible assurance does not belong to the essence of faith, but that a true believer may wait long and conflict with many difficulties before he partake of it, yet being enabled by the Spirit to know the things which are freely given him by God, he may, without extraordinary revelation, in the right use of ordinary means attain thereunto.   And, therefore, it is the duty of each one to give diligence to make his calling and election sure."   It is agreed by all that a true faith can not admit of any doubt as to its object. What is believed is assuredly believed. But the object of saving faith is Christ and his work as Mediator guaranteed to us in the promises of the gospel on the condition of faith. True faith does, therefore, essentially include the assurance—1st. That Christ is able to save us. 2d. That he is faithful and will save us if *we believe.* It is meant that this is of the essence of faith, not that every true believer always enjoys a state of mind which excludes all doubt as to Christ's power or love; because the spiritual illumination upon which faith rests is often imperfect in degree and variable in exercise. Faith may be weak, or it may be limited by doubt, or it may alternate with doubt. Yet all such doubt is of sin, and is alien to the essential nature of faith. But the condition, *if we believe*, upon which all assurance of our own salvation is suspended, is a matter not of revelation, but of experience, not of faith, but of consciousness.

Theologians have, therefore, made a distinction between the assurance of faith, Heb. x. 22, and the assurance of hope, Heb. vi. 11. The first is of the essence of saving faith, and is the assurance that Christ is all that he professes to be, and will do all that he promises. The second is the assurance of our own personal salvation, is a fruit of faith, and one of the higher attainments of the Christian life.

33. *How may it be proved that assurance of our own personal salvation is not essential to saving faith?*

1st. From the true object of saving faith as given above. 2d. From the examples given in the Scriptures of eminent saints who doubted with regard to themselves.—1 Cor. ix. 27. 3d. from the exhortations addressed to those who were already believers to attain to assurance as a degree of faith beyond that which they already enjoyed. 4th. From the experience of God's people in all ages.

34. *How may it be proved that assurance is attainable in this life?*

1st. This is directly asserted.—Rom. viii. 16; 2 Pet. i. 10; 1 John ii. 3; iii. 14; v. 13. 2d. Scriptural examples are given of its attainment.—2 Tim. i. 12; iv. 7, 8. 3d. Many eminent Christians have enjoyed an abiding assurance, of the genuineness of which their holy walk and conversation was an indubitable seal.

35. *On what grounds may a man be assured of his salvation?*

"It is an infallible assurance of faith, founded, 1st, upon the divine truth of the promises of salvation; 2d, the inward evidence of those graces unto which those promises are made, and, 3d, the testimony of the spirit of adoption, Rom. viii. 15, 16, witnessing with our spirits that we are the children of God. Which Spirit, Eph. i. 13, 14; 2 Cor. i. 21, 22, is the earnest of our inheritance whereby we are sealed to the day of redemption."—"Con. of Faith," Chap. xviii.

This genuine assurance may be distinguished from that presumptuous confidence which is a delusion of Satan, chiefly by these marks. True assurance, 1st, begets unfeigned humility, 1 Cor. xv. 10; Gal. vi. 14; 2d, leads to ever-increasing diligence in practical religion, Ps. li. 12, 13, 19; 3d, to candid self-examination, and a desire to be searched and corrected by God, Ps. cxxxix. 23, 24; 4th, to constant aspirations after nearer conformity, and more intimate communion with God.—1 John iii. 2, 3.

36. *How may it be shown that a living faith necessarily leads to good works?*

1st. From the nature of faith. It is the spiritual apprehension and the voluntary embrace of the whole truth of God,—the promises, the commands, the threatenings of the Scripture,—viewed as true and as good. This faith occasions, of course, the exercise of the renewed affections, and love acted out is obedience. Each separate truth thus apprehended produces its appropriate effect upon the heart, and consequently upon the life.

2d. The testimony of Scripture.—Acts xv. 9; xxvi. 18; Gal. v. 6; James ii. 18; 1 John v. 4.

3d. The experience of the universal church.

AUTHORITATIVE STATEMENTS.

St. Augustine.—"Quid est fides nisi credere quod non vides?"

ROMISH DOCTRINE.—"*Cat. Counc. Trent*," i. 1.—1. "We here speak of that faith, by force of which we yield our entire assent to whatsoever has been divinely delivered, ... by virtue of which we hold that as fixed whatsoever the authority of our holy mother the church teaches us to have been delivered from God."

Bellarmin, "Justif.," 1, 4.—"(Catholics) teach that historic faith, both of miracles and of promises, is one and the same thing, and that this one thing is not properly a knowledge or assurance, but a certain and most fixed assent, on the authority of the ultimate verity. . . . The object of justifying faith, which heretics restrict to the single object of special (personal) mercy, Catholics wish to extend as broadly as the word of God extends; nay, they contend that the promise of special mercy belongs not so much to faith as to presumption. Hence they differ (from Protestants) as to the faculty and power of mind which is the seat of faith. Inasmuch as they (Protestants) locate faith in the will, they define it to be assurance (*fiducia*) (or trust), and so confound it with hope, for trust (or assurance) is nothing more than strong hope, as holy Thomas teaches. Catholics teach that faith has its seat in the intellect. Lastly (they differ) as to the act itself of the intellect (in which faith consists). They (Protestants), indeed, define faith as a form of knowledge; we (Catholics) as assent. For we assent to God, although he proposes things to us to be believed which we do not understand. Ch. 7.—In him, who believes, there are two things, apprehension, and judgment or assent. But apprehension is not faith, but something that precedes faith. Besides apprehension is not properly called knowledge. For it may happen that an unlearned Catholic may only very confusedly apprehend the three names (of the Trinity), and nevertheless may truly believe in them. But judgment or assent is twofold, the one follows reason and the evidence of a thing, the other follows the authority of the propounder; the first is called knowledge, the latter faith. Therefore the mysteries of faith, which transcend the reason, we believe but do not understand, so that·faith is distinguished as opposite to science, and is better defined as ignorance than as knowledge."

"*Cans. Counc. Trent,*" Sess. 6, ch. 9.—"For even as no pious person ought to doubt of the mercy of God, of the merits of Christ, and of the virtue and efficacy of the sacraments, even so each one, when he regards himself and his own weakness and indisposition, may have fear and apprehension touching his own grace; seeing that no one can know with a certainty of faith, which can not be subject to error, that he has obtained the grace of God."

Bellarmin, "*Justif.,*" 3, 3, says, "The question in debate between Romanists and the Reformed was, Whether any one should or could, without a special revelation, be certain with the certainty of a divine faith, to which error can in no way pertain, that his sins are remitted?"

THE PROTESTANT DOCTRINE OF FAITH AND ASSURANCE.

Calvin's "*Institutes,*" B. 3, ch. 2, § 7.—"We shall have a complete definition of faith, if we say that it is a steady and certain knowledge of the divine benevolence towards us, which, being founded on the truth of the gratuitous promise in Christ, is both revealed to our minds and confirmed to our hearts by the Holy Spirit."

"*Heidelberg Cat.,*" Ques. 21.—"What is true faith? It is not a mere knowledge, by which I firmly assent to all that God has revealed to us in his word, but it is also an assured confidence kindled in my heart by the Holy Ghost through the gospel, whereby I acquiesce in God, certainly knowing, that not to others only, but to me also, remission of sins, eternal righteousness and life, is given gratuitously, of the mercy of God, on account of the merit of Christ alone."

"*Apol. Augb. Conf.,*" p. 68.—"But that faith which justifies is not merely a knowledge of history; but it is assent to the promise of God in which is freely, for Christ's sake, offered the remission of sins and justification. . . . This special faith, therefore, whereby each one believes that his own sins are remitted to him for Christ's sake, and that God is reconciled and propitious through Christ, (is the faith that) attains remission of sins, and (that) justifies."

"*West. Conf. Faith,*" ch. 18, § 2.—"This certainly is not a bare conjectural and probable persuasion, grounded upon a fallible hope, but an infallible assurance of faith, founded on (*a*) the divine truth of the promises, (*b*) the inward evidence of those graces to which the promises are made, and (*c*) the testimony of the Holy Spirit . . . . § 3.—This infallible assurance doth not so belong to the essence of faith, but that a true believer may wait long and conflict with many difficulties before he partake thereof. . . Yet he may, without extraordinary revelation, in the right use of ordinary means attain thereto. And, therefore, it is the duty of every one to give all diligence to make his calling and election sure."

Turretin, L. 15, Q. 10.—"The diversity (of expression) which occurs between the orthodox has arisen from a different usage of the word *fiducia* (confidence), which may be taken in three senses : 1. For *confident assent*, or persuasion, which arises from the practical judgment of the understanding, concerning the truth and goodness of the evangelical promises, and concerning the power, willingness, and faithfulness of God promising. In which sense $\pi\varepsilon\iota\delta\mu o\nu\dot{\eta}$ (persuasion), Gal. v. 8, is used synonymously with it, and $\pi\lambda\eta\rho o\varphi o\rho\iota\alpha$ (full assurance) is attributed to faith, Col. ii. 2, and Heb. x. 22. 2. For *the act of fleeing to, and of receiving Christ,* by which the believer, the truth and goodness of the promises being known, flees to Christ, receives and embraces him, and reclines alone on his merits. 3. For *confidence, satisfaction, and tranquillity of mind,* which arise from the refuge of the mind to Christ and reception of him. For he who firmly reclines on Christ and embraces him, can not fail to acquiesce in him securely, and to consider himself to have found and to have received that which he sought. In the *first* and *second* sense *confidence (fiducia)* is of the essence of faith, is rightly said by theologians to be its *form;* because, as afterwards proved against the Papists, it is a confidential (trusting) apprehension of Christ and of all the benefits offered in the word of the gospel. But in the *third* sense it is by others rightly said not to be the *form,* but the *fruit,* of faith; because it is born from it, but does not constitute it.

CHAPTER XXXI.

UNION OF BELIEVERS WITH CHRIST.

1. *To whom are all men united in their natural estate?*

To Adam. Our union with him includes, 1st, his federal headship under the covenant of works.—Rom. v. 12–19. 2d. His natural headship, as per force of ordinary generation, the source of our nature, and of its moral corruptions.—Gen. v. 3; 1 Cor. xv. 49.

But the law upon which rested the covenant of works, whereby we were held in union with Adam, having been slain by Christ, "that being dead wherein we were held," we were "married to another," that is, to Christ.—Rom. vii. 1–4.

2. *What is the general nature of our union with Christ?*

It is a single, ineffable, and most intimate union, presenting to our view two different aspects, and giving rise to two different classes of consequents.

1st. The first aspect of this union is its federal and representative character, whereby Christ, as the second Adam (1 Cor. xv. 22), assumes in the covenant of grace those broken obligations of the covenant of works which the first Adam failed to discharge, and fulfils them all in behalf of all his "sheep," "they whom the Father has given him." The consequences which arise from our union with Christ under this aspect of it are such as the imputation of our sins to him, and of his righteousness to us, and all of the forensic benefits of justification and adoption, etc.—See Chaps. XXXIII., XXXIV.

2d. The second aspect of this union is its spiritual and vital character, the nature and consequences of which it is our business to discuss under the present head.

3. *What is the foundation of this union?*

(1.) The eternal purpose of the triune God, expressed in the decree of election (we were chosen *in him* before the foundation of the world.—Eph. i. 4), providing for its own fulfilment in the covenant of grace between the Father as God absolute, and the Son as Mediator.—John xvii. 2–6; Gal. ii. 20; (2) in the incarnation of the Son, whereby he assumed fellowship with us in community of nature, and became our brother.—Heb. ii. 16, 17; and (3) in the mission and official work of the Spirit of Christ (1 John iv. 13), through the powerful operation of whom in the bodies and souls of his people the last Adam is made a quickening spirit (1 Cor. xv. 45), and they are all constituted the body of Christ and members in particular. 1 Cor. xii. 27.

4. *By what analogies drawn from earthly relations is this union of believers with Christ illustrated in Scripture?*

The technical designation of this union in theological language is "mystical," because it so far transcends all the analogies of earthly relationships, in the intimacy of its communion, in the transforming power of its influence, and in the excellence of its consequences. Yet Holy Scripture illustrates different aspects of this fountain of graces by many apt though partial analogies.

As, 1st, foundation of a building and its superstructure.—1 Pet. ii. 4, 6. 2d. Tree and its branches.—John xv. 5. 3d. Head and members of the body.—Eph. iv. 15, 16. 4th. Husband and wife.—Eph. v. 31, 32; Rev. xix. 7–9. 5th. Adam and his descendants, in both their federal and natural relations.—Rom. v. 12–19; 1 Cor. xv. 22, 49.

5. *What is the essential nature of this union?*

On the one hand, this union does not involve any mysterious confusion of the person of Christ with the persons of his people; and, on the other hand, it is not such a mere association of separate persons as exists in human societies. But it is a union which, 1st, determines our legal status on the same basis with his. 2d. Which revives and sustains, by the influence of his indwelling Spirit, our spiritual life, from the fountain of his life, and which transforms our bodies and souls into the likeness of his glorified humanity.

It is, therefore—

1st. A spiritual union. Its actuating source and bond is the Spirit of the head, who dwells and works in the members. 1 Cor. vi. 17; xii. 13; 1 John iii. 24; iv. 13.

2d. A vital union, *i. e.*, our spiritual life is sustained and determined in its nature and movement by the life of Christ, through the indwelling of his Spirit.—John xiv. 19; Gal. ii. 20.

3d. It embraces our entire persons, our bodies through our spirits.—1 Cor. vi. 15, 19.

4th. It is a legal or federal union, so that all of our legal or covenant responsibilities rest upon Christ, and all of his legal or covenant merits accrue to us.

5th. It is an indissoluble union.—John x. 28; Rom. viii. 35, 37; 1 Thess. iv. 14, 17.

6th. This union is between the believer and the person of the God-man in his office as Mediator. Its immediate organ is the Holy Spirit, who dwells in us, and through him we are virtually united to and commune with the whole Godhead, since he is the Spirit of the Father as well as of the Son.—John xiv. 23; xvii. 21, 23.

6. *How is this union between Christ and the Christian established?*

It was established in the purpose and decree of God, and in the Covenant of the Father with the Son from eternity.—Eph. i. 4; John xvii. 2, 6. Nevertheless, the elect, as to personal character and present relations, before their effectual calling by the Spirit, are born and continued "by nature children of wrath even as others," and "strangers to the covenants of promise." Eph. ii. 3, 12. In God's appointed time, with each individual of his chosen, this union is established mutually—1st. By the commencement of the effectual and permanent workings of the Holy Spirit within them (they are quickened together with Christ); in the act of the new birth opening the eyes and renewing the will, and thus laying in their natures the foundation of the exercise of saving faith. 2d. Which faith is the second bond by which this mutual union is established, by the continued actings of which their fellowship with Christ is sustained, and its blessed consequences developed.—Eph. iii. 17. Thus we "come to him," "receive him," "eat of his flesh and drink of his blood," etc.

7. *What are the consequences of this union to the believer?*

1st. They have a community with him in his covenant standing, and rights. Forensically they are rendered "complete in him." His righteousness and his Father is theirs. They receive the adoption in him, and are accepted as to both their persons and services in the beloved. They are sealed by his Holy Spirit of promise; in him obtain an inheritance; sit with him on his throne and behold his glory.—Rom. viii. 1; Col. ii. 10; Eph. i. 6, 11, 13; Phil. iii. 8, 9.

As Mediator, Jesus is "the Christ," the anointed one, and the believer is the Christian, or receiver of "the unction."—Acts

xi. 26; 1 John ii. 20. His mediatorial office embraces three principal functions—(1.) That of prophet, and in fellowship with him the believer is a prophet.—John xvi. 13; 1 John ii. 27. (2.) That of priest, and the believer also is a priest in him. Isa. lxi. 6; 1 Pet. ii. 5; Rev. xx. 6. (3.) That of king, and in him the believer is a king.—1 Pet. ii. 9; Rev. iii. 21; v. 10.

2d. They have fellowship with him in the transforming, assimilating power of his life, making them like him; every grace of Jesus reproducing itself in them; "of his fulness we have all received, and grace for grace." This holds true, (1) with regard to our souls, Rom. viii. 9; Phil. ii. 5; 1 John iii. 2; (2) with regard to our bodies, causing them to be *now* the temples of the Holy Ghost, 1 Cor. vi. 17, 19; and his resurrection to be the cause of ours, and his glorified body to be the type of ours.—Rom. vi. 5; 1 Cor. xv. 47, 49; Phil. iii. 21. And thus believers are made to bear fruit in Christ, both in their bodies and spirits, which are his.—John xv. 5; 2 Cor. xii. 9; 1 John i. 6.

3d. This leads to their fellowship with Christ in their experience, in their labors, sufferings, temptations, and death.—Gal. vi. 17; Phil. iii. 10; Heb. xii. 3; 1 Pet. iv. 13. Thus rendering sacred and glorious even our earthly life.

4th. Also to Christ's rightful fellowship with them in all they possess.—Prov. xix. 17; Rom. xiv. 8; 1 Cor. vi. 19, 20.

5th. Also to the consequence that, in the spiritual reception of the holy sacraments, they do really hold fellowship with him. They are "baptized into Christ."—Gal. iii. 27. "The bread which we break, is it not the communion of the body of Christ; the cup of blessing which we bless, is it not the communion of the blood of Christ."—1 Cor. x. 16; xi. 26; John vi. 51–56.

6th. This leads also to the fellowship of believers with one another through him, that is, to the communion of saints.

8. *What is the nature of that "communion of saints" which springs from the union of each saint with the Lord?*

See "Confession of Faith," Chapter xxvi. Believers being all united to one head are, of course, through him mutually related in the same community of·spirit, life, status, and covenanted privileges with one another.

This involves upon the part of all believers—

1st. Reciprocal obligations and offices according to the special grace vouchsafed to each. Like the several organs of the body all have part in the same general life, yet each has his own individual difference of qualification, and consequently of

duty; "for the body is not one member but many."—1 Cor. xii.
4–21; Eph. iv. 11–13.

2d. They have fellowship in each other's gifts and complementary graces, each contributing his special loveliness to the
beauty of the whole.—Eph. iv. 15, 16.

3d. These reciprocal duties have respect to the bodies and
temporal interests of the brethren, as well as to those which
concern the soul.—Gal. ii. 10; 1 John iii. 16–18.

4th. They have fellowship in faith and doctrine.—Acts ii. 42;
Gal. ii. 9.

5th. In mutual respect and subordination.—Rom. xii. 10;
Eph. v. 21; Heb. xiii. 17.

6th. In mutual love and sympathy.—Rom. xii. 10; 1 Cor.
xii. 26.

7th. This fellowship exists unbroken between believers on
earth and in heaven. There is one "whole family in heaven
and on earth."—Eph. iii. 15.

8th. In glory this communion of saints shall be perfected,
when there is "one fold and one shepherd," when all saints
shall be one as Father and Son are one.—John x. 16; xvii. 22.

CHAPTER XXXII.

1. *What are the words used in the original to express this change of mind and feeling?*

1st. μεταμέλεσθαι, from μέλομαι, to care for; combined with μετα, to change one's care. This is used only five times in the New Testament.

2d. μετανοεῖν, from νοέω, to perceive, understand, consider; combined with μετά, to change one's mind or purpose. This is the verb constantly used in, the New Testament to designate this change.

3d. From the same source comes the noun μετάνοια, repentance, change of mind or purpose. In the New Testament usage of these words the idea of sorrow and contrition is included.

2. *What is saving repentance?*

See "Con. Faith," Chap. xv.; "Larger Cat.," Q. 76; "Shorter Cat.," Q. 87.

It includes—1st. A sense of personal guilt, pollution, and helplessness. 2d. An apprehension of the mercy of God in Christ. 3d. Grief and hatred of sin, a resolute turning from it unto God, and a persistent endeavor after a new life of holy obedience.

3. *Prove that repentance is a grace or gift of God.*

1st. This is evident from the nature of repentance itself. It includes, (1) sense of the hatefulness of sin, (2) sense of the beauty of holiness, (3) apprehension of the mercy of God in Christ. It, therefore, presupposes faith, which is God's gift. Gal. v. 22; Eph. ii. 8.

2d. The Scriptures expressly affirm it.—Zech. xii. 10; Acts v. 31; xi. 18; 2 Tim. ii. 25.

4. *What is the nature of that sense of sin which is an essential element of repentance?*

That spiritual illumination and renewal of the affections

which is effected in regeneration, brings the believer to see and appreciate the holiness of God as revealed alike in the law and the gospel, Rom. iii. 20; Job xlii. 6, and in that light to see and feel also the exceeding sinfulness of all sin, and the utter sinfulness of his own nature just as it is in truth. This sense of sin, thus corresponding to the facts of the case, includes, 1st, consciousness of guilt, *i. e.*, exposure to righteous punishment, as opposed to the justice of God.—Ps. li. 4, 9.   2d. Consciousness of pollution as opposed to the holiness of God, Ps. li. 5, 7, 10; and, 3d, consciousness of helplessness.—Ps. li. 11; cix. 22.   See "Way of Life."

5. *What are the fruits and evidences of this sense of sin?*

A sense of guilt, especially when coupled with a sense of helplessness, will naturally excite apprehension of danger. This painful feeling is experienced in infinitely various degrees and modifications, as determined by natural temperament, education, and the special dealings of the Holy Spirit. These legal fears, however, are common both to false and to true repentance, and possess no sanctifying influence.

A sense of pollution leads to shame when we think of God, and to self-loathing when we think of ourselves.

Confession of sin, both in private to God and before men, is a natural and indispensable mode in which this sense of sin will give genuine expression to itself.—Ps. xxxii. 5, 6; Prov. xxviii. 13; James v. 16; 1 John i. 9.

The only indubitable test of the genuineness of such a sense of sin, however, is an earnest and abiding desire and endeavor to be delivered from it.

6. *Show that an apprehension of the mercy of God in Christ is essential to repentance.*

1st. The awakened conscience echoes God's law, and can be appeased by no less a propitiation than that demanded by divine justice itself, and until this is realized in a believing application to Christ, either indifference must stupefy, or remorse must torment the soul.

2d. Out of Christ God is a consuming fire, and an inextinguishable dread drives the soul away.—Deut. iv. 24; Heb. xii. 29.

3d. A sense of the amazing goodness of God to us in the gift of his Son, and of our ungrateful requital of it, is necessary to excite in the repentant soul the proper shame and sorrow for sin as committed against God.—Ps. li. 4.

4th. This is proved by the teachings and examples furnished in Scripture.—Ps. li. 1; cxxx. 4.

7. *What is the nature of that "turning unto God" which constitutes the essence of genuine repentance?*

It is a voluntary forsaking of sin as evil and hateful, with sincere sorrow, humiliation, and confession; and a returning unto God, because he has a right to us, and because he is merciful and willing to forgive, together with a determination to live, by the help of his grace, in obedience to his commandments.

8. *What are the evidences of genuine repentance?*

1st. The agreement of our own internal experience with the teachings of the word of God on this subject. This is to be determined by the prayerful study of the Scriptures in connection with self-examination. 2d. The permanent effects realized in the life. These are the hatred and forsaking of secret as well as of open sins, the choice of God's service as both right and desirable, public confession, and entire practical consecration. "These things must be in us and abound."—2 Cor. vii. 11.

9. *What are the relations which the ideas represented by the terms "faith," "repentance," "regeneration" and "conversion" mutually sustain to one another?*

Regeneration is the ineffable act of God implanting a new nature. The term conversion is used generally to express the first exercises of that new nature in ceasing from the old life and commencing the new. Faith designates the primary act of the new nature, and also that permanent state or habit of mind which continues the essential condition of all other graces. It is the spiritual apprehension of the truth by the mind, and the loyal embrace of the truth by the will, without which there can be neither love, hope, peace, joy, nor repentance. The common sense attached to the word *repentance* is very similar to that attached to the word *conversion*, but it differs from it as to its usage in two particulars—1st. Conversion is the more general term, and is used to include the first exercises of faith, as well as all those experiences of love, of holiness, and hatred of sin, etc., which are consequent upon it. Repentance is more specific, and expresses that hatred and renunciation of sin, and that turning unto God, which accompanies faith as its consequent. 2d. Conversion is generally used to designate only the *first* actings of the new nature at the commencement of a religious life, or at most the first steps of a return to God after a notable backsliding.—Luke xxii. 32. While repentance is applied to that constant bearing of the cross which is one main characteristic of the believer's life on earth.—Ps. xix. 12, 13; Luke ix. 23; Gal. vi. 14; v. 24.

10. *What doctrine concerning repentance was taught by many of the Reformers?*

Some of them defined repentance as consisting, 1st, of mortification, or dying unto sin; and, 2d, of vivification, or living unto God. This corresponds to our view of sanctification. The Lutherans make repentance to consist in, 1st, contrition, or sorrow for sin; and, 2d, in faith in the gospel, or absolution.— "Augsburg Conf.," Art 12. This, although a peculiar phraseology, is the true view.

11. *What is the Romish doctrine of Penance?*

In their scheme of salvation the true analogy to the Protestant doctrine of justification is not to be found in the Romish doctrine of justification (so called), but in their doctrine of penance. By justification Protestants understand a change of relation to the divine law, from condemnation to favor with our Judge and King, on the ground of the satisfaction rendered by Christ. By "justification" Romanists mean "not remission of sin merely, but also the sanctification and renewal of the inward man, through the voluntary reception of the grace and of the gifts whereby man of unjust becomes just, and of an enemy a friend." "For although no one can be just, but he to whom the merits of the passion of Christ, of our Lord Jesus Christ, are communicated, yet is this done in the said justification of the impious, when by the merit of that same most holy passion, the charity of God is poured forth by the Holy Spirit in the hearts of those that are justified, and is inherent therein." "*Conc. Trent*," Sess. 6, ch. 7. This is effected by baptism, and in all its stages presupposes the satisfaction and merit of Christ. His satisfaction atones for all sins committed before baptism, and for the eternal punishment of all sins of the baptized. His merits secure prevenient grace, baptismal regeneration, and are the basis on which the gracious obedience and the temporal sufferings of the believer merit forgiveness of sins and continuance, restoration, and increase of grace, and the rewards of heaven.

Having been thus justified and made friends of God, they advance from virtue to virtue, and are renewed from day to day through the observance of the commandments of God and of the Church, which good works truly merit and receive, as a just reward, increase of grace and more and more perfect justification (sanctification). The Christian man's *first* justification, effected in baptism, was for Christ's sake without co-operation of his own merit, though by co-operation of his own will (if adult). His *continued* and *increasing* justification (sanctification) is for Christ's sake through and in proportion to-his own merit, which merit increases in proportion (*a*) to his holiness, (*b*) to his obedience to moral and ecclesiastical rules.—"Conc. Trent," Sess. 6, ch. 10, and can. 32.

In case of those who have by sin fallen from the received grace of "justification," the grace lost is, through the merits of Christ, restored by the SACRAMENT OF PENANCE, provided as a second plank, after the shipwreck of grace lost. This penance includes (1) sorrow for sin, (2) confession of those sins, (3) sacerdotal absolution, (4) satisfaction rendered (*a*) in this world by fasts, alms, prayers, etc., and (*b*) after death by the fires of purgatory.

They distinguish penance—1st. As a virtue, equivalent to the Protestant doctrine of the grace of repentance. 2d. As a sacrament. Penance, as a virtue, is internal, or a change of mind, including sorrow for sin and turning unto God. External penance, or the outward expression of the internal state, is that which constitutes the SACRAMENT OF PENANCE. The *matter* of this sacrament is constituted by the acts of the penitent in the way of contrition, of confession, and of satisfaction. *Contrition* is sorrow and detestation of past sins, with a purpose of sinning no more. *Confession* is self-accusation to a priest having jurisdiction and the power of the keys. *Satisfaction* is some painful work imposed by the priest, and performed by the penitent to satisfy justice for sins committed. These effect (*a*) the expiation of the guilt of past sins, and (*b*) the discipline and increase of the spiritual life of the soul. The *form* of the sacrament is the absolution pronounced judicially, and not merely declaratively, by the priest. They hold "that it is only by means of this sacrament that sins committed after baptism can be forgiven."—"Cat. Rom.," Part II., Chap. V., Qu. 12 and 13; "Conc. Trent," Sess. 6, chs. 14–16; Sess. 14, chs. 1–9; Sess. 6, can. 30.

12. *How may it be proved that it is not a sacrament?*

1st. It was not instituted by Christ. The Scriptures teach nothing concerning it. 2d. It is an essential consequent of the false theory of baptismal regeneration. 3d. It does not either signify, seal, or convey the benefits of Christ and the new covenant.—See below, Chap. XLI., Questions 2–5.

13. *What is their doctrine concerning confession?*

Confession is self-accusation to a priest having jurisdiction and the power of the keys. All sins must be confessed without reserve, and in all their details and qualifying circumstances. If any mortal sin is not confessed, it is not pardoned, and if the omission is wilful, it is sacrilege, and greater guilt is incurred.—"Cat. Rom.," Pt. II., Chap. V., Qu. 33, 34 and 42.

14. *What are the Protestant arguments against auricular confession?*

1st. It has no warrant in Scripture. The command is to "confess one to another."

2d. It perverts the whole plan of salvation, by making necessary the mediation of the priest between the Christian and Christ, which has been refuted above, Chap. XXIV., Questions 8 and 21.

3d. We are commanded to confess to God immediately. Matt. xi. 28; 1 Tim. ii. 5; 1 John i. 9.

4th. The practical results of this system have always been evil, and this gross invasion of all the sacred rights of personality is revolting to every refined soul.

15. *What is the nature of that absolution which the Romish priests claim the power to grant?*

It absolves judicially, not merely declaratively, from all the penal consequences of the sins confessed by the authority of Jesus Christ. They appeal to Matt. xvi. 19; xviii. 18; John xx. 22, 23. "Cat. Rom.," Part II., Chap. V., Qu. 13 and 17; "Council of Trent," Sess. 14, De Pœnitentia, can. 9.

16. *What are the arguments against the possession, upon the part of the Christian ministry, of such a power to absolve?*

1st. The Christian ministry is not a priesthood.—See above, Chap. XXIV., Question 21.

2d. But even if it were, the conclusion which the Papists draw from it would not follow. Absolution is a sovereign, not a priestly act. This is plain, from the definition of the priesthood given (Heb. v. 1–6), from the Levitical practice, and from the very nature of the act itself.

3d. The grant of the power of the keys, whatever it was, was not made to the ministry as such, for in Matt. xviii. 1–18, Christ was addressing the body of the disciples, and the primitive ministers never either claimed or exercised the power in question.

4th. The power of absolute forgiveness is incommunicable in itself, and was not granted as a matter of fact; the words in question will not bear that sense, and were not so understood. The practice of the apostles shows that their understanding of the words was that they conveyed merely the power of declaring the conditions on which God would pardon sin, and in accordance with that declaration, of admitting or excluding men from sealing ordinances.

5th. This one false principle makes Christ of none effect, and perverts the whole gospel.—"Bib. Rep.," Jan., 1845.

17. *What is the Romish doctrine concerning satisfaction as a part of penance?*

By satisfaction is meant such works as are enjoined by the priest upon confession, which being set over against the sins confessed, for which contrition has been professed, are supposed to constitute a compensation for the breach of God's law, and in consideration of which the sins are forgiven.—"Cat. Rom.," Part II., Chap. V., Qu. 52 and 53. "Council of Trent," Sess. XIV., "De Pœnitentia," Chs. I–IX.

18. *What are the objections to that doctrine?*

1st. It is not supported by any Scriptural authority. 2d. It does dishonor to the one perfect satisfaction offered by our High Priest once for all.—Heb. x. 10–14. 3d. The distinction they make between the temporal and eternal punishments of sin is unauthorized. The penalty of sin is the judicial wrath of God—while that lasts there is no peace. When that is propitiated there is no more condemnation (Rom. viii. 1). The temporal sufferings of believers in Christ are *chastisements,* not punishments, nor satisfactions. 4th. The pretended "satisfactions" are either commanded or not. If commanded, they are simple duties. Their performance can have no merit. The performance of one duty can never "satisfy" for the neglect or violation of another. If not commanded, they are a form of will-worship which God abhors.—Col. ii. 20–23.

19. *What is the Papal doctrine of Indulgences?*

The Papal doctrine of INDULGENCES—1st. Rests upon the same principles with their doctrine of PENANCE. (1.) The distinction between the eternal and the temporal penalties demanded for the satisfactions for sins. (2.) The superabundant merit acquired by and belonging to the Head of the Church and his members (Christ, the Virgin Mary, and the saints), which constitute a Treasury of Merit, disposable at the discretion of competent authority to the relief of any repentant believer not in mortal sin. (3.) The dispensing power of the church, whereby a church officer possessing competent jurisdiction has authority to dispense in behalf of God and of the church any or all temporal satisfactions due from the penitent, either on earth or in purgatory, not as yet discharged by him personally.

2d. These indulgences are to be granted for "reasonable

causes," *i. e.*, "the cause must be pious, that is, not a work which is merely temporal, or vain, or in no respect appertaining to the divine glory, but any work whatsoever which tends to the honor of God, or the service of the church." They "do not depend for their efficacy on consideration of the work enjoined, but on the infinite treasure of the merits of Christ and the saints." These "causes" are payments of money for pious purposes, special prayers, visit to certain shrines, etc., etc.

3d. Indulgences are of various kinds. (1.) General for the whole church, granted only by the pope himself, to all the faithful throughout the world; or particular, granted by due authority to certain persons. (2.) They may be *plenary*, granting remission from *all* temporal punishments in this world and in purgatory; or *partial*, remitting only some part of the penalty due. (3.) They may be *temporary*, for a specified number of days or months. (4.) *Perpetual*, without any limitation of time. (5.) *Local*, attached to certain churches or other places. (6.) *Real*, attached to certain movable things as rosaries, medals, etc. (7.) *Personal*, granted to particular persons, or communities.— See M'Clintock and Strong's "Encyclopædia," and below, the "Counc. of Trent," etc.

Authoritative Statements.

"Counc. Trent," Sess. 14, ch. 1.—"But the Lord then principally instituted the Sacrament of Penance, when being raised from the dead, he breathed upon his disciples saying, 'Receive ye the Holy Ghost, whose sins ye shall forgive, they are forgiven them, and whose sins ye retain, they are retained.' By which action so signal, and words so clear, the consent of all the Fathers has ever understood, that the power *of forgiving and retaining sins* was communicated to the apostles and their lawful successors, for the reconciling of the faithful who have fallen after baptism."

Ib., ch. 3.—"The holy synod doth furthermore teach, (1) that the FORM of the Sacrament of Penance, wherein its force principally consists, is placed in those words of the minister, 'I ABSOLVE THEE, ETC.' . . . . But (2) the acts of the penitent himself, to wit, *contrition, confession*, and *satisfaction*, are as it were the MATTER of this sacrament, which acts, inasmuch as they are, by God's institution, required in the penitent for the integrity of the sacrament, and for the full and perfect remission of sins, are for this reason called the parts of penance. But (3) the thing signified indeed, and the effect of this sacrament, as far as regards its force and efficacy, is reconciliation with God."

Ib., ch. 4.—"*Contrition*, which holds the first place amongst the aforesaid acts of the penitent, is a sorrow of mind, and a detestation for sin committed, with the purpose of not sinning for the future."

Ib., ch. 5.—"All mortal sins of which, after a diligent examination of themselves, they are conscious, must needs be by penitents enumerated in confession, even though those sins be most hidden, and committed only against the two last precepts of the decalogue. . . Venial sins, whereby we are not excluded from the grace of God, and into which we fall more frequently, although they be rightly and profitably and without presumption declared in confession, yet they may be omitted without guilt, and be expiated by many other remedies. . . . . Other sins (mortal) which do not occur to him (the penitent) after diligent thought, are understood to be included as a whole in that same confession; for which sins we confidently say with the prophet. 'From my secret sins cleanse me, O Lord.'"

Ib., ch. 6.—"It also teaches, that even priests, who are in mortal sin, exercise through the virtue of the Holy Ghost, which God has bestowed in ordination, the office of forgiving sins. . . . But although the absolution of the priest is the dispensation of another's bounty, yet it is not a bare ministry only, or declarative act, but of the nature of a judicial act, whereby sentence is pronounced by the priest as by a judge. . . Neither would faith without penance bestow any remission of sins; nor would he be otherwise than most careless of his own salvation, who knowing that a priest but absolved him in jest, should not carefully seek for another who would act in earnest."

Ib., ch. 8.—"Finally, as regards *Satisfaction,* which as it is, of all the parts of Penance, that which has been at all times recommended to the Christian people by our Fathers. Ch. 9.—We are able through Jesus Christ to make satisfaction to God the Father, not only by pains voluntarily undertaken by ourselves for the punishment of sin, or by those imposed at the discretion of the priest according to the measure of our delinquency,—but also, which is a very great proof of love, by the temporal scourges inflicted of God and borne patiently by us."

"*Counc. Trent,*" Sess. 6, Can. 29.—"If any one saith, that he, who has fallen after baptism, is not able by the grace of God to rise again; or that he is able indeed to recover the justice which he has lost, but by faith alone without the sacrament of penance. . . . . Let him be accursed. Can. 30.—If any one saith that after the grace of Justification (sanctification) has been received, to every penitent sinner the guilt is remitted, and the debt of eternal punishment is blotted out in such wise, that there remains not any debt of temporal punishment to be discharged either in this world, or in the next in Purgatory, before entrance to the kingdom of heaven can be opened (to him); Let him be accursed."

INDULGENCES.—"*Conc. Trent,*" Sess. 25, "*De Indulgentiis.*"

Pope Leo X., "*Bull De Indulgentiis*" (1518).—"That no one in future may allege ignorance of the doctrine of the Roman Church respecting indulgences and their efficacy . . . the Roman pontiff, vicar of Christ on earth, can, for reasonable causes, by the powers of the keys, grant to the faithful, whether in this life or in Purgatory, indulgences, out of the superabundance of the merits of Christ, and of the saints (expressly called a treasure); and that those who have truly obtained those indulgences are released from so much of the temporal punishment due for their actual sins to the divine justice as is equivalent to the indulgence granted and obtained."

CHAPTER XXXIII.

JUSTIFICATION.

1. *What is the sense in which the word δικαιος, just, is used in the New Testament?*

Its fundamental idea is that of perfect conformity to all the requirements of the moral law.

1st. Spoken of things or actions.—Matt. xx. 4; Col. iv. 1.

2d. Spoken of persons (1.) as personally holy, conformed to the law in character.—Matt. v. 45; ix. 13. (2.) In respect to their possessing eminently some one quality demanded by the law.—Matt. i. 19; Luke xxiii. 50. (3.) As forensically just, *i. e.*, as conformed to the requirements of the law as the condition of the covenant of life.—Rom. i. 17. (4.) Spoken of God in respect to his possession of the attribute of distributive justice in administering the provisions of the law and the covenants. Rom. iii. 26; 1 John i. 9. (5.) Spoken of Christ in respect to his character as the only perfect man, and to his representative position in satisfying all the demands of the law in behalf of his people.—Acts iii. 14; vii. 52; xxii. 14.

2. *What is the usage of the verb δικαιόω, to justify, in the New Testament?*

It means to declare a person to be just.

1st. Personally conformed to the law as to moral character. Luke vii. 29; Rom. iii. 4.

2d. Forensically, that is, that the demands of the law as a condition of life are fully satisfied with regard to him.—Acts xiii. 39; Rom. v. 1, 9; viii. 30–33; 1 Cor. vi. 11; Gal. ii. 16; iii. 11.

3. *How can it be proved that the word δικαιόω is used in a forensic sense when the Scriptures use it with reference to the justification of sinners under the gospel?*

1st. In many instances it can bear no other sense. The ungodly are said to be justified without the deeds of the law, by the blood of Christ, by faith, freely, and of grace, through the agency of an advocate, by means of a satisfaction and of imputed righteousness.—Rom. iii. 20-28; iv. 5-7; v. 1; Gal. ii. 16; iii. 11; v. 4; 1 John ii. 2.

2d. It is used as the contrary of condemnation.—Rom. viii. 33, 34.

3d. The same idea is conveyed in many equivalent and interchangeable expressions.—John iii. 18; v. 24; Rom. iv. 6, 7; 2 Cor. v. 19.

4th. If it does not bear this meaning, there is no distinction between justification and sanctification.—Turretin, L. XVI., Quæstio 1.

4. *What is the usage of the term δικαιοσύνη, righteousness, and of the phrase "righteousness of God," in the New Testament?*

The term "just" is concrete, designating the person who is perfectly conformed to the law, or in respect to whom all the demands of the law are completely satisfied. The term "righteousness," on the other hand, is abstract, designating that quality or that obedience or suffering which satisfies the demands of the law, and which constitutes the ground upon which justification proceeds.

Consequently, it sometimes signifies, 1st, holiness of character, Matt. v. 6; Rom. vi. 13; 2d, that perfect conformity to the law in person and life which was the original ground of justification under the covenant of works, Rom. x. 3, 5; Phil. iii. 9; Titus iii. 5; 3d, the vicarious obedience and sufferings of Christ our substitute, which he wrought in our behalf, and which, when imputed to us, becomes our righteousness, or the ground of our justification, Rom. iv. 6; x. 4; 1 Cor. i. 30; which is received and appropriated by us through faith, Rom. iii. 22; iv. 11; x. 5-10; Gal. ii. 21; Heb. xi. 7.

The phrase, "righteousness of God," occurs in Matt. vi. 33; Rom. i. 17; iii. 5, 21, 22, 25, 26; x. 3; 2 Cor. v. 21; Phil. iii. 9; James i. 20; 2 Pet. i. 1. It evidently means that perfect righteousness or satisfaction to the whole law, precept, and penalty alike, which God provides, and which God will accept, in contrast to our own imperfect services or self-inflicted penances, which God will reject, if offered as a ground of justification.

5. *What is the usage of the term δικαίωσις, justification, in the New Testament?*

It occurs only in Rom. iv. 25; v. 16, 18. It signifies that relation to the law into which we are brought in consequence of the righteousness of Christ being made legally ours. We are absolved from all liability to the penalty, and the rewards promised to obedience are declared to belong to us.

6. *Define justification in its gospel sense.*

God, as sovereign, elected his chosen people, and gave them to his Son in the covenant of grace, and as sovereign he executes that covenant when he makes the righteousness of Christ theirs by imputation. Justification, on the other hand, is a judicial act of God proceeding upon that sovereign imputation, declaring the law to be perfectly satisfied in respect to us. This involves, 1st, pardon; 2d, restoration to divine favor, as those with regard to whom all the promises conditioned upon obedience to the commands of the law accrue. It is most strictly legal, although he sovereignly admits and credits to us a vicarious righteousness, since this vicarious righteousness is precisely in all respects what the law demands, and that by which the law is fulfilled.—See below, Question 28.

7. *What does the law require in order to the justification of a sinner?*

The law consists essentially of a rule of duty, and of a penalty attached to take effect in case of disobedience. In the case of the sinner, therefore, who has already incurred guilt, the law demands that, besides the rendering of perfect obedience, the penalty also should be suffered.—Rom. x. 5; Gal. iii. 10–13.

8. *Prove that works can not be the ground of a sinner's justification.*

Paul repeatedly asserts this (Gal. ii. 16), and declares that we are not justified by our own righteousness, which comes by obedience to the law.—Phil. iii. 9. He also proves the same by several arguments—

1st. The law demands perfect obedience. All works not perfect, therefore, lead to condemnation, and no act of obedience at one time can atone for disobedience at another.—Gal. iii. 10, 21; v. 3.

2d. If we are justified by works, then Christ is dead in vain. Gal. ii. 21; v. 4.

3d. If it were of works it would not be of grace.—Rom. xi. 6; Eph. ii. 8, 9.

4th. It would afford cause for boasting.—Rom. iii. 27; iv. 2.

5th. He also quotes the Old Testament to prove that all men are sinners, Rom. iii. 9, 10; that consequently they can not be justified by works.—Ps. cxliii. 2; Rom. iii. 20. He quotes

Hab. ii. 4, to prove that "the just by faith shall live"; and he cites the example of Abraham.—Gal. iii. 6.

9. *What are the different opinions as to the kind of works which the Scriptures teach are not sufficient for justification?*

The Pelagians admit that works of obedience to the ceremonial law are of this nature, but affirm that works of obedience to the moral law are the proper and only ground of justification. The Romanists admit that works wrought in the natural strength, previous to regeneration, are destitute of merit, and unavailable for justification, but they maintain that original sin and previous actual transgressions having been forgiven in baptism for Christ's sake, good works afterwards performed through grace have, in consequence of the merits of Christ, the virtue, 1st, of meriting heaven; 2d, of making satisfaction for sins. We are justified, then, by evangelical obedience.—"Cat. Rom.," Part II., Chapter v.; "Council of Trent," Sess. VI., Can. xxiv., and xxxii. Protestants deny the justifying efficiency of all classes of works equally.

10. *How may it be shown that no class of works, whether ceremonial, moral, or spiritual, can justify?*

1st. When the Scriptures deny that justification can be by works, the term "works" is always used generally as obedience to the whole revealed will of God, however made known. Works of obedience rendered to one law, as a ground of justification, are never contrasted with works wrought in obedience to another law, but with grace.—Rom. xi. 6; iv. 4. God demands perfect obedience to his whole will as revealed to any individual man. But since every man is a sinner, justification by the law is equally impossible for all.—Rom. ii. 14, 15; iii. 9, 10.

2d. The believer is justified without the deeds of the law, Rom. iii. 28, and God justifies the ungodly in Christ.—Rom. iv. 5.

3d. Justification is asserted to rest altogether upon a different foundation. It is "in the name of Christ," 1 Cor. vi. 11; "by his blood," Rom. v. 9; "freely," "by his grace," "by faith." Rom. iii. 24, 28.

4th. Paul proves that instead of our being justified by good works, such works are rendered possible to us only in that new relation to God into which we are introduced by justification. Eph. ii. 8–10; Rom. 6th and 7th chapters.

11. *How can* James ii. 14–26, *be reconciled with this doctrine?*

James is not speaking of the meritorious ground of justification, but of the relation which good works sustain to a genuine faith as its fruit and evidence. The meritorious ground of justification is the righteousness of Christ.—Rom. x. 4; 1 Cor. i. 30. Faith is the essential prerequisite and instrument of receiving that righteousness.—Eph. ii. 8. James, in the passage cited, simply declares and argues the truth that the faith which is thus the instrumental cause of justification, is never a dead, but always a living and fruitful principle. Paul teaches the same truth often, "Faith works by love," Gal. v. 6, and "love is the fulfilling of the law," Rom. xiii. 10.

12. *What do the Scriptures declare to be the true and only ground of justification?*

Justification is a declaration on the part of the infinitely wise and holy God that the law is satisfied. The law is, like its Author, absolutely unchangeable, and can be satisfied by nothing else than an absolutely perfect righteousness, at once fulfilling the precept, and suffering the penalty. This was rendered by Christ as our representative, and his perfect right-eousness, as imputed to us, is the sole and strictly legal ground of our justification. Thus he is made for us the end of the law for righteousness, and we are made the righteousness of God in him.—Rom. iii. 24; v. 9, 19; viii. 1; x. 4; 1 Cor. i. 30; vi. 11; 2 Cor. v. 21; Phil. iii. 9.

13. *How can it be proved that Christ's active obedience to the precepts of the law is included in that righteousness by which we are justified?*

1st. The condition of the covenant of works was perfect obedience. This covenant having failed in the hands of the first Adam must be fulfilled in the hands of the second Adam, since in the covenant of grace Christ assumed all of the undis-charged obligations of his people under the covenant of works. His suffering discharges the penalty, but only his active obe-dience fulfills the condition.

2d. All the promises of salvation are attached to obedience, not to suffering.—Matt. xix. 16, 17; Gal. iii. 12.

3d. Christ came to fulfil the whole law.—Is. xlii. 21; Rom. iii. 31; 1 Cor. i. 30.

4th. The obedience of Christ is expressly contrasted with the disobedience of Adam.—Rom. v. 19.

14. *How may it be shown that Christ's obedience was free?*

Although Christ was made under the law by being born of the woman, and rendered obedience to that law in the exercises of his created human nature, yet he did not owe that obedience for himself, but rendered it freely that its merits might be imputed to his people, because the claims of law terminate not upon nature, but upon persons; and he was always a divine person. As he suffered, the just for the unjust, so he obeyed, the Lawgiver in the place of the law-subject.

15. *In what sense is Christ's righteousness imputed to believers?*

Imputation is an act of God as sovereign judge, at once judicial and sovereign, whereby (1) he makes the guilt and legal responsibilities of our sins really Christ's, and punishes him for them. "He was wounded for our transgression, the punishment of our peace was upon him."—Is. liii. 5 and 11. "Christ hath redeemed us from the curse of the law, being made a curse for us."—Gal. iii. 13. "For he hath made him to be sin for us, who knew no sin, that we might be made the righteousness of God in him."—2 Cor. v. 21; John i. 29. (2.) He makes the righteousness of Christ ours (that is, the legal right to reward, by the gracious covenant conditioned on righteousness), and then treats us as persons legally invested with those rights. "Even as David also describeth the blessedness of the man to whom the Lord imputeth righteousness without works."—Rom. iv. 6. "For Christ is the end of the law for righteousness to every one that believeth."—Rom. x. 4; 1 Cor. i. 30; 2 Cor. v. 21; Phil. iii. 9.

"Imputation" is the charging or crediting to one's account as the ground of judicial treatment.

"Guilt" is the just obligation to punishment. The *reatus pœnæ*, or "guilt of punishment," is imputed to Christ in our stead. The *reatus culpæ*, or guilt of fault, remains ours.

"Righteousness imputed" is the vicarious fulfillment of all the covenant demands on which eternal life is conditioned.

"Merit" is that which deserves on the ground of covenant promise a reward. The merit of reward is imputed to us from Christ, the merit of praiseworthiness remains his forever.

As Christ is not made a sinner by the imputation to him of our sins, so we are not made holy by the imputation to us of his righteousness. The transfer is only of guilt from us to him, and of merit from him to us. He justly suffered the punishment due to our sins, and we justly receive the rewards due to his righteousness.—1 John i. 9. For explanation of "Imputation," see above, Chap. XXI., Ques. 12, and Chap. XXV., Ques. 9.

16. *Upon what ground does this imputation proceed?*

Upon the union federal, spiritual, and vital, which subsists between Christ and his people. Which union, in turn, rests upon the eternal decree of election common to all the persons of the Godhead, and upon the eternal covenant of grace formed between the Father as God absolute and the Son as Mediator. Thus the ultimate ground of imputation is the eternal nature and imperial will of God, the fountain of all law and all right.

17. *How may the fact of this imputation be proved from Scripture?*

See Rom. v. 12–21. Compare Rom. iv. 6; iii. 21, with Rom. v. 19.

The doctrine of imputation is essentially involved in the doctrine of substitution. If Christ obeyed and suffered in our place it can only be because our sins were imputed to him, which is directly asserted in Scripture, Isa. liii. 6; 2 Cor. v. 21; 1 Pet. ii. 24; and, if so, the merit of that obedience and suffering must accrue to us, Matt. xx. 28; 1 Tim. ii. 6; 1 Pet. iii. 18. See above, Chapter XXI., Question 12.

This doctrine is also taught by those passages which affirm that Christ fulfilled the law, Rom. iii. 31; x. 4; and by those which assert that we are justified by the righteousness of Christ, 1 Cor. vi. 11; Rom. viii. 1, etc.

This doctrine, moreover, stands or falls with the whole view we have presented of the priesthood of Christ, of the justice of God, of the covenants of works and of grace, and of the nature of the atonement; to which subjects, under their respective heads, the reader is referred.

18. *What are the two effects ascribed to the imputation of Christ's righteousness?*

Christ's righteousness satisfies, 1st, the penalty of the law; 2d, then the positive conditions of the covenant of works, *i. e.*, obedience to the precepts of the law. The imputation of that righteousness to the believer, therefore, secures, 1st, the remission of the penalty, pardon of sins; 2d, the recognition and treatment of the believer as one with respect to whom the covenant is fulfilled, and to whom all its promises and advantages legally accrue.—See below, Question 28.

19. *Are the sins of believers, committed subsequently to their justification, included in the pardon which is consequent to the imputation of Christ's righteousness; and, if so, in what way?*

The elect, although embraced in the purpose of God, and in his covenant with his Son from eternity, are not effectively united to Christ until the time of their regeneration, when, in consequence of their union with him, and the imputation of his righteousness to them, their relation to the law is permanently changed. Although the immutable law always continues their perfect standard of experience and of action, it is no longer to them a condition of the covenant of life,.because that covenant has been fully discharged for them by their sponsor. God no longer imputes sin to them to the end of judicial punishment. Every suffering which they henceforth endure is of the nature of chastisement, designed for their correction and improvement, and forms, in its relation to them, no part of the penalty of the law.

20. *What are the different opinions as to the class of sins which are forgiven when the sinner is justified?*

Romanists teach that original sin and all actual transgressions prior to baptism are forgiven for Christ's sake, through the reception of that sacrament, and that after baptism, sins, as they are committed, are through the merits of Christ forgiven in the observance of the sacrament of penance. See above, Chapter XXXII., Question 11.

Dr. Pusey has revived an ancient doctrine that in baptism all past sins, original and actual, are forgiven; but his system makes no provision for sins subsequently committed.

Many Protestants have held that only past and present sins are forgiven in the first act of justification, and that sins after regeneration, as they occur, are forgiven upon renewed acts of faith.

The true view, however, is, that in consequence of the imputation to him of Christ's righteousness, the believer is emancipated from his former *federal* relation to the law, and consequently henceforth no sin is charged to him to the end of judicial condemnation. This follows from the nature of justification, as stated above, and it is illustrated by the recorded experience of Paul, who, while complaining of the law of sin, still warring in his members, yet never doubted of his filial relation to God, nor of the forgiveness of his sins.

21. *What are the different opinions as to the relation between faith and justification?*

Socinians hold that faith, including obedience, is the proper meritorious ground of justification.—"Cat. Rac.," Quest. 418–421, and 453.

Arminians teach that although faith has no merit in itself, since it is the gift of God, yet, as a living principle, including evangelical obedience, it is graciously, for Christ's merits' sake, imputed to us for righteousness, *i. e.*, accepted as righteousness, upon the ground of which we are declared just.—Limborch, "Theol. Christ.," 6, 4, 22, and 6, 4, 46.

The orthodox view is that the active and passive obedience

of Christ satisfying both the precept and penalty of the law as a covenant of life, and thus constituting a perfect righteousness, is, upon being appropriated by the believer in the act of faith, actually made his, in a legal sense, by imputation. Faith, therefore, is the mere instrument whereby we partake in the righteousness of Christ, which is the true ground of our justification.

22. *Prove from Scripture that faith is only the instrumental cause of justification.*

1st. From the nature of faith itself. (1.) It is not of ourselves, it is the gift of God.—Eph. ii. 8; Phil. i. 29. (2.) It is one of the fruits of the Spirit, and, therefore, not the meritorious ground of spiritual blessings.—Gal. v. 22. (3.) It is an act of the soul, and therefore a work, but though, by means of faith, justification is not by works.—Rom. iv. 2–5; xi. 6. (4.) Justifying faith terminates on or in Christ, in his blood and sacrifice, and in the promises of God; in its very essence, therefore, it involves trust, and, denying its own justifying value, affirms the sole merit of that on which it trusts.—Rom. iii. 25, 26; iv. 20, 22; Gal. iii. 26; Eph. i. 12, 13; 1 John v. 10. (5.) The law necessarily demands a perfect righteousness, but faith, even when combined with the evangelical obedience which springs from it, is not a perfect righteousness.

2d. The Scriptures, when referring to the relation of justification to faith, use the terms ἐκ πίστεως, *by faith*, and διὰ πίστεως, *by or through faith*, but never διὰ πίστιν, on account of faith, Gal. ii. 16.

3d. Faith is distinguished from the righteousness which it apprehends.—Rom i. 17; Phil. iii. 8–11. Turretin, L. 16, Q. 7.

23. *What is the specific object of justifying faith?*

The Socinians, denying the divinity of Christ, make the act of justifying faith to terminate "in God through Christ."—"Rac. Cat.," Sec. 5., Ch. 9.

The Romanists, confounding justification and sanctification, make the whole revelation of God the object of the faith that justifies.—"Cat. Rom." Part 1, Chap. 1.

The Scriptural doctrine is, that while the renewed heart believes equally every ascertained word of God, the specific act of faith, whereby we are justified, terminates upon the person and work of Christ as Mediator.

This is proved, 1st, from express declarations of Scripture. Rom. iii. 22, 25; Gal. ii. 16; Phil. iii. 9. 2d. By the declaration that we are saved by believing in him.—Acts x. 43; xvi. 31; John iii. 16, 36. 3d. By those figurative expressions which illustrate the act of saving faith as "looking to Christ," etc.—Is. xlv. 22; John i. 12; vi. 35, 37; Matt. xi. 28. 4th. Unbelief is the refusing the righteousness which God provides, *i. e.,* Christ.—Rom. x. 3, 4.

24. *What is the nature of that peace which flows from justification?*

1st. Peace with God, his justice being completely satisfied through the righteousness of Christ.—Rom. v. 1; 2 Cor. v. 19; Col. i. 21; Eph. ii. 14. In witness whereof his Holy Spirit is given to us.—Rom. viii. 15, 16; Heb. x. 15, 17. His love shed abroad in our hearts, Rom. v. 5, and our habitual fellowship with him established, 1 John i. 3. 2d. Inward peace of conscience, including consciousness of our reconciliation with God through the operation of his Spirit, as above, and the appeasement of our self-condemning conscience through the apprehension of the righteousness by which we are justified.—Heb. ix. 14; x. 2, 22.

25. *What other benefits flow from justification?*

Being justified on the ground of a perfect righteousness, our whole relation to God and the law is changed; the gift of the Holy Ghost, adoption, sanctification, perseverance, the working of all things together for good in this life, deliverance in death, the resurrection of the body, and the final glorification, all result.

OBJECTIONS ANSWERED.

26. *State and Refute the principal objections made to the Protestant doctrine of justification.*

1st. That it is legal, and therefore excludes grace.

We ANSWER—that it is transcendently gracious. 1. The admission of a substitute for guilty sinners was an act of grace. 2. The vicarious obedience and sufferings of the God-man were of infinite grace. 3. The imputation of his righteousness to an individual elected out of the mass of fallen humanity is an act of pure grace. Hence, 4, the entire subsequent regarding and treating the believer as righteous, is a work of grace.

2d. That it is impious because it declares the sinner to be righteous with the very righteousness of Christ.

We ANSWER. It is not impious because—1. This righteousness was freely wrought out with the intention it should be ours, and it is freely given to us. 2. It is not Christ's personal subjective righteousness which is incommunicable, but his vicarious fulfillment of the covenant of life under which we were created which is imputed to us. 3. The merit of praiseworthiness is retained by Christ, only its merit of rewardableness is given to us. 4. It is given to us gratuitously, that the praise of glorious grace may redound to Christ alone.

3d. That gratuitous justification by faith leads to licentiousness.

PAUL ANSWERS, Rom. vi. 2–7:

Prop. 1st. Where sin abounded grace did much more abound. Rom. v. 20.

Prop. 2d. Shall we conclude, therefore, that we are to continue in sin that grace may abound? God forbid.—Rom. vi. 1, 2.

Prop. 3d. The federal union of the believer with Christ, which secures our justification, is the foundation of, and is inseparable from, that vital spiritual union with him, which secures our sanctification.

Prop. 4th. This method of justification, so far from leading to licentiousness, secures the only conditions under which we could be holy. (1.) This method of justification, by changing our relation to God, enables us to return to him in a way of a free, loving service.—Rom. vi. 14; vii. 1–6. (2.) It alone delivers us from the spirit of bondage and fear, and gives us that of adoption and love.—Rom. viii. 1–17; xiii. 10; Gal. v. 6; 1 John iv. 18; 2 John 6.

27. *In what respect did the doctrine of Piscator on this subject differ from that of the Reformed Churches?*

Piscator, a Protestant divine, Prof. at Herborn (1584–1625), taught, 1st, that, as to his human nature, Christ was under the law in the same sense as any other creature, and that, therefore, he could only obey the law for himself; 2d, that if Christ had obeyed the law in our place, the law could not claim a second fulfillment of us, and, consequently, Christians would be under no obligations to obey the law of God; 3d, that if Christ had both obeyed the precept of the law and suffered its penalty, then the law would have been doubly fulfilled, since the claims of the precept and the penalty of the law are alternative, not coincident.

This doctrine was expressly condemned in the Reformed Churches of Switzerland and Holland, and by the French synods held in the years 1603, 1612, and 1614. In 1615, however, the Synod tacitly allowed these views to pass without condemnation.—Mosheim's " Hist."

28. *How may it be shown that justification is not mere pardon?*

Piscator erred, from failing to distinguish—1st. That the claims of law terminate not upon natures, but upon persons. Christ was a divine person, and, therefore, his obedience was free. 2d. That there is an evident difference between a federal relation to the law as a condition of salvation, and a natural relation to law as a rule of life. Christ discharged the former as our federal representative. The latter necessarily attaches to the believer as to all moral agents forever.

Justification is more than pardon—1st. Because the very word "to justify" proves it. To "pardon" is, in the exercise of sovereign prerogative, to waive the execution of the penal sanctions of the law. "To justify" is to declare that the demands of the law are satisfied, not waived. Pardon is a sovereign act—justification is a judicial act. 2d. As we proved under Chap. XXV., Christ did in strict rigor of justice satisfy vicariously for us the demands of the law, both the obedience demanded and the penalty denounced. His satisfaction is the *ground* of our justification. But pardon is remission of penalty *in absence* of satisfaction. 3d. If justification were mere pardon it would simply release us from penal suffering, but would provide no further good for us. But "justification through faith in Christ," secures not pardon only, but also peace, grace, reconciliation, adoption of sons, coheirship, etc., etc.—See above, Ques. 13. Rom. v. 1–10; Acts xxvi. 18; Rev. i. 5, 6.

In the case of justified believers "justification" includes "pardon." Our justification proceeds on the ground of a "satisfaction," and, therefore, is not mere pardon. But it is a "vicarious" satisfaction graciously set to the credit of the unworthy, and, therefore, it effects pardon to us sinners who believe in Christ.

29. *Did not Calvin often use language to the effect that justification and pardon are the same?*

He did. But his language is to be interpreted—1st. By the fact that he was arguing with Romanists who taught that "justification consists in remission of sins and infusion of grace." He argued in opposition that justification consists in the former but does not include the latter. 2d. By the conclusive fact that his full definitions of justification comprehend the full truth more accurately defined in the Symbols of the Lutheran and Reformed Churches.

Calvin's "Institutes," Bk. 3, ch. 11, § 2.—"A man is said to be justified in the sight of God, when in the judgment of God he is decreed righteous, and is accepted on account of his righteousness. . . . In the same manner a man will be said to be *justified by works,* if in his life, or by the perfection of his works, he can answer and satisfy the divine justice. On the contrary a man will be justified by faith, when excluded from the righteousness of works, he by faith lays hold of the righteousness of Christ, and clothed in it appears in the sight of God not as sinner, but as righteous. Thus we simply interpret justification, as the acceptance with which God receives us into his favor as if we were righteous, and we say that this justification consists in the forgiveness of sins, *and* the imputation of the righteousness of Christ."

Calvin's "Com.," 1 Cor. i. 30.—"'Christ is made unto us righteousness,' by which, he (the apostle) understood that we are accepted by God in his name (Christ's), because he expiated our sins, and his obedience is imputed to us for righteousness. For since the righteousness of faith consists in remission of sins, *and* in gratuitous acceptance, we ,obtain *both* through Christ."

30. *In what respect does the governmental theory of the atonement modify the doctrine of justification?*

See above, Chap. XXV., Question 27.

1st. It follows, from that theory, that justification is a sovereign, not a judicial act of God. Christ has not satisfied the law, but merely made it consistent with the government of God to set aside the law in the case of believing men. It is mere pardon, an act of executive clemency.

2d. As Christ did not die as a substitute, it follows that his righteousness is not imputed; it is the occasion, not the ground of justification.

3d. As Christ did not die as a substitute, there is no strictly federal union between Christ and his people, and faith can not be the instrument of salvation by being the means of uniting us to Christ, but only the arbitrary condition of justification, or the means of recommending us to God.

4th. As justification is mere pardon, it only sets aside condemnation, and renders, so far forth, future salvation possible. It does nothing to secure the future standing and relations of the believer, under the covenant of salvation, to God.

Dr. Emmons (1745–1840), one of the ablest theologians of the New England School, says ("Sermons," Vol. III., p. 3–67)— (1.) "Justification, in a gospel sense, signifies no more nor less than pardon or remission of sin." (2.) "Forgiveness is the only favor which God bestows upon men on Christ's account." (3.) "The full and final justification of believers, or their title to their eternal inheritance, is conditional. They must perform certain things, which he has specified as terms or conditions of their taking possession of their several legacies." (4.) "God does promise eternal life to all who obey his commands or exercise those holy and benevolent affections which his commands require."

31. *How does the Arminian theory as to the nature and design of the satisfaction of Christ modify the doctrine of justification?*

They hold—1st. As to the nature of Christ's satisfaction.

that although it was a real propitiation rendered to justice for us, it was not in the rigor of justice perfect, but was graciously accepted and acted on as such by God.—Limborch, "Apol. Theo.," 3, 22, 5. 2d. That it was not strictly the substitution of Christ in place of his elect, but rather that he suffered the wrath of God in behalf of all men, in order to make it consistent with justice for God to offer salvation to all men upon condition of faith.

Therefore they regard justification as a sovereign, not a judicial act—1st. In accepting the sufferings of Christ as sufficient to enable God consistently to offer to men salvation on the terms of the new covenant of grace, *i. e.*, on the condition of faith. 2d. In imputing to the believer his faith for righteousness for Christ's sake.

This faith they make—1st. To include evangelical obedience, *i. e.*, the whole principle of religion in heart and life. 2d. They regard it as the graciously admitted ground, rather than the mere instrument of justification; faith being counted for righteousness, because Christ died. — Limborch, "Theo. Christ.," 6, 4, 22, and 6, 4, 46.

This theory, besides being opposed by all the arguments we have above presented in establishing the orthodox doctrine, labors under the further objections—

1st. It fails to render a clear account as to how the satisfaction of Christ makes it consistent with divine justice to save men upon the condition of faith. If Christ did not obey and suffer strictly as the substitute of his people, it is difficult to see how the justice of God, as it respects them, could have been appeased; and if he did so fulfil the demands of justice in their place, then the orthodox view, as above stated, is admitted.

2d. It fails to render a clear account of the relation of faith to justification—(1.) Because faith in Christ, including trust, necessarily implies that the merits of Christ upon which the trust terminates is the ground of justification. (2.) Faith must be either the ground or the mere instrument of justification. If it be the latter then the righteousness of Christ, which is the object of faith, is that ground. If it be the former, then what is made of the merits of Christ upon which faith rests?

32. *How do the Romanists define justification?*

They confound justification with sanctification. It is, 1st, the forgiveness of sins; 2d, the removal of inherent sin for Christ's sake; 3d, the positive infusion of grace.

Of this justification they teach that the final cause is the glory of God and eternal life. The efficient cause is the power of the Holy Ghost. The meritorious cause the work of Christ. The instrumental cause baptism. The formal cause the influence of grace, whereby we are made not merely forensically but inherently righteous.—"Council of Trent," Sess. vi., Chapter vii.

They define faith in its relation to justification to be the beginning of human salvation, the fountain and root of all justification, *i. e.*, of spiritual life. They consequently hold that justification is progressive, and that when a man receives a new nature in baptism, and the work of justification is commenced in him with the forgiveness and the removal of sin, the work is to be carried on by the exercise of the grace implanted, *i. e.*, by good works. Since they confound justification with sanctification, they necessarily deny that men are justified by the imputation of the righteousness of Christ, or by mere faith without works.—Sess. 6, Can. 9th and 11th, "de Justificatione."

They admit that justification is entirely gracious, *i. e.*, of the mere mercy of God, and for the sake of the merits of Jesus Christ, as neither the spiritual exercises nor the works of men previous to justification have any merit whatsoever.—"Council of Trent," Sess. vi., Chapter viii.

A careful distinction must be made between (*a*) that which in the case of an adult prepares for justification, (*b*) the realization of justification in the first instance, (*c*) its subsequent progressive realization in the advance of the gracious soul in justification towards perfection, and (*d*) the restoration to a state of grace of the baptized Christian after backsliding into sin.

1st. The *preparation* of the sinner for justification proceeds from the prevenient grace of God, without any merit on the part of the subject. This grace acting through the hearing of the word leads to conviction of sin, repentance, apprehension of the mercy of God in Christ (the church), and hence to a determination to receive baptism and lead a new life ("Conc. Trent," Sess. vi., chaps. v. and vi).

2d. The actual justification of the sinner is the infusion of gracious habits, the pollution of sin having been washed away by the power of God, on account of the merits of Christ, through the instrumentality of baptism, which operates its effects by an energy made inherent in it, by the institution of God. After this, inherent sin being removed, remission of guilt necessarily follows as its immediate effect. Guilt is the relation which sin sustains to the justice of God. The thing being removed, the relation ceases *ipso facto* (Bellarmin, "De Amiss. Gratiæ," etc., v. 7.

3d. Having thus been justified and made a friend of God, the baptized Christian advances from virtue to virtue, and is renewed from day to day, through the observance of the commandments of God and of the church, faith co-operating with good works, now made possible in virtue of the previous justification, and which truly merit, and receive as a just reward, increase of grace, and more and more perfect justification. His *first* justification was for Christ's sake, without any co-operation of his own merit, but by consent of his own will. His *second* or continued and increasing justification is for Christ's sake, through and in proportion to his own merit, which deserves increase of grace and acceptance in proportion (*a*) to his personal holiness, and (*b*) to his obedience to ecclesiastical rules ("Conc. Trent," Sess. 6, Chap. x. and Can. 32).

4th. In the case of those who having been justified, have sinned, the lost grace of justification is restored, for the merits of Christ, through the sacrament of Penance, which is provided as a second plank to rescue those who have shipwrecked grace. This penance includes (*a*) sorrow for sin, (*b*) confession to a priest having jurisdiction, (*c*) sacerdotal absolution, (*d*) satisfaction by alms, prayers, fasts, etc., and this justification if not rendered perfect by these means on earth is completed by purgatorial fires. All these satisfactions, earthly and purgatorial, are meritorious satisfactions to divine justice, cancelling the *temporal* punishments attaching to the sins for which they are undergone, the *eternal* punishment whereof has been at once and freely remitted, either through the sacrament itself, or the honest desire for it ("Conc. Trent," Sess. 6, Chaps. xiv. and xvi., and Can. 30, and Sess. 14, Chaps. i.–ix).

33. *What are the points of difference between Protestants and Romanists on this whole subject?*

1st. As to the nature of justification. We regard it as a judicial act of God, declaring the believer to be forensically just, on the ground of the righteousness of Christ made his by imputation. They regard it as the infusion of inherent grace.

2d. As to its meritorious ground. Both say the merits of Christ. But they say these merits are made ours by sanctification. We, by imputation, through the instrumentality of faith.

3d. As to the nature and office of faith. We say that it is the instrument; they the beginning and root of justification.

4th. They say that justification is progressive.

5th. That it may be lost by mortal sin and regained and increased through the sacrament of Penance, and completed in Purgatory.—See above, Chapter XXXII., on "Repentance and Penance."

34. *What are the leading arguments against the Romanist view on this subject?*

1st. This whole doctrine is confused. (1.) It confounds under one definition two matters entirely distinct, namely, the forensic remission of the condemnation due to sin with the washing away of inherent sin, and the introduction to a state of covenant favor with God with the infusion of inherent grace. (2.) It renders no sensible account as to the manner in which the merit of Christ propitiates divine justice.

2d. Their definition is refuted by all the evidence above exhibited, that the terms "justification" and "righteousness" are used in Scripture in a forensic sense.

3d. Their view, by making our inherent grace wrought in us by the Holy Ghost for Christ's sake the ground of our acceptance with God, subverts the whole gospel. It is of the very essence of the gospel that the ground of our acceptance with the Father is the mediatorial work of the Son, who is for us the end of the law for righteousness, and not our own graces.

4th. Their view of the merit of works performed by divine grace after baptism is inconsistent with what Scripture teaches and the Romish Church itself teaches as to original sin and guilt, and as to the essential graciousness of the salvation wrought by Christ. Thomas Aquinas himself ("Summa.," Q. 114, Art. 5) says, "If grace be considered in the sense of a gratuitous gift, all merit is excluded by grace." Therefore the entire system of Papist justification falls.

5th. It is legal in its spirit and method, and consequently induces either spiritual pride or despair, but never can nourish true evangelical assurance at once humble and confident.

6th. The Scriptures declare that on the ground of the propitiation of Christ God justifies the believer as *ungodly*, not as sanctified. It certainly could not require an atonement to render God both just and the *sanctifier* of the ungodly. Rom. iv. 5.

7th. The phrases to impute, reckon, count sin or righteousness are absolutely consistent only with a forensic interpretation. To impute righteousness without works in the forensic sense, in the 4th chapter of Romans, is reasonable. To impute inherent grace without works is nonsense.

8th. Their definition is refuted by all those arguments which establish the true view with respect to the nature and office of justifying faith.—See above, Questions 21-23.

AUTHORITATIVE STATEMENTS.

ROMISH DOCTRINE. —For statement of the *nature, ground, and means* of justification, see above, under Ch. XXIX. For statement of Romish Doctrine of Good Works and Works of Supererogation, see below, under Ch. XXXV., and see Doctrine of Penance, above, under Ch. XXXII.

"*Counc. Trent,*" Sess. 6, ch. 8.—"We are said to be justified by faith, because faith is the beginning of human salvation, the foundation and the root of all justification." *Ib.*, can. 23.—"If any one saith that a man once justified can sin no more nor lose grace, and therefore he that falls and sins was never truly justified; or on the other hand, that he is able during his whole life to avoid all sins, even those that are venial, except by a special privilege from God, as the church holds in regard of the Blessed Virgin, let him be accursed." Can. 24.—"If any one say that righteousness received is not preserved and also increased before God through good works; but that the said works are merely the fruits and signs of justification obtained, but not a cause of the increase thereof; let him be accursed." Can. 29.—"If any one saith that he, who has fallen after baptism, is not able by the grace of God to rise again; or, that he is able indeed to recover the righteousness which he has lost, but by faith alone, without the sacrament of penance . . . . let him be accursed." Can. 30.—"If any one saith, that, after the grace of Justification has been received, to every penitent sinner the guilt is remitted and the debt of eternal punishment is blotted out in such wise, that there remains not any debt of temporal punishment to be discharged either in this world, or in the next in Purgatory, before he can enter the kingdom of heaven; let him be accursed." Can. 32.—"If any one saith, that the good works of one that is justified are in such manner the gifts of God, as that they are not also the good merits of him that is justified; or that the justified man, by the good works which he performs through the grace of God and the merit of Jesus Christ, whose living member he is, does not truly merit increase of grace, eternal life, and the attainment of eternal life if he die in grace, and also an increase of glory; let him be accursed."

BELLARMIN, "*De Justificatione,*" 5, 1.—"The common opinion of all Catholics holds that all the good works of justified persons are truly and properly meritorious, and deserving not merely of a reward of some sort, but of eternal life itself. 4, 7.—We say that good works are necessary to a justified man in order to his salvation, not only in the way of being present, but also in the way of efficiency, since they effect salvation, and faith without them does not effect it. *Ib.* 5, 5.—The merits of justified persons do not stand opposed to the merits of Christ, but they spring from these, and whatever praise those merits of the justified have, redounds entire to the praise of the merits of Christ."

LUTHERAN DOCTRINE.—"*Apologia Confessionis.*"—"To justify in this place (Rom. v. 1), signifies in a forensic sense to absolve an accused person and pronounce him righteous, but on account of another's righteousness, *i. e.*, of Christ; which other's righteousness is made over to us through faith."

"*Formula Concordiæ*" (Hase Ed.), p. 685.—"The term justification in this transaction means to pronounce righteous, to absolve from sins, and from the eternal punishment of sinners, on account of the righteousness of Christ, which is imputed by God to faith." *Ib.* p. 684.—"Man a sinner may be justified before God . . without any merits or worthiness of ours, and apart from any works, preceding, accompanying, or following, out of mere grace." *Ib.* p. 584.—"We confess that faith alone is that means and instrument by which we apprehend Christ our Saviour, and in Christ of that righteousness, which can stand the judgment of God." *Ib.* p. 689.—"Neither repentance, nor love, nor any other virtue, but faith alone, is the single means and instrument by which we are able to apprehend and accept the grace of God, the merit of Christ, and the remission of sins."

REFORMED DOCTRINE.

"*Westminster Confession of Faith*," Ch. 11.

"*Heidelberg Cat.*," Ques. 60.—"Nevertheless I may now embrace all these benefits with a true boldness of mind; without any merit of mine, of the mere mercy of God, the perfect satisfaction, righteousness, and holiness of Christ is imputed and given to me, as if I had myself committed no sin, nor incurred any stain; yea, as if I had myself perfectly performed that obedience which Christ performed for me."

REMONSTRANT DOCTRINE.—*Limborch, "Christ. Theol.*," 6, 4, 22.—"Let it be understood that, when we say we are justified by faith, we do not exclude works, which faith requires, and as a fruitful mother produces, but we include them . . . nor by faith is a bare faith to be understood, as contradistinguished from the works which faith produces, but together with the faith, all that obedience which God in the New Testament appoints, and which is supplied by faith in Jesus Christ. . . . 31.—But faith is a condition in us and is required of us in order that we may obtain justification. It is therefore an act which, although viewed in itself it is by no means perfect, but in many respects defective, is yet received as full and perfect by God graciously and freely, and on account of it God graciously bestows remission of sins and the reward of eternal life. . . 29.—The object of faith (justifying) we declare to be Jesus Christ entire, as prophet, priest, and king; not only his propitiation, but his precepts, promises, and threatenings; by it therefore we embrace the entire Christ, his word, and all his saving benefits."

SOCINIAN DOCTRINE.—"*Racovian Catechism*," Sec. 5, ch. 9.—"The faith which is by itself followed by salvation, is such an assent to the doctrine of Christ that we apply it to its proper object; that is, that we trust in God through Christ, and give ourselves up wholly to obey his will, whereby we obtain his promises. . . . . If piety and obedience, when life is continued after the acknowledgment of Christ, be required as indispensable to salvation, it is necessary that the faith to which alone and in reality salvation is ascribed, should comprehend obedience. . . *Ib.* ch. 11.—Justification is, when God regards us as just, or so deals with us as if we were altogether just and innocent. This he does in the New Covenant, in forgiving our sins and conferring upon us eternal life."

CHAPTER XXXIV.

ADOPTION, AND THE ORDER OF GRACE IN THE APPLICATION OF
REDEMPTION, IN THE SEVERAL PARTS OF JUSTIFICATION,
REGENERATION, AND SANCTIFICATION.

1. *To what classes of creatures is the term "sons," or "children
of God," applied in the Scriptures, and on what grounds is that
application made?*

1st. In the singular it is applied, in a supreme and incommunicable sense, to the Second Person of the Trinity alone.

2d. In the plural, to angels, (1) because they are God's
favored creatures, (2) because as holy intelligences they are
like him.—Job i. 6; xxxviii. 7.

3d. To human magistrates, because they possess authority
delegated from God, and in that respect resemble him.—Ps.
lxxxii. 6.

4th. To good men as the subjects of a divine adoption.

This adoption, and the consequent sonship it confers is twofold, (1) general and external, Ex. iv. 22; Rom. ix. 4; (2) special, spiritual and immortal.—Gal. iv. 4, 5; Eph. i. 4–6.

2. *What is the Adoption of which believers are the subjects in
Christ; and what relation does the conception which this word represents in Scripture sustain to those represented by the terms justification, regeneration, and sanctification?*

Turretin makes adoption a constituent part of justification.
He says that in execution of the covenant of grace God sovereignly imputes to the elect, upon their exercise of faith, the
righteousness of Christ, which was the fulfilling of the whole
law, precept as well as penalty, and therefore the legal ground,
under the covenant of works, for securing to his people both
remission of the penalty and a legal right to all the promises
conditioned upon obedience. Upon the ground of this sovereign imputation God judicially pronounces the law, in its
federal relations, to be perfectly satisfied with regard to them,
i. e., he justifies them, which involves two things, 1st, the re-

mission of the penalty due to their sins, 2d, the endowing them with all the rights and relations which accrue from the positive fulfilment of the covenant of works by Christ in their behalf. This second constituent of justification he calls adoption, which essentially agrees with the definition of adoption given in our "Con. Faith," Chapter xii.; "L. Cat.," Q. 74; "S. Cat.," Q. 34. Turretin, L. 16, Q. 4 and 6.

The great Amesius (†1633), in his "Medulla Theologica," ch. 28, represents Adoption as a new grace in advance of justification, and not an element in it. A gracious sentence of God, whereby a believer, having been justified, is accepted for Christ's sake into the relation and rights of sonship.

It appears, however, to us that the words "Adoption" and "Sonship," as used in Scripture, express more than a change of relation, and that they are more adequately conceived of as expressing a complex view, including the change of nature together with the change of relation, and setting forth the new creature in his new relations.

The instant a sinner is united to Christ in the exercise of faith, there is accomplished in him simultaneously and inseparably, 1st, a total change of relation to God, and to the law as a covenant; and, 2d, a change of *inward condition or nature.* The change of relation is represented by justification; the change of nature is represented by the term regeneration. REGENERATION is an act of God originating by a new creation a new spiritual life in the heart of the subject. The first and instant act of that new creature, consequent upon his regeneration, is FAITH, or a believing, trusting embrace of the person and work of Christ. Upon the exercise of faith by the regenerated subject, JUSTIFICATION is the instant act of God, on the ground of that perfect righteousness which the sinner's faith has apprehended, declaring him to be free from all condemnation and to have a legal right to the relations and benefits secured by the covenant which Christ has fulfilled in his behalf. SANCTIFICATION is the progressive growth toward the perfected maturity of that new life which was implanted in regeneration. ADOPTION presents the new creature in his new relation; his new relations entered upon with a congenial heart, and his new life developing in a congenial home, and surrounded with those relations which foster its growth, and crown it with blessedness. Justification is wholly forensic, and concerns only relations, immunities, and rights. Regeneration and sanctification are wholly spiritual and moral, and concern only inherent qualities and states. Adoption comprehends the complex condition of the believer as at once the subject of both.

3d. *What is the order of grace in the application of Redemption?*

I. The two principles which fundamentally characterize Protestant Soteriology are—1st. The clear distinction between the change of relation signalized by justification, and the change of character signalized by regeneration and sanctification. 2d. That the change of relation, the remission of penalty, and the restoration to favor involved in justification, necessarily precedes, and renders possible, the real moral change expressed by regeneration and sanctification. The continuance of judicial condemnation precludes the exercise of grace. Remission of punishment must precede the work of the Spirit. We are pardoned in order that we may be good, never made good in order that we may be pardoned.

"It is evident that God must himself already have been secretly favorable and gracious to a man, and must already have pardoned him *forum divinum*, for the sake of Christ and his relation to human nature, to be able to bestow upon him the grace of regeneration. In fact viewed as *actus Dei forensis* there was of necessity that it should be regarded as existing prior to man's consciousness of it, nay prior to faith."—Dr. J. A. Dorner's "Hist. Prot. Theo.," Vol. II., pp. 156, 160.

II. Hence the apparent circle in the order of grace. The righteousness of Christ is said to be imputed to the *believer*, and justification to be *through faith*. Yet *faith* is an act of a soul already regenerated, and regeneration is possible only to a soul to whom God is reconciled by the application of Christ's satisfaction.

Thus the satisfaction and merit of Christ is the antecedent cause of regeneration, and on the other hand the participation of the believer in the satisfaction and merit of Christ (his justification) is conditioned on his faith, which is the effect of his regeneration. We must have part in Christ so far forth as to be regenerated, in order to have part in him so far forth as to be justified.

This is not a question of order in time, because regeneration and justification are gracious acts of God absolutely synchronous. The question is purely as to the true order of causation; Is the righteousness of Christ imputed to us that we may believe, or is it imputed to us because we believe? Is justification an analytic judgment, that the man is justified as a believer though a sinner, or is it a synthetic judgment, that this sinner is justified for Christ's sake?

III. The solution is to be sought in the fact that Christ impetrated the application of his salvation to his "own," and all the means, conditions, and stages thereof, and that this was done in pursuance of a covenant engagement with the Father, which provided for the application of redemption to specific persons at certain times and under certain conditions. The relation from birth of an elect person to Adam, and to sin and its condemnation, is precisely the same with that of all his fellow-men. But his relation to the satisfaction and merits of Christ, and to the graces they impetrate, is analogous to that of an heir to an inheritance secured to him by will. As long as he is under age the will secures the inchoate right of the heir *de jure.* It provides for his education at the expense of the estate in preparation for his inheritance. It determines the previous instalments of his patrimony to be given him by his trustees. It determines in some sense his present status as a prospective heir. It determines the precise time and conditions of his being inducted into absolute possession. He possesses certain rights and enjoys certain benefits from the first. But he has absolute rights and powers of ownership only when he reaches the period and fulfils the conditions prescribed therefor in the will. Thus the merits of Christ are imputed to the elect heir from his birth so far forth as they constitute the basis of the gracious dealing provided for him as preparatory to his full possession.

Justification is assigned by Protestant theologians to that final mental act of God as Judge whereby he declares the heir in full possession of the *rights* of his inheritance, henceforth to be recognized and treated as the heir in possession, although the actual consummation of that possession is not effected until the resurrection. Christ and his righteousness are not given to the believer because of faith. Faith is the conscious trusting receiving of that which is already given. Our Catechism, Ques. 33, says, "Justification is an act of God's free grace, wherein he pardoneth all our sins, and accepteth us as righteous in his sight only for the righteousness of Christ (1) imputed to us, and (2) received by faith alone."

Regeneration and consequently faith are wrought in us for Christ's sake and as the result conditioned on a previous imputation of his righteousness to that end. Justification supervenes upon faith, and implies such an imputation of Christ's righteousness as effects a radical and permanent change of relationship to the law as a condition of life.

4. *What is represented in Scripture as involved in being a child of God by this adoption?*

1st. Derivation of nature from God.—John i. 13; James i. 18; 1 John v. 18.

2d. Being born again in the image of God, bearing his likeness.—Rom. viii. 29; 2 Cor. iii. 18; Col. iii. 10; 2 Pet. i. 4.

3d. Bearing his name.—1 John iii. 1; Rev. ii. 17; iii. 12.

4th. Being the objects of his peculiar love.—John xvii. 23; Rom. v. 5–8; Titus iii. 4; 1 John iv. 7–11.

5th. The indwelling of the Spirit of his Son (Gal. iv. 5, 6), who forms in us a filial spirit, or a spirit becoming the children of God, *obedient*, 1 Pet. i. 14; 2 John 6; *free from sense of guilt, legal bondage, fear of death*, Rom. viii. 15, 21; 2 Cor. iii. 17; Gal. v. 1; Heb. ii. 15; 1 John v. 14; and *elevated with a holy boldness and royal dignity*, Heb. x. 19, 22; 1 Pet. ii. 9; iv. 14.

6th. Present protection, consolations, and abundant provisions.—Ps. cxxv. 2; Isa. lxvi. 13; Luke xii. 27–32; John xiv. 18; 1 Cor. iii. 21, 23; 2 Cor. i. 4.

7th. Present fatherly chastisements for our good, including both spiritual and temporal afflictions.—Ps. li. 11, 12; Heb. xii. 5–11.

8th. The certain inheritance of the riches of our Father's glory, as heirs with God and joint heirs with Christ, Rom. viii. 17; James ii. 5; 1 Pet. i. 4; iii. 7; including the exaltation of our bodies to fellowship with him.—Rom. viii. 23; Phil. iii. 21.

5. *What relation do the three persons of the Trinity sustain to this adoption, and into what relation does it introduce us to each of them severally?*

This adoption proceeds according to the eternal purpose of the Father, upon the merits of the Son, and by the efficient agency of the Holy Ghost.—John i. 12, 13; Gal. iv. 5, 6; Titus iii. 5, 6. By it God the Father is made our Father. The incarnate God-man is made our elder brother, and we are made—(1) like him; (2) intimately associated with him in community of life, standing, relations, and privileges; (3) joint heirs with him of his glory.—Rom. viii. 17, 29; Heb. ii. 17; iv. 15. The Holy Ghost is our indweller, teacher, guide, advocate, comforter, and sanctifier. All believers, being subjects of the same adoption, are brethren.—Eph. iii. 6; 1 John iii. 14; v. 1.

CHAPTER XXXV.

SANCTIFICATION.

1. *What sense do the words ἅγιος, holy and ἁγιάζειν, to sanctify, bear in the Scriptures?*

The verb ἁγιάζειν is used in two distinct senses in the New Testament:

1st. To make clean physically, or morally. (1.) Ceremonial purification.—Heb. ix. 13. (2.) To render clean in a moral sense.—1 Cor. vi. 11; Heb. xiii. 12. Hence the phrase "them that are sanctified" is convertable with believers.—1 Cor. i. 2.

2d. To set apart from a common to a sacred use, to devote, (1) spoken of things, Matt. xxiii. 17; (2) spoken of persons, John x. 36; (3) to regard and venerate as holy, Matt. vi. 9; 1 Pet iii. 15.

ἅγιος, as an adjective, *pure, holy*, as a noun, *saint*, is also used in two distinct senses, corresponding to those of the verb.

1st. Pure, clean; (1) ceremonially, (2) morally, Eph. i. 4, (3) as a noun, saints, sanctified ones, Rom. i. 7; viii. 27.

2d. Consecrated, devoted.—Matt. iv. 5; Acts vi. 13; xxi. 28; Heb. ix. 3. This word is also used in ascriptions of praise to God.—John xvii. 11; Rev. iv. 8.

2. *What are the different views entertained as to the nature of sanctification?*

1st. Pelagians denying original sin and the moral inability of man, and holding that sin can be predicated only of acts of the will, and not of inherent states or dispositions, consequently regard sanctification as nothing more than a moral reformation of life and habits, wrought under the influence of the truth in the natural strength of the sinner himself.

2d. The advocates of the "exercise scheme" hold that we can find nothing in the soul other than the agent and his exercises. Regeneration, therefore, is nothing more than the cessation from a series of unholy, and the inauguration of a series of holy exercises; and sanctification the maintenance of these holy exercises. One party, represented by Dr. Emmons, say that God immediately effects these holy exercises. Another party, represented by Dr. Taylor, of New Haven, held that the man himself determines the character of his own exercises by choosing God as his chief good; the Holy Spirit in some unexplained way assisting.—See above, Chap. XXIX., Questions 5 and 6.

3d. Many members of the Church of England, as distinguished from the evangelical party, hold that a man conforming to the church, which is the condition of the Gospel covenant, is introduced to all the benefits of that covenant, and in the decent performance of relative duties and observance of the sacraments, is enabled to do all that is now required of him, and to attain to all the moral good now possible or desirable.

4th. The orthodox doctrine is that the Holy Ghost, by his constant influences upon the whole soul in all its faculties, through the instrumentality of the truth, nourishes, exercises, and develops those holy principles and dispositions which he implanted in the new birth, until by a constant progress all sinful dispositions being mortified and extirpated, and all holy dispositions being fully matured, the subject of this grace is brought immediately upon death to the measure of the stature of perfect manhood in Christ.

"Con. Faith," Chap. xiii.; " L. Cat.," Question 75; "S. Cat.," Question 35.

3. *How can it be shown that sanctification involves more than mere reformation?*

See above, Chap. XXIX., Question 12.

4. *How may it be shown that it involves more than the production of holy exercises?*

See above, Chap. XXIX., Questions 7–10.

Besides the arguments presented in the chapter above referred to, this truth is established by the evidence of those passages of Scripture which distinguish between the change wrought in the heart and the effects of that change in the actions.—Matt. xii. 33–35; Luke vi. 43–45.

5. *What relation does sanctification sustain to regeneration?*

Regeneration is the creative act of the Holy Spirit, implanting a new principle of spiritual life in the soul. Conversion is the first exercise of that new gracious principle, in the spontaneous turning of the new-born sinner to God. Sanctification is

the sustaining and developing work of the Holy Ghost, bringing all the faculties of the soul more and more perfectly under the
purifying and regulating influence of the implanted principle
of spiritual life.

6. *What is the relation which justification and sanctification
sustain to each other?*

In the order of nature, regeneration precedes justification,
although as to time they are always necessarily contemporaneous. The instant God regenerates a sinner he acts faith in
Christ. The instant he acts faith in Christ he is justified, and
sanctification, which is the work of carrying on and perfecting
that which is begun in regeneration, is accomplished under the
conditions of those new relations into which he is introduced
by justification. In justification we are delivered from all the
penal consequences of sin, and brought into such a state of
reconciliation with God, and communion of the Holy Ghost,
that we are emancipated from the bondage of legal fear, and
endued with that spirit of filial confidence and love which is
the essential principle of all acceptable obedience. Our justification, moreover, proceeds on the ground of our federal union
with Christ by faith, which is the basis of that vital and spiritual union of the soul with him from whom our sanctification
flows.—See above, Chap. XXXI., Question 3.

7. *How can it be shown that this work extends to the whole
man, the understanding, will, and affections?*

The soul is a unit, the same single agent alike, thinking,
feeling, and willing. A man can not love that loveliness which
he does not perceive, nor can he perceive that beauty, whether
moral or natural, which is uncongenial to his own heart. His
whole nature is morally depraved, 1st, blind or insensible to
spiritual beauty; 2d, averse, in the reigning dispositions of the
will, to moral right, and therefore disobedient. The order in
which the faculties act is as follows: The intellect perceives the
qualities of the object concerning which the mind is engaged;
the heart loves those qualities which are congenial to it; the
will chooses that which is loved.

This is proved, 1st, by experience. As the heart becomes
more depraved the mind becomes more insensible to spiritual
light. On the other hand, as the eyes behold more and more
clearly the beauty of the truth, the more lively become the
affections, and the more obedient the will. 2d. From the testimony of Scripture. By nature the whole man is depraved.
The understanding darkened, as well as the affections and will
perverted.—Eph. iv. 18.

If this be so, it is evident that sanctification must also be effected throughout the entire nature. 1st. From the necessity of the case. 2d. From the testimony of Scripture.—Rom. vi. 13; 2 Cor. iv. 6; Eph. i. 18; Col. iii. 10; 1 Thess. v. 23; 1 John iv. 7.

8. *In what sense is the body sanctified?*

1st. As consecrated, (1) as being the temple of the Holy Ghost, 1 Cor. vi. 19; (2) hence as being a member of Christ.— 1 Cor. vi. 15. 2d. As sanctified, since they are integral parts of our persons, their instincts and appetites act immediately upon the passions of our souls, and consequently these must be brought subject to the control of the sanctified soul, and all its members, as organs of the soul, made instruments of righteousness unto God.—Rom. vi. 13; 1 Thess. iv. 4. 3d. It will be made like Christ's glorified body.—1 Cor. xv. 44; Phil. iii. 21.

9. *To whom is the work of sanctification referred in Scripture?*

1st. To the Father.—1 Thess. vi. 23; Heb. xiii. 21. 2d. To the Son.—Eph. v. 25, 26; Titus ii. 14. 3d. To the Holy Ghost.— 1 Cor. vi. 11; 2 Thess. ii. 13.

In all external actions the three Persons of the Trinity are always represented as concurring, the Father working through the Son and Spirit, and the Son through the Spirit. Hence the work of sanctification is with special prominence attributed to the Holy Spirit, since he is the immediate agent therein, and since this is his special office work in the plan of redemption.

10. *What do the Scriptures teach as to the agency of the truth in the work of sanctification?*

The whole process of sanctification consists in the development and confirmation of the new principle of spiritual life implanted in the soul in regeneration, conducted by the Holy Ghost in perfect conformity to, and through the operation of the laws and habits of action natural to the soul as an intelligent, moral and free agent. Like the natural faculties both of body and mind, and the natural habits which modify the actions of those faculties, so Christian graces, or spiritual habits, are developed by exercise; the truths of the gospel being the objects upon which these graces act, and by which they are both excited and directed. Thus the divine loveliness of God presented in the truth, which is his image, is the object of our complacent love; his goodness of our gratitude; his promises of our trust; his judgments of our wholesome awe, and his commandments variously exercise us in the thousand forms of filial obedience. John xvii. 19; 1 Pet. i. 22; ii. 2; 2 Pet. i. 4; James i. 18.

11. *What efficiency do the Scriptures ascribe in this work to the Sacraments?*

There are three views entertained on this subject by theologians—

1st. The lowest view is, that the sacraments simply, as symbols, present the truth in a lively manner to the eye, and are effective thus only as a form of presenting the gospel objectively.

2d. The opinion occupying the opposite extreme is, that they, of their own proper efficiency, convey sanctifying grace *ex opere operato,* "because they convey grace by the virtue of the sacramental action itself, instituted by God for this very end, and not through the merit either of the agent (priest) or the receiver."—Bellarmin, "De Sac.," 2, 1.

3d. The true view is, "that the sacraments are efficacious means of grace, not merely exhibiting but actually conferring upon those who worthily receive them the benefits which they represent;" yet this efficacy does not reside properly in them, but accompanies their proper use in virtue of the divine institution and promise, through the accompanying agency of the Holy Ghost, and as suspended upon the exercise of faith upon the part of the recipient, which faith is at once the condition and the instrument of the reception of the benefit.—Matt. iii. 11; Acts ii. 41; x. 47; Rom. vi. 3; 1 Cor. xii. 13; Titus iii. 5; 1 Pet. iii. 21.

12. *What office do the Scriptures ascribe to faith in sanctification?*

Faith is the first grace in order exercised by the soul consequent upon regeneration, and the root of all other graces in principle.—Acts xv. 9; xxvi. 18. It is instrumental in securing sanctification therefore—

1st. By securing the change of the believer's relation to God and to the law, as a condition of life and favor.—See above, Question 6.

2d. By securing his union with Christ.—1 Cor. xiii.; Gal. ii. 20; Col. iii. 3.

3d. It is sanctifying in its own nature, since, in its widest sense, faith is that spiritual state of the soul in which it holds living active communion with spiritual truth. "By this faith a Christian believeth to be true, whatsoever is revealed in the word, for the authority of God himself speaking therein; and acteth differently, upon that which every particular passage thereof containeth; yielding obedience to the commands, trembling to the threatenings, and embracing the promises of God for this life, and that which is to come."—"Conf. Faith," ch. 14, § 2.

13. *What, according to Scripture, is necessary to constitute a good work?*

1st. That it should spring from a right motive, *i. e.*, love for God's character, regard for his authority, and zeal for his glory; love as a fruit of the Spirit, if not always consciously present, yet reigning as a permanent and controlling principle in the soul.

2d. That it be in accordance with his revealed law.—Deut. xii. 32; Isa. i. 11, 12; Col. ii. 16–23.

14. *What is the Popish doctrine as to "the counsels" of Christ, which are not included in the positive precepts of the law?*

The positive commands of Christ are represented as binding on all classes of Christians alike, and their observance necessary in order to salvation. His counsels, on the other hand, are binding only upon those who, seeking a higher degree of perfection and a more excellent reward, voluntarily assume them. These are such as celibacy, voluntary poverty, etc., and obedience to rule (monastic).—Bellarmin, "de Monachis," Cap. vii.

The wickedness of this distinction is evident—

1st. Because Christ demands the entire consecration of every Christian: after we have done all we are only unprofitable servants. Works of supererogation, therefore, are impossible.

2d. All such will worship is declared abhorrent to God.—Col. ii. 18–23; 1 Tim. iv. 3.

15. *What judgment is to be formed of the good works of unrenewed men?*

Unrenewed men retain some dispositions and affections in themselves relatively good, and they do many things in themselves right, and according to the letter of God's law. Yet—

1st. As to his person, every unrenewed man is under God's wrath and curse, and consequently can do nothing pleasing to him. The rebel in arms is in every thing a rebel until he submits and returns to his allegiance.

2d. Love for God and regard to his authority are never his supreme motive in any of his acts. Thus while many of his actions are civilly good as respects his fellow-men, none of them can be spiritually good as it respects God. There is an obvious distinction between an act viewed in itself, and viewed in connection with its agent. The sinner, previous to justification and renewal, is a rebel; each one of his acts is the act. of a rebel, though as considered in itself any single act may be either good, bad, or indifferent.

16. In what sense are good works necessary for salvation?

As the necessary and invariable fruits of both the change of relation accomplished in justification, and of the change of nature accomplished in regeneration, though never as the meritorious grounds or conditions of our salvation.

This necessity results, 1st, from the holiness of God; 2d, from his eternal purpose, Eph. i. 4; ii. 10; 3d, from the design and redemptive efficacy of Christ's death, Eph. v. 25–27; 4th, from the union of the believer with Christ, and the energy of his indwelling Spirit, John xv. 5; Gal. v. 22; 5th, from the very nature of faith, which first leads to and then works by love, Gal. v. 6; 6th, from the command of God, 1 Thes. iv. 6; 1 Pet. i. 15; 7th, from the nature of heaven, Rev. xxi. 27.

17. What is the theory of the Antinomians upon this subject?

Antinomians are, as their name signifies, those who deny that Christians are bound to obey the law. They argue that, as Christ has in our place fulfilled both the preceptive and the penal departments of God's law, his people must be delivered from all obligation to observe it, either as a rule of duty or as a condition of salvation.—See above, Question 3, Chap. XXV.

It is evident that all systems of Perfectionism, which teach (as the Pelagian and Oberlin theories) that men's ability to obey is the measure of their responsibility, or (as the Papal and Arminian theories) that God, for Christ's sake, has graciously reduced his demand from *absolute* moral perfection to faith and evangelical obedience, are essentially Antinomian. Because they all agree in teaching that Christians in this life are no longer under obligations to fulfil the Adamic law of absolute moral perfection.

Paul, in the 6th chapter of Romans, declares that this damnable heresy was charged as a legitimate consequent upon his doctrine in that day. He not only repudiates the charge, but, on the contrary, affirms that free justification through an imputed righteousness, without the merits of works, is the only possible condition in which the sinner can learn to bring forth holy works as the fruits of filial love. The very purpose of Christ was to redeem to himself a peculiar people, zealous of good works, and this he accomplished by delivering them from the federal bondage of the law, in order to render them capable as the Lord's freedmen of moral conformity to it, ever increasingly in this life, absolutely in the life to come.

18. *What are the different senses which have been applied to the term "merit"?*

It has been technically used in two different senses. 1st. Strictly, to designate the common quality of all services to which a reward is due, *ex justiciâ,* on account of their intrinsic value and dignity. 2d. Improperly, it was used by the Fathers as equivalent to that which results in or attains to a reward or consequent, without specifying the ground or virtue on account of which it is secured.—Turretin, L. xvii., Quæstio 5.

19. *What distinction does the Romish Church design to signalize by the terms "merit of condignity" and the "merit of congruity"?*

The "merit of condignity" they teach attaches only to works wrought subsequently to regeneration by the aid of divine grace, and is that degree of merit that intrinsically, and in the way of equal right, not by mere promise or covenant, deserves the reward it attains at God's hands. The "merit of congruity" they teach attaches to those good dispositions or works which a man may, previously to regeneration, realize without the aid of divine grace, and which makes it congruous or specially fitting for God to reward the agent by infusing grace into his heart.

It is extremely difficult to determine the exact position of the Romish Church on this subject, since different schools of theologians in her midst differ widely, and the decisions of the Council of Trent are studiously ambiguous. The general belief appears to be that ability to perform good works springs from grace infused into the sinner's heart for Christ's sake, through the instrumentality of the sacraments, but that afterwards these good works merit, that is, lay for us the foundation of a just claim to salvation and glory. Some say, like Bellarmin, "De Justific.," 5, 1, and 4, 7, that this merit attaches to the good works of Christians intrinsically, as well as in consequence of God's promise; others that these works deserve the reward only because God has promised the reward on the condition of the work.—"Coun. Trent," Sess. vi., Cap. xvi., and canons 24 and 32.

20. *What is necessary that a work should be in the proper sense of the term meritorious?*

Turretin makes five conditions necessary to that end. 1st. That the work be not of debt, or which the worker was under obligation to render.—Luke xvii. 10. 2d. That it is our own, *i. e.,* effected by our own natural energy. 3d. That it be perfect. 4th. That it be equal to the reward merited. 5th. That the reward be of justice due to such an act.—Turretin, L. xvii., Quæstio 5.

According to this definition, it is evident, from the absolute dependence and obligation of the creature, that he can never merit any reward for whatever obedience he may render to the commands of his Creator. 1st. Because all the strength he works with is freely given by God. 2d. All the service he can render is owed to God. 3d. Nothing he can do can equal the reward of God's favor and eternal blessedness.

Under the covenant of works, God graciously promised to reward the obedience of Adam with eternal life. This was a reward, however, not of merit, but of free grace and promise. Every thing under that constitution depended upon the standing of the person before God. As long as Adam continued without sin, his services were accepted and rewarded according to promise. But from the moment he forfeited the promise, and lost his standing before God, no work of his, no matter of what character, could merit any thing at the hand of God.

21. *How can it be proved that our good works, even after the restoration of our person to God's favor by justification, do not merit heaven?*

1st. Justification proceeds upon the infinite merits of Christ, and on that foundation rests our title to the favor of God and all the infinite consequences thereof. Christ's merit, lying at the foundation and embracing all, excludes the possibility of our meriting any thing. 2d. The law demands perfect obedience.— Rom. iii. 23; Gal. v. 3. 3d. We are saved by grace not by works.—Eph. ii. 8, 9. 4th. All good dispositions are graces or gifts of God.—1 Cor. xv. 10; Phil. ii. 13; 1 Thess. ii. 13. 5th. Eternal life itself is declared to be the gift of God.—1 John v. 11.

22. *What do the Scriptures teach concerning the good works of believers, and the rewards promised to them?*

Both the work and its reward are branches from the same gracious root. The covenant of grace provides alike for the infusion of grace in the heart, the exercise of this grace in the life, and the rewards of that grace so exercised. It is all of grace, grace for grace, grace added to grace, presented to us in this form of a reward: 1st. That it may act upon us as a rational motive to diligent obedience. 2d. To mark that the gift of heaven and eternal blessedness is an act of strict legal justice (1) in respect to the perfect merits of Christ, (2) in respect to God's faithful adherence to his own free promise.—1 John i. 9. 3d. To indicate that the heavenly reward stands in a certain gracious proportion to the grace given in the obedience on earth; (1) because God so wills it, Matt. xvi. 27; 1 Cor. iii. 8; (3) because the grace given on earth prepares the soul to receive the grace given in heaven, 2 Cor. iv. 17.

Is Perfect Sanctification attainable by Believers in Christ in this Life?

23. *What, in general terms, is perfectionism?*

The various theories of perfectionism all agree in maintaining that it is possible for a child of God in this world to become, 1st, perfectly free from sin, 2d, conformed to the law under which they now live. They differ very variously among themselves, however, 1st, as to what sin is; 2d, as to what law we are now obliged to fulfil; 3d, as to the means whereby this perfection may be attained, whether by nature or by grace.

24. *How does the Pelagian theory of the nature of man and of grace lead to perfectionism?*

Pelagians maintain, 1st, as to man's nature, that it was not radically corrupted by the fall, and that every man possesses sufficient power to fulfil all the duties required of him, since God can not in justice demand that which man has not full power to do. 2d. As to God's grace, that it is nothing more than the favorable constitution of our own minds, and the influence exerted on them by the truth he has revealed to us, and the propitious circumstances in which he has placed us. Thus in the Christian church, and with the Christian revelation, men are, in fact, placed in the most propitious circumstances possible to persuade them to perform their duties. It follows from this system directly that every one who wishes may certainly attain perfection by using his natural powers and advantages of position with sufficient care.—"Wigger's Historical View of Augustinianism and Pelagianism."

25. *What, according to the Pelagian theory, is the nature of the sin from which man may be perfectly free; what the law which he may perfectly fulfil, and what are the means by which this perfection may be attained?*

They deny original and inherent corruption of nature, and hold that *sin* is only voluntary transgression of known law, from which any man may abstain if he will.

As to the *law* which man in his present state may perfectly fulfil, they hold that it is the single and original law of God, the requirements of which, however, in the case of every individual subject, are measured by the individual's ability, and opportunities of knowledge. As to the *means* whereby this perfection may be attained, they maintain the plenary ability of man's natural will to discharge all the obligations resting upon him, and they admit the assistance of God's grace only in the sense of the influence of the truth, and other propitious circumstances in persuading man to use his own power. Thus the means of perfect sanctification are, 1st, man's own volition, 2d, as helped by the study of the Bible, prudent avoidance of temptation, etc.

26. *In what sense do Romanists hold the doctrine of perfection?*

The decisions of the Council of Trent upon the subject, as upon all critical points, are studiously ambiguous. They lay down the principle that the law must be possible to them upon whom it is binding, since God does not command impossibilities. Men justified (sanctified) may by the grace of God dwelling in them satisfy the divine law, *pro hujus vitœ statu, i. e.,* as graciously for Christ's sake adjusted to our present capacities. They confess, nevertheless, that the just may fall into venial sins every day, and that while in the flesh no man can live entirely without sin (unless by a special privilege of God); yet that in this life the renewed can fully keep the divine law; and even by the observance of the evangelical counsels do more than is commanded; and thus, as many saints have actually done, lay up a fund of supererogatory merit.—"Council of Trent," Session vi. Compare Chap. xi. and xvi., and Canons 18, 23, and 32. See above, Question 14.

27. *In what sense do they hold that the renewed may, in this life live without sin; in what sense fully satisfy the law; and by the use of what means do they teach that this perfection may be attained?*

As to sin, they hold the distinction between mortal and venial sins, and that the concupiscence that remains in the bosom of the renewed, as the result of original and the fuel of actual sin, is not itself sin, since sin consists only in the consent of the will to the impulse of concupiscence. In accordance with these views they hold that a Christian in this life may live without committing mortal sins, but that he never can be free from the inward movements of concupiscence, nor from liability to fall through ignorance, inattention, or passion, into venial sins.

As to the law, which a believer in this life may fully satisfy, they hold that as God is just and can not demand of us what is impossible, his law is graciously adjusted to our present capacities, as assisted by grace, and that it is this law *pro hujus vitæ statu,* which we may fulfil.

As to the means whereby this perfection may be attained, they hold that divine grace precedes, accompanies, and follows all of our good works, which divine grace is to be sought through those sacramental and priestly channels which Christ has instituted in his church, and especially in the observance of works of prayer, fasting, and alms deeds, and the acquisition of supererogatory merit by the fulfilment of the counsels of Christ to chastity, obedience, and voluntary poverty.—"Council of Trent," Sess. xiv., Chapter v., Sess. vi., Chapters xi. and xii., Sess. v., Canon 5; "Cat. Rom.," Part II., Chapter ii., Question 32, and Part II., Chapter v., Question 59, and Part III., Chapter x., Questions 5–10.

28. *In what form was the doctrine taught by the early Arminians?*

Arminius declared that his mind was in suspense upon this subject ("Writings of Arminius," translated by Nichols, Vol. I., p. 256). His immediate successors in the theological leadership of the remonstrant party, developed a theory of perfectionism apparently identical with that taught by Wesley, and professed by his disciples. "A man can, with the assistance of divine grace, keep all the commandments of God perfectly, according to the gospel or covenant of grace. The highest evangelical perfection (for we are not teaching a legal perfection, which includes sinlessness entire in all respects and in the highest degree, and excludes all imperfection and infirmity, for this we believe to be impossible), embraces two things, 1st, a perfection proportioned to the powers of each individual; 2d, a desire of making continual progress and increasing one's strength more and more."—Episcopius, quoted by Dr. G. Peck, "Christian Perfection," pp. 135 and 136.

29. *What is the Wesleyan doctrine on this subject?*

1st. That although every believer as soon as he is justified is regenerated, and commences the incipient stages of sanctification, yet this does not exclude the remains of much inherent sin, nor the warfare of the flesh against the Spirit, which may continue for a long time, but which must cease at some time before the subject can be fit for heaven.

2d. This state of progressive sanctification is not itself perfection, which is properly designated by the phrases "entire," or "perfect santification." This, sooner or later, every heir of glory must experience; although the majority do not reach it long before death, it is the attainment of some in the midst of life, and consequently it is the duty and privilege of all to desire, strive for, and expect its attainment now.

3d. This state of evangelical perfection does not consist in an ability to fulfil perfectly the original and absolute law of holiness under which Adam was created, nor does it exclude all liability to mistake, or to the infirmities of the flesh, and of natural temperament, but it does exclude all inward disposition to sin as well as all outward commission of it, since it consists in a state in which perfect faith in Christ and perfect love for God fills the whole soul and governs the entire life, and thus fulfils all the requirements of the "law of Christ," under which alone the Christian's probation is now held.

30. *In what sense do they teach that men may live without sin?*

Mr. Wesley did not himself use, though he did not object to, the phrase "sinless perfection." He distinguished between "sin, properly so called, *i. e.*, a voluntary transgression of a known law, and sin, improperly so called, *i. e.*, an involuntary trangression of a divine law, known or unknown," and declared "I believe there is no such perfection in this life as excludes these involuntary transgressions, which I apprehend to be naturally consequent on the ignorance and mistakes inseparable from mortality." He also declares that the obedience of the perfect Christian "can not bear the rigor of God's justice, but needs atoning blood," and consequently the most perfect "must continually say, 'forgive us our trespasses,'" and Dr. Peck says that the holier men are here "the more they loathe and abhor themselves." On the other hand they hold that a Christian may in this life attain to a state of perfect and constant love, which fulfils perfectly all the requirements of the gospel covenant. Violations of the original and absolute law of God are not counted to the believer for sin, since for him Christ has been made the end of that law for righteousness, and for Christ's sake he has been delivered from that law and been made subject to the "law of Christ," and that only is sin to the Christian which is a violation of this law of love. See Mr. Wesley's "Tract on Christian Perfection," in the volume of "Methodist Doctrinal Tracts," pp. 294, 310, 312, and Dr. Peck's "Christian Doc. of Perfection," p. 204.

31. *What law do they say the Christian can in this life perfectly obey?*

Dr. Peck says, p. 244, "To fallen humanity, though renewed by grace, perfect obedience to the moral law is inpracticable during the present probationary state. And consequently Christian perfection does not imply perfect obedience to the moral law."—Peck, p. 244.

This moral law they hold to be universal and unchangeable, all moral agents are under perpetual obligations to fulfil it, and they are in no degree released therefrom by their loss of ability through sin.—Peck, p. 271. This law sustains, however, a twofold relation to the creature. 1st. It is a rule of being and acting. 2d. It is a condition of acceptance. In consequence of sin, it became impossible for men to obtain salvation by the law, and therefore Christ appeared and rendered to this law perfect satisfaction in our stead, and thus is for us the end of the law for righteousness. This law, therefore, remaining forever as a rule of duty, is abrogated by Christ as a condition of our acceptance. "Nor is any man living bound to observe the Adamic more than the Mosaic law (I mean it is not the condition either of present or future salvation.)"—"Doctrinal Tracts," p. 332. "The gospel, which is the law of love, the 'law of liberty,' offers salvation upon other terms, and yet provides the vindication of the broken law. The condition of justification at first is *faith alone*, and the condition of continued acceptance is *faith working by love*. There are degrees of faith, and degrees of love. . . . Perfect faith and perfect love is Christian perfection." "Christian character is estimated by the conditions of the gospel; Christian perfection implies the perfect performance of these conditions and nothing more."

32. *By what means do they teach this perfection is to be attained?*

Wesley says, "I believe this perfection is always wrought in the soul by a simple act of faith, consequently in an instant. But I believe there is a gradual work, both preceding and following that instant."—Quoted by Dr. Peck, pp. 47, 48.

They hold that this entire sanctification is not to be effected through either the strength or the merit of man, but entirely of grace, for Christ's sake, by the Holy Ghost, through the instrumentality of faith in the Lord Jesus Christ, which faith involves our believing, 1st, "in the sufficiency of the provisions of the gospel for the complete deliverance of the soul from sin." 2d. "That these provisions are made for *us*." 3d. "That this blessing is for us *now*."—Peck, "Ch. Doc. Sanc.," pp. 405–407.

33. *What is the Oberlin doctrine of perfection?*

"It is a full and perfect discharge of our entire duty, of all existing obligations to God, and all other beings. It is perfect obedience to the moral law." This is God's original and universal law, which, however, always, not because of grace, but of sheer justice, adjusts its demands to the measure of the present ability of the subject. The law of God can not now justly demand that we should love him as we might have done if we had always improved our time, etc. Yet a Christian may now attain to a state of "perfect and disinterested benevolence," may be, "according to his knowledge, as upright as God is," and as "perfectly conformed to the will of God as is the will of the inhabitants of heaven." And this, Mr. Finney appears to teach, is essential for even the lowest stage of genuine Christian experience. The amount of the matter appears to be, God has a right to demand only that which we have the power to render; therefore, it follows that we have full power to render all that God demands, and, therefore, we may be as perfectly conformed to his will *as it regards us*, as the inhabitants of heaven are to his will *as it regards them.*"

Pres. Mahan, "Scripture Doctrines of Christian Perfection," and Prof. Finney, "Oberlin Evangelist," Vol. IV., No. 19, and Vol. IV., No. 15, as quoted by Dr. Peck.

34. *State the points of agreement and disagreement between these several theories, Pelagian, Romish, Arminian, and Oberlin?*

1st. They all agree in maintaining that it is possible for men in this life to attain a state in which they may habitually and perfectly fulfil all their obligations, *i. e.*, to be and do perfectly all that God requires them to be or do at present.

2d. The Pelagian theory differs from all the rest, in denying the deterioration of our natural and moral powers, and consequently, in denying the necessity of the intervention of supernatural grace to the end of making men perfect.

3d. The Pelagian and Oberlin theories agree in making the original moral law of God the standard of perfection. The Oberlin theologians, however, admitting that our powers are deteriorated by sin, hold that God's law, as a matter of sheer justice, adjusts its demands to the present ability of the subject. The Romish theory regards the same law as the standard of perfection, but differs from the Pelagian theory in maintaining that the demands of this law are adjusted to man's deteriorated powers; and on the other hand, it differs from the Oberlin theory, by holding that the lowering of the demands of this law in adjustment to the enfeebled powers of man, instead of being of sheer justice, is of grace for the merits of Christ. The Arminian theory differs from all the rest in denying that the original law is the standard of evangelical perfection; in holding that that law having been fulfilled by Christ, the Christian is now required only to fulfil the requirements of the gospel covenant of grace. This, however, appears to differ more in form than essence from the Romish position in this regard.

4th. The Romish and Arminian theories *agree*—1st. In admitting that the perfect Christian is still liable to transgress the provisions of the original moral law, and that he is subject to mistakes and infirmities. The Romanist calls them venial sins; the Arminian, mistakes or infirmities. 2d. In referring all the work of making man perfect to the efficiency of the Holy Ghost, who is given for Christ's sake. But they differ, on the other hand, 1st, as to the nature of that faith by which sanctification is effected, and, 2d, as to the merit of good works.

35. *What are the arguments upon which perfectionists sustain their theory, and how may they be answered?*

1st. They argue that this perfection is *attainable* in this life, (1.) From the commands of God, who never will command impossibilities.—Matt. v. 48.   (2.) From the fact that abundant provision has already been made in the gospel for securing the perfect sanctification of God's people; in fact, all the provision that ever will be made. (3.) From the promises of God to redeem Israel from all his iniquities, etc.—Ps. cxxx. 8; Ezek. xxxvi. 25–29; 1 John i. 7, 9. (4.) From the prayers of saints recorded in Scripture with implied approval.—Ps. li. 2; Heb. xiii. 21.

2d. They argue that this perfection has in *fact* been attained, (1.) From biblical examples, as David.—Acts xiii. 22. See also Gen. vi. 9; Job i. 1; Luke i. 6. (2.) Modern examples—Peck's "Christian Perfection," pp. 365–396.

We ANSWER—

1st. The Scriptures never assert that a Christian may in this life attain to a state in which he may live without sin.

2d. The meaning of special passages must be interpreted in consistency with the entire testimony of Scripture.

3d. The language of Scripture never implies that man may here live without sin. The commands of God are adjusted to man's responsibility, and the aspirations and prayers of the saints to their duties and ultimate privileges, and not to their present ability. Perfection is the true aim of the Christian's effort in every period of growth and in every act. The terms "perfect" and "blameless" are often relative, or used to signify simple genuineness or sincerity. This is evident from the recorded fact—

4th. That all the perfect men of the Scriptures sometimes sinned; witness the histories of Noah, Job, David, Paul, and compare Gen. vi. 9, with Gen. ix. 21, and Job i. 1, with Job iii. 1, and ix. 20; also see Gal. ii. 11, 14; Ps. xix. 12; Rom. vii.; Gal. v. 17; Phil. iii. 12–14.

36. *What special objections bear against the Pelagian theory of perfection?*

This is a part of a wholly Anti-Christian system. Its constituent elements are a denial of the Scripture testimony with regard to original sin, and the work of the Spirit of grace in effectual calling, and an assertion of man's ability to save himself. It involves low views of the guilt and turpitude of sin, and of the extent, spirituality, and unchangeableness of God's holy law. This is the only perfectly consistent theory of perfection ever ventilated, and in the same proportion it is the most thoroughly unchristian.

37. *What special objections bear against the Romish theory?*

This theory is inconsistent—

1st. With the true nature of sin. It denies that concupiscence is sin, and admits as such only those deliberate acts of the will which assent to the impulse of concupiscence. It distinguishes between mortal and venial sins. The truth is that every sin is mortal, and concupiscence, "sin dwelling in me," "law in my members," is of the very essence of sin.—Rom. vii. 8–23.

2d. It is inconsistent with the nature of God's holy law, which is essentially immutable, and the demands of which have never been lowered in accommodation to the weakened faculties of men.

3d. It is essentially connected with their theory of the merit of good works, and of the higher merit of works of supererogation which is radically subversive of the essentials of the gospel.

38. *What special objections bear against the Oberlin theory?*

This theory appears to assimilate more nearly than the others with the terrible self-consistency and the Anti-Christian spirit of the Pelagian view. It differs from that heresy, however, in holding—1st. That the law of God is, as a matter of sheer justice, accommodated to the weakened faculties of men. 2d. That the shortcomings of men in the present life, as measured by the original law of God, are not sin, since a man's duty is measured only by his ability. 3d. In making the principle of this perfection to consist in "perfect and disinterested benevolence." In all these respects, also, this theory is inconsistent with the true nature of God's law, the true nature of sin, and the true nature of virtue.

39. *What special objections bear against the Arminian theory?*

This view, as presented by the Wesleyan standard writers, is far less inconsistent with the principles and spirit of Christianity than either of the others, and consequently it is precisely in the same proportion less self-consistent as a theory, and less accurate in its use of technical language. These Christian brethren are to be honored for their exalted views, and earnest advocacy of the duty of pressing forward to the highest measures of Christian attainment, while it is to be forever lamented that their great founder was so far misled by the prejudices of system as to bind in unnatural alliance so much precious truth with a theory and terminology proper only to radical error. I will make here, once for all, the general explanation, that when stating the Arminian doctrine on any point, I have generally preferred to refer to the form in which the doctrine was explicitly defined by the Dutch Remonstrants, rather than to the modified, and, as it seems to me, far less logically definite form in which it is set forth by the authorities of the Wesleyan churches, who properly style themselves *"Evangelical* Arminians." I attribute the peculiar theoretical indefiniteness which appears to render their definitions obscure, especially on the subjects of justification and of perfection, to the spirit of a warm, loving, working Christianity struggling with the false premises of an Arminian philosophy.

1st. While over and over insisting upon the distinction as to the twofold relation sustained by the original law of God to man (1) as a rule of being and acting, (2) as a condition of divine favor, their whole theory is based upon a logical confusion of these two things so distinct. Dr. Peck teaches earnestly, and confirms by many Wesleyan testimonies, excellent Calvinistic doctrine upon the following points: The original law of God is universal and unchangeable, its demands never can be changed nor compromised. Obedience to this law was the condition of the original covenant of works. This condition was broken by Adam, but, in our behalf, perfectly fulfilled by Christ, and thus the integrity of God's changeless law was preserved. Therefore, he goes on to argue, the believer is no longer under the law, but under the covenant of grace, *i. e.,* to use Wesley's own qualifying parenthesis, "as the condition of either present or future salvation." Certainly, we *answer,* Christ is the end of the law for us for righteousness, in its *forensic* sense, that is, to secure our justification, but surely Christ did not satisfy that changeless law, in our place, in such a sense that it does not remain our rule of action, to which it is our duty to be *personally* conformed. The question of perfection is one which relates to our personal character, not to our relations; it is moral and inherent, and not forensic. To prove, therefore, what we also rejoice to believe, that the original law of God, under the gospel covenant, is no longer our *condition* of salvation, does not avail one iota towards proving that God, under the gospel, demands an obedience adjusted to any easier standard than was required before.

2d. This theory is part of the Arminian view of the covenant of grace, which we regard so inconsistent with the gospel, and which Mr. Watson (see "Institutes," Part II., Chap. xxiii.) appears to attempt to avoid while refusing to admit the imputation to the believer of Christ's righteousness. This view is. that by Christ's propitiation, he having fulfilled the original law of God, it is made consistent with divine justice to present salvation upon easier conditions, *i. e.*, faith and evangelical obedience; Christian perfection requiring nothing more than the perfect fulfilment of these new gracious conditions. Now this view, besides confounding the ideas of law, and of covenant, of a rule, and of a condition, of a ground of justification, and of a standard of sanctification, is inconsistent with the broad teachings of the gospel concerning the righteousness of Christ, and the office of faith in justification. It makes the merit of Christ only in some uncertain and distant way the *occasion* of our salvation, and faith, and evangelical obedience, in the place of perfect obedience under the old covenant, the *ground* instead of the mere *instrument* and fruit of our justification. Logically developed, this theory must lead to the Romish doctrine as to the merit of good works.

3d. This theory denies that mistakes and infirmities resulting from the effects of original sin, are themselves sin, yet admits that they are to be confessed, forgiveness implored for them, and the atonement of Christ's blood applied to them, and that the more perfect a man becomes the more he abhors his own internal state. Surely this is a confusion of language, and abuse of the word sin. What is sin but (1) that which transgresses God's original law, (2) which needs Christ's atonement, (3) which should be confessed, and must be forgiven, (4) which lays a proper foundation for self-abhorrence.

40. *What express declarations of Scripture are contradicted by every possible modification of the theory of Christian perfection?*

1 Kings viii. 46; Prov. xx. 9; Eccle. vii. 20; James iii. 2; 1 John i. 8.

41. *How may it be shown to be in opposition to the experience of saints, as recorded in the Scriptures?*

See Paul's account of himself, Rom. vii. 14–25; Phil. iii. 12–14. See case of David, Ps. xix. 12; Ps. li.; of Moses, Ps. xc. 8; of Job, Job xlii. 5, 6; of Daniel, ix. 20. See Luke xviii. 13; Gal. ii. 11–13; vi. 1; James v. 16.

42. *How does it conflict with the ordinary experience of God's people?*

The more holy a man is, the more humble, self-renouncing, self-abhorring, and the more sensitive to every sin he becomes, and the more closely he clings to Christ. The moral imperfections which cling to him he feels to be sins, laments and strives to overcome them. Believers find that their life is a constant warfare, and they need to take the kingdom of heaven by storm, and watch while they pray. They are always subject to the constant chastisement of their Father's loving hand, which can only be designed to correct their imperfections, and to confirm their graces. And it has been notoriously the fact that the best Christians have been those who have been the least prone to claim the attainment of perfection for themselves.

43. *What are the legitimate practical effects of perfectionism?*

The tendency of every such doctrine must be evil, except in so far as it is modified or counteracted by limiting or inconsistent truths held in connection, which is pre-eminently the case with respect to the Wesleyan view, from the amount of pure gospel which in that instance the figment of perfectionism alloys. But perfectionism, by itself, must tend, 1st, to low views of God's law; 2d, to inadequate views of the heinousness of sin; 3d, to a low standard of moral excellence; 4th, to spiritual pride and fanaticism.

AUTHORITATIVE STATEMENTS OF CHURCH DOCTRINE.

ROMISH DOCTRINE AS TO THE MORAL PERFECTION OF THE REGENERATE, AS TO GOOD WORKS, AND WORKS OF SUPEREROGATION. As to their view of the MERIT OF GOOD WORKS, see above, Chap. XXXIII.

"*Conc. Trident.*," Sess. 5, can. 5.—"If any one denies, that, by the grace of our Lord Jesus Christ, which is conferred in baptism, the guilt of original sin is remitted; or even asserts that the whole of that which has the true and proper nature of sin is not taken away; but says that it is only rased, or not imputed; let him be anathema. . . . . But this holy Synod confesses and is sensible, that in the baptized there remains concupiscence, or an incentive (to sin). . . . This concupiscence, which the Apostle sometimes calls sin, the holy Synod declares that the Catholic Church has never understood it to be called sin, as being truly and properly sin in those *born again*, but because it is of sin, and inclines to sin. If any man is of a contrary sentiment, let him be anathema."

"*Conc. Trident.*," Sess. 6, can. 18.—"If any one says that the commandments of God, even for one that is justified and constituted in grace, are impossible to keep, let him be anathema."

Bellarmin, "*De Justific.*," iv. 10, *sqq.*—"If precepts are impossible, they oblige no one, and hence the precepts are not precepts. Neither is it possible to devise wherein any one sins in respect to that which it is impossible to avoid."

Ibid, "*De Monachis,*" cap. 7.—"A 'council of perfection' we call a good work, not commanded us by Christ, but declared; not appointed but commended. But it differs from a precept in respect to its matter, subject, form, and end. (1.) In respect to their *matter* (the difference) is twofold. *First,* because the matter of the precept is easier, that of the counsel more difficult, for the former is derived from the principles of nature, while the latter in some sense exceeds nature, *e. g.*, for nature inclines to the preservation of conjugal fidelity, but not to abstaining from the conjugal relation. *Secondly,* because the matter of the precept is good . . . for the council includes the precept, which relates to the same matter, and adds something beyond the precept. (2.) In respect to the *subject,* precepts and counsels differ, because the precept binds all men in common, while the counsel does not. (3.) In respect to their *form* they differ, because the precept binds of its own inherent obligation, but the counsel through the will of man. (4.) In respect to their *end* or *effects* they differ, because the precept observed has a reward, but when not observed a penalty, but the counsel when not observed has no penalty, but when observed has the greater reward." Cap. 8.—"It is the opinion of all Catholics that there are many true and proper evangelical counsels, but especially, viz., celibacy, poverty, and obedience (monastic), which are neither commanded to all, nor matters of indifference, but grateful to God and by him commended (Matt. xix. 11, sq., 21; 1 Cor. vii. 1–7)."

Lutheran Doctrine.

"*Apology for Augburg Conf.*," p. 91.—"The entire Scripture and the whole church declare that the Law can not be satisfied (by any thing within man's power since the fall). This incomplete fulfilling of the law is accepted, not on its own account, but only through faith in Christ. Otherwise the Law always accuses us. . . In this infirmity there is always sin, which may be charged to our account (for condemnation)."

"*Formula Concordiæ,*" p. 678.—"The papal and monastic doctrine, that a man after he is regenerated is able perfectly to fulfil the law of God in this life, is to be rejected."

Ib., p. 589.—"Our Confession is, that good works most surely and indubitably follow a true faith, as the fruits of a good tree. We also believe that good works are entirely to be left out of account, not only when we are treating of justification, but even when we are debating concerning our eternal life."

Ib., p. 700.—"Because those are not good works, which any one himself devises with good intention, or which are done according to human traditions; but those which God himself has prescribed and ordered in his own word. Because works truly good can be performed, not by the proper natural powers, but then only when the person is, by faith, reconciled with God, and is renewed by the Spirit, and is created anew to good works, in Jesus Christ."

Reformed Doctrine.

"*Heidelberg Catechism,*" Q. 62.—"Our best works in the present life are all imperfect and stained with sin."

"*Thirty-nine Articles of the Church of England,*" Art. 12.—"Albeit that Good Works, which are the fruits of faith, and follow after Justification, can not put away our sins, and endure the severity of God's judgment; yet are they pleasing and acceptable to God in Christ, and do spring out necessarily of a true.and lively faith; insomuch that by them a lively faith may be as evidently known as a tree discerned by the fruit."

Ib., Art. 14.—"Voluntary works besides, over and above, God's commandments, which they call Works of Supererogation, can not be taught without arrogancy and impiety; for by them men do declare that they do not only render unto God as much as they are bound to do, but that they do more for his sake, than of bounden duty is required: whereas Christ saith plainly, When ye have done all that are commanded to you, say, We are unprofitable servants."

"*Confess. Helvetica posterior,*" p. 498.—"We teach that God gives an ample reward to those doing good works. Yet we refer this reward that the Lord gives, not to the merit of the men receiving it, but to the goodness, liberality, and truth of God, who promises and bestows it; who, while he owes nothing to any one, yet has promised that he will give a reward to his faithful worshippers."

"*West. Conf. of Faith,*" ch. 16, § 4.—"They who in their obedience attain to the greatest height which is possible in this life, are so far from being able to supererogate, and to do more than God requires, that they fall short of much, which in their duty they are bound to do" (see the whole chapter).

Ib., chap. 13, § 2.—"This sanctification is throughout in the whole man, yet imperfect in this life: there abideth still some remnants of corruption in every part, whence ariseth a continual and irreconcilable war, the flesh lusting against the Spirit, and the Spirit against the flesh." § 3.—"In which war, although the remaining corruption for a time may much prevail, yet, through the continual supply of strength from the sanctifying Spirit of Christ, the regenerate part doth overcome: and so the saints grow in grace, perfecting holiness in the fear of God."

CHAPTER XXXVI.

PERSEVERANCE OF THE SAINTS.

1. *What is the Scriptural doctrine as to the perseverance of the saints?*

"They whom God hath accepted in his beloved, effectively called and sanctified by his Spirit, can neither totally nor finally fall away from the state of grace; but shall certainly persevere therein to the end, and be eternally saved."—"Con. Faith," Chap. xvii.; "L. Cat.," Question 79.

2. *By what arguments may the certainty of the final perseverance of the saints be established.*

1st. The direct assertions of Scripture.—John x. 28, 29; Rom. xi. 29; Phil. i. 6; 1 Pet. i. 5.

2d. This certainty is a necessary inference, from the Scriptural doctrine (1) of election, Jer. xxxi. 3; Matt. xxiv. 22–24; Acts xiii. 48; Rom. viii. 30; (2) of the covenant of grace, wherein the Father gave his people to his Son as the reward of his obedience and suffering, Jer. xxxii. 40; John xvii. 2–6; (3) of the union of Christians with Christ, in the federal aspect of which Christ is their surety, and they can not fail (Rom. viii. 1), and in the spiritual and vital aspect of which they abide in him, and because he lives they must live also, John xiv. 19; Rom. viii. 38, 39; Gal. ii. 20; (4) of the atonement, wherein Christ discharged all the obligations of his people to the law as a covenant of life, and purchased for them all covenanted blessings; if one of them should fail, therefore, the sure foundation of all would be shaken, Is. liii. 6, 11; Matt. xx. 28; 1 Pet. ii. 24; (5) of justification, which declares all the conditions of the covenant of life satisfied, and sets its subject into a new relation to God for all future time, so that he can not fall under condemnation, since he is not under the law, but under grace, Rom. vi. 14; (6) of the indwelling of the Holy Ghost, (*a*) as a seal by which we are marked as belonging to God, (*b*) as an earnest, or first instalment of the promised redemption, in pledge of complete fulfilment, John xiv. 16; 2 Cor. i. 21, 22; v. 5; Eph. i. 14; (7) of the prevalency of Christ's intercession. John xi. 42; xvii. 11, 15, 20; Rom. viii. 34.

3. *What is the doctrine of the Romish Church on this subject?*

"Council of Trent," Sess. vi., Canon 23. "If any one maintain that a man once justified can not lose grace, and, therefore, that he who falls and sins never was truly justified, let him be accursed."—See below, under Romish doctrine in this chapter, their view as to "venial sins."

4. *What is the Arminian doctrine on this point?*

It is an inseparable part of the Arminian system, flowing necessarily from their views of election, of the design and effect of Christ's death, and of sufficient grace and free will, that those who were once justified and regenerated may, by neglecting grace and grieving the Holy Spirit, fall into such sins as are inconsistent with true justifying faith, and continuing and dying in the same, may consequently finally fall into perdition.—"Confession of the Remonstrants," xi. 7. The Lutherans and the Arminians agree on this point. They both believe that the "elect" (those whom God has chosen to eternal life because he has certainly foreseen their perseverance in faith and obedience to the end) can not finally apostatize. The true question between them and the Calvinists, therefore, is *not* whether the "elect," *but* whether those once truly "regenerate and justified" can finally apostatize and perish.

5. *What objection is urged against the orthodox doctrine on the ground of the free agency of man?*

Those who deny the certainty of the final perseverance of the saints hold the false theory that liberty of the will consists in indifference, or the power of contrary choice, and consequently that certainty is inconsistent with liberty. This fallacy is disproved above, Chap. XV., see especially Ques. 25, 26.

That God does govern the free acts of his creatures, as a matter of fact, is clear from history and prophecy, from universal Christian consciousness and experience, and from Scripture.—Acts ii. 23; Eph. i. 11; Phil. ii. 13; Prov. xxi. 1.

That he does secure the final perseverance of his people in a manner perfectly consistent with their free agency is also clear. He changes their affections and thus determines the will by its own free spontaneity. He brings them into the position of children by adoption, surrounding them with all of the sources and instruments of sanctifying influence, and when they sin he carefully chastises and restores them. Hence the doctrine of Scripture is *not* that a man who has once truly believed is secure of ultimate salvation, subsequently feel and act as he may; but, on the contrary, that God secures the ultimate salvation of every one who is once truly united to his Son by faith, by securing, through the power of the Holy Ghost, his most free perseverance in Christian feeling and obedience to the end.

6. *What objection is urged against the orthodox doctrine upon the ground of its supposed unfavorable influence upon morality?*

The objection charged is, that this doctrine, "once in grace always in grace," must naturally lead to carelessness, through a false sense of security in our present position, and of confidence that God will secure our final salvation independently of our own agency.

Although it is certain, on the part of God, that if we are elected and called, we shall be saved; yet it requires constant watchfulness, and diligence, and prayer to make that calling and election sure to us.—2 Pet. i. 10. That God powerfully works with us, and therefore secures for us success in our contest with sin, is in Scripture urged as a powerful reason not for sloth, but for diligence.—Phil. ii. 13. The orthodox doctrine does not affirm certainty of *salvation* because we have *once* believed, but certainty of *perseverance in holiness* if we have *truly* believed, which perseverance in holiness, therefore, in opposition to all weaknesses and temptations, is the only sure evidence of the genuineness of past experience, or of the validity of our confidence as to our future salvation, and surely such an assurance of certainty can not encourage either carelessness or immorality.

7. *What objection to this doctrine is founded on the exhortations to diligence; and on the warnings of danger in case of carelessness, addressed to believers in the Scriptures?*

The objection alleged is, that these exhortations and warnings necessarily imply the contingency of the believer's salvation, as conditioned upon the believer's continued faithfulness, and consequently involving liability to apostasy.

We answer—

1st. The outward word necessarily comes to all men alike, addressing them in the classes in which they regard themselves as standing; and as professors, or "those who think they stand," are many of them self-deceived, this outward word truly implies the uncertainty of their position (as far as man's knowledge goes), and their liability to fall.

2d. That God secures the perseverance in holiness of all his true people by the use of means adapted to their nature as rational, moral, and free agents. Viewed in themselves they are always, as God warns them, unstable, and therefore, as he exhorts them, they must diligently cleave to his grace. It is always true, also, that if they apostatize they shall be lost; but by means of these very threatenings his Spirit graciously secures them from apostasy.

8. *What special texts are relied upon to rebut the arguments of the orthodox upon this subject?*

Ezek. xviii. 24; Matt. xiii. 20, 21; 2 Pet. ii. 20, 21, and especially Heb. vi. 4–6; x. 26.

All of these passages may be naturally explained in perfect consistency with the orthodox doctrine which is supported upon that wide range of Scripture evidence we have set forth above, Question 2. They present either, 1st, hypothetical warnings of the consequences of apostasy with the design of preventing it, by showing the natural consequences of indifference and of sin, and the necessity for earnest care and effort; or, 2d, they indicate the dreadful consequences of misimproving or of abusing the influences of *common grace*, which, although involving great responsibility, nevertheless come short of a radical change of nature or genuine conversion.

9. *What argument do the opponents of this doctrine urge from Bible examples and from our own daily experience of apostates?*

They cite from the Scriptures such instances as that of David and Peter, and they refer to the many examples of the apostasy of well-accredited professors, with which, alas! we are all familiar.

All these examples, however, fall evidently under one of two classes, either, 1st, they were from the beginning without the real power of godliness, although bearing so fair an appearance of life in the sight of their fellow-men, Rom. ii. 28; ix. 6; 1 John ii. 19; Rev. iii. 1; or, 2d, they are true believers who, because of the temporary withdrawal of restraining grace, have been allowed to backslide for a time, while in every such case they are graciously restored, and that generally by chastisement.—Rev. iii. 19. Of this class were David and Peter. No true Christian is capable of deliberate apostasy; his furthest departure from righteousness being occasioned by the sudden impulse of passion or fear.—Matt. xxiv. 24; Luke xxii. 31.

Authoritative Statements of Church Doctrine.

Romish Doctrine.

"Conc. Trident.," Sess. 6, ch. 15.—"It is to be maintained that the received grace of justification is lost, not only by infidelity, whereby even faith itself is lost, but also by any other mortal sin whatever, though faith be not lost."

Ib., can. 23.—"If any one saith, that a man once justified can sin no more, nor lose grace, and that therefore he that falls and sins was never truly justified . . . let him be anathema."

Ib., chap. 11.—"For, although, during this mortal life, men how holy and just soever, at times fall at least into light and daily sins, which are also called venial, not therefore do they cease to be just."

Ib., Sess. 14, ch. 5.—"For venial sins, whereby we are not excluded from the grace of God, and into which we fall more frequently, although they be rightly and profitably, and without any presumption, declared in confession, as the custom of pious persons demonstrates, yet may they be omitted without guilt, and be expiated by many other remedies. But, whereas all mortal sins, even those of thought, render men children of wrath, and enemies of God, it is necessary to seek also for the pardon of them all from God, with a modest and open confession."

Bellarmin, "*De Amiss. Gra.,*" Sess. 14, cap. 5.—"(1.) Venial sin is distinguished from mortal sin, as of its own nature, and without any relation to the predestination or the mercy of God, or to the state of the regenerate, deserving a certain but not an eternal punishment. (2.) These sins are either venial from their own nature, having for their object a thing evil and inordinate, but which does not oppose the love of God and of our neighbor—as an idle word, or they are venial from the imperfection of the action, *i. e.,* (*a*) such as are not perfectly voluntary (deliberate), as arising from a sudden movement of cupidity or anger, and (*b*) such as relate to trifles, as the theft of one obolus."

Lutheran Doctrine.

"Formula Concordiæ," p. 705.—"That false opinion is to be earnestly confuted and rejected, which certain feign, that faith, and realized justification, and salvation itself, can not be lost by any sins or crimes whatsoever."

Ib., p. 591.—"We condemn that dogma, that faith in Christ is not lost, and that the Holy Spirit continues to dwell none the less in a man, although he knowingly and willingly sins, and that the sanctified and elect retain the Holy Spirit, although they fall into adulteries or other crimes, and persevere in them."

"Apol. Aug. Conf.," p. 71.—"Faith can not coexist with mortal sin."

Ib., p. 86.—"That faith, which receives remission of sins . . does not remain in those who indulge their lusts, neither can it coexist with mortal sin."

Reformed Doctrine.

"*Can. of the Synod of Dort,*" ch. 5, c. 3.—"Because of the remains of indwelling sin . . . the converted could not continue in this grace, if they were left to their own strength. But God is faithful, who confirms them in the grace once mercifully conferred on them, and powerfully preserves them in the same, even unto the end. Can. 4.—But though that power of God, confirming the truly faithful in grace, and preserving them, is greater than what can be overcome by the flesh, yet the converted are not always so influenced and moved by God, that they can not depart in certain particular actions, from the leading of grace, and be seduced by the lusts of the flesh, and obey them. They may fall even into grievous and atrocious sins. . . . . Can. 5.—But by such enormous sins they exceedingly offend God, they incur the guilt of death, they grieve the Holy Spirit, they interrupt the exercise of faith, they most grievously wound conscience, and they sometimes lose for a time the sense of grace, until by serious repentance returning into the way, the paternal countenance of God again shines upon them. Can. 6. For God, who is rich in mercy, from his immutable purpose of election, does not wholly take away his Holy Spirit from his own, even in lamentable falls, nor does he so permit them to glide down that they should fall from the grace of adoption, and the state of justification, or commit the sin unto death, or against the Holy Spirit, that being deserted by him, they should cast themselves headlong into eternal destruction. . . Can. 8.—So that not by their own merits or strength, but by the gratuitous mercy of God they (the elect) obtain it, that they neither totally fall from faith and grace, nor finally continue in their falls and perish."

"*West. Conf. Faith,*" ch. 17, § 1.—"They whom God hath accepted in his Beloved, effectually called and sanctified by his Spirit, can neither totally nor finally fall away from the state of grace; but shall certainly persevere therein to the end, and be eternally saved. § 2.—This perseverance of the saints depends not upon their own free-will, but upon the immutability of the decree of election, flowing from the free and unchangeable love of God the Father; upon the efficacy of the merit and intercession of Jesus Christ; the abiding of the Spirit and of the seed of God within them, and the nature of the covenant of grace: from all which ariseth also the certainty and infallibility thereof."

XXXVII.

DEATH, AND THE STATE OF THE SOUL AFTER DEATH.

1. *What department of theology are we now entering, and what subjects are embraced in it?*

The department of ESCHATOLOGY or the discussion of *last things* τὰ ἔσχατα. It embraces the subjects of death, the state of the soul after death, the second advent of Christ, the resurrection of the dead, the final judgment, the end of the world, heaven and hell.

2. *By what forms of expression is death described in the Bible?*

A departure out of this world.—2 Tim. iv. 6. A going the way of all the earth.—Josh. xxiii. 14. A being gathered to one's fathers, Judges ii. 10; and to one's people, Deut. xxxii. 50. A dissolving the earthly house of this tabernacle.—2 Cor. v. 1. A returning to the dust.—Eccle. xii. 7. A sleep.—John xi. 11. A giving up the ghost.—Acts v. 10. A being absent from the body and present with the Lord.—2 Cor. v. 8. Sleeping in Jesus.—1 Thess. iv. 14.

3. *What is death?*

The suspension of the personal union between the body and the soul, followed by the resolution of the body into its chemical elements, and the introduction of the soul into that separate state of existence which may be assigned to it by its Creator and Judge.—Eccle. xii. 7.

4. *How does death stand related to sin?*

The entire penalty of the law, including all the spiritual, physical, and eternal penal consequences of sin, is called death in Scripture. The sentence was, "The day thou eatest thereof thou shalt surely die."—Gen. ii. 17; Rom. v. 12. That this included natural death is proved by Rom. v. 13, 14; and from the fact that when Christ bore the penalty of the law it was necessary for him to die.—Heb. ix. 22.

5. *Why do the justified die?*

Justification changes the entire federal relation of its subject to the law, and raises him forever above all the penal consequences of sin. Death, therefore, while remaining a part of the penalty of the unsatisfied law in relation to the unjust, is like all other afflictions changed, in relation to the justified, into an element of improving discipline. It is made necessary for them from the present constitution of the body, while it is to both body and soul the gateway of heaven. They are made free from its sting and fear.—1 Cor. xv. 55, 57; Heb. ii. 15. They are now "blessed" in death because they die "in the Lord," Rev. xiv. 13, and they shall at last be completely delivered from its power when the last enemy shall be destroyed. 1 Cor. xv. 26.

6. *What evidence have we of the immateriality of the soul, and what argument may be derived from that source in proof of its continued existence after death?*

For the evidence establishing the immateriality of the soul see Chap. II., Question 18.

Now although the continued existence of any creature must depend simply upon the will of its Creator, that will may either be made known by direct revelation, or inferred in any particular instance by analogical reasoning from what is known of his doings in other cases. As far as this argument from analogy goes it decidedly confirms the belief that a spiritual substance is, as such, immortal. The entire range of human experience fails to make us acquainted with a single instance of the annihilation of an atom of matter, *i. e.*, of matter as such. Material *bodies*, organized or chemically compounded, or mere mechanical aggregations, we observe constantly coming into existence, and in turn passing away, yet never through the annihilation of their elementary constituents or component parts, but simply from the dissolution of that relation which these parts had temporarily sustained to each other. Spirit, however, is essentially simple and single, and therefore incapable of that dissolution of parts to which material bodies are subject. We infer, therefore, that spirits are immortal since they can not be subject to that only form of death of which we have any knowledge.

7. *What argument in favor of the immortality of the soul may be derived from its imperfect development in this world?*

In every department of organized life every individual creature, in its normal state, tends to grow toward a condition of complete development, which is the perfection of its kind. The acorn both prophesies and grows toward the oak. Every human being, however, is conscious that in this life he never attains that completeness which the Creator contemplated in the ideal of his type; he has faculties undeveloped, capacities unfulfilled, natural desires unsatisfied; he knows he was designed to be much more than he is, and to fill a much higher sphere. As the prophetic reason of the Creator makes provision for the butterfly through the instinct of the caterpillar, so the same Creator reveals the immortal existence of the soul in a higher sphere by means of its conscious limitations and instinctive movements in this.

8. *What argument on this subject may be derived from the distributive justice of God?*

It is an invariable judgment of natural reason, and a fundamental doctrine of the Bible, that moral good is associated with happiness, and moral evil with misery, by the unchangeable nature and purpose of God. But the history of all individuals and communities alike establishes the fact that this life is not a state of retribution; that here wickedness is often associated with prosperity, and moral excellence with sorrow; we must hence conclude that there is a future state in which all that appears at present inconsistent with the justice of God shall be adjusted.—See Ps. lxxiii.

9. *How do the operations of conscience point to a future state?*

Conscience is the voice of God in the soul, which witnesses to our sinfulness and ill-desert, and to his essential justice. Except in the case of those who have found refuge in the righteousness of Christ, every man feels that his moral relations to God are never settled in this life, and hence the characteristic testimony of the human conscience, in spite of great individual differences as to light, sensibility, etc., has always been coincident with the word of God, that "after death comes the JUDGMENT."

10. *How is this doctrine established by the general consent of mankind?*

This has been the universal faith of all men, of all races, and in all ages. Universal consent, like every universal effect, must be referred to an equally universal cause, and this consent, uniform among men differing in every other possible respect, can be referred to no common origin other than the constitution of man's common nature, which is the testimony of his Maker.

11. *Show that the Old Testament teaches the same distinction between soul and body that is taught in the New Testament.*

1st. In the account of the creation. The body was formed of the dust of the earth, and the soul in the image of the Almighty.—Gen. i. 26; ii. 7.

2d. In the definition of death.—Eccle. xii. 7. "Then shall the dust return to the earth as it was, and the spirit shall return to God who gave it."—See also Eccle. iii. 21.

12. *What does the Old Testament teach concerning Sheol? and how is it shown, from the usage of that word, that the immortality of the soul was a doctrine of the ancient covenant?*

Sheol is derived from the verb שָׁאַל, *to ask*, expressing the sense of our English proverb, that the "grave crieth give, give." It is used in the Old Testament to signify, in a vague and general sense, the state of the departed, both the good and bad, intermediate between death and the resurrection of the righteous (Hosea xiii. 14), generally invested with gloomy associations, and indefinitely referred to the lower parts of the earth. Deut. xxxii. 22; Amos ix. 2. Thus it is used for grave as the receptacle of the body after death (Gen. xxxvii. 35; Job xiv. 13), but principally to designate the receptacle of departed spirits, without explicit reference to any division between the stations allotted to the righteous and the wicked. That they were active and conscious in this state appears to be indicated by what is revealed of Samuel.—1 Sam. xxviii. 7–20; Is. xiv. 15–17. With regard to the good, however, the residence in Sheol was looked upon only as intermediate between death and a happy resurrection.—Ps. xlix. 15. In their treatment of this whole subject, the Old Testament Scriptures rather take the continued existence of the soul for granted, than explicitly assert it.—Fairbairn's "Herm. Manual"; "Josephus' Ant.," xviii., 1.

13. *What is the purport of our Saviour's argument on this subject against the Sadducees?*

Luke xx. 37, 38. Long after the death of Abraham, Isaac, and Jacob, Jehovah designated himself to Moses as their God. Ex. iii. 6. But, argues Christ against the Sadducee who denied the resurrection of the dead, "he is the God, not of the dead, but of the living." This more immediately proves the immortality of their souls, but as God is the covenant God of persons, and as the persons of these patriarchs included alike body and soul, this argument likewise establishes the ultimate immortality of the body also, *i. e.*, of the entire person.

14. *What passages of the Old Testament assert or imply the hope of a state of blessedness after death?*

Num. xxiii. 10; Job xix. 26, 27; Ps. xvi. 9–11; xvii. 15; xlix. 14, 15; lxxiii. 24–26; Is. xxv. 8; xxvi. 19; Hosea xiii. 14; Dan. xii. 2, 3, 13.

15. *What other evidence does the Old Testament afford of the continued existence of the soul?*

1st. The translations of Enoch and Elijah, and the temporary reappearance of Samuel.—Gen. v. 24; Heb. xi. 5; 2 Kings ii. 11; 1 Sam. xxviii. 7–20.

2d. The command to abstain from the arts of necromancy implies the prevalent existence of a belief that the dead still continue in being in another state.—Deut. xviii. 11, 12.

3d. In their symbolical system Canaan represents the permanent inheritance of Christ's people, and the entire purpose of the whole Old Testament revelation, as apprehended by Old Testament believers, had respect to a future existence and inheritance after death. This is directly asserted in the New Testament.—Acts xxvi. 6–8; Heb. xi. 10–16; Eph. i. 14.

16. *What does the New Testament teach of the state of the soul immediately after death?*

"The souls of the righteous, being made perfect in holiness, are received into the highest heavens, where they behold the face of God in light and glory, waiting for the full redemption of their bodies."—Luke xxiii. 43; 2 Cor. v. 6, 8; Phil. i. 23, 24. "And the souls of the wicked are cast into hell, where they remain in torment and utter darkness, reserved to the judgment of the great day."—Luke xvi. 23, 24; Jude v. 6, 7. "Confession of Faith," Chap. xxxii., § 1.

This statement represents the doctrine of the Lutheran and Reformed churches.

It includes the following points: 1st. The state of souls between death and the resurrection may properly be called intermediate when viewed with relation to the states which precede and follow. 2d. Whether there be also an intermediate place or not the Scriptures do not definitely declare, but they suggest it.—See below, Ch. XL., Ques. 3. 3d. The souls both of the righteous and the lost continue during this state active and conscious. 4th. The moral and spiritual character and destiny of each is irrevocably decided at death either for good or evil. 5th. The righteous are immediately made perfect in holiness. 6th. They pass at once and remain during the whole period in the presence of Christ. 7th. This intermediate differs from the final state of the redeemed—(1.) Because of the absence of the body. (2.) Because redemption is not yet realized in its final stage.

17. *What is the signification and usage of the word ἅιδης, Hades, in Scripture?*

῞Αιδης, from α primitive, and ἰδειν, designates generally the invisible world inhabited by the spirits of dead men. Among the ancient classical heathen, this invisible world was regarded as consisting of two contrasted regions, the one called Elysium, the abode of the blessed good, and the other Tartarus, the abode of the vicious and miserable.

It was used by the authors of the Septuagint to translate the Hebrew word Sheol, compare Acts ii. 27, and Ps. xvi. 10. In the New Testament this word occurs only eleven times. Matt. xi. 23; xvi. 18; Luke x. 15; xvi. 23; Acts ii. 27, 31; 1 Cor. xv. 55; Rev. i. 18; vi. 8; xx. 13, 14. In every case, except 1 Cor. xv. 55, where the more critical editions of the original substitute the word θάνατε in the place of ᾅδη, hades is translated hell, and certainly always represents the invisible world as under the dominion of Satan, as opposed to the kingdom of Christ, and as finally subdued under his victorious power. See Fairbairn's "Herm. Manual."

18. *What is the signification and usage of the words παράδεισος and γέεννα?*

Παράδεισος, *Paradise*, derived from some oriental language, and adopted into both the Hebrew and Greek languages, signifies parks, pleasure gardens.—Neh. ii. 8; Eccle. ii. 5. The Septuagint translators use this word to represent the garden of Eden.—Gen. ii. 8, etc. It occurs only three times in the New Testament, Luke xxiii. 43; 2 Cor. xii. 4; Rev. ii. 7; where the context proves that it refers to the "third heavens," the garden of the Lord, in which grows the "tree of life," which is by the river which flows out of the throne of God and of the Lamb. Rev. xxii. 1, 2.

Γέεννα is a compound Hebrew word, expressed in Greek letters, signifying "Valley of Hinnom, Josh. xv. 8, skirting Jerusalem on the south, running westward from the valley of Jehosaphat, under Mount Zion. Here was established the idolatrous worship of Moloch, to whom infants were burned in sacrifice.—1 Kings xi. 7. This worship was broken up and the place desecrated by Josiah, 2 Kings xxiii. 10–14, after which it appears to have become the receptacle for all the filth of the city, and of the dead bodies of animals, and of malefactors, to consume which fires would appear to have been from time to time kept

up, hence called Tophet, an abomination, a vomit, Jer. vii. 31."
Robinson's "Greek Lex." By a natural figure, therefore, this
word was used to designate the place of final punishment, forci-
bly carrying with it the idea of pollution and misery. It occurs
twelve times in the New Testament, and always to signify the
place of final torment.—Matt. v. 22, 29, 30; x. 28; xviii. 9;
xxiii. 15, 33; Mark ix. 43, 47; Luke xii. 5; James iii. 6.

19. *What various views are maintained as to the intermediate
state of the souls of men between death and the judgment?*

1st. Many Protestants, especially of the Church of England,
retaining the classical sense of the word Hades, as equivalent
to the Jewish Sheol (as given above, Question 12), hold that
there is an intermediate region, consisting of two distinct departments, in one or other of which the disembodied souls, both
of the lost and of the redeemed, respectively await the resurrection of their bodies, the award of judgment, and their translation to their final abodes of bliss or misery. They differ from
the common Protestant doctrine chiefly—(1.) In *positively* asserting that the place as well as the state is intermediate.
(2.) In asserting that it is situated "under" in respect to this
world. (3.) In holding that it is not the "highest heavens"
where God manifests his special presence, and where Christ
habitually abides.—See the Rev. E. H. Bickersteth's "Yesterday,
To-day, and Forever," and "Hades and Heaven, or State of the
Blessed Dead."

2d. For the complete statement of the doctrine of the Romanists, see below, Question 22.

3d. Materialists and some Socinians hold that the souls of
men remain in a state of unconsciousness or suspended life from
death until the moment of the resurrection.

This opinion is also held by the advocates of the ultimate
annihilation of the wicked, and advocated most ably by C. F.
Hudson in America, and as probable by the late Archbishop
Whately in England ("View of Sc. Concerning a Future State").

The arguments are—(1) We have no experience and can
form no conception of conscious mental activity in a disembodied state. (2.) That the Scriptural evidence relied upon for
the support of the church doctrine is obscure and inconclusive.
(3.) That the original and simple meaning of the word death is
"extinction of being." God said to Adam, "The day thou eatest thereof thou," not thy body, but thyself, "shall surely die.'
Matt. x. 28. (4.) That the great prominence afforded in the
New Testament to the future resurrection of the body, as the
effect of redemption, and the object of Christian hope, proves
that the only future life the apostles expected was subsequent

to and dependent upon that event.—1 Cor. xv. 14. (5.) They quote many passages to prove that the Scriptures teach that the dead remain at present in a state of bodily and spiritual inactivity.—Ps. vi. 5. " For in death there is no remembrance of thee, in the grave who shall give thee thanks."—Ps. cxlvi. 4; Jer. li. 57.

This doctrine was first taught by certain heretics in Arabia in the time of Origen, called Thnetopsychites. It was revived as an opinion of some theologians in the thirteenth and fourteenth centuries, but condemned by the University of Paris, 1240, and by Pope Benedict XII., 1366. It was revived by some Anabaptist and refuted by Calvin in his "Psychopannychia, etc." It has never been held by any church or permanent school of theologians.

Isaac Taylor, in his "Physical Theory of Another Life," ch. 17, concludes, purely on Biblical grounds, that the intermediate state of redeemed souls is one "not of unconsciousness indeed, but of comparative inaction, or of suspended energy. A transition state during the continuance of which the passive faculties of our nature rather than the active are to awake."

20. *State the Scriptural grounds upon which the Protestant doctrine stated above, Ques. 16, rests.*

1st. The reappearance of Samuel in the use of all his faculties.—1 Sam. xxviii. 7–20. The appearance of Moses and Elias at the transfiguration of Christ on the mount.—Matt. xvii. 3. Christ's address to the thief upon the cross.—Luke xxiii. 43. The parable of the rich man and Lazarus.—Luke xvi. 23, 24. The prayer of dying Stephen.—Acts vii. 59. In 2 Cor. v. 1–8 Paul declares that to be at home in the body is to be absent from the Lord, and to be absent from the body is to be present with the Lord, and hence he says (Phil. i. 21–24) that for him to die is gain, and that he was in a strait betwixt two, "having a desire to depart and be with Christ, which is far better, nevertheless to abide in the flesh is more needful for you." He declares (1 Thess. v. 10) that the sleep of death is a living together with Christ.—See also Eph. iii. 15; Heb. vi. 12–20; Acts i. 25; Jude 6, 7; Heb. xii. 23; Rev. v. 9; vi. 9–11; vii. 9, and xiv. 1, 3.

21. *How can it be shown that the Intermediate State does not afford a further probation for those who depart from this life out of Christ?*

An opinion is becoming prevalent among some classes of Protestants that another opportunity for repentance and faith will be afforded to Christless souls between death and the resurrection. That this is unfounded appears—1st. From the fact that it is nowhere taught in Scripture. It is a hope at best suggested by the wish, but without any foundation in the word of God. Even if the "preaching to the spirits in prison" (1 Pet. iii. 19) is rightly referred to Christ's personal ministry in the sphere of the intermediate state, it certainly did not apply to those who had rejected him on earth, and it would, in that case, probably apply only to true believers under the Old Testament Dispensation, as the Catholic Church has always taught. 2d. The assumption is built upon the grossly unchristian principle that God owes to all men a favorable opportunity of knowing and of receiving Christ. If this were true the gospel would be of *debt* and not of GRACE. 3d. All the teaching of Christ and his apostles implies the contrary. "It is appointed unto men once to die, but after this the judgment."—Heb. ix. 27. "I go my way, and ye shall seek me, and shall die in your sins; whither I go ye can not come."—John viii. 21. "And besides all this, between us and you there is a great gulf fixed, so that they which would pass from hence to you, can not, neither can they pass to us, that would come from thence."—Luke xvi. 26; Rev. xxii. 11. 4th. The law of habit, and of confirmed moral character would, of course, even if conditions of repentance were offered, render the moral state of the sinner far more obdurate and hopeless in the intermediate state, than it was during the earthly life. The "Hope," is as much unwarranted by reason as it is by revelation.

22. *What do Romanists teach with regard to the souls of men after death?*

1st. That the souls of unbaptized infants go to a place prepared expressly for them, called the "*limbus infantum*," where they endure no positive suffering, although they do not enjoy the vision of God. This is placed in a higher part of the Infernus which the fires can not reach, and they suffer only a *pœnam damni* (penalty of loss), and have no share in the *pœnam sensûs* (penalty of actual suffering), which afflicts adult sinners.

2d. That all unbaptized adults, and all those who subsequently have lost the grace of baptism by mortal sin, and die unreconciled to the church, go immediately to hell.

3d. That those believers who have attained to a state of Christian perfection go immediately to heaven.

4th. That the great mass of partially sanctified Christians dying in fellowship with the church, yet still encumbered with imperfections, go to purgatory, where they suffer, more or less intensely, for a longer or shorter period, until their sins are both atoned for and purged out, when they are translated to heaven, during which intermediate period they may be efficiently assisted by the prayers and labors of their friends on earth.

5th. That Old Testament believers were gathered into a region called "*limbus patrum,*" called "Abraham's bosom," where they remained without the beatific vision of God, yet without suffering, until Christ, during the three days in which his body lay in the grave, came and released them.—1 Pet. iii. 19, 20. "Cat. Rom." Part I., Chapter vi., Question 3; "Council of Trent," Sess. xxv., de Purgatorio.

As to purgatory the Council of Trent settled only two points, 1st, that there is a purgatory; 2d, that souls therein may be benefited by the prayers and mass of the church on earth.

It is generally held, however, that its pains are both negative and positive. That the instrument of its sufferings is material fire. That these are dreadful and indefinite in extent. That satisfaction may be rendered in this world on much easier terms. That while there their souls can neither incur guilt nor merit any thing, they can alone render satisfaction for their sins by means of passive sufferings.

They confess that this doctrine is not taught directly in Scripture, but maintain, 1st, that it follows necessarily from their general doctrine of the satisfaction for sins; 2d, that Christ and the apostles taught it incidentally as they did infant baptism, etc. They refer to Matt. xii. 32; 1 Cor. iii. 15.

23. *How may the Anti-Christian character of this doctrine be shown?*

1st. It confessedly has no direct, and obviously no real foundation in Scripture. This consideration alone suffices.

2d. It proceeds upon an entirely unchristian view of the method of satisfying divine justice for sins. (1.) That while Christ's merits are infinite, they atone only for original sins. (2.) That each believer must make satisfaction in his own person for sins which he commits after baptism, either in the pains of penance or of purgatory. This is contrary to all the Scriptures teach, as we have above shown under their respective heads, (1) as to the satisfaction rendered to justice by Christ; (2) the nature of justification; (3) nature of sin; (4) relation of the sufferings and good works of the justified man to the law; (5) state of the souls of believers after death, etc., etc.

3d. It is a heathen doctrine derived from the Egyptians through the Greeks and Romans, and currently received through the Roman empire.—Virgil's "Eneid," vi. 739, 43.

4th. Its practical effects have always been, 1st, the abject subjection of the people to the priesthood; 2d, the gross demoralization of the people. The church is the self-appointed depository and dispenser of the superabundant merits of Christ, and the supererogatory merits of her eminent saints. On this foundation she dispenses the pains of purgatory to those who pay for past sins, or sells indulgences to those who pay for the liberty to sin in the future. Thus the people sin and pay, and the priest takes the money and remits the penalty. The figment of a purgatory under the control of the priest is the main source of his hold upon the fears of the people.—See Ch. XXXII., Q. 19

AUTHORITATIVE STATEMENTS OF CHURCH DOCTRINE.

ROMISH DOCTRINE.

"*Cat. of Conc. Trident,*" Pt. 1, ch. 6, § 3.—"There is also the fire of purgatory, in which the souls of the just are purified by punishment for a stated time, to the end that they may be admitted into their eternal country, into which *nothing that defileth entereth.* And of the truth of this doctrine which holy Councils declare to be confirmed by the testimonies of Scripture, and by apostolic tradition, the pastor will have occasion to treat more diligently and frequently, as we are fallen on times when men endure not sound doctrine."

Bellarmin, "*Purgator,*" ii. 10.—"It is certain that in purgatory, as there is also in hell, there is punishment by fire, whether that fire is understood literally or metaphorically." His own opinion is that it is corporeal fire.

DOCTRINE OF THE GREEK CHURCH.—"*The Longer Catechism of the Orthodox Catholic, Eastern Church,*" now the most authoritative standard of the Orthodox Græco-Russian Church. On the 11th Article, Ques. 372–377.—"From death till the general resurrection the souls of the righteous are in light and rest, with a foretaste of eternal happiness; but the souls of the wicked are in a state the reverse of this. We know this because it is ordained that the perfect retribution according to works shall be received by the perfect man after the resurrection of the body and God's last judgment.—2 Tim. ii. 8 and 2 Cor. v. 10. But that they have a foretaste of bliss is shown on the testimony of Jesus Christ, who says in the parable that the righteous Lazarus was immediately after death carried into Abraham's bosom.—Luke xvi. 22; Phil. i. 23. But we remark of such souls as have departed with faith, but without having had time to bring forth fruits worthy of repentance, that they may be aided towards the attainment of a blessed resurrection by prayers offered in their behalf, especially such as are offered in union with the oblation of the bloodless sacrifice of the Body and Blood of Christ, and by works of mercy done in faith for their memory."

PROTESTANT DOCTRINE.

"*Articles of Smalcald*" (*Lutheran*), p. 307.—"Purgatory, and whatever of religious rites, worship, or business pertains to it, is a mere disguise of the Devil."

"*Thirty-nine Articles of the Church of England,*" Art. 22.—"The Romish doctrine concerning purgatory, pardons, worshipping and adoration as well as of images as of relics, and also invocation of saints, is a fond thing, vainly invented, and grounded upon no warranty of Scripture, but rather repugnant to the word of God."

"*Shorter Catechism of West. Assembly,*" Ques. 37.—"The souls of believers are at their death made perfect in holiness and do immediately pass into glory; and their bodies being still united to Christ, do rest in their graves till the resurrection.

CHAPTER XXXVIII.

THE RESURRECTION.

1. *What is the meaning of the phrase, "resurrection of the dead," and "from the dead," as used in Scripture?*

Ἀνάστασις signifies etymologically "a rising or raising up." It is used in Scripture to designate the future general raising, by the power of God, of the bodies of all men from the sleep of death.

2. *What Old Testament passages bear upon this subject?*

Job xix. 25–27; Ps. xlix. 15; Is. xxvi. 19; Dan. xii. 1–3.

3. *What are the principal passages bearing upon this subject in the New Testament?*

Matt. v. 29; x. 28; xxvii. 52, 53; John v. 28, 29; vi. 39; Acts ii. 25–34; xiii. 34; Rom. viii. 11, 22, 23; Phil. iii. 20, 21; 1 Thess. iv. 13–17, and 15th chap. of 1 Cor.

4. *What is the meaning of the phrases, σῶμα ψυχικὸν, natural body, and σῶμα πνευματικόν, spiritual body, as used by Paul, 1 Cor. xv. 44?*

The word ψυχή, when contrasted with πνεῦμα, always designates the principle of animal life, as distinguished from the principle of intelligence and moral agency, which is the πνεῦμα. A σῶμα ψυχικὸν, translated *natural body*, evidently means a body endowed with animal life, and adapted to the present condition of the soul, and to the present physical constitution of the world it inhabits. A σῶμα πνευματικόν, translated *spiritual body*, is a body adapted to the use of the soul in its future glorified estate, and to the moral and physical conditions of the heavenly world, and to this end assimilated by the Holy Ghost, who dwells in it, to the glorified body of Christ.—1 Cor. xv. 45–48.

5. *How does it appear that the same body is to rise that is deposited in the grave?*

The passages of Scripture which treat of this subject make

it plain that the same bodies are to be raised that are deposited in the grave, by the phrases by which they designate the bodies raised: 1st, "our bodies," Phil. iii. 21; 2d, "this corruptible," 1 Cor. xv. 53, 54; 3d, "all who are in their graves," John v. 28; 4th, "they who are asleep," 1 Thess. iv. 13–17; 5th, "our bodies are the members of Christ," 1 Cor. vi. 15; 6th, our resurrection is to be because of and like that of Christ, which was of his identical body.—John xx. 27.

6. *How does it appear that the final resurrection is to be simultaneous and general?*

See below, Chap. XXXIX., Questions 9 and 10.

7. *What do the Scriptures teach concerning the nature of the resurrection body?*

1st. It is to be spiritual.—1 Cor. xv. 44. See above, Question 4. 2d. It is to be like Christ's body.—Phil. iii. 21. 3d. Glorious, incorruptible, and powerful.—1 Cor. xv. 54. 4th. It shall never die.—Rev. xxi. 4. 5th. Never be given in marriage. Matt. xxii. 30.

8. *How may it be proved that the material body of Christ rose from the dead?*

1st. Christ predicted it.—John ii. 19–21. 2d. His resurrection is referred to as a miraculous attestation of the truth of his mission, but unless his body rose literally there was nothing miraculous in his continued life. 3d. The whole language of the inspired narratives necessarily implies this, the rolling away of the stone, the folding up of the garments, etc. 4th. He did not rise until the third day, which proves that it was a physical change, and not a mere continuance of spiritual existence.—1 Cor. xv. 4. 5th. His body was seen, handled, and examined, for the space of forty days, in order to establish this very fact.—Luke xxiv. 39. Dr. Hodge.

9. *How can the materiality of Christ's resurrection body be reconciled with what is said as to the modes of its manifestation, and of its ascension into heaven?*

The events of his suddenly appearing and vanishing from sight, recorded in Luke xxiv. 31; John xx. 19; Acts i. 9, were accomplished through a miraculous interference with the ordinary laws regulating material bodies, of the same kind precisely with many miracles which Jesus wrought in his body before his death, *e. g.*, his walking on the sea.—Matt. xiv. 25; John vi. 9–14.

10. *How does the resurrection of Christ secure and illustrate that of his people?*

Body and soul together constitute the one person, and man in his entire person, and not his soul separately, is embraced in both the covenants of works and of grace, and in federal and vital union with both the first and the second Adam. Christ's resurrection secures ours—1st. Because his resurrection seals and consummates his redemptive power; and the redemption of our persons involves the redemption of our bodies.—Rom. viii. 23. 2d. Because of our federal and vital union with Christ. 1 Cor. xv. 21, 22; 1 Thess. iv. 14. 3d. Because of his Spirit which dwells in us (Rom. viii. 11), making our bodies his members.—1 Cor. vi. 15. 4th. Because Christ by covenant is Lord both of the living and the dead.—Rom. xiv. 9. This same federal and vital union of the Christian with Christ (see above, Chap. XXXI.) likewise causes the resurrection of the believer to be similar to, as well as consequent upon that of Christ.—1 Cor. xv. 49; Phil. iii. 21; 1 John iii. 2.

11. *How far are objections of a scientific character against the doctrine of the resurrection of the body entitled to weight?*

All truth is one, and of God, and necessarily consistent, whether revealed by means of the phenomena of nature or of the words of inspiration. On the other hand, it follows from our partial knowledge and often erroneous interpretation of the data both of science and revelation, that we often are unable to discern the harmonies of truths in reality intimately related. Nothing can be believed to be true which is clearly seen to be inconsistent with truth already certainly established. But, on the other hand, in the present stage of our development, the largest proportion of the materials of our knowledge rests upon independent evidence, and are received by us all as certain on their own respective grounds, although we fail as yet to reconcile each fact with every other in the harmonies of their higher laws. The principles of physical science are to be taken as true upon their own ground, *i. e.*, so far as they are matured, and the testimony of revelation is to be taken as infallible truth on its own ground. The one may modify our interpretation of the other, but the most certain of all principles is that a matured science will always corroborate rightly interpreted revelation.

12. *How may the identity of our future with our present bodies be reconciled with 1 Cor. xv. 42–50?*

In verses 42–44 this identity is expressly asserted. The

body is to be the same, though changed in these several particulars. 1st. It is *now* subject to corruption, *then* incorruptible. 2d. It is now dishonored, it will then be glorified. 3d. It is now weak, it will then be powerful. 4th. It is now *natural, i. e.*, adapted to the present condition of the soul and constitution of the world. It will then be *spiritual, i. e.*, adapted to the glorified condition of the soul, and constitution of the "new heavens and new earth."

Verse 50 declares simply that "flesh and blood," that is, the present corruptible, weak, and depraved constitution of the body can not inherit heaven. Yet the passage as a whole clearly teaches, not the substitution of a new body, but the transformation of the old.

13. *What facts does physiological science establish with respect to the perpetual changes that are going on in our present bodies, and what relation do these facts sustain to this doctrine?*

By a ceaseless process of the assimilation of new material and excretion of the old, the particles composing our bodies are ceaselessly changing from birth to death, effecting, as it is computed, a change in every atom of the entire structure every seven years. Thus there will not be a particle in the organism of an adult which constituted part of his person when a boy, nor in that of the old man of that which belonged to him when of middle age. The body from youth to age is universally subject to vast changes in size, form, expression, condition, and many times to total change of constituent particles. All this is certain; but it is none the less certain that through all these changes the man possesses identically the same person from youth to age. This proves that neither the identity of the body of the same man from youth to age, nor the identity of our present with our resurrection bodies, consists in sameness of particles. If we are sure of our identity in the one case, we need not stumble at the difficulties attending the other.

14. *What objection to this doctrine is derived from the known fact of the dispersion and assimilation into other organisms of the particles of our bodies after death?*

The instant the vital principle surrenders the elements of the body to the unmodified control of the laws of chemical affinity, their present combinations are dissolved and distributed throughout space, and they are taken up and assimilated by other animal and vegetable organisms. Thus the same particles have formed, at different times, part of the bodies of myriads of men, in the successive periods of the growth of individuals, and in successive generations. Hence it has been objected to the scriptural doctrine of the resurrection of the body, that it will be impossible to decide to which of the thousand bodies which these particles have formed part in turn, they should be assigned in the resurrection; or to reinvest each soul with its own body, when all the constituent elements of every body have been shared in common by many. We *answer* that bodily identity does not consist in sameness of constituent particles. See above, Question 13. Just as God has revealed to us through consciousness that our bodies are identical from infancy to age, although their constituent elements often change, he has, with equal certainty and reasonableness, revealed to us in his inspired word that our bodies, raised in glory, are identical with our bodies sown in dishonor, although their constituent particles may have been scattered to the ends of the earth.

15. *What is essential to identity?*

1st. "It is evident that identity depends upon different conditions in different cases. The identity of a stone or any other portion of unorganized matter consists in its substance and form. On the other hand, the identity of a plant from the seed to its maturity is, in a great measure, independent of sameness of substance or of form. Their identity appears to consist in each plant's being one organized whole, and in the continuity of the succession of its elements and parts. The identity of a picture does not depend upon the sameness of the particles of coloring matter of which it is composed, for these we may conceive to be continually changing, but upon the drawing, the tints, the light and shade, the expression, the idea which it embodies," etc.

2d. Bodily identity is not a conclusion drawn from the comparison, or combination of other facts, but it is itself a single irresolvable fact of consciousness. The child, the savage, the philosopher, are alike certain of the sameness of their bodies at different periods of their lives, and on the same grounds. This intuitive conviction, as it is not the result of science, so it is no more bound to give an account of itself to science, *i. e.*, we are no more called upon to explain it before we believe it than we are to explain any other of the simple data of consciousness.

3d. The resurrection of our bodies, although a certain fact of revelation, is to us, as yet, an unrealized experience, an unobserved phenomenon. The *physical conditions*, therefore, of the identity of our "spiritual bodies" with our "natural bodies," we can not now possibly comprehend, since we have neither the experience, the observation, nor the revelation of the facts involved in such knowledge. This much, however, is certain as to the result—1st. The body of the resurrection will be as strictly identical with the body of death, as the body of death is with the body of birth. 2d. Each soul will have an indubitable intuitive consciousness that its new body is identical with the old. 3d. Each friend shall recognize the individual characteristics of the soul in the perfectly transparent expression of the new body.—Dr. Hodge.

16. *How far was the doctrine of the resurrection of the body held by the Jews?*

With the exception of some heretical sects, as the Sadducees, the Jews held this doctrine in the same sense in which we hold it now. This is evident—1st. Because it was clearly revealed in their inspired writings, see above, Question 2. 2d. It is affirmed in their uninspired writings.—Wisdom, iii. 6, 13; iv. 15; 2 Maccabees vii. 9, 14, 23, 29. 3d. Christ in his discourses, instead of proving this doctrine, assumes it as recognized.—Luke xiv. 14; John v. 28, 29. 4th. Paul asserts that both the ancient Jews (Heb. xi. 35), and his own contemporaries (Acts xxiv. 15), believed this doctrine.

17. *What early heretical sects in the Christian church rejected this doctrine?*

All the sects bearing the generic designation of gnostic, and under various specific names embodying the leaven of oriental philosophy, which infested the church of Christ from the beginning for many centuries, believed, 1st, that matter is essentially vile, and the source of all sin and misery to the soul; 2d, that complete sanctification is consummated only in the dissolution of the body and the emancipation of the soul; 3d, that consequently any literal resurrection of the body is repugnant to the spirit, and would be destructive to the purpose of the whole gospel.

18. *What is the doctrine taught by Swedenborg on this subject?*

It is substantially the same with that set forth by Professor Bush in his once famous book, "Anastasia." They teach that the literal body is dissolved, and finally perishes in death. But by a subtle law of our nature an etherial, luminous body is eliminated out of the ψυχή (the seat of the nervous sensibility, occupying the middle link between matter and spirit), so that the soul does not go forth from its tabernacle of flesh a bare power of thought, but is clothed upon at once by this psychical body. *This* resurrection of the body, they pretend, takes place in every case immediately at death, and accompanies the out-going soul.—See "Religion and Philosophy of Swedenborg," Theophilus Parsons.

19. *How do modern rationalists explain the passages of Scripture which relate to this subject?*

They explain them away, denying their plain sense, either, 1st, as purely allegorical modes of inculcating the truth of the continued existence of the soul after death; or, 2d, as conces-sions to the prejudices and superstitions of the Jews.

CHAPTER XXXIX.

THE SECOND ADVENT AND GENERAL JUDGMENT.

1. *What is the meaning of the expressions "the coming," or "the day of the Lord," as used in both the Old and New Testaments?*

1st. For any special manifestation of God's presence and power.—John xiv. 18, 23; Is. xiii. 6; Jer. xlvi. 10. 2d. By way of eminence. (1.) In the Old Testament, for the coming of Christ in the flesh, and the abrogation of the Jewish economy. Malachi iii. 2; iv. 5. (2.) In the New Testament, for the second and final coming of Christ.

The several terms referring to this last great event are, 1st, ἀποκάλυψις, *revelation.*—1 Cor. i. 7; 2 Thess. i. 7; 1 Pet. i. 7, 13; iv. 13. 2d. παρουσία, *presence, advent.*—Matt. xxiv. 3, 27, 37, 39; 1 Cor. xv. 23; 1 Thess. ii. 19; iii. 13; iv. 15; v. 23; 2 Thess. ii. 1–9; James v. 7, 8; 2 Pet. i. 16; iii. 4, 12; 1 John ii. 28. 3d. ἐπιφάνεια, *appearance, manifestation.*—2 Thess. ii. 8; 1 Tim. vi. 14; 2 Tim. iv. 1, 8; Titus ii. 13.

The *time* of that coming is designated as "the day of God." 2 Pet. iii. 12. "The day of the Lord."—1 Thess. v. 2. "The day of the Lord Jesus, and of Jesus Christ."—1 Cor. i. 8; Phil. i. 6, 10; 2 Pet. iii. 10. "That day."—2 Thess. i. 10; 2 Tim. i. 12, 18. "The last day."—John vi. 39–54. "The great day," "the day of wrath," and "of judgment," and "of revelation."— Jude 6; Rev. vi. 17; Rom. ii. 5; 2 Pet. ii. 9.

Christ is called ὁ ἐρχόμενος, *the coming one*, with reference to both advents.—Matt. xxi. 9; Luke vii. 19, 20; xix. 38; John iii. 31; Rev. i. 4; iv. 8; xi. 17.

2. *Present the evidence that a literal personal advent of Christ still future is taught in the Bible.*

1st. The analogy of the first advent. The prophecies relating to the one having been literally fulfilled by a personal coming, we may be certain that the perfectly similar prophecies relating to the other will be fulfilled in the same sense.

2d. The language of Christ predicting such advent admits

of no other rational interpretation. The coming itself, its manner and purpose are alike defined. He is to be attended with the hosts of heaven, in power and great glory. He is to come upon the occasion of the general resurrection and judgment, and for the purpose of consummating his mediatorial work, by the final condemnation and perdition of all his enemies, and by the acknowledgment and completed glorification of all his friends.—Matt. xvi. 27; xxiv. 30; xxv. 31; xxvi. 64; Mark viii. 38; Luke xxi. 27.

3d. The apostles understood these predictions to relate to a literal advent of Christ in person. They teach their disciples to form the habit of constantly looking forward to it, as a solemnizing motive to fidelity, and to encouragement and resignation under present trials. They teach that his coming will be visible and glorious, accompanied with the abrogation of the present gospel dispensation, the destruction of his enemies, the glorification of his friends, the conflagration of the world, and the appearance of the "new heaven and new earth." See the passages quoted under the preceding chapter, and Acts. i. 11; iii. 19–21; 1 Cor. iv. 5; xi. 26; xv. 23; Heb. ix. 28; x. 37.— Dr. Hodge's "Lecture."

3. *What three modes of interpretation have been adopted in reference to* Matt. xxiv. *and* xxv.?

"It is to be remarked that these chapters contain an answer to three distinct questions. 1st. When the temple and city were to be destroyed. 2d. What were to be the signs of Christ's coming? 3d. The third question related to the end of the world. The difficulty consists in separating the portions relating to these several questions. There are three methods adopted in the explanation of these chapters. 1st. The first assumes that they refer exclusively to the overthrow of the Jewish polity, and the establishment and progress of the gospel. 2d. The second assumes that what is here said has been fulfilled in one sense in the destruction of Jerusalem, and is to be fulfilled in a higher sense at the last day. 3d. The third supposes that some portions refer exclusively to the former event and others exclusively to the latter. It is plain that the *first* view is untenable, and whether the *second* or *third* view be adopted, the obscurity resting upon this passage can not properly be allowed to lead us to reject the clear and constant teaching of the New Testament with regard to the second personal and visible advent of the Son of God."—Dr. Hodge.

4. *In what passages is the time of Christ's second advent declared to be unknown?*

Matt. xxiv. 36; Mark xiii. 32; Luke xii. 40; Acts i. 6, 7; 1 Thess. v. 1–3; 2 Pet. iii. 3, 4, 10; Rev. xvi. 15.

5. *What passages are commonly cited in proof that the apostles expected the second advent during their lives?*

Phil. i. 6; 1 Thess. iv. 15; Heb. x. 25; 1 Pet. i. 5; James v. 8.

6. *How may it be shown that they did not entertain such an expectation?*

1st. The apostles, as individuals, apart from their public capacity as inspired teachers, were subject to the common prejudices of their age and nation, and only gradually were brought to the full knowledge of the truth. During Christ's life they expected that he would establish his kingdom in its glory at that time, Luke xxiv. 21; and after his resurrection the first question they asked him was, "Wilt thou at this time restore the kingdom to Israel?"

2d. In their inspired writings they have never taught that the second coming of their Lord was to occur in their lifetime, or at any fixed time whatever. They only taught (1) that it ought to be habitually desired, and (2) since it is uncertain as to time, that it should always be regarded as imminent.

3d. As further revelations were vouchsafed to them, they learned, and explicitly taught, that the time of the second advent was not only uncertain, but that many events, still future, must previously occur, *e. g.*, the anti-Christian apostasy, the preaching of the gospel to every nation, the fulness of the Gentiles, the conversion of the Jews, the millennial prosperity of the church, and the final defection.—Rom. xi. 15–32; 2 Cor. iii. 15, 16; 2 Thess. ii. 3. This is clear, because the coming of Christ is declared to be attended with the resurrection of the dead, the general judgment, the general conflagration, and the restitution of all things. See below, Question 9.

7. *What is the Scriptural doctrine concerning the millennium?*

1st. The Scriptures, both of the Old and New Testament, clearly reveal that the gospel is to exercise an influence over all branches of the human family, immeasurably more extensive and more thoroughly transforming than any it has ever realized in time past. This end is to be gradually attained through the spiritual presence of Christ in the ordinary dispensation of Providence, and ministrations of his church.—Matt. xiii. 31, 32; xxviii. 19, 20; Ps. ii. 7, 8; xxii. 27, 29; lxxii. 8–11; Is. ii. 2, 3; xi. 6–9; lx. 12; lxvi. 23; Dan. ii. 35, 44; Zech. ix. 10; xiv. 9; Rev. xi. 15.

2d. The period of this general prevalency of the gospel will continue a thousand years, and is hence designated the millennium.—Rev. xx. 2–7.

3d. The Jews are to be converted to Christianity either at the commencement or during the continuance of this period. Zech. xii. 10; xiii. 1; Rom. xi. 26–29; 2 Cor. iii. 15, 16.

4th. At the end of these thousand years, and before the coming of Christ, there will be a comparatively short season of apostasy and violent conflict between the kingdoms of light and darkness.—Luke xvii. 26–30; 2 Pet. iii. 3, 4; Rev. xx. 7–9.

5th. Christ's advent, the general resurrection and judgment, will be simultaneous, and immediately succeeded by the burning of the old, and the revelation of the new earth and heavens. "Confession of Faith," Chaps. xxxii. and xxxiii.

8. What is the view of those who maintain that Christ's coming will be "premillennial," and that he will reign personally upon the earth a thousand years before the judgment?

1st. Many of the Jews, mistaking altogether the spiritual character of the Messiah's kingdom, entertained the opinion that as the church had continued two thousand years before the giving of the law, so it would continue two thousand years under the law, when the Messiah would commence his personal reign, which should, in turn, continue two thousand years to the commencement of the eternal Sabbath. They expected that the Messiah would reign visibly and gloriously in Jerusalem, as his capital, over all the nations of the earth, the Jews, as his especial people, being exalted to pre-eminent dignity and privilege.

2d. The Apostolical Fathers of the Jewish Christian branch of the church, such as Barnabas, Hermes, and Papias, adopted it. It prevailed generally throughout the church from A. D. 150, to A. D. 250, being advocated by Irenæus and Tertullian. Since that time the doctrine taught in this chapter has been the one generally recognized by the whole church, while *Millenarianism* or *Chilianism* has been confined to individuals and transient parties. Its advocates based their doctrine on the literal interpretation of Rev. xx. 1–10, and held—1st. That after the development of the anti-Christian apostasy, at some time very variously estimated, Christ was suddenly to appear and commence his personal reign of a thousand years in Jerusalem. The dead in Christ (some say only the martyrs) were then to rise and reign with him in the world, the majority of whose inhabitants shall be converted, and live during this period in great prosperity and happiness, the Jews in the mean time being converted, and restored to their own land. (2.) That after the thousand years there shall come the final apostasy for a little season, and then the resurrection of the rest of the dead, *i. e.*, the wicked and their judgment and condemnation at the last day, the final conflagration, and new heavens and earth.

3d. Modern premillenarians, while differing among themselves as to the details of their interpretations, agree substantially with the view just stated. Hence they are called premillenarians, because they believe the advent of Christ will occur *before* the *Millennium.*

9. *What are the principal Scriptural arguments against this view?*

1st. The theory is evidently Jewish in its origin and Judaizing in its tendency.

2d. It is not consistent with what the Scriptures teach. (1.) As to the nature of Christ's kingdom, *e. g.*, (*a*) that it is not of this world but spiritual, Matt. xiii. 11–44; John xviii. 36; Rom. xiv. 17; (*b*) that it was not to be confined to the Jews, Matt. viii. 11, 12; (*c*) that regeneration is the condition of admission to it, John iii. 3, 5; (*d*) that the blessings of the kingdom are purely spiritual, as pardon, sanctification, etc., Matt. iii. 2, 11; Col. i. 13, 14. (2.) As to the fact that the kingdom of Christ has already come. He has sat upon the throne of his Father David ever since his ascension.—Acts ii. 29–36; iii. 13–15; iv. 26–28; v. 29–31; Heb. x. 12, 13; Rev. iii. 7–12. The Old Testament prophecies, therefore, which predict this kingdom, must refer to the present dispensation of grace, and not to a future reign of Christ on earth in person among men in the flesh.

3d. The second advent is not to occur until the resurrection, when all the dead, both good and bad, are to rise at once. Dan. xii. 2; John v. 28, 29; 1 Cor. xv. 23; 1 Thess. iv. 16; Rev. xx. 11, 15. Only one passage (Rev. xx. 1–10) is even apparently inconsistent with the fact here asserted. For the true interpretation of that passage, see next question.

4th. The second advent is not to occur until the simultaneous judgment of all men, the good and the bad together. Matt. vii. 21, 23; xiii. 30–43; xvi. 24, 27; xxv. 31–46; Rom. ii. 5, 16; 1 Cor. iii. 12–15; 2 Cor. v. 9–11; 2 Thess. i. 6–10; Rev. xx. 11–15.

5th. The second advent is to be attended with the general conflagration and the generation of the "new heavens and the new earth."—2 Pet. iii. 7–13; Rev. xx. 11; xxi. 1. "Brown on the Second Advent."

10. *What considerations favor the spiritual and oppose the literal interpretation of* Rev. xx. 1–10.

The spiritual interpretation of this difficult passage is as follows: Christ has in reserve for his church a period of universal expansion and of pre-eminent spiritual prosperity, when the spirit and character of the "noble army of martyrs" shall be reproduced again in the great body of God's people in an unprecedented measure, and when these martyrs shall, in the general triumph of their cause, and in the overthrow of that of their enemies, receive judgment over their foes and reign in the earth; while the party of Satan, "the rest of the dead," shall not flourish again until the thousand years be ended, when it shall prevail again for a little season.

The considerations in favor of this interpretation of the passage are—

1st. It occurs in one of the most highly figurative books of the Bible.

2d. This interpretation is perfectly consistent with all the other more explicit teachings of the Scriptures on the several points involved.

3d. The same figure, viz., that of life again from the dead, is frequently used in Scripture to express the idea of the spiritual revival of the church.—Is. xxvi. 19; Ezek. xxxvii. 12–14; Hosea vi. 1–3; Rom. xi. 15; Rev. xi. 11.

The considerations bearing against the literal interpretation of this passage are—

1st. That the pretended doctrine of two resurrections, *i. e.*, first of the righteous, and then, after an interval of a thousand years, of the wicked, is taught nowhere else in the Bible, and this single passage in which it occurs is an obscure one. This is a strong presumption against the truth of the doctrine.

2d. It is inconsistent with what the Scriptures uniformly teach as to the nature of the resurrection body, *i. e.*, that it is to be "spiritual," not "natural," or "flesh and blood."—1 Cor. xv. 44. It is, on the contrary, an essential part of the doctrine associated with the literal interpretation of this passage, that the saints, or at least the martyrs, are to rise and reign a thousand years in the flesh, and in this world as at present constituted.

3d. The literal interpretation of this passage contradicts the clear and uniform teaching of the Scriptures, that all the dead, good and bad, are to rise and be judged together at the second coming of Christ, and the entire revolution of the present order of creation. See the Scripture testimonies collected under the preceding question.

11. *Show that the future general conversion of the Jews is taught in Scripture?*

This Paul, in Rom. xi. 15–29, both asserts and proves from

Old Testament prophecies, *e. g.*, Isa. lix. 20; Jer. xxxi. 31. See also Zech. xii. 10; 2 Cor. iii. 15, 16.

12. *State the argument for and against the opinion that the Jews are to be restored to their own land?*

The arguments *in favor* of that return are—

1st. The literal sense of many old Testament prophecies. Isa. xi. 11, 12; Jer. iii. 17; xvi. 14, 15; Ezek. xx. 40–44; xxxiv. 11–31; xxxvi. 1–36; Hosea iii. 4, 5; Amos ix. 11–15; Zech. x. 6–10; xiv. 1–20; Joel iii. 1–17.

2d. That the whole territory promised by God to Abraham has never at any period been fully possessed by his descendants, Gen. xv. 18–21; Num. xxxiv. 6–12, and renewed through Ezekiel, Ezek. xlvii. 1–23.

3d. The land, though capable of maintaining a vast population, is as preserved unoccupied, evidently waiting for inhabitants.—See Keith's "Land of Israel."

4th. The Jews, though scattered among all nations, have been miraculously preserved a separate people, and evidently await a destiny as signal and peculiar as has been their history.   The arguments *against* their return to the land of their fathers are—

1st. The New Testament is entirely silent on the subject of any such return, which would be an inexplicable omission in the clearer revelation, if that event is really future.

2d. The literal interpretation of the Old Testament prophecies concerned in this question would be most unnatural— (1.) Because, if the interpretation is to be consistent, it must be literal in all its parts. Then it would follow that David himself, in person, must be raised to reign again in Jerusalem. Ezek. xxxvii. 24, etc.   Then the Levitical priesthood must be restored, and bloody sacrifices offered to God.—Ezek. xl. to xlvi.; Jer. xvii. 25, 26   Then must Jerusalem be the centre of government, the Jews a superior class in the Christian church, and all worshippers must come monthly and from Sabbath to Sabbath, from the ends of the earth to worship at the Holy City.—Isa. ii. 2, 3; lxvi. 20–23; Zech. xiv. 16–21.   (2.) Because the literal interpretation thus leads to the revival of the entire ritual system of the Jews, and is inconsistent with the spirituality of the kingdom of Christ.—See above, Question 9.   (3.) Because the literal interpretation of these passages is inconsistent with what the New Testament plainly teaches as to the abolition of all distinctions between the Jew and Gentile; the Jews, when converted, are to be grafted back into the same church. Rom. xi. 19–24; Eph. ii. 13–19.   (4.) Because this interpretation is inconsistent with what the New Testament teaches as to the temporary purpose, the virtual insufficiency, and the final abolition of the Levitical priesthood and their sacrifices, and of the infinite sufficiency of the sacrifice of Christ, and the eternity of his priesthood.—Gal. iv. 9, 10; v. 4–8; Col. ii. 16–23; Heb. vii. 12–18; viii. 7–13; ix. 1–14.

3d. On the other hand, the spiritual interpretation of these Old Testament prophecies—which regards them as predicting the future purity and extension of the Christian church, and as indicating these spiritual subjects by means of those persons, places, and ordinances of the old economy which were typical of them—is both natural and accordant to the analogy of Scripture. In the New Testament, Christians are called Abraham's seed, Gal. iii. 29; Israelites, Gal. vi. 16; Eph. ii. 12, 19; comers to Mount Zion, Heb. xii. 22; citizens of the heavenly Jerusalem, Gal. iv. 26; the circumcision, Phil. iii. 3; Col. ii. 11, and in Rev. ii. 9, they are called Jews. There is also a Christian priesthood and spiritual sacrifice.—1 Pet. ii. 5, 9; Heb. xiii. 15, 16; Rom. xii. 1. See Fairbairn's "Typology Appendix," Vol. I.

13. *Who is to be the judge of the world?*

Jesus Christ, in his official character as Mediator, in both natures, as the God-man. This is evident, 1st, because as judge he is called the "Son of Man," Matt. xxv. 31, 32, and the "man ordained by God."—Acts xvii. 31. 2d. Because all judgment is said to be *committed* to him by the Father.—John v. 22, 27. 3d. Because it pertains to him as Mediator to complete and publicly manifest the salvation of his people, and the overthrow of his enemies, together with the glorious righteousness of his work in both respects, 2 Thess. i. 7–10; Rev. i. 7; and thus accomplish the "restitution of all things."—Acts iii. 21. And this he shall do in his own person, that his glory may be the more manifest, the discomfiture of his enemies the more humiliating, and the hope and joy of his redeemed the more complete.

14. *Who are to be the subjects of the judgment?*

1st. The whole race of Adam, without exception, of every generation, condition, and character, each individual appearing in the integrity of his person, "body, soul, and spirit." The dead will be raised, and the living changed simultaneously. Matt. xxv. 31–46; 1 Cor. xv. 51, 52; 2 Cor. v. 10; 1 Thess. iv. 17; 2 Thess. i. 6–10; Rev. xx. 11–15. 2d. All evil angels. 2 Pet. ii. 4; Jude 6. Good angels appearing as attendants and ministers.—Matt. xiii. 41, 42.

15. *In what sense is it said that the saints shall judge the world ?*

See Matt. xix. 28; Luke xxii. 29, 30; 1 Cor. vi. 2, 3; Rev. xx. 4.

In virtue of the union of believers with Christ, his triumph and dominion is theirs. They are joint heirs with him, and if they suffer with him they shall reign with him.—Rom. viii. 17; 2 Tim. ii. 12. He will judge and condemn his enemies as head and champion of his church, all his members assenting to his judgment and glorying in his triumph.—Rev. xix. 1–5. Hodge's "Com. on 1st Cor."

16. *Upon what principles will his judgment be dispensed ?*

The judge is figuratively represented (Rev. xx. 12), after the analogy of human tribunals, as opening "books" in judgment, according to the things written in which the dead are to be judged, and also "another book," "which is the book of life." The books first mentioned doubtless figuratively represent the law or standard according to which each one was to be judged, and the facts in his case, or "the works which he had done." The "book of life" (see also Phil. iv. 3; Rev. iii. 5; xiii. 8; xx. 15) is the book of God's eternal electing love. Those whose names are found written in the "book of life" will be declared righteous on the ground of their participation in the righteousness of Christ. Their holy characters and good deeds, however, will be publicly declared as the *evidences* of their election, of their relation to Christ, and of the glorious work of Christ in them.—Matt. xiii. 43; xxv. 34–40.

Those whose names are not found written in "the book of life" will be condemned on the ground of the evil "deeds they have done in the body," tried by the standard of God's law, not as that law has been ignorantly conceived of by each, but as it has been more or less fully and clearly revealed by the Judge himself to each severally. The heathen who has sinned without the written law "shall be judged without the law," *i. e.*, by the law written upon his heart, which made him a law unto himself.—Luke xii. 47, 48; Rom. ii. 12–15. The Jew, who "sinned in the law, shall be judged by the law."—Rom. ii. 12. Every individual dwelling under the light of the Christian revelation shall be judged in strict accordance with the whole will of God as made known to him, all of the special advantages of every kind enjoyed by him individually modifying the proportion of his responsibility.—Matt. xi. 20–24; John iii. 19.

The secrets of all hearts, the inward states and hidden springs of action, will be brought in as the subject matter of judgment, as well as the actions themselves, Eccle. xii. 14; 1

Cor. iv. 5; and publicly declared to vindicate the justice of the Judge, and to make manifest the shame of the sinner.—Luke viii. 17; xii. 2, 3; Mark iv. 22. Whether the sins of the saints will be brought forward at the judgment or not is a question not settled by the Scriptures, though debated by theologians. If they should be, we are sure that it will be done only with the design and effect of enhancing the glory of the Saviour and the comfort of the saved.

17. *What do the Scriptures reveal concerning the future conflagration of our earth?*

The principal passages bearing upon this point are Ps. cii. 26, 27; Is. li. 6; Rom. viii. 19–23; Heb. xii. 26, 27; 2 Pet. iii. 10–13; Rev. xx. and xxi.

Many of the older theologians thought that these passages indicated that the whole existing physical universe was to be destroyed. This view is now universally discarded. Some held that this earth is to be annihilated.

The most common and probable opinion is that at "the restitution of all things," Acts. iii. 21, this earth, with its atmosphere, is to be subjected to intense heat, which will radically change its present physical condition, introducing in the place of the present an higher order of things, which shall appear as a "new heavens and a new earth," wherein "the creature itself, also, shall be delivered from the bondage of corruption into the glorious liberty of the children of God," Rom. viii. 19–23, and wherein the constitution of the new world will be adapted to the "spiritual" or resurrection bodies of the saints, 1 Cor. xv. 44, to be the scene of the heavenly society, and, above all, to be the palace-temple of the God-man forever.—Eph. i. 14; Rev. v. 9, 10; xxi. 1–5. See also Fairbairn's "Typology," Vol. I., Part II., Chap. ii., sec. 7.

18. *What should be the moral effect of the Scripture doctrine of Christ's second advent?*

Christians ought thereby to be comforted when in sorrow, and always stimulated to duty.—Phil. iii. 20; Col. iii. 4, 5; James v. 7; 1 John iii. 2, 3. It is their duty also to *love, watch, wait for*, and *hasten unto* the coming of their Lord.—Luke xii. 35, 37; 1 Cor. i. 7, 8; Phil. iii. 20; 1 Thess. i. 9, 10; 2 Tim. iv. 8; 2 Pet. iii. 12; Rev. xxii. 20.

Unbelievers should be filled with fearful apprehension, and with all their might they should seek place for immediate repentance.—Mark xiii. 35, 37; 2 Pet. iii. 9, 10; Jude 14, 15. Brown's "Second Advent."

Authoritative Statements of Church Doctrine.

Augustine ("*De Civitate Dei*," 20, 7) states, that he once held the doctrine of a millenarian sabbath, but then rejected it and advocates the doctrine of this chapter, which has thenceforward prevailed in the Roman Church.

"*Augsburg Confession*," Pt. 1, Art. 17.—"They also teach that Christ will appear at *the end of the world* for judgment, and that he will resuscitate all the dead, and that he will give to the pious elect eternal life and perpetual joy, but condemn wicked men and devils, that they shall be tormented without end. They condemn the Anabaptists, who believe that there will be an end of the future punishment of lost men and devils. And they condemn others who scatter Jewish opinions, to the effect that before the resurrection of the dead the pious will occupy the kingdom of the world, and the wicked be everywhere in subjection."

"*The English Confession of Edward VI.*"—"Those who endeavor to recall the fable of the Millenarians, oppose the sacred Scriptures, and precipitate themselves into Jewish insanities."

"*Belgic Confession*," Art. 37.—"Lastly, we believe, from the word of God, that our Lord Jesus Christ will return from heaven bodily and visibly, and with the highest glory, when the time predetermined by God, but unknown to all creatures, shall arrive, and *the number of the elect be complete.* . . . At that time all who have heretofore died on the earth shall arise."

"*Westminster Conf.* Chaps. 32 and 33; "*Larger Cat.*," Ques. 87–89.— These teach—1. At the last day shall be a general resurrection of the dead both of the just and of the unjust. 2. All found alive shall be immediately changed. 3. Immediately after the resurrection shall follow the general and final judgment of all angels and men, good and bad. 4. That the date of this day and hour is purposely kept secret by God. In *Ques.* 53–56, we are further taught, that Christ's second coming will not occur until "the last day," "the end of the world," and that he will then come "to judge the world in righteousness."

CHAPTER XL.

HEAVEN AND HELL.

1. *What is the New Testament usage as to the terms* ὀυρανός, *" heaven," and* τά ἐπουράνια, *" heavenly places ? "*

Ὀυρανός is used chiefly in three senses. 1st. The upper air where the birds fly.—Matt. viii. 20; xxiv. 30. 2d. The region in which the stars revolve.—Acts vii. 42; Heb. xi. 12. 3d. The abode of Christ's human nature, the scene of the special manifestation of divine glory, and of the eternal blessedness of the saints.—Heb. ix. 24; 1 Pet. iii. 22. This is sometimes called the "third heaven."—2 Cor. xii. 2. The phrases "new heaven," and " new earth," in contrast with "first heavens," and "first earth," 2 Pet. iii. 7, 13; Rev. xxi. 1, refer to some unexplained change which will take place in the final catastrophe, by which God will revolutionize our portion of the physical universe, cleansing it from the stain of sin, and qualifying it to be the abode of blessedness.

For the usage with regard to the phrase "kingdom of heaven," see above, Chap. XXVII., Question 5.

The phrase τά ἐπουράνια is translated sometimes, "heavenly things," John iii. 12, where it signifies the mysteries of the unseen spiritual world; and sometimes "heavenly places," Eph. i. 3, and ii. 6, where it means the state into which a believer is introduced at his regeneration; see also Eph. i. 20, where it means the "third heavens"; and Eph. vi. 12, where it signifies indefinitely the supermundane universe.

2. *What are the principal terms, both literal and figurative, which are used in Scripture to designate the future blessedness of the saints ?*

Literal terms: "life, eternal life, and life everlasting.—Matt. vii. 14; xix. 16, 29; xxv. 46. Glory, the glory of God, an eternal weight of glory.—Rom. ii. 7, 10; v. 2; 2 Cor. iv. 17. Peace. Rom. ii. 10. Salvation, and eternal salvation.—Heb. v. 9."

Figurative terms: "Paradise.—Luke xxiii. 43; 2 Cor. xii. 4; Rev. ii. 7.   Heavenly Jerusalem.—Gal. iv. 26; Rev. iii. 12. Kingdom of heaven, heavenly kingdom, eternal kingdom, kingdom prepared from the foundation of the world.—Matt. xxv. 34; 2 Tim. iv. 18; 2 Pet. i. 11.   Eternal inheritance.—1 Pet. i. 4; Heb. ix. 15.   The blessed are said to sit down with Abraham, Isaac, and Jacob, to be in Abraham's bosom, Luke xvi. 22; Matt. viii. 11; to reign with Christ, 2 Tim. ii. 11, 12; to enjoy a Sabbath or rest, Heb. iv. 10, 11."—Kitto's "Bib. Ency."

3. *What is revealed with respect to heaven as a place?*

All the Scripture representations of heaven involve the idea of a definite place, as well as of a state of blessedness.   Of that place, however, nothing more is revealed than that it is defined by the local presence of Christ's finite soul and body, and that it is the scene of the pre-eminent manifestation of God's glory. John xvii. 24; 2 Cor. v. 9; Rev. v. 6.

From such passages as Rom. viii. 19–23; 2 Pet. iii. 5–13; Rev. xxi. 1, it appears not improbable that after the general destruction of the present form of the world by fire, which shall accompany the judgment, this world will be reconstituted, and gloriously adapted to be the permanent residence of Christ and his church.   As there is to be a "spiritual body," there may be in the same sense a spiritual world, that is, a world adapted to be the theatre of the glorified spirits of the saints made perfect.   As nature was cursed for man's sake, and the creature, through him, made subject to vanity, it may be that they shall share in his redemption and exaltation.—See Fairbairn's "Typology," Part II., Chap. ii., sec. 7.

4. *Wherein does the blessedness of heaven consist as far as revealed?*

1st. Negatively, in perfect deliverance from sin, and from all its evil consequences, physical, moral, and social.—Rev. vii. 16, 17; xxi. 4, 27.

2d. Positively.   (1.) In the perfection of our nature, both material and spiritual; the full development and harmonious exercise of all our faculties, intellectual and moral, and in the unrestrained progress thereof to eternity.—1 Cor. xiii. 9–12; xv. 45–49; 1 John iii. 2.   (2.) In the sight of our blessed Redeemer, communion with his person, and fellowship in all his glory and blessedness, and through him with saints and angels. John xvii. 24; 1 John i. 3; Rev. iii. 21; xxi. 3, 4, 5.   (3.) In that "beatific vision of God," which, consisting in the ever increasingly clear discovery of the divine excellence lovingly apprehended, transforms the soul into the same image, from glory unto glory.—Matt. v. 8; 2 Cor. iii. 18.

In meditating upon what is revealed of the conditions of heavenly existence two errors are to be avoided: 1st, the extreme of regarding the mode of existence experienced by the saints in heaven as too nearly analogous to that of our earthly life; 2d, the opposite extreme of regarding the conditions of the heavenly life as too widely distinguished from that of our present experience. The evil effect of the first extreme will, of course, be to degrade by unworthy associations our conceptions of heaven; while the evil effect of the opposite extreme will be in great measure to destroy the moral power which a hope of heaven should naturally exert over our hearts and lives, by rendering our conceptions of it vague, and our sympathy with its characteristics consequently distant and feeble. To avoid both of these extremes, we should fix the limits within which our conceptions of the future existence of the saints must range, by distinguishing between those elements of man's nature, and of his relations to God and other men, which are essential and unchangeable, and those elements which must be changed in order to render his nature in his relations perfect. 1st. The following must be changed: (1) all sin and its consequences must be removed; (2) "spiritual bodies" must take the place of our present flesh and blood; (3) the new heavens and the new earth must take the place of the present heavens and earth, as the scene of man's life; (4) the laws of social organization must be radically changed, since in heaven there will be no marriage, but a social order analogous to that of the "angels of God" introduced.

2d. The following elements are essential, and therefore unchangeable. (1.) Man will continue ever to exist, as compounded of two natures, spiritual and material. (2.) He is essentially intellectual, and must live by knowledge. (3.) He is essentially active, and must have work to do. (4.) Man can, as a finite creature, know God only mediately, *i. e.*, through his works of creation and providence, the experience of his gracious work upon our hearts, and through his incarnate Son, who is the *image* of his person, and the fulness of the Godhead *bodily*. God will therefore in heaven continue to teach man through his works, and to act upon him by means of motives addressed to his will through his understanding. (5.) The memory of man never finally loses the slightest impression, and it will belong to the perfection of the heavenly state that every experience acquired in the past will always be within the perfect control of the will. (6.) Man is essentially a social being. This, taken in connection with the preceding point, indicates the conclusion that the associations, as well as the experience of our earthly life, will carry all of their natural consequences with them into the new mode of existence, except as far as they are necessarily modified (not lost) by the change. (7.) Man's life is essentially an eternal progress towards infinite perfection. (8.) All the known analogies of God's works in creation, in his providence in the material and moral world, and in his dispensation of grace (1 Cor. xii. 5–28), indicate that in heaven saints will differ among themselves both as to inherent capacities and qualities, and as to relative rank and office. These differences will doubtless be determined (*a*) by constitutional differences of natural capacity, (*b*) by gracious rewards in heaven corresponding in kind and degree to the gracious fruitfulness of the individual on earth, (*c*) by the absolute sovereignty of the Creator.—Matt. xvi. 27; Rom. ii. 6; 1 Cor. xii. 4–28.

5. *What are the principal terms, literal and figurative, which are applied in Scripture to the future condition of the reprobate?*

As a *place*, it is sometimes literally designated by ἅιδης, *Hades*, and sometimes by γεέννα, both translated hell.—Matt. v. 22, 29, 30; Luke xvi. 23. Also by the phrase, "place of torment."—Luke xvi. 28. As a *condition* of suffering, it is literally designated by the phrases, "wrath of God," Rom. ii. 5, and "second death," Rev. xxi. 8.

Figurative terms.—Everlasting fire, prepared for the devil and his angels.—Matt. xxv. 41. The hell of fire, where the worm dieth not, and the fire is not quenched.—Mark ix. 44. The lake which burneth with fire and brimstone.—Rev. xxi. 8. Bottomless pit.—Rev. ix. 2. The dreadful nature of this abode of the wicked is implied in such expressions as "outer darkness," the place "where there is weeping and gnashing of teeth," Matt. viii. 12; "I am tormented in this flame," Luke xvi. 24; "unquenchable fire," Luke iii. 17; "furnace of fire," Matt. xiii. 42; "blackness of darkness," Jude 13; "torment in fire and brimstone," Rev. xiv. 10; "the smoke of their torment ascendeth forever and ever, and they have no rest day nor night," Rev. xiv. 11.—Kitto's "Bib. Ency."

6. *What do the Scriptures teach as to the nature of future punishments?*

The terms used in Scripture to describe these sufferings are evidently figurative, yet they certainly establish the following points. These sufferings will consist—1st. In the loss of all good, whether natural, as granted through Adam, or gracious, as offered through Christ. 2d. In all the natural consequences of unrestrained sin, judicial abandonment, utter alienation from God, and the awful society of lost men and devils.—2 Thess. i. 9. 3d. In the positive infliction of torment, God's wrath and curse descending upon both the moral and physical nature of its objects. The Scriptures also establish the fact that these sufferings must be—1st. Inconceivably dreadful in degree. 2d. Endless in duration. 3d. Various in degree, proportionately to the deserts of the subject.—Matt. x. 15; Luke xii. 48.

7. *What is the usage of the words, ἀιών, eternity, and ἀιώνιος, eternal, in the New Testament, and the argument thence derived establishing the endless duration of future punishment?*

1st. The Greek language possesses no more emphatic terms with which to express the idea of endless duration than these. 2d. Although they are sometimes employed in the New Testament to designate limited duration, yet, in the vast majority of instances, they evidently designate unlimited duration. 3d. They are used to express the endless duration of God. (1.) ἀιών is thus used, 1 Tim. i. 17, and as applied to Christ, Rev. i. 18. (2.) ἀιώνιος is thus used, Rom. xvi. 26, and as applied to the Holy Ghost.—Heb. ix. 14. 4th. They are used to express the endless duration of the future happiness of the saints. (1.) ἀιών is thus used.—John vi. 57, 58; 2 Cor. ix. 9. (2.) ἀιώνιος is thus used.—Matt. xix. 29; Mark x. 30; John iii. 15; Rom. ii. 7. 5th. In Matt. xxv. 46, the very same word is used in a single clause to define at once the duration of the future happiness of the saints, and the misery of the lost. Thus the Scriptures do expressly declare that the duration of the future misery of the lost is to be in precisely the same sense unending, as is either the life of God, or the blessedness of the saints. See the learned, independent, and conclusive critical examination of the New Testament usage of these words by the late Prof. Moses Stuart, "Stuart's Essays on Future Punishment," published Presby. Board of Publication.

8. *What evidence for the truth on this subject is furnished by the New Testament usage of the word ἀΐδιος?*

This word, formed from ἀεί, always, forever, signifies, in classical Greek, eternal. It occurs only twice in the New Testament, Rom. i. 20, "even his *eternal* power and Godhead," and Jude 6, "Angels reserved in *everlasting* chains." But lost men share the fate of lost angels.—Matt. xxv. 41; Rev. xx. 10. Thus the same word expresses the duration of the Godhead and of the sufferings of the lost.

9. *What other evidence do the Scriptures furnish on this subject?*

1st. There is nothing in the Scriptures which, even by the most remote implication, suggests that the sufferings of the lost shall ever end.

2d. The constant application to the subject of such figurative language as, "fire that shall not be quenched," "fire unquenchable," "the worm that never dies," "bottomless pit," the necessity of paying the "uttermost farthing," "the smoke of their torment arising forever and ever," Luke iii. 17; Mark ix. 45, 46; Rev. xiv. 10, 11, is consistent only with the conviction that God wills us to believe on his authority that future punishments are literally endless. It is said of those who commit the unpardonable sin that they shall never be forgiven, "neither in this world nor in that which is to come."—Matt. xii. 32.

It is argued that this language is figurative, and the dictum is quoted "*Theologia symbolica non est demonstrativa.*" This is true. But of what are these the figures? What does God intend to signify by such symbols? They may unquestionably be pulled to pieces severally, and their meaning brought into doubt in detail. But it must be remembered—(1.) That this language is characteristic of all God's revelations to us of the future of those who die impenitent. Such descriptions color uniformly the whole presentation. (2.) The Bible was intended for popular instruction. Hence the obvious meaning must have been the one intended to be conveyed, and hence the one to which the divine veracity is pledged. This is especially a weighty consideration in the case of this doctrine, because— (*a.*) It is a practical one of personal concernment. (*b.*) The language occurs frequently, and strikes the eye of every reader. (*c.*) The entire historical church (with only individual exceptions) have, as a matter of fact, interpreted it in the sense of endless suffering. And this in spite of the constant and tremendous pressure of human desires toward the opposite conclusion.

10. *What presumption on this subject is afforded by reason and experience?*

The Scriptures teach us—(1.) That man is dead in sin and morally impotent. (2.) That repentance and faith are wrought in the soul by the Holy Ghost. Experience teaches us that repentance and faith are as duties exceedingly difficult under the most favorable conditions. Reason and experience unite in teaching us that they become more difficult and unusual the longer a person lives and the more definitely his moral character and habits are fixed.

1st. The most favorable possible conditions are afforded in

this life. Youth, immature character, the word and the Spirit, and the providence of God and the Christian Church. Supernatural demonstrations and purgatorial sufferings would have no equal moral effect. "If they hear not Moses and the prophets, neither will they be persuaded though one rose from the dead."—Luke xvi. 31.

2d. The law of habit and fixed moral character leads to the conclusion, that the hope of a favorable change must rapidly decrease in proportion as it is delayed.

11. *What two views on this subject have been held by different parties in opposition to the faith of the whole Christian Church, and the clear teaching of God's word?*

I. That of the total extinction of the being of the finally reprobate, as the sentence of the "second death," after the last Judgment. This doctrine is styled popularly "The Annihilation of the Wicked," and by its advocates "Conditional Immortality." It has been advocated ably in "Debt and Grace as related to the Doctrine of a Future Life," by C. F. Hudson, and in "The Duration and Nature of Future Punishment," by Henry Constable, and "View of Scripture Revelation concerning a Future State," by Archb. Whately, and in "Life in Christ," by Edward White.

They argue that the word "death" means always "cessation of being," and "eternal destruction" means always the "putting out of existence."

We *answer*—(1.) They fail utterly in their attempt to show that the words and phrases cited ever have, and much more that they always have, the sense contended for. (2.) Their doctrine is in plain contradiction of the uniform representation of Scripture as to the ultimate state of the finally impenitent as illustrated above, Ques. 9. (3.) Their doctrine is in contradiction of the natural and universal instinct of immortality witnessed to by the religions and literatures of all nations, whether heathen, Jewish, or Christian.

II. The opinion of those who agree in general in teaching the future restoration of sinners after an indefinite period of purifying discipline subsequent to death, whether in the intermediate state or after the judgment (see above, Ch. XXXVII., Ques. 21). This view rests, (1) upon a class of texts presumed to teach the restitution of all things as Acts iii. 21; Eph. i. 10; Col. i. 19, 20, etc. (2.) Upon what they claim to be a moral intuition that endless punishment would be unworthy of God.

We ANSWER—1st. The passages of Scripture upon which the argument is based would be consistent with this view of ultimate universal salvation, if there were no explicit statements of Scripture to the contrary.   Each class of Scripture must be interpreted in view of the other.   And it is self-evident that the general and indefinite must be ruled by the definite and explicit.   It is an axiom that the phrase "all" and "all things" include more or less according to the subject.   We gladly admit—(1) that ALL *in Christ* shall be made alive, and (2) that he will be made head of ALL THINGS absolutely without exception, in the sense that the entire universe, including friends and foes, shall be subjected to his royal supremacy, all revolt subdued, and each class put into its own sphere.—See below, Ques. 14.

2d. The "intuitions" upon which the doctrine is founded are shown below, Ques. 12 and 13, not to be trustworthy.

3d. See above, Ques. 10, as the hope of moral reformation in another life is not accordant with the representations of Scripture, so it is not confirmed by the lessons of reason and experience.

12. *What objections are urged against this doctrine derived from the justice of God?*

The justice of God requires—(1.) That none should suffer for that for which they are not responsible.   (2.) That punishment should in every case be exactly proportioned to the guilt of the subject.

But it is objected—1st. Multitudes in Christian as well as in heathen lands are not responsible for their impenitency, because they have never in their whole lives had an opportunity of knowing or of receiving Christ.

We ANSWER—that the direct statements of the Bible, the whole analogy of the Christian system, and the experience of all Christians, unite in affirming that all human ·nature is guilty and deserving of the wrath and curse of God anterior to the gift or the rejection of Christ.   If it were not so Christ need not have been given to *expiate* guilt.   If it were not so Christ would be "dead in vain," and salvation would be of *debt* and not of GRACE.

It is objected—2d. No sin of a finite creature can deserve an infinite punishment, but all endless punishment is infinite.

We ANSWER—that the word infinite in this connection is misleading.   It is plain that *endless* sin deserves *endless* punishment, and that is all the Scriptures or the Church teach.   One sin deserves the wrath and curse of God.   He is under no obligation in justice to provide a redemption.   The instant a soul sins it is cut off from the communion and life of God.   As long as it continues in that state it will continue to sin.   As long as it continues to sin, it will continue to deserve his wrath and curse.   It is obvious that the sinful tempers and conduct indulged in hell will deserve and receive punishment as strictly as those previously indulged in this life. Otherwise the monstrous principle would be true that the worse a sinner becomes the less is he worthy of blame or punishment.

It is objected—3d. The infinite does not admit of degrees, yet the guilt of different sinners is various.

We ANSWER—this is a dishonest cavil. It is plain that sufferings alike endless may vary indefinitely in degree.

It is objected—4th. That the moral difference between the lowest saint saved and the most amiable sinner lost may be imperceptible, yet the difference of destiny is infinite.

We ANSWER—that this is all true, but the ground of the treatment of the most unworthy believer is the righteousness of Christ, and the ground of the treatment of the least unworthy unbeliever is his own character and conduct.

13. *What objection drawn from the benevolence of God is urged against this doctrine?*

It is claimed—1st. That the benevolence of God prompts him to do all in his power to promote their happiness. And as we have no right to limit that power, we are warranted to hope that he will ultimately secure the happiness of all.

We ANSWER—(1.) God's benevolence prompts him to secure the happiness of all his creatures as far as that is consistent with his other attributes of wisdom, holiness, and justice. (2.) We have constant experience that he does inflict upon his creatures evils which have no tendency and no influence in promoting the ultimate happiness of the individuals concerned. (3) The benevolence of the supreme Moral Governor, as concerned for the peace and purity of the universe, concurs with his justice in demanding the execution of the full penalty of the law upon all law-breakers, especially upon all who have aggravated their guilt by the rejection of his crucified Son.

It is claimed—2d. That the cultivated intuitions of Christian men assure them that it is inconsistent with the moral perfections of God *first* to bring into existence immortal beings under conditions common to the majority of men, and *then* to doom them to an after-life of endless misery.

We ANSWER—(1.) The permission of sin in general is a mystery. The ante-natal forfeiture of human beings in Adam is a mystery. But every enlightened human being knows himself to be without excuse, and worthy of God's wrath. (2.) God has shown his sense of the terrible guilt of men by the penalty he executed upon his own Son, when he suffered in our place. (3.) It is absurd for us to claim that our intuitions are adequate to determine what it will be right for the Moral Governor of all the universe to do with finally impenitent sinners. Doubtless righteousness in him is precisely what righteousness is in a perfectly righteous man. But we do not know all the conditions of the case, and our "intuitions" are darkened by sin (Heb. iii. 13). Hence our only source of reliable knowledge is the word of God, and that, as we have seen, gives us no ground to hope for repentance beyond the grave. (2.) It is absolutely cruel to follow the example of the devil with Eve in persuading the people that after all God may be more benevolent than the language of his word implies (Gen. iii. 3, 4).

14. *What argument for the future restoration of all rational creatures to holiness and happiness is founded upon* Rom. v. 18, 19; 1 Cor. xv. 22–28; Eph. i. 10; Col. i. 19, 20?

In regard to Rom. v. 18, it is argued that the phrase "all men" must have precisely the same extent of application in the one clause as in the other. We answer, 1st, the phrase "all men" is often used in Scripture in connections which necessarily restrict the sense.—John iii. 26; xii. 32. 2d. In this case the phrase "all men" is evidently defined by the qualifying phrase, ver. 17, "who have received abundance of grace and the gift of righteousness." 3d. This contrast between the "all men" in Adam and the "all men" in Christ is consistent with the analogy of the whole gospel.

In regard to 1 Cor. xv. 22, the argument is the same as that drawn from Rom. v. 18. From verses 25–28 it is argued that the great end of Christ's mediatorial reign must be the restoration of every creature to holiness and blessedness. To this we answer, 1st, this is a strained interpretation put upon these words, which they do not necessarily bear, and which is clearly refuted by the many direct testimonies we have cited from Scripture above. 2d. It is inconsistent with the scope of Paul's subject in this passage. He says that from eternity to the ascension God reigned absolutely. From the ascension to the restitution of all things God reigns in the person of the God-man as Mediator. From the restitution to eternity God will again reign directly as absolute God.

The ultimate salvation of all creatures is argued also from Eph. i. 10; Col. i. 19, 20. In both passages, however, the "all things" signify the whole company of angels and redeemed men, who are gathered under the dominion of Christ. Because, 1st, in both passages the subject of discourse is the church, not the universe; 2d, in both passages the "all things" is limited by the qualifying phrases, "the predestinated," "we who first trusted in Christ," "the accepted in the beloved," "if ye continue in the faith," etc., etc. See Hodge's "Commentaries on Romans, 1st Corinthians, and Ephesians."

15. *What opinions have prevailed among extreme Arminians on this subject?*

From their fundamental principles as to the relation of ability to responsibility, they must hold that none can perish who have not in some form and degree or another had an opportunity of availing themselves of salvation through Christ.

In order to avoid the obvious inferences from the broad facts of the case, some have supposed that God may extend the probation of some beyond this life.—Scot's "Christian Life."

Limborch (Lib. iv., c. xi.) says, that probably all who make a good use of their light in this world will be saved, but if we reject this, rather than believe that the divine goodness could condemn to hell fire *these* (the ignorant) it appears better to hold that as there is a threefold estate of mankind in this life,—of believers, of unbelievers, and of the ignorant,—so there is also a threefold estate after this life: of eternal life for believers, of infernal sufferings for unbelievers, and besides these the *status ignorantium.*

CHAPTER XLI.

SACRAMENTS.

1. *What is the etymology and what the classical and patristic usage of the word "sacramentum?"*

1st. It is derived from *sacro, āre, to make sacred*, dedicate to gods or sacred uses.

2d. In its classical usage it signified—(1.) That by which a person binds himself to another to perform any thing. (2.) Thence a sum deposited with the court as pledge, and which, if forfeited, was devoted to sacred uses. (3.) Also an oath, especially a soldier's oath of faithful consecration to his country's service.—Ainsworth's "Dic."

3d. The Fathers used this word in a conventional sense as equivalent to the Greek μυστήριον, *a mystery*, i. e., something unknown until revealed, and hence an emblem, a type, a rite having some latent spiritual meaning known only to the initiated, or instructed.

The Greek fathers applied the term μυστήριον to the Christian ordinances of baptism and the Lord's Supper, inasmuch as these rites had a spiritual significance, and were thus a form of revelation of divine truth.

The Latin fathers used the word "sacramentum" as a Latin word, in its own proper sense, for any thing sacred in itself, or having the power of binding, or consecrating men, and in addition they used it as the equivalent of the Greek word μυστήριον, i. e., in the entirely different sense of a revealed truth, or a sign or symbol revealing a truth otherwise hidden. This fact has given to the usage of this word "sacramentum," in the scholastic theology, an injurious latitude and indefiniteness of meaning. Thus in Eph. iii. 3, 4, 9; v. 32; 1 Tim. iii. 16; Rev. i. 20, the word μυστήριον truly bears the sense of "the revelation of a truth undiscoverable by reason," and it is translated in such passages in the English version, *mystery*, and in the Latin vulgate, "*sacramentum.*" Thus the Romish church uses the same word in two entirely different senses, applying it indifferently to baptism and the Lord's Supper "as binding ordinances," and to the union of believers with Christ as a *revealed* truth.—Eph. v. 32. And hence they absurdly infer that matrimony is a sacrament.

2. *What is the definition of a sacrament, as given by the Fathers, the Schoolmen, the Romish Church, the Church of England, and in our own Standards?*

1st. Augustine's definition is "Signum rei sacræ," or "Sacramentum est invisibilis gratiæ visibile signum, ad nostram justificationem institutum;" "accedit verbum ad elementum, et fit sacramentum."

2d. Victor of St. Hugo: "Sacramentum est visibilis forma invisibilis gratiæ in eo collatæ."

3d. The Council of Trent: "A sacrament is something presented to the senses, which has the power, by divine institution, not only of signifying, but also of efficiently conveying grace."—"Cat. Rom.," Part II., Chap. i., Q. 6.

4th. The Church of England, in the 25th article of religion, affirms that "Sacraments instituted by Christ are not only the badges and tokens of the profession of Christian men, but rather they be certain sure witnesses and effectual signs of grace, and of God's good will towards us, by the which he doth work inwardly in us, and doth not only quicken, but also strengthen and confirm our faith in him."

5th. The "Westminster Assembly's Larger Cat.," Q. 162 and 163, affirms that a "Sacrament is a holy ordinance instituted by Christ in his church, to signify, seal, and exhibit to those who are within the covenant of grace the benefits of his mediation, to increase their faith and all other graces, to oblige them to obedience, to testify and cherish their love and communion with one another, and to distinguish them from those that are without." "The parts of a sacrament are two, the one an outward and sensible sign used according to Christ's own appointment; the other an inward spiritual grace thereby signified."

3. *On what principles is such a definition to be constructed?*

1st. It is to be remembered that the term "sacrament" does not occur in the Bible.

2d. From the extreme latitude with which this term has been used, both in the sense proper to it as a Latin word, and in that attributed to it as the conventional equivalent of the

Greek word μνστήριον, it is evident that no definition of a gospel ordinance can be arrived at by a mere reference either to the etymology or ecclesiastical usage of the word "sacramentum."

3d. The definition of a class of gospel ordinances can be properly formed only by a comparison of all the Scriptures teach concerning the origin, nature, and design of those ordinances universally recognized as belonging to that class, and thus by determining those essential elements which are common to each member of the class, and which distinguish them as a class from all other divine ordinances.

4th. Those ordinances which are "universally recognized" as sacraments are baptism and the Lord's Supper. "Thomas Aquinas agreed with other theologians, 'Summa,' P. III., Qu. 62, Art. 5, in regarding baptism and the Lord's Supper as '*potissima sacramenta.*'"—Hagenbach. The true question then is, *Are there any other divine ordinances having the essential characteristics which are common to baptism and the Lord's Supper?*

4. *How many sacraments do Romanists make, and how may the controversy between them and the Protestants be decided?*

The Roman church teaches that there are seven sacraments, viz., baptism, confirmation, the Lord's Supper, penance, extreme unction, orders, marriage.

We maintain, however, that only baptism and the Lord's Supper can be properly embraced under either the Protestant or the Catholic definitions of a sacrament, as given above, Question 2.

1st. Confirmation, penance, and extreme unction are not divine institutions, having no warrant whatever in Scripture.

2d. That marriage instituted by God in Paradise, and ordination to the gospel ministry instituted by Christ, although both divine institutions, are evidently not ordinances of the same kind with baptism and the Lord's Supper, and do not meet the conditions of either definitions of a sacrament, since they neither signify nor convey any inward grace.

5. *What two things are included in every sacrament?*

1st. "An outward visible sign used according to Christ's own appointment; 2d, an inward spiritual grace thereby signified."—"L. Cat.," Q. 163. See below, "Apol. Aug. Conf." (Hase), p. 267.

The Romanists, in the language of the Schoolmen, distinguish between the *matter* and the *form* of a sacrament. The *matter* is that part of the sacrament subjected to the senses, and significant of grace, *e. g.*, the water, and the act of applying the water in baptism, and the bread and wine, and the acts of breaking the bread, and pouring out the wine in the Lord's Supper. The *form* is the divine word used by the minister in administering the elements, devoting them thus to the office of signifying grace.

6. *What, according to the Romanists, is the relation between the sign and the grace signified?*

They hold that in consequence of the divine institution, and in virtue of the "power of the Omnipotent which exists in them," the grace signified is contained in the very nature of the sacraments themselves, so that it is always conferred, *ex opere operato* (*i. e.*, ex vi ipsius actionis sacramentalis), upon every receiver of them who does not oppose a positive obstacle thereto. Thus they understand the "sacramental union," or relation between the sign and the grace signified to be *physical*, or that which subsists between a substance and its properties, *i. e.*, the virtue of conferring grace is, in the sacraments, *as* the virtue of burning is in fire.—"Council of Trent," Sess. 7, Cans. 6 and 8. "Cat. Rom.," Part II., Chap. i., Q. 18. Bellarmin, "De Sacram.," 2, 1.

7. *What is the Zwinglian doctrine on this subject?*

Zwingle, the reformer of Switzerland, held a position at the opposite extreme to that of the Romish church, viz., that the sign simply represents by appropriate symbols, and symbolical actions, the grace to which it is related. Thus the sacraments are only effective means of the objective presentation of the truth symbolized.

8. *In what 'sense is the word "exhibit" used in our standards in reference to this subject?*

Compare "Con. of Faith," Chap. xxvii., Sec. 3, and Chap. xxviii., Sec. 6, and "L. Cat.," Q. 162.

This word is derived from the Latin word "exhibeo," which bore the twofold sense of *conveying* and of *disclosing*. It is evident that the term "exhibit" has retained in our standards the former sense of *conveying, conferring*. As in medical language, "to exhibit a remedy" is to administer it.

9. *What is the common doctrine of the Reformed churches as to the relation of the sign to the grace signified?*

The Reformed confessions agree in teaching that this relation is, 1st, simply moral, *i. e.*, it is established only by the institution and promise of Christ, and it depends upon the right administration of the ordinance, and upon the faith and knowledge of the recipient. And, 2d, that it is real, that is, when rightly administered, and when received by the recipient with knowledge and faith they do really, because of the promise of Christ, seal the grace signified, and convey it to the recipient, *i. e.,* the recipient does receive the grace with the sign.

This doctrine, therefore, includes, 1st, the Zwinglian view, that the outward visible sign truly signifies the grace. And, 2d, that they are, as ordinances of God's appointment, seals attached to the promise to authenticate it, as the natural phenomenon of the rainbow was made a seal of God's promise to Noah in virtue of the divine appointment. 3d. That as seals thus accompanying a divine promise by divine authority, they do actually convey the grace they signify to those for whom that grace is intended, and who are in a proper spiritual state to receive it, "as a key conveys admission, a deed an estate, the ceremony of marriage the rights of marriage." See Turretin, L. xix., Question 4; "Conf. of Faith," Chap. xxvii.; "L. Cat.," Questions 162, 163; "Cat. Gene.," sec. 5th, "de Sacramentis;" "Conf. Faith of the French Church," article 34; "Old Scotch Conf.," section 21.

10. *What is the design of the sacraments?*

1st. That they should signify, seal, and exhibit to those within the covenant of grace the benefits of Christ's redemption, and thus as a principal means of grace edify the church. Matt. iii. 11; Gen. xvii. 11, 13; 1 Cor. x. 2–21; xi. 23–26; xii. 13; Rom. ii. 28, 29; iv. 11; vi. 3, 4; Gal. iii. 27; 1 Pet. iii. 21.

2d. That they should be visible badges of membership in the church, to put a visible difference between the professed followers of Christ and the world, Gen xxxiv. 14; Ex. xii. 48; Eph. ii. 19; "Conf. Faith," Chap. xxvii., section 1.

THE ROMISH DOCTRINE AS TO THE EFFICACY OF THE SACRAMENTS.

11. *What is the Romish doctrine as to the efficacy of the Sacraments?*

1st. As shown above, under Question 6, they hold that the sacraments contain the grace which they signify. That this grace-conferring energy is inseparable from a genuine sacrament, and that as an objective fact, they contain it at all times, and present it alike to all subjects irrespective of character.

2d. In every case of their application, except when positively opposed and nullified, they effect the grace they signify, as an *opus operatum, i. e.*, by the mere inherent power of the sacramental action itself.

12. *Upon what conditions on the part of the administrator do they believe that the efficacy of the sacrament depends?*

The genuineness of a sacrament on the part of the administrator, depends, according to the Romanists—

1st. On his being canonically authorized. In case of the sacraments of orders and confirmation he must be a bishop in communion with the pope. In the case of the other sacraments he must be a regular popish priest. The personal character of the bishop or priest, even though he be in mortal sin, does not prevent the effect.—"Con. Trident," Sess. can. 12.

2d. The administrator must, in the act, exercise the positive intention of effecting what the church intends to be effected by each sacrament.

Dens (Vol. V., p. 127) says, "To the valid performance of the sacrament is required the intention upon the part of the officiating minister of doing that which the church does. The necessary intention in the minister consists in an act of his will, by which he wills the external action with the intention of doing what the church does;" that is, of performing a valid sacrament. Otherwise, although every external action may be regularly performed, the whole is void. See "Con. Trent," Sess. 7, canon 11. This leaves the recipient entirely at the mercy of the minister, since the validity of the whole service depends upon his secret intention, and is evidently one of the devices of that anti-Christian church to make the people dependent upon the priesthood.

13. *What is the sense in which Protestants admit "intention" to be necessary?*

They admit that in order to render the outward service a valid sacrament, it must be performed with the ostensible professed design of complying thereby with the command of Christ, and of doing what he requires to be done by those who accept the gospel covenant.

14. *What condition do the Romanists hold to be essential to the efficacy of a sacrament, on the part of the subject?*

1st. In the case of infant baptism no condition upon the part of the subject is necessary.

2d. On the part of adults, the only condition is that they shall not positively oppose them by absolute infidelity or resistance of will (*non ponentibus obicem*). Faith and repentance, as these are possible to the unregenerate soul, are also required as necessary to the effect of baptism ("Cat. Rom.," Pt. II., Chap. ii., Ques. 39). Bellarmin, "De Sacramentis," 2, 1, says that the will to be baptized, faith, and penitence, are necessary dispositions enabling the sacrament to produce its effect, just as dryness on the part of wood is the condition of the fire burning it when applied, but never the cause of the burning.

15. *What according to the Papal Church are the effects produced by the sacraments?*

1st. Justifying (sanctifying) grace.

2d. Three of the sacraments, baptism, confirmation, and orders, also impress upon the subject "a character." This "sacramental character" (from the Greek word χαρακτήρ, *a mark, or device, engraved or impressed by a seal*) is a distinctive and indelible impression stamped on the soul, "the twofold effect of which is, that it qualifies us to receive or perform something sacred, and distinguishes one from another." It is upon this account that baptism and confirmation are never repeated, and that the authority and privileges of the priesthood can never be alienated.—"Cat. Rom.," Part II., Chap. i., Q. 21–25; "Council Trent," Sess. 7, can. 9.

16. *How may this doctrine be disproved?*

That the sacraments have not the power of conveying grace to all, whether they are included within the covenant of grace or not, or whether they possess faith or not, is certain, because—

1st. They are seals of the gospel covenant (see below, Question 14). But a seal merely ratifies a covenant as a covenant. It can convey the grace promised only on the supposition that the conditions of the covenant are fulfilled. But salvation and every spiritual blessing is by that covenant declared to depend upon the condition of faith.

2d. Knowledge and faith are required as the prerequisite conditions necessary to be found in all applicants, as the essential qualification for receiving the sacraments.—Acts ii. 41; viii. 37; x. 47; Rom. iv. 11.

3d. Faith is essential to render the sacraments efficacious. Rom. ii. 25–29; 1 Cor. xi. 27–29; 1 Pet. iii. 21.

4th. Many who receive the sacraments are notoriously without the grace they signify. Witness the case of Simon Magus, Acts viii. 9–21, and of many of the Corinthians and Galatians, and of the majority of nominal Christians in the present day.

5th. Many have had the grace without the sacraments. Witness Abraham, the thief upon the cross, and Cornelius the centurion, and a multitude of eminent Christians among the Society of Friends.

6th. This doctrine blasphemously ties down the grace of the ever living and sovereign God, and puts its entire disposal into the hands of fallible and often wicked men.

7th. This doctrine is an essential element of that ritualistic and priestly system which prevailed among the Pharisees, and against which the whole New Testament is a protest.

8th. The uniform effect of this system has been to exalt the power of the priests, and to confound all knowledge as to the nature of true religion. As the baptized, as a matter of fact, do not always nor generally bear the fruits of the Spirit, all ritualists agree in regarding these fruits as not essential to salvation. Where this system prevails vital godliness expires.

DOCTRINE OF PROTESTANT CHURCHES AS TO THE EFFICACY OF THE SACRAMENTS.

17. *What is the Lutheran doctrine as to the efficacy of the sacraments?*

1st. They reject the popish doctrine that the sacraments effect grace *ex opere operato.*

2d. They maintain that their grace-conferring efficacy resides in the sacraments intrinsically.

3d. That as an objective fact it is communicated to every recipient, whether he have faith or not.

4th. But it takes effect only in those who have true faith to receive it. As the healing virtue resided in Christ whether the woman touched or not (Matt. ix. 20), yet it would not have availed her unless she had believed and touched.

5th. They hold that this efficacy resides not in the sign or ceremony, but in the Word which accompanies the sign and constitutes it a sacrament. The efficacy is not due to the mere moral power of the truth, nor to the faith of the recipient, but it is supernatural, residing in the power of the Holy Ghost. But not the power of the Holy Ghost as extrinsic to the truth, but as dwelling in it, and inseparable from it—the *virtus Spiritus Sancti* intrinsicus *accedens.* See Krauth's "Conservative Reformation," pp. 825–830.

18. *What is the Zwinglian and Remonstrant view as to the same?*

The tendency of thought on this subject first developed by Zwingle was afterward carried out more fully by the Remonstrants of the next century, and to a greater extent by the

Socinians. Low views as to the nature and efficacy of the sacraments have also largely prevailed in this century among all evangelical churches, in reaction from the extreme views of the Romanists and Ritualists. For a general statement of this mode of thought see above, Ques. 7.

19. *State the doctrine of the Reformed churches on this subject.*

As to their doctrine of the relation of the sign to the grace signified, see above, Ques. 9.

Hence as to the efficacy of the sacraments the Reformed— 1st. Deny that they confer grace as an *opus operatum.* 2d. They affirm that they convey no grace to the unworthy recipient. 3d. That their efficacy is not of the mere moral power of the truth they symbolize. 4th. That they do really confer grace upon the worthy recipient. 5th. But they do this instrumentally, because the supernatural efficiency is not due to them, nor to him that administers them, but to the Holy Spirit who as a free personal agent uses them sovereignly as his instruments to do his will (*virtus Spiritus Sancti* extrinsicus *accedens*). 6th. That as seals of the covenant of grace they convey and confirm grace to those to whom it belongs, *i. e.*, that is to those who are within that covenant, and in the case of adults, only through a living faith. 7th. That the grace conferred by the sacraments often is conferred upon true believers before and without their use.

20. *By what evidence is the truth of the Reformed Doctrine established?*

The truth of the Reformed doctrine is established on the one hand by the evidence disproving the truth of the Romish doctrine, set forth under Ques. 16. Its truth as opposed to the meagre Zwinglian view, on the other hand, is established as follows: (1.) That the sacraments are not only *signs* of the grace of Christ, but also *seals* of the gospel covenant offering us that grace upon the condition of faith, "is evident from the fact that Paul says that circumcision is the seal of the righteousness of faith.—Rom. iv. 11. And that the apostle regarded baptism in the same light is evident from Col. ii. 11. In reference to the Lord's Supper, the Saviour said, 'this cup is the new covenant in my blood,' *i. e.*, the new covenant was ratified by his blood. Of that blood the cup is the appointed memorial, and it is, therefore, both the memorial and the confirmation of the covenant itself. . . . . The gospel is represented under the form of a covenant. The sacraments are the seals of that covenant. God, in their appointment, binds himself to the fulfilment of his promises; his people, by receiving them, bind themselves to trust and serve him. This idea is included in the representation given (Rom. vi. 3, 4) in the formula of baptism, and in all those passages in which a participation of Christian ordinances is said to include a profession of the gospel." (2.) As seals attached to the covenant, it follows that they actually convey the grace signified, as a legal form of investiture, to those to whom, according to the terms of the covenant, it belongs. Thus a deed, when signed and sealed, is said to convey the property it represents, because it is the legal form by which the intention of the original possessor is publicly expressed, and his act ratified. It is on this ground that in Scripture, as in common language, the names and attributes of the graces sealed are ascribed to the sacraments by which they are sealed and conveyed to their rightful possessors.—"Conf. Faith," Chap. xxvii., section 2. They are said to wash away sin, to unite to Christ, to save, etc.—Acts ii. 38; xxii. 16; Rom. vi. 2, 6; 1 Cor. x. 16; xii. 13; Gal. iii. 27; Titus iii. 5. "Way of Life."

THE NECESSITY OF THE SACRAMENTS.

21. *What doctrine do the Romanists maintain as to the necessity of the Sacraments?*

The Romanists distinguish, 1st, between a condition absolutely necessary to attain an end, and one which is only highly convenient and helpful in order to it. And, 2d, between the necessity which attaches to essential means, and that obligation which arises from the positive command of God. Accordingly, they hold that the several sacraments are necessary in different respects.

BAPTISM they hold to be absolutely necessary, either its actual reception, or the honest purpose to receive it, alike for infants and adults, as the sole means of attaining salvation.

PENANCE they hold to be absolutely necessary in the same sense, but only for those who have committed mortal sin subsequently to their baptism.

ORDERS they hold to be absolutely necessary in the same sense, yet not for every individual, as a means of personal salvation, but in respect to the whole church as a community.

CONFIRMATION, the EUCHARIST, and EXTREME UNCTION are necessary only in the sense of having been commanded, and of being eminently helpful.

MARRIAGE they hold to be necessary only in this second sense, and only for those who enter into the conjugal relation.—"Cat. Rom.," Part II., Chap. i., Q. 13.

Puseyites, and high churchmen generally, hold the dogma of baptismal regeneration, and of course the consequence that baptism is absolutely necessary as the sole means of salvation.

22. *What is the Protestant doctrine as to the necessity of the sacraments?*

1st. That the sacraments of baptism and the Lord's Supper were instituted by Christ, and that their perpetual observance is obligatory upon the church upon the ground of the divine precept. This is evident (1) from the record of their institution, Matt. xxviii. 19; 1 Cor. xi. 25, 26; (2) from the example of the apostles.—Acts ii. 41; viii. 37; 1 Cor. xi. 23–28; x. 16–21.

2d. That nevertheless the grace offered in the gospel covenant does not reside in these sacraments physically, nor is it tied to them inseparably, so that, although obligatory as duties, and helpful as means to those who are prepared to receive them, they are in no sense the essential means, without which salvation can not be attained. This is proved by the arguments presented above, under Q. 16.

The Validity of the Sacraments.

This includes whatever is essential to the genuineness of a sacrament, in order that it may avail to the end of its institution.

23. *What are the various opinions on this subject?*

All church parties agree that there must be—1st. The right "matter," the proper elements, and actions. 2d. The right "form," the prescribed words which attend its administration, and added to the "form" constitute the sacrament. 3d. The right "intention," the serious design of doing what Christ commanded in the institution of the rite.

Different churches differ as to what are the proper "matter," "form," and "intention." It appears certain that no one not sincerely believing in the supreme deity of Christ and in his office as Redeemer, and in the personality of the Holy Ghost, can possibly have the right "intention." Hence the General Assembly, 1814 ("Moore's Digest.," p. 660), decided, "It is the deliberate and unanimous opinion of the Assembly, that those who renounce the fundamental doctrines of the Trinity, and deny that Jesus Christ is the same in substance, equal in power and glory with the Father, can not be recognized as ministers of the gospel, and that their ministrations (baptism, etc.) are wholly invalid." All churches agree that "the efficacy of a sacrament does not depend upon the piety of him that doth administer it."—"Conf. Faith," Ch. xxvii., § 3, "Can. Conc. Trident," Sess. 7, can. 11. And the "Gallic Conf.," Art. 28, states the common opinion and practice of all the Protestant churches with respect to Romish baptism. "Because, nevertheless, that in the papacy some scant vestiges of the true church remain, and especially the substance of baptism, the efficacy of which does not depend on him that administers it, we acknowledge those baptized by them, not to need to be rebaptized, although on account of the corruptions adhering, no one can offer his infants to be baptized by them, without suffering pollution himself."

In respect to the qualifications of the person administrating the Papists maintain that it is essential to the validity of a sacrament that it should be administered by a canonically ordained minister. For orders and confirmation a bishop, for the rest a priest. But on account of the absolute necessity (as they hold) of baptism for salvation, they admit "all, even from among the laity, whether men or women, whatever sect they profess (to baptize). For this is permitted, if necessity compels, even to Jews, infidels or heretics, provided, however, they intend to perform what the Catholic Church performs in that act of her ministry."—"Cat. of Conc. Trident," and "Conc. Trident," Sess. 7, "On Bapt.," can. 4.

Protestants regard the sacraments both as a preaching of the Word, and as authoritative seals, and badges of church membership. Their administration consequently must be confined to those church officers who possess by divine commission the office of teaching and ruling, "neither of which (sacraments) may be dispensed by any, but by a minister of the Word, lawfully ordained."—"Conf. Faith," Ch. xxvii., § 4. Not regarding baptism as essential to salvation, Protestants generally make no exception in favor of lay-baptism.—"Directory for Worship," Ch. vii., § 1, Calvin's "Instit.," Bk. IV., Ch. xv., § 20.

The Authoritative Statements of various Churches.

Romish Doctrine.—"*Cat. Conc. Trident*," Pt. 2, ch. i., Ques. 8.—"A sacrament is a thing lying open to the senses, which from the institution of God, has the power both of signifying and of effecting holiness and righteousness."

"*Conc. Trident*," Sess. 7, can. 1.—"If any one saith that the sacraments of the New Law, were not all instituted by Jesus Christ, our Lord, or that they are more or less than seven, to wit, Baptism, Confirmation, the Eucharist, Penance, Extreme Unction, Order, and Matrimony; or even that any one of these seven is not truly and properly a sacrament; let him be anathema."

Can. 4.—"If any one saith that the sacraments of the New Law are not necessary unto salvation, but superfluous; and that, without them, or without the desire thereof, men obtain of God, through faith alone, the grace of justification (though all the sacraments are not necessary for every individual); let him be anathema."

Can. 6.—"If any one saith that the sacraments of the New Law do not contain the grace which they signify; or that they do not confer that grace on those who do not place an obstacle thereunto; as though they were merely outward signs of grace or justice received through faith, and certain marks of the Christian profession, whereby believers are distinguished amongst men from unbelievers; let him be anathema."

Can. 8.—"If any one saith that by the sacraments of the New Law grace is not conferred *ex opere operato*, but that faith alone in the divine promise suffices for the obtaining of grace; let him be anathema."

Can. 9.—"If any one says that in the three sacraments, of Baptism, Confirmation, and Orders, there is not imprinted in the soul a character, that is a certain spiritual and indelible sign, on account of which they can not be repeated; let him be anathema."

Can. 11.—"If any one saith that in ministers, when they effect and confer the sacraments, there is not required the intention, at least, of doing what the Church does; let him be anathema."

"*Cat. Conc. Trident.*," Pt. 2, ch. i., Ques. 24, 25.—"The other effect of Baptism, Confirmation, and Orders is the character which they impress on the soul. This character is, as it were, a certain distinctive mark impressed on the soul, which inhering, as it does perpetually, can never be blotted out   .   .   .   it has a twofold effect: it both renders us fit to undertake and perform something sacred; and it serves to distinguish us one from another by some mark."

Bellarmin "*De Sac.*," 2, 1.—"That which actively, proximately, and instrumentally effects the grace of justification is that sole external action which is called a sacrament, and this is called an *opus operatum*, being received passively (operatum), so that it is the same for a sacrament to confer grace *ex opere operato*, that it is to confer grace by virtue of the sacramental action itself, instituted by God for this end, and not from the merit either of the agent or of the receiver.   .   .   .   The will of God, which uses the sacrament, concurs indeed actively, but is the principal cause. The sufferings of Christ concur, but is the meritorious cause, not however the efficient (cause), since it is not in the act, but has passed away, although it remains objectively in the mind of God. The power and will of the minister necessarily concur, but they are remote causes, for they are required to effect the sacramental action itself, which afterwards acts immediately.   .   .   .   Will, faith, and repentance in the adult recipient are necessarily required as dispositions on the part of the subject, not as active causes, for not even faith and repentance can either effect sacramental grace, or give efficacy to the sacrament, but only remove obstacles, which would hinder the sacraments from exercising their own efficacy, hence in the case of children, where disposition is not required, justification is effected without these things. If in order to burn wood, the wood is first dried, the fire struck out from the flint, and then applied to the wood, and then combustion ensues, no one would say that the immediate cause of the combustion was either the dryness, or the striking of fire from the flint, or its application to the wood, but that the primary cause is the fire alone, and the instrumental cause is the heating alone."

THE LUTHERAN DOCTRINE. "*Aug. Conf.*," p. 13. (Hase).—"Sacraments have been instituted not only that they might be marks of profession among men, but more that they may be signs and testimonies of the will of God toward us set forth to excite and confirm faith in those who use them."

"*Apol. Augs. Conf.*," p. 267.—"And because that in a sacrament there are two things, the sign and the word; the word is the New Testament promise of the remission of sin . . .   and the ceremony is as it were a picture of the word or a seal showing the promise. Therefore as the promise is ineffective if it be not accepted by faith, so the ceremony is ineffective unless faith accedes. And as the word is given to excite this faith; so the sacrament is instituted, that this representation meeting the eyes may move the heart to believe."

Ib., p. 203.—" We condemn the whole class of scholastic doctors, who teach that to one presenting no obstacle the sacraments confer grace *ex opere operato*, without any good movement of the partaker. But sacraments are signs of promises, therefore in the use of them faith should be present. . .   We here speak of the special faith which trusts a present promise, which not only believes in general that God is, but believes that remission of sins is offered."

Quenstedt (Wittenburg †1688), Vol. I., p. 169.—"The word of God has, from the will and ordination of God himself, even before and beyond all legitimate use, an intrinsic power divine and common to all men, and sufficient for producing immediately and properly spiritual and divine effects, both gracious and punitive."

"*Aug. Conf.*," Art. 9.—"They condemn the Anabaptists who disapprove of the baptism of children, and who affirm that children can be saved without baptism."

"*Apol. Aug. Conf.*," p. 156.—"The ninth article is approved in which we confess, that Baptism is necessary for salvation, and that children are to be baptized, and that the baptism of children is not void, but necessary and efficacious to salvation."

"*Art. Smalcald*," pars. 3, ch. 8.—"And in respect to these things which concern the spoken and outward word, it is steadfastly to be maintained, that God grants to no one his Spirit or grace, unless through the word and with the word outward and preceding. . .   Wherefore in this we must constantly persevere, because God does not wish to act otherwise with us than through the spoken word and sacraments, and because whatever is boasted of, as the Spirit, without the word and sacraments, is the devil himself."

The Reformed Doctrine. "*Catech. Genev.*," p. 519.—"A sacrament is an outward attestation of the divine benevolence towards us, which by a visible sign figures spiritual graces, for sealing the promises of God to our hearts, whereby their virtue may be the better confirmed. Do you think that the power and efficacy of the sacrament are embraced not in the outward element, but flow only from the Spirit of God ? I think so, truly, as it would be pleasing to the Master to exercise his own force through his own instrumentalities, to whatever design he destined them."

"*Cat. Heidelb.*," Fr. 66.—"Sacraments are visible, sacred signs and seals appointed by God that in their use we may have the promise of the gospel made clearer and sealed; to wit, that God for the sake of the one oblation of Christ bestows on us forgiveness of sins and eternal life."

"*Thirty-nine Articles*," Art. 25.—"Sacraments ordained of Christ be not only badges or tokens of Christian men's profession, but rather they be certain sure witnesses and effectual signs of grace, and God's good-will towards us, by the which he doth work invisibly in us, and doth not only quicken, but also strengthen and confirm our faith in him. . . . And in such only as worthily receive the same they have a wholesome effect or operation; but they that receive them unworthily, purchase to themselves damnation, as St. Paul saith."

"West. Conf. Faith," ch. 27; *"L. Cat.,"* Ques. 161–168; *"S. Cat.,"* Ques. 91–93. See above, page 589.

ZWINGLIAN AND REMONSTRANT DOCTRINE. *Limborch, "Christ. Theo.,"* 5, 66, 31.—"It remains to say that God, through the sacraments, exhibits to us his grace, not by conferring it in fact through them, but by representing it and placing it before our eyes through them as clear and evident signs. . . And this efficacy is no other than objective, which requires a cognitive faculty rightly disposed that it may be able to apprehend that which the sign offers objectively to the mind. . . They operate upon us, as signs representing to the mind the thing whose sign they are. No other efficacy ought to be sought for in them."

CHAPTER XLII.

THE NATURE AND DESIGN OF BAPTISM.

1. *State the facts with regard to the prevalence of washing with water, as a symbol of spiritual purification, among the Jews and Gentile nations before the advent of Christ.*

No other religious symbol is so natural and obvious, and none has been so universally practiced. Its usage is distinctly traced among the disciples of Zoroaster, the Brahmen, the Egyptians, Greeks, and Romans, and especially the Jews. In the original tabernacle, the pattern of which God showed Moses on the mount, a large laver stood between the altar on which expiation was made for sin, and the Holy House. At which laver the priests continually washed ere they entered the presence of God. This symbolism penetrated all their religious services and language (Ps. xxvi. 6; Heb. ix. 10), and at the time of Christ it was carried into all the details of secular life (Mark vii. 3, 4).

The religious washing of the body with water lay, therefore, ready to the use of John the Baptist, and the disciples of our Lord.

2. *Was John's baptism Christian baptism?*

The "Council of Trent" (Sess. 7, "De Baptismo," can. 1) decided, "If any one should say that the baptism of John had the same effect with the baptism of Christ; let him be anathema." For controversial reasons Protestants, especially those of the school of Zwingle and Calvin, took the opposite side, and decided that the two were identical (Calvin's "Instit.," Bk. IV., Ch. xv., § 7–18, Turretin's "Instit.," L. 19, Quæ. 16).

We believe Calvin, etc., to have been wrong, for the following reason—

1st. John belonged to the Old and not to the New Testament economy. He came "in the spirit and power of Elias,"

Luke i. 17, in the garb, with the manners, and teaching the doctrine of the ancient prophets (Matt. xi. 13, 14; Luke i. 17).

2d. His was the "baptism of repentance," binding its subjects to repentance, but not to the faith and obedience of Christ.

3d. The Jewish Church yet remained in its old form. The Christian Church, as such, did not exist. John preached that "the kingdom of heaven was at hand," but he did not by baptism gather and seal the subjects of that kingdom into a separate visible society. While he lived his personal disciples were never merged with those of Christ.

4th. It was not administered in the name of the Trinity.

5th. Those baptized by John were rebaptized by Paul (Acts xviii. 24–xix. 7).

3. *Were the baptisms practiced by the disciples of Christ previous to his crucifixion identical with that practiced by the apostles after his ascension?*—See John iii. 22 and iv. 1 and 2.

Up to the time of his death Christ, like John, conformed to the usages and taught the doctrines of the Jewish dispensation. His crucifixion and resurrection mark the actual transition of the new out of the old dispensation. The nature of his kingdom and his own divinity, and hence the doctrine of the Trinity, was not clearly discerned, and the Christian Church as a distinct communion was not yet organized. He preached like John, "Repent for the kingdom of heaven is at hand," Matt. iv. 17, and he commissioned his disciples to say "the kingdom of God has come nigh unto you."—Luke x. 9.

We, therefore, believe that this baptism practiced by his disciples before his crucifixion was, like that of John, simply a preparatory purifying rite binding to repentance.

4. *Where is the record of the real institution of Christian baptism contained?*

Matt. xxviii. 19, 20.—"Go ye therefore, and disciple ($\mu\alpha\theta\eta$-$\tau\epsilon\dot{\upsilon}\sigma\alpha\tau\epsilon$) all nations, baptizing them in the name of the Father, and of the Son, and of the Holy Ghost; teaching them to observe all things, whatsoever I have commanded you; and lo, I am with you alway, even unto the end of the world."

5. *Prove that its observance is of perpetual obligation.*

This has been denied by Socinians on rationalistic grounds, and by Quakers (Barclay, "Apol. Prop.," 12, comm. § 6), on the ground of a false spiritualism, and by some parties of Anti-Baptists, who hold baptism to have been exclusively designed for the initiation of aliens to the church, and therefore not to be applied to those born within the church, in established Christian communities.

That it was designed to be observed everywhere and always is plain—1st. From the command given in the words of institution. (1.) "All nations," and (2) "alway, even unto the end of the world." 2d. The commands and practice of the apostles. Acts ii. 38; x. 47; xvi. 33, etc. 3d. The reason of and necessity for the ordinance which determined its existence at the first, remains and is universal. 4th. The uniform practice of the entire church in all its branches from the beginning.

6. *How is baptism defined in our standards?*

"Con. of Faith," Chap. xxviii.; "L. Cat.," Q. 165; "S. Cat.," Q. 94.

The essential points of this definition are—1st. It is a washing with water. 2d. A washing in the name of the Father, Son, and Holy Ghost. 3d. It is done with the design to "signify and seal our ingrafting into Christ, and partaking of the benefits of the covenant of grace, and our engagement to be the Lord's."

7. *What is essential to the "matter" of baptism?*

As to its "matter," baptism is essentially *a washing with water.* No particular mode of washing is essential—1st. Because no such mode is specified in the command.—See below, Questions 12–21. 2d. Because no such mode of administration is essential to the proper symbolism of the ordinance.—See below, Question 11. On the other hand, water is necessary—1st. Because it is commanded. 2d. Because it is essential to the symbolism of the rite. It is the natural symbol of moral purification, Eph. v. 25, 26; and it was established as such in the ritual of Moses.

8. *What is necessary as to the form of words in which baptism is administered?*

It is essential to the validity of the ordinance that it should be administered "in the name of the Father, and of the Son, and of the Holy Ghost." This is certain—1st. Because it is included in the command.—Matt. xxviii. 19. 2d. From the significancy of the rite. Besides being a symbol of purification, it is essentially, as a rite of initiation into the Christian church, a covenanting ordinance whereby the recipient recognizes and pledges his allegiance to God in that character and in those relations in which he has revealed himself to us in the Scriptures. The formula of baptism, therefore, is a summary statement of the whole Scripture doctrine of the Triune Jehovah as he has chosen to reveal himself to us, and in all those relations which the several Persons of the Trinity graciously sustain in the scheme of redemption to the believer. Hence the baptism of all those sects which reject the scriptural doctrine of the Trinity is invalid.

The frequent phrases, to be baptized in "the name of Jesus Christ," or "in the name of the Lord Jesus," or "in the name of the Lord" (Acts ii. 38; x. 48; xix. 5), do not at all present the form of words which the apostles used in administering this sacrament, but are simply used to designate Christian baptism in distinction from that of John, or to indicate the uniform effect of that spiritual grace which is symbolized in baptism, viz., union with Christ.—Gal. iii. 27.

9. *What is the meaning of the formula "to baptize in the name* (εἰς τό ὄνομα) *of any one"?*

To be baptized "in the name of Paul" (εἰς τὸ ὄνομα), 1 Cor. i. 13, or "unto Moses" (εἰς τὸν Μωϋσῆν), 1 Cor. x. 2, is, on the part of the baptized, to be made the believing and obedient disciples of Paul and Moses, and the objects of their care, and the participants in whatever blessings they have to bestow. To be baptized in the name of the Trinity (Matt. xxviii. 19), or "in the name of the Lord Jesus" (Acts xix. 5), or "into Jesus Christ," (Rom. vi. 3), is by baptism, or rather by the grace of which ritual baptism is the sign, to be united to Christ, or to the Trinity through Christ, as his disciples, believers in his doctrine, heirs of his promises, and participants in his spiritual life.

10. *What is the design of baptism?*

Its design is—

1st. *Primarily,* to signify, seal, and convey to those to whom they belong the benefits of the covenant of grace. Thus— (1.) It symbolizes "the washing of regeneration," "the renewing of the Holy Ghost," which unites the believer to Christ, and so makes him a participant in Christ's life and all other benefits.—1 Cor. xii. 13; Gal. iii. 27; Titus iii. 5. (2.) Christ herein visibly seals his promises to those who receive it with faith, and invests them with the grace promised.

2d. Its design was, *secondarily,* as springing from the former, (1) to be a visible sign of our covenant to be the Lord's, *i. e.,* to accept his salvation, and to consecrate ourselves to his service. (2.) And, hence, to be a badge of our public profession, our separation from the world, and our initiation into the visible church. As a badge it marks us as belonging to the Lord, and consequently (*a*) distinguishes us from the world, (*b*) symbolizes our union with our fellow-Christians.—1 Cor. xii. 13.

11. *What is the emblematic import of baptism?*

In every sacrament there is a visible sign representing an invisible grace. The sign represents the grace in virtue of Christ's authoritatively appointing it thereto, but the selection by Christ of the particular sign is founded on its fitness as a natural emblem of the grace which he appoints it to represent. Thus in the Lord's supper the bread broken by the officiating minister, and the wine poured out, are natural emblems of the body of Christ broken, and his blood shed as a sacrifice for our sins. And in like manner in the sacrament of baptism the application of water to the person of the recipient is a natural emblem of the "washing of regeneration."—Titus iii. 5. Hence we are said to be "born of water and of the Spirit," John iii. 5, *i. e.*, regenerated by the Holy Spirit, of which new birth baptism with water is the emblem; and to be baptized "by one Spirit into one body," *i. e.*, the spiritual body of Christ; and to be "baptized into Christ," so as "to have put on Christ," Gal. iii. 27; and to be "baptized into his death," and to be "buried with him in baptism . . . so that we should walk with him in newness of life," Rom. vi. 3, 4, because the sacrament of baptism is the emblem of that spiritual regeneration which unites us both federally and spiritually to Christ, so that we have part with him both in his life and in his death, and as he died unto sin as a sacrifice, so we die unto sin in its ceasing to be the controlling principle of our natures; and as he rose again in the resumption of his natural life, we rise to the possession and exercise of a new spiritual life.

Baptist interpreters, on the other hand, insist that the Bible teaches that the outward sign in this sacrament, being the immersion of the whole body in water, is an emblem both of purification *and* of our death, burial, and resurrection with Christ. Dr. Carson says, p. 381, "The immersion of the whole body is essential to baptism, not because nothing but immersion can be an emblem of purification, but because immersion is the thing commanded, and because that, without immersion, there is no emblem of death, burial, and resurrection, which are in the emblem equally with purification." He founds his assumption that the outward sign in the sacrament of baptism was designed to be an emblem of the death, burial, and resurrection of the believer in union with Christ, upon Rom. vi. 3, 4, and Col. ii. 12.

We object to this interpretation—1st. In neither of these passages does Paul say that our baptism *in water* is an emblem of our burial with Christ. He is evidently speaking of that spiritual baptism of which water baptism is the emblem; by which spiritual baptism we are caused to die unto sin, and live unto holiness, in which death and new life we are conformed unto the death and resurrection of Christ. We are said to be "baptized into Christ," which is the work of the Spirit, not "into the name of Christ," which is the phrase always used when speaking of ritual baptism.—Matt. xxviii. 19; Acts ii. 38; xix. 5. 2d. To be "baptized into his death" is a phrase perfectly analogous to baptism "into repentance," Matt. iii. 11, and "into remission of sins," Mark i. 4, and "into one body," 1 Cor. xii. 13, *i. e.*, in order that, or to the effect that, we participate in the benefits of his death.

3d. The Baptist interpretation involves an utter confusion in reference to the emblem. Do they mean that the outward sign of immersion is an emblem of the death, burial, and resurrection of Christ, or of the spiritual death, burial, and resurrection of the believer? But the point of comparison in the passages themselves is plainly "not between our baptism and the burial and resurrection of Christ, but between our death to sin and rising to holiness, and the death and resurrection of the Redeemer."

4th. Baptists agree with us that baptism with water is an emblem of spiritual purification, *i. e.*, regeneration, but insist that it is *also* an emblem (in the mode of immersion) of the death of the believer to sin and his new life of holiness.—Dr. Carson, p. 143. But what is the distinction between regeneration and a death unto sin, and life unto holiness.

5th. Baptists agree with us that water baptism is an emblem of purification. But surely it is impossible that the same action should at the same time be an *emblem* of a washing, and of a burial and a resurrection. One idea may be associated with the other in consequence of their spiritual relations, but it is impossible that the same *visible sign* should be emblematical of both.

6th. Our union with Christ through the Spirit, and the spiritual consequences thereof, are illustrated in Scripture by many various figures, *e. g.*, the substitution of a heart of flesh for a heart of stone, Ezek. xxxvi. 26; the building of a house, Eph. ii. 22; the ingrafting of a limb into a vine, John xv. 5; the putting off of filthy garments, and the putting on of clean, Eph. iv. 22–24; as a spiritual death, burial, and resurrection, and as a being planted in the likeness of his death, Rom. vi. 3–5; as the application of a cleansing element to the body, Ezek. xxxvi. 25. Now baptism with water represents all these, because it is an emblem of spiritual regeneration, of which all of these are analogical illustrations. Hence we are said to be "baptized into one body," 1 Cor. xii. 13, and by baptism to "have put on Christ," Gal. iii. 27. Yet it would be absurd to regard water baptism as a literal emblem of all these, and our Baptist brethren have no scriptural warrant for assuming that the outward sign in this sacrament is an emblem of the one analogy more than of the other.—See Dr. Armstrong's "Doctrine of Baptisms," Part II., Chap. ii.

The Mode of Baptism.

12. *What are the words which, in the original language of Scripture, are used to convey the command to baptize?*

The primary word βάπτω occurs four times in the New Testament (Luke xvi. 24; John xiii. 26; Rev. xix. 13), but never in connection with the subject of Christian baptism. Its classical meaning was, 1st, to dip; 2d, to dye; 3d, to wash by dipping or pouring.

The word βαπτίζω, in form, though not in usage, the frequentative of βάπτω, occurs seventy-six times in the New Testament, and is the word used by the Holy Ghost to convey the command to baptize. Its classical meaning was, (1) dip, submerge, sink; (2) to wet thoroughly; (3) to pour upon, to drench; (4) to overwhelm. Besides these, we have the nouns of the same root and usage, βάπτισμα occurring twenty-two times, translated *baptism*, and βαπτισμός occurring four times, translated *baptism*, Heb. vi. 2, and *washing*, Mark. vii. 4, 8; Heb. ix. 10. The only question with which we are concerned, however, is as to the *scriptural* usage of these words. It is an important and universally recognized principle, that the biblical and classical usage of the same word is often very different. This effect is to be traced to the influence of three general causes.—See *"Baptism, its Modes and Subjects,"* by Dr. Alex. Carson; *"Meaning and Use of the Word Baptizein,"* by Rev. Dr. Conant, and *"Classic, Judaic, Johannic, and Christian Baptism,"* by Rev. James W. Dale, D.D.

1st. The principal classics of the language were composed in the Attic dialect. But the general language used by the Greek-speaking world at the Christian era was the "common, or Hellenic dialect of the later Greek," resulting from the fusion of the different dialects previously existing.

2d. The language of the writers of the New Testament was again greatly modified by the fact that their vernacular was a form of the Hebrew language (Syro-Chaldaic); that their constant use of the Septuagint translation of the Hebrew Scriptures had largely influenced their usage of the Greek language, especially in the department of religious thought and expression; and that, in the very act of composing the New Testament Scriptures, they were engaged in the statement of religious ideas, and in the inauguration of religious institutions which had their types and symbols in the ancient dispensation, as revealed in the sacred language of the Hebrew Scriptures.

3d. The New Testament writings are a revelation of new ideas and relations, and hence the words and phrases through which these new thoughts are conveyed must be greatly modified in respect to their former etymological sense and heathen usage, and "for the full depth and compass of meaning belonging to them in their new application we must look to the New Testament itself, comparing one passage with another, and viewing the language used in the light of the great things which it brings to our apprehension."

As examples of this contrast between the scriptural and classical usage of a word, observe, ἄγγελος, *angel;* πρεσβύτερος, *presbyter* or *elder;* ἐκκλησία, *church;* βασιλεία τοῦ θεοῦ, or *τῶν οὐρανῶν, kingdom of God,* or *of heaven;* παλιγγενεσία, *regeneration;* χάρις, *grace,* etc., etc.—Fairbairn's "Herm. Manual," Part I., section 2.

13. *What is the position of the Baptist churches as to the meaning of the Scriptural word* βαπτίζω, *and by what arguments do they seek to prove that immersion is the only valid mode of baptism?*

"That it always signifies to dip, never expressing any thing but mode."—"Carson on Baptism," p. 55. He confesses: "I have ALL the lexicographers and commentators against me." Baptists insist, therefore, upon always translating the words βαπτίζω and βάπτισμα by the words immerse and immersion.

They argue that immersion is the only valid mode of baptism—1st. From the constant meaning of the word βαπτίζω. 2d. From the symbolical import of the rite, as emblematic of burial and resurrection. 3d. From the practice of the apostles. 4th. From history of the early church.

14. *What is the position occupied upon this point by all other Christians?*

1st. It is an established principle of scriptural usage that the names and attributes of the things signified by sacramental signs are attributed to the signs, and on the other hand that the name of the sign is used to designate the grace signified. Thus, Gen. xvii. 11, 13, the name of covenant is given to circumcision; Matt. xxvi. 26–28, Christ called the bread his body, and the wine his blood; Titus iii. 5, baptism is called the washing of regeneration. Thus also the words BAPTIZE and BAPTISM are often used to designate that work of the Holy Ghost in regeneration, which the sign, or water baptism, signifies.—Matt. iii. 11; 1 Cor. xii. 13; Gal. iii. 27; Deut. xxx. 6. It follows consequently that these words are often used in a *spiritual sense.*

2d. These words when relating to ritual baptism, or the sign representing the thing signified, imply the application of water in the name of the Trinity, as an emblem of purification or spiritual regeneration, and never, in their scriptural usage, signify any thing whatever as to the *mode* in which the water is applied.

The precise question in debate is to be stated thus. Baptists insist that Christ's command to baptize is a command to "immerse." All other Christians hold that it is a command to "wash with water" as a symbol of spiritual purification.

I have answered, under Question 11, above, the *second* Baptist argument, as stated under Question 13. Their *first* and *third* arguments, as there stated, I will proceed to answer now.

15. *How may it be proved from their scriptural usage that the words βαπτίζω and βάπτισμα do not signify immersion, but* WASHING *to effect* PURIFICATION, *without any reference to mode?*

1st. The word occurs four times in the Septuagint translation of the Old Testament, in three of which instances it refers to baptism with water. 2 Kings v. 14—The prophet told Naaman to "wash and be clean," and "he baptized himself in Jordan, and he was clean." Eccle. xxxiv. 25—"He that baptizeth himself after the touching of a dead body." This purification according to the law was accomplished by *sprinkling the water of separation.*—Num. xix. 9, 13, 20. Judith xii. 7, Judith "baptized herself in the camp at a fountain of water." Bathing was not performed among those nations by immersion; and the circumstances in which Judith was placed increase the improbability in her case. It was a purification, for she "baptized herself," and "so came in *clean.*"

2d. The question agitated between some of John's disciples and the Jews, John iii. 22–30, and iv. 1–3, concerning baptism, is called a question concerning *purification,* περὶ καθαρισμοῦ.

3d. Matt. xv. 2; Mark vii. 1–5; Luke xi. 37–39. The word βαπτίζω is here used (1) for the customary washing of the hands before meals, which was designed to purify, and was habitually performed by pouring water upon them, 2 Kings iii. 11; (2) it is interchanged with the word νίπτω, which always signifies a partial washing; (3) its effect is declared to be to purify, καθαρίζειν; (4) the baptized or washed hands are opposed to the unclean, κοιναῖς.

4th. Mark vii. 4, 8, "Baptism of pots and cups, brazen vessels, and of tables," κλίναι, couches upon which Jews reclined at their meals, large enough to accommodate several persons at once. The object of these baptisms was purification, and the mode could not have been immersion in the case of the tables, couches, etc.

5th. Heb. ix. 10, Paul says the first tabernacle "stood only in meats, and drinks, and divers baptisms." In verses 13, 19, 21, he specifies some of these "divers baptisms" or washings, "For if the blood of bulls and goats, and the ashes of an heifer sprinkling the unclean, sanctifieth to the purifying of the flesh," and "Moses sprinkled both the book and all the people, and the tabernacle, and all the vessels of the ministry."—Dr. Armstrong's "Doc. of Bapt.," Part I.

16. *What argument in favor of this view of the subject may be drawn from what is said of baptism with the Holy Ghost?*

Matt. iii. 11; Mark i. 8; Luke iii. 16; John i. 26, 33; Acts i. 5; xi. 16; 1 Cor. xii. 13.

If the word βαπτίζω only means to immerse, it would be incapable of the figurative use to which, in these passages, it is actually subjected. But if, as we claim, it signifies to purify, to cleanse, then water baptism, as a washing, though never as an immersion, may fitly represent the cleansing work of the Holy Ghost. See next Question.

17. *What argument may be drawn from the fact that the blessings symbolized by baptism are said to be applied by sprinkling and pouring?*

The gift of the Holy Ghost was the grace signified.—Acts ii. 1–4, 32, 33; x. 44–48; xi. 15, 16. The fire which did not immerse them, but appeared as cloven tongues, and "sat upon each one of them," was the sign of that grace. Jesus was himself the baptizer, who now fulfilled the prediction of John the Baptist that he should baptize with the Holy Ghost and with fire. This gift of the Holy Ghost is set forth in such terms as "came from heaven," "poured out," "shed forth," "fell on them."

These very blessings were predicted in the Old Testament by similar language.—Is. xliv. 3; lii. 15; Ezek. xxxvi. 25–27; Joel ii. 28, 29. Hence we argue that if these spiritual blessings were predicted in the Old Testament by means of these figures of sprinkling and pouring, and if in the New Testament they were symbolically set forth under the same form, they may, of course, be symbolized by the church now by the same emblematical actions.

18. *What argument may be drawn from the mode of purification adopted under the Old Testament?*

The rites of purification prescribed by the Levitical law were in no case commanded to be performed by immersion in the case of persons. Washing and bathing is prescribed, but there is no indication given by the words used, or otherwise, that these were performed by immersion, which was *not* the usual mode of bathing practiced in those countries. The hands and feet of the priests, whenever they appeared to minister before the Lord, were washed, Ex. xxx. 18–21, and their personal ablutions were performed at the brazen laver, 2 Chron. iv. 6, from which the water poured forth through spouts or cocks.—1 Kings vii. 27–39. On the other hand, purification was freely ordered to be effected by sprinkling of blood, ashes, or water.—Lev. viii. 30; xiv. 7 and 51; Ex. xxiv. 5–8; Num. viii. 6, 7; Heb. ix. 12–22. Now, as Christian baptism is a purification, and as it was instituted among the Jews, familiar with the Jewish forms of purification, it follows that a knowledge of those forms must throw much light upon the essential nature and proper mode of the Christian rite.

19. *How may it be shown from 1 Cor. x. 1, 2, and from 1 Pet. iii. 20, 21, that to baptize does not mean to immerse?*

1 Cor. x. 1, 2. The Israelites are said to have been "baptized unto Moses in the cloud and in the sea."—Compare Ex. xiv. 19–31. The Israelites were baptized, yet went over dryshod. The Egyptians were immersed, yet not baptized. Dr. Carson, p. 413, says, Moses "got a dry dip."

1 Pet. iii. 20, 21. Peter declares that baptism is the antitype of the salvation of the eight souls in the ark. Yet their salvation consisted in their *not* being immersed.

20. *What argument as to the proper mode of baptism is to be drawn from the record of the baptisms performed by John?*

1st. John's baptism was not the Christian sacrament, but a rite of purification administered by a Jew upon Jews, under Jewish law. From this we infer (1) that it was not performed by immersion, since the Levitical purification of persons was not performed in that way; yet (2) that he needed for his purpose either a running stream as Jordan, or much water as at Ænon (or the springs), because under that law whatsoever an unclean person touched previous to his purification became unclean, Num. xix. 21, 22, with the exception of a "fountain or pit in which is plenty of water," Lev. xi. 36, which he could not find in the desert in which he preached. After the gospel dispensation was introduced we hear nothing of the apostles baptizing in rivers, or needing "much water" for that purpose.

2d. In no single instance is it stated in the record that John baptized by immersion. All the language employed applies just as naturally and as accurately to a baptism performed by affusion (the subject standing partly in the water, the baptizer pouring water upon the person with his hand). The phrases "baptized in Jordan," "coming out of the water," would have been as accurately applied in the one case as in the other. That John's baptism was more probably performed by affusion appears (1) from the fact that it was a purification performed by a Jewish prophet upon Jews, and that Jewish washings were performed by affusion. The custom was general then, and has continued to this day. (2.) This mode better accords with the vast multitudes baptized by one man.—Matt. iii. 5, 6; Mark i. 5; Luke iii. 3–21. (3.) The very earliest works of Christian art extant represent the baptism of Christ by John as having been performed by affusion.—Dr. Armstrong's "Doctrine of Baptisms," Part II., Chap. iii.

21. *What evidence is afforded by the instances of Christian baptism recorded in the New Testament?*

1st. It has been abundantly shown above that the command to baptize is a command to purify by washing with water, and it hence follows that even if it could be shown that the apostles baptized by immersion, that fact would not prove that particular mode of washing to be essential to the validity of the ordinance, unless it can be proved also that, according to the analogies of gospel institutions, the mere mode of obeying a command is made as essential as the thing itself. But the reverse is notoriously the fact. The church was organized on certain general principles, and the public worship of the gospel ordained, but the details as to the manner of accomplishing those ends are not prescribed. Christ instituted the Lord's supper at night, reclining on a couch, and with unleavened bread. Yet in none of these respects is the "mode" essential.

2d. But, in fact, there is not one instance in which the record makes it even probable that the apostles baptized by immersion, and in the great majority of instances it is rendered in the last degree improbable.

(1.) The baptism of the eunuch by Philip, Acts viii. 26–39, is the only instance which even by appearance favors immersion. But observe (*a*) the language used by Luke, *even as rendered in our version*, applies just as naturally to baptism performed by affusion as by immersion. (*b*.) The Greek prepositions, εἰς, here translated *into*, and ἐκ, here translated *out of*, are in innumerable instances used to express motion, *toward*, *unto*, and *from*.—Acts xxvi. 14; xxvii. 34, 40. They probably descended from the chariot to the brink of the water. Philip is also said to have "descended to" and to have "ascended from the water," but surely he was not also immersed. (*c.*) The very passage of Isaiah, which the eunuch was reading, Is. lii. 15, declared that the Messiah, in whom he believed, should "*sprinkle* many nations." (*d.*) Luke says the place was "a desert," and no body of water sufficient for immersion can be discovered on that road. (2.) Every other instance of Christian baptism recorded in the Scriptures bears evidence positively against immersion. (*a.*) The baptism of three thousand in Jerusalem on one occasion on the day of Pentecost.—Acts ii. 38–41. (*b.*) The baptism of Paul.—Acts ix. 17, 18; xxii. 12–16. Ananias said to him "standing up, be baptized," ἀναστὰς βάπτισαι, and, "standing up, he was baptized." (*c.*) The baptism of Cornelius.—Acts x. 44–48. (*d.*) The baptism of the jailor, at Philippi.—Acts xvi. 32–34. In all these instances baptism was administered on the spot, wherever the convert received the gospel. Nothing is said of rivers, or much water, but vast multitudes at a time, and individuals and families were baptized in their houses, or in prisons, wherever they happened to be at the moment.

22. *What has been in the past, and what is in the present, the usage of the churches as to the mode of baptism?*

In the early church the prevalent mode was to immerse the naked body. For several ages trine-immersion was practiced, or the dipping the head of the person standing in the water three times. In cases of extreme danger of death, and when water was scarce, affusion or sprinkling was considered valid (Bingham's "Christ. Antiquities," Bk. II., ch. xi.; Neander's "Ch. Hist.," Vol. I., Torrey's Trans., p. 310; Schaff's "Ch. Hist.," Vol. II., § 92). The Greek Church has insisted on immersion. The Romish and Protestant churches admit either form. The modern customs favor sprinkling.

The Baptists maintain that immersion is the only valid baptism. All other western churches deny this and maintain the equal validity of pouring and of sprinkling.—"Con. Faith," ch. xxviii., § 3.

No advocate of sprinkling can, in consistency with his own fundamental principles or with the historical usages of the Christian Church, outlaw immersion. The opposition of most churches to immersion arises from the narrow and arrogant claims of the Baptists, and from their false views with respect to the emblematic import of baptism, making it a "burying" instead of a "washing"; against THIS we mean to protest.

SUBJECTS OF BAPTISM.

23. *Who are the proper subjects of baptism ?*

"Conf. Faith," Chap. xxviii., Section 4; "L. Cat.," Question 166; "S. Cat.," Question 95.

All those, and those only, who are members of the visible church, are to be baptized. These are, 1st, they who make a credible profession of their faith in Christ; 2d, the children of one or both believing parents.

24. *What in the case of adults are the prerequisites of baptism?*

Credible profession of their faith in Jesus as their Saviour. This is evident—1st. From the very nature of the ordinance as symbolizing spiritual gifts, and as sealing our covenant to be the Lord's. 2d. From the uniform practice of the apostles and evangelists.—Acts ii. 41; viii. 37. For a full answer to this question, see below Ch. XLIII., Ques. 25, for conditions of admission to Lord's table, which are identical with those requisite for baptism.

25. *Upon what essential constitutional principle of human nature does this institution rest? and show how that principle is recognized in all God's providential and gracious dealing with the race.*

The grand peculiarity of humanity is that while each individual is a free responsible moral agent, yet we constitute a race, reproduced under the law of generation, and each new-born agent is educated and his character formed under social conditions. Hence everywhere the "free-will of the parent becomes the destiny of the child." Hence results the representative character of progenitors, and the inherited character and destiny of all races, nations, and families.

This principle runs through all God's dealing with the human race under the economy of redemption. The family and not the individual is the unit embraced in all covenants and dispensations. This may be traced in all God's dealings with Adam, Noah (Gen. ix. 9), Abraham (Gen. xvii. 7, and Gal. iii. 8), and the nation of Israel (Ex. xx. 5; Deut. xxix. 10–13). The same principle is continued in the Christian dispensation as asserted by Peter in the first sermon.—Acts ii. 38–39.

26. *What is the visible church, to which baptism is the initiating rite?*

1st. The word church, ἐκκλησία, is used in Scripture in the general sense of the company of God's people, called out from the world, and bound to him in covenant relations.

2d. The true spiritual church, therefore, in distinction to the phenomenal church organized on earth, consists of the whole company of the elect, who are included in the eternal covenant of grace formed between the Father and the second Adam.—Eph. v. 27; Heb. xii. 23.

3d. But the visible church universal consists of "all those throughout the world that profess the true religion, together with their children, and is the kingdom of the Lord Jesus Christ, the house and family of God, out of which there is no ordinary possibility of salvation."—"Conf. Faith," chap. xxv., section 2. This visible kingdom, Christ, as Mediator of the covenant of grace, has instituted, as an administrative provision, for the purpose of administering thereby the provisions of that covenant; and this kingdom, as an outward visible society of professors, he established by the covenant he made with Abraham.—Gen. xii. 1–3; xvii. 1–14.

4th. Christ has administered this covenant in three successive modes or dispensations. (1.) From Abraham to Moses, during which he attached to it the ratifying seal of circumcision. (2.) From Moses to his advent (for the law which was temporarily added did not make the promise of none effect, but rather administered it in a special mode, Gal. iii. 17), he added a new seal, the passover, emblematic of the atoning work of the promised seed, as set forth in the clearer revelation then vouchsafed. (3.) From Christ to the end of the world, when the promise being unfolded in an incomparably fuller revelation, the original seals are superseded by baptism and the Lord's Supper. See below, Question 26.

5th. That the Abrahamic covenant was designed to embrace the visible church of Christ, and not his mere natural seed in their family or national capacity, is plain. (1.) It pledged salvation by Christ on the condition of faith.—Compare Gen. xii. 3, with Gal. iii. 8, 16; Acts iii. 25, 26. (2.) The sign and seal attached to it symbolized spiritual blessings, and sealed justification by faith.—Deut. x. 15, 16; xxx. 6; Jer. iv. 4; Rom. ii. 28, 29; iv. 11. (3.) This covenant was made with him as the representative of the visible church universal. (*a.*) It was made with him as the "father of many nations." Paul said it constituted him the "heir of the world," "the father of all them that believe," Rom. iv. 11, 13, and that all believers in Christ now, Jew or Gentile, are "Abraham's seed and heirs according to the promise."—Gal. iii. 29. (*b.*) It contained a provision for the introduction to its privileges of those who were not born of the natural seed of Abraham.—Gen. xvii. 12. Multitudes of such proselytes had been thus introduced before the advent of Christ, and many such were present in Jerusalem as members of the church under its old form on the day of Pentecost "out of every nation under heaven."—Acts ii. 5–11.

6th. That the church thus embraced in this administrative covenant is not the body of the elect, as such, but the visible church of professors and their children, is evident, because, (1.) the covenant contains the offer of the gospel, including the setting forth of Christ, and the offer of his salvation to all men (all the families of the earth) on the condition of faith. Gal. iii. 8. But this belongs to the visible church, and must be administered by means of inspired oracles and a visible ministry. (2.) As an indisputable fact, there was such a visible society under the old dispensation; and under the new dispensation all Christians, whatever theories they may entertain, attempt to realize the ideal of such a visible society, for Christian and ministerial communion. (3.) Under both dispensations Christ has committed to his church, as to a *visible kingdom,* written records, sacramental ordinances, ecclesiastical institutions, and a teaching and ruling ministry. Although these are all designed to minister the provisions of the covenant of grace, and to effect as their ultimate end the ingathering of the elect, it is evident that visible signs and seals, a written word and a visible ministry, can, as such, attach only to a visible church. Rom. ix. 4; Eph. iv. 11. (4.) The same representation of the church is given in the New Testament, in the parable of the tares, etc.—Matt. xiii. 24–30 and 47–50; xxv. 1–13. It was to consist of a mixed community of good and evil, true and merely professed believers, and the separation is not to be made until the "end of the world."

7th. This visible church from the beginning has been transmitted and extended in a twofold manner. (1.) Those who are born "strangers from the covenants of promise," or "aliens from the commonwealth of Israel," Eph. ii. 12, were introduced to that relation only by profession of faith and conformity of life. Under the old dispensation these are called *proselytes.* Acts ii. 10; Num. xv. 15. (2.) All born within the covenant had part in all of the benefits of a standing in the visible church by inheritance. The covenant was with Abraham and his *"seed after him, in all their generations, as an everlasting covenant,"* and consequently they received the sacrament which was the sign and seal of that covenant. Hence the duty of teaching and training was engrafted on the covenant, Gen. xviii. 18, 19; and the church made a school, or training institution, Deut. vi. 6–9. In accordance with this, Christ commissioned his apostles to disciple all nations, baptizing and teaching them. Matt. xxviii. 19, 20. Thus the church is represented as a flock, including the lambs with the sheep, Is. xl. 11, and as a vineyard in which the scion is trained, the barren tree cultivated, and, if incurable, cut down.—Is. v. 1–7; Luke xiii. 7, 8.

27. *How may it be shown that this visible church is identical under both dispensations, and what argument may be thence derived to prove that the infant children of believers should be baptized?*

1st. The church, under both dispensations, has the same nature and design. The Old Testament church, embraced in the Abrahamic covenant, rested on the gospel offer of salvation by faith.—Gal. iii. 8; Heb. xi. Its design was to prepare a spiritual seed for the Lord. Hence—(1.) Its foundation was the same—the sacrifice and mediation of Christ. (2.) Conditions of membership were the same. (*a.*) Every true Israelite was a true believer.—Gal. iii. 7. (*b.*) *All* Israelites were at least professors of the true religion. (3.) Its sacraments symbolized and sealed the same grace as those of the New Testament church. Thus the passover, as the Lord's Supper, represented the sacrifice of Christ.—1 Cor. v. 7. Circumcision, as baptism, represented "the putting off the body of the sins of the flesh," and baptism is called by Paul "the circumcision of Christ." Col. ii. 11, 12. Even the ritual of the Mosaic law was only a symbolical revelation of the gospel.

2d. They bear precisely the same name. ἐκκλησία κυρίου, *the church of the Lord*, is an exact rendering in Greek of the Hebrew קְהַל יְהוָה translated in our version the "congregation of the Lord."—Compare Ps. xxii. 22, with Heb. ii. 12. Thus Stephen called the congregation of Israel before Sinai "the *church* in the wilderness."—Compare Acts vii. 38, with Ex. xxxii. Thus also *Christ* is the Greek form of the Hebrew *Messiah*, and the *elders* of the New Testament church are identical in function and name with those of the synagogue.

3d. There is no evidence whatever furnished by the apostolical records that the ancient church was abolished and a new and a different one organized in its place. The apostles never say one word about any such new organization. The pre-existence of such a visible society is everywhere taken for granted as a fact. Their disciples were always *added* to the "church" or "congregation" previously existing.—Acts ii. 47. The Mosaic ritual law, by means of which the Abrahamic character of the church had been administered for about fifteen hundred years, was indeed abolished. But Paul argues that the introduction of this law, four hundred and thirty years after, could not make the promise of none effect, Gal. iii. 17, and consequently the disannulling of the law could only give place to the more perfect execution of the covenant, and development of the church embraced within it.

4th. There is abundant positive evidence that the ancient church, resting upon its original charter, was not abolished by the new dispensation. (1.) Many of the Old Testament prophecies plainly declare that the then existing *visible* church, instead of being abrogated by the advent of the Messiah, should thereby be gloriously strengthened and enlarged, so as to embrace the Gentiles also.—Is. xlix. 13–23, and lx. 1–14. They declare also that the federal constitution, embracing the child with the parent, shall continue under the new dispensation of the church, after "the Redeemer has come to Zion."—Is. lix. 21, 22. Peter, in Acts iii. 22, 23, expounds the prophecy of Moses, Deut. xviii. 15–19, to the effect that every soul which will not hear that prophet (the Messiah) shall be cut off from among the people, *i. e.*, from the church, which of course implies that the church from which they are cut off continues. (2.) In precise accordance with these prophecies Paul declares that the Jewish church was not abrogated, but that the unbelieving Jews were cut off from their own olive-tree, and the Gentile branches grafted in in their place; and he foretells the time when God will graft the Jews back again into their own stock and not into another. Rom. xi. 18–26. He says that the alien Gentiles are made fellow-citizens with believing Jews in the old household of the faith.—Eph. ii. 11–22. (3.) The covenant which constituted the ancient church also constituted Abraham the father of many nations. The promise of the covenant was that God would "be a God unto him and to his seed after him." This covenant, therefore, embraced the "many nations" with their father Abraham. Hence it never could have been fulfilled until the advent of the Messiah, and the abolishment of the restrictive law. Hence the Abrahamic covenant, instead of having been superseded by the gospel, only now begins to have its just accomplishment. Hence, on the day of Pentecost, Peter exhorts all to repent and be BAPTIZED, BECAUSE the Abrahamic covenant still held in force for all Jews and for their children, and for all those afar off, *i. e.*, Gentiles, as many as God should call. Acts ii. 38, 39. Hence also Paul argued earnestly that since the Abrahamic covenant is still in force, therefore, from its very terms, the Gentiles who should believe in Christ had a right to a place in that ancient church, which was founded upon it, on equal terms with the Jews. "In thee shall all nations be blessed, so THEN," says Paul, "they which be of faith are blessed with faithful Abraham," and all who believe in Christ, Jew or Gentile indiscriminately, ":are," to the full intent of the covenant, "Abraham's seed, and heirs according to the promise," Gal. iii. 6–29, which promise was, "I will be a God to thee, and TO THY SEED AFTER THEE."

The bearing of this argument upon the question of infant baptism is direct and conclusive.

Ist. Baptism now occupies the same relation to the covenant and the church which circumcision did. (1.) Both rites represent the same spiritual grace, namely, regeneration.—Deut. xxx. 6; Col. ii. 11; Rom. vi. 3, 4. (2.) Baptism is now what circumcision was, the seal, or confirming sign, of the Abrahamic covenant. Peter says, "be baptized FOR the PROMISE is to you and to your children."—Acts ii. 38, 39. Paul says explicitly that baptism is the sign of that covenant, "for as many as have been baptized into Christ are Abraham's seed, and heirs according to the promise," Gal. iii. 27, 29; and that baptism is the circumcision of Christ.—Col. ii. 10, 11. (3.) Both rites are the appointed forms, in successive eras, of initiation into the church, which we have proved to be the same church under both dispensations.

2d. Since the church is the same, in the absence of all explicit command to the contrary, the members are the same. Children of believers were members then. They ought to be recognized as members now, and receive the initiatory rite. This the apostles took for granted as self-evident, and universally admitted; an explicit command to baptize would have implied doubt in the ancient church rights of infants.

3d. Since the covenant, with its promise to be "a God to the believer and his seed," is expressly declared to stand firm under the gospel, the believer's seed have a right to the seal of that promise.—Dr. John M. Mason's "Essays on the Church."

28. *Present the evidence that Christ recognized the church standing of children.*

1st. Christ declares of little children (Matthew, παιδία, Luke βρέφη, *infants*) that "of such is the kingdom of heaven."—Matt. xix. 14; Luke xviii. 16. The phrase "kingdom of God and of heaven" signifies the visible church under the new dispensation.—Matt. iii. 2; xiii. 47.

2d. In his recommission of Peter, after his apostasy, our Lord commanded him, as under shepherd, to feed the *lambs*, as well as the sheep of the flock.—John xxi. 15–17.

3d. In his general commission of the apostles, he commanded them to disciple *nations* (which are always constituted of families) by baptizing, and then teaching them.—Matt. xxviii. 19, 20.

29. *Show that the apostles always acted on the principle that the child is a church member if the parent is.*

The apostles were not settled pastors in the midst of an established Christian community, but itinerant missionaries to an unbelieving world, sent not to baptize, but to preach the gospel.—1 Cor i. 17. Hence we have in the Acts and Epistles the record of only ten separate instances of baptism. In two of these, viz., of the eunuch and of Paul, Acts viii. 38; ix. 18, there were no families to be baptized. In the case of the three thousand on the day of Pentecost, the people of Samaria, and the disciples of John at Ephesus, crowds were baptized on the very spot on which they professed to believe. Of the remaining five instances, in the four cases in which the family is mentioned at all, it is expressly said they were baptized, viz., the households of Lydia of Thyatira, of the jailer of Philippi, of Stephanas, and of Crispus.—Acts xvi. 15, 32, 33; xviii. 8; 1 Cor. i. 16. In the remaining instance of Cornelius, the record implies that the family was also baptized. Thus the apostles, in every case, without a single recorded exception, baptized believers on the spot, and whenever they had families, they also baptized their households, *as such.*

They also addressed children in their epistles as members of the church.—Compare Eph. i. 1, and Col. i. 1, 2, with Eph. vi. 1–3, and Col. iii. 20. And declared that even the children of only one believing parent were to be regarded "holy," or consecrated to the Lord, *i. e.*, as church members.—1 Cor. vii. 12–14.

30. *What argument may be inferred from the fact that the blessings symbolized in baptism are promised and granted to children?*

Baptism represents regeneration in union with Christ. Infants are born children of wrath, even as others. They can not be saved, therefore, unless they are born again, and have part in the benefits of Christ's death. They are evidently, from the nature of the case, in the same sense capable of being subjects of regeneration as adults are. "Of such is the kingdom of heaven."—Matt. xxi. 15, 16; Luke i. 41, 44.

31. *What argument may be drawn from the practice of the early church?*

The practice of infant baptism is an institution which exists as a fact, and prevails throughout the universal church, with the exception of the modern Baptists, whose origin can be definitely traced to the Anabaptists of Germany, about A. D. 1537. Such an institution must either have been handed down from the apostles, or have had a definite commencement as a novelty, which must have been signalized by opposition and controversy. As a fact, however, we find it noticed in the very *earliest* records as a *universal custom,* and an *apostolical* tradition. Justin Martyr, writing A. D. 138, says that "There were among Christians of his time, many persons of both sexes, some sixty and some seventy years old, who had been made disciples of Christ from their infancy." Irenæus, born about A. D. 97, says, "He came to save all by himself; all I say who by him are *born again* unto God, infants, and little children and youths." It is acknowledged by Tertullian, born in Carthage, A. D. 160, or only sixty years after the death of the apostle John. Origen, born of Christian parents in Egypt, A. D. 185, declares that it was "the usage of the church to baptize infants," and that "the church had received the tradition from the apostles." Cyprian, bishop of Carthage from A. D. 248 to 258, together with an entire synod over which he presided, decided that baptism should be administered to infants before the eighth day. St. Augustine, born A. D. 358, declared that this "doctrine is held by the whole church, not instituted by councils, but always retained." This Pelagius admitted, after having visited all parts of the church from Britain to Syria, although the fact was so repugnant to his system of doctrine.—See Wall's "Hist. of Infant Baptism," and Bingham's "Christ. Antiquities," Bk. XI., Ch. iv.

Our argument is that infant baptism has prevailed (*a*) from the apostolic age, (*b*) in all sections of the ancient church, (*c*) uninterruptedly to the present time, (*d*) in every one of the great historical churches of the Reformation. While its impugners (*a*) date since the Reformation, (*b*) and are generally guilty of the gross schismatical sin of close communion.

32. *How is the objection, that faith is a prerequisite to baptism, and that infants can not believe, to be answered?*

The Baptists argue—1st. From the commission of the Lord, "Go preach—he that believeth and is baptized shall be saved; he that believeth not shall be damned," Mark xvi. 16, that infants ought not to be baptized because they can not believe. 2d. From the nature of baptism, as a sign of a spiritual grace and seal of a covenant, that infants ought not to be baptized, since they are incapable of understanding the sign, or of contracting the covenant.

We answer—1st. The requisition of faith evidently applies only to the adult, because faith is made the essential prerequisite of salvation, and yet infants are saved, though they can not believe. 2d. Circumcision was a sign of a spiritual grace; it required faith in the adult recipient, and it was the seal of a covenant; yet, by God's appointment, infants were circumcised. The truth is that faith is required, but it is the faith of the parent acting for his child. The covenant of which baptism is the seal is contracted with the parent, in behalf of the child upon whom the seal is properly applied.

It is besides to be remembered that the infant is not a thing, but a person born with an unholy moral nature, and fully capable of present regeneration, and of receiving from the Holy Ghost the "habit" or state of soul of which faith is the expression. Hence Calvin says ("Instit.," Bk. 4, ch. xvi., § 20), "The seed of both repentance and faith lies hid in them by the secret operation of the Spirit."

33. *How can we avoid the conclusion that infants should be admitted to the Lord's Supper, if they are admitted to baptism?*

The same reason and the same precedents do not hold in relation to both sacraments. 1st. Baptism recognizes and seals church membership, while the Lord's Supper is a commemorative act. 2d. In the action of baptism the subject is passive, and in that of the Lord's Supper active. 3d. Infants were never admitted to the Passover until they were capable of comprehending the nature of the service. 4th. The apostles baptized households, but never admitted households as such to the Supper.

34. *Whose children ought to be baptized?*

"Infants of such as are members of the visible church," "S. Cat.," Q. 95; that is, theoretically, "infants of one or both believing parents," "Con. of Faith," Chap. xxviii., sec. 4; and practically, "of parents, one or both of them professing faith in Christ."—"L. Cat.," Q. 166. Roman Catholics, Episcopalians, the Protestants of the continent, the Presbyterians of Scotland (and formerly of this country), act upon the principle that every baptized person, not excommunicated, being himself a member of the visible church, has a right to have his child regarded and treated as such also. Even when parents are unbelievers Catholics and Episcopalians will baptize their infants upon the faith of sponsors.

It is evident, however, that only the children of such parents, or actual guardians, as make a credible profession of personal faith ought to be baptized. 1st. Because of the nature of the act. Faith is the condition of the covenant of which baptism is the seal. The Gen. Assembly of 1794 decided that our "Directory for Worship" demands that the parent enters before God and the Church into an express engagement," "that they pray with and for the child, that they set an example of piety and godliness before it," etc. And the Gen. Synod of 1735 asserts that if other than parents professing piety are encouraged to take these engagements "the seal would be set to a blank"

("Moore's Digest," pp. 665 and 666). Hence it is evident that the conditions prerequisite for having one's children baptized are precisely the same with those prerequisite for being baptized or admitted to the Lord's Supper one's self, *i. e.*, credible profession of a true faith.

2d. Sponsors who are neither parents nor actual and permanent guardians are evidently neither the providentially constituted representatives of the child, nor in a position to make good their engagements.

3d. Those who, having been baptized, do not by faith and obedience discharge their baptismal vows when they are of mature age, are *ipso facto* in a state of suspension from covenant privileges, and can not, therefore, plead them for their children.

4th. The apostles baptized the households only of those who professed faith in Christ.

The Efficacy of Baptism.

35. *What is the Romish and Ritualistic doctrine as to the efficacy of baptism.*

The Romish doctrine, with which the "Tractarian" doctrine essentially agrees, is, 1st, that baptism confers the merits of Christ and the power of the Holy Ghost, and therefore (1) it cleanses from inherent corruption; (2) it secures the remission of the penalty of sin; (3) it secures the infusion of sanctifying grace; (4) it unites to Christ; (5) it impresses upon the soul an indelible character; (6) it opens the portals of heaven. Newman, "Lectures on Justification," p. 257; "Cat. Rom.," Pt. II., Chap. ii., Q. 32–44. 2d. That the efficacy of the ordinance is inherent in itself in virtue of the divine institution. Its virtue does not depend either on the merit of the officiating minister, nor on that of the recipient, but in the sacramental action itself as an *opus operatum.* In the case of infants, the only condition of its efficiency is the right administration of the ordinance. In the case of adults its efficiency depends upon the additional condition that the recipient is not in mortal sin, and does not resist by an opposing will.—Dens "De Baptismo," N. 29.

36. *What is the Lutheran doctrine on this subject?*

The Lutherans agreed with the Reformed churches in repudiating the Romish doctrine of the magical efficacy of this sacrament as an *opus operatum.* But they went much further than the Reformed in maintaining the sacramental union between the sign and the grace signified. Luther, in his "Small

Cat.," Pt. iv., sec. 2, says baptism, "worketh forgiveness of sins, delivers from death and the devil, and confers everlasting salvation on all who believe," and, in sec. 3, that "it is not the water indeed which produces these effects, but the word of God which accompanies, and is connected with the water, and our faith, which relies on the word of God connected with the water. For the water without the word is simply water and no baptism. But when connected with the word of God, it is a baptism, that is, a gracious water of life, and a washing of regeneration." This efficacy depends upon true saving faith in the adult subject: "Moreover, faith being absent, it remains only a naked and inoperative sign."

Hence they hold—1st. Baptism is an efficient means of conferring the forgiveness of sins and the grace of Christ. 2d. It contains the grace it confers. 3d. Its efficacy resides not in the water but in the word, and in the Holy Spirit in the word. 4th. Its efficacy, in the case of the adult, depends upon the faith of the subject. Krauth's "Conservative Reformation," pp. 545–584.

37. *What was the Zwinglian doctrine on this subject?*

That the outward rite is a mere sign, an objective representation by symbol of the truth, having no efficacy whatever beyond that due to the truth represented.

38. *What is the doctrine of the Reformed churches, and of our own among the number, on this subject?*

They all agree, 1st, that the Zwinglian view is incomplete.

2d. That besides being a sign, baptism is also the seal of grace, and therefore a present and sensible conveyance and confirmation of grace to the believer who has the witness in himself, and to all the elect a seal of the benefits of the covenant of grace, to be sooner or later conveyed in God's good time.

3d. That this conveyance is effected, not by the bare operation of the sacramental action, but by the Holy Ghost, which accompanies his own ordinance.

4th. That in the adult the reception of the blessing depends upon faith.

5th. That the benefits conveyed by baptism are not peculiar to it, but belong to the believer before or without baptism, and are often renewed to him afterwards.

Our "Conf. Faith," Chap. xxviii., sections 5 and 6, affirms, "1st. 'That by the right use of this ordinance the grace promised is not only offered, but really exhibited and conferred by the Holy Ghost to such (whether of age or infants), as that grace belongeth unto.'

"2d. That baptism does not in all cases secure the blessings of the covenant.

"3d. That in the cases in which it does the gift is not connected necessarily in time with the administration of the ordinance.

"4th. That these blessings depend upon two things: (1) the right use of the ordinance; (2) the secret purpose of God."— Dr. Hodge.

39. *What in general is the doctrine known as Baptismal Regeneration? On what ground does it rest? and how can it be shown to be false?*

The Protestant advocates of Baptismal Regeneration, without committing themselves to the Romish theory of an *opus operatum*, hold that baptism is God's ordained instrument of communicating the benefits of redemption in the first instance. That whatever gracious experiences may be enjoyed by the unbaptized, are uncovenanted mercies. That by baptism the guilt of original sin is removed, and the Holy Ghost is given, whose effects remain like a seed in the soul, to be actualized by the free-will of the subject, or neglected and hence rendered abortive. Every infant is regenerated when baptized. If he dies in infancy the seed is actualized in paradise. If he lives to adult age, its result depends upon his use of it (Blunt's "Dict. of Theology," Art. Baptism). See above, Ch. XXIX., Ques. 4.

They rest their doctrine on a large class of Scripture passages like the following, "Christ gave himself for the church that he might sanctify and cleanse it by the washing of water, by the word," Eph v. 26, "Arise and be baptized, and wash away thy sins."—Acts xxii. 16. Also John iii. 5; 1 Pet. iii. 21; Gal. iii. 27, etc.

The Reformed explain these passages on the following principles. 1st. In every sacrament there are two things (*a*) an outward visible sign, and (*b*) an inward invisible grace thereby signified. There is between these a sacramental or symbolical relation that naturally gives rise to a *usus loquendi*, whereby the properties and effects of the grace are attributed to the sign. Yet it never follows that the two are inseparable, any more than it proves the absurdity that the two are identical.

2d. The sacraments are badges of religious faith, and necessarily involve the profession of that faith. In all ordinary language, therefore, that faith is presumed to be present, and to be genuine, in which case the grace signified by the sacrament is, of course, always not only offered but conveyed ("S. Cat.," Ques. 91 and 92).

That baptism can not be the only or even the ordinary means of conveying the grace of regeneration (*i. e.*, for initiating the soul into a state of grace) is plain.—1st. Faith and repentance are the fruits of regeneration. But faith and repentance are required as conditions prerequisite to baptism.— Acts ii. 38; viii. 37; x. 47, and xi. 17.

2d. This doctrine is identical with that of the Pharisees, which Christ and his apostles constantly rebuked.—Matt. xxiii. 23-26. "For in Christ Jesus neither circumcision availeth any thing, nor uncircumcision, but faith that worketh by love—but a new creature."—Gal. v. 6, and vi. 15; Rom. ii. 25-29. Faith alone is said to save, the absence of faith alone to damn.—Acts xvi. 31, and Mark xvi. 16.

3d. The entire spirit and method of the gospel is ethical not magical. The great instrument of the Holy Ghost is the TRUTH, and all that is ever said of the efficacy of the sacraments is said of the efficacy of the truth. They are means of grace therefore in common with the word and as they contain and seal it (1 Pet. i. 23, and John xvii. 17, 19). Our Saviour says "*by their fruits ye shall know them.*"—(Matt. vii. 20).

4th. This doctrine is disproved by experience. Vast multitudes of the baptized of all ages and nations bring forth none of the fruits of regeneration. Multitudes who were never baptized have produced these fruits. The ages and communities in which this doctrine has been most strictly held have been conspicuous for spiritual barrenness.

5th. The great evil of the system of which the doctrine of baptismal regeneration is a part, is that it tends to make religion a matter of external and magical forms, and hence to promote rationalistic skepticism among the intelligent, and superstition among the ignorant and morbid, and to dissociate among all classes religion and morality.

THE NECESSITY OF BAPTISM.

40. *What is the Romish doctrine as to the necessity of baptism?*

That it is by the appointment of God the one means, *sine qua non*, of justification (regeneration, etc.) both for infants and adults. In the case of adults they except only the case of those who have formed a sincere purpose of being baptized, which has been providentially hindered. In the case of infants there is no exception.

41. *What is the Lutheran view?*

Their standards state the necessity of the sacraments without apparent qualification (See "Aug. Conf.," Art. 9, and "Apol.

Aug. Conf.," p. 156, quoted under last chapter). But Dr. Krauth has shown from the writings of Luther and their standard theologians, that their actual view was that (1) baptism is not *essential* (as *e. g.*, Christ's atonement is), but that (2) it is *necessary*, as the ordained ordinary means of conferring grace, yet (3) not *unconditionally*, because the "necessity" is limited (*a*) by the possibility of having it, so that not the deprivation of baptism, but the contempt of it condemns a man, and (*b*) by the fact that all the blessings of baptism are conditioned on faith. (4) Baptism is not always followed by regeneration, and regeneration is not always preceded by baptism, and men may be saved though unbaptized. (5) That within the church all infants are saved although unbaptized. (6) As to infants of heathen, the point undecided, because unrevealed, but hopeful views entertained.—Krauth's "Conserv. Reform.," pp. 557–564.

42 *What is the Reformed doctrine?*

That it is "necessary" because commanded, and universally obligatory, because it is a divinely ordained and most precious means of grace, which it would be impious knowingly and willingly to neglect. And because it is the *appointed* and *commonly recognized* badge whereby our allegiance to Christ is openly acknowledged. Under the circumstances, intelligent neglect of the sacraments looks very like treason.

But baptism does not ordinarily confer grace in the first instance, but presupposes it, and the grace it symbolizes and seals is often realized both before and without their use.— "Conf. Faith," Ch. xxviii., "Cal. Instit.," Bk. IV., ch. xvi., § 26.

The Authoritative Creed Statements.

Romish Doctrine.

"Cat. Conc. Trident.," Pt. 2, Ch. 2, Ques. 5.—"It follows that baptism may be accurately and appositely defined to be *the sacrament of regeneration by water in the word.* For by nature we are born from Adam children of wrath, but by baptism we are regenerated in Christ children of mercy."

Ib., Pt. 2, Ch. 2, Ques. 33.—"For as no other means of salvation remains for infant children except baptism, it is easy to comprehend the enormity of the guilt under which they lay themselves, who suffer them to be deprived of the grace of the sacrament longer than necessity requires."

Bellarmin, *"Bapt.,"* 1, 4.—"The church has always believed that infants perish if they depart this life without baptism. For although little children fail of baptism without any fault of their own, yet they do not perish without their own fault, since they have original sin."

Lutheran Doctrine.—See quotations under last chapter.

Quenstedt, iv., 147.—"By baptism and in baptism the Holy Ghost excites in infants a true, saving, life-giving, and actual faith, whence also baptized infants truly believe."

"*Art. Smalcald*," pt. 3, art. 5, "*De Baptismo.*"—"Baptism is nothing else than the word of God with dipping in water, according to his institution and command. . . . The word is added to the element and it becomes a sacrament."

"*Cat. Minor*," iv., Ques. 3.—"Baptism effects remission of sins, liberates from death and the devil, and gives eternal blessedness to all and each who believe this which the word and divine promises hold forth."

REFORMED DOCTRINE.

"*Cat. Genev.*," p. 522.—"The signification of baptism has two parts, for therein is represented remission of sins. . . . Do you attribute nothing else to the water, than that it is only a figure of washing? I think it is such a figure, that at the same time a truth is joined with it. For God does not disappoint us in promising to us his gifts. Hence it is certain that pardon of sins and newness of life are offered and received by us in baptism."

Calvin's "*Instit.*," B. iv., Ch. 16, ¿ 26.—"I would not be understood as insinuating that baptism may be contemned with impunity. So far from excusing this contempt, I hold that it violates the covenant of the Lord. The passage (John v. 24) only serves to show that we must not deem baptism so necessary as to suppose that every one who has lost the opportunity of obtaining it has forthwith perished."

"*Thirty-nine Art. of Ch. of England*," Art. 27.—"Baptism is not only a sign of profession, and mark of difference, whereby Christian men are discerned from others that are not christened, but it is also a sign of regeneration or new birth, whereby, as by an instrument, they that receive baptism rightly are grafted into the church: the promises of the forgiveness of sin, and of our adoption to be the sons of God by the Holy Ghost, are visibly signed and sealed; faith is confirmed, and grace increased by virtue of prayer unto God."

"The baptism of young children is in any wise to be retained in the church, as most agreeable with the institution of Christ."

"*Conf. Faith*," Ch. 28; "*L. Cat.*," Q. 165–167; "*S. Cat.*," Q. 94, 95.

¿ 1.—"Baptism is a sacrament of the New Testament, ordained by Jesus Christ, not only for the solemn admission of the party baptized into the visible church, but also to be unto him a sign and seal of the covenant of grace, of his ingrafting into Christ, of regeneration, of remission of sins, and of his giving up unto God, through Jesus Christ, to walk in newness of life."

¿ 5.—"Although it be a great sin to contemn or neglect this ordinance, yet grace and salvation are not so inseparably annexed unto it, as that no person can be regenerated or saved without it, or that all that are baptized are undoubtedly regenerated."

¿ 6.—"The efficacy of baptism is not tied to that moment of time wherein it is administered; yet, notwithstanding, by the right use of this ordinance the grace promised is not only offered, but really exhibited and conferred by the Holy Ghost, to such (whether of age or infants) as that grace belongeth unto, according to the council of God's own will, in his appointed time."

SOCINIAN DOCTRINE.—Socinus believed baptism to have been practiced by the apostles after the death of Christ, and to have been applicable only to converts from without the church. Socinians generally held baptism to be only a badge of public profession of adherence to Christ, and maintained that immersion is the only proper mode, and adults the only proper subjects.—"*Racovian Cat.*," Section 5, Ch. 3.

CHAPTER XLIII.

THE LORD'S SUPPER.

1. In what passages of the New Testament is the institution of the Lord's Supper recorded?

Matt. xxvi. 26–28; Mark xiv. 22–24; Luke xxii. 17–20; 1 Cor. x. 16, 17; and xi. 23–30.

2. Prove that its observance is a perpetual obligation.

1st. From the words of institution, "Do this in remembrance of me," and again "this do as oft as ye drink it in remembrance of me." 2d. Paul's word.—1 Cor. xi. 26. "For as often as ye eat this bread and drink this cup ye do show the Lord's death *till he come.*" 3d. The apostolic example (Acts ii. 42 and 46; xx. 7, etc). 4th. The frequent reference to it as of perpetual obligation in the apostolical writings (1 Cor. x. 16–21, etc). 5th. The practice of the entire Christian church in all its branches from the first.

3. What are the various phrases used in Scripture to designate the Lord's Supper, and their import?

1st. "Lord's Supper."—1 Cor. xi. 20. The Greek word δεῖπνον, translated supper, designated the dinner, or principal meal of the Jews, taken towards or in the evening. Hence this sacrament received this name because it was instituted at that meal. It was called the "Lord's," because it was instituted by him, to commemorate his death, and signify and seal his grace.

2d. "Cup of blessing."—1 Cor. x. 16. The cup was blessed by Christ, and the blessing of God is now invoked upon it by the officiating minister.—Matt. xxvi. 26, 27.

3d. "Lord's Table."—1 Cor. x. 21. Table here stands by a usual figure for the provisions spread upon it. It is the table at which the Lord invites his guests, and at which he presides.

4th. "Communion."—1 Cor. x. 16. In partaking of this sacrament, the fellowship of the believer with Christ is established and exercised in a mutual giving and receiving, and consequently also the fellowship of believers with one another, through Christ.

5th. "Breaking of bread."—Acts ii. 42. Here the symbolical action of the officiating minister is put for the whole service.

4. *By what other terms was it designated in the early church?*

1st. "Eucharist," from ἐυχαριστέω, *to give thanks.* See Matt. xxvi. 27. This beautifully designates it as a thanksgiving service. It is both the cup of thanksgiving, whereby we celebrate the grace of God and pledge our gratitude to him, and the cup of blessing, or the consecrated cup.

2d. "Σύναξις," a *coming together,* because the sacrament was administered in the public congregation.

3d. "Λειτουργία," a *sacred ministration,* applied to the sacrament by way of eminence. From this word is derived the English word liturgy.

4th. "Θυσία," *sacrifice offering.* "This term was not applied to the sacrament in the proper sense of a propitiatory sacrifice. But (1) because it was accompanied with a collection and oblation of alms; (2) because it commemorated the true sacrifice of Christ on the cross; (3) because it was truly a eucharistical sacrifice of praise and thanksgiving, Heb. xiii. 15; (4) because, in the style of the ancients, every religious action, whereby we consecrate any thing to God for his glory and our salvation, is called a sacrifice."

5th. Ἀγάπη. The Agapæ, or love feasts, were meals at which all the communicants assembled, and in connection with which they received the consecrated elements. Hence the name of the feast was given to the sacrament itself.

6th. Μυστήριον, *a mystery,* or a symbolical revelation of truth, designed for the special benefit of initiated Christians. This was applied to both sacraments. In the Scriptures it is applied to all the doctrines of revelation.—Matt. xiii. 11; Col. i. 26.

7th. Missa, *mass.* The principal designation used by the Latin church. The most probable derivation of this term is from the ancient formula of dismission. When the sacred rites were finished the deacons called out, "Ite, missa est," *go, it is discharged.*—Turretin, L. 19, Q. 21.

5. *How is this sacrament defined, and what are the essential points included in the definition?*

See "L. Cat.," Q. 168; "S. Cat.," Q. 96.

The essential points of this definition are, 1st, the elements, bread and wine, given and received according to the appointment of Jesus Christ. 2d. The design of the recipient of doing this in obedience to Christ's appointment, in remembrance of him, to show forth his death till he come. 3d. The promised presence of Christ in the sacrament by his Spirit, "so that the worthy receivers are not after a corporeal and carnal manner, but by faith, made partakers of Christ's body and blood, with all his benefits, to their spiritual nourishment and growth in grace."

6. *What kind of bread is to be used in the sacrament, and what is the usage of the different churches on this point?*

Bread of some kind is essential, 1st, from the command of Christ; 2d, from the significancy of the symbol; since bread, as the principal natural nourishment of our bodies, represents his flesh, which, as living bread, he gave for the life of the world.—John vi. 51. But the kind of bread, whether leavened or unleavened, is not specified in the command, nor is it rendered essential by the nature of the service.

Christ used unleavened bread because it was present at the Passover. The early Christians celebrated the Communion at a common meal, with the bread of common life, which was leavened. The Romish Church has used unleavened bread ever since the eighth century, and commands the use of the same as the only proper kind, but does not make it essential ("Cat. Conc. Trident.," Pt. 2, ch. iv., §§ 13 and 14). The Greek Church insists upon the use of leavened bread. The Lutheran Church uses unleavened bread. The Reformed Church, including the Church of England, regards the use of leavened bread, as the food of common life, to be most proper, since bread in the Supper is the symbol of spiritual nourishment. The use of sweet cake, practiced in some of our churches, is provincial and arbitrary, and is without any support in Scripture, tradition, or good taste.

7. *What is the meaning of the term* ὄινος, *wine, in the New Testament, and how does it appear that wine and no other liquid must be used in the Lord's Supper?*

It is evident from the usage of this word in the New Testament that it was designed by the sacred writers to designate the fermented juice of the grape.—Matt. ix. 17; John ii. 3–10; Rom. xiv. 21; Eph. v. 18; 1 Tim. iii. 8; v. 23; Titus ii. 3.

This is established by the unanimous testimony of all competent scholars and missionary residents in the East.—See Dr. Lindsay W. Alexander's article in Kitto's "Cyclopædia";

and Dr. Wm. L. Bevan's art. on "Wine" in "Smith's Bible Dict."; and Dr. Ph. Schaff in Lange's "Com. on John," ch. ii. 1–11, note p. 111; and Rev. Dr. T. Laurie, missionary, in the "Bibliotheca Sacra," Jan., 1869; and Dr. Justin Perkins' "Residence of Eight Years in Persia," p. 236; and Dr. Eli Smith in the "Bib. Sacra," 1846, pp. 385, etc.; and Rev. J. H. Shedd (missionary), in "Interior," of July 20, 1871.

The Romish Church contends, on the authority of tradition, that water should be mingled with the wine ("Cat. Conc. Trident., Pt. II., Ch. iv., Ques. 16 and 17). But this has not been commanded, nor is it involved in any way in the symbolical significancy of the rite. That wine and no other liquid is to be used is clear from the record of the institution, Matt. xxvi. 26–29, and from the usage of the apostles.

8. *How does it appear that breaking the bread is an important part of the service?*

1st. The example of Christ in the act of institution, which is particularly noticed in each inspired record of the matter. Matt. xxvi. 26; Mark xiv. 22; Luke xxii. 19; 1 Cor. xi. 24.

2d. It is prominently set forth in the reference made by the apostles to the sacrament in the epistles.—1 Cor. x. 16. The entire service is designated from this one action.

3d. It pertains to the symbolical significancy of the sacrament. (1.) It represents the breaking of Christ's body for us. 1 Cor. xi. 24. (2.) It represents the communion of believers, being many in one body.—1 Cor. x. 17. This is denied by the Lutheran Church, which holds that the "breaking" is only a preparation for distribution (see Krauth's "Conservative Reformation," pp. 719–722).

9. *What is the proper interpretation of* 1 Cor. x. 16, *and in what sense are the elements to be blessed or consecrated?*

The phrase *to bless* is used in Scripture only in three senses, 1st. To bless God, *i. e.*, to declare his praises, and to utter our gratitude to him. 2d. To confer blessing actually, as God does upon his creatures. 3d. To invoke the blessing of God upon any person or thing.

The "cup of blessing which we bless" is the consecrated cup upon which the minister has invoked the divine blessing. As the blessing of God is invoked upon food, and it is thus consecrated unto the end of its natural use, 1 Tim. iv. 5, so the elements are set apart as sacramental signs of an invisible spiritual grace, to the end of showing forth Christ's death, and of ministering grace to the believing recipient. by the invocation by the minister of God's blessing in the promised presence of Christ through his Spirit.

The Romish Church teaches that when the priest pronounces the words of consecration with the due intention, he really effects the transubstantiation of the bread and wine into the body and blood of Christ. The form to be used in the consecration of the bread is, "This is my body." The form to be used in consecrating the wine is, "For this is the chalice of my blood, of the new and eternal testament, the mystery of faith, which shall be shed for you and for many for the remission of sins" ("Cat. Conc. Trident.," Pt. II., Ch. iv., Ques. 19–26).

10. *Show that the distribution of the elements to the people and their reception by them is an essential part of this sacrament?*

Since the Romish Church has perfectly developed the doctrines of transubstantiation, and of the sacrifice of the mass, they have logically come to regard the essential design of the ordinance to be effected when the act of consecration has been performed, and hence the distribution of the elements to the people is considered non-essential. Hence they preserve the bread as the veritable body of the Lord shut up in the pyx, carry it about in processions and worship it. Hence they also maintain the right of the priest in the mass to communicate without the people, and to carry the wafer to the sick who are absent from the place of communion.—"Conc. Trident.," Sess. 13, Ch. 6, and cans. 4–7, and Sess. 22, can. 8.

Protestants, on the contrary, hold that it is of the *essence* of this holy ordinance that it is an *action*, beginning and ending in the appointed use of the elements. "*Take eat*," said Christ. "*This do* in remembrance of me." It is a "breaking of bread," an "eating and drinking" in remembrance of Christ, it is a "communion." Protestants all hold, consequently, that the distribution and reception of the elements are essential parts of the service, and that when these are accomplished the sacrament ends. The Lutherans hold that the presence of the flesh and blood of Christ in the sacrament is confined to the time of the sacramental use of the elements, that is to the time of their distribution and reception, and that what remains afterwards is common bread and wine.—"Form. Concord.," Pt. 2, Ch. 7, 82, and 108; "Conf. Faith," Ch. 29, § 4.

The Reformed Church holds that the elements should be put into the hands of the communicant, and not as Catholics, into his mouth. Christ said, "take eat," and the act is symbolical of personal self-appropriation.

Since this sacrament is a "communion" (1 Cor. x. 16, 17) of the members with one another and with Christ together, the rite is abused when the elements are sent to persons absent from the company among whom it is celebrated, and all private communion of ministers or laymen is absurd. In case of need all Reformed Churches allow the pastor and elders to go, with as many Christian friends as the case admits of, and hold a communion in the chamber of sick believers, who otherwise would be unable to attend (Gen. Assem. O. S., 1863, "Moore's Digest.," p. 668).

11. *What should be the nature of the exercises during the distribution of the elements?*

"The Sacraments are seals of the Covenant of Grace" formed between Christ and his people, and in the Lord's Supper "the worthy receivers really and truly receive and apply *unto themselves* Christ crucified," each believer being made "a priest unto God" (1 Pet. ii. 5; Rev. i. 6), "having liberty to enter into the holiest by the blood of Jesus" (Heb. x. 19). From all this it necessarily follows that *in this sacrament the communicants are to act immediately in their covenanting with the Lord.*

The minister ought never, therefore, to throw the communicants into a passive attitude as the recipients of instructions or exhortations. All such didactic and hortatory exercises being assigned to the "preparatory" services, and to the sermon before communion, the minister should confine himself to leading the communicants *in the act of communion in exercises of direct worship*, such as suitable prayers and hymns. And all the prayers and hymns associated with this holy ordinance should be specifically appropriate to it, and not merely of a general religious character.

The Relation of the Sign and the Grace Signified.

12. *What is the Romish doctrine on this subject? And how is it expressed by the term Transubstantiation?*

The early fathers spoke of the presence of Christ in the Supper in indefinite language, and with a general tendency to exaggeration. Their metaphorical language tended to a confusion between the symbols of religious service and the spiritual ideas represented. As the ministry came to be regarded as a priesthood, and the only channels of grace to the people, the sacraments were more and more exalted into the necessary instruments through which they acted. With the conception of a real priesthood necessarily emerged the need of a real sacrifice; and for the reality of the sacrifice the real presence of a divine incarnate victim also was necessarily provided.

The doctrine in its present form was first brought out explicitly by Paschasius Radbert, abbot of Corbet (A. D. 831). It was opposed by Ratramnus, but gradually gained ground. The term *transubstantiatio, conversion of substance*, was used to define it in the first instance by Hildebert of Tours (†1134). It was first decreed as an article of faith, at the instance of Innocent III., by the fourth "Lateran Council," A. D. 1215.

Their doctrine is that when the words of consecration are pronounced by the priest—1st. The whole substance of the bread is changed into the very body of Christ which was born of the Virgin, and is now seated at the right hand of the Father in heaven, and the whole substance of the wine is changed into the blood of Christ. 2d. That as in his theanthropic person the soul is inseparable from the body, and the divinity from the soul, so in the sacrament the soul and body of the Redeemer is present with his flesh and blood. 3d. That only the species, or sensible qualities of the bread and wine remain, *accidentia sine subjecto*, and that the substance of the flesh and blood is present without their accidents. 4th. This conversion of substance is permanent, so that the flesh and blood remain permanently and are to be preserved and adored as such. They rest their doctrine on Scripture (*Hic est corpus meum*), tradition, and the authority of councils.

13. *On what grounds does the Romish Church withhold the use of the cup from all except the officiating priest? and what is their doctrine of 'concomitance'?*

The Early Church for ages, and the Greek and all Protestant Churches to the present time, follow the example of Christ and his apostles in distributing among all communicants both the bread and the wine, "*sub utraque forma.*" The Romish Church however, for fear that some portion of the Lord's person might be unintentionally desecrated, has restricted the cup to the officiating minister alone. The only exception allowed is when the cardinals receive the cup from the pope officiating on Holy Thursday. The Hussite War had for its principal object the gaining for the people the privilege of communicating in both kinds. To defend their custom theologians advanced the doctrine that the whole Christ is present in each of the elements, to which Thomas Aquinas first gave the name *concomitantia.* The body includes the nerves, sinews, and all else that is necessary to a complete body; and as the blood is inseparable from the flesh, and the soul from the body, and the divinity from the soul, it follows that the entire person of the Redeemer is present in each particle of both elements, separation having been made. He, therefore, who receives any fraction of the bread receives blood as well as flesh, because he receives the whole Christ.

14. *Present the arguments proving the Romish doctrine of the relation of the sign to the thing signified to be unscriptural as well as irrational.*

1st. The sole Scriptural argument of the Romanists is derived from the words of institution, "This is my body" (Matt. xxvi. 26). Protestants answer. This phrase in this place *must* mean, "this bread represents, or symbolizes, my body." This is evident—(1.) Because such language in Scripture must often be so interpreted, *e. g.*, Gen. xli. 26, 27—"The seven good kine are seven years: and the seven good ears are seven years." Dan. vii. 24—"And the ten horns are ten kings." Ex. xii. 11; Ezek. xxxvii. 11—"These bones are the whole house of Israel." Matt. xiii. 19, 37; Rev. i. 20—"The seven stars are the angels of the seven churches, and the seven candlesticks are the seven churches." (2.) In this case any other interpretation is rendered impossible by the fact that Christ was sitting present in the body when he spoke the words, and that he also eat the bread. (3.) Also by what Christ says of the cup. Matt., "This *cup* is my blood." Luke, "This cup is the New Testament in my blood." Paul (1 Cor. x. 16) says the cup is the κοινωνία of the blood, and the bread is the κοινωνία of the body of Christ.

2d. Paul calls one of the elements bread, as well after as before its consecration.—1 Cor. x. 16; xi. 26–28.

3d. This doctrine is inconsistent with their own definition of a sacrament. They agree with Protestants and with the fathers in distinguishing, in every sacrament, two things, viz., the sign and the thing signified. See above, Chap. XLI., Question 2. But the doctrine of transubstantiation confounds these together.

4th. The senses, when exercised in their proper sphere, are as much a revelation from God as any other. No miracle recorded in the Bible contradicted the senses, but, on the contrary, the reality of the miracle was established by the testimony of the senses. See the transubstantiation of water into wine.—John ii. 1–10, and Luke xxiv. 36–43. But this doctrine flatly contradicts our senses, since we see, smell, taste, and touch the bread and wine as well after their consecration as before.

5th. Reason also, in its proper sphere, is a divine revelation, and though it may be transcended, never can be contradicted by any other revelation, supernatural or otherwise. See above, Chap. III., Question 14. But this doctrine contradicts the principles of reason (1) with respect to the nature of Christ's body, by supposing that, although it is material, it may be, without division, wholly present in heaven, and at many different places on earth at the same time. (2.) In maintaining that the body and blood of Christ are present in the sacrament, yet without any of their sensible qualities, and that all the sensible qualities of the bread and wine are present, while the bodies to which they belong are absent. But qualities have no existence apart from the substances to which they belong.

6th. This doctrine is an inseparable part of a system of priestcraft entirely anti-Christian, including the worship of the host, the sacrifice of the mass, and hence the entire substitution of the priest and his work in the place of Christ and his work. It also blasphemously subjects the awful divinity of our Saviour to the control of his sinful creatures, who at their own will call him down from heaven, and withhold or communicate him to the people.

15. *State the Lutheran view as to the nature of Christ's presence in the Eucharist.*

The Lutherans hold—1st. The *communicatio idiomatum,* or that the personal union of the divine and human natures involve the sharing of the humanity at least with the omnipresence of the divinity. The entire person of the incarnate God, body, soul, and divinity are everywhere. 2d. That the language of our Lord in the institution, "This (bread) is my body," is to be understood literally.

They, therefore, hold—1st. That the entire person, body and blood of Christ are really and corporeally present in, with, and under the sensible elements. 2d. That they are received by the mouth. 3d. That they are received by the unbeliever as well as by the believer. But the unbeliever receives them to his own condemnation.

On the other hand they deny—1st. Transubstantiation; holding that the bread and wine remain (as to their substance) what they appear. 2d. That the presence of Christ in the sacrament is effected by the officiating minister. 3d. That the presence of Christ in the elements is permanent; being sacramental, it ceases when the sacrament is over. 4th. That the bread and wine only represent Christ's body and blood. 5th. That the presence of the true body and blood is "spiritual," in the sense of being mediated either (*a*) through the Holy Ghost, or (*b*) through the faith of the recipient.

16. *State the doctrine of the Reformed Church.*

Luther's activity as a reformer extended from 1517 to 1546; Melanchthon's from 1521 to 1560; Zwingle's from his appearance at Zurich, 1518, to his death, 1531; Calvin's from 1536 to 1564. The Marburg Colloquy was held October, 1529; the Augsburg Confession published June, 1530; and the first edition of "Calvin's Institutes" was published at Basle, 1536, and the finished work was published by him in Geneva, 1559.

I. Zwingle held that the bread and wine are mere memorials of the body of Christ absent in heaven. His view at first prevailed among the Reformed churches, and was embodied in Zwingle's "Fidei Ratio," sent to the diet at Augsburg, 1530; the "Confessio Tetrapolitana," by Martin Bucer, 1530; the "First Basle Confession," by Oswald Myconius, 1532; and the "First Helvetic Confession," by Bullinger, Myconius, etc., 1536.

II. Calvin occupied middle ground between the Zwinglians and Lutherans. He held—(1.) In common with Zwingle and all the Reformed that the words "This is my body," means "this bread represents my body." (2.) That God in this sacrament offers to all, and gives to all believing recipients, through the eating and drinking the bread and wine, all the sacrificial benefits of Christ's redemption. (3.) He also taught that besides this the very body and blood of Christ, though absent in heaven, communicate a life-giving influence to the believer in the act of receiving the elements. But that this influence though real and vital is (a) mystical not physical, (b) mediated through the Holy Ghost, (c) conditioned upon the act of faith by which the communicant receives them. This view is set forth chiefly in his "Institutes," Bk. 4, Ch. 17, and in the "Gallic Confession," Art. 36, prepared by a Synod in Paris, 1559; in the "Scottish Confession," Art. 21, by John Knox, 1560; and the "Belgic Confession," Art. 35, by Von Bres, 1561.

III. After all hope of reconciling the Lutherans with the Reformed branches of the church on this subject was exhausted, Calvin drew up the *Consensus Tigurinus* in 1549 for the purpose of uniting the Zurich-Zwinglian with the Genevan-Calvinistic party in one doctrine of the Eucharist. It was accepted by both parties, and the doctrine it presents has ever since been received as the consensus of the Reformed churches. It prevails in the "Second Helvetic Confession," by Bullinger, 1564; the "Heidelberg Catechism," by Ursinus, a student of Melanchthon, 1562; the "Thirty-nine Articles of the Church of England," 1562; and the "Westminster Confession of Faith," 1648.

These all agree—1st. As to the "presence" of the flesh and blood of Christ. (1.) His human nature is in heaven only. (2.) His Person as God-man is omnipresent everywhere and always, our communion is with his entire person rather than with his flesh and blood (see above, Ch. XIII., Ques. 13 and 16).

(3.) The presence of his flesh and blood in the sacrament is neither physical nor local, but only through the Holy Spirit, affecting the soul graciously. 2d. As to *that* which the believer feeds upon, they agreed that it was not the "substance" but the virtue or efficacy of his body and blood, *i. e.*, their sacrificial virtue, as broken and shed for sin. 3d. As to the "feeding" of believers upon this "body and blood," they agreed—(1.) It was not with the mouth in any manner. (2.) It was by the soul alone. (3.) It was by faith, the mouth or hand of the soul. (4.) By or·through the power of the Holy Ghost. (5.) It is not confined to the Lord's Supper. It takes place whenever faith in him is exercised.—"Bib. Ref.," April, 1848.

THE EFFICACY OF THIS SACRAMENT.

17. *What is the Romish doctrine as to the efficacy of the Eucharist, and in what sense and on what ground do they hold that it is also a sacrifice?*

They distinguish between the eucharist as a sacrament, and as a sacrifice. As a sacrament its effect is that *ex opere operato* the receiver who does not present an obstacle, is nourished spiritually, sanctified and replenished with merit by the actual substance of the Redeemer eaten or drunk.

On the other hand—"The sacrifice of the mass is an external oblation of the body and blood of Christ offered to God in recognition of his supreme Lordship, under the appearance of bread and wine visibly exhibited by a legitimate minister, with the addition of certain prayers and ceremonies prescribed by the church for the greater worship of God and edification of the people."—Dens, Vol. v., p. 358.

With respect to its end it is to be distinguished into, 1st, Latreuticum, or an act of supreme worship offered to God. 2d. Eucharisticum, thanksgiving. 3d. Propitiatorium, atoning for sin, and propitiating God by the offering up of the body and blood of Christ again. 4th. Imperatorium, since through it we attain to many spiritual and temporal blessings.—Dens, Vol. v., p. 368.

The difference between the eucharist as a sacrament and a sacrifice is very great, and is twofold; as a sacrament it is perfected by consecration, as a sacrifice all its efficacy consists in its oblation. As a sacrament it is to the worthy receiver a source of merit, as a sacrifice it is not only a source of merit, but also of satisfaction, expiating the sins of the living and the dead.—"Cat. Rom.," Pt. II., Chap. iv., Q. 55; "Council Trent," Sess. 22.

They found this doctrine upon the authority of the church, and absurdly appeal to Mal. i. 11, as a prophecy of this perpetually recurrent sacrifice, and to the declaration, Heb. vii. 17, that Christ is "a priest forever, after the order of Melchizedec," who, say they, discharged his priestly functions in offering bread and wine to Abraham.—Gen. xiv. 18.

18. *How may this doctrine be refuted?*

1st. It has no foundation whatever in Scripture. Their appeal to the prophecy in Malachi, and to the typical relation of Melchizedec to Christ, is self-evidently absurd.

2d. It rests wholly upon the fiction of transubstantiation, which was disproved above, Question 14.

3d. The sacrifice of Christ on the cross was perfect, and from its essential nature excludes all others.—Heb. ix. 25–28; x. 10–14 and 18, 26, 27.

4th. It is inconsistent with the words of institution pronounced by Christ.—Luke xxii. 19, and 1 Cor. xi. 24–26. The sacrament commemorates the sacrifice of Christ upon the cross, and consequently can not be a new propitiatory sacrifice itself. For the same reason the essence of a sacrament is different from that of a sacrifice. The two can not coexist in the same ordinance.

5th. It belonged to the very essence of all propitiatory sacrifices, as well to the typical sacrifices of the Old Testament, as to the all-perfect one of Christ, that life should be taken, that blood should be shed, since it consisted in vicariously suffering the penalty of the law.—Heb. ix. 22. But the Papists themselves call the mass a bloodless sacrifice, and it is wholly without pain or death.

6th. A sacrifice implies a priest to present it, but the Christian ministry is not a priesthood.—See above, Chap. XXIV., Question 21.

19. *What is the Lutheran view as to the efficacy of the sacrament?*

The Lutheran view on this point is that the efficacy of the sacrament resides not in the signs, but in the word of God connected with them, and that it is operative only when there is true faith in the receiver. This effect is identical with that of the word, and through faith includes the benefits of vital communion with Christ and all the fruits thereof. It, however, lays stress upon the virtue of the literal body and blood of Christ as present in, with, and under, the bread and wine. This body and blood, being physically received equally by the believer and unbeliever, but being of gracious avail only in the case of the believer.—Luther's "Small Cat.," Part V., Krauth's "Conserv. Reform.," pp. 825–829.

20. *What is the so-called Zwinglian and Remonstrant and So-cinian view as to the efficacy of the Eucharist?*

Zwingle died prematurely. He undoubtedly took too low a view of the sacraments. If he had lived he would, doubtless, have accompanied his disciples in their union with Calvin in the adoption of the *Consensus Tigurinus.* The doctrine ever since known by his name, and really held by the Socinians and Remonstrants, differs from the Reformed—1st. In making the elements mere signs; and in denying that Christ is in any special sense present in the eucharist. 2d. In denying that they are means of grace, and holding that they are bare acts of commemoration and badges of profession.

21. *What is the view of the Reformed churches upon this subject?*

They rejected the Romish view which regards the efficacy of the sacrament as inhering in it physically as its intrinsic property, as heat inheres in fire. They rejected also the Lutheran view as far as it attributes to the sacrament an inherent supernatural power, due indeed not to the signs, but to the word of God which accompanies them, but which, nevertheless, is always operative, provided there be faith in the receiver. And, thirdly, they rejected the doctrine of the Socinians and others, that the sacrament is a mere badge of profession, or an empty sign of Christ and his benefits. They declared it to be an efficacious means of grace; but its efficacy, as such, is referred neither to any virtue in it, nor in him that administers it, but solely to the attending operation of the Holy Ghost (virtus Spiritus Sancti extrinsecus accedens), precisely as in the case of the word. It has indeed the moral objective power of a significant emblem, and as a seal it really conveys to every believer the grace of which it is a sign, and it is set apart with especial solemnity as a meeting point between Christ and his people; but its power to convey grace depends entirely, as in the case of the word, on the co-operation of the Holy Ghost. Hence the power is in no way tied to the sacrament. It may be exerted without it. It does not always attend it, nor is it confined to the time, place, or service.—"Bib. Ref.," April, 1848; see "Gal. Conf.," Arts. 36 and 37; "Helv.," ii., c. 21; "Scotch Conf.," Art. 21; 28th and 29th "Articles of Church of England"; also our own standards, "Conf. Faith," Chapter xxix., section 7.

22. *What do our standards teach as to the qualifications for admission to the Lord's Supper?*

1st. Only those who are truly regenerated by the Holy Ghost are qualified, and only those who profess faith in Christ and walk consistently are to be admitted.

2d. Wicked and ignorant persons, and those who know themselves not to be regenerate, are not qualified, and ought not to be admitted by the church officers.—" Conf. Faith," Ch. xxix., section 8; " L. Cat.," Question 173.

3d. But since many who doubt as to their being in Christ are nevertheless genuine Christians, so if one thus doubting unfeignedly desires to be found in Christ, and to depart from iniquity, he ought to labor to have his doubts resolved, and, so doing, to come to the Lord's Supper, that he may be further strengthened.—" L. Cat.," Question 172.

4th. " Children born within the pale of the visible church, and dedicated to God in baptism, when they come to years of discretion, if they be free from scandal, appear sober and steady, and to have sufficient knowledge to discern the Lord's body, they ought to be informed it is their duty and their privilege to come to the Lord's Supper." " The years of discretion in young Christians can not be precisely fixed. This must be left to the prudence of the eldership."—" Direct. for Worship," Chap. ix.

23. *What is the practice which prevails in the different churches on this subject, and on what principles does such practice rest?*

1st. The Romanists make the condition of salvation to be union with and obedience to the church, and, consequently, admit all to the sacraments who express their desire to conform and obey. " No one," however, " conscious of mortal sin, and having an opportunity of recurring to a confessor, however contrite he may deem himself, is to approach the holy eucharist, until he is purified by sacramental confession."—" Coun. Trent," sess. 13, canon 11. The Lutherans agree with them in admitting all who conform to the external requirements of the church.

2d. High Church prelatists, and others who regard the sacraments as in themselves effective means of grace, maintain that even those who, knowing themselves to be destitute of the fruits of the Spirit, nevertheless have speculative faith in the gospel, and are free from scandal, and desire to come, should be admitted.

3d. The faith and practice of all the evangelical churches is that the communion is designed only for believers, and therefore, that a credible profession of faith and obedience should be required of every applicant. (1.) The Baptist churches, denying altogether the right of infant church membership, receive all applicants for the communion as from the world, and therefore demand *positive* evidences of the new birth of all. (2.) All the Pedobaptist churches, maintaining that all children baptized in infancy are already members of the church, distinguish between the admission of the children of the church to the communion, and the admission *de novo* to the church of the unbaptized alien from the world. With regard to the former, the presumption is that they should come to the Lord's table when they arrive at "years of discretion, if they be free from scandal, appear to be sober and steady, and to have sufficient knowledge to discern the Lord's body." In the case of the unbaptized worldling, the presumption is that they are aliens until they bring a credible profession of a change.

24. *How may it be proved that the Lord's Supper is not designed for the unrenewed?*

It can, of course, be designed only for those who are spiritually qualified to do in reality what every recipient of the sacrament does in form and professedly. But this ordinance is essentially—

1st. A profession of Christ.

2d. A solemn covenant to accept Christ and his gospel, and to fulfil the conditions of discipleship.

3d. An act of spiritual communion with Christ.

The qualifications for acceptable communion, therefore, are such knowledge, and such a spiritual condition, as shall enable the recipient intelligently and honestly to discern in the emblems the Lord's body as sacrificed for sin, to contract with him the gospel covenant, and to hold fellowship with him through the Spirit.

25. *What have the church and its officers a right to require of those whom they admit to the Lord's Supper?*

"The officers of the church are the judges of the qualifications of those to be admitted to sealing ordinances." "And those so admitted shall be examined as to their knowledge and piety."—"Direct. for Worsh.," Chap. ix. As God has not endowed any of these officers with the power of reading the heart, it follows that the qualifications of which they are the judges are simply those of competent knowledge, purity of life, and credible profession of faith. [By "credible" is meant not that which convinces, but that which can be believed to be genuine.] It is their duty to examine the applicant as to his knowledge, to watch and inquire concerning his walk and conversation, to set before him faithfully the inward spiritual qualifications requisite for acceptable communion, and to hear his profession of that spiritual faith and purpose. The responsibility of the act then rests upon the individual professor, and not upon the session, who are never to be understood as passing judgment upon, or as indorsing the validity of his evidences.

26. *What is the difference between the Presbyterian and the Congregational churches upon this point?*

There exists a difference between the traditional views and practice of these two bodies of Christians with respect to the ability, the right, and the duty of church officers, of forming and affirming a positive official judgment upon the inward spiritual character of applicants for church privileges. The Congregationalists understand by "credible profession" the positive evidence of a religious experience which satisfies the official judges of the gracious state of the applicant. The Presbyterians understand by that phrase only an intelligent *profession* of true spiritual faith in Christ, which is not contradicted by the life.

Dr. Candlish, in the "Edinburgh Witness," June 8th, 1848, says, "The principle (of communion), as it is notorious that the Presbyterian church has always held it, does not constitute the pastor, elders, or congregation, judges of the actual conversion of the applicant; but, on the contrary, lays much responsibility upon the applicant himself. The minister and kirk session must be satisfied as to his competent knowledge, credible profession, and consistent walk. They must determine negatively that there is no reason for pronouncing him not to be a Christian, but they do not undertake the responsibility of positively judging of his conversion. This is the Presbyterian rule of discipline, be it right or wrong, differing materially from that of the Congregationalists. In practice there is room for much dealing with the conscience under either rule, and persons destitute of knowledge and of a credible profession are excluded."

AUTHORITATIVE STATEMENTS OF CHURCH DOCTRINE.

ROMISH DOCTRINE.—DOCTRINE OF THE EUCHARIST BOTH AS A SACRAMENT AND AS A SACRIFICE.

"*Conc. Trident.,*" Sess. 13, can. 1.—"If any one denieth, that, in the sacrament of the most holy Eucharist, are contained truly, really, and substantially, the body and blood together with the soul and divinity of our Lord Jesus Christ, and consequently the whole Christ; but saith that he is only therein as in a sign, or in figure, or virtue; let him be anathema."

Can. 2.—"If any one saith, that, in the sacred and holy sacrament of the Eucharist, the substance of the bread and wine remains conjointly with the body and blood of our Lord Jesus Christ, and denieth that wonderful and singular conversion of the whole substance of the bread into the body, and the whole substance of the wine into the blood—the species (accidents) of the bread and wine remaining—which conversion indeed the Catholic Church most aptly calls Transubstantiation; let him be anathema."

Can. 3.—"If any one denieth, that, in the venerable sacrament of the Eucharist, the whole Christ is contained under each species, and under every part of each species, when separation has been made; let him be anathema."

Can. 4.—"If any one saith, that, after the consecration has been completed, the body and blood of our Lord Jesus Christ are not in the admirable sacrament of the Eucharist, but (are there) only during the use, whilst it is being taken, and not either before or after; and that in the host, or consecrated particles, which are received or remain after communion, the true body remaineth not; let him be anathema."

Can. 6.—"If any one saith, that, in the holy sacrament of the Eucharist, Christ, the only begotten Son of God, is not to be adored with the worship, even external, of latria; and is, consequently, neither to be venerated with special festive solemnity, nor to be solemnly borne about in processions, according to the laudable and universal rite and custom of holy church; or, is not to be exposed publicly to the people to be adored, and that the adorers thereof are idolaters; let him be anathema."

Can. 7.—"If any one shall say that it is not lawful for the sacred Eucharist to be reserved in the *sacrarium*, but that immediately after consecration, it must necessarily be distributed amongst those present; or, that it is not lawful that it be carried with honor to the sick; let him be anathema."

Can. 8.—"If any one saith that Christ, given in the Eucharist, is eaten spiritually only, and not also sacramentally and really; let him be anathema."

Can. 10.—"If any one saith, that it is not lawful for the celebrating priest to communicate by himself; let him be anathema."

Sess. 21, Can. 1.—"If any one saith, that, by the precept of God, or by necessity of salvation, all and each of the faithful of Christ ought to receive both species of the most holy sacrament of the Eucharist; let him be anathema."

Can. 2.—"If any one saith that the holy Catholic Church was not induced, by just causes and reasons, to communicate under the species of bread only, laymen and also clerics when not consecrating; let him be anathema."

Can. 3.—"If any one denieth that Christ whole and entire—the fountain and author of all graces—is received under the one species of bread; because that—as some falsely assert—he is not received according to the institution of Christ himself under both species; let him be anathema."

Sess. 22, Can. 1.—"If any one saith, that in the mass, a true and proper sacrifice is not made to God; or, that to be offered is nothing else but that Christ is given us to eat; let him be anathema."

Can. 2.—"If any one saith, that by those words, *Do this for the commemoration of me* (Luke xxii. 19), Christ did not institute the apostles priests; or did not ordain that they and other priests should offer his own body and blood; let him be anathema."

Can. 3.—"If any one saith that the sacrifice of the mass is only a sacrifice of praise and of thanksgiving; or, that it is a bare commemoration of the sacrifice consummated on the cross, but not a propitiatory sacrifice; or, that it profits him only that receives; and that it ought not to be offered for the living and for the dead, for sins, pains, satisfactions, and other necessities; let him be anathema."

Can. 8.—"If any one saith, that masses, wherein the priest alone communicates sacramentally, are unlawful . . let him be anathema."

Chap. 2.—"Forasmuch as in this divine sacrifice which is celebrated in the mass, that same Christ is contained and immolated in an unbloody manner, who once offered himself in a bloody manner on the altar of the cross . . . therefor, not only for the sins, punishments, satisfactions, and other necessities of the faithful who are living, but also for those who are departed in Christ, and who are not as yet fully purified, is it rightly offered agreeably to a tradition of the apostles."

Bellarmin, "*Controv. de Euchar.*," v. 5.—"The sacrifice of the mass has not an efficacy *ex opere operato* after the manner of a sacrament. The sacrifice does not operate efficiently and immediately, nor is it properly the instrument of God for making just. It does not make just immediately as baptism and absolution do, but it impetrates the gift of penitence, through which a sinner is made willing to approach the sacrament, and by this be justified. . . The sacrifice of the mass is the procurer not only of spiritual but also of temporal benefits, and therefore it can be offered for sins, for punishments, and for any other necessary uses."

LUTHERAN DOCTRINE.

"*Augsburg Confession,*" Pars 1, Art. 10; "*Apol. Augs. Conf.*," p. 157 (Hase); "*Formula Concordiæ,*" Pars 1, ch. 7, § 1.—"We believe, teach, and profess that in the Lord's Supper the body and blood of Christ are truly and substantially present, and that together with the bread and wine they are truly distributed and received. § 2.—The words of Christ (this is my body) are to be understood only in their strictly literal sense; so that neither the bread signifies the absent body of Christ, nor the wine the absent blood of Christ, but so that on account of the sacramental union the bread and wine truly are the body and blood of Christ. § 3.—As to what pertains to the consecration we believe, etc., that no human act, nor any utterance of the minister of the church, is the cause of the presence of the body and blood of Christ in the Supper, but that this is to be attributed solely to the omnipotent power of our Lord Jesus Christ. § 5.—The grounds, however, on which, in this matter, we contend against the Sacramentarians, are these. . . The *first* ground is an article of our Christian faith, namely, Jesus Christ is true, essential, natural, perfect God and man, in unity of person inseparable and undivided. The *second* is that the right hand of God is everywhere; but *there* Christ has, truly and in very deed, been placed, in respect to his humanity, and therefore being present he rules, and holds in his hands and under his feet all things which are in heaven and on earth. The *third* is that the word of God can not be false. The *fourth* is that God knows and has in his power various modes in which it is possible to be in a place (present), and he was not restricted to that single mode of presence which philosophers have been accustomed to call *local* or *circumscribed.* § 6.—We believe, etc., that the body and blood of Christ are received not only spiritually through faith, but also by the mouth, not after a capernaitish, but a supernatural and celestial manner, by virtue of a sacramental union. . . § 7.—We believe, etc., that not only those who believe in Christ, and worthily approach the Lord's Supper, but also the unworthy and unbelievers receive the true body and blood of Christ, so that, however, they shall not thence derive either consolation or life, but rather that this receiving shall fall out to judgment to them, unless they be converted and exercise repentance."

DOCTRINE OF THE REFORMED CHURCHES.

" *Gallic Conf.*," Art. 36.—"Although Christ is now in heaven, there also to remain till he shall come to judge the world, yet we believe that he, by the hidden and incomprehensible power of his Spirit, nourishes and vivifies us with the substance of his body and blood, apprehended by faith."

"*Scottish Conf.*"—"And although there is great distance of place between his now glorified body in heaven and us mortals now upon the earth, yet we nevertheless believe that the bread which we break is the communion of his body, and the cup which we bless is the communion of his blood. . . So we confess that believers in the right use of the Lord's Supper do thus eat the body and drink the blood of Jesus Christ; and we surely believe that he remains in them and they in him, yea, so become flesh of his flesh and bone of his bones, that as the eternal divinity gives life and immortality to the flesh of Jesus Christ, so also, his flesh and blood, when eaten and drunk by us, confer on us the same privileges."

"*Belgic Conf.*," Art. 35.

Calvin's "*Institutes*," Bk. iv., Ch. 17, § 10.—"The sum is, that the flesh and blood of Christ feed our souls just as bread and wine maintain and support our corporeal life. . . But though it seems an incredible thing that the flesh and blood of Christ, while at such a distance from us in respect of place, should be food to us, let us remember how far the secret virtue of the Holy Spirit surpasses all our conceptions, and how foolish it is to measure its immensity by our feeble capacity. Therefore what our mind does not comprehend, let faith conceive; viz., that the Spirit truly unites things separated by space. That sacred communion of flesh and blood whereby Christ transfuses his life into us, just as if it penetrated our bones and marrow, he testifies and seals in his supper, and that not by presenting a vain or empty sign, but by there exerting an efficacy of the Spirit by which he fulfils what he promises. And truly the thing there signified he exhibits and offers to all who sit down at that spiritual feast, although it is beneficially received by believers only."

"*Thirty-nine Articles*," Art. 28.—"The Supper of the Lord is a sacrament of the redemption by Christ's death: insomuch that to such as rightly, worthily, and with faith receive the same, the bread which we break is a partaking of the body of Christ, and likewise the cup of blessing is a partaking of the blood of Christ. . . The body of Christ is given, taken, and eaten in the Supper only after an heavenly and spiritual manner. And the mean whereby the body of Christ is received and eaten in the Supper is faith. The sacrament of the Lord's Supper was not by Christ's ordinance reserved, carried about, lifted up, or worshipped."

"*Heidelberg Cat.*," Ques. 76.—"What is it to eat the crucified body of Christ and to drink his shed blood? It means, not only with thankful hearts to appropriate the passion of Christ, and thereby receive forgiveness of sins and eternal life, but also and therein, through the Holy Ghost who dwelleth in Christ and in us, to be more and more united to his blessed body, so that, although he is in heaven, and we are upon earth, we nevertheless are flesh of his flesh, and bone of his bones, and live forever one spirit with him."

"*West. Conf. Faith,*" Ch. 29, § 5.—"The outward elements in this sacrament, duly set apart to the uses ordained by Christ, have such a relation to him crucified, as that truly, yet sacramentally only, they are sometimes called by the names of the things they represent, to wit, the body and blood of Christ, albeit in substance and nature they still remain truly and only bread and wine. § 7.—Worthy receivers, outwardly partaking of the visible elements in this sacrament, do then also inwardly by faith, really and indeed, but not carnally and corporeally, but spiritually receive and feed upon Christ crucified and all the benefits of his death: the body and blood of Christ being then not corporeally or carnally in, with, or under the bread and wine; yet as really but spiritually present to the faith of believers in that ordinance, as the elements themselves are to the outward senses."—See "*Consensus Tigurinus,*" in Appendix.

APPENDIX.

THE CONSENSUS TIGURINUS

AND

THE FORMULA CONSENSUS HELVETICA.

I.

THE CONSENSUS TIGURINUS.

WRITTEN BY CALVIN, 1549, FOR THE PURPOSE OF UNITING ALL
BRANCHES OF THE REFORMED CHURCH IN A COMMON
DOCTRINE AS TO THE LORD'S SUPPER.

HEADS OF CONSENT.

The whole Spiritual regimen of the Church leads us to Christ.

I. Since Christ is the end of the Law, and the knowledge of Him
comprehends in itself the entire sum of the Gospel, there is no doubt
but that the whole spiritual regimen of the Church is designed to lead
us to Christ; as through Him alone we reach God, who is the ultimate
end of a blessed (holy) life; and so whoever departs in the least from
this truth will never speak rightly or fitly respecting any of the ordinances of God.

A true knowledge of the Sacraments from a knowledge of Christ.

II. Moreover since the Sacraments are auxiliaries (appendices) of the
Gospel, he certainly will discuss both aptly and usefully their nature,
their power, their office and their fruit, who weaves his discourse from
Christ; not merely touching the name of Christ incidentally, but truth-
fully holding forth the purpose for which He was given to us by the
Father, and the benefits which He has conferred upon us.

Knowledge of Christ, what it involves.

III. Accordingly it must be held, that Christ, being the eternal Son
of God, of the same essence and glory with the Father, put on our flesh
in order that, by right of adoption, He might communicate to us what
by nature was solely His own, to wit, that we should be sons of God.
This takes place when we, ingrafted through faith into the body of
Christ, and this by the power of the Holy Spirit, are first justified by
the gratuitous imputation of righteousness, and then regenerated into a
new life, that, new-created in the image of the Heavenly Father, we may
put off the old man.

Christ, Priest and King.

IV. We must therefore regard Christ in His flesh as a *Priest*, who has expiated our sins by His death, the only Sacrifice, blotted out all our iniquities by His obedience, procured for us a perfect righteousness, and now intercedes for us that we may have access to God; as an expiatory *Sacrifice* whereby God was reconciled to the world; as a *Brother*, who from wretched sons of Adam has made us blessed sons of God; as a *Restorer* (Reparator), who by the power of His Spirit transforms all that is corrupt (*vitiosum*) in us, that we may no longer live unto the world and the flesh, and God himself may live in us; as a *King*, who enriches us with every kind of good, governs and preserves us by His power, establishes us with spiritual arms, delivers us from every evil, and restrains and directs us by the sceptre of His mouth; and He is to be so regarded, that He may lift us up to Himself, very God, and to the Father, until that shall be fulfilled which is to be at last, that God be all in all.

How Christ communicates Himself to us.

V. Moreover in order that Christ may manifest Himself such a one to us and produce such effects in us, it behooves us to be made one with Him and grow together in His body. For He diffuses His life in us in no other way than by being our Head; "from whom the whole body fitly joined together, and compacted by that which every joint supplieth, according to the effectual working in the measure of every part, maketh increase of the body " (Eph. iv. 16).

Communion spiritual. Sacraments instituted.

VI. This communion which we have with the Son of God, is spiritual; so that He, dwelling in us by His Spirit, makes all of us who believe partakers of all the good that resides in Him. To bear witness of this, both the preaching of the Gospel and the use of the Sacraments, Holy Baptism and the Holy Supper were instituted.

The Ends of the Sacraments.

VII. The Sacraments, however, have also these ends:—to be marks and tokens of Christian profession and (Christian) association, or brotherhood; to incite gratitude (thanksgiving), and to be exercises of faith and a pious life, in short, bonds (sealed contracts) making these things obligatory. But among other ends this one is chief, that by these Sacraments God attests, presents anew, and seals to us His grace. For while they indeed signify nothing more than is declared in the word itself, yet it is no small matter that they are presented to our eyes as lively symbols which better affect our feeling, leading us to the reality (*in rem*), while they recall to memory Christ's death and all the benefits thereof, in order that faith may have more vigorous exercise; and finally, it is of no little moment that what was proclaimed to us by the mouth of God, is confirmed and sanctioned by seals.

Thanksgiving.

VIII. Moreover, since the testimonials and seals of His grace, which the Lord has given us, are verities, surely He himself will beyond all doubt make good to us inwardly, by His Spirit, what the Sacraments symbolize to our eyes and other senses, viz., possession of Christ as the fountain of all blessings, then reconciliation to God by virtue of His death, restoration by the Spirit unto holiness of life, and finally attainment of righteousness and salvation; accompanied with thanksgiving for these mercies, which were formerly displayed on the cross, and through faith are daily received by us.

The signs and the things signified are not separated, but distinct.

IX. Wherefore, though we rightly make a distinction between the signs and the things signified, yet we do not separate the verity from the signs; but we believe, that all who by faith embrace the promises therein offered, do spiritually receive Christ and His spiritual gifts, and so also they who have before been made partakers of Christ, do continue and renew their communion.

In the Sacraments the promise is chiefly to be kept in view.

X. For not to the bare signs, but rather to the promise which is annexed to them, it becomes us to look. As far then as our faith advances in the promise offered in the Sacraments, so far will this power and efficacy of which we speak exert itself. Accordingly the matter *(materia)* of the water, bread or wine, by no means present Christ to us, nor makes us partakers of His spiritual gifts; but we must look rather to the promise, whose office it is to lead us to Christ by the right way of faith, and this faith makes us partakers of Christ.

The Elements are not to be superstitiously worshipped.

XI. Hence the error of those who superstitiously worship *(obstupescunt)* the elements, and rest therein the assurance of their salvation, falls to the ground. For the Sacraments apart from Christ are nothing but empty masks; and they themselves clearly declare to all this truth, that we must cling to nothing else but Christ alone, and in nothing else must the free gift of salvation be sought.

The Sacraments (per se) have no efficacy.

XII. Furthermore, if any benefit is conferred upon us by the Sacraments, this does not proceed from any virtue of their own, even though the promise whereby they are distinguished be included. For it is God alone who works by His Spirit. And in using the instrumentality of the Sacraments, He thereby neither infuses into them His own power, nor abates in the least the efficiency of His Spirit; but in accordance with the capacity of our ignorance *(ruditas)* He uses them as instruments in such a way that the whole efficiency *(facultas agendi)* remains solely with Himself.

God uses the instrument but in such a way that all the power (virtus) is His.

XIII. Therefore, as Paul advises us that "neither is he that planteth any thing, neither he that watereth, but God that giveth the increase" (1 Cor. iii. 7); so also it may be said of the Sacraments, that they are nothing, for they will be of no avail except God work the whole to completion *(in solidum omnia efficiat)*. They are indeed instruments with which God works efficiently, when it pleases Him, but in such a manner that the whole work of our salvation must be credited solely to Him.

XIV. We have therefore decided that it is solely Christ who verily baptizes us within, who makes us partakers of Him in the Supper, who, in fine, fulfils what the Sacraments symbolize, and so uses indeed, these instruments, that the whole efficiency resides in His Spirit.

How the Sacraments confirm.

XV. So the Sacraments are sometimes called seals, are said to nourish, confirm, and promote faith; and yet the Spirit alone is properly the seal, and the same Spirit is the originator and perfecter of our faith. For all these attributes of the Sacraments occupy a subordinate place, so that not even the least portion of the work of our salvation is transferred from its sole author to either the creature or the elements.

Not all who participate in the Sacraments partake also of the verity.

XVI. Moreover, we sedulously teach that God does not exert His power promiscuously in all who receive the Sacraments, but only in the elect. For just as he enlightens unto faith none but those whom He has foreordained unto life, so by the hidden power of His spirit He causes only the elect to receive what the Sacraments offer.

The Sacraments do not confer grace.

XVII. This doctrine refutes that invention of sophists which teaches that the Sacraments of the New Covenant confer grace on all who do not interpose the impediment of a mortal sin. For besides the truth that nothing is received in the Sacraments except by faith, it is also to be held that God's grace is not in the least so linked to the Sacraments themselves that whoever has the sign possesses also the reality (*res*); for the signs are administered to the reprobate as well as to the elect, but the verity of the signs comes only to the latter.

God's gifts are offered to all; believers alone receive them.

XVIII. It is indeed certain that Christ and His gifts (*dona*) are offered to all alike, and that the verity of God is not so impaired by the unbelief of men that the Sacraments do not always retain their proper virtue (*vim*); but all persons are not capable of receiving Christ and His gifts (*dona*). Therefore on God's part there is no variableness, but on the part of men each one receives according to the measure of his faith.

Believers have communion with Christ, before and without the use of the Sacraments.

XIX. Moreover, as the use of the Sacraments confers on unbelievers nothing more than if they had abstained therefrom, indeed, is only pernicious to them; so without their use the verity which they symbolize endures to those who believe. Thus in Baptism were washed away Paul's sins, which had already been washed away before. Thus also Baptism was to Cornelius the washing of regeneration, and yet he had already received the gift of the Holy Spirit. So in the Supper Christ communicates himself to us, and yet He imparted himself to us before, and abides continually in us forever. For since each one is commanded to examine himself, it hence follows that faith is required of each before he comes to the Sacraments. And yet there is no faith without Christ; but in so far as in the Sacraments faith is confirmed and grows, God's gifts are confirmed in us, and so in a measure Christ grows in us and we in Him.

Grace is not so joined to the act of the Sacraments, that their fruit is received immediately after the act.

XX. The benefit also which we derive from the Sacraments should by no means be restricted to the time in which they are administered to us; just as if the visible sign when brought forward into view, did at the same moment with itself bring God's grace. For those who are baptized in early infancy, God regenerates in boyhood, in budding youth, and sometimes even in old age. So the benefit of Baptism lies open to the whole course of life; for the promise which it contains is perpetually valid. It may, also, sometimes happen, that a partaking of the Supper, which in the act itself brought us little good because of our inconsiderateness or dullness, afterward brings forth its fruit.

Local imagination should be suppressed.

XXI. Especially should every conception of local (bodily) presence be suppressed. For while the signs are here in the world seen by the eyes, and felt by the hands, Christ, in so far as He is man, we must contemplate as in no other place but heaven, and seek Him in no other way than with the mind and faith's understanding. Wherefore it is a preposterous and impious superstition to enclose Him under elements of this world.

Exposition of the words of the Lord's Supper, " This is my body."

XXII. We therefore repudiate as absurd interpreters, those who urge the precise literal sense, as they say, of the customary words in the Supper, "This is my body," "This is my blood." For we place it beyond all controversy that these words are to be understood figuratively, so that the bread and the wine are said to be that which they signify. And verily it ought not to seem novel or unusual that the name of the thing signified be transferred by metonomy to the sign, for expressions of this kind are scattered throughout the Scriptures; and saying this we assert nothing that does not plainly appear in all the oldest and most approved writers of the Church.

Concerning the eating of the body of Christ.

XXIII. Moreover, that Christ, through faith by the power of His Holy Spirit, feeds our souls with the eating of His flesh and the drinking of His blood, is not to be understood as if any commingling or transfusion of substance occurred, but as meaning that from flesh once offered in sacrifice and blood once poured out in expiation we derive life.

Against Transubstantiation and other silly conceits..

XXIV. In this way not only is the invention of Papists about transubstantiation refuted, but also all the gross fictions and futile subtleties which are either derogatory to His divine glory or inconsistent with the verity of His human nature. For we consider it no less absurd to locate Christ under the bread, or conjoin Him with the bread, than to transubstantiate the bread into His body.

Christ's body is in heaven as in a place.

XXV. But in order that no ambiguity may remain, when we say that Christ should be contemplated as in heaven, the phrase implies and expresses a difference of place (a distance between places). For though, philosophically speaking, "above the heavens" is not a locality, yet because the body of Christ—as the nature and the limitation of the human body show—is finite, and is contained in heaven as in a place, it is therefore necessarily separated from us by as great an interval as lies between heaven and earth.

Christ is not to be worshipped in the bread.

XXVI. But if it is not right for us in imagination to affix Christ to the bread and wine, much less is it lawful to worship Him in the bread. For though the bread is presented to us as a symbol and pledge of our communion with Christ, yet because it is the sign, not the reality, neither has the reality enclosed in it or affixed to it, they therefore who bend their minds upon it to worship Christ, make it an idol.

II.

FORMULA CONSENSUS HELVETICA.

COMPOSED AT ZURICH, A. D. 1675, BY JOHN HENRY HEIDEGGER, OF ZURICH, ASSISTED BY FRANCIS TURRETINE, OF GENEVA, AND LUKE GERNLER, OF BASLE, AND DESIGNED TO CONDEMN AND EXCLUDE THAT MODIFIED FORM OF CALVINISM, WHICH, IN THE SEVENTEENTH CENTURY, EMANATED FROM THE THEOLOGICAL SCHOOL AT SAUMUR, REPRESENTED BY AMYRAULT, PLACÆUS, AND DAILLE; ENTITLED "FORM OF AGREEMENT OF THE HELVETIC REFORMED CHURCHES RESPECTING THE DOCTRINE OF UNIVERSAL GRACE, THE DOCTRINES CONNECTED THEREWITH, AND SOME OTHER POINTS."

CANONS.

I. God, the Supreme Judge, not only took care to have His word, which is the "power of God unto salvation to every one that believeth" (Rom. i. 16), committed to writing by Moses, the Prophets, and the Apostles, but has also watched and cherished it with paternal care ever since it was written up to the present time, so that it could not be corrupted by craft of Satan or fraud of man. Therefore the Church justly ascribes it to His singular grace and goodness that she has, and will have to the end of the world, a "sure word of prophecy" and "Holy Scriptures" (2 Tim. iii. 15), from which, though heaven and earth perish, "one jot or one tittle shall in no wise pass" (Matt. v. 18).

II. But, in particular, the Hebrew Original of the Old Testament, which we have received and to this day do retain as handed down by the Jewish Church, unto whom formerly "were committed the oracles of God" (Rom. iii. 2), is, not only in its consonants, but in its vowels—either the vowel points themselves, or at least the power of the points —not only in its matter, but in its words, inspired of God, thus forming, together with the Original of the New Testament, the sole and complete rule of our faith and life; and to its standard, as to a Lydian stone, all extant versions, oriental and occidental, ought to be applied, and wherever they differ, be conformed.

III. Therefore we can by no means approve the opinion of those who declare that the *text* which the Hebrew Original exhibits was determined by man's will alone, and do not scruple at all to remodel a Hebrew reading which they consider unsuitable, and amend it from the Greek Versions of the LXX and others, the Samaritan Pentateuch, the Chaldee Targums, or even from other sources, yea, sometimes from their own reason alone; and furthermore, they do not acknowledge any other reading to be genuine except that which can be educed by the critical power of the human judgment from the collation of editions with each other and with the various readings of the Hebrew Original itself—which, they maintain, has been corrupted in various ways; and finally, they affirm that besides the Hebrew edition of the present time, there are in the Versions of the ancient interpreters which differ from our Hebrew context other Hebrew Originals, since these Versions are also indicative of ancient Hebrew Originals differing from each other. Thus they bring the foundation of our faith and its inviolable authority into perilous hazard.

IV. Before the foundation of the world God purposed in Christ Jesus, our Lord, an eternal purpose (Eph. iii. 11), in which, from the mere good pleasure of His own will, without any prevision of the merit of works or of faith, unto the praise of His glorious grace, out of the human race lying in the same mass of corruption and of common blood, and, therefore, corrupted by sin, *He elected a certain and definite number* to be led, in time, unto salvation by Christ, their Surety and sole Mediator, and on account of His merit, by the mighty power of the regenerating Holy Spirit, to be effectually called, regenerated, and gifted with faith and repentance. So, indeed, God, determining to illustrate His glory, decreed to create man perfect, in the first place, then, permit him to fall, and at length pity some of the fallen, and therefore elect those, but leave the rest in the corrupt mass, and finally give them over to eternal destruction.

V. In that gracious decree of Divine Election, moreover, Christ himself is also included, not as the meritorious cause, or foundation anterior to Election itself, but as being Himself also elect (1 Peter ii. 4, 6), foreknown before the foundation of the world, and accordingly, as the first requisite of the execution of the decree of Election, chosen Mediator, and our first born Brother, whose precious merit God determined to use for the purpose of conferring, without detriment to His own justice, salvation upon us. For the Holy Scriptures not only declare that Election was made according to the mere good pleasure of the Divine counsel and will (Eph. i. 5, 9; Matt. xi. 26), but also make the appointment and giving of Christ, our Mediator, to proceed from the *strenuous love* of God the Father toward the world of the elect.

VI. Wherefore we can not give suffrage to the opinion of those who teach:—(1) that God, moved by philanthropy, or a sort of special love for the fallen human race, to *previous election*, did, in a kind of conditioned willing—willingness—first moving of pity, as they call it—inefficacious desire—purpose the salvation of all and each, at least, conditionally, *i. e.*, if they would believe; (2) that He appointed Christ Mediator for all and each of the fallen; and (3) that, at length, certain ones whom He regarded, not simply as sinners in the first Adam, but as redeemed in the second Adam, He *elected, i. e.,* He determined to graciously bestow on these, in time, the saving gift of faith; and in this sole act Election properly so called is complete. For these and all other kindred teachings are in no wise insignificant deviations from the form of sound words respecting Divine Election; because the Scriptures do not extend unto all and each God's purpose of showing mercy to man, but restrict it to the elect alone, the reprobate being excluded, even by name, as Esau, whom God hated with an eternal hatred (Rom. ix. 10–13). The same Holy Scriptures testify that the counsel and the will of God change not, but stand immovable, and God in the heavens *doeth* whatsoever he will (Ps. cxv. 3; Isa. xlvi. 10); for God is infinitely removed from all that human imperfection which characterizes inefficacious affections and desires, rashness, repentance, and change of purpose. The appointment, also, of Christ, as Mediator, equally with the salvation of those who were given to Him for a possession and an inheritance that can not be taken away, proceeds from one and the same Election, and does not underly Election as its foundation.

VII. As all His works were known unto God from eternity (Acts xv. 18), so in time, according to His infinite power, wisdom, and goodness, He made man, the glory and end of His works, in His own image, and, therefore, upright, wise, and just. Him, thus constituted, He put under the Covenant of Works, and in this Covenant freely promised him communion with God, favor, and life, if indeed he acted in obedience to His will.

VIII. Moreover that promise annexed to the Covenant of Works was not a continuation only of earthly life and happiness, but the possession especially of life eternal and celestial, a life, namely, of both body and soul in heaven—if indeed man ran the course of perfect obedience—with unspeakable joy in communion with God. For not only did the Tree of Life prefigure this very thing unto Adam, but the power of the law, which, being fulfilled by Christ, who went under it in our stead, awards to us no other than celestial life in Christ who kept the righteousness of the law (Rom. ii. 26), manifestly proves the same, as also the opposite threatening of death both temporal and eternal.

IX. Wherefore we can not assent to the opinion of those who deny that a reward of *heavenly* bliss was proffered to Adam on condition of obedience to God, and do not admit that the promise of the Covenant of Works was any thing more than a promise of perpetual life abounding in every kind of good that can be suited to the body and soul of man in a state of *perfect* nature, and the enjoyment thereof in an *earthly* Paradise. For this also is contrary to the sound sense of the Divine Word, and weakens the power (*potestas*) of the law in itself considered.

X. As, however, God entered into the Covenant of Works not only with Adam for himself, but also, in him as the head and root (*stirps*), with the whole human race, who would, by virtue of the blessing of the nature derived from him, inherit also the same perfection, provided he continued therein; so Adam by his mournful fall, not only for himself, but also for the whole human race that would be born of bloods and the will of the flesh, sinned and lost the benefits promised in the Covenant. We hold, therefore, that the sin of Adam is imputed by the mysterious and just judgment of God to all his posterity. For the Apostle testifies that *in Adam all sinned, by one man's disobedience many were made sinners* (Rom. v. 12, 19), and *in Adam all die* (1 Cor. xv. 21, 22). But there appears no way in which hereditary corruption could fall, as a spiritual death, upon the whole human race by the just judgment of God, unless some sin (*delictum*) of that race preceded, incurring (*inducens*) the penalty (*reatum*, guilt) of that death. For God, the supremely just Judge of all the earth, punishes none but the guilty.

XI. For a double reason, therefore, man, because of sin (*post peccatum*) is by nature, and hence from his birth, before committing any actual sin, exposed to God's wrath and curse; first, on account of the transgression and disobedience which he committed in the loins of Adam; and, secondly, on account of the consequent hereditary corruption implanted in his very conception, whereby his whole nature is depraved and spiritually dead; so that original sin may rightly be regarded as twofold, viz., *imputed sin* and *inherent hereditary sin*.

XII. Accordingly we can not, without harm to Divine truth, give assent to those who deny that Adam represented his posterity by appointment of God, and that his sin is imputed, therefore, *immediately* to his posterity; and under the term *imputation mediate and consequent* not only destroy the imputation of the first sin, but also expose the doctrine (*assertio*) of hereditary corruption to great danger.

XIII. As Christ was from eternity elected the Head, Prince, and Lord (*Hæres*) of all who, in time, are saved by His grace, so also, in time, He was made Surety of the New Covenant only for those who, by the eternal Election, were given to Him as His own people (*populus peculii*), His seed and inheritance. For according to the determinate counsel of the Father and His own intention, He encountered dreadful death instead of the elect alone, restored only these into the bosom of the Father's grace, and these only he reconciled to God, the offended Father, and delivered from the curse of the law. For our Jesus saves *His people* from their sins (Matt. i. 21), who gave His life a ransom for *many sheep* (Matt. xx. 28; John x. 15), His own, who hear His voice (John x. 27, 28), and for these only He also intercedes, as a divinely appointed Priest, and not for the world (John xvii. 9). Accordingly in the death of Christ, only the elect, who in time are made new creatures (2 Cor. v. 17), and for whom Christ in His death was substituted as an expiatory sacrifice, are regarded as having died with Him and as being justified from sin; and thus, with the counsel of the Father who gave to Christ none but the elect to be redeemed, and also with the working of the Holy Spirit, who sanctifies and seals unto a living hope of eternal life none but the elect, the will of Christ who died so agrees and amicably conspires in perfect harmony, that the sphere of the Father's election (*Patris eligentis*), the Son's redemption (*Filii redimentis*), and the Spirit's sanctification (*Spiritus S. sanctificantis*) is one and the same (*æqualis pateat*).

XIV. This very thing further appears in this also, that Christ merited for those in whose stead He died the *means of salvation*, especially the regenerating Spirit and the heavenly gift of faith, as well as salvation itself, and actually confers these upon them. For the Scriptures testify that Christ, the Lord, came *to save the lost sheep of the house of Israel* (Matt. xv. 24), and sends the same Holy Spirit, the fount of regeneration, as His own (John xvi. 7, 8); that among the better promises of the New Covenant of which He was made Mediator and Surety this one is pre-eminent, *that He will write His law*, i. e., the law of faith, *in the hearts of his people* (Heb. viii. 10); that *whatsoever the Father has given to Christ will come to Him*, by faith, surely; and finally, that we are *chosen in Christ to be holy and without blame*, and, moreover, *children by Him* (Eph. i. 4, 5); but our being holy and children of God proceeds only from faith and the Spirit of regeneration.

XV. But *by the obedience of his death* Christ instead of the elect so satisfied God the Father, that in the estimate, nevertheless, of His vicarious righteousness and of that obedience, all of that which He rendered to the law, as its just servant, during the whole course of His life, whether by doing or by suffering, ought to be called obedience. For Christ's life, according to the Apostle's testimony (Philip. ii. 7, 8), was nothing but a continuous emptying of self, submission and humiliation, descending step by step to the very lowest extreme, even the death of the Cross; and the Spirit of God plainly declares that Christ in our stead satisfied the law and Divine justice by His most holy life, and makes that ransom with which God has redeemed us to consist not in His sufferings only, but in His whole life conformed to the law. The Spirit, however, ascribes our redemption to the death, or the blood, of Christ, in no other sense than that it was consummated by sufferings; and from that last terminating and grandest act derives a name (*denominationem facit*) indeed, but in such a way as by no means to separate the life preceding from His death.

XVI. Since all these things are entirely so, surely we can not approve the contrary doctrine of those who affirm that of His own intention, by His own counsel and that of the Father who sent Him, Christ died for all and each upon the impossible condition, provided they believe; that He obtained for all a salvation, which, nevertheless, is not applied to all, and by His death merited salvation and faith for no one individually and certainly (*proprie et actu*), but only removed the obstacle of Divine justice, and acquired for the Father the liberty of entering into a new covenant of grace with all men; and finally, they so separate the active and passive righteousness of Christ, as to assert that He claims His *active* righteousness for himself as His own, but gives and imputes only His *passive* righteousness to the elect. All these opinions, and all that are like these, are contrary to the plain Scriptures and the glory of Christ, who is *Author and Finisher* of our faith and salvation; they make His cross of none effect, and under the appearance of augmenting His merit, they really diminish it.

XVII. The call unto salvation was suited to its *due time* (1 Tim. ii. 6); since by God's will it was at one time more restricted, at another, more extended and general, but never absolutely universal. For, indeed, in the Old Testament God *showed His word unto Jacob, His statutes and His judgments unto Israel; He dealt not so with any nation* (Ps. cxlvii. 19, 20). In the New Testament, peace being made in the blood of Christ and the inner wall of partition broken down, God so extended the limits (*pomœria*) of Gospel preaching and the external call, that there is no longer any *difference between the Jew and the Greek; for the same Lord over all is rich unto all that call upon Him* (Rom. x. 12). But not even thus is the call universal; for Christ testifies that *many are called* (Matt. xx. 16), not all; and when Paul and Timothy essayed to go into Bithynia to preach the Gospel, *the Spirit suffered them not* (Acts xvi. 7); and there have been and there are to-day, as experience testifies, innumerable myriads of men to whom Christ is not known even by rumor.

XVIII. Meanwhile God *left not himself without witness* (Acts xiv. 17) unto those whom He refused to call by His Word unto salvation. For He divided unto them the spectacle of the heavens and the stars (Deut. iv. 19), and *that which may be known of God*, even from the works of nature and Providence, *He hath showed unto them* (Rom. i. 19), for the purpose of attesting His long suffering. Yet it is not to be affirmed that the works of nature and Divine Providence were means (*organa*), sufficient of themselves and fulfilling the function of the external call, whereby He would reveal unto them the mystery of the good pleasure or mercy of God in Christ. For the Apostle immediately adds (Rom. i. 20), "The invisible things of Him from the creation are clearly seen, being understood by the things that are made, even *His eternal power and Godhead;*" not His hidden good pleasure in Christ, and not even to the end that thence they might learn the mystery of salvation through Christ, but that they might be *without excuse,* because they did not use aright the knowledge that was left them, but *when they knew God, they glorified Him not as God, neither were thankful.* Wherefore also Christ glorifies God, His Father, because *He had hidden these things from the wise and the prudent, and revealed them unto babes* (Matt. xi. 25); and the Apostle teaches, moreover, that God has made known unto us the mystery of His will according to His good pleasure which He hath purposed in Himself (*in Christo*), (Eph. i. 9).

XIX. Likewise the external call itself, which is made by the preaching of the Gospel, is on the part of God also, who calls, earnest and sincere. For in His Word He unfolds earnestly and most truly, not, indeed, His secret intention respecting the salvation or destruction of each individual, but what belongs to our duty, and what remains for us if we do or neglect this duty. Clearly it is the will of God who calls, that they who are called come to Him and not neglect so great salvation, and so He promises eternal life also in good earnest, to those who come to Him by faith; for, as the Apostle declares, "it is a faithful saying:—For if we be dead with Him, we shall also live with Him; if we suffer, we shall also reign with Him; if we deny Him, He also will deny us; if we believe not, yet He abideth faithful; He can not deny Himself." Nor in regard to those who do not obey the call is this will inefficacious; for God always attains that which He intends in His will (*quod volens intendit*), even the demonstration of duty, and following this, either the salvation of the elect who do their duty, or the inexcusableness of the rest who neglect the duty set before them. Surely the spiritual man in no way secures (*conciliat*) the internal purpose of God to produce faith (*conceptum Dei internum, fidei analogum*) along with the externally proffered, or written Word of God. Moreover, because God approved every verity which flows from His counsel, therefore it is rightly said to be His will, that *all who see the Son and believe on Him may have everlasting life* (John vi. 40). Although these "all" are the elect alone, and God formed no plan of universal salvation without any selection of persons, and Christ therefore died not for every one but for the elect only who were given to Him; yet He intends this in any case to be universally true, which follows from His special and definite purpose. But that, by God's will, the elect alone believe in the external call thus universally proffered, while the reprobate are hardened, proceeds solely from the discriminating grace of God: election by the same grace to them that believe; but their own native wickedness to the reprobate who remain in sin, and after their hardness and impenitent heart treasure up unto themselves wrath against the day of wrath, and revelation of the righteous judgment of God (Rom. ii. 5).

XX. Accordingly we have no doubt that they err who hold that the call unto salvation is disclosed not by the preaching of the Gospel solely, but even by the works of nature and Providence without any further proclamation; adding, that the call unto salvation is so indefinite and universal that there is no mortal who is not, at least objectively, as they say, sufficiently called either *mediately*, namely, in that God will further bestow the light of grace on him who rightly uses the light of nature, or *immediately*, unto Christ and salvation; and finally denying that the external call can be said to be serious and true, or the candor and sincerity of God be defended, without asserting the absolute universality of grace. For such doctrines are contrary to the Holy Scriptures and the experience of all ages, and manifestly confound nature with grace, that which may be known of God with His hidden wisdom, the light of reason, in fine, with the light of Divine Revelation.

XXI. They who are called unto salvation through the preaching of the Gospel can neither believe nor obey the call, unless they are raised up out of spiritual death by that very power whereby God commanded the light to shine out of darkness, and God shines into their hearts with the soul-swaying grace of His Spirit, to give *the light of the knowledge of the glory of God in the face of Jesus Christ* (2 Cor. iv. 6). *For the natural man receiveth not the things of the Spirit of God; for they are foolishness unto him: neither can he know them, because they are spiritually discerned* (1 Cor. ii. 14); and this utter inability the Scripture demonstrates by so many direct testimonies and under so many emblems that scarcely in any other point is it surer (*locupletior*). This inability *may*, indeed, be called *moral* even in so far as it pertains to a moral subject or object; but it *ought* at the same time to be also called *natural*, inasmuch as man by nature, and so by the law of his formation in the womb, and hence from his birth, is *the child of disobedience* (Eph. ii. 2); and has that inability so innate (*congenitam*) that it can be shaken off in no way except by the omnipotent heart-turning grace of the Holy Spirit.

XXII. We hold therefore that they speak with too little accuracy and not without danger, who call this inability to believe *moral* inability, and do not hold it to be *natural*, adding that man in whatever condition he may be placed is able to believe if he will, and that faith in some way or other, indeed, is self-originated ; and yet the Apostle most distinctly calls it the gift of God (Eph. ii. 8).

XXIII. There are two ways in which God, the just Judge, has promised justification : either by one's own works or deeds in the law ; or by the obedience or righteousness of another, even of Christ our Surety, imputed by grace to him that believes in the Gospel. The former is the method of justifying man perfect ; but the latter, of justifying man a sinner and corrupt. In accordance with these two ways of justification the Scripture establishes two covenants: the Covenant of Works, entered into with Adam and with each one of his descendants in him, but made void by sin; and the Covenant of Grace, made with only the elect in Christ, the second Adam, eternal, and liable to no abrogation, as the former.

XXIV. But this later Covenant of Grace according to the diversity of times had also different dispensations. For when the Apostle speaks of the dispensation of the fulness of times, *i. e.*, the administration of the last time, he very clearly indicates that there had been another dispensation and administration for the times which the προθεσμίαν (Gal. iv. 2), or appointed time. Yet in each dispensation of the Covenant of Grace the elect have not been saved in any other way than by the *Angel of his presence* (Is. lxiii. 9), *the Lamb slain from the foundation of the world* (Rev. xiii. 8), Christ Jesus, through the knowledge of that just Servant and faith in Him and in the Father and His Spirit. For Christ is *the same yesterday, to-day, and forever* (Heb. xiii. 8); and by His grace we believe that we are saved (*servari*) in the same manner as the Fathers also were saved (*salvati sunt*), and in both Testaments these statutes remain immutable: "Blessed are all they that put their trust in Him," the Son (Ps. ii. 12); "He that believeth in Him is not condemned, but he that believeth not is condemned already" (John iii. 18); "Ye believe in God," even the Father, "believe also in me" (John xiv. 1). But if, moreover, the sainted Fathers believed in Christ as their Goël, it follows that they also believed in the Holy Spirit, without whom no one can call Jesus Lord. Truly so many are the clearest exhibitions of this faith of the Fathers and of the necessity thereof in either Covenant, that they can not escape any one unless he wills it. But though this saving knowledge of Christ and the Holy Trinity was necessarily derived, according to the dispensation of that time, both from the promise and from shadows and figures and enigmas, with greater difficulty (*operosius*) than now in the New Testament; yet it was a true knowledge, and, in proportion to the measure of Divine Revelation, was sufficient to procure for the elect, by help of God's grace, salvation and peace of conscience.

XXV. We disapprove therefore of the doctrine of those who fabricate for us three Covenants, the Natural, the Legal, and the Gospel Covenant, different in their whole nature and pith; and in explaining these and assigning their differences, so intricately entangle themselves that they obscure not a little, or even impair, the nucleus of solid truth and piety; nor do they hesitate at all, with regard to the necessity, under the Old Testament dispensation, of knowledge of Christ and faith in Him and His satisfaction and in the whole sacred Trinity, to theologize much too loosely and not without danger.

XXVI. Finally, both unto us, to whom in the Church, which is God's house, has been entrusted the dispensation for the present, and unto all our Nazarenes, and unto those who under the will and direction of God will at any time succeed us in our charge, in order to prevent the fearful enkindling of dissensions with which the Church of God in different places is disturbed (*infestatur*) in terrible ways, *we earnestly wish* (*volumus,* will) *this to be a law:*—

That in this corruption of the world, with the Apostle of the Gentiles as our faithful monitor, *we all keep faithfully that which is committed to our trust, avoiding profane and vain babblings* (1 Tim. vi. 20); and religiously guard the purity and simplicity of that knowledge which is according to piety, constantly clinging to that beautiful pair, Charity and Faith, unstained.

Moreover, in order that no one may be induced to propose either publicly or privately some doubtful or new dogma of faith hitherto unheard of in our churches, and contrary to God's Word, to our Helvetic Confession, our Symbolical Books, and to the Canons of the Synod of Dort, and not proved and sanctioned in a public assembly of brothers according to the Word of God, let it also be a law:—

That we not only hand down sincerely in accordance with the Divine Word, the especial necessity of the sanctification of the Lord's Day, but also impressively inculcate it and importunately urge its observation; and, in fine, that in our churches and schools, as often as occasion demands, we unanimously and faithfully hold, teach, and assert the truth of the Canons herein recorded, truth deduced from the indubitable Word of God.

The very God of peace in truth sanctify us wholly, and preserve our whole spirit and soul and body blameless unto the coming of our Lord Jesus Christ! to whom, with the Father and the Holy Spirit be eternal honor, praise and glory. AMEN!

INDEX.

JACOBI, 51
JAMBLICUS, 51
JANSENIUS, 99
JANSENISTS, 100, 449
JESUITS, 99, 271
JEWS, future Conversion and Restoration of, 571–573
JOHN Ascusnages, 197
JOHN Philoponus, 197
JOSEPHUS, 297
JOWETT, Prof., 58, 422
JULIAN, 96
JUDGMENT, final, 573–576
JUSTIFICATION, 496–514
  New Testament usage of δικαίοω, etc., 496, 497
  Doctrine defined and proved, 498–502
  Not grounded on works, 498, 499
  But upon the righteousness, active and passive, of Christ, 500
  Imputation of righteousness proved 501, 502
  Relation of Faith to, 503, 504
  Specific object of justifying faith, 504
  Its effects, 505
  Objections stated and answered, 505
  Erroneous views of, 505–512
  Piscator's view, 506
  As modified by Governmental theory of the Atonement, 508, and by the Arminian theory, 508, 509
  Calvin vindicated, 507, 508
  Romish doctrine of Justification stated and refuted, 509–512
  Authoritative Church statements, 513, 514

KAHNIS, 58
KANT, 63
KINGSHIP of Christ. (See *Christ.*)
KITTO, 249, 578, 580
KNOX, John, 640
KRAUTH, Dr., C. P., 49, 123, 362, 595, 626, 629, 634, 643
KURTZ, 27

LAMPE, 352
LEATHES, Stanley, 61
LE CLERC, 105
LEIBNITZ, 63, 244
LEIPSIC Conference, 448
LELAND, 48
LEO the Great, 388
LESSING, 48
LIMBORCH, 105, 307, 337, 347, 353, 413, 425, 447, 503, 509, 514, 587, 602
LOCKE, John, 63

LORD'S SUPPER, 631–650
  Its institution and perpetual obligation, 631
  Scriptural and Ecclesiastical designations, 631, 632
  Kind of bread and wine to be used, 633, 634
  The breaking of bread, 634
  Distribution of elements essential, 635, 636
  Proper manner of conducting services, 636
  Relation of the sign to the grace signified, 636–641
  Romish view of (Transubstantiation) stated and refuted, 636, 639
  Doctrine of "Concomitance," 637
  Reasons for withholding the cup, 637
  Lutheran view of the presence of Christ in, 639
  The Reformed view of same, 639–641
  Efficacy of, 641–647
  Romish Doctrine of same as a Sacrament and as a Sacrifice (Mass) stated and refuted, 641, 642
  Lutheran view of same, 642, 643
  Zwinglian view of, 643
  Reformed view of, 643
  Qualification for admission to, 644–646
  Authoritative Statements, 646–650
LOYOLA Ignatius, 99
LUTHER, 100, 102, 354, 384, 404, 405, 444, 625, 626, 639
LUTHERAN Churches, 102
LUTHERANISM, 100–102, 122, 123, 271
  Of Original Sin, 336, 337
  Of Predestination, 234, 235
  Of Original Righteousness, 307
  Of Inability, 346
  Of Person of Christ, 384, 389, 390
  Of the "Descent into Hell," 439, 443, 444
  Of Effectual Calling, 447
  Of Regeneration, 464
  Of Justification, 513
  Of Perseverance, 546
  Of Efficacy of Sacraments, 595, 600, 601
  Of Necessity of Baptism, 625, 629
  Of Christ's presence in the Eucharist, 639, 648, 649
  Of Efficacy of same, 64, 643, 648, 649

M'CLINTOCK, Dr. John, 26, 27, 28, 494
M'COSH, Dr. James, 142, 283, 286, 315
MACEDONIUS, 174